Guide to the Birds of Madagascar

Birds of

GUIDE TO THE

Madagascar

OLIVIER LANGRAND

Illustrated by Vincent Bretagnolle

Translated by Willem Daniels

Foreword by H.R.H. Prince Philip

Yale University Press   New Haven & London

The publication of the English-language version of this book was made possible by a grant from the Smithsonian Institution Atherton Seidell Endowment Fund.

Published with assistance from the Kingsley Trust Association Publication Fund established by the Scroll and Key Society of Yale College.

Designed by Richard Hendel.
Set in Ehrhardt type by G & S Typesetters, Austin, Texas.
Printed in the United States of America by Vail-Ballou Press, Binghamton, New York.

Library of Congress Cataloging-in-Publication Data
Langrand, Olivier.
[Guide des oiseaux de Madagascar. English]
Guide to the birds of Madagascar / Olivier Langrand ; illustrated by Vincent Bretagnolle ; translated by Willem Daniels.
   p.   cm.
Translation of: Guide des oiseaux de Madagascar.
ISBN 0-300-04310-4 (alk. paper)
1. Birds—Madagascar.   I. Title.
QL692.M28L3613   1990
598.29691—dc20   90-30668
                          CIP

Contents

Foreword by H.R.H. Prince Philip   vii

Acknowledgments   ix

Notes by the Illustrator   xi

Introduction   1

Map of Madagascar: Geographic Location   2

Overview of the Natural Habitats of Madagascar   3
    Forest Habitats   3
    Other Habitats   6
    Map of Floristic Domains   8

The Avifauna of Madagascar   9
    Taxonomic Composition   9
    Extinct Species   11
    Introduced Species   11
    Migratory Movements   12
    Diagram of the Composition of Resident Species   13

Analysis of the Bird Community   15
    The Bird Community Specific to the Eastern Region   15
    The Bird Community Specific to the Western Region   22

Diagram of the Distribution of Species by Domain   27

Protected Areas System   29
    List of Protected Areas   29
    Map of Protected Area Locations   30
    Diagram of Species Distribution in Protected Areas   31

Recommended Sites for Observing the Avifauna
    of Madagascar   33

List of Birds at Recommended Observation Sites   38

Map of the Western Indian Ocean around Madagascar   45

Potential Species in the Vicinity of the
    Coast of Madagascar   47
    List of Potential Species   47
    Identification of Potential Species   48
    Brief Guide to the Identification of Potential Species   49

Organization of the Field Identification Guide   53

Topography of a Bird   54

Taxonomic List of Scientific, English, and French Names   57

Locator Map   68

Alphabetical List of Places   69

Guide to the Birds of Madagascar   71

Distribution Maps   315

Alphabetical and Etymological Key to Malagasy Names   341

Index of English Names   353

Index of Scientific Names   357

Foreword

All islands hold a special fascination for naturalists and particularly for ornithologists. The absence of any physical boundaries on the continents means that birds can move about freely, migration is easier and species tend to merge with one another. Islands are isolated, and the principles of evolution dictate that, whatever their origin, island species develop along their own lines.

It was this feature that attracted Darwin's attention when he visited the Galápagos Islands, but had fate taken him to Madagascar, he would have noticed exactly the same thing. Madagascar has been cut off from the rest of the world for so long that it now contains an exceptionally high proportion of endemic species in its rich endowment of flora and fauna. A cursory glance at the taxonomic list at the end of this book is enough to reveal the proportion of names that start with "Madagascar . . . ."

I am quite sure that this thoroughly researched and beautifully illustrated book will be greatly welcomed by people interested in birds all over the world, from the academic ornithologist to the enthusiastic bird-watcher. We all owe a debt of gratitude to the author, Olivier Langrand, to his translator, Willem Daniels, and to Vincent Bretagnolle for his excellent illustrations.

H.R.H. Prince Philip

Acknowledgments

I begin by thanking Lucienne Wilmé, both for her fruitful participation throughout these years of fieldwork and for her highly valuable contribution in gathering and processing the collected data, particularly the vocalizations.

My special gratitude goes to Dominique Halleux, who awakened my interest in Madagascar and who, through his friendship and his exceptional knowledge of that country's avifauna, has done much to make the publication of this book possible.

I extend warm appreciation to Michel Gunther for his trust and kindness throughout the writing of this book, to Dr. Martin E. Nicoll for his valuable advice in organizing the data, and to Georges Randrianasolo for his support since our first meeting.

Many thanks are owed all those who have contributed directly or indirectly to the completion of this book; their names include my parents, as well as a long list of friends and coworkers: Dr. George Angehr, Otto Appert, Patrick Bassand, Dr. Alain and Béatrice Bosshardt, Jacqueline and Jean Bretagnolle, José Bronfman, Danièle and Hubert Charpentier, Dr. Nigel Collar, Victoria B. Cevey, Jean De Heaulme, Catherine Deulofeu, Dr. Robert E. Dewar, Charles Domergue, Christian Dronneau, Lee and Gerald Durrell, Dr. Christian Erard, Dr. Armand Fayard and the staff of the Muséum d'Histoire Naturelle de Grenoble, Dr. John Fitzpatrick, Patrick Gateron, Sylvie and Denis Gerber, Michel Gissy, Pétronille Gunther, Pierre Huguet, Dr. Jean-Claude and Chantal Humbert, Christian John, Dr. Alison Jolly, Elisabeth Lang, Madeleine and Philippe Langrand, Christine, Colette, and Jean-Philippe Langrand, Benjamin Lenormand, Dr. Porter P. Lowry, Dr. Roderic B. Mast, Dr. Bernd U. and Christiane Meyburg, Dany Meyer, Raymonde and Christan Meyer, Dr. Russell Mittermeier, Dr. François Moutou, Dr. Sheila O'Connor, Dr. Storrs L. Olson, Simon Peers, Mark Pidgeon, Jean Priard, Francine and Francis Pink, Michael Putnam, Françoise and Caleb Rakotoarivelo, Dr. Voara and Bodo Randrianasolo, Dr. Claude Ratsimandresy, Marion Regan, Dr. Alison F. Richard, Jeffrey A. Sayer, Dr. George E. Schatz, Frank Schmidt, Dr. Roland Seitre, Josef Shea, Jean-Pierre Sorg, Dr. Jean-Claude Stahl, Gillian and François Steimer, Max Vigreux, and Marie-Antoinette and Jean-Pierre Wilmé.

I would especially like to thank the Smithsonian Institution and Marsha Sitnik for arranging the translation from the French.

Notes by the Illustrator

The plates were done entirely in water-colors. To execute them, I made two visits to Madagascar, October–December 1982 and August–September 1983. Field observation, notes, and sketches alone, however, though indispensable, would not have sufficed to achieve the accuracy and precision required for such work. I therefore used, whenever necessary, material from the comprehensive collections of the Muséum d'Histoire Naturelle de Paris, and I take pleasure here in thanking Dr. Christian Erard, Assistant Director of the museum, for his unhesitating generosity in allowing me to borrow specimens.

The plates are designed for convenient field use. Thus, classification is sometimes disregarded in grouping species that frequent the same terrain or closely resemble each other. Similarly, except as otherwise indicated, birds on a given plate are all represented on the same scale. Species that are difficult to identify are shown in similar postures so as to emphasize the features by which they can be recognized. Every plumage that might be encountered (male, female, juvenile, immature, and molting) has been identified.

Introduction

The chief purpose of this guide is to enable general readers as well as scientists to identify all the birds found in Madagascar. The presentation of each species in a text divided into concise sections with colored illustrations of every species covered and their distribution throughout the island should make this guide easy to use. Since the last decades of the nineteenth century studies of the avifauna of Madagascar have given rise not only to numerous articles but also to quite a few books, of which the two best known are: A. Milne-Edwards and A. Grandidier, *Histoire physique, naturelle et politique de Madagascar*, vols. XII, XIV, and XV: *Histoire naturelle des oiseaux*, vols. I, III, and IV (Paris, 1879, 1881, 1882, 1885), and P. Milon, J. J. Petter, and G. Randrianasolo, *Faune de Madagascar*, vol. 35: *Oiseaux* (Antananarivo and Paris: ORSTOM and CNRS, 1973). None of these, however, was designed for field use. This practical guide fills that gap. The data included in it, many not previously published, were collected in the course of expeditions undertaken from 1980 to 1988 by the author, among others, the few ornithologists living in Madagascar, O. Appert, D. Halleux, G. Randrianasolo, L. Wilmé, and by passing multidisciplinary scientific field missions. Material on the Procellariiformes was prepared by Vincent Bretagnolle, a task made possible by field experience gained in the course of research expeditions to the French Southern and Antarctic Territories. For rare species, whether or not exclusive to Madagascar, the old data have also been taken into account. Eight authors have published scientific reference works on Malagasy ornithology: O. Appert, "Zur Biologie der Vangawürger (Vangidae) Südwest-Madagaskars," *Orn. Beob.* 67 (1970); O. Appert, "Zur Biologie einiger Kua-arten Madagaskars (Aves, Cuculi)," *Zool. Jb. Syst.* 97 (1970); O. Appert, "Zur Biologie der Mesitornithiformes (Nakas oder 'Stelzenrallen') Madagaskars und erste fotographishe Dokumente von Vertretern der Ordnung," *Orn. Beob.* 82 (1982); C. W. Benson and J. F. R. Colebrook-Robjent, "Contribution à l'ornithologie de Madagascar," *Oiseau et R.F.O.* 46, 47 (1976, 1977); N. J. Collar and S. N. Stuart, *Threatened Birds of Africa and Related Islands: The ICBP Red Data Book*, pt. 1, 3d ed. (Cambridge: ICBP, 1985); T. Dee, *The Endemic Birds of Madagascar* (Cambridge: ICBP, 1986); J. Delacour, "Les Oiseaux de la mission franco-anglo-américaine à Madagascar," *Oiseau et R.F.O.* 2 (1932); A. L. Rand, "The Distribution and Habits of Madagascar Birds," *Bull. Amer. Mus. Nat. Hist.* 72 (1936); and the authors of the two volumes already listed.

Map 1. Madagascar: Geographic Location

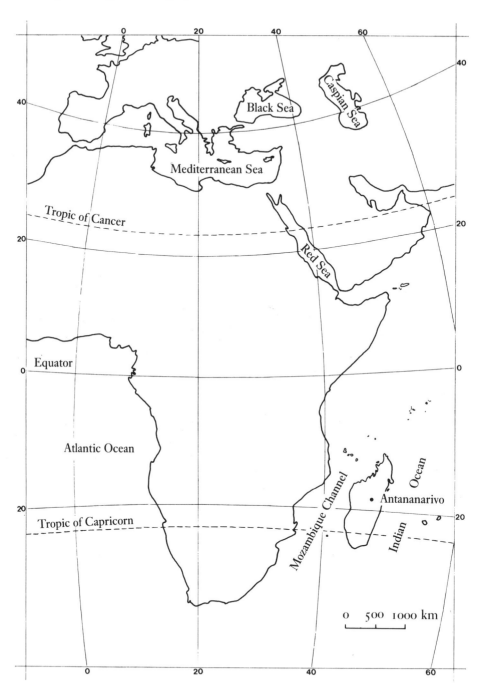

Overview of the Natural Habitats of Madagascar

The geographic position of Madagascar between 11°57′ and 25°37′ latitude south combines with a large surface area (587,000 km²) and mountainous terrain running from north to south in the path of the eastern trade winds to endow this Indian Ocean island continent with a great variety of natural habitats. It was generally assumed until recently that Madagascar was continuously covered by forest before the arrival of humans. Recent studies based on the stratigraphic analysis of pollen and charcoal of the Holocene, however, indicate that the High Plateau was subjected to climatic variation and hence underwent dynamic fluctuations between forest and savanna vegetation types. Before the first human presence was established 1,500–2,000 years ago, fires occurred naturally. The considerable increase in the frequency of fires that seems to have accompanied the arrival of people led to the almost complete transformation of the High Plateau into grassland savanna. Today, the great original natural habitats of Madagascar are primarily forest habitats, to which must be added less widespread original natural environments, such as reefs and wetlands. The altered environments of anthropic origin like the grassland savanna, which nearly completely covers the High Plateau, as well as secondary forest formations, now dominate the landscape.

Forest Habitats

The classification of F. White (*The Vegetation of Africa*, UNESCO, 1983), distinguishes two biogeographic regions in Madagascar, the Eastern Malagasy Region and the Western Malagasy Region. In distinguishing among vegetation zones within these biogeographic regions, White follows H. Humbert (*Les Territoires phytogéographiques de Madagascar: Leur cartographie*, Paris: CNRS, 1954, pp. 439–48). The Eastern Malagasy Region is further divided into four domains: Eastern, Central, High Mountain, and Sambirano. The Western Region is divided into two domains: Western and Southern. Specific types of vegetation can be identified within these domains.

Eastern Malagasy Region

Approximately 5,500 species of vascular plants have been recorded in this region, of which 4,500 are endemic; 22 percent are generically endemic and 82 percent are specifically endemic.

EASTERN DOMAIN
Location: Extends along the east coast from north of Sambava to Tolagnaro; elevations range from sea level to approximately 800 m.
Climate: Average annual precipitation 2,000–3,000 mm; no dry season.
Diversity and level of endemism: Great species diversity; variable floristic composition; high level of endemism.
General structure: Height of the evergreen canopy averages 25–30 m, with no emergent trees. The understory con-

sists of small trees whose leaves are more coriaceous and broader than those of the canopy trees. The herbaceous stratum is little developed. Epiphytic plants abound.

Level of threat: The most endangered type of vegetation; chief threats are slash-and-burn itinerant cultivation and exploitation for firewood.

CENTRAL DOMAIN

Location: Extends parallel to the east coast from north of Sambava to Tolagnaro, at elevations of roughly 800–1,300 m, rising locally to 2,000 m.

Climate: High average annual rainfall, in excess of 1,500 mm, some of it in the form of drizzle; no dry season.

Diversity and level of endemism: As diverse as the Eastern Domain, but with a higher level of endemism.

General structure: Differs from that of the Eastern Domain by its lower canopy, which averages 20–25 m, and by the texture of its leaves, which are of a more marked xerophytic character. The epiphytic vegetation is more plentiful and the herbaceous stratum more developed.

Level of threat: Chief threats are slash-and-burn itinerant cultivation and exploitation for firewood.

HIGH MOUNTAIN DOMAIN

Location: Extends from north of Sambava to Tolagnaro, parallel to the east coast, at elevations of 2,000–2,876 m, locally lower than 2,000 m.

Climate: Substantial rainfall throughout the year; considerable diurnal and seasonal temperature variation.

Diversity and level of endemism: Not very diverse, but with a high level of endemism.

General structure: A dense single stratum up to 6 m in height of evergreens with narrow, coriaceous leaves. The Ericaceae are the best-represented family.

Level of threat: Chief threat, given its inflammable nature, is the high risk of fire. Fires are usually human in origin, either criminal or accidental, but some are caused by lightning.

SAMBIRANO DOMAIN

Location: This domain has limited distribution, being found only in the Sambirano, which, with the Tsaratanana Massif, constitutes the northern end of the island's central mountain range. It lies roughly between Maromandia and Ambanja and consists of elevations from sea level to 1,876 m.

Climate: Year-round heavy rainfall in excess of 2,000 mm a year; average annual temperature is 26° C.

Diversity and level of endemism: High specific diversity and high level of endemism. The Sambirano Domain shares many features with the Eastern and Central domains and some with the Western Domain.

General structure: Similar to that of the Eastern Domain forest. The canopy is 30 m in height, with trees emerging to 35 m locally. The shrub stratum is substantial and epiphytic plants and creepers are common.

Level of threat: Along with the High Mountain Domain, it is the most threatened domain. Clearing carried out for rain-fed rice growing and coffee is the leading cause. The limited area of this domain intensifies the threat.

ANTHROPIC GRASSLAND OF EASTERN MADAGASCAR

Location: Secondary vegetation widely distributed over the Eastern Region and varying in terms of floristic composition according to elevation. It manifests itself as coastal grassland savanna, close to sea level, the grassland savanna of the hill country, 1,200–1,500 m, the grassland savanna of the Tampoketsa, 1,600–1,900 m, the grassland of the western slopes, 800–1,600 m, where the Eastern and Western regions meet, and the highland savanna on the slopes of some mountain ridges of over 2,000 m.

Climate: Varies chiefly according to the altitudinal zone of this type of vegetation, which grows from sea level to more than 2,000 m elevation.

Diversity and level of endemism: Little diversity; extremely low level of endemism. Diversity has been further diminished by repeated fire.

General structure: Grasses are about 50 cm in height, except in the highland savanna, where they are much shorter.

Level of threat: Impoverished by fire, which may occur several times a year. Also threatened by overgrazing, which can be locally very severe. The combined effects of fires and overgrazing accelerate erosion, particularly in the grassland savannas that are subject to heavy rainfall, such as the coastal savanna. This process transforms the savanna environments into steppe.

Western Malagasy Region

Approximately 1,800 species of vascular plants comprising 200 genera have been recorded here. The level of generic endemism is 38 percent and that of specific endemism 89 percent.

WESTERN DOMAIN

Western Malagasy Deciduous Dry Forest

Location: Except the Montagne d'Ambre Massif and the Sambirano Domain, it covers the entire area from Antsiranana in the north to Morombe in the southwest and the high valley of the Mandrare in the south, excluding the Southern Domain. Elevation ranges from sea level to 800 m.

Climate: Annual rainfall ranges 500–2,000 mm along a south-north gradient, most of it recorded November–March; dry season lasts almost seven months; annual temperature averages 25–27° C.

Diversity and level of endemism: Species diversity, though very high, is lower than in Eastern Region forest types, but the level of endemism is higher.

General structure: Canopy averages 12–15 m, sometimes reaching 25 m. Almost all its trees lose their leaves during the dry season. The shrub layer is well developed and vines are common. There is little or no herbaceous stratum and epiphytic plants are rare. Three principal subtypes, based on edaphic factors, exist: (1) on clay lateritic soil—this substratum generates the most luxuriant type of dry deciduous forest, one marked by large trees and a thick litter; (2) on sandy soil—this differs by the smaller size of its trees and its shallower litter; at the outermost bounds of the Southern Domain, it changes to scrub; (3) on limestone plateaus—this differs from the type on a clay lateritic substratum by the smaller size of its trees and their special adaptation to drought; it has a well-developed shrub stratum and fewer vines than the other subtypes.

Level of threat: Considerable; slash-and-burn cultivation is the chief menace, followed by illicit and irrational exploitation of the forest, roaming cattle and goats, and uncontrolled or intentionally set pasture fires that spread to the forest.

SOUTHERN DOMAIN

Deciduous Thicket of Western Madagascar or Subarid Thorn Scrub

Location: Runs southward from Morombe along the coastal strip and covers the entire south to 50 km west of Tolagnaro; limited altitudinal distribution ranges from sea level to 400 m.

Climate: Sparse and irregular annual rainfall of 300–800 mm; long, very marked dry season and strong evapotranspiration.

Diversity and level of endemism: Considerable species diversity with a very high level of endemism.

General structure: Height and density varies with climatic and edaphic factors. In some zones its height averages 2 m, in others 8–10 m; averages 3–6 m. Usually impenetrable, and all its plants are highly adapted to drought, as manifested by their thorns, small, coriaceous leaves, or short-lived broad leaves. The Didiereaceae, an endemic family of four genera, characterizes this vegetation and, along with the arborescent *Euphorbia* species, dominates and typifies this habitat, the floristic composition of which varies greatly.

Level of threat: Because it is found on very poor substrates that are usually unsuited to cultivation, slash-and-burn cultivation is not often attempted. Clearing is associated with the search for firewood and the production of charcoal, particularly near major urban areas, and with the search for materials to make cattle pens. Roaming cattle and goats cause substantial damage, directly by consuming the vegetation or indirectly by creating means of penetration. Excessive and irrational picking of medicinal or ornamental plants is also harming this habitat.

Anthropic Grassland and Woodland Savanna of Western Madagascar

Location: Covers almost 80 percent of the Western Malagasy Region.

Climate: Varies in accordance with location of this vegetation within the region.

Diversity and level of endemism: Little diversity; very low level of endemism.

General structure: This habitat presents great variations linked to climatic and edaphic factors. Trees rarely exceeding 8–12 m in height are locally scattered over the savanna. Locally, this woodland savanna is dominated by a single species of palm—*Borassus madagascariensis, Bismarckia nobilis,* or *Hyphaene shatan.*

Level of threat: Impoverished by fire, which may occur several times a year. Also threatened by overgrazing, which can be locally very severe.

Other Habitats

Coastal and Lake Ecosystems

MANGROVES

Location: Of the total area of mangrove—330,000 ha—97 percent is found along the west coast. Here mangroves of more than 15,000 ha are common, with the largest measuring 46,000 ha. In the east, the largest mangrove covers 2,220 ha. Madagascar has the largest total area of the western Indian Ocean covered by mangroves.

Diversity and level of endemism: Lacks species diversity, being dominated by just nine species; low level of endemism. Richer in species than African mangroves, however, with a floristic composition similar to that of other western Indian Ocean mangroves.

General structure: Typically homogeneous and evergreen. Canopy height ranges 2–12 m, averaging 5–6 m.

Level of threat: Infrequently exploited, unlike African mangrove, which is overexploited for firewood. In view of rapid deforestation, however, it is probably only a matter of years before Madagascar's mangroves undergo the same fate.

CORAL REEFS

Location: Generously distributed along the western coastline, locally forming a continuous barrier. Much less common along the east coast, where they are mainly found by Ile Sainte-Marie and in the Antsiranana region. The total length of the reefs along the west coast is estimated at 1,000 km. The best-known large reefs are those of Toliara and Nosy Be. Numerous islands scattered off the west coast are also ringed with coral reefs.

Importance of the environment: Coral reefs form an important habitat for many groups of animals, many of which are used as sources of food and for industrial purposes.

Level of threat: Environmental impact of exploitation is unknown. Local overexploitation of fishery resources has been recorded. Intense erosion from deforestation is causing tremendous amounts of sediment to be carried by rivers, which poses a potential threat to coral reefs, particularly by causing currents to change direction.

LAKE ECOSYSTEMS

Madagascar possesses five large lakes: Alaotra in the east, Itasy on the High Plateau, and Kinkony, Ihotry, and Tsimanampetsotsa in the west.

Alaotra, situated at an elevation of 750m, is the largest, covering 22,000 ha.

Adjoining marshes increase this area to 35,000 ha. It is shallow, with an average depth of 2 m. Its water is heavily laden with sediments because of the intense erosion affecting the neighboring hills. Since 1923 it has been undergoing a transformation for agricultural purposes; it is a rice producing center of national importance. The original environment is threatened by drainage, fishery resources are irrationally exploited, and poaching is commonplace. Alaotra is an important site for the aquatic avifauna of the east and the High Plateau, particularly for the Aloatra little grebe *(Tachybaptus rufolavatus)* and the Madagascar pochard *(Aythya innotata)*, two endemic species whose range is limited to Alaotra Lake. The ichthyofauna counts at least four endemic species.

Itasy, at 1,221 m elevation, has a surface of 3,500 ha and a maximum depth of 6.5m. It is an important site for aquatic birds from the High Plateau. Local activity is limited to fishing.

Kinkony, at 8 m elevation, has a surface area that varies between 10,000 and 14,900 ha. It is fairly shallow, with a maximum depth of 4 m. Kinkony is an important site for the aquatic avifauna of western Madagascar and for migratory avifauna, principally of Palearctic origin. The ichthyofauna comprises at least four endemic species. Local economic activity is limited to fishing, which has been allowed to develop haphazardly.

Ihotry, at 50 m elevation, has a surface area that varies from 865 to as many as 9,400 ha. Its salinity changes in accordance with the rate of freshwater replenishment. It is fairly shallow, with a maximum depth of 3.8 m. Ihotry is a very important site for aquatic avifauna from the west and south of Madagascar and from the Ethiopian and the Palearctic regions. Economic activity is limited to crop production around the lake.

Tsimanampetsotsa, at 40 m elevation, has a surface area that varies between 1,600 and 2,900 ha. Its shallow waters are saturated with calcium and magne-sium sulfates. It is a fairly important site for aquatic fauna from the south of Madagascar. The lake is reported to contain no species of fish, and it is of no particular economic interest.

Map 2. Floristic Domains

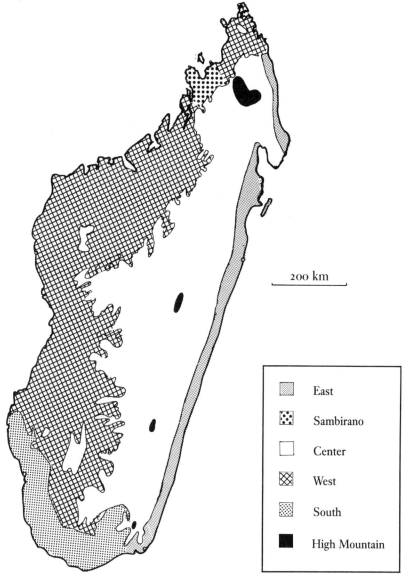

200 km

	East
	Sambirano
	Center
	West
	South
	High Mountain

The Avifauna of Madagascar

The fourth largest island in the world (587,000 km²), Madagascar has been isolated for at least 120 million years. A large number of endemic taxa belonging to the plant and animal kingdoms attest to that long history. Many of these endemic taxa belong to lines that disappeared many years ago from the African subcontinent. The great diversity of ecological niches that have resulted from the island's spectacular geologic and climatic variety have given rise to remarkable evolutionary adaptations. These factors make Madagascar one of the most important living laboratories of evolution in existence.

The vegetation of Madagascar changed rapidly after humans arrived about 1,500 to 2,000 years ago. Now only 20 percent of Madagascar's original cover remains unaltered, these areas being confined mainly to outer portions of the island. Three principal classes of vegetation can be identified within the two biogeographic regions: evergreen rain forest, deciduous dry forest, and subarid thorn scrub. Within those three major classes, of course, specific vegetative communities often harbor species with restricted ranges. It is imperative to protect the full spectrum of habitats to ensure that biological diversity is maintained. The system of protected areas must include the greatest possible number of different habitats and emphasize the protection of those that are threatened with total destruction, isolation, or fragmentation. The exceptional diversity and unique character of the life forms found on Madagascar have, in recent years, led to the island's being accorded the highest international conservation priority.

Taxonomic Composition

The inventorying of the avifauna of Madagascar began in the seventeenth century with mention of the "vorompatra," a giant flightless bird, in the account of the voyage of Etienne de Flacourt. Research intensified in the nineteenth century, and today the inventory can be considered almost complete, at least as far as nesting species are concerned. The inventory accounts for 256 species, of which 201 are resident (including 3 introduced species), 105 of these are endemic, and 25 are endemic to the Malagasy Region (Madagascar, the Comoros, Mauritius, Réunion, and their satellite islands).

The first characteristic of Madagascar's avifauna is its relative poverty in number of species, not only in comparison with the continental bird communities at the same latitude but also in comparison with the bird populations of such Indo-Oceanic islands as Borneo. Second is the very high level of endemism, in terms of both genera (24.6 percent) and species (53 percent). Three families are endemic and two others are limited to the Malagasy Region. And third is that almost all the endemic avifauna consists of forest species, which supports the hypothesis that Madagascar had little savanna before the arrival of humans.

The oldest and most archaic colonization of birds is reflected by the survival, until the seventeenth century, of giant flightless birds. Several species have been identified, but all have been classified under the genus *Aepyornis*, family Aepyornithidae, order Aepyornithiformes. Some taxonomists, however, distinguish two genera, *Aepyornis* and *Mullerornis*. All species were tall and massive of build. Their lower limbs were particularly strong. The heaviest species, comparable in stature to the Ostrich *(Struthio camelus)*, weighed 450–500 kg. Some species attained a height of 3 m, similar to that of the Moa *(Dinornis maximus)* of New Zealand. The *Aepyornis* egg is considered the largest cell of the animal kingdom. Its volume ranges from 7 to 9 liters, or seven times that of an Ostrich egg. Shell fragments, and more rarely intact eggs, can still be found today. The best-known discovery sites are in the south, near Amboasary and Faux Cap, but the traditional use to which these eggs used to be put, service as water tanks, caused them to be dispersed along the south and west coasts, as far as Antsiranana in the north. What caused these giant birds to disappear is uncertain, but it seems likely that they were relicts unable to adapt to new biological pressures and that hunting by humans led to their demise.

The three endemic families and the two endemic to the Malagasy Region comprise the oldest living core of the island's avifauna. All the representatives of these families are forest species.

The family Mesitornithidae has three representatives. This family is assigned to the order Gruiformes, but the lack of obvious links to that or any other order has led to the proposal to create a new order, the Mesitornithiformes. The Mesitornithidae constitute a veritable taxonomic enigma, for they possess morphological features common to several orders.

The family Brachypteraciidae has five representatives, of which four occur in the evergreen rain forest and one in the subarid thorn scrub. Differential use of the habitat of the four sympatric species is marked.

The family Philepittidae has four representatives, three of which inhabit the evergreen rain forest exclusively. Differential use is marked between the two species of the genus *Neodrepanis*.

The family Leptosomatidae is a monospecific family endemic to the region.

The Cuckoo roller *(Leptosomus discolor)* has the peculiar property of being a forest species without a highly specialized diet.

The family Vangidae has fourteen representatives, of which one is also found in the Comoros. The spectacular evolutionary diversification of this regionally endemic family has given rise to eleven genera. The astonishing divergence of the vanga beak is comparable to better-known cases of adaptive radiation, such as that of the Geospizinae of the Galapagos Islands or that of the Drepanidae of the Hawaiian Islands. The Vangidae are close to the African Laniidae and occur in all of Madagascar's forest types.

The subfamily Couinae is endemic to Madagascar and comprises ten species, one of which, the Snail-eating coua *(Coua delalandei)*, is considered extinct. The subfamily shows various adaptations that have enabled it to colonize Madagascar's different forest environments. The Couinae's spatial use of the forest environments is complete: three of the species are strictly arboreal and seven are terrestrial. Their relation to an equivalent taxonomic group on the African or Asian continent is not obvious.

Analysis of the avian community of Madagascar shows that, except for the Leptosomatidae, the families that are not endemic and broadly diversified are poorly represented, often by a single representative. Thus, in Madagascar, among the forty-seven distinct genera of the order Passeriformes, thirty-five have only one species, eleven have two to four species, and just one has more than four species. The scanty specific diversity within the orders is particularly striking for the Psittaciformes, which have only three species, with no representative of the genera *Psittacula* (found, however, on Mauritius) or *Mascarinus* (formerly found on Réunion). The order Apodiformes has four resident species, of which only one is a forest species, though one might have expected far more diversified speciation, given the variety of vegetation zones found throughout the island. Certain orders, such as the Galliformes, are poorly represented, even though, as is the case with the Galliformes, they can be very diversified in the Afro-tropical zone. This is explained by the chiefly forest setting originally offered by Madagascar. However, the existence of such highly specialized species as the Madagascar sandgrouse *(Pterocles personatus)* in savanna environments proves that Madagascar formerly had natural savanna zones. The arrival of humans caused that habitat to expand and furthered the extension of the range of that endemic species.

The affinities of Madagascar's avifauna are primarily Afro-tropical, but certain species—the Réunion harrier *(Circus maillardi)*, the Madagascar lesser cuckoo *(Cuculus rochii)*, the White-browed owl *(Ninox superciliaris)*, the Madagascar nightjar *(Caprimulgus madagascariensis)*, the Madagascar magpie-robin *(Copsychus albospecularis)*, the Madagascar bulbul *(Hypsipetes madagascariensis)*, and the Madagascar starling *(Hartlaubius auratus)*—belong to the Oriental region.

Extinct Species

Apart from the giant flightless species classified under the genus *Aepyornis*, few species have become extinct on Madagascar. Based on IUCN (International Union for Conservation of Nature and Natural Resources) criteria, a species is considered extinct if it has not been observed for more than fifty years. Although this applied to several species on Madagascar until as recently as a few years ago, the main reason was that they had not been sought out. Among them are the Slender-billed flufftail *(Sarothrura wa-*

tersi), the Madagascar red owl *(Tyto soumagnei)*, the Yellow-bellied sunbird-asity *(Neodrepanis hypoxantha)*, and the Dusky greenbul *(Phyllastrephus tenebrosus)*. Only the Madagascar serpent-eagle *(Eutriorchis astur)*, the Snail-eating coua *(Coua delalandei)*, and the Red-tailed newtonia *(Newtonia fanovanae)* have not been observed for more than fifty years. Hope of finding the Madagascar serpent-eagle is justified by the fact that the sites where it was captured in the past are still intact. The same is not true for the Snail-eating coua, which used to live on Ile Sainte-Marie, now completely deforested. The Red-tailed newtonia is also associated with a single site that, though now degraded, lies near a still-intact tract of forest. Only the Snail-eating coua is treated as extinct in this book.

The outlook is bleak for numerous species whose range is limited and whose habitat is threatened with destruction. If no additional protective measures are taken within the next ten years, five species are threatened with extinction: the Alaotra little grebe *(Tachybaptus rufolavatus)*, the Madagascar pochard *(Aythya innotata)*, Subdesert mesite *(Monias benschi)*, the Long-tailed ground-roller *(Uratelornis chimaera)*, and Appert's greenbul *(Phyllastrephus apperti)*.

Introduced Species

Madagascar was not subjected to the wholesale introduction of exotic species as occurred on other islands, such as New Zealand, the Hawaiian Islands, or, closer to home, Mauritius and Réunion. Only four species have been introduced, three of which have established themselves.

The introduction of the Helmeted guineafowl *(Numida meleagris)*, though widely suspected, has been neither dated nor proved. It must have been carried out with specimens collected in Mozambique during the period when regular trade existed between Madagascar and that part of Africa. The Helmeted guineafowl is well suited to secondary forest environments.

The Rock dove *(Columba livia)* was introduced as a domestic species. It is distributed throughout the island but is confined to towns and villages and has not established itself in original environments. The first attempts at acclimatization must date from the arrival of the European settlers in Madagascar.

The Common myna *(Acridotheres tristis)* was introduced at Toamasina, in the form of specimens from Réunion whose initial place of origin was India, in the second half of the nineteenth century as part of an anti-locust campaign. Fragmentation of surrounding forests, which, while unbroken, constituted an insurmountable barrier to this opportunistic species, furthered the expansion of its range. The Common myna is now distributed over the entire east coast, in the south, and locally on the High Plateau and in the northwest.

The House sparrow *(Passer domesticus)* has been introduced recently, the first specimens having been observed in 1984 at Toamasina. It may have been unintentionally carried on board ship from Europe, or more probably from Réunion or Mauritius, where the species was introduced in the nineteenth century. At present confined to the port of Toamasina, this opportunistic species may extend its range in coming years, to the detriment of endemic granivorous species.

The Common waxbill *(Estrilda astrild)* has been observed at only one site, Nosy Be, in 1983, and has not been sighted since. This introduction, probably voluntary, can be assumed to have failed.

Some Malagasy species have been introduced into Réunion, Mauritius, Seychelles, or the Comoros. They are Meller's duck *(Anas melleri)*, the Madagascar partridge *(Margaroperdrix madagascariensis)*, the Madagascar buttonquail *(Turnix nigricollis)*, and the Madagascar red fody *(Foudia madagascariensis)*.

Migratory Movements

Intercontinental Migrations

Intercontinental migrants can be placed in three major categories: antarctic or subantarctic migrants, Palearctic migrants, and Afro-tropical migrants.

The antarctic and subantarctic migrants are principally pelagic species, nine in number, belonging to the order Procellariiformes. Maritime observations on Madagascar are too rare to permit firm estimates of their occurrence. They appear during the austral winter.

The Palearctic migrants consist primarily of Charadriiformes, as well as two Falconiformes, Eleonora's falcon *(Falco eleonorae)* and the Sooty falcon *(Falco concolor)*, which winter almost exclusively in Madagascar. Palearctic migrants number thirty, of which six make occasional appearances. Some migratory species of Charadriiformes remain on Madagascar in small numbers during the austral winter, although this corresponds to their nesting season in the Northern Hemisphere. The birds involved are mostly immatures and nonbreeding birds.

The Afro-tropical migrants consist of species breeding in Madagascar and wintering in Africa, as well as species nesting in Africa and coming to Madagascar outside the nesting period. Three species that nest in Madagascar migrate to eastern Africa: the Malagasy pond heron *(Ardeola idae)*, the Madagascar pratincole *(Glareola ocularis)*, and the Broad-billed

Figure 1. Composition of Resident Species

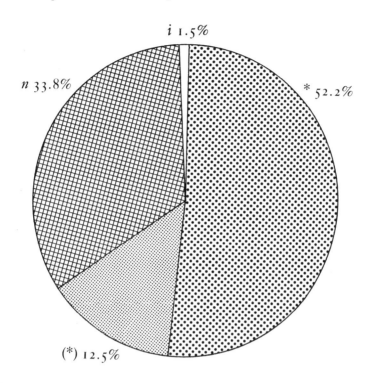

KEY:
* 52.2% endemic species
(*) 12.5% species endemic to the region
n 33.8% other species not endemic and not introduced
i 1.5% introduced species

roller *(Eurystomus glaucurus)*. Other species reproducing in Madagascar are suspected of traveling to Africa, but no hard evidence to this effect has been produced. This applies particularly to the African black swift *(Apus barbatus)* and the Madagascar bee-eater *(Merops superciliosus)*. Several species travel to Madagascar from Africa more or less regularly. A population of Lesser flamingos *(Phoeniconaias minor)* is permanently present in Madagascar but has never been observed to breed there. Also noted are the sporadic appearance of the Harlequin quail *(Coturnix delegorguei)* and the occasional

appearance of the Black-headed heron *(Ardea melanocephala)* and the Goliath heron *(Ardea goliath)*.

Regional Migrations

Regional migrations principally involve some marine species, including the Greater frigatebird *(Fregata minor)*, the Lesser frigatebird *(Fregata ariel)*, the Red-footed booby *(Sula sula)*, the Lesser noddy *(Anous tenuirostris)*, and the White tern *(Gygis alba)*, but also the Mascarene swiftlet *(Collocalia francica)*. These species reproduce on such islands near Madagascar as the Seychelles, Tromelin, Europa, Aldabra, Mauritius, and Réunion.

Internal Migrations

Little is known about internal migratory movements, because there are so few resident observers in Madagascar. The most apparent phenomenon is the departure from the High Plateau during the austral winter of most insectivorous species. This affects especially those species not exclusively confined to forest, such as the African black swift *(Apus barbatus)*, the Madagascar bee-eater *(Merops superciliosus)*, the Mascarene martin *(Phedina borbonica)*, the Madagascar wagtail *(Motacilla flaviventris)*, and the Madagascar brush-warbler *(Nesillas typica)*. The movements of forest species are much more difficult to ascertain, but if they are occurring they must be hampered considerably by the fragmentation of the forests. Each cleared area presents numerous forest species with an impassable barrier.

Analysis of the
Bird Community

The Bird Community Specific to the Eastern Region

The Eastern Malagasy Region contains four of the six floristic domains recognized in Madagascar. The Eastern and Central domains represent by far the greatest part of this biogeographic region, the Sambirano and High Mountain domains comprising much less territory. This region harbors the greatest diversity of resident avifauna. Of the 165 nesting species listed in the Eastern Region, 42 are found nowhere else. These 42 include many species belonging to endemic families, among them 1 of the 3 species of Mesitornithidae, 4 of the 5 species of Brachypteraciidae, 3 of the 4 species of Philepittidae, 3 of the 10 species of the endemic subfamily of the Couinae, and 4 of the 14 species of the Vangidae, a family endemic to the Madagascar Region. In addition, an entire family, the Timaliidae, as well as 13 genera, are represented only in this region. This wealth of avifauna is due to the exceptional floristic diversity found here.

The species bound to the wetlands environment and strictly local to the Eastern Malagasy Region number six: the Alaotra little grebe *(Tachybaptus rufolavatus)*, the Madagascar pochard *(Aythya innotata)*, the Madagascar rail *(Rallus madagascariensis)*, the Slender-billed flufftail *(Sarothrura watersi)*, the Madagascar snipe *(Gallinago macrodactyla)*, and the Brown-throated sand martin *(Riparia paludicola)*. The Alaotra little grebe and Madagascar pochard are limited to Alaotra Lake. They are threatened directly by the alteration of their environment for agricultural purposes, by intensive poaching and hunting, and, in the case of the grebe, by hybridization. Of the birds endemic to Madagascar, these two are the most threatened. The Madagascar pochard is on the verge of extinction. Other threats of more uncertain impact should also be kept in mind. These include the introduction of exotic plants *(Eichhornia crassipes)* and exotic herbivorous or carnivorous fish *(Tilapia* spp., *Micropterus salmonoides)*, as well as the use, over many years, of organochloride pesticides. The range of these two species includes no currently protected areas. The Madagascar rail is widely distributed in the Eastern Region. It has been listed in Strict Nature Reserve 12 of Marojejy, Manombo Special Reserve, and Analamazaotra Special Reserve. It has probably found refuge in other reserves, but its shyness makes it difficult to spot. The Slender-billed flufftail is a rare species with few recent data. It is known from four sites scattered between Andapa and Ranomafana, two of which are included in the reserve system. These are Analamazaotra Special Reserve and the proposed Ranomafana National Park. The marshes outside Antananarivo comprise the fourth site. The Madagascar snipe is widely distributed in the Eastern Region and has been observed in many reserves (Strict Nature Reserves 5 of Andringitra, 3 of Zahamena, and 4 of Tsaratanana and Analamazaotra Special Reserve). Its two principal threats are hunting pressure and the alteration of its habitat. The Brown-throated sand martin is a rather common species distributed over much of the Eastern Region. It faces no particular threat.

Thirty-six forest species, only one of which is not endemic, are restricted to the Eastern Malagasy Region. The Madagascar serpent-eagle *(Eutriorchis astur)* belongs to a monospecific genus. It is known only from ten specimens collected before 1935 in the Mangoro Valley west of Anosibe An'Ala, in the Sihanaka Forest near Fito, at Rogez, at Analamazaotra, and near Maroantsetra. Of these five sites, only Analamazaotra Special Reserve is protected. The forest sector of Anosibe An'Ala has already been greatly degraded, as has Rogez to a lesser extent. The Fito region adjoining the expanse of forest of Strict Nature Reserve 3 of Zahamena, that of Maraoantsetra with the forests of the Masoala Peninsula, of Makira, and of Antsahamena, and the expanse of forest surrounding Analamazaotra Special Reserve, which has recently been expanded and elevated to the status of national park, provide this large forest-dwelling predator with its best chances of survival.

The Brown mesite *(Mesitornis unicolor)* is one of the three species that make up the endemic family Mesitornithidae, which is distributed in the Eastern Region. Its shyness has kept knowledge of its range fragmentary, but it is known from many sightings, including four in the protected areas system. It was recently observed in Strict Nature Reserve 12 of Marojejy, on the Masoala Peninsula, in Ranomafana Forest, and in the Biosphere Reserve of Mananara, and it has been collected in Analamazaotra Special Reserve. The Madagascar fluff-tail *(Sarothrura insularis)* is distributed over the entire Eastern Region and commonly frequents degraded areas and secondary forests. The Madagascar blue pigeon *(Alectroenas madagascariensis)* is

distributed in all domains of the Eastern Region and is present in many protected areas. The Thick-billed cuckoo *(Cuculus audeberti)* is the only nonendemic species whose distribution is limited to the Eastern Region. Just five sightings—at Maroantsetra, Mananara, Rogez, and the Sihanaka Forest—are on record for this species, the most recent dating from 1922. The Snail-eating coua *(Coua delalandei)* is known only from thirteen specimens, all collected at Ile Sainte-Marie. The last capture dates from 1834. In view of the destruction of the original forests of Ile Sainte-Marie and the absence of any reported sighting for more than a century, the Snail-eating coua is considered extinct. The Red-breasted coua *(Coua serriana)* is located in the northern part of the region but is present in many of the protected areas. It has been observed in Strict Nature Reserve 12 of Marojejy, in Mananara Biosphere Reserve, and in Strict Nature Reserve 3 of Zahamena. The Red-fronted coua *(Coua reynaudii)* is the third Couinae limited to the region. It is widely distributed, present in many reserves and adaptable to secondary forests.

The Madagascar red owl *(Tyto soumagnei)* is a rare species on which few data are available, most pre-dating 1934. The only recent sighting, of one individual, took place near Analamazaotra in 1973. Specimens have been collected in Sihanaka Forest and at Analamazaotra, as well as near Toamasina and Antananarivo, but this information is unaccompanied by further details. Of these various sites, only Analamazaotra Special Reserve enjoys legally protected status.

The Short-legged ground-roller *(Brachypteracias leptosomus)* is distributed over almost the entire region, and its apparent rareness may stem only from its shyness. It has been observed in numerous reserves, including Strict Nature Reserve

12 of Marojejy, Analamazaotra Special Reserve, and the Forests of Ranomafana, Masoala, and Mananara Biosphere Reserve. The distribution of the Scaly ground-roller *(Brachypteracias squamiger)* is limited to the northern half of the region. It has been sighted in Strict Nature Reserve 12 of Marojejy, Mananara Biosphere Reserve, Strict Nature Reserve 3 of Zahamena, and Analamazaotra Special Reserve. It is the most localized of the rain forest ground-rollers. The Pitta-like ground-roller *(Atelornis pittoides)* is the family's most common and best distributed representative. It is known in many reserves, including National Park 1 of Montagne d'Ambre, Strict Nature Reserves 3 of Zahamena and 5 of Andringitra, Analamazaotra and Kalambatritra Special Reserves, Mananara Biosphere Reserve, and Forest of Ranomafana. This species is, moreover, the only member of its family to occur in the Sambirano Domain. The Rufous-headed ground-roller *(Atelornis crossleyi)* seems less common and its range does not extend into the Sambirano and Montagne d'Ambre areas. It has been observed in several reserves, including Strict Nature Reserves 4 of Tsaratanana, 12 of Marojejy, and 5 of Andringitra, Analamazaotra Special Reserve, and the Forest of Ranomafana.

The Velvet asity *(Philepitta castanea)* is distributed almost throughout the entire region, including the Sambirano Domain, where it is common. The Sunbird-asity *(Neodrepanis coruscans)* has the same distribution, except for the Sambirano Domain, which it does not seem to frequent. The Yellow-bellied sunbird-asity *(Neodrepanis hypoxantha)* is the rarest representative of this endemic family. It is known from thirteen specimens collected in the forests of the Central Domain. It was observed. however, near Analamazaotra Special Reserve in 1973 and in Strict Nature Reserve 5 of Andringitra in

1987. Since the only recent sightings took place within the protected areas system, it is hoped that this rare species will survive.

The Spectacled greenbul *(Phyllastrephus zosterops)* is widely distributed in the Eastern Region and occurs in numerous reserves. The Dusky greenbul *(Phyllastrephus tenebrosus)* is known only from eight specimens in three locations; one came from Analamazaotra Special Reserve. Since 1974 it has been seen again regularly in Analamazaotra Special Reserve and it was sighted in 1982 on the Masoala Peninsula. Of the four sites, only one enjoys legal protection status. It is one of the rarest and most vulnerable species of the Eastern Region. The rather less rare Gray-crowned greenbul *(Phyllastrephus cinereiceps)* is known from four sites, of which one, Strict Nature Reserve 4 of Tsaratanana, is a reserve.

The Forest rock-thrush *(Pseudocossyphus sharpei)* is found in all domains of the Eastern Region except the Sambirano. It is represented in numerous reserves, including those of the Central Domain, such as Ambohitantely Special Reserve, and those of the High Mountain Domain, such as Manjakatompo Forest Station in the Ankaratra Massif. The Brown emutail *(Dromaeocercus brunneus)* is widely distributed in the Central Domain. It is known in some reserves, among them Strict Nature Reserve 4 of Tsaratanana, Analamazaotra Special Reserve, and Ranomafana Forest. Its shyness has probably permitted it to go unnoticed in many sites. The Gray emutail *(Dromaeocercus seebohmi)* is distributed in the Eastern, Central, and High Mountain domains. Although often hard to detect, it has been sighted in Strict Nature Reserves 4 of Tsaratanana and 5 of Andringitra, Analamazaotra Special Reserve, Ranomafana Forest, and Manjakatompo Forest Station.

Rand's warbler *(Randia pseudozosterops)* escapes detection easily by spending most of its time in the canopy. Its range covers the Eastern and Central domains, which contain Strict Nature Reserve 3 of Zahamena, Analamazaotra Special Reserve, and Ranomafana Forest. It has also been observed in such major forest sites as the Masoala Peninsula and the Andapa region. The Dark newtonia *(Newtonia amphichroa)* is distributed all over the Eastern and Central domains, including National Park 1 of Montagne d'Ambre, Strict Nature Reserves 12 of Marojejy and 3 of Zahamena, Analamazaotra Special Reserve, and Ranomafana Forest. The Red-tailed newtonia *(Newtonia fanovanae)* is known only from a single specimen collected in 1931 at Fanovana in the Eastern Domain. If this is not just an aberrant form of *N. brunneicauda* or *N. amphichroa*, then the Red-tailed newtonia must certainly be a canopy species. The forest in the environs of Fanovana is very degraded, but the vegetation that once existed there is represented in Analamazaotra Special Reserve 20 kilometers away, at a 100-meter higher elevation. If the taxon is accepted as valid, it is Madagascar's rarest bird species. The Green jery *(Neomixis viridis)* is distributed in the Eastern and Central domains; it frequents numerous reserves. The Wedgetailed jery *(Hartertula flavoviridis)* is a little-known species distributed in the Eastern and Central domains. It has been sighted in Strict Nature Reserves 4 of Tsaratanana and 3 of Zahamena, Analamazaotra Special Reserve, and Ranomafana Forest. Ward's flycatcher *(Pseudobias wardi)* is common in the Eastern and Central domains. It has been sighted in many reserves of the Eastern Region.

The family Timaliidae of Madagascar includes three representatives strictly associated with the Eastern and Central domains. The White-throated oxylabes *(Oxylabes madagascariensis)* is also found in the Sambirano Domain. The Yellowbrowed oxylabes *(Crossleyia xanthophrys)* is the rarest of the three. Knowledge of its range is fragmentary, since it has been recorded only at four widely scattered sites in the region. These include three protected areas, Strict Nature Reserve 4 of Tsaratanana, Analamazaotra Special Reserve, and Ranomafana Forest, and one extensive forest area, the Sihanaka Forest. Crossley's babbler *(Mystacornis crossleyi)* is common and well represented within the protected areas system. Pollen's vanga *(Xenopirostris polleni)* is distributed in the Eastern and Central domains. It has been recorded in some reserves and, though rare, is not threatened. It is known from Strict Nature Reserve 12 of Marojejy, Analamazaotra Special Reserve, and Ranomafana Forest, as well as from such forested areas as those of the Masoala Peninsula and Sihanaka. The range of Bernier's vanga *(Oriolia bernieri)* is restricted to the north and center of the Eastern Domain. It is a fairly rare species but nevertheless well represented within the reserves system. It has been recorded in Strict Nature Reserves 12 of Marojejy and 3 of Zahamena. It also occupies the great tracts of forest of the Masoala Peninsula and the Sihanaka Forest. The Helmet vanga *(Euryceros prevostii)* is distributed over the same range as Bernier's vanga and has been observed in the same reserves. These two species, each belonging to a monospecific genus, are among the most localized of the Vangidae. Only Van Dam's vanga *(Xenopirostris damii)* and Lafresnaye's vanga *(Xenopirostris xenopirostris)* have an equally or more restricted range. The lowland eastern Madagascar rain forest that constitutes their favorite biotope is the type of vegetation most threatened with destruction by slash-and-burn cultivation and cutting for firewood. Of all the species of this family endemic to the Malagasy Region and occupying the Eastern Region, Bernier's vanga and the Helmet vanga are the most threatened.

The Nelicourvi weaver *(Ploceus nelicourvi)* is distributed in the Eastern, Central, and Sambirano domains. It is a common species, well represented in the protected areas system. The Forest fody *(Foudia omissa)* is found throughout the Eastern, Central, and High Mountain domains and is well represented in the reserves system. It is threatened by hybridization with *F. madagascariensis* (Madagascar red fody). This hybridization process was set in motion by the extensive fragmentation of the forest cover of the entire Eastern Region, which has encouraged the penetration and establishment of the Madagascar red fody at the edge of and sometimes well inside the forests that used to be the Forest fody's favored habitat. Keeping large tracts of forest intact is the only way to prevent this species from disappearing. The Tsaratanana and Marojejy mountain ranges, the forests of the Masoala Peninsula and Zahamena with the adjacent tract of the Sihanaka Forest, and the forested sector of Midongy to the north of Strict Nature Reserve 11 of Andohahela may still contain pure populations of the Forest fody.

The protected area system of the Eastern Malagasy Region consists of twenty-four sites, including three national parks (PN), seven strict nature reserves (RNI), and fourteen special reserves (RS). The creation of a national park is planned in the context of the biosphere reserve. See the accompanying list of sites (p. 20).

Outside the protected area system, few tracts of forest remain intact. Most affected is the Eastern Domain, deforested by slash-and-burn clearing for cultiva-

tion. The only large tracts left are those surrounding the Bay of Antongil and south of Mananara. The Central Domain has been largely transformed into grassland savanna. Large tracts remain on the Masoala Peninsula, in Sihanaka Forest, and in Midongy Forest. The Sambirano Domain has been much degraded outside the reserves. Some patches of forest on steep mountainsides as well as the western slopes of the Tsaratanana Massif remain intact. The High Mountain Domain is not extensive. It is well protected within the present system, but sites other than Marojejy (Tsaratanana, Ankaratra, and Andringitra) are no longer intact after being ravaged by fires. To safeguard the genetic diversity of the Eastern Malagasy Region and to protect the forest avifauna specific to that region, the remaining large tracts of forest must be safeguarded: those around Maroantsetra, the Masoala Peninsula, the forest situated between Strict Nature Reserve 3 of Zahamena and Analamazaotra Special Reserve, known as Sihanaka Forest, and the forest lying between Midongy and Strict Nature Reserve 11 of Andohahela. Lake habitats, which offer significant and often very specific genetic diversity, should also be included in the protected areas system. Alaotra Lake and the great marshes of the Central Domain are threatened by their transformation into rice paddies. This is also true of the Andapa basin marsh, the Didy marsh, and the Torotorofotsy marsh near Andasibe.

The six specific species of the Eastern Region that require wetland environment are all threatened by the lack of official protection of their natural habitat. The situation regarding the thirty-six forest species is more favorable, thanks to the reserves system now in place. The danger exists, however, that the viability of the system will be jeopardized in a few years if the unprotected forests that still link

| | | | Domains | | |
Reserves	Total Surface (ha)	East	Central	Sambirano	High Mountain
PN (National Park)					
Montagne d'Ambre	18,200		18,200		
Isalo	81,540		81,540		
Mantady	10,000		10,000		
RNI (Strict Nature Reserve)					
Zahamena	73,160	5,120	68,040		
Andohahela	63,100	6,300	56,800		
Marojejy	60,150	12,030	42,105		6,015
Tsaratanana	48,622	8,270	36,952		3,400
Andringitra	31,160	1,600	21,860		7,700
Betampona	2,228	2,228			
Lokobe	740			740	
RS (Special Reserve)					
Ambatovaky	60,050	51,050	9,000		
Marotandrano	42,200		42,200		
Manongarivo	35,250			35,250	
Anjanaharibe	32,100	1,600	30,500		
Kalambatritra	28,250		28,250		
Ambohijanahary	24,750		24,750		
Analamaitso	17,150		17,150		
Ambohitantely	5,600		5,600		
Manombo	5,020	5,020			
Forêt d'Ambre	4,810		4,810		
Pic d'Ivohibe	3,450				3,450
Analamazaotra	810		810		
Mangerivola	800	800			
Nosy Mangabe	520	520			
RB (Biosphere Reserve)					
Mananara	23,000	23,000			
TOTAL	672,660	117,538	498,567	35,990	20,565

the protected areas disappear. Of the thirty-six species, four are particularly vulnerable because they reside principally in the northeast of the island: the Red-breasted Coua, the Scaly ground-roller, Bernier's vanga, and the Helmet vanga. The Yellow-bellied sunbird-asity, if its predilection for the Central Domain forests is confirmed, is highly threatened, as is the subspecies of Forest rock-thrush *Pseudocossyphus sharpei salomonseni*, which inhabits the highland forests of the Central and High Mountain domains.

Species Specific to the Eastern Malagasy Region by Domain

	Domains			
Species	East	Central	Sambirano	High Mountain
Tachybaptus rufolavatus		X		
Aythya innotata		X		
Eutriorchis astur	X	X		
Mesitornis unicolor	X	X		
Rallus madagascariensis	X	X		
Sarothrura insularis	X	X	X	X
Sarothrura watersi		X		
Gallinago macrodactyla	X	X		X
Alectroenas madagascariensis	X	X	X	X
Cuculus audeberti	X	X		
Coua delalandei	X			
Coua serriana	X	X		
Coua reynaudii	X	X		
Tyto soumagnei		X		
Brachypteracias leptosomus	X	X		
Brachypteracias squamiger	X	X		
Atelornis pittoides	X	X	X	
Atelornis crossleyi	X	X		
Philepitta castanea	X	X	X	
Neodrepanis coruscans	X	X		
Neodrepanis hypoxantha		X		
Riparia paludicola	X	X	X	X
Phyllastrephus zosterops	X	X		
Phyllastrephus tenebrosus	X	X		
Phyllastrephus cinereiceps		X		
Pseudocossyphus sharpei	X	X		X
Dromaeocercus brunneus	X	X		
Dromaeocercus seebohmi		X		X
Randia pseudozosterops	X	X		
Newtonia amphichroa	X	X		
Newtonia fanovanae		X		
Neomixis viridis	X	X		
Hartertula flavoviridis		X		
Pseudobias wardi	X	X		
Oxylabes madagascariensis	X	X	X	
Crossleyia xanthophrys		X		
Mystacornis crossleyi	X	X		
Xenopirostris polleni	X	X		
Oriolia bernieri	X	X		
Euryceros prevostii	X	X		

Species Specific to the Eastern Malagasy Region by Domain (*continued*)

| | Domains | | | |
Species	East	Central	Sambirano	High Mountain
Ploceus nelicourvi	X	X	X	
Foudia omissa	X	X		X
Total of 42	32	41	7	7
Specific Species	1	10	0	0

The Bird Community Specific to the Western Region

The Western Region of Madagascar en-compasses two vegetation domains, the Western and the Southern. Twenty-five species occur there exclusively.

Avifauna Specific to the Western Domain

Of the 186 nonintroduced, nonmarine resident species listed for Madagascar, 145 frequent the Western Region. Of those, 131 frequent the Western Domain, 8 of them exclusively (not including 2 marine species). These birds comprise species bound to the lake habitat, such as the Pink-backed pelican *(Pelecanus rufescens)*, the African openbill stork *(Anastomus lamelligerus)*, the Sacred ibis *(Threskiornis aethiopicus)*, Bernier's teal *(Anas bernieri)*, the Madagascar fish eagle *(Haliaeetus vociferoides)*, and the Sakalava rail *(Amaurornis olivieri)*, as well as such forest species as the White-breasted mes-ite *(Mesitornis variegata)*, Appert's green-bul *(Phyllastrephus apperti)*, and Van Dam's vanga *(Xenopirostris damii)*.

Species tied to a lake environment are distributed throughout the lakes and rivers of the domain, except for Bernier's

teal, which is by and large local to Be-mamba and Masama lakes and to those of the Masoarivo region, and the Saka-lava rail, which is known only from a few specimens observed from three sites—Bemamba and Masama lakes, Kinkony Lake, and Nosy Ambositra on the Man-goky River. The Pink-backed Pelican bred sometime in Madagascar in the 1960s and has not been seen since then.

The forest species local to the Western Domain have limited or fragmented ranges. The White-breasted mesite is known only from four sites, two of them discovered only in 1987: the forest north of Morondava and the forests of Ankara-fantsika, Ankarana, and Analamera. Two of those four sites are Special Reserves and one is a Strict Nature Reserve, giving this species some legal protection. Ap-pert's greenbul is a recently discovered species with a range limited to two con-tiguous forests: Zombitse near Sakaraha and Vohibasia north of Sakaraha. Al-though they have "classified" but not protected status with respect to fauna, these two forests are highly threatened by illegal and irrational exploitation of their resources, frequent unlawful fires, cattle that stray into the understory and cause considerable damage, and intensive poaching. Originally known from a loca-tion in the northwest of Madagascar, Van

Dam's Vanga is now known in Ankarafantsika Forest, which is within Strict Nature Reserve 7, and in Analamera Special Reserve. Burning within the forest and illegal logging for firewood threaten this extremely local species.

The forested areas most essential to the avifauna of the Western Domain comprise Zombitse and Vohibasia forests, the tract of forest between Morondava and Belo-sur-Tsiribihina, the lake and forest complex of the Tsimembo and Bemamba-Masama region, the forest of Ankarafantsika, and the Bora, Ankarana, and Analamera forests, where the Western and Eastern regions meet. The forests of Zombitse; Ankazoabo, the north of Morondava, and the Tsimembo and Bemamba-Masama region are still without legal protection. Introducing such a system would ensure the protection of all known species in the Western Domain.

The avifauna of the wetlands of the Western Domain is highly diversified and its level of endemism fairly low. Some endemic species, however, are noted in taxonomic groups whose distribution is usually continental if not cosmopolitan. These include Humblot's heron *(Ardea humbloti)*, Bernier's teal, Meller's duck, and the Madagascar plover *(Charadrius thoracicus)*. The major sites for lake avifauna consist of such large rivers and their satellite lakes as the Mangoky, the Tsiribihina, the Manombolo, the Betsiboka, and the Mahajamba, as well as such lakes as Bemamba and Masama, Kinkony, Mitsinjo, Sahaka, and those of the Tsimembo region. These sites currently face transformation for agricultural purposes, exploitation of marsh plants, and irrational exploitation of fishery resources and poaching. The lakes and rivers are indirectly affected by deforestation, which, by causing intense erosion, is rapidly increasing the rate of sedimentation. The introduction of exotic

plant-eating or carnivorous species of fish *(Tilapia* spp., *Micropterus salmoides)* is undermining certain species of lake avifauna by altering the original characteristics of the environment and favoring certain opportunistic bird species. Thus the Madagascar little grebe *(Tachybaptus pelzelnii)* is declining in relation to the Little grebe *(T. ruficollis)*, a species better adapted to the changes. The proliferation of introduced exotic plant species, such as *Eichhornia crassipes* (Pontederiaceae), is rendering some lakes unsuitable for many bird species. This is particularly true for the White-backed duck *(Thalassornis leuconotus)*, whose population has declined most drastically of all the marsh species in recent decades. Raiding of nests, poaching, and hunting all contribute to the decline of aquatic avifauna. Colonial species are severely affected by the often systematic raids on their nests. Some, the Glossy ibis *(Plegadis falcinellus)*, for example, have become rare over roughly the past two decades because of the intensification of such practices, which are linked to population pressure. Poaching, which has been carried on for generations on a traditional scale, now shows signs of becoming a business. It is often practiced blindly without regard to avian reproductive cycles. In addition to reducing bird populations, it leads birds to avoid otherwise prime habitats, forcing them to move to other areas and try to establish breeding grounds in rice paddies, thereby causing damage that arouses the farmers' ire. This pattern involves ducks in particular. Hunting has declined in recent years because of a shortage of cartridges and as a consequence has become a pastime for the rich and for the international community. Hunting is not effectively controlled, hunters do not know which species are legally protected, and hunting activity commonly occurs out of season or within legally protected areas.

The protected areas system of the Western Domain contains 10 sites, of which 3 are Strict Nature Reserves (RNI) and 7 are Special Reserves (RS). Analabe Private Reserve is not included here, given its present degraded state and the bleak prospects for its future monitoring and management. The reserves are the following:

RNI (Strict Nature Reserve)
9 Tsingy de Bemaraha   152,000 ha
7 Ankarafantsika   60,520 ha
8 Tsingy de Namoroka   21,742 ha

RS (Special Reserve)
Analamera   34,700 ha
Kasijy   18,800 ha
Ankarana   18,200 ha
Bemarivo   11,570 ha
Maningozo   7,900 ha
Andranomena   6,420 ha
Bora   4,780 ha

TOTAL   336,652 ha

The current system does not ensure the protection of lake habitats (Bemamba, Masama, and Kinkony lakes and those of the Tsimembo region), which provide considerable genetic diversity. The species associated with those habitats enjoy no official protection, even though Hunting Reserve status has been conferred on some lakes, for this label does not entail any concrete measure for wildlife monitoring or management. Some forested areas straddling the two domains of protection or the two biogeographic regions, such as Zombitse and Vohibasia, enjoy no protection. No coastal forests or mangroves of this domain are protected. Nor is any sanctuary extended the sandy and rocky islands scattered throughout the Mozambique Channel along the Malagasy coast, which are often important nesting sites for marine avifauna. The rational harvesting that still took place a few years ago has given way to outright pillaging of rookeries and a consequent exodus of the remaining populations to areas farther from the coast. This process heightens the vulnerability of those species by increasing the populations concentrated at one location and decreasing the number of occupied sites. Granting official protection to the rocky islets of the northwest would safeguard almost the entire Madagascar fish-eagle population in the rocky island ecosystem.

Avifauna Specific to the Southern Domain

The avifauna of the Southern Domain has many affinities with that of the Western but is also unique in some ways. Eight species of the 118 recorded there occur in the Southern Domain exclusively, as do 3 marine species: the Wedge-tailed shearwater *(Puffinus pacificus)*, the Red-tailed tropicbird *(Phaethon rubricauda)*, and the Kelp gull *(Larus dominicanus)*. The Wedge-tailed shearwater breeds on the two rocky islets near Morombe, and the Red-tailed tropicbird nests on a sandy islet south of Toliara. None of those three islets enjoys reserve status. Although the Red-tailed tropicbird is protected naturally by a local taboo, the Wedge-tailed shearwater is not similarly privileged and its rookeries are regularly raided. The Kelp gull enjoys worldwide distribution south of the Tropic of Capricorn. On Madagascar it is not particularly threatened, although its population is small.

The eight species exclusive to the Southern Domain are all forest species, three—Subdesert mesite *(Monias benschi)*, the Running coua *(Coua cursor)*, and the Long-tailed ground-roller *(Uratelornis chimaera)*—terrestrial. The other five are Verreaux's Coua *(Coua verreauxi)*, the Littoral rock-thrush *(Pseudocossyphus im-*

erinus), the Thamnornis warbler *(Thamnornis chloropetoides)*, Archbold's newtonia *(Newtonia archboldi)*, and Lafresnaye's vanga *(Xenopirostris xenopirostris)*.

Among the forest species typical of the Southern Domain, two have a limited range: the Subdesert mesite and the Long-tailed ground-roller are distributed along a narrow strip of forest 200 kilometers long, paralleling the coast between the Mangoky River to the north and the Fiherenana to the south and bounded by uplands to the east. These two species, each belonging to a monospecific genus, are representatives of two of the three families endemic to Madagascar. The forest areas they occupy enjoy no legal protection. Their restricted range leaves them at the mercy of unfavorable ecological developments. Illicit and irrational exploitation of the forest in the quest for firewood has caused local destruction of their biotope. Uncontrolled pasture fires that spread inside the forest pose another threat. This problem has been noted around Ihotry Lake, where considerable populations of the two species reside. The Subdesert mesite and the Long-tailed ground-roller are also directly threatened by poaching and, near villages, by roving dogs and proliferating rat *(Rattus rattus)* populations.

The Running coua is distributed over the entire Southern Domain. It has been sighted in the various protected areas of the domain. Along with the Thamnoris warbler, Archbold's newtonia, and Verreaux's coua, the Running coua is one of the eight species exclusive to the Southern Domain that are not endangered. Verreaux's coua was originally known from the region between the Onilahy River and the Menarandra. Recent finds outside that area prove that its range formerly extended far to the east of the Menarandra, to Amboasary. Although its preferred biotope consists of vegetation

dominated by Didiereaceae and Euphorbiaceae, it makes do locally with secondary brush cover. The original biotope of this species is under little threat; the region is thinly populated and difficult of access, while the calcareous substratum underlying most of it is unsuited to agriculture. Degradation caused chiefly by goats has been noted around villages. Strict Nature Reserve 10 of Tsimanampetsotsa harbors a large population of Verreaux's coua; the forest, moreover, extends nearly 85 kilometers south of the reserve to Itampolo. Verreaux's coua has also been observed in Cap Sainte-Marie Special Reserve and Berenty Private Reserve.

The Littoral rock-thrush is local to the coastal strip between Morombe and Anony Lake. It is particularly fond of scrub on a sandy substratum. This is one of the most degraded habitats in the Southern Domain because it contains many villages. Clearing of land for agriculture, logging for firewood, and roaming cattle and goats, both of which are present in large numbers, all pose threats. This species has been observed in Cap Sainte-Marie Special Reserve along the western boundary of Strict Nature Reserve 10 of Tsimanampetsotsa, but its preferred biotope, the coastal scrub on a sandy substratum, enjoys no legal protection.

The Thamnornis warbler is the least threatened typical species of the Southern Domain. It is found from the borders of the Western Domain throughout the Southern Domain, parts of which, such as the Ihotry Lake area, harbor dense populations of it. It has been recorded in all the protected areas of the Southern Domain. Archbold's newtonia has the same range as the Thamnornis warbler. It is common in some locations, such as Ihotry Lake and Strict Nature Reserve 10 of Tsimanampetsotsa. Lafresnaye's vanga is distributed throughout the

Species Specific to the Western
Malagasy Region by Domain

| | *Domains* | |
Species	Western	Southern
Pelecanus rufescens	x	
Anastomus lamelligerus	x	
Threskiornis aethiopicus	x	
Phoenicopterus ruber	x	x
Anas bernieri	x	
Haliaeetus vociferoides	x	
Mesitornis variegata	x	
Monias benschi		x
Amaurornis olivieri	x	
Charadrius thoracicus	x	x
Pterocles personatus	x	x
Coua gigas	x	x
Coua cursor		x
Coua ruficeps	x	x
Coua verreauxi		x
Uratelornis chimaera		x
Phyllastrephus apperti	x	
Pseudocossyphus imerinus		x
Thamnornis chloropetoides		x
Newtonia archboldi		x
Xenopirostris xenopirostris		x
Xenopirostris damii	x	
Ploceus sakalava	x	x
Total of 23	15	14
Number of Specific Species	9	8

Figure 2. Distribution of Species by Domain

201 nesting species
− 3 introduced species
− 12 pelagic species (1 Procellaridae, 2 Phaethontidae, 1 Sulidae, 7 Sternidae, 1 Laridae)
186

  165 Number of species of the REGION or the DOMAIN
  42 Number of endemic species of the REGION or the DOMAIN

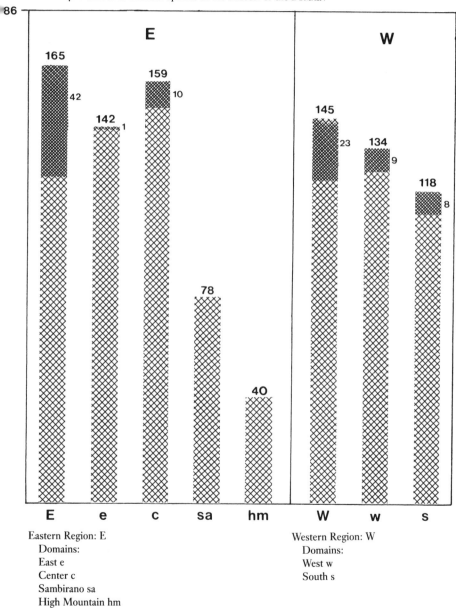

Eastern Region: E
 Domains:
 East e
 Center c
 Sambirano sa
 High Mountain hm

Western Region: W
 Domains:
 West w
 South s

Southern Domain, in original or slightly degraded habitats. It has been sighted in Strict Nature Reserves 10 of Tsimanampetsotsa and 11 of Andohahela, Beza-Mahafaly Special Reserve, and Berenty Private Reserve.

The reserves are the following:

RNI (Strict Nature Reserve)
10 Tsimanampetsotsa   43,200 ha
11 Andohahela (parcelle 2)   12,420 ha

RS (Special Reserve)
Beza-Mahafaly   600 ha
Cap Sainte-Marie   1,750 ha

RP (Private Reserve)
Berenty   265 ha

TOTAL   58,335 ha

The current system extends no protection to the coastal strip, the areas of scrub north of the Tropic of Capricorn, and patches of forest located at the borders of the Western Domain. Of the eight species exclusively local to the Southern Domain, two—the Subdesert mesite and the Long-tailed ground-roller—enjoy no protection within the protected areas system, and a third, the Littoral rock-thrush, is only partially protected.

Protected Areas System

Madagascar's system of protected areas was initiated in 1927. Since then it has grown to encompass 3 national parks, 11 strict nature reserves, and 23 special reserves. One private reserve and one biosphere reserve are also part of the system. The Ministry of Waters and Forests supervises all reserves, except those of Beza-Mahafaly and Ambohitantely, which it supervises jointly with the Ministry of Higher Education. These protected areas represent 1.8 percent of the total area of Madagascar. They provide fairly good protection of the various forest environments, except mangroves. In contrast, wetlands, coasts, and the rocky or sandy islands close to the coast enjoy no legal protection. Although access to the strict nature reserves is restricted to Ministry of Waters and Forests personnel and to authorized researchers, the national parks and some special reserves are open to visitors. Visitors must, however, obtain passes from Service de la Protection de la Nature, Direction des Eaux et Forêts, B.P. 243, Antananarivo (101), or, in some cases, from Services Provinciaux des Eaux et Forêts.

New reserves are planned for the near future in the form of the National Park of Masoala Peninsula and the National Park of Ranomafana.

Protected Areas
PN (National Parks)

1 Montagne d'Ambre   2 Isalo
3   Mantady

RNI (Strict Nature Reserves)

1 Betampona   3 Zahamena
4 Tsaratanana   5 Andringitra
6 Lokobe   7 Ankarafantsika
8 Namoroka   9 Bemaraha
10 Tsimanampetsotsa   11 Andohahela
12 Marojejy

RS (Special Reserves)

1 Analamera   2 Anjanaharibe
3 Ankarana   4 Ambre
5 Manongarivo   6 Kalambatritra

7 Manombo   8 Ivohibe
9 Ambohijanahary   10 Bemarivo
11 Bora   12 Kasijy
13 Maningozo   14 Marotandrano
15 Analamaitso   16 Ambatovaky
17 Mangerivola   18 Nosy Mangabe
19 Analamazaotra   20 Andranomena
21 Cap Sainte-Marie   22 Beza
                                    Mahafaly
23 Ambohitantely   24 Pic d'Ivohibe

RP (Private Reserve)

Berenty

RB (Biosphere Reserve)

Mananara

Map 3. Locations of Protected Areas

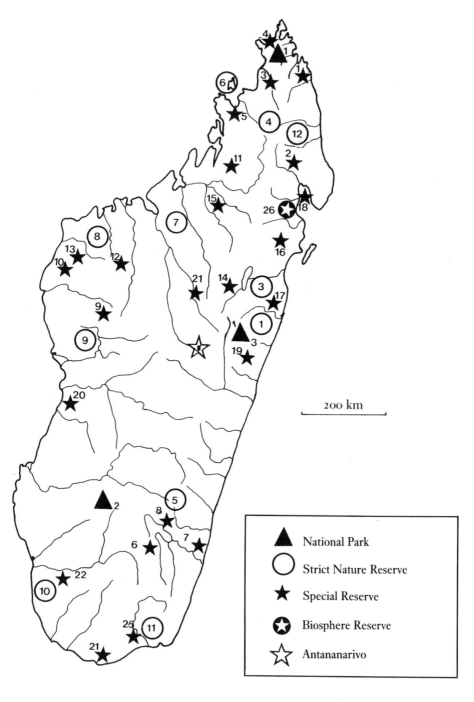

200 km

National Park

Strict Nature Reserve

Special Reserve

Biosphere Reserve

Antananarivo

Figure 3. Number of Species in Protected Areas

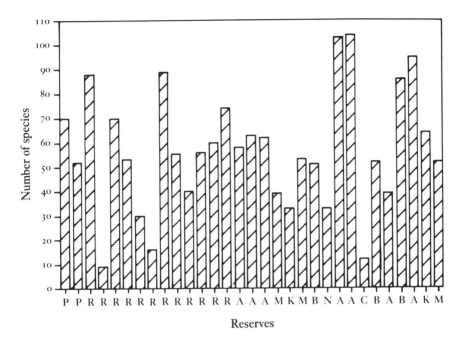

Recommended Sites for Observing the Avifauna of Madagascar

Whereas residents, be they Malagasy or foreign, have time to discover for themselves the many sites from which the avifauna of Madagascar can be observed, this approach will generally prove impractical for visitors. In the course of a three or four weeks' stay, however, visitors can go to three or four locations in different floristic domains and observe many of the endemic species that constitute the principal wealth of Malagasy avifauna.

The seventeen sites described below provide those staying in Madagascar for one month or less with a range of choices that are all fairly easy of access, with or without authorization. The strict nature reserves have been deliberately omitted, as access to them is contingent upon research approved by the Ministry of Waters and Forests.

Site 1

Name: Montagne d'Ambre National Park 1.

Forest type: Central Domain.

Accessibility: Year-round, but difficulties may be encountered along the last seven kilometers preceding arrival at the Roussettes Forest Station in the rainy season. The park is 39 km (1 hr) from Antsiranana and is connected by a good paved road to Ambohitra (Joffreville).

Authorization requirements: Yes. Issued by Service de la Protection de la Nature, Direction des Eaux et Forêts, BP 243, Antananarivo (101), or by Service Provincial des Eaux et Forêts, Antsiranana.

Accommodations: There are a number of hotels and shops at Antsiranana. Ambohitra has one hotel and a few shops. There is a shelter at the Roussettes Forest Station that can accommodate up to ten persons in rudimentary fashion. Permission to use it must be requested from the Service Provincial des Eaux et Forêts at Antsiranana.

Observation facilities: There is a good network of marked footpaths; their condition varies depending on the maintenance they receive at various seasons of the year.

Avifauna: Seventy-three species have been listed in the park to date. Star attractions are the endemic subspecies of the Forest rock-thrush and the Spectacled greenbul. The Madagascar crested ibis, the Pitta-like ground-roller, the Dark newtonia, and the White-throated oxylabes are commonly seen. The Madagascar fish-eagle and the Madagascar little grebe may be spotted on the lakes in the forest.

Site 2

Name: Isalo National Park 2.

Forest type: Central Domain.

Accessibility: Year-round. The park is easily accessible from Ranohira, which is situated 245 km (4 hrs) from Toliara and 90 km (1½ hrs) from Ihosy.

Authorization requirements: Yes. Issued by the Cantonnement Forestier de Ranohira.

Accommodations: Ranohira has a hotel that offers rudimentary amenities and some shops. Guides can be hired here.

Observations: There is an extensive network of footpaths, but the use of guides is strongly advised.

Avifauna: Fifty-five species have been

listed, including Benson's rock-thrush, whose range is almost wholly limited to this massif, as well as the Réunion harrier and the White-browed owl.

Site 3

Name: Ranomafana (national park under development).
Forest type: Central Domain.
Accessibility: Year-round. The site is easily reached from Fianarantsoa by a paved road (65 km, 2 hrs).
Authorization requirements: No permission will be necessary until the park is officially inaugurated. It is expected that from then on passes will be issued by Service de la Protection de la Nature, Direction des Eaux et Forêts, BP 243, Antananarivo (101), and/or by Service Provincial des Eaux et Forêts, Fianarantsoa.
Accommodations: Ranomafana has one hotel and some shops.
Observation facilities: There are no readily discernible footpaths. It is strongly recommended that visitors engage a guide at Ranomafana or Vohiparara. Many species can be very satisfactorily observed from the paved highway.
Avifauna: Ninety-eight species have been recorded in Ranomafana Forest, including numerous rare species such as Henst's goshawk, the Brown mesite, the Slender-billed flufftail, the Madagascar snipe, the Short-legged ground-roller, the Rufous-headed ground-roller, the Gray-crowned greenbul, the Brown emutail, the Gray emutail, the Yellow-browed oxylabes, and Pollen's vanga.

Site 4

Name: Analamazaotra Special Reserve (Périnet/Analamazaotra).
Forest type: Central Domain.
Accessibility: Year-round. The reserve can be reached from Antananarivo by road

(145 km, 3 hrs) or by train (5 hrs, one train daily).
Authorization requirements: Yes. Issued by Service de la Protection de la Nature, Direction des Eaux et Forêts, BP 243, Antananarivo (101).
Accommodations: There is a hotel not far (20 minutes' walk) from the Forest Station. Food is available at Périnet/Andasibe.
Observation facilities: There is a very good system of well-marked footpaths.
Avifauna: One hundred and ten species have been listed, including such rare ones as the Short-legged ground-roller, the Rufous-headed ground-roller, the Yellow-bellied sunbird-asity, the Wedge-tailed jery, and Pollen's vanga. Other very rare species, such as the Madagascar serpent-eagle, the Brown mesite, the Slender-billed flufftail, and the Madagascar red owl, have been collected in the past at Analamazaotra or its environs.

Site 5

Name: Beza-Mahafaly Special Reserve.
Forest type: Southern Domain.
Accessibility: Year-round. The reserve can be reached from Toliara (190 km, 5 hrs) by paved and dirt road.
Authorization requirements: Yes. Issued by the Etablissement d'Enseignement Supérieur des Sciences Agronomiques, Antananarivo (101), or by the Service de la Protection de la Nature, Direction des Eaux et Forêts, BP 243, Antananarivo (101).
Accommodations: There is a rudimentary hotel at Betioky, and camping is possible near the base camp of the reserve. There are some small shops at Betioky.
Observation facilities: There is a network of well-marked footpaths.
Avifauna: Sixty-three species have been listed, including some typical of the Southern Domain, such as the Run-

ning coua, the Thamnornis warbler, Archbold's newtonia, and Lafresnaye's vanga, as well as the Madagascar sparrowhawk, the Giant coua, and the White-browed owl.

Site 6
Name: Ambohitantely Special Reserve.
Forest type: Central Domain.
Accessibility: Year-round. The reserve can be reached from Antananarivo (120 km, 3 hrs) by paved road.
Authorization: Yes. Issued by the Service de la Protection de la Nature, Direction des Eaux et Forêts, BP 243, Antananarivo (101).
Accommodations: There are hotels and shops at Ankazobe (25 km, 30 mins). There is an overnight shelter in the reserve.
Observation facilities: There is a good network of footpaths in the patches of forest in the southern part of the reserve.
Avifauna: Forty-nine species have been listed, among them the Madagascar crested ibis, Meller's duck, the Bat hawk, the Pitta-like ground-roller, the Forest rock-thrush, and the Tylas vanga.

Site 7
Name: Berenty Private Reserve.
Forest type: Southern Domain.
Accessibility: Year-round. The reserve can be reached from Tolagnaro (80 km, 2 hrs) by paved road.
Authorization requirements: The Berenty Private Reserve is part of a hotel complex operated by Mr. J. de Heaulme, BP 37, Tolagnaro.
Accommodations: The hotel service relieves visitors of any concern of a logistic nature.
Observation facilities: There are numerous very well laid-out and marked footpaths, even suitable for nocturnal birding walks.

Avifauna: Ninety-eight species have been listed in this reserve, including several species exclusive to the Southern Domain, such as the Running coua, Verreaux's coua, the Thamnornis warbler, Archbold's newtonia, and Lafresnaye's vanga. Other species, such as Humblot's heron, the Madagascar sparrowhawk, the Madagascar sandgrouse, the Giant coua, the Malagasy scops-owl, the White-browed owl, and the Malagasy kingfisher, can be observed.

Site 8
Name: Ampijoroa Forest Station.
Forest type: Western Domain.
Accessibility: Year-round. The station can be reached from Antananarivo (425 km, 8 hrs) or from Mahajanga (120 km, 2½ hrs) by paved road.
Authorization requirements: Yes. Issued by Service de la Protection de la Nature, Direction des Eaux et Forêts, BP 243, Antananarivo (101).
Accommodations: There are no hotel facilities, but camping is permitted in the forest station. There are a few shops at Andranofasika (4 km).
Observation facilities: There is a very good network of footpaths in the station, which is directly adjacent to Strict Nature Reserve 7 of Ankarafantsika.
Avifauna: One hundred and three species have been listed, including some species exclusive to the Western Domain, such as the Madagascar fish-eagle, the White-breasted mesite, and Van Dam's vanga. Other unusual species, such as Coquerel's coua, the Red-capped coua, Schlegel's asity, the Rufous vanga, and the Sickle-billed vanga, have been observed.

Site 9
Name: Forest North of Toliara.
Forest type: Southern Domain.

Accessibility: Year-round. The section of the forest of interest here is on the unpaved road between Toliara and Morombe from the 28 km to the 32 km markers. Boundary markings have been set up along the road. The site can be reached in an hour from Toliara.

Authorization requirements: None required.

Accommodations: There are several hotels at Toliara and one at the 28 km point very near the forest.

Observation facilities: At the 32 km point, the subarid thorn scrub can be entered by a footpath leading east. Other small footpaths can be followed from the road. Some aquatic species can be observed at Andranobe Lake a few kilometers northeast of the 32 km point.

Avifauna: Seventy-nine species have been observed at this site, among them several local to the Southern Domain, such as the Subdesert mesite, the Running coua, the Long-tailed ground-roller, the Thamnornis warbler, Archbold's newtonia, and Lafresnaye's vanga. Other interesting species, such as the Banded kestrel, the Madagascar plover, and the Sickle-billed vanga, are easily observable.

Site 10

Name: Forest North of Morondava (Kirindy).

Forest type: Western Domain.

Accessibility: May be inaccessible for some weeks during the rainy season. The section of forest of interest is situated 30 km (45 mins) north of Morondova on the unpaved road leading to Belo-sur-Tsiribihina.

Authorization requirements: This forest sector is subject to selective logging, so that permission must be requested to enter and stay in the concession.

Apply to the Centre de Formation Professionnelle Forestière (CFPF) de Morondava.

Accommodations: There are several hotels and numerous shops at Morondava.

Observation facilities: There is a very good network of footpaths within the concession, and the road itself is excellent for purposes of observation, particularly of aquatic species.

Avifauna: One hundred and fourteen species have been listed at this site, including aquatic species frequenting temporary forest ponds, areas subject to flooding, the mangroves, and the coastal strip. The forest species include such unusual birds as Henst's goshawk, the Banded kestrel, and the White-breasted mesite, as well as more common ones, such as the Giant coua, the Red-capped coua, and the Sickle-billed vanga. The wetlands attract some interesting aquatic species, including the Madagascar little grebe, the African openbill stork, the Greater flamingo, the African pygmy goose, the Madagascar plover, and the Madagascar jacana.

Site 11

Name: Alaotra Lake.

Accessibility: Alaotra Lake lies at 160 km (4 hrs) from Moramanga by dirt road. Road access is almost impossible during the rainy season. There is daily rail service from Antananarivo via Moramanga (275 km, 9 hrs). The only rapid means of access is by air (airport at Ambatondrazaka).

Authorization requirements: None required.

Accommodations: There are several hotels and numerous shops at Ambatondrazaka.

Observation facilities: Observation is possible from the shore, particularly from the paved road northwest of the lake, but it is preferable to rent a canoe so that one can approach the islands of vegetation. The best lacustrine sites are near the villages of Ambatosoratra, east of the lake, and Anororo, west of the lake.

Avifauna: Eighty-eight species have been listed, including two rare species known only at this lake, the Alaotra little grebe and the Madagascar pochard. Other endemic or regionally endemic species observed here include Meller's duck, the Malagasy pond heron, Humblot's heron, the Réunion harrier, the Madagascar rail, and the Madagascar snipe. During the austral summer, Eleonora's falcon and the Sooty falcon are common sights.

Because tours can be organized around short stays in the principal cities of Madagascar, some urban sites suited to ornithological observation are listed below.

Site 12

Location: Antananarivo.

Site: Botanical and Zoological Park of Tsimbazaza.

Visitor information: Tsimbazaza Park is open to the public Thursday, Saturday, and Sunday afternoons. Located in the center of town, it is easy to find.

Avifauna: Fifty species have been observed in the park, which has long been known especially for the heronries around its ponds. Nine species of heron are found there, including the Malagasy pond heron, Black-crowned night-heron, and Great egret. Other species, such as the Darter, Glossy ibis, Madagascar cuckoo-falcon, Madagascar long-eared owl, Madagascar brush-warbler, and Common jery can also be observed here.

Site 13

Location: Antananarivo.

Site: Alarobia Lake.

Visitor information: The lake is the property of the Ranarivelo family. Visitors should conduct themselves in a manner appropriate to a bird sanctuary. The lake is in the Alarobia area, at the end of the Route des Hydrocarbures, and can be reached by taxi.

Avifauna: Forty-nine species have been listed around Lake Alarobia. The main attraction, as in the case of Tsimbazaza Park, is a heronry, which in this case supports seven species, including a fairly large population of the Malagasy pond heron. During the hunting season the lake may be frequented by more than a thousand ducks, mostly White-faced whistling duck and Red-billed teal. Four other species, including Meller's duck, can be found here as well. Other species, such as the African spoonbill and Red-knobbed coot, have occasionally been sighted. Several raptor species, such as the Madagascar cuckoo-falcon and Réunion harrier, have been recorded regularly, and less frequently reported species include the Banded kestrel and the Madagascar buzzard. During the austral summer, sightings of Eleonora's falcon and the Sooty falcon are common.

Site 14

Location: Antananarivo.

Site: Ivato Lake.

Visitor information: No authorization is necessary. The lake lies next to the runway of Ivato International Airport, which contains army facilities. It is therefore advisable not to approach the part of the lake near which the army camp is situated. The site is easily accessible on foot from the airport.

Avifauna: Forty species have been recorded here. The number of birds and the variety of species depend on the lake's water level. The lake attracts such regular visitors as the Gray heron, the Common greenshank, and the Gray-headed gull. It provides a resting-place for ducks, including Meller's duck and especially the Red-billed teal, which congregate in large numbers. A few nesting species, among them the Whiskered tern, are worth noting. Many domestic ducks feed on the lake.

Site 15

Location: Antsiranana.

Site: Ramena Beach.

Visitor information: Ramena Beach lies 18 km (20 mins) by paved road northeast of Antsiranana. It can be reached by taxi. The southern end of the beach ends in a long spit frequented by many shore species. Next to the spit is a small mangrove whose salt marshes teem with birds at low tide.

Avifauna: Twenty-seven species have been observed here, among them the Caspian tern, Roseate tern, Lesser-crested tern, and Greater-crested tern. A group of Crab plovers resides here year-round, and it is a good place to observe Palearctic shore birds. The White-tailed tropicbird and the Lesser frigatebird are regularly observed here.

Site 16

Location: Toliara.

Site: Coastal mud flats of Toliara.

Visitor information: The coastal mud flats of Toliara are in the middle of town, just north of the harbor. The best time for observation, which can be conducted from a stone jetty projecting into the sea, is at low tide.

Avifauna: Twenty-three species have been observed, among them a large number of Palearctic migrants, including the Greater sand plover and the Terek sandpiper. Tern roosts, primarily of Greater-crested terns, may be established on nearby coral reefs.

Site 17

Location: Tolagnaro.

Site: Port of Tolagnaro.

Visitor information: The port is in town.

Avifauna: This site permits easy observation of the Kelp gull, and such subantarctic or antarctic oceanic species as the Southern giant petrel may be encountered during the austral winter.

Birds at Recommended Observation Sites

								Sites									
Species	1	2	3	4	5	6	7	8	9	10	11	12	13	14	15	16	17
1 *Eudyptes chrysocome*																	
2 *Diomedea melanophrys*																	
3 *Macronectes giganteus*																	
4 *Daption capense*																	
5 *Pachyptila desolata*																	
6 *Pachyptila salvini*																	
7 *Puffinus pacificus*																	
8 *Oceanites oceanicus*																	

Species		Sites																
		1	2	3	4	5	6	7	8	9	10	11	12	13	14	15	16	17
9	*Fregetta tropica*																	
10	*Tachybaptus ruficollis*	•	•					•	•		•			•				
11	*Tachybaptus pelzelnii*	•		•				•	•		•	•	•					
12	*Tachybaptus rufolavatus*											•						
13	*Phaethon aetherus*																	
14	*Phaethon rubricauda*																	
15	*Phaethon lepturus*															•		
16	*Fregata minor*																	
17	*Fregata ariel*															•		
18	*Phalacrocorax africanus*	•		•				•	•		•		•	•	•			
19	*Anhinga melanogaster*	•							•			•	•	•				
20	*Sula sula*																	
21	*Sula leucogaster*																	
22	*Pelecanus rufescens*																	
23	*Ixobrychus minutus*										•	•						
24	*Nycticorax nycticorax*					•		•	•			•	•	•				
25	*Ardeola ralloides*	•			•			•	•			•	•	•				
26	*Ardeola idae*	•			•			•					•	•				
27	*Bubulcus ibis*		•	•	•	•		•	•		•	•	•	•				
28	*Butorides striatus*				•			•	•			•					•	•
29	*Egretta ardesiaca*					•		•				•	•					
30	*Egretta dimorpha*				•		•	•	•			•	•	•				•
31	*Casmerodius albus*				•			•	•			•	•	•				
32	*Ardea purpurea*			•	•			•	•			•	•	•				
33	*Ardea cinerea*							•	•			•	•	•				
34	*Ardea melanocephala*																	
35	*Ardea humbloti*				•			•	•			•						
36	*Ardea goliath*																	
37	*Scopus umbretta*	•	•	•	•	•				•								
38	*Mycteria ibis*										•	•						
39	*Anastomus lamelligerus*								•			•	•					
40	*Threskiornis aethiopicus*																	
41	*Plegadis falcinellus*											•	•					
42	*Lophotibis cristata*	•				•	•	•			•							
43	*Platalea alba*								•			•	•			•		
44	*Phoenicopterus ruber*										•							
45	*Phoeniconaias minor*										•							•
46	*Dendrocygna bicolor*							•				•		•				
47	*Dendrocygna viduata*			•				•	•			•	•	•				
48	*Sarkidiornis melanotos*						•		•	•				•				
49	*Nettapus auritus*										•							
50	*Anas bernieri*										•							
51	*Anas melleri*					•		•				•		•	•			

		Sites															
Species	1	2	3	4	5	6	7	8	9	10	11	12	13	14	15	16	17
52 Anas erythrorhyncha		•					•			•	•	•	•				
53 Anas hottentota											•		•				
54 Aythya innotata											•						
55 Thalassornis leuconotus										•	•						
56 Aviceda madagascariensis	•		•	•			•	•				•	•				
57 Machaeramphus alcinus						•	•	•									
58 Milvus migrans	•	•	•	•	•	•	•	•	•	•	•	•	•	•	•	•	•
59 Haliaeetus vociferoides	•							•		•							
60 Eutriorchis astur			•														
61 Polyboroides radiatus		•	•	•	•	•	•	•	•		•		•				
62 Circus maillardi	•										•		•				
63 Accipiter henstii			•	•					•								
64 Accipiter madagascariensis	•		•	•	•		•	•			•						
65 Accipiter francesii	•		•	•	•	•	•	•	•		•						
66 Buteo brachypterus	•	•	•	•	•	•	•	•	•		•		•				
67 Falco newtoni	•	•	•			•	•	•	•		•	•	•	•			•
68 Falco zoniventris			•				•	•	•		•			•			
69 Falco eleonorae	•						•				•	•	•				
70 Falco concolor	•	•	•	•			•				•	•	•	•		•	
71 Falco peregrinus							•					•					
72 Margaroperdix madagascarensis	•	•			•	•	•	•	•								
73 Coturnix coturnix	•						•	•			•			•			
74 Corturnix delegorguei								•									
75 Numida meleagris	•	•	•	•	•		•	•	•								
76 Mesitornis variegata								•		•							
77 Mesitornis unicolor			•	•													
78 Monias benschi								•									
79 Turnix nigricollis		•				•	•	•	•	•	•						
80 Rallus madagascariensis											•						
81 Dryolimnas cuvieri	•	•	•	•	•		•	•		•	•		•	•			
82 Canirallus kioloides			•	•													
83 Porzana pusilla								•			•						
84 Amaurornis olivieri																	
85 Sarothrura insularis	•		•	•		•				•							
86 Sarothrura watersi			•	•													
87 Gallinula chloropus		•		•			•	•	•	•	•		•	•	•		
88 Porphyrula alleni							•				•						
89 Porphyrio porphyrio						•				•	•						
90 Fulica cristata								•			•		•	•			
91 Actophilornis albinucha							•				•						
92 Rostratula benghalensis							•				•						
93 Himantopus himantopus							•			•	•						

Species	\<th colspan=17\>Sites																
	1	2	3	4	5	6	7	8	9	10	11	12	13	14	15	16	17
94 Recurvirostra avosetta																	
95 Dromas ardeola										•					•		
96 Glareola ocularis			•	•		•				•	•						
97 Pluvialis fulva																	
98 Pluvialis squatarola															•	•	
99 Charadrius hiaticula										•					•	•	
100 Charadrius thoracicus										•							
101 Charadrius pecuarius							•	•	•	•	•			•	•	•	
102 Charadrius tricollaris		•					•	•	•	•	•			•	•	•	
103 Charadrius leschenaultii										•					•	•	
104 Charadrius marginatus								•	•	•					•	•	
105 Limosa limosa																•	
106 Limosa lapponica										•					•	•	
107 Numenius phaeopus							•		•	•					•	•	
108 Numenius arquata																	
109 Tringa stagnatilis																	
110 Tringa nebularia							•	•		•	•				•	•	•
111 Tringa ochropus																	
112 Tringa glareola																	
113 Xenus cinereus										•					•	•	
114 Actitis hypoleucos						•	•			•	•			•	•	•	•
115 Arenaria interpres										•					•	•	
116 Gallinago macrodactyla			•	•						•							
117 Calidris alba										•					•	•	
118 Calidris minuta								•									
119 Calidris ferruginea							•		•	•					•	•	•
120 Philomachus pugnax																	
121 Catharacta antarctica																	
122 Stercorarius parasiticus																	
123 Larus dominicanus						•											•
124 Larus cirrocephalus								•			•		•				
125 Chlidonias hybridus											•		•				
126 Chlidonias leucopterus																	
127 Chlidonias niger																	
128 Sterna nilotica																	
129 Sterna caspia						•	•	•							•	•	
130 Sterna hirundo																	
131 Sterna dougallii										•					•		
132 Sterna anaethetus																	
133 Sterna fuscata																	
134 Sterna saundersi																•	
135 Sterna bergii															•	•	
136 Sterna bengalensis															•	•	

Species	1	2	3	4	5	6	7	8	9	10	11	12	13	14	15	16	17
137 Anous stolidus																	
138 Anous tenuirostris																	
139 Gygis alba																	
140 Pterocles personatus		•				•		•	•	•							
141 Columba livia																	
142 Streptopelia picturata	•	•		•	•			•	•		•	•					
143 Oena capensis	•	•			•			•	•	•	•						
144 Treron australis	•			•	•	•			•	•	•						
145 Alectroenas madagascariensis	•			•	•		•										
146 Coracopsis vasa	•			•	•	•		•	•	•							
147 Coracopsis nigra	•	•		•	•	•	•	•	•	•	•	•					
148 Agapornis cana		•			•		•	•				•					
149 Cuculus audeberti																	
150 Cuculus rochii	•	•	•	•	•	•	•	•	•	•	•			•			•
151 Coua delalandei																	
152 Coua gigas					•		•		•	•							
153 Coua coquereli							•		•								
154 Coua serriana																	
155 Coua reynaudii			•	•													
156 Coua cursor					•		•		•								
157 Coua ruficeps					•		•	•	•								
158 Coua cristata	•	•	•	•	•			•	•	•							
159 Coua verreauxi							•										
160 Coua caerulea			•	•													
161 Centropus toulou	•	•		•	•	•		•	•		•	•	•	•		•	•
162 Tyto soumagnei				•													
163 Tyto alba			•	•		•	•				•	•		•	•		
164 Otus rutilus	•		•	•	•	•	•	•	•		•		•				
165 Ninox superciliaris		•			•		•		•	•							
166 Asio madagascariensis	•		•	•										•			
167 Asio capensis											•		•				
168 Caprimulgus madagascariensis	•	•	•	•	•	•	•		•		•		•	•			
169 Caprimulgus enarratus	•		•	•													
170 Collocalia francica																	
171 Zoonavena grandidieri	•	•	•	•	•		•	•	•		•						
172 Cypsiurus parvus		•	•	•			•			•	•					•	
173 Apus melba	•		•	•		•				•							
174 Apus barbatus	•	•			•	•		•		•	•	•	•	•			
175 Corythornis vintsioides	•	•	•	•	•	•	•	•	•	•	•	•	•	•		•	•
176 Ispidina madagascariensis	•		•	•		•	•	•									
177 Merops superciliosus	•	•	•	•	•	•	•	•	•	•	•	•	•	•			

Species	Sites																
	1	2	3	4	5	6	7	8	9	10	11	12	13	14	15	16	17
178 Eurystomus glaucurus	•	•	•	•	•	•	•	•	•	•	•	•					
179 Brachypteracias leptosomus			•	•													
180 Brachypteracias squamiger																	
181 Atelornis pittoides	•		•	•		•											
182 Atelornis crossleyi			•	•													
183 Uratelornis chimaera									•								
184 Leptosomus discolor	•	•	•	•	•	•	•	•	•	•	•	•	•	•			
185 Upupa epops	•	•			•		•	•	•	•	•		•				
186 Philepitta castanea			•	•													
187 Philepitta schlegeli									•								
188 Neodrepanis coruscans			•	•													
189 Neodrepanis hypoxantha				•													
190 Mirafra hova	•	•				•	•	•	•	•	•				•		
191 Riparia paludicola			•	•		•					•			•			
192 Riparia riparia																	
193 Phedina borbonica	•	•	•	•			•	•		•	•	•	•				•
194 Hirundo rustica																	
195 Motacilla flaviventris	•	•	•	•					•	•		•	•	•			
196 Coracina cinerea	•	•	•	•	•	•	•	•	•	•							
197 Phyllastrephus madagascariensis	•		•	•		•		•	•								
198 Phyllastrephus zosterops	•		•	•													
199 Phyllastrephus apperti																	
200 Phyllastrephus tenebrosus				•													
201 Phyllastrephus cinereiceps			•														
202 Hypsipetes madagascariensis	•	•	•	•	•	•	•	•	•	•	•	•	•				
203 Copsychus albospecularis	•	•	•	•	•	•	•	•	•								
204 Saxicola torquata	•	•	•	•		•	•	•	•					•	•		
205 Pseudocossyphus sharpei	•		•	•		•											
206 Pseudocossyphus imerinus																	
207 Pseudocossyphus bensoni		•															
208 Acrocephalus newtoni			•	•			•	•					•	•			
209 Nesillas typica	•	•	•	•					•				•	•	•		
210 Thamnornis chloropetoides					•		•		•								
211 Cisticola cherina	•		•	•	•		•	•	•	•	•	•		•	•		
212 Dromaeocercus brunneus			•	•													
213 Dromaeocercus seebohmi			•														
214 Randia pseudozosterops			•	•													
215 Newtonia amphichroa	•		•	•													
216 Newtonia brunneicauda	•	•	•	•	•	•	•	•	•	•							
217 Newtonia archboldi					•		•		•								
218 Newtonia fanovanae																	

Species	Sites																
	1	2	3	4	5	6	7	8	9	10	11	12	13	14	15	16	17
219 Neomixis tenella	•	•		•	•		•	•	•	•				•	•		
220 Neomixis viridis				•	•												
221 Neomixis striatigula				•	•	•		•	•	•							
222 Hartertula flavoviridis				•	•												
223 Pseudobias wardi				•	•												
224 Terpsiphone mutata	•	•		•	•	•	•	•	•	•	•	•	•				
225 Oxylabes madagascariensis	•			•	•												
226 Crossleyia xanthophrys				•													
227 Mystacornis crossleyi				•	•												
228 Nectarinia souimanga	•	•		•	•	•	•	•	•	•	•			•	•		
229 Nectarinia notata	•			•	•			•	•	•	•						
230 Zosterops maderaspatana	•			•	•	•	•	•	•	•	•			•	•		
231 Oriolus oriolus																	
232 Calicalicus madagascariensis	•			•	•		•	•	•	•							
233 Schetba rufa				•	•			•	•								
234 Vanga curvirostris	•			•	•			•	•	•							
235 Xenopirostris xenopirostris						•		•		•							
236 Xenopirostris damii								•									
237 Xenopirostris polleni				•	•												
238 Falculea palliata						•		•	•	•	•						
239 Leptopterus viridis		•	•	•	•			•	•	•	•						
240 Leptopterus chabert	•	•		•	•	•		•	•	•	•						
241 Cyanolanius madagascariensis	•			•	•			•	•								
242 Oriolia bernieri																	
243 Euryceros prevostii					•												
244 Hypositta corallirostris					•												
245 Tylas eduardi				•	•		•										
246 Dicrurus forficatus	•	•		•	•	•	•	•	•	•			•				
247 Corvus albus	•	•		•	•	•	•	•	•	•	•	•				•	
248 Hartlaubius auratus	•			•	•		•										
249 Acridotheres tristis				•	•			•					•				
250 Passer domesticus																	
251 Ploceus nelicourvi	•			•	•												
252 Ploceus sakalava						•		•	•	•	•						
253 Foudia madagascariensis		•	•	•	•	•	•	•	•	•	•	•	•	•	•		
254 Foudia omissa				•	•												
255 Lonchura nana	•	•		•			•	•	•			•	•	•	•		
256 Estrilda astrild																	

Map 4. The Western Indian Ocean around Madagascar

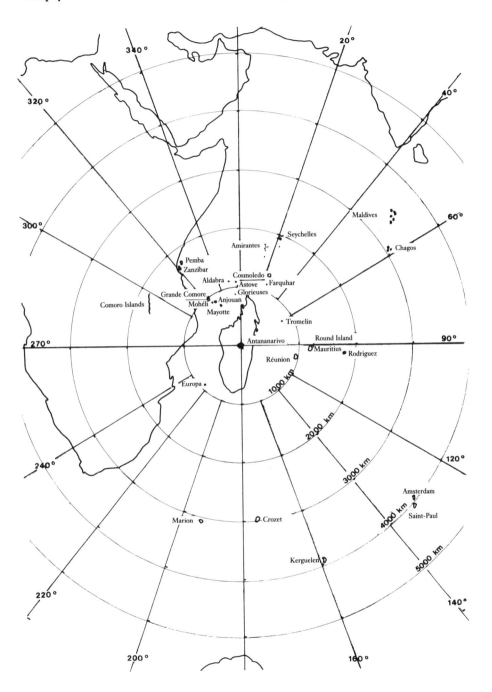

Potential Species in the Vicinity of the Coast of Madagascar

A program of regular, frequent ornithological investigation has been conducted for many years by scientists of the French southern and antarctic territories, in the southern Indian Ocean. Data collected especially on the Réunion-Amsterdam island and Réunion-Crozet island transects indicate that some twenty oceanic species can be considered potentially present near the coast of Madagascar although never yet observed. This is explained by the very small number of resident ornithologists and the limited time they spend observing the marine environment. The proposed list of potential species is speculative and should not be regarded as exhaustive.

The species classified as potential are those that have been observed north of Lat. 32°S, the southernmost point of Madagascar (Cap Sainte-Marie) being on Lat. 25°37′S. The species listed north of Lat. 25°S, such as *Macronectes halli* and *Puffinus carneipes*, which have already been observed at the Mascarene Islands, are briefly described. The period they frequent the zone is mentioned for each. *Sula dactylatra* and *Sterna sumatrana* are added to the list in view of the proximity of some of their breeding grounds (Cosmoledo, Aldabra) to Madagascar.

Two shorebirds, *Charadrius dubius* and *C. mongolus*, considered regular winter visitors to the Seychelles, are also included on the list of potential species.

Potential Species

(Data obtained during observations carried out south of Réunion)
Diomedea exulans (Lat. 25°S, Sept.) regular movement
Diomedea cauta cauta (Lat. 28°S, July–Aug.) regular movement
Diomedea chlororhynchos (Lat. 26°S, June–Sept.) regular movement
Phoebetria fusca (Lat. 28°S, June–July) regular movement
Macronectes halli (Lat. 29°S, July–Sept.) regular movement
Pterodroma macroptera (Lat. 23°S, Sept.) regular movement
Pterodroma aterrima (Lat. 21°S) species known only from Réunion
Pterodroma arminjoniana species breeds on Round Island near Mauritius
Pterodroma mollis (Lat. 22°S, July–Sept.) regular movement
Pterodroma baraui (Lat. 21°S, Sept.) regular movement
Pachyptila belcheri (Lat. 26°S, July–Sept.) regular movement
Pachyptila turtur (Lat. 26°S, July–Aug.) regular movement
Bulweria bulwerii (Lat. 21°S) regular movement
Bulweria fallax (Lat. 21°S, Nov.–Feb.) regular movement
Procellaria aequinoctialis (Lat. 28°S, Apr.) regular movement
Puffinus carneipes (Lat. 29°S, Dec.–Mar.) regular movement
Puffinus griseus (Lat. 32°S, Apr.) regular movement
Puffinus lherminieri breeds on Réunion *(P. l. bailloni)* and the Comoros *(P. l. temptator)*

Fregetta grallaria (Lat. 23°S, Apr.) regular movement
Oceanodroma matsudairae regularly observed in the Seychelles
Sula dactylatra breeds at Cosmoledo
Sterna sumatrana breeds at Aldabra, Chagos, and Amirantes
Charadrius dubius winters regularly in the Seychelles
Charadrius mongolus winters regularly in the Seychelles

Identification of Potential Species

The observation and identification of oceanic species, particularly those of the Procellariiformes, is not easy. Considerable distance often separates bird and observer, the bird seldom remains visible for long, and observing conditions are frequently poor. Following some simple criteria, however, may facilitate identification. Those are the size of the bird under observation, which must be compared with those of an oceanic species well known to the observer, and the color pattern (single color, two colors, white belly, white rump). Other characteristics, including general appearance or behavioral traits, may also help to determine the species. The identification key that follows should enable the observer to recognize the potential oceanic species included on the list. The key covers oceanic species observed on Madagascar. Vincent Bretagnolle, who has had much experience identifying oceanic species on missions conducted in the French southern and antarctic territories, has created the identification key.

Identification Key

1. Great wingspan (more than 2 m); slow, steady flight with almost no wingbeats
    1.1. Generally dark coloring
        1.1.1. Long, thin bill, slender body, sometimes with white feathers on the wing: *Diomedea exulans* (immature)
        1.1.2. Narrow, angled wings; long, wedge-shaped tail: *Phoebetria fusca*
        1.1.3. Stocky body, stout bill, head sometimes white: *Macronectes* spp.
    1.2. White coloring with only the remiges black: *Diomedea exulans* (adult)
    1.3. Two-color pattern, upperparts black and underparts white, undersides of wings edged with black
        1.3.1. Very narrow black edge: *Diomedea cauta*
        1.3.2. Wide leading edge, narrow trailing edge: *Diomedea chlororhynchos*
        1.3.3. Very wide edge: *Diomedea melanophrys*

2. Average or small wingspan, swift or fluttering flight occasionally punctuated by wingbeats
    2.1. Speckled black and white: *Daption capense*
    2.2. Fairly large, all-dark plumage; bird circles low in flight using only occasional wingbeats: *Procellaria aecquinoctialis*
    2.3. All-black or two-tone plumage, swift and powerful flight with or without wingbeats
        2.3.1. Plumage entirely dark
            2.3.1.1. Rather long tail with rounded end; face and chin gray in close view: *Pterodroma macroptera*

2.3.1.2. Rather short tail with squared end, dark head: *Pterodroma aterrima*

2.3.2. Two-tone plumage (white belly or white spots on wings, dark upperparts)

2.3.2.1. Very swift flight, medium size, white body contrasts with gray wings: *Pterodroma mollis*

2.3.2.2. Powerful, heavy flight, rather large size, underside of wing almost entirely white: *Pterodroma baraui*

2.3.2.3. Fairly large size, underside of wing marked with white diamond in both color morphs: *Pterodroma arminjoniana*

2.4. Flight at water level, rather direct with frequent wingbeats

2.4.1. Small size, blue-gray coloring, black W on upper side of wings, hesitant flight: *Pachyptila* spp.

2.4.2. Small size, two-tone (dark above, white below): *Puffinus lherminieri*

2.4.3. Small size, entirely dark plumage, wings sharply angled, long pointed tail: *Bulweria* spp.

2.4.4. Medium size, very dark plumage, long bill

2.4.4.1. Narrow wings partly white or gray underneath, stocky body and small head: *Puffinus griseus*

2.4.4.2. Long, narrow wings, long, wedge-shaped tail: *Puffinus pacificus*

2.4.4.3. Long, rather wide wings, short tail, stocky silhouette: *Puffinus carneipes*

2.5. Fluttering flight, very small size

2.5.1. Entirely black plumage: *Oceanodroma matsudairae*

2.5.2. Entirely black plumage except for white rump: *Oceanite oceanicus*

2.5.3. Black plumage except for white rump and belly, which may be crossed by a black bar: *Fregetta* spp.

Brief Guide to the Identification of Potential Species

Northern Giant Petrel

Macronectes halli Mathews, 1912

DESCRIPTION: Length 81–94 cm, wingspan 180–200 cm.
Adult. Sexes similar. Species is distinguished from the Southern giant petrel only by the coloring of the bill, which is yellow with a reddish-orange hook. This field mark can also be used in identifying immature individuals. There is no white morph in this species.

DISTRIBUTION: Breeds in subantarctic islands. The breeding area nearest Mad-agascar is Crozet. It has occasionally been observed near Réunion.

Great-winged Petrel

Pterodroma macroptera (Smith, 1840)

DESCRIPTION: Length 41 cm, wingspan 97 cm.
Adult. Sexes similar. Species is large for its genus. Coloring is dark brown all over, except for a lighter area around the bill. The Great-winged petrel is difficult to distinguish from the Mascarene petrel but differs by its larger size and short, rounded tail. Observed from nearby, the bill appears less massive.

DISTRIBUTION: Breeds in the subantarctic islands. Crozet is the nesting site nearest Madagascar.

Mascarene Petrel

Pterodroma (Pseudobulweria) aterrima
(Bonaparte, 1857)

DESCRIPTION: Length 33 cm, wingspan 88 cm.
Adult. Sexes similar. Entirely black
plumage, small size for its genus, stoutly
built with long wings and squared tail.
Difficult to distinguish from the Great-
winged petrel, but differs by its smaller
size and longer, squared tail.

DISTRIBUTION: Only currently known
breeding site is Réunion. Dispersion of
species outside breeding period not
known.

Herald Petrel

Ptreodroma arminjoniana
(Giglioli and Salvadori, 18)
Dark Morph Illustrated

DESCRIPTION: Length 37 cm, wingspan 95 cm.
Adult. Sexes similar. Polymorphic species
that always presents white diamonds on
the underside of the wings at the base of
the primary remiges regardless of the
plumage morph.

DISTRIBUTION: A nesting site exists
near Madagascar, on Round Island, near
Mauritius. Most individuals in the colony, which consists of about 150 pairs,
are dark morphs.

Soft-plumaged Petrel

Pterodroma mollis (Gould, 1844)

DESCRIPTION: Length 34 cm, wingspan 89 cm.
Adult. Sexes similar. Small size for its
genus, with white belly contrasting with
gray underside of wings, which seem
black at a distance. Very swift flight. Differs from Barau's petrel by dark underside of wings and bigger size.

DISTRIBUTION: Breeds in the subantarctic islands. Crozet and Amsterdam,
where it is represented by the subspecies
P. m. dubia, provide the breeding sites
nearest Madagascar.

Bulwer's Petrel

Bulweria bulweri
(Jardine and Selby, 1828)
Not Illustrated

DESCRIPTION: Length 26 cm, wingspan 67 cm.
Adult. Sexes similar. Plumage entirely
dark brown, wings long, pointed, and
usually angled. Long, wedge-shaped tail
is often held tight and generally appears
pointed. Flight is very choppy, with frequent changes of direction. Species is
very similar to Jouanin's petrel but can be
distinguished by its smaller size, thinner
bill, and pale upper wing coverts.

DISTRIBUTION: Distribution of this
species in the Indian Ocean was noted
only recently, and a breeding site has
been discovered on Mauritius.

Jouanin's Petrel

Bulweria fallax Jouanin, 1955

DESCRIPTION: Length 31 cm, wingspan 79 cm.
Adult. Sexes similar. Plumage entirely
dark brown, wings long, pointed, and
usually angled. Very long, wedge-shaped
tail is held tight and generally appears
pointed. Flight is choppy, with frequent
changes of direction. Species is very
similar to Bulwer's petrel but can be distinguished by its larger size, stouter bill
and the absence of pale markings on the
upper wing coverts.

DISTRIBUTION: Appears limited to the
w Indian Ocean. No nesting site known
at present. Suspected to breed in the islands of the Gulf of Oman.

Audubon's Shearwater

Puffinus lherminieri (Lesson, 1839)

DESCRIPTION: Length 30 cm, wingspan 69 cm.
Adult. Sexes similar. Small shearwater with brown upperparts contrasting with light underparts. Flight typical of shearwaters, rapid wing beats alternating with brief glides.

DISTRIBUTION: Breeds on Réunion, where it is represented by the subspecies *P. l. bailloni*, and on the Comoros, where it is represented by the recently described subspecies *P. l. temptator.*

White-bellied Storm Petrel

Fregetta grallaria (Vieillot, 1817)

DESCRIPTION: Length 20 cm, wingspan 46 cm.
Adult. Sexes similar. Identical to the Black-bellied storm petrel, except for the absence of a black abdominal median bar.

DISTRIBUTION: The nesting site nearest Madagascar is on the Ile de Saint-Paul, where it breeds in small numbers.

Matsudaira's Storm Petrel

Oceanodroma matsudairae Kuroda, 1922

DESCRIPTION: Length 25 cm, wingspan 56 cm.
Adult. Sexes similar. Rather large petrel characterized by entirely dark plumage and long, forked tail.

DISTRIBUTION: Breeds in Japan and regularly frequents the w Indian Ocean. Regularly observed in the Seychelles.

Masked Booby

Sula dactylatra Lesson, 1831

DESCRIPTION: Length 86 cm, wingspan 152 cm.
Adult. Sexes similar. Large black-and-white booby. Differs from the Red-footed booby by its much larger size, black face, and yellow bill. Immatures closely resemble the Brown booby but are distinguishable by their white collar and the white stripe running along the leading edge on the lower side of the wings.

DISTRIBUTION: Breeds on Round Island, on Saint-Brandon, and in the Seychelles, which constitute the nesting sites nearest Madagascar, where the species is represented by the subspecies *S. d. melanops.*

Black-naped Tern

Sterna sumatrana Raffles, 1822

DESCRIPTION: Length 31 cm, wingspan 61 cm.
Adult. Sexes similar. Small tern with a long, forked tail and almost entirely white plumage, except the black back of the head, a black bar starting behind the eye, and the black outer edge of the first primary remige.

DISTRIBUTION: Breeds at Aldabra, the nesting site nearest Madagascar.

Little Ringed Plover

Charadrius dubius Scopoli, 1786

DESCRIPTION: Length 16 cm.
Adult. Sexes similar. Plumage varies seasonally. Medium-sized species halfway between the Common ringed plover and the Madagascar plover in size. Can be distinguished from the Madagascar plover by white belly and yellow orbital ring and by the absence of a wing bar.

DISTRIBUTION: Breeds in the Palearctic Region and normally winters north of the Equator. Considered a regular winter visitor to the Seychelles.

Lesser Sand Plover

Charadrius mongolus Pallas, 1776

DESCRIPTION: Length 20 cm.
Adult. Sexes similar. Plumage varies seasonally. Fairly large species closely resembling the Greater sand plover, from which it differs by its slightly smaller size and smaller bill, black tarsi, and shorter legs, which give it a stockier appearance.

DISTRIBUTION: Breeds in the n Palearctic region. Winters regularly on the e coast of Africa and the Seychelles.

Organization of the Field Identification Guide

Discussion of each of the 256 species is divided into nine sections.

Name of Species: *Numbering*—The species are numbered from 1 to 256. Each number is also used for the color plates and distribution maps. *French names*—French names are based on P. Devillers, "Projet de nomenclature française des oiseaux du monde" (1976, 1977, 1978, 1980), *Le Gerfaut* 66, 67, 68, 70, partly modified for species either endemic to or associated with the region for which the names proposed were considered as inadapted and partly modified for some species endemic to or associated with the region for which the taxonomy was developed in recent work, as for the Procellariiformes and Sphenisciformes. *Scientific names*—These are based on R. Howard and A. Moore, *A Complete Checklist of the Birds of the World* (Oxford: Oxford University Press, 1984). The name of the describer and the year of description follow the Latin binomial identification. *English names*—These are based on Howard and Moore, *A Complete Checklist of the Birds of the World,* partly modified for some species endemic to or associated with the region for which the names provided were considered unsuitable. *Malagasy names*—The Malagasy have an acute sense of observation, and as a result almost all resident species have specific names. These names are rooted in calls or songs (Katrakatraka—*Pterocles personatus,* Deho—*Streptopelia picturata),* morphological features (Sotrovava, spoonbill—*Platalea alba),* or behavioral traits (Sakaizamboay, friend of the crocodiles—*Phalacrocorax africanus;* Talapiotany,

ground singer—*Mystacornis crossleyi).* Some species are named after the most common species of the taxonomic group to which they belong (Kilandry—*Bubulcus ibis* and Kilandry be, the large cattle egret—*Casmerodius albus),* (Vintsy—*Corythornis vintsoides* and Vintsimena, red kingfisher, or Vintsiala, forest kingfisher—*Ispidina madagascariensis).* The names vary between regions with the different dialects used by the eighteen principal tribes that inhabit Madagascar. Some of these peoples, who were or still are primarily forest dwellers (such as the Tanala or the Betsimisaraka), have specific names for most of the species that frequent their regions. Only very similar species do not have separate names (Kimitsy for *Neomixis tenella* and *N. striatigula).* Nonresident species generally lack specific names. Such is the case with the small shorebirds, which are lumped together under the name Viky-Viky, and the terns, which all go by the name Samby. The Malagasy names have been gleaned in the field in the presence of local guides knowledgeable about the avifauna of their areas and familiar with fine distinctions between species of the same taxonomic group. The spellings in the various dialects are not standardized, and several spellings of a given word may be possible, particularly because some letters or combinations of letters are phonetically interchangeable. This applies to *v* and *b, d* and *l, j* and *dz, z* and *ts,* and *tr* and *dr.* Their pronunciation is rather easy, but the tonic accent often determines the meaning. As a general rule, it falls on the penultimate syllable. With respect to the vowels, note that the *e* is always fully

Figure 4. Topography of a Bird

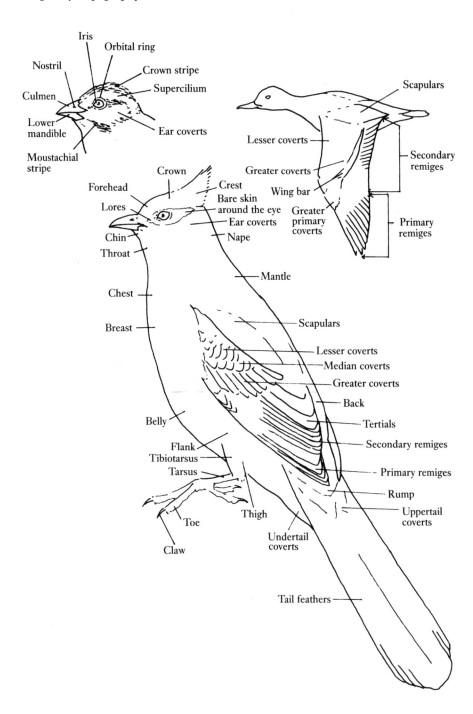

enunciated, approximately rhyming with *say* or resembling a French *é*, and that the *o* is pronounced *oo* as in *roost*. The etymology of the Malagasy names here set down, reviewed together with their spelling by Georges Randrianasolo, an expert from the University of Antananarivo, provides insight into their local significance and facilitates their memorization. The use of local names in the field will help considerably in identifying birds when working with locals.

Description: This is based on detailed observation of the kind possible with a captive bird or one observed at close range. This section covers different plumages of given species, as well as differences linked to polymorphism, sexual dimorphism, seasonal changes, or stages of development. Body length and, when possible, wingspan are given in centimeters (1 inch = 2.54 centimeters).

Identification: The main morphological criteria used in examining the species under observation are described here. Comparative identification of similar species helps avoid confusion.

Behavior: The species is examined in its own habitat and its principal behavioral characteristics are outlined here.

Voice: Vocal emissions are excellent guides to identification and location. Some morphologically very similar species can be easily distinguished by their song, good examples being the Common newtonia, Archbold's newtonia, and the Dark newtonia. Certain secretive species betray their presence only by their song or call, as do most owls or such furtive species as most rails. A phonetic approach is used in describing the most common or most characteristic vocal

emissions. An identification guide to the voices of the birds of Madagascar complete with sonograms produced by Lucienne Wilmé will soon be available. This tool will be useful not only for recognizing species in situ but also for investigating in the field.

Habitat: The natural environment in which the species is most often encountered is briefly described here. The different types of vegetation encountered in the six floristic domains, which themselves belong to two biogeographic regions, are detailed at the beginning of the guide. Other information to describe the biotope frequented is furnished when necessary. The scientific names of plants mentioned in the text are taken from the list published by J. C. Willis, revised by H. K. Airy Shaw, *A Dictionary of the Flowering Plants and Ferns* (1985). The elevation range is given in meters (1 meter = 39.37 inches) for each species.

Diet: All the known data on diets are summarized here.

Breeding: This section sums up the reproductive biology of each species. Descriptions include the situation and features of the nest, the number and nature of the eggs, the average size of the eggs in millimeters (1 inch = 25.4 millimeters), the characteristics of the chicks, and the nesting period based on direct observation.

Distribution and status: The guide uses the toponymy used by the Institut National de Géodésie et de Cartographie de Madagascar in the 1:500,000 mapping project begun in 1980. Some names and spellings have been changed, with the old versions, italicized, indicated in parentheses. A list presented earlier in

the guide includes all the geographic features mentioned in the text, with a locator to pinpoint them on an accompanying grid map. All the distribution maps—one for each resident species—are found at the end of the guide. The range of each nesting species is shown in gray. A large white star indicates a site where a species has been sighted only once. A small black star indicates where an observation has been made outside the normally accepted range. These maps reflect recent and older data wherever the sites are still intact. However, although a great deal of work and ambitious, fruitful ornithological missions were carried out until the mid-twentieth century, recent data are sparse. Internal migrations and migrations to the African continent, as well as exchanges with Africa, are still too little understood to be shown on the maps.
The distribution maps provide an overall picture based on the affinity of given species with various vegetations. The maps and the texts complement each other and are best consulted in tandem. No maps are presented for non-nesting species, among which are recorded migrants from the Palearctic Region, the Afrotropical Region, and the subantarctic or antarctic regions, as well as occasional visitors. The species involved include most of the Procellariiformes and Charadriiformes, which are generally observed from or off the coast of Madagascar.

Taxonomic List of Scientific, English, and French Names

Sphenisciformes

    Spheniscidae

	1	Eudyptes chrysocome	Gorfou sauteur	Rockhopper Penguin

Procellariiformes

    Diomedeidae

	2	Diomedea melanophrys	Albatros à sourcils noirs	Black-browed Albatross

    Procellariidae

	3	Macronectes giganteus	Pétrel géant	Southern Giant Petrel
	4	Daption capense	Damier du Cap	Cape Petrel
	5	Pachyptila desolata	Prion de la Désolation	Antarctic Prion
	6	Pachyptila salvini	Prion de Salvin	Salvin's Prion
n	7	Puffinus pacificus	Puffin du Pacifique	Wedge-tailed Shearwater

    Hydrobatidae

	8	Oceanites oceanicus	Océanite de Wilson	Wilson's Storm Petrel
	9	Fregetta tropica	Océanite à ventre noir	Black-bellied Storm Petrel

Podicipediformes

    Podicipedidae

n	10	Tachybaptus ruficollis	Grèbe castagneux	Little Grebe
(*)*	11	Tachybaptus pelzelnii	Grèbe malgache	Madagascar Little Grebe

*	12 Tachybaptus rufolavatus	Grèbe de Delacour	Alaotra Little Grebe

Pelecaniformes

Phaethontidae

	13 Phaethon aetherus	Phaéton à bec rouge	Red-billed Tropicbird
n	14 Phaethon rubricauda	Phaéton à queue rouge	Red-tailed Tropicbird
n	15 Phaethon lepturus	Phaéton à queue blanche	White-tailed Tropicbird

Fregatidae

	16 Fregata minor	Frégate du Pacifique	Greater Frigatebird
	17 Fregata ariel	Frégate ariel	Lesser Frigatebird

Phalacrocoracidae

n	18 Phalacrocorax africanus	Cormoran africain	Reed Cormorant

Anhingidae

n	19 Anhinga melanogaster	Anhinga d'Afrique	Darter

Sulidae

	20 Sula sula	Fou à pieds rouges	Red-footed Booby
n	21 Sula leucogaster	Fou brun	Brown Booby

Pelecanidae

n	22 Pelecanus rufescens	Pélican gris	Pink-backed Pelican

Ciconiiformes

Ardeidae

n	23 Ixobrychus minutus	Blongios nain	Little Bittern
n	24 Nycticorax nycticorax	Héron Bihoreau à calotte noire	Black-crowned Night-Heron
n	25 Ardeola ralloides	Héron crabier chevelu	Squacco Heron
*	26 Ardeola idae	Héron crabier blanc	Malagasy Pond Heron
n	27 Bubulcus ibis	Héron garde-boeufs	Cattle Egret
n	28 Butorides striatus	Héron à dos vert	Green-backed Heron
n	29 Egretta ardesiaca	Héron ardoisé	Black Heron
(*)	30 Egretta dimorpha	Aigrette dimorphe	Dimorphic Egret
n	31 Casmerodius albus	Grande Aigrette	Great Egret
n	32 Ardea purpurea	Héron pourpré	Purple Heron
n	33 Ardea cinerea	Héron cendré	Gray Heron
	34 Ardea melanocephala	Héron à tête noire	Black-headed Heron
*	35 Ardea humbloti	Héron de Humblot	Humblot's Heron
	36 Ardea goliath	Héron goliath	Goliath Heron

Scopidae

n	37 Scopus umbretta	Ombrette	Hamerkop

Ciconiidae

	38	Mycteria ibis	Tantale africain	Yellow-billed Stork
n	38	Mycteria ibis	Tantale africain	Yellow-billed Stork
n	39	Anastomus lamelligerus	Cigogne à bec-ouvert africaine	African Openbill Stork

Threskiornithidae

n	40	Threskiornis aethiopicus	Ibis sacré	Sacred Ibis
n	41	Plegadis falcinellus	Ibis falcinelle	Glossy Ibis
*	42	Lophotibis cristata	Ibis huppé de Madagascar	Madagascar Crested Ibis
n	43	Platalea alba	Spatule africaine	African Spoonbill

Phoenicopteridae

n	44	Phoenicopterus ruber	Flamant rose	Greater Flamingo
	45	Phoeniconaias minor	Flamant nain	Lesser Flamingo

Anseriformes

Anatidae

n	46	Dendrocygna bicolor	Dendrocygne fauve	Fulvous Whistling Duck
n	47	Dendrocygna viduata	Dendrocygne veuf	White-faced Whistling Duck
n	48	Sarkidiornis melanotos	Canard à bosse	Knob-billed Duck
n	49	Nettapus auritus	Anserelle naine	African Pygmy Goose
*	50	Anas bernieri	Sarcelle de Bernier	Bernier's Teal
*	51	Anas melleri	Canard de Meller	Meller's Duck
n	52	Anas erythrorhyncha	Canard à bec rouge	Red-billed Teal
n	53	Anas hottentota	Sarcelle hottentote	Hottentot Teal
*	54	Aythya innotata	Fuligule de Madagascar	Madagascar Pochard
n	55	Thalassornis leuconotus	Erismature à dos blanc	White-backed Duck

Falconiformes

Accipitridae

*	56	Aviceda madagascariensis	Baza malgache	Madagascar Cuckoo-Falcon
n	57	Machaeramphus alcinus	Milan des Chauves-Souris	Bat Hawk
n	58	Milvus migrans	Milan noir	Black Kite
*	59	Haliaeetus vociferoides	Pygargue de Madagascar	Madagascar Fish-Eagle
*	60	Eutriorchis astur	Aigle serpentaire de Madagascar	Madagascar Serpent-Eagle
*	61	Polyboroides radiatus	Polyboroide rayé	Madagascar Harrier-Hawk

(*)	62 Circus maillardi	Busard de Maillard	Réunion Harrier
*	63 Accipiter henstii	Autour de Henst	Henst's Goshawk
*	64 Accipiter madagascariensis	Epervier de Madagascar	Madagascar Sparrowhawk
(*)	65 Accipiter francesii	Epervier de Frances	Frances's Sparrowhawk
*	66 Buteo brachypterus	Buse de Madagascar	Madagascar Buzzard

Falconidae

(*)	67 Falco newtoni	Faucon de Newton	Madagascar Kestrel
*	68 Falco zoniventris	Faucon à ventre rayé	Banded Kestrel
	69 Falco eleonorae	Faucon d'Eléonore	Eleonora's Falcon
	70 Falco concolor	Faucon concolore	Sooty Falcon
n	71 Falco peregrinus	Faucon pélerin	Peregrine Falcon

Galliformes

Phasianidae

*	72 Margaroperdix madagascarensis	Caille de Madagascar	Madagascar Partridge
	73 Coturnix coturnix	Caille des blés	Common Quail
	74 Coturnix delegorguei	Caille arlequine	Harlequin Quail

Numididae

| n(i) | 75 Numida meleagris | Pintade mitrée | Helmeted Guineafowl |

Gruiformes

Mesitornithidae

*	76 Mesitornis variegata	Mésite variée	White-breasted Mesite
*	77 Mesitornis unicolor	Mésite unicolore	Brown Mesite
*	78 Monias benschi	Monias de Bensch	Subdesert Mesite

Turnicidae

| * | 79 Turnix nigricollis | Turnix de Madagascar | Madagascar Buttonquail |

Rallidae

*	80 Rallus madagascariensis	Râle de Madagascar	Madagascar Rail
(*)	81 Dryolimnas cuvieri	Râle de Cuvier	White-throated Rail
*	82 Canirallus kioloides	Râle à front gris	Madagascar Wood Rail
n	83 Porzana pusilla	Marouette de Baillon	Baillon's Crake
*	84 Amaurornis olivieri	Râle d'Olivier	Sakalava Rail
*	85 Sarothrura insularis	Râle insulaire	Madagascar Flufftail
*	86 Sarothrura watersi	Râle de Waters	Slender-billed Flufftail
n	87 Gallinula chloropus	Poule d'eau commune	Common Moorhen
n	88 Porphyrula alleni	Poule d'Allen	Allen's Gallinule
n	89 Porphyrio porphyrio	Poule sultane	Purple Swamphen
n	90 Fulica cristata	Foulque à crêtes	Red-knobbed Coot

Charadriiformes

    Jacanidae
*   91 Actophilornis albinucha   Jacana malgache   Madagascar Jacana

    Rostratulidae
n   92 Rostratula benghalensis   Rhynchée peinte   Greater Painted Snipe

    Recurvirostridae
n   93 Himantopus   Echasse à manteau noir   Black-winged Stilt
           himantopus
    94 Recurvirostra avosetta   Avocette à tête noire   Eurasian Avocet

    Dromadidae
    95 Dromas ardeola   Drome ardéole   Crab Plover

    Glareolidae
*   96 Glareola ocularis   Glaréole malgache   Madagascar Pratincole

    Charadriidae
    97 Pluvialis fulva   Pluvier doré du   Pacific Golden Plover
                           Pacifique
    98 Pluvialis squatarola   Pluvier argenté   Black-bellied Plover
    99 Charadrius hiaticula   Grand Gravelot   Common Ringed
                                           Plover
* 100 Charadrius thoracicus   Gravelot de   Madagascar Plover
                           Madagascar
n 101 Charadrius pecuarius   Pluvier de Kittlitz   Kittlitz's Plover
n 102 Charadrius tricollaris   Gravelot à triple collier   Three-banded Plover
  103 Charadrius   Gravelot de   Greater Sand Plover
           leschenaultii   Leschenault
n 104 Charadrius marginatus   Pluvier pâtre   White-fronted Plover

    Scolopacidae
  105 Limosa limosa   Barge à queue noire   Black-tailed Godwit
  106 Limosa lapponica   Barge rousse   Bar-tailed Godwit
  107 Numenius phaeopus   Courlis corlieu   Whimbrel
  108 Numenius arquata   Courlis cendré   Eurasian Curlew
  109 Tringa stagnatilis   Chevalier stagnatile   Marsh Sandpiper
  110 Tringa nebularia   Chevalier aboyeur   Common Greenshank
  111 Tringa ochropus   Chevalier cul-blanc   Green Sandpiper
  112 Tringa glareola   Chevalier sylvain   Wood Sandpiper
  113 Xenus cinereus   Bargette de Terek   Terek Sandpiper
  114 Actitis hypoleucos   Chevalier guignette   Common Sandpiper
  115 Arenaria interpres   Tournepierre à collier   Ruddy Turnstone
* 116 Gallinago macrodactyla   Bécassine malgache   Madagascar Snipe
  117 Calidris alba   Bécasseau Sanderling   Sanderling
  118 Calidris minuta   Bécasseau minute   Little Stint
  119 Calidris ferruginea   Bécasseau cocorli   Curlew Sandpiper
  120 Philomachus pugnax   Combattant   Ruff

Stercorariidae

	121	Catharacta antarctica	Grand labbe subantarctique	Subantarctic Skua
	122	Stercorarius parasiticus	Labbe parasite	Parasitic Jaeger

Laridae

n	123	Larus dominicanus	Goéland dominicain	Kelp Gull
n	124	Larus cirrocephalus	Goéland à tête grise	Gray-headed Gull

Sternidae

n	125	Chlidonias hybridus	Guifette moustac	Whiskered Tern
	126	Chlidonias leucopterus	Guifette leucoptère	White-winged Tern
	127	Chlidonias niger	Guifette noire	Black Tern
	128	Sterna nilotica	Sterne hansel	Gull-billed Tern
n	129	Sterna caspia	Sterne caspienne	Caspian Tern
	130	Sterna hirundo	Sterne pierregarin	Common Tern
n	131	Sterna dougallii	Sterne de Dougall	Roseate Tern
n	132	Sterna anaethetus	Sterne bridée	Bridled Tern
n	133	Sterna fuscata	Sterne fuligineuse	Sooty Tern
	134	Sterna saundersi	Sterne de Saunders	Saunders's Tern
n	135	Sterna bergii	Sterne huppée	Greater-crested Tern
	136	Sterna bengalensis	Sterne voyageuse	Lesser-crested Tern
n	137	Anous stolidus	Noddi brun	Brown Noddy
	138	Anous tenuirostris	Noddi à bec grèle	Lesser Noddy
	139	Gygis alba	Gygis blanc	White Tern

Columbiformes

Pteroclididae

*	140	Pterocles personatus	Ganga masqué	Madagascar Sandgrouse

Columbidae

n(i)	141	Columba livia	Pigeon biset	Rock Dove/ Feral Pigeon
(*)	142	Streptopelia picturata	Tourterelle peinte	Madagascar Turtledove
n	143	Oena capensis	Tourterelle à masque de fer	Namaqua Dove
(*)	144	Treron australis	Pigeon vert de Madagascar	Madagascar Green Pigeon
*	145	Alectroenas madagascariensis	Pigeon bleu de Madagascar	Madagascar Blue Pigeon

Psittaciformes

Psittacidae

(*)	146	Coracopsis vasa	Grand perroquet Vasa	Greater Vasa Parrot
(*)	147	Coracopsis nigra	Petit perroquet noir	Lesser Vasa Parrot
*	148	Agapornis cana	Inséparable à tête grise	Gray-headed Lovebird

Cuculiformes

    Cuculidae

n	149	Cuculus audeberti	Coucou d'Audebert	Thick-billed Cuckoo
*	150	Cuculus rochii	Coucou de Madagascar	Madagascar Lesser Cuckoo
*	151	Coua delalandei	Coua de Delalande	Snail-eating Coua
*	152	Coua gigas	Coua géant	Giant Coua
*	153	Coua coquereli	Coua de Coquerel	Coquerel's Coua
*	154	Coua serriana	Coua de Serre	Red-breasted Coua
*	155	Coua reynaudii	Coua de Reynaud	Red-fronted Coua
*	156	Coua cursor	Coua coureur	Running Coua
*	157	Coua ruficeps	Coua à tête rousse	Red-capped Coua
*	158	Coua cristata	Coua huppé	Crested Coua
*	159	Coua verreauxi	Coua de Verreaux	Verreaux's Coua
*	160	Coua caerulea	Coua bleu	Blue Coua
(*)	161	Centropus toulou	Coucal malgache	Madagascar Coucal

Strigiformes

    Tytonidae

| * | 162 | Tyto soumagnei | Effraie de Soumagne | Madagascar Red Owl |
| n | 163 | Tyto alba | Chouette effraie | Common Barn Owl |

    Strigidae

(*)	164	Otus rutilus	Petit duc de Madagascar	Malagasy Scops-Owl
*	165	Ninox superciliaris	Ninox à sourcils	White-browed Owl
*	166	Asio madagascariensis	Hibou de Madagascar	Madagascar Long-eared Owl
n	167	Asio capensis	Hibou du cap	Marsh Owl

Caprimulgiformes

    Caprimulgidae

| (*) | 168 | Caprimulgus madagascariensis | Engoulevent de Madagascar | Madagascar Nightjar |
| * | 169 | Caprimulgus enarratus | Engoulevent à collier | Collared Nightjar |

Apodiformes

    Apodidae

	170	Collocalia francica	Salangane des Mascareignes	Mascarene Swiftlet
(*)	171	Zoonavena grandidieri	Martinet de Grandidier	Malagasy Spine-tailed Swift
n	172	Cypsiurus parvus	Martinet des palmes	African Palm Swift
n	173	Apus melba	Martinet à ventre blanc	Alpine Swift
n	174	Apus barbatus	Martinet noir africain	African Black Swift

Coraciiformes

   Alcedinidae

(*) 175 Corythornis vintsioides   Martin-pêcheur   Malagasy Kingfisher
                            malachite

*   176 Ispidina   Martin-chasseur   Madagascar Pygmy
          madagascariensis   malgache   Kingfisher

   Meropidae

n   177 Merops superciliosus   Guêpier de   Madagascar Bee-eater
                            Madagascar

   Coraciidae

n   178 Eurystomus glaucurus   Rollier malgache   Broad-billed Roller

   Brachypteraciidae

*   179 Brachypteracias   Rollier terrestre   Short-legged
          leptosomus   leptosome   Ground-Roller

*   180 Brachypteracias   Rollier terrestre   Scaly Ground-Roller
          squamiger   écailleux

*   181 Atelornis pittoides   Rollier terrestre   Pitta-like
                          pittoide   Ground-Roller

*   182 Atelornis crossleyi   Rollier terrestre de Rufous-headed
                          Crossley   Ground-Roller

*   183 Uratelornis chimaera Rollier terrestre à Long-tailed
                          longue queue   Ground-Roller

   Leptosomatidae

(*) 184 Leptosomus discolor   Courol   Cuckoo-Roller

   Upupidae

n   185 Upupa epops   Huppe fasciée   Hoopoe

Passeriformes

   Philepittidae

*   186 Philepitta castanea   Philépitte veloutée Velvet Asity

*   187 Philepitta schlegeli   Philépitte de Schlegel Schlegel's Asity

*   188 Neodrepanis coruscans Philépitte faux-   Sunbird-Asity
                          souimanga
                          caronculée

*   189 Neodrepanis   Philépitte   Yellow-bellied
          hypoxantha   faux-souimanga de Sunbird-Asity
                          Salomonsen

   Alaudidae

*   190 Mirafra hova   Alouette malgache   Madagascar Bush Lark

   Hirundinidae

n   191 Riparia paludicola   Hirondelle paludicole Brown-throated Sand
                            Martin

	192	Riparia riparia	Hirondelle de rivages	Sand Martin/Bank Swallow
(*)	193	Phedina borbonica	Hirondelle des Mascareignes	Mascarene Martin
	194	Hirunda rustica	Hirondelle de cheminées	Swallow/Barn Swallow

Motacillidae

*	195	Motacilla flaviventris	Bergeronnette malgache	Madagascar Wagtail

Campephagidae

(*)	196	Coracina cinerea	Echenilleur malgache	Ashy Cuckoo-Shrike

Pycnonotidae

*	197	Phyllastrephus madagascariensis	Bulbul de Madagascar	Long-billed Greenbul
*	198	Phyllastrephus zosterops	Bulbul zosterops	Spectacled Greenbul
*	199	Phyllastrephus apperti	Bulbul d'Appert	Appert's Greenbul
*	200	Phyllastrephus tenebrosus	Bulbul fuligineux	Dusky Greenbul
*	201	Phyllastrephus cinereiceps	Bulbul à tête grise	Gray-crowned Greenbul
n	202	Hypsipetes madagascariensis	Bulbul noir	Madagascar Bulbul

Turdidae

*	203	Copsychus albospecularis	Dyal malgache	Madagascar Magpie-Robin
n	204	Saxicola torquata	Traquet pâtre	Stonechat
*	205	Pseudocossyphus sharpei	Merle de roche de forêt	Forest Rock-Thrush
*	206	Pseudocossyphus imerinus	Merle de roche du sub-désert	Littoral Rock-Thrush
*	207	Pseudocossyphus bensoni	Merle de roche de Benson	Benson's Rock-Thrush

Sylviidae

*	208	Acrocephalus newtoni	Rousserole de Newton	Madagascar Swamp-Warbler
(*)	209	Nesillas typica	Fauvette de Madagascar	Madagascar Brush-Warbler
*	210	Thamnornis chloropetoides	Thamnornis	Thamnornis Warbler
(*)	211	Cisticola cherina	Cisticole de Madagascar	Madagascar Cisticola
*	212	Dromaeocercus brunneus	Dromaeocerque brun	Brown Emutail

*	213 Dromaeocercus seebohmi	Dromaeocerque de Seebohm	Gray Emutail
*	214 Randia pseudozosterops	Fauvette de Rand	Rand's Warbler
*	215 Newtonia amphichora	Newtonie sombre	Dark Newtonia
*	216 Newtonia brunneicauda	Newtonie commune	Common Newtonia
*	217 Newtonia archboldi	Newtonie d'Archbold	Archbold's Newtonia
*	218 Newtonia fanovanae	Newtonie de Fanovana	Red-tailed Newtonia
*	219 Neomixis tenella	Petite Eroesse	Common Jery
*	220 Neomixis viridis	Eroesse verte	Green Jery
*	221 Neomixis striatigula	Grande Eroesse	Stripe-throated Jery
*	222 Hartertula flavoviridis	Eroesse à queue étagée	Wedge-tailed Jery

Monarchidae

| * | 223 Pseudobias wardi | Gobe-mouche de Ward | Ward's Flycatcher |
| (*) | 224 Terpsiphone mutata | Gobe-mouche de paradis de Madagascar | Madagascar Paradise Flycatcher |

Timaliidae

*	225 Oxylabes madagascariensis	Oxylabe à gorge blanche	White-throated Oxylabes
*	226 Crossleyia xanthophrys	Oxylabe à sourcils jaunes	Yellow-browed Oxylabes
*	227 Mystacornis crossleyi	Mystacornis	Crossley's Babbler

Nectariniidae

| (*) | 228 Nectarinia souimanga | Souimanga malgache | Souimanga Sunbird |
| (*) | 229 Nectarinia notata | Souimanga angaladian | Long-billed Green Sunbird |

Zosteropidae

| (*) | 230 Zosterops maderaspatana | Zosterops malgache | Madagascar White-Eye |

Oriolidae

| | 231 Oriolus oriolus | Loriot d'Europe | European Golden Oriole |

Vangidae

*	232 Calicalicus madagascariensis	Vanga à queue rousse	Red-tailed Vanga
*	233 Schetba rufa	Artamie rousse	Rufous Vanga
*	234 Vanga curvirostris	Vanga écorcheur	Hook-billed Vanga
*	235 Xenopirostris xenopirostris	Vanga de Lafresnaye	Lafresnaye's Vanga
*	236 Xenopirostris damii	Vanga de Van Dam	Van Dam's Vanga
*	237 Xenopirostris polleni	Vanga de Pollen	Pollen's Vanga
*	238 Falculea palliata	Falculie mantelée	Sickle-billed Vanga
*	239 Leptopterus viridis	Artamie à tête blanche	White-headed Vanga

*	240	Leptopterus chabert	Artamie de Chabert	Chabert's Vanga
(*)	241	Cyanolanius madagascarinus	Artamie azurée	Blue Vanga
*	242	Oriolia bernieri	Oriolie de Bernier	Bernier's Vanga
*	243	Euryceros prevostii	Eurycère de Prévost	Helmet Vanga
*	244	Hypositta corallirostris	Vanga-Sittelle	Nuthatch Vanga
*	245	Tylas eduardi	Tylas	Tylas Vanga
		Dicruridae		
(*)	246	Dicrurus forficatus	Drongo malgache	Crested Drongo
		Corvidae		
n	247	Corvus albus	Corbeau pie	Pied Crow
		Sturnidae		
*	248	Hartlaubius auratus	Etourneau de Madagascar	Madagascar Starling
n(i)	249	Acridotheres tristis	Martin triste	Common Myna
		Ploceidae		
n(i)	250	Passer domesticus	Moineau domestique	House Sparrow
*	251	Ploceus nelicourvi	Tisserin nelicourvi	Nelicourvi Weaver
*	252	Ploceus sakalava	Tisserin sakalave	Sakalava Weaver
*	253	Foudia madagascariensis	Foudi de Madagascar	Madagascar Red Fody
*	254	Foudia omissa	Foudi de forêt	Forest Fody
		Estrildidae		
*	255	Lonchura nana	Mannikin de Madagascar	Madagascar Mannikin
(i)	256	Estrilda astrild	Astrild à bec de corail	Common Waxbill

Map 5. Locator Map

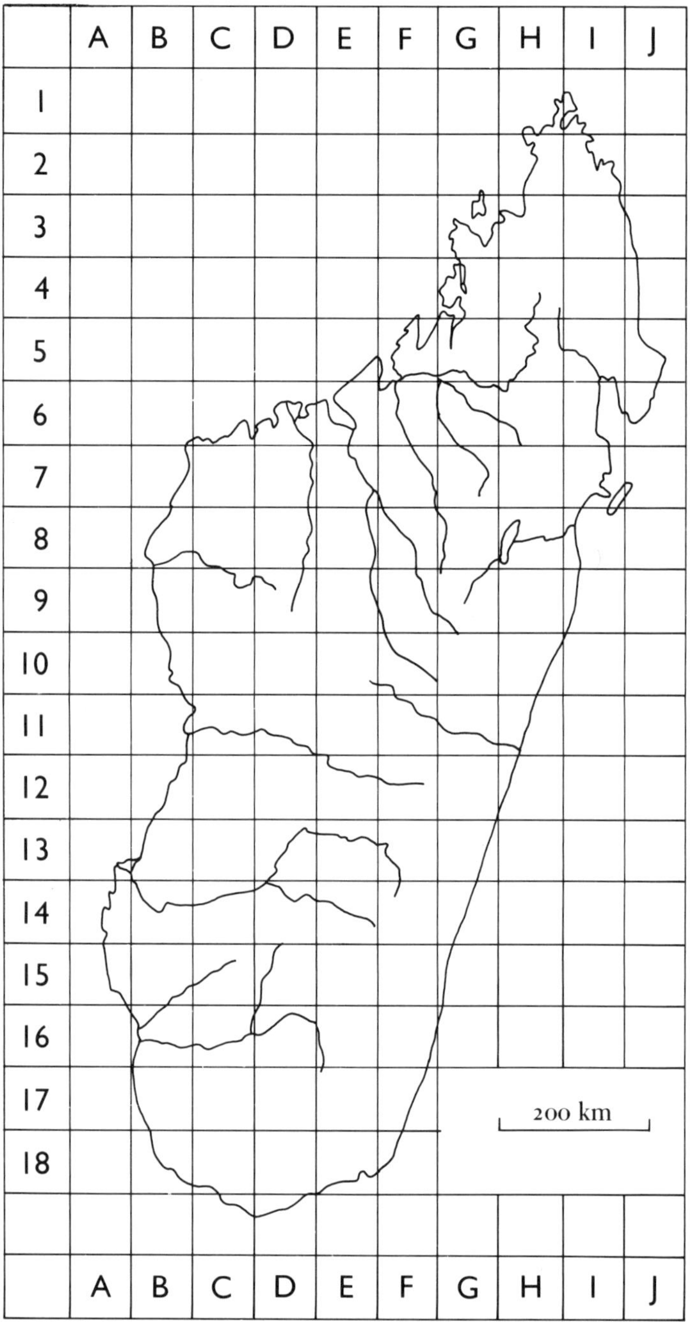

Alphabetical List of Places

Alaotra (lake) H8
Ambalavao F14
Ambanja G3
Ambararatabe D6
Ambato Boeny E7
Ambatondrazaka H8
Ambatosoratra H8
Ambazoana (valley)
G3
Ambilobe H2
Amboasary E18
Ambohitantely
(Special Reserve)
Ambohitra
(Joffreville) H2
Amboromalandy
(lake) E7
Ambre (National
Park 1) H2, I2
Ambre (Special
Reserve) H2
Ampasimanolotra
(Brickaville) H10
Ampasindava (bay
of) G3
Ampijoroa E7
Anaborano H3
Anakao A16
Analamazaotra
Périnet (Special
Reserve) G10
Analamera (Special
Reserve) I2
Andapa I4
Andasibe (*Périnet*)
G10
Andekaleka G10
Andoany (*Hell-Ville*)
G3
Andohahela (RNI no.
11) E17
Andranobe (lake)
B16
Andranofasika E7
Andringitra (RNI no.
5) F14
Androka B18
Anivorano I2
Anjozorobe G9
Ankarafantsika (RNI
no. 7) F6
Ankarana (Special
Reserve) H2
Ankaratra F11
Ankazoabo C14
Ankazobe F9
Ankerika (lake) E18
Anony (lake) B10

Anororo H8
Anosibe An'Ala G11
Antainambalana
(river) H5, I5
Antalaha J5
Antananarivo
(*Tananarive*) F10
Antongil (bay of the)
I6
Antsahamena G10
Antsalova C10
Antsirabe F11
Antsiranana (*Diego-
Suarez*) I1
Antsohihy G5
Bealanana (marsh)
G4
Befandriana B14
Befotaka (lake) B10
Belo-sur-mer B12
Belo-sur-Tsiribihina
B10
Beloha C18
Bemamba (lake) B10
Bemangidy F17
Bemaraha (Strict
Nature Reserve 9)
C10
Berenty E18
Beroboka C11
Besalampy B7
Betampona (Strict
Nature Reserve 1)
H9
Betanty (*Faux Cap*)
D18
Betioky B16
Betsiboka (river) G9,
F9, F8, F7, E7, E6
Betsileo (southeast)
E13, E14, F13,
F14
Bevoay (lake) B10
Beza-Mahafaly
(Special Reserve)
C17
Bora (Special
Reserve) G5
Cap Sainte-Marie
(Special Reserve)
C19
Didy H9
Doany I4
Ejeda C17
Erombo (lake) E18
Fanovana G10
Farafangana G15

Fenoarivo (*Fénérive*)
I8
Fianarantsoa F13
Fiherenana (river)
C15, B15, B16
Fito H9
Horombe (plateau)
D15
Hatokaliotsy B18
Iharanä (*Vohémar*) I3
Ihosy D15
Ihotry (lake) A14
Ikopa (river) F10,
F9, E9, E8, E7
Ile Sainte-Marie I7,
I8
Iles Barren B9
Ilots des Quatre
Fréres H2
Isalo (National Park
2) D14, D15
Itampolo B18
Itasy (lake) E10
Itremo (massif) F12
Ivohibe (Special
Reserve) E15
Kinkony (lake) D6
Linta (river) C17,
B17, B18
Lokobe (Strict
Nature Reserve 6)
G3
Maevatanana E7
Mahajamba (river)
G8, F8, F7, F6
Mahajanga (*Majunga*)
E6
Mahovavy (river) D9,
D8, D7, D6
Maintirano B9
Makira G10
Manakara G14
Manambolo (river)
D9, C9, C8, B8
Mananara I6
Mandrare (river)
E17, E18
Mandroseza (lake
and marsh)
Mangoky (river)
D13, D14, C14,
B14, A13
Mangoro (river) G9,
G10, G11, H11
Maningory (river)
H8, I8
Manja B13
Manjakatompo F10

Manombo (Special
Reserve) F15
Manongarivo
(Special Reserve)
B18
Mantady (National
Park) G10
Maroantsetra I5
Marojejy (Strict
Nature Reserve
12) I4
Maromandia (marsh)
G4
Marovoay E6
Masama (lake) B10
Masoala (peninsula)
I6, J6
Masoarivo B10
Menarandra (river)
D17, C17, C18
Midongy E16
Mitsinjo D6
Moramanga G10
Morombe A14
Morondava B12
Namoroka (Strict
Nature Reserve 8)
D7
Nosimborona B18
Nosy Ambositra B14
Nosy Andranombala
A14
Nosy Be G3
Nosy Jamanjaky A14
Nosy Mangabe
(Special Reserve)
I6
Nosy Manitra B18
Nosy Mitsio H2
Nosy Satrana A16
Nosy Ve A16
Onilahy (river) C16,
B16
Pangalanes (canal)
I9, H10, H11,
H12, G12, G13,
G14, G15
Pointe-à-Larrée I7
Port-Bergé F6
Ranohira D15
Ranomafana F13
Rogez G10
Sahaka (lake) I3
Sakaraha C15
Sambava J4
Sambirano (massif)
G3
Sihanaka (forest)

Soalala D6
Soanirara-Ivingo I7
Sofia (river) H4, H5, H6, G6, G5, F5
Tabiky B14
Toamasina (*Tamatave*) I9
Tolognaro (*Fort-Dauphin*) F18

Toliara (*Tuléar*) B16
Tritriva (lake) F11
Tsaramandroso F7
Tsaratanana (massif) H4
Tsiandro C10
Tsimanampetsotsa (lake, Strict

Nature Reserve) B17
Tsiombe D18
Tsiribihina (river) D11, C11, B11
Vangaindrano F16
Vohibasia C15
Vohiparara F13

Vondrozo G15
Zahamena (RNI no. 3) H8
Zombitse (forest) C15

Guide to the
Birds of Madagascar

Sphenisciformes

Spheniscidae – Penguin

Flightless birds adapted to oceanic life, with wings shaped like narrow, flattened paddles. The short, abundant, and dense plumage is black on top and white underneath, and the head is generally colored or ornamented. Seventeen species classified into 6 genera are distributed in the S Hemisphere. Only 1 species has been captured on the s tip of Madagascar.

1. *Rockhopper Penguin*

Eudyptes chrysocome (Forster, 1781)
French: Gorfou sauteur
No Map

DESCRIPTION: Length 60 cm.
Adult. Sexes similar. Massive head, black with occipital crest made of erectile black feathers, and long tufts of yellow feathers growing from the sides of the head. White chin and throat. Brownish red bill, more massive in the male than in the female. Red iris. Black upperparts and tail, white underparts. Pink feet with black soles. Outer surface of flippers black with a fine white border, inner surface white with more or less pronounced black markings at the tip, depending on the

subspecies (of which there are 3).
Immature. Differs from adult by thinner body and absence both of yellow tufts and of white chin and throat.

DISTRIBUTION AND STATUS: Nests on many subantarctic islands. Breeding sites nearest Madagascar are Saint-Paul and Amsterdam islands, where subspe-cies *E. c. moseleyi* (regarded by some authors as a species) breeds. In Madagascar an individual was taken at s tip of Betanty, Jan. 1956. This event may be linked to the fact that sailors from Saint-Paul and Amsterdam bound for Réunion sometimes used to take living individuals, which later were released or escaped.

Procellariiformes

Diomedeidae – Albatross

The largest members of the order Procellariiformes, albatrosses are excellent gliders. They are characterized by nostrils that extend from each side of the culmen through a short tube, their 3 anterior toes connected by a web and the absence of a hind toe. The family is represented by 14 species comprising 2 genera mainly distributed in the South Seas. One species regularly frequents the coasts of Madagascar.

2. *Black-browed Albatross*

Diomedea melanophrys Temminck, 1823
French: Albatros à sourcils noirs
No Map

DESCRIPTION: Length 80–95 cm, wingspan 213–46 cm.
Adult. Sexes similar. White head and neck, except for black eyebrow stripe. Yellow bill with orange tip. Brown iris. Gray mantle, dark gray back, white rump and undertail coverts. White underparts. Fleshy tarsi, toes, and webs. Wings slate gray on upper surfaces, white with broad black borders below. Slate gray remiges and tail.
Immature. Distinguished from adult by gray collar, dark or two-tone (dirty yellow with black tip) bill, and dusky underside of wings, which may appear black from a distance.

IDENTIFICATION: Largest seabird in this zone. Very long, narrow wings; short, squared tail; long, stout, yellow bill. Plumage shows strong contrasts: dark gray back, topside of wings, and tail, rest of upperparts white, underside of wings white with black border.

BEHAVIOR: Strictly oceanic species; sometimes comes within close range of fishing boats and coast. Usually observed in flight, gliding most of the time and beating its wings only occasionally. Stays on water when there is no wind. Takes its food from water's surface.

VOICE: Silent at sea.

HABITAT: Strictly oceanic species.

DIET: Fish and cephalopods; sometimes carrion.

DISTRIBUTION AND STATUS: Migrating species breeding on subantarctic islands. Nesting sites nearest Madagascar are Crozet (2,500 km away) and especially Kerguelen (3,500 km away). Commonly ventures as far as the Tropic of Capricorn. It is the only species of albatross officially identified in Malagasy waters.

Procellaridae – Petrels, Prions, Shearwater

These oceanic birds vary greatly in size. The structure of the nostrils varies among genera, but in all cases the nasal tubes extend side-by-side on the bill. Various taxonomies divide the family into 55–60 species that are classified into 12 genera. Only 1 species nests in Madagascar, and 4 species have been observed or captured along its coasts.

3. *Southern Giant Petrel*
Macronectes giganteus (Gmelin, 1789)
Malagasy: Vorompamono
French: Pétrel géant
No Map

DESCRIPTION: Length 86–99 cm, wingspan 185–205 cm.
Adult. Sexes similar. Male slightly larger than female. Color of plumage lightens with age. Polymorphic species.
Dark Morph. Whitish head, throat, and upper chest. Stout bill, yellow with light green hook. Gray or brown iris. Upper- and underparts dark brownish gray, gradually lightening toward the head. Sooty gray tarsi and toes. Wings have dark brownish gray uppersides and lighter undersides with a white border in front and a black border along the rear. Dark brownish gray tail.
White Morph. Plumage uniformly white, lightly speckled with brown on back and wings.
Immature Dark Morph. Uniformly sooty, bill same as in all adult morphs, iris brown. The first light-colored feathers appear at age 8–10.
Immature White Morph. Differs from

adult white morph by absence of sparse brown feathers.

IDENTIFICATION: This very large oceanic species is distinguishable from the albatrosses by its plumper silhouette, shorter wings, longer neck, larger head, and stouter bill. Individuals in the white morph cannot be confused with any other species, whereas those in the dark morph are difficult to distinguish from the Northern giant petrel *(Macronectes halli)*. The dark adult morph is distinguished from the Northern giant petrel by the contrast between the generally light head and darker body and by the yellow bill with green angular ridge (*M. halli* has a red and black bill).

BEHAVIOR: Species observed in isolation in Malagasy waters. Skims water surface with powerful wingbeats in alternation with long periods of gliding flight. May follow ships for several days, willingly feeding on refuse. At sea it catches its prey on the surface. Most encounters in Madagascar have involved exhausted immature individuals on beaches or near the shore that were approached and captured without resistance.

VOICE: Generally silent at sea.

HABITAT: Oceanic species.

DIET: Carrion, refuse, crustaceans, cephalopods, and mollusks.

DISTRIBUTION AND STATUS: Nests on many antarctic and subantarctic islets. Breeding sites nearest Madagascar are Crozet (2,500 km away) and Kerguelen (3,500 km away). Numerous data from observation or capture have been collected at Toliara and Morombe on w coast and at Vangaindrano, Manakara, and Maroantsetra on e coast: Toliara (Aug. 1949, July 1957, Mar. 1970), Morombe (July 1983), Toamasina (Sept. 1950), Vangaindrano (July 1958—indi-vidual ringed in Feb. 1958 in Signey Islands, S Orkneys [60°43'S, 45°36'E]), Manakara (July 1987—individual ringed in Feb. 1987 on Elephant Island, S Shetlands [61°20'S, 55°20'E]).

4. Cape Petrel
Daption capense (Linnaeus, 1758)
French: Damier du Cap
No Map

DESCRIPTION: Length 38–40 cm, wingspan 81–91 cm.
Adult. Sexes similar. Black head and neck, black bill, brown iris. Black mantle, rest of upper body white speckled with black. White underparts. Black tarsi and toes. Wings black and white on upper surface, white with broad black borders below. Tail black with white base.
Immature. Similar to adult.

IDENTIFICATION: Medium-sized Procellaridae with black and white plumage.

BEHAVIOR: Oceanic species fond of following boats; frequents coasts during stormy weather.

VOICE: Silent at sea.

HABITAT: Oceanic species.

DIET: Mainly crustaceans, but also refuse and carrion.

DISTRIBUTION AND STATUS: Distributed over most subantarctic islands. Crozet (2,500 km away) and Kerguelen (2,500 km away) provide nearest nesting sites. Range extends to Tropic of Capricorn. An occasional migrant, it has been captured only once at Manakara, in Aug. 1986.

5 and 6. Prions *Pachyptila* spp.
Antarctic Prion, Salvin's Prion

Pachyptila desolata, Pachyptila salvini
French: Prion de la Désolation, Prion de
Salvin
No Map

The specific determination of the prions,
both at sea and in the hand, dead or alive,
is usually impossible outside breeding
areas. If the conditions for observation at
sea or the state of the specimen are satis-

factory, the subgenus or group of species
can be determined. There are 3 such
groups:

   1. *P. salvini, P. vittata, P. desolata*
   2. *P. turtur, P. crassirostris*
   3. *P. belcheri*

IDENTIFICATION: The genus is distinguished from other petrels (in the
absence of *Pachyptila*, which does not frequent tropical seas) by its blue-gray color
and the black **W** on its wings. Fluttering
flight. Brown iris and blue tarsi and toes.

Key to identification (of the groups of species):

	P. salvini, P. vittata and *P. desolata*	*P. turtur* and *P. crassirostris*	*P. belcheri*
IN HAND			
Bill	*P. vittata*, all black, the other two black and blue.	Blue with a black stripe where the patches meet.	Ditto, but bill is more delicate.
Head	More or less marked black supercilium. Dark head with faint collar.	No black supercilium. Very light head. No collar.	Clear black stripe at eye level, with clear black supercilium. Light coloring.
IN FLIGHT			
	Dark appearance, with the black **W** rather wide. Underparts dirty white. Fairly narrow black band on tail.	Rather light in appearance, with the **W** rather narrow and well defined. Underparts white. Wide black band on tail.	Light coloring, very well defined **W**. Underparts white. Outside tail feathers white.

BEHAVIOR: Oceanic species that sometimes accompany boats for short
distances.

HABITAT: Oceanic species.

DIET: Crustaceans and cephalopods.

DISTRIBUTION AND STATUS: All
prions but *P. vittata* breed on subantarctic
islands of Indian Ocean. Their distribution at sea differs according to species,

however, and not all appear, even occasionally, in tropical zone. Most probable
are *P. turtur* and *P. salvini*, which does
not rule out presence of others. Prions
are rarely sighted. The capture of *P. desolata* has been reported along coasts of
Madagascar, and 2 carcasses found at

Nosy Satrana in Aug. 1985 are thought to have been *P. salvini.*

7. Wedge-tailed Shearwater

Puffinus pacificus (Gmelin, 1789)
Malagasy: Vorotomany
French: Puffin du Pacifique

DESCRIPTION: Length 41–46 cm, wingspan 99–106 cm.
Adult. Sexes similar. Polymorphic species; light morph occurs only in the Hawaii sector and is not described here.
Dark Morph. Plumage brown all over, with tail and primary remiges darker. Dark gray bill, brown iris, fleshy tarsi and toes.
Immature. Similar to adult.

IDENTIFICATION: Large shearwater with dark plumage, narrow wings, wedge-shaped tail, and characteristically elastic flight.

BEHAVIOR: Oceanic species that comes to land only to breed. Occasionally follows ships. Solitary flier but sometimes feeds in groups that may include brown and lesser noddies. Flies low over the water and usually seizes its prey in flight, but can also feed on the surface.

VOICE: Silent at sea but very vocal at nesting sites. Utters repeated long, modulated, powerful wails.

HABITAT: Oceanic species.

DIET: Cephalopods, crustaceans, and fish.

NESTING: Nests in narrow natural cavities under large rock formations protected by thorny bushes (*Euphorbia stenoclada*—Euphorbiaceae, *Salvadora angustifolia*—Salvadoraceae). Lays 1 dull white egg in a small hollow. Nesting has been observed in Nov.

DISTRIBUTION AND STATUS: Distributed in intertropical zone of Indian and Pacific oceans. Only 1 nesting site known in Madagascar, on 3 small rocky calcareous islands lying 11–30 km sw of Morombe (Nosy Jamanjaky and Nosy Andranombala). Species has also been observed near Tolagnaro and along sw coast. Only shearwater officially recorded in Madagascar. Nesting population estimated at about 125 pairs. It is threatened by local people who each year take unfledged young and brooding adults from accessible nests. Only birds nesting in deep caves or protected by spiny vegetation survive this predation.

Hydrobatidae – Petrels

Small oceanic birds, the smallest of the
order Procellariiformes, with generally
dark plumage, sometimes very long-
legged. Characteristic fluttering flight.
Family represented by approximately 20
species constituting 8 genera and distributed over all seas of the planet. Two species are regular visitors to Madagascar's
coasts.

VOICE: Soft, high-pitched call while
feeding.

HABITAT: Oceanic species.

DIET: Small crustaceans, fish, and
cephalopods.

DISTRIBUTION AND STATUS: Breeds
in subantarctic islands. Nearest nesting
site to Madagascar is Crozet (2,500 km
away). During its biannual transequato-
rial migration, it is regularly found in
large flocks along the Malagasy coast.

8. *Wilson's Storm Petrel*

Oceanites oceanicus (Kuhl, 1820)
French: Océanite de Wilson
No Map

DESCRIPTION: Length 15–19 cm,
wingspan 38–42 cm.
Adult. Sexes similar. Dark brown head,
black bill, brown iris. Upperparts brown,
except for white rump. Underparts
brown, except for white sides of undertail
coverts. Black tarsi and toes, yellow web.
Upper side of wing dark brown with
grayish diagonal stripe over greater coverts, underside of wing dark brown. Dark
brown tail.
Immature. Similar to adult.

IDENTIFICATION: Small, dark petrel
characterized by short wings with round
tips, white rump, squared tail, and long
legs extending past tail. Supple, direct
flight just over the water. Feeds while
running at the surface of the water, wings
held high over its back. Species is distinguished from Black-bellied storm petrel
by its small size and entirely dark underparts and underside of wings.

BEHAVIOR: Oceanic species, gregarious, forming loose groups of hundreds of
individuals. Given to following ships. Often flies in troughs of waves.

9. *Black-bellied Storm Petrel*

Fregetta tropica (Gould, 1844)
French: Océanite à ventre noir
No Map

DESCRIPTION: Length 20 cm, wingspan 46 cm.
Adult. Sexes similar. Sooty head, black
bill, brown iris. Upperparts dark brown,
except for white rump. Chin sometimes
dull white; throat, chest, and undertail
coverts black. Belly and flanks white, except for black ventral median stripe.
Black tarsi, toes, and webs. Upper side of
wing dark brown with a lighter diagonal
stripe over the greater coverts, underside black and with white axillaries and
greater coverts. Black tail.
Immature. Similar to adult.

IDENTIFICATION: Small petrel with
white rump, characterized by partly white
underside of wings and underparts and
squared tail. In irregular, zigzagging,
choppy flight legs hang down and each
flank is exposed in turn. Often drops into
water in search of food. Distinguished
from Wilson's petrel by its slightly larger
size, white belly, and contrasting underparts and underside of wings.

BEHAVIOR: Oceanic species that sometimes accompanies ships, usually staying
ahead of them.

VOICE: Silent at sea.

HABITAT: Oceanic species.

DIET: Small crustaceans, fish, and cephalopods.

DISTRIBUTION AND STATUS: Breeds in subantarctic islands. Nesting sites nearest Madagascar are Crozet (2,500 km away) and Kerguelen (3,500 km away). Has often been seen near Malagasy coasts during austral winter.

Podicipediformes

Podicipedidae – Grebes

Aquatic birds readily distinguished by their lobed webs and small tails, which consist of small feathers instead of the usual tail feathers. Grebes have difficulty moving about on land because their legs are set so far back. When alarmed, they dive or swim to safety, rarely flying. They take off after a long run on the water, whirring their wings. Simultaneous molting of primary and secondary remiges prevents them from flying for a brief period. The family is cosmopolitan, represented by 20 species. Of the 3 species of the genus *Tachybaptus*, small grebes, that nest in Madagascar, 2 are endemic.

10. *Little Grebe*

Tachybaptus ruficollis (Pallas, 1764)
Malagasy: Kiborano, Vivy, Tsiriry, Fanaliandro
French: Grèbe castagneux

DESCRIPTION: Length 15–19 cm, wingspan 40–45 cm.
Adult. Sexes similar. Plumage varies seasonally.
Breeding Plumage. Dark brown forehead, crown, back of neck, and chin. Rufous cheeks and sides and front of neck. Bill black, except for lighter tip, with bright yellow markings at the commissure of the two mandibles. Dark red iris. Upperparts dark brown, underparts dull white, except for rust-tinged flanks. Greenish gray tarsi and toes. Wings: upper side brownish, underside dull white. Fluffy dark brown tail.
Nonbreeding Plumage. Lighter and drabber plumage overall. Dull brown forehead, front and top of head, back of neck, and chin. Light tan cheeks and sides and front of neck.

Immature. Similar to adult in nonbreeding plumage.

IDENTIFICATION: Small, compact, short-necked species, characterized in breeding plumage by its brown crown, chin, and back of neck contrasting with rufous cheeks and sides and front of neck. Straight, short, rather stout bill marked with a conspicuous yellow patch created by the commissural folds. Swift flight and rapid wingbeats. In breeding plumage distinguished from Madagascar little grebe by its lighter build, shorter dark bill set off with a yellow commissural fold, rufous cheeks not separated from dark cap by white line, short wings, and rust-tinged flanks. Differs from Alaotra little grebe by its shorter bill, dark eyes, rufous tinge of cheeks and neck, russet flanks, light-colored underparts, and longer wings.

BEHAVIOR: Aquatic species found in pairs or family groups or, outside the breeding season, in flocks of 5–300. Commonly seen foraging for food in the company of Madagascar little grebe, Alaotra little grebe, or various species of ducks: African pygmy goose, Red-billed teal, White-backed duck, and White-faced whistling duck. It feeds throughout the day, diving for its prey. When alarmed, it often flees by diving several times; it may also remain immobile amid floating vegetation or take flight for a short distance.

VOICE: Vocal, with characteristic loud, piercing call resembling *Heeheeheehee . . . .* Also utters clipped, piercing alarm call suggesting the word *tick;* sometimes repeated.

HABITAT: Frequents bodies of fresh or brackish water, generally shallow, lined, and partially covered with vegetation (*Nymphaea* spp—Nymphaeaceae). Also occasionally found in running water, including rivers, and temporary bodies of water (rice paddies, lakes, pools). Observed at elevations from sea level to 1,500 m.

DIET: Chiefly small fish but also batrachians and aquatic insects.

NESTING: Anchored to aquatic vegetation near the bank, the nest is a floating structure made of aquatic plants. Clutch numbers 2–4 rather shiny whitish eggs that turn brownish during incubation (average size: 35.6 mm × 23.8 mm). Both parents incubate. Chicks are nidifugous and covered with brownish down; they frequently ride on backs of parents. Nesting has been observed Aug.–Mar.

DISTRIBUTION AND STATUS: Distributed in Europe, Africa, Asia, and Oceania. Represented in Madagascar by subspecies *T. r. capensis* (Salvadori, 1884), common in sub-Saharan Africa. In Madagascar its appearance is recent, first references dating from about 1930, but it is now common throughout Madagascar, except in e and s, where it is unusual. Its adaptation in Madagascar seems to have been helped by the introduction of herbivorous fish *(Tilapia melanopleura, T. zillii)* that have altered bodies of water by considerably limiting the development of aquatic vegetation. This change has given rise to a competition that has reduced the numbers of the Madagascar little grebe.

11. *Madagascar Little Grebe*

Tachybaptus pelzelnii (Hartlaub, 1861)
Malagasy: Kiborano, Vivy, Tsiriry
French: Grèbe malgache

DESCRIPTION: Length 19 cm, wingspan 45 cm.
Adult. Sexes similar. Plumage varies seasonally.
Breeding Plumage. Sooty forehead, crown, and back of neck. Rest of head grayish, except for the partly russet cheeks, which

are separated from the black crown by a white line. Sides and front of neck grayish. Light-colored bill with black mark at base of lower mandible. Dark red iris. Dark brown upperparts. Underparts whitish, except for grayish breast and flanks. Yellow-green tarsi and toes. Dark brown wings. Fluffy dark brown tail. *Nonbreeding Plumage.* Differs by generally paler and duller hue of plumage and by absence of white line between black crown and rest of head.
Immature. Similar to adult in nonbreeding plumage.

IDENTIFICATION: Small, compact, short-necked grebe with straight, short, rather stout bill. Species is characterized by black crown and back of neck, which contrast with rest of neck and rufous-flecked grayish head and by clear bill without commissural patches. In breeding plumage distinguished from Little grebe by heavier build, longer light-colored bill without commissural patches, white line between cheeks and cap, longer wings, and grayish flanks. Differs from Alaotra little grebe by its light-colored bill, dark eye, rufous-tinged cheeks and neck, light-colored underparts, and longer wings.

BEHAVIOR: Very similar to that of Little grebe and Alaotra little grebe. Flocks of up to 150 have been observed (Ihotry Lake, Aug. 1983).

VOICE: Similar to Little grebe, but lower-pitched.

HABITAT: Frequents bodies of fresh, less often brackish water, generally shallow, permanent or temporary, lined and abundantly covered with aquatic vegetation (*Nymphaea* spp.—Nymphaeaceae). Seen on running water. Observed at elevations from sea level to 2,000 m.

DIET: Chiefly small fish, also aquatic insects.

NESTING: Anchored to aquatic vegetation near the bank, the nest is a floating structure made of aquatic plants. Clutch numbers 3–4 slightly bluish white eggs that, from contact with decaying plants, gradually turn brownish. They are round to elliptical in shape (average size: 35.5 mm × 24.0 mm). Both parents incubate, covering eggs with aquatic plants when they leave nest. Chicks are nidifugous. Nesting has been observed Aug.–Mar.

DISTRIBUTION AND STATUS: Endemic to Madagascar, distributed throughout island. Common in w and n and on High Plateau but uncommon in e and rather rare in s, where it is observed locally (Anony and Erombo lakes). Its decline in numbers, noted some 30 years ago, has been continuous. It is due to hybridization with Little grebe and introduction of herbivorous fish *(Tilapia melanopleura, T. zillii)*, which, by considerably limiting development of aquatic vegetation, have favored implantation of Little grebe.

12. *Alaotra Little Grebe*

Tachybaptus rufolavatus (Delacour, 1932)
Malagasy: Kiborano, Vivy
French: Grèbe de Delacour

DESCRIPTION: Length 19 cm, wingspan 40 cm.
Adult. Sexes similar. Plumage varies seasonally.
Breeding Plumage. Forehead, crown, and back of neck black, slightly tinged with green. Feathers on nape are longer and slightly erectile. Rest of head, neck, and throat are pale tan. Whitish chin. Narrow sooty stripe from the base of the bill to the black crown, crossing the eye. Bill black with light tip. Pale yellow iris. Upperparts dark brown, underparts dusky brown, except for lighter patch in middle

of belly. Yellow-green tarsi and toes, dark brown wings, fluffy dark brown tail. *Nonbreeding Plumage.* Paler and duller hues overall.

Immature. Few data. Similar to adult in nonbreeding plumage, with dark patches on sides of neck.

IDENTIFICATION: Small, compact, short-necked grebe with straight, fairly stout bill. Crown and back of neck black, chin white, rest of head and neck tan, bill black without commissural patches, and eye pale yellow. Distinguished from Little grebe by its pale eyes, tan cheeks and neck, fine sooty eye-line, dark underparts, and short wings. Differs from Madagascar little grebe by its dark bill, pale eyes, absence of rufous tinge on cheeks and neck, fine sooty eye-line, dark underparts, and short wings.

BEHAVIOR: Little-known aquatic species whose behavior generally resembles that of Little grebe and Madagascar little grebe. Most often found in pairs, sometimes in association with Little grebe.

VOICE: Not known.

DIET: Fish almost exclusively.

NESTING: No data.

DISTRIBUTION AND STATUS: Species is endemic to Madagascar and exclusively local to Lake Alaotra, but some sparse data exist on its presence at other lakes and ponds of the High Plateau around Antananarivo. Reports on its presence farther w (Mahajanga, Antsalova) or in s (Isalo Massif) are doubtful and may stem from sightings of hybrid individuals displaying intermediate characteristics. The Alaotra little grebe is a rare species whose population can hardly exceed 20 pairs; along with the Madagascar pochard, it is one of the island's most threatened species. Its steady decline since its discovery in 1929 forebodes early extinction from several factors: hybridization with the Little grebe, intensive hunting and trapping on Lake Alaotra, transformation of the lake into a rice-growing area, and introduction of herbivorous fish.

Pelecaniformes

Phaethonidae – Tropicbirds

Oceanic birds of tropical seas, with long wings and tails. The two central tail feathers are thin and very long. A web connects the 4 toes, but the hind toe is very small. The nostrils are shaped like open slits and placed high, near the base of the culmen. Tropicbirds are fast, strong fliers. They generally fly high and seize their prey by diving into the water from a certain height. The family is represented by only 3 species; 2 nest in Madagascar and the third has been captured there.

13. *Red-billed Tropicbird*

Phaethon aetherus Linnaeus, 1758
French: Phaéton à bec rouge
No Map

DESCRIPTION: Length 46–50 cm + 46–56-cm streamers, wingspan 99–106 cm.
Adult. Sexes similar. Head white, except for black eye stripe starting at base of bill and continuing to back of nape. Nape and neck white, lightly flecked with gray. Bright red bill, dark brown iris. Upperparts white streaked with black, underparts white, flanks grayish. White scapulars streaked with black. Yellow tarsi and toes, black webs. Wings: upper side white, except for primary coverts and 4 outer remiges, which are black. White underside of wings, white wedge-shaped tail with 2 very long (46–56 cm), stiff, white central tail feathers.
Immature. Differs from adult by yellowish, sometimes black tip of its bill, white tail with black-tipped tail feathers, and absence of elongated central tail feathers.

IDENTIFICATION: Adult is readily identifiable by its size (this is the biggest tropicbird), striped back, 2 long, white central tail feathers, black primary remiges, and bright red bill. Immature is distinguished by its large size, more marked streaking of upperparts than on other species, black tip of tail, and black nape collar.

BEHAVIOR: Oceanic bird.

DISTRIBUTION AND STATUS: Frequents intertropical zones of Pacific, Atlantic, and Indian oceans. Nesting sites nearest Madagascar are in the Red Sea and Persian Gulf. Sole report concerning Madagascar involves an individual captured near Antsirabe. It was unverified (no reference) and is regarded as doubtful.

14. Red-tailed Tropicbird

Phaethon rubricauda Boddaert, 1785
Malagasy: Vorompano
French: Phaéton à queue rouge

DESCRIPTION: Length 46 cm + 30–35-cm streamers, wingspan 104 cm. *Adult.* Sexes similar. Head white, except for a black eye-stripe wider in front of the eye than behind. Stout, sharp, bright red bill. Dark brown iris. Rest of plumage entirely white, sometimes tinged with pink. Scapulars and primary remiges sometimes edged with black. Black tarsi, toes, and webs. White, wedge-shaped tail, prolonged by 2 thin but stiff red central tail feathers 30–35 cm long. *Immature.* Differs from adult by its sooty bill and crown and neck slightly streaked with black. Upperparts streaked with dark gray, underparts white. Primary remiges edged with black. Black-tipped white tail without elongated central tail feathers.

IDENTIFICATION: The adult is readily distinguished by its large size, stocky body, almost entirely white plumage, long, red central tail feathers, and stout, bright red bill. The immature stands out by the delicate black borders of its primary remiges and sooty bill.

BEHAVIOR: Most pelagic of the 3 tropicbird species. Hunts for surface fish alone or in small groups far offshore. Often flies in wide circles, alternating glides with powerful wingbeats.

VOICE: Silent at sea. On land, when nesting, adults utter consistently dissonant, raucous, harsh cries, the most common of which is a guttural, bisyllabic *kuh-ek,* usually emitted in flight. In the nest, the young utter a very loud *kia kia kia.*

HABITAT: Oceanic bird.

DIET: Chiefly flying fish and squid.

NESTING: Nests in loose-knit colonies. The nest is built on the sand, under a low shrub close to shore. The single egg is reddish mottled with brown, laid at ground level in a slight hollow made in the cover of dead leaves. Both parents incubate. Chicks are covered with white down. Nesting has been observed year-round with a peak June–Oct.

DISTRIBUTION AND STATUS: Distributed on islands and islets of intertropical zone of Pacific and Indian oceans. Has nested for many years on Aldabra, Europa, and Round islands. Nesting was first recorded in Madagascar in 1980 on a sandy islet near the coast s of Toliara (Nosy Ve). Two pairs occupied the site in 1980, 12 pairs were recorded nesting in 1983, 16 pairs in 1985. Taboo forbids villagers to kill species or to remove its eggs.

15. *White-tailed Tropicbird*

Phaethon lepturus Daudin, 1802
Malagasy: Kafotsy
French: Phaéton à queue blanche

DESCRIPTION: length 38–40 cm +
33–40 cm streamers, wingspan 89–96 cm.
Adult. Sexes similar. Head white, except
for a black stripe in front of and behind
eyes. Yellow bill, brown iris. Upperparts
white, except for black-tipped scapulars.
Underparts white. Yellow tarsi and toes,
black webs. Wings: upperside white, except for white-tipped black primary remiges and black internal secondary remiges
and secondary coverts. Underside white.
White wedge-shaped tail prolonged by
2 very slender but stiff white central tail
feathers, 33–40 cm long.
Immature. Differs from adult by less pronounced black headband, black-streaked
nape, neck, and upperparts, and yellowish, often black-tipped bill.

IDENTIFICATION: Smallest of the
tropicbirds. Characterized by very agile
and graceful flight, long, narrow wings,
and showy plumage. Additional distinguishing features are black wingtips and
two diagonal black stripes from secondary coverts to scapulars, which set off
white from rest of body. Distinguished
from Red-billed tropicbird by yellow bill
and absence of black stripes on upperparts, and from Red-tailed tropicbird by
yellow bill, white central tail feathers, and
more extensive black markings on its upperparts. The immature differs from the
Red-billed immature by its size and the
lesser black stripes on its upperparts, and
from the Red-tailed by its size, yellow
bill, and black primary remiges. All species subject to both central tail feathers
breaking or tattering during nesting
season.

BEHAVIOR: Least oceanic of 3 tropicbird species. Though it usually fishes on
the open sea, it will also fish close to
shore. Hunts alone or in small groups,
circling over the water and swooping to
seize its prey.

VOICE: Vocal only at breeding sites.
Adults utter a call resembling that of the
Red-tailed tropicbird but shriller and
more drawn out.

HABITAT: Oceanic bird frequenting
land areas near the coast during nesting
period.

DIET: Fish (chiefly flying fish) and
squid.

NESTING: Nests in loose-knit colonies
(15 nests at Nosy Tanikely, July 1987).
Nest is situated in a cliff, in a rock cavity
or in a hole created in the dense vegetation. Single reddish egg is laid on the
ground. Both parents incubate. Chick is
covered with white down. Nesting has
been observed Mar.–Sept.

DISTRIBUTION AND STATUS: Spe-
cies breeds on islands and islets of intertropical zone of Pacific, Atlantic, and Indian oceans (nests in Comoros, Réunion,
Mauritius, Aldabra, and Seychelles). In
Madagascar, it is represented by the
nominate subspecies *P. l. lepturus.* Breeds
on rocky n and nw coasts, especially at
Antsiranana, Nosy Be, Nosy Tanikely,
and Nosy Mitsio, where it is fairly common. Local populations remove eggs,
young, and brooding adults of accessible
colonies.

Fregatidae – Frigatebirds

Oceanic birds of tropical seas, rather large, with decurved bill, short legs, webbed toes, black plumage with white at least on the throat, and characterized by long wings and forked tail. Frigatebirds seize their prey on the water's surface but often attack other seabirds, pursuing them until they disgorge their prey, which the frigatebird then grabs on the wing before the prey falls into the sea. Five species are generally recognized. Two visit Malagasy waters but none nests there.

16. *Greater Frigatebird*

Fregata minor (Gmelin, 1789)
Malagasy: Bomomandry
French: Frégate du Pacifique

DESCRIPTION: Length 86–100 cm, wingspan 206–30 cm.
Adult. Sexes differ. Male slightly larger than female.
Male. Black head with metallic green sheen. Black neck, scarlet throat pouch, blue-gray bill, dark brown iris. Upperparts black with metallic green sheen on mantle, underparts black. Red tarsi, toes, and webs. Black wings and tail.
Female. Black head and neck. Whitish chin and throat, blue-gray bill, dark brown iris, and red orbital ring. Upperparts sooty brown, underparts black, except for white upper chest. Pinkish red tarsi, toes, and webs. Wings dark brown, except for brownish gray upper wing coverts. Black tail.
Immature. Differs from female by the head, chin, throat, and chest, which are white more or less mottled or striped with light brown.

IDENTIFICATION: Very large seabird with characteristic highly aerodynamic silhouette, long, narrow, sharply angled wings, very long forked tail (not always evident, the tail feathers often held close together), and very long hooked bill. Plumage is entirely black (male) or black with white markings on throat and upper chest (female). Greater frigatebird can be confused only with Lesser frigatebird, from which it differs by its considerably larger size. Male Greater frigatebird is distinguished from male Lesser frigatebird by uniformly black underparts. Female is distinguished from female Lesser frigatebird by white throat and black middle and lower belly, and immature differs from immature Lesser frigatebird by lighter hue of head.

BEHAVIOR: Very aerial oceanic species found alone, in pairs, or in small groups of 3–6, rarely more. It may associate with Lesser frigatebird, which is almost always in the majority in mixed groups. Greater frigatebird seeks its food in flight, as a surface feeder or by harassing other species (Brown booby, Greater crested tern, Lesser crested tern) to make them disgorge their prey. Because its plumage is not perfectly waterproof, it does not alight on the water but rests on rocks, cliffs, or island shrubbery. It often soars high in the sky, sometimes beating its wings slowly, and steers with its extremely mobile tail.

VOICE: Silent at sea.

HABITAT: Oceanic species.

DIET: Chiefly fish, squid, and jellyfish, but also young sea turtles and chicks or eggs taken from bird colonies.

DISTRIBUTION AND STATUS: Species breeds in intertropical zone of Atlantic, Pacific, and Indian oceans. Nesting sites nearest Madagascar are Europa, Aldabra, and Tromelin, where the subspecies *F. m. aldabrensis* breeds. Observed most frequently on Madagascar's n and w coasts.

17. *Lesser Frigatebird*

Fregata ariel (Gray, 1845)
Malagasy: Bomomandry
French: Frégate ariel

DESCRIPTION: Length 71–81 cm, wingspan 175–93 cm.
Adult. Sexes differ.
Male. Head and neck black with blue or green metallic sheen. Scarlet throat pouch, grayish bill, dark brown iris. Upperparts black with blue metallic sheen, underparts black, except for a white mark on the flanks extending under the wings. Red-brown tarsi, toes, and webs. Upper side of wings black, underside black, except for white axillaries. Black tail.
Female. Sooty head, brownish nape and back of neck, with whitish borders. Sooty chin and throat, gray to blue-gray bill, brown iris, red orbital ring. Upperparts sooty, underparts sooty, except for white upper chest and flanks. Reddish tarsi, toes, and webs. Upper side of wings sooty with whitish borders at median coverts, underside sooty, except for white axillaries. Black tail.
Immature. Differs from female by its rust-brown head and brownish upperparts edged with fawn and by the rust-brown upper chest, separated from belly and flanks by a dark brown pectoral stripe.

IDENTIFICATION: Very large seabird with characteristic highly aerodynamic silhouette, long, narrow, sharply angled wings, very long forked tail, and very long hooked bill. Plumage entirely black, except for a white mark on the flanks extending to axillaries (male) or sooty with white chest, flanks, and axillaries. Species is distinguished from Greater frigatebird by its considerably smaller size and lighter build. Difference shows clearly in mixed groups. The male is distinguished from male Greater frigatebird by its black throat and white mark on flanks and axillaries. Immature is distinguished from immature Greater frigatebird, with difficulty, by russet head and white mark on axillaries.

BEHAVIOR: Similar to that of Greater frigatebird, with which Lesser frigatebird can be observed.

VOICE: Silent at sea.

HABITAT: Oceanic species.

DIET: Chiefly fish, squid, and jellyfish, but also young sea turtles and chicks or eggs taken from bird colonies.

DISTRIBUTION AND STATUS: Species breeds principally in intertropical zone of Indian and Pacific oceans and to a lesser extent in Atlantic. Nesting sites nearest Madagascar are Aldabra, Tromelin, and Chagos, where the subspecies *F. a. iredalei* (Mathews, 1914), local to the w Indian Ocean, breeds. In Madagascar it is fairly common in nw, around Nosy Be. A rookery numbering several hundred individuals has been found on Quatre Frères Islands near Nosy Mitsio.

Phalacrocoracidae – Cormorant

Aquatic birds that frequent fresh or salt-water, with black or almost black plumage, short tarsi, webbed toes, and stiff tail feathers. The body is more slender than that of the boobies (Sulidae) or pelicans (Pelecanidae), with a long neck, silky head, often crested, and a slender hooked bill. The neck is extended in flight, and wingbeats are rapid with stiff movements. The cormorant's feathers, unlike those of most aquatic birds, quickly get wet when they are in prolonged contact with water, and representatives of this family are often seen drying themselves by opening their wings to the sun. Excellent swimmers and divers, they feed on fish, which they pursue underwater. The family is cosmopolitan and is represented by 32 species. Only 1 species nests in Madagascar.

18. *Reed Cormorant*

Phalacrocorax africanus (Gmelin, 1789)
Malagasy: Fangalamotamboay, Kontonboay, Vadimboay, Ramangarana, Sakaizamboay, Razamboay, Manaramboalavo, Vorondrano
French: Cormoran africain

DESCRIPTION: Length 50–55 cm, wingspan 80–90 cm.
Adult. Sexes similar. Plumage varies seasonally.
Breeding Plumage. Head, neck, chin, and throat smooth black, except for feathers of forehead, which stand up in a short crest with a white base and very light white feathers over and behind the eyes. Pink facial skin. Bill pinkish red, except for black upper ridge. Bright red iris. Upperparts black with green sheen, un-derparts black. Black tarsi, toes, and webs. Wings: upper side silvery gray with black borders, remiges black, underside black. Glossy black tail.
Nonbreeding Plumage. Brown head and nape, whitish chin, dull light brown throat and front of neck. Yellowish bill, dull red iris. Upperparts brown edged with fawn; underparts pale brown, except for brownish flanks and undertail coverts. Brown wings edged with fawn. Sooty tail.
Immature. Differs from adult in non-breeding plumage by more uniform hue of upperparts, whitish underparts, and reddish brown bill and iris.

IDENTIFICATION: Small cormorant with short neck and bill. Long, wedged tail with black and silvery plumage on top, black underneath. Only cormorant in Madagascar. Easily distinguished from the Darter by its considerably smaller size, black plumage, and short hooked bill.

BEHAVIOR: Aquatic species found alone or in small groups, perched on a tree at water's edge. Solitary feeder, swimming very low in the water and seizing its prey at depths to 2 m by means of dives lasting 5–20 seconds. Fishing activity alternates with periods of display out of water to dry plumage, which is not waterproof. Rests in small groups, often with Darters, on dead or withered trees, stumps, or, more rarely, floating islands of vegetation or the bank.

VOICE: Silent outside nesting sites.

HABITAT: Fresh or saltwater (lakes, ponds, rivers, mangroves). Observed at elevations from sea level to 1,500 m.

DIET: Chiefly fish.

NESTING: Usually nests in small numbers (1–5 pairs) amid heron colonies. At Antananarivo, in Apr. 1982, 3 Reed cormorant pairs in a tree that harbored some 10 Great egret pairs. The entire colony included 3 Reed cormorant pairs, 35 Great egret pairs, 2 Squacco heron pairs, and 2 Black-crowned night-heron pairs. Nest is built of woven twigs in a tree. Clutch numbers 3 chalky pale blue to light green eggs. Both parents incubate. Nesting is most common Apr.–Dec. but has been observed all year.

DISTRIBUTION AND STATUS: Distributed in sub-Saharan Africa and Madagascar. In Madagascar it is represented by endemic subspecies *P. a. pictilis* (Bangs, 1918). Ranges over entire island. Common in e, n, and w, less common on High Plateau, and rather rare in s.

Anhingidae – Darter

Darters resemble cormorants in their behavior and habitat. They differ by their pointed bill, stiff, longer tail feathers and longer, thinner neck, but they have the same webs and short tarsi adapted for swimming. The family is represented by 5 species distributed in tropical regions. Only 1 species occurs in Madagascar.

19. *Darter*

Anhinga melanogaster Pennant, 1769
Malagasy: Vadimboay, Ragniboay, Manarana, Manaranomby, Vorona lava ambozona
French: Anhinga d'Afrique

DESCRIPTION: Length 94 cm.
Adult. Sexes differ. Plumage of male varies seasonally.
Male Breeding Plumage. Brown crown, nape, and back of neck. Front and sides of neck fawn, separated from back of neck by thin whitish lateral stripe. Tan chin and throat, fleshy facial skin and bill. Golden yellow iris, eye surrounded by whitish area. Upper- and underparts glossy black. Black tarsi, toes, and webs. Wings: upper side glossy black finely speckled with white, remiges and underside black. Glossy black tail.
Male Nonbreeding Plumage. Differs by faded white lateral neck stripe and dull black of upperparts, underparts, wings, and tail.
Female. Differs from male in nonbreeding plumage by brown crown, back of neck, and mantle and by less speckled wings.
Immature. Differs from female by pale brown underparts.

IDENTIFICATION: Large, somber aquatic species characterized by its very long neck, very small head, slender, straight, sharp bill, and long, wedged tail. Easily distinguished from Reed cormorant by its considerably larger size, black plumage marked with fawn on sides of neck and speckled with white on upper side of wings, and its long, straight bill. In flight its dark silhouette is typical: neck almost completely extended, forming a coil in its posterior part, heavy body, wide wings and long, wedged tail. Powerful wingbeats. Only representative of family in Madagascar.

BEHAVIOR: Aquatic species most often encountered alone. To feed, swims almost completely immersed, with only head and neck above water. Seizes its prey during dives of 20–60 seconds. Frequently seen on a stump or tree near its fishing ground, wings open and drooping and tail spread out to enable its plumage, which is hardly water-resistant, to dry. Roosts in groups of 5–50, sometimes with Reed cormorants. Flies swiftly, skimming the water, for short trips, but frequently soars to great heights.

VOICE: Silent outside nesting sites.

HABITAT: Frequents calm, fairly deep bodies of freshwater surrounded by aquatic vegetation or with wooded banks (lakes and ponds), or more rarely running water (Betsiboka), brackish waters, or mangroves. Observed at elevations from sea level to 1,500 m.

DIET: Chiefly fish but also amphibians.

NESTING: Generally nests in small numbers in heron colonies. The nest, a sort of platform of woven twigs, is built in a tree. Clutch numbers 2–3 chalky pale green or pale blue eggs. Both parents incubate. Nesting has been observed in March and June but probably occurs throughout the year.

DISTRIBUTION AND STATUS: Distributed in Africa, Asia, and Oceania. Represented in Madagascar by endemic subspecies *A. m. vulsini* (Bangs, 1918). Distributed in w from Antsiranana to Morondava (Kinkony, Mitsinjo, Soalala, Masama, Befotaka, Ankerika lakes) and in n (Montagne d'Ambre, Anivorano, Port-Bergé lakes), where it is common, and on High Plateau (Itasy, Tsimbazaza, and Alarobia lakes at Antananarivo), where it is uncommon. Rather rare in e, s, and sw (Ihotry Lake). Once common on Lake Alaotra, it has, like most aquatic birds of that area, dwindled in numbers at an alarming rate.

Sulidae – Boobies

Sea birds with long wings, totipalmate feet, and pointed bill. Nostrils are not visible. Tail feathers are less stiff than those of cormorants and pelicans. Boobies often follow schools of fish, seizing their prey after diving from high up. They nest in colonies. The family is represented by 9 species, 1 of which nests along the coast of Madagascar, while another is an occasional visitor.

20. *Red-footed Booby*

Sula sula (Linnaeus, 1766)
French: Fou à pieds rouges
No Map

DESCRIPTION: Length 66–77 cm, wingspan 91–101 cm.
Adult. Sexes similar. Female larger than male. Polymorphic species. Following morphs may be observed in Madagascar: *White Morph.* Head and neck white, somewhat tinged with yellow. Blue bare periocular area, pale blue bill, brown iris. Upperparts white; underparts white, somewhat tinged with yellow about the chest. Bright red tarsi, toes, and webs. Upper side of wings white with black remiges; underside white with black mark at lesser coverts, black remiges. White tail.
Dark Morph with White Head and Tail. Head and neck white. Upperparts white, except for brown back; underparts white. Brown wings, white tail.
Dark Morph. Plumage brownish all over, except for yellowish patch on crown and neck.
Dark Morph with White Tail. Differs from dark morph only by white tail.
Immature. All immatures are brownish

with mauvish facial area, brownish bill, and yellow legs.

IDENTIFICATION: Large oceanic species with distinctive silhouette characterized by long, narrow wings, wedge-shaped tail, and stout, conical bill. All morphs of Red-footed booby are distinguished from Brown booby by absence of contrast between head and belly (which are always the same color) and by bright red webs. Red-footed also differs from Brown by lighter build and swifter, more agile, and graceful flight.

BEHAVIOR: Oceanic species that feeds in manner typical of boobies.

VOICE: Silent at sea.

HABITAT: Oceanic species.

DIET: Chiefly fish and squid.

DISTRIBUTION AND STATUS: Breeds mainly in intertropical area of Atlantic, Pacific, and Indian oceans. Nesting areas nearest Madagascar are Europa, Aldabra, Cosmoledo, Farquhar, and Tromelin, where subspecies *S. s. rubripes* breeds. In Madagascar, can be seen occasionally on w and n coasts.

21. *Brown Booby*

Sula leucogaster (Boddaert, 1783)
Malagasy: Ngovo
French: Fou brun

DESCRIPTION: Length 64–74 cm, wingspan 132–50 cm.
Adult. Sexes similar. Head and neck chocolate brown. Bare skin of face and throat blue-green to turquoise in male and pale green in female. Yellow bill, pale yellow to straw-colored iris. Upperparts chocolate brown; underparts white, except for chocolate brown upper chest. Yellow-green tarsi, toes, and webs. Upper side of wings chocolate brown. Underside

of wings white with wide brown borders. Brown remiges, chocolate brown tail. *Immature.* Differs from adult by brownish mottling of white parts and generally duller hue of chocolate brown plumage. Bare parts of face and throat gray.

IDENTIFICATION: Large oceanic species with distinctive silhouette characterized by long, narrow wings, wedge-shaped tail, and stout, conical bill. Plumage is strongly contrasted: upperparts dark brown and underparts white, except for brown throat, neck, upper chest, borders of wing, undersides, and remiges. Readily distinguished from Red-footed booby by strongly contrasting brown-and-white plumage of underparts and uniformly brown upperparts.

BEHAVIOR: Oceanic species generally encountered alone, in small numbers, or in a larger flock near roosting or nesting sites or places where food is abundant. Feeds by diving like all other boobies. Dives at very slight angle to surface, which results in shallow penetration of water. Sometimes alights amid school of fish at surface and seizes prey by immersing head. At the end of the day commonly forms ragged line or V-formation of several dozen individuals to return to roost, skimming over waves. Powerful, direct flight in which vigorous wingbeats alternate with long periods of gliding.

VOICE: Silent at sea, moderately vocal at nesting sites.

HABITAT: Oceanic species.

DIET: Chiefly surface fish, also squid and shrimp.

NESTING: Establishes colonies on rocky islets. Nesting observed June–July.

DISTRIBUTION AND STATUS: Breeds mainly in intertropical zone of Pacific, Atlantic, and Indian oceans. Common in Madagascar in vicinity of Nosy Be, where it has recently been found nesting on rocky islets of Nosy Mitsio. Nosy Mitsio also contains several extensive roosts where several hundred individuals may gather.

Pelecanidae – Pelican

Large aquatic birds that frequent fresh or salty waters and are characterized by a thickset body, short tarsi, a rather long neck, a long bill, and a fleshy pouch suspended from the lower mandible and upper throat. Pelicans feed on fish captured either individually by diving from some height to modest depths or in groups by forming lines to drive fish to shallows, where they are then taken. They are good gliders and are fond of soaring. The fairly cosmopolitan family is represented by 8 species, 1 of which used to nest in Madagascar.

22. *Pink-backed Pelican*

Pelecanus rufescens Gmelin, 1789
Malagasy: Gisandrano
French: Pélican gris

DESCRIPTION: Length 125–32 cm, wingspan 265–90 cm.
Adult. Sexes similar. Male larger than female. Slight seasonal variation of plumage.
Nonbreeding Plumage. White head with upright gray feathers on back of head and nape. Gray or pink bill with orange or pink hook, fleshy pouch, dark brown iris, eyes surrounded by gray skin. Upperparts white, tinged with pink on back and uppertail coverts, underparts whitish. Legs yellowish, wings white with black primary remiges and gray secondary remiges edged with gray. Grayish tail.
Breeding Plumage. Feathers of crest grow longer, eye is surrounded by black area, facial skin turns pink, pouch becomes yellow with black stripes, and legs turn red.
Immature. Differs from adult in nonbreeding plumage by its brownish neck, scapulars, and tail. Gray bill, yellowish legs, gray facial skin. White back, brownish wings with sooty primary remiges and brownish secondary remiges edged with white.

IDENTIFICATION: Its enormous size sets the Pink-backed pelican off from all other species.

BEHAVIOR: Aquatic species, gregarious at breeding time and other periods with exception of feeding, which is engaged in alone or in small groups, generally early in the morning or at end of the day, even at night under full moon. When not feeding, species gathers at roosting sites—sandbanks, lakeshores—often with other aquatic birds. Spends much time soaring, at which it excels, often in large flocks.

VOICE: Rather silent outside nesting sites.

HABITAT: Aquatic environments.

DIET: Fish.

NESTING: Used to nest in Madagascar, but there are no data describing the discovered colony. In Africa nests in large colonies in trees, and much more rarely on the ground among reeds.

DISTRIBUTION AND STATUS: Nests in sub-Saharan Africa and s half of Red Sea. Known as accidental visitor to Madagascar before 1958, when a colony was found in w, in Antsalova lakes region. Colony still existed in 1960, but no sighting has been recorded since then. Species is given to nesting fearlessly near humans, and colony was certainly wiped out by villagers.

Ciconiiformes

Ardeidae – Bittern, Herons, Egrets

Large waders with graceful silhouettes, fine long feathers, long pointed bill, and long slender legs with long decurved claws. They frequent shallow waters, marshes, and sometimes meadows and cropland in search of prey. In flight their necks are held in a vertical S-curve. All species utter a harsh call when alarmed, and most nest in sometimes very large colonies that can contain several species. The family is cosmopolitan and is represented by some 60 species. Twelve nest in Madagascar, of which 3 (or 2) are endemic (cf. *Egretta dimorpha* or *E. garzetta dimorpha*). Two other African species occasionally visit the island.

23. *Little Bittern*

Ixobrychus mitutus (Linnaeus, 1766)
Malagasy: Fiandrivoditatratra, Godrano, Mpiandravoditra, Zafimbano, Voromalemy, Tambakoratsy
French: Blongios nain

DESCRIPTION: Length 35 cm, wingspan 53–55 cm.
Adult. Sexes differ. Plumage varies seasonally.
Male Breeding Plumage. Head pale yellow to rufous, sides of neck pale ocher. Bill reddish with brown ridge. Yellowish lores, yellow-orange iris. Upperparts black with greenish sheen; underparts rusty, paler on chest. Greenish tarsi and toes. Wings russet, except for black remiges with green sheen. Black tail.
Female Breeding Plumage. Differs from male by duller plumage. Head pale yellow, except for black cap. Sides of neck

pale ocher spotted with brown. Upperparts yellowish-speckled brown, except for black uppertail coverts; underparts rather similar to male but with conspicuous dark brown stripes on flanks. Tan wings with black-brown remiges.
Adult Nonbreeding Plumage. Plumage of each sex more subdued, with no gloss. Greenish yellow bill with brown ridge.
Immature. Differs from female in nonbreeding plumage by generally browner overall hue and conspicuous yellowish mottling of plumage on head, neck, and underparts.

IDENTIFICATION: Tiny heron (smallest of Madagascar), with thick neck and contrasting plumage. Cannot be confused with any other species. In flight shows wide, rounded black wings marked with large light area, neck bulges and toes extend beyond tail. Rather rapid wingbeats alternate with glides.

BEHAVIOR: Found alone or in pairs. Very secretive. Active during day, especially early and at twilight. Difficult to observe; generally seen flying swiftly over marshlands at morning or nightfall. Waits, usually concealed among reeds at edge of open area, for prey to come within range and then seizes quarry with quick stab of bill. Moves about confidently on its long legs in dense vegetation. If disturbed, it melts into reeds or flies a few meters, letting its legs hang down. When surprised, it freezes in absolutely vertical stance, bill pointing straight up, blending perfectly with surrounding vegetation.

VOICE: Largely silent, except for brief cawing *kreh-eh* uttered in flight.

HABITAT: Frequents marshlands, lakes, even small bodies of water with reeds along bank or a belt of islands of dense vegetation. Observed at elevation from sea level to 1,500 m.

DIET: Small fish, batrachians (tadpoles and frogs), crayfish, and insects.

NESTING: Very few data in Madagascar; species nests in isolation. Nest is built in reeds a few decimeters above water. No information on number of eggs, which are white. Nesting has been observed Nov.–Dec.

DISTRIBUTION AND STATUS: Distributed in Europe, Africa, Asia, and Oceania. Represented in Madagascar by endemic subspecies *I. m. podiceps* (Bonaparte, 1855), which breeds in Madagascar but seems to migrate to E Africa (sightings at Zanzibar). Uncommon, it is known from a few points scattered throughout Madagascar, except s: Ihotry, Kinkony, Sambirano, Mandroseza (Antananarivo), Itasy, Alaotra, Maroantsetra, and Andapa lakes. Subspecies *I. m. minutus*, which breeds in Europe and winters in sub-Saharan Africa, is thought to frequent Madagascar during boreal winter.

24. *Black-crowned Night-Heron*

Nycticorax nycticorax (Linnaeus, 1758)
Malagasy: Goaka, Goadrano, Doaka, Koaka, Rahoaka
French: Héron Bihoreau à calotte noire

DESCRIPTION: Length 58–62 cm, wingspan 95–110 cm.
Adult. Sexes similar. Plumage varies seasonally.
Breeding Plumage. Crown and nape black, with 2–3 long, narrow white feathers extending to the back. Forehead, eyebrow, and rest of head white. Neck white, except ashen gray in back. Black bill, green-blue lores, red iris. Upperparts: upper back and scapulars black, except for gray-tinted flanks. Tarsi and toes straw-colored to red. Pale gray wings with dark gray remiges. Dark gray tail.

Nonbreeding Plumage. Differs from adult in breeding plumage by absence of ornamental head feathers, greenish bill and lores, and pale yellow tarsi and toes. *Immature.* Head and upperparts dark brown streaked with yellow. Grayish pink bill, tan iris. Scapulars end in large yellowish patch. Underparts: chest and flanks brown with yellowish streaks, belly whitish streaked with brown, undertail coverts whitish. Gray-green tarsi and toes. Wings brown with large light tan patches, remiges dark brown with light tan tips. Gray-brown tail.

IDENTIFICATION: Squat, medium-sized, dark gray and white heron, with large head and short, thick neck. Other distinguishing features are short, thick black bill, long ornamental feathers sweeping down to the back, and red iris. In flight, its silhouette is characteristic, with large rounded wings, stocky body, and toes barely extending beyond tail. Gray wings contrast with black upperparts. Its flight is graceful and its wingbeats are rapid for a medium-sized heron.

BEHAVIOR: Gregarious, mainly nocturnal aquatic species found in small groups of 3–10 perched on floating vegetation, banks, or trees at water's edge. Frequently seen flying in pairs or small groups at dusk. Hunts stealthily in shallow water, from a perch rising out of the water, or while walking slowly. Feeds almost exclusively at night, except during breeding period, when it also feeds during the day and final hours of daylight. Daytime roosts of several dozen birds, occasionally several hundred (120 at Alarobia Lake, May 1982; 380 at Bemamba Lake, Oct. 1985), are established in dense vegetation of marshlands, lakes, rivers, and mangroves. Moves about gracefully in branches of trees or bushes of these roosts.

VOICE: Its call, a solemn, resonant *Gwok,* uttered frequently during its nocturnal flights, helps identify and locate species. No other sound has been recorded outside nesting sites.

HABITAT: Frequents fresh and brackish waters of lakes, rivers, river mouths, rice paddies, and mangroves. Rests near its feeding grounds when they offer dense cover. Observed at elevations from sea level to 1,500 m.

DIET: Varied; fish, reptiles, batrachians, small mammals, birds, insects, and crustaceans.

NESTING: Gregarious, it usually nests in mixed heron colonies (30 pairs of Black-crowned night-herons, 500 of Squacco herons, 50 of Malagasy pond herons, 1,000 of Cattle egrets, 400 of Dimorphic egrets, and 30 of Great egrets at Antananarivo, Dec. 1981). Nest of interlaced branches and twigs is built in low shrubs, reedbeds, or bamboo stands, or in bushes or trees, at a height that varies 0.5–20.0 m. Clutch numbers 3 green-blue eggs (average size: 49.5 mm × 35.6 mm). Both parent incubate. Chicks are covered with brownish down. Nesting has been observed Aug.–Jan., peaking Nov.–Dec.

DISTRIBUTION AND STATUS: Distributed in Europe, Africa, Asia, and N and S America. Represented in Madagascar by nominate subspecies *N. n. nycticorax,* common to Europe and Africa. Its range covers the island, and it is fairly common everywhere except s. Like other species of herons that nest in colonies, it is subject to regular nest-raiding by villagers.

25. *Squacco Heron*

Ardeola ralloides (Scopoli, 1769)
Malagasy: Mpiandrivoditatatra,

Fiandrivoditatratra, Andevondangoro
French: Héron crabier chevelu

DESCRIPTION: Length 45–48 cm,
wingspan 80–90 cm.
Breeding Plumage. Crown and back of
neck yellowish with a crest of long
plumes with sooty edges. Whitish throat,
rest of head and neck yellowish. Black-
tipped blue bill, green or blue lores,
bright yellow iris. Upperparts: feathers of
mantle and scapulars brownish, very long,
with fine separate barbs, sweeping back
over wings and tail; rest of upperparts
whitish tinged with yellow. Underparts:
ocher chest, white belly. Red tarsi and
toes. White wings tipped with ocher on
wing coverts. White tail.
Nonbreeding Plumage. No crest and ornamental feathers. Head and neck have
brown stripes. Brownish back, yellow-
green black-tipped bill, yellow iris, yellow-green tarsi and toes.
Immature. Differs from nonbreeding
adult by more sustained brownish tinge,
more pronounced stripes on chest, grayish belly, and brown-tinged wings.

IDENTIFICATION: Stocky, short-
legged ocher heron with short, tapering
bill. In flight its silhouette is even more
hunched than when it is settled, toes extending slightly beyond tail. White wings
and ocher upperparts contrast conspicuously. From below it appears white
with dark chest. Wingbeats are rapid and
light, and it glides more rapidly than
Dimorphic and Cattle egrets. Distinguished from Cattle egret by smaller size,
ocher-brown color, much more horizontal posture, and most of all, habitat. Distinguished from Malagasy pond heron in
breeding plumage by ocher-brown coloring. Distinction between Squacco heron
and Malagasy pond heron is very subtle
in the field. Squacco will be seen as more
lightly built, with less thick neck and less

conspicuous black streaks. Wing profiles
differ in flight: tip is more pointed in
Squacco, squarer in Malagasy pond
heron.

BEHAVIOR: Secretive, usually sighted
as solitary stalker, more rarely in small
groups of 3–8. Activity is strictly diurnal
and tends to occur in early morning or
at dusk. Usually stands immobile at edge
of aquatic vegetation, often slightly concealed, on floating vegetation or in shallow water. Gregarious at roosts, often
associating with other heron species
(Malagasy pond heron, Cattle egret, Dimorphic egret).

VOICE: Quiet, sometimes uttering a sort
of hoarse and stifled *kah* at nightfall.

HABITAT: Frequents shallow bodies of
water ringed by dense vegetation (reeds)
or offering floating vegetation: marshes,
ponds, lakes, flooded meadows, or rice
paddies, as well as river or marine mud
flats and mangroves. Observed at elevations from sea level to 1,800 m.

DIET: Chiefly small fish and insects, but
also batrachians, crabs, and spiders.

NESTING: Gregarious at nesting sites.
Usually nests in mixed heron colonies
than can accommodate several hundred
pairs (500 Squacco heron pairs at Antananarivo, Dec. 1981). Nest of interlaced
twigs, reeds, and grasses is built low off
ground (rarely higher than 0.5–1.0 m),
on or in thick brush at water's edge.
Clutch numbers 3 green-blue eggs. Both
parents incubate. Chick is covered in
mixed gray, rust, and white down. Nesting has been observed Oct.–Mar., peaking Nov.–Dec.

DISTRIBUTION AND STATUS: Widely
distributed in Europe, Africa, and Asia.
Found throughout Madagascar, where
it is common, except in s, where it is
rather rare.

26. *Malagasy Pond Heron*

Ardeola idae (Hartlaub, 1860)
Malagasy: Mpiandrivoditatatra,
Fiandrivoditatratra
French: Héron crabier blanc

DESCRIPTION: Length 45–48 cm.
Adult. Sexes similar. Plumage varies
seasonally.
Breeding Plumage. Pure white all over.
Plumes on crown and very long ornamental feathers with fine separate barbs
on upperparts and chest give plumage
slightly puffy appearance. Black-tipped
bright blue bill, greenish lores, and yellow
iris. Pink tarsi and toes.
Nonbreeding Plumage. Crown and nape
tan, heavily streaked with black. Sides of
head and throat yellow, lightly streaked
with dark brown. Black-tipped gray bill
tinged with green, greenish lores, yellow
iris. Upperparts: brown mantle and scapulars with tan streaks widening at tips of
feathers. Brownish back, whitish rump.
Underparts: yellow chest slightly streaked
with dark brown, whitish belly. Greenish
to yellowish tarsi and toes. Wings: white
remiges. Whitish tail.
Immature. Differs from adult in nonbreeding plumage by external remiges
and tail finely marked with dark brown.
Orange bill with sooty tip, pale green iris.

IDENTIFICATION: Small, stocky heron
with uniformly white breeding plumage,
short pink legs, and short, tapered, black-
tipped bright blue bill. Easy to identify in
breeding plumage. Distinguished from
Cattle egret by smaller bill and from
Squacco heron by its white coloring. For
identification in nonbreeding plumage,
see Squacco heron.

BEHAVIOR: Resembles that of Squacco
heron. Secretive and solitary, even during
daytime rest periods. Groups of several
individuals are rarely sighted. Hunts
stealthily, standing immobile at water's
edge, in shallow water, or perched on
floating vegetation. Tends to seek refuge
on nearby tree when disturbed.

VOICE: Quiet, utters a sort of brief,
hoarse, rather soft *keh-eh* when disturbed.

HABITAT: Frequents shallow bodies of
water ringed by vegetation or located in
woodlands or offering floating vegetation
(marshes, lakes, slow-moving rivers, rice
paddies). Seldom seen in mangroves or
mud flats near the sea. Observed at elevations from sea level to 1,800 m.

DIET: Chiefly batrachians and fish, also
insects.

NESTING: Gregarious at nesting sties.
Usually nests in mixed heron colonies (10
pairs of Malagasy pond herons, 50 of
Black-crown night-herons, and 30 of
Squacco herons at Maroantsetra, Jan.
1982; 50 pairs of Malagasy pond herons,
30 of Black-crowned night-herons, 500
of Squacco herons, 1,000 of Cattle egrets,
and 400 of Dimorphic egrets at Antananarivo, Dec. 1981). Nest of interlaced
twigs is built low off ground (0.5–1.5 m)
on a bush or in shrubbery near water.
Clutch numbers 2–4 (generally 3) greenish white eggs. Both parents incubate.
Chicks are covered with yellowish down.
Nesting has been observed Oct.–Mar.,
peaking Nov.–Dec.

DISTRIBUTION AND STATUS: Migratory species endemic to Malagasy region,
having also bred at Aldabra since 1967.
Leaves Madagascar May–Oct. to spend
austral winter in e and central Africa
(s half of Kenya, Tanzania, Rwanda, e of
Zaire, and more seldom the e half of
Zambia, ne Zimbabwe, n half of Mozambique, s of Uganda). Ranges throughout
Madagascar, where it is fairly common,
except in s, where it is rather rare. Population has declined over past 50 years in

favor of Squacco heron, which is better adapted to new human-made environments (creation of rice paddies is accompanied by disappearance of woodlands, which species likes to have near feeding grounds). This decline is much more pronounced on High Plateau than in other regions.

27. Cattle Egret

Bubulcus ibis (Linnaeus, 1758)
Malagasy: Vorompotsy, Kilandry, Rainibao
French: Héron garde-boeufs

DESCRIPTION: Length 50–55 cm, wingspan 90 cm.
Adult. Sexes similar. Plumage varies seasonally.
Breeding Plumage. Entirely white, except for crest of orange erectile feathers on crown and nape, and orange ornamental feathers with fine separate barbs on upper chest and back. Orange to coral red bill, orange, pink, or red lores, orange-red iris. Orange-yellow to orange-red tarsi and toes.
Nonbreeding Plumage. No orange coloring or ornamental feathers. Yellow bill, lores, and iris. Yellowish tarsi and yellow-gray toes.
Immature. Similar to adult in nonbreeding plumage with sooty bill, tarsi, and toes.

IDENTIFICATION: Small, stocky, short-necked white species with yellow-orange short, stout bill. Distinguished from Dimorphic egret by plump silhouette, short neck, short yellow bill, short yellow or orange tarsi, and orange coloring of ornamental feathers (breeding plumage). Differs from Squacco heron and Malagasy pond heron in nonbreeding plumage by its much more vertical posture and especially by its behavior and habitat. Distinguished from Malagasy

pond heron in breeding plumage by same features, as well as yellow or orange bill and yellow or orange tarsi. In flight it differs from Dimorphic egret by its shorter, rounded wings and more rapid wingbeats and from Malagasy pond heron in breeding plumage by its shorter, lighter-colored bill and slower wingbeats.

BEHAVIOR: Gregarious species closely linked to presence of cattle, found in pastures in groups of 5–30. Larger gatherings may be seen in places where food is abundant (several hundred attracted by a bushfire at Antsiranana, Sept. 1985). Least aquatic of all herons in Madagascar. Feeds in daylight, seizing prey disturbed by grazing zebus. Often seen on backs of cattle. At dusk, flocks of 10–200 in line or V-formation return to roosts, which are established in trees or sometimes on ground, usually near water (lakes, rivers, mangroves), sometimes near a village.

VOICE: Silent outside nesting or roosting sites.

HABITAT: Open land frequented by cattle: pasture, grass savanna, lakeshores and riverbanks, outskirts of towns and villages. Less inclined to frequent wetlands. Observed at elevations from sea level to 1,700 m.

DIET: Chiefly insects (mostly Orthoptera); also amphibians, reptiles, and young birds.

NESTING: Colonies of this very gregarious species often attract other heron species—Squacco heron, Malagasy pond heron, Dimorphic egret, Great egret. Colonies may accommodate several hundred nests (1,000 pairs of Cattle egrets at Antananarivo, Dec. 1982). Nest of twigs, branches, and reeds is built 2–3 m above ground or water in a tree, bush, bamboo stand, or shrub. Nesting sites are often away from feeding sites. Clutch numbers

3 bluish eggs. Both parents incubate. Chick is covered in white down. Nesting has been observed Aug.–Feb., peaking Sept. –Nov.

DISTRIBUTION AND STATUS: Cosmopolitan species with expanding worldwide range. Found in Europe, Africa, Asia, N and S America, and Oceania. Represented in Madagascar by nominate subspecies *B. i. ibis,* common to sub-Saharan Africa, Comoros, Aldabra, Réunion, and Mauritius. Very common throughout Madagascar.

28. *Green-backed Heron*

Butorides striatus (Linnaeus, 1758)
Malagasy: Tambakoratsy, Koaky, Kisanjy, Keho, Vorompantsika, Voromaty, Ambaramaty
French: Héron à dos vert

DESCRIPTION: Length 40 cm.
Adult. Sexes similar. Plumage varies seasonally.
Breeding Plumage. Crown and nape green-tinged glossy black, ending in long crest on neck. White stripe from forehead to over eye and heavy white stripe from white chin to cheek, framing a black stripe crossing the eye. Rest of head gray. Shiny black bill, yellow lores, orange-yellow iris. Upperparts gray, except for long, tapering, glossy dark green scapulars. Underparts: sides and back of neck gray, front of neck and upper chest grayish mottled with rust brown, lower chest and belly grayish. Orange-yellow to red-orange tarsi and toes. Wings: gray remiges, greenish upper wing coverts, gray underside. Dark gray tail.
Nonbreeding Plumage. Duller plumage, no ornamental feathers. Orange tarsi and toes. Dull sooty bill, greenish lores, yellow iris.
Immature. Differs from adult in non-

breeding plumage by brownish upperparts, grayish underparts heavily streaked with brown, and brownish wings mottled with white. Light brown bill.

IDENTIFICATION: Small, stocky heron with short, thick neck and long, sharp bill. Characterized by dark green cap and scapulars, grayish neck and underparts. Distinguished from Little bittern by larger size, long erectile head feathers, dark wings, and especially behavior and habitat. When at rest, its horizontal silhouette, head drawn back or leaning forward, is distinctive. In flight it appears as a small, somber heron, neck slightly stretched, orange legs extending past tail.

BEHAVIOR: Solitary and secretive. Spends long periods immobile, in wait for prey in shallow water. Commonly observed in this position on a stump, rock, or muddy or sandy bank barely emerging from water, body held horizontal, bill poised a few centimeters from water's surface. Moves about easily among low branches of wooded banks or mangroves. When alarmed, it draws itself up, stretches its neck, and walks away or takes flight, uttering a brief call before settling again a short distance away, always blending perfectly into its surroundings. Diurnal and nocturnal roosts are established in trees near feeding grounds or rocks along the coast.

VOICE: Silent except for brief, loud, dissonant call suggesting a *kiah* accompanying its flight when alarmed.

HABITAT: Shallow fresh, brackish, or salt waters (ponds, lakes, river mouths, waterways, mudbanks, mangroves, rocky coasts). Often seen in rice paddies and drainage and irrigation ditches. Particularly fond of wooded banks or wetlands covered with dense undergrowth. Observed at elevations from sea level to 1,500 m.

DIET: Chiefly small fish (Mud skip-per—*Perioptalmus* sp. in mangroves), crabs, batrachians, and insects.

NESTING: Nests in isolation. Nest is a platform of interlaced twigs built in a tree or shrub near feeding grounds, usually 1–2 m above water, occasionally higher (4 m in a clove tree on bank of rice paddy at Maroantsetra, Jan. 1982). Clutch num-bers 3 light green-blue eggs (average size: 37 mm × 27 mm). Both parents incu-bate. Chick is covered in light gray down. Nesting has been observed Oct.–Jan.

DISTRIBUTION AND STATUS: Distrib-uted in Africa, Asia, N and S America, and Oceania. Thirty subspecies recog-nized. Represented in Madagascar by subspecies *B. s. rutenbergi* (Hartlaub, 1880), local to Madagascar and Réunion. Ranges throughout island. Rare on High Plateau (first mentioned at Antananarivo, Oct. 1983), uncommon in s, and common elsewhere.

29. Black Heron

Egretta ardesiaca (Wagler, 1827)
Malagasy: Salobokomana, Lombokoma, Ombikomana, Rafanopoka
French: Héron ardoisé

DESCRIPTION: Length 48–50 cm.
Adult. Sexes similar. Plumage entirely black, tinged with slate gray or blue. Long plumes on crown, nape, neck, and mantle. Black bill and lores. Bright yellow iris. Black tarsi and yellow to orange-yel-low toes.
Immature. Differs from adult by duller plumage, black tinged with brown, and absence of plumes.

IDENTIFICATION: Small heron with all black plumage setting off yellow toes and bright yellow eyes. Swift flight with vigorous wingbeats. Habit of spreading wings to cover water surface to feed is unmistakable field mark. Distinguished from Dimorphic egret in dark morph by smaller size, shorter tarsi, and lack of any white in its plumage.

BEHAVIOR: Very gregarious aquatic species found in groups of 5–40, some-times more (250 at Bemamba Lake, Oct. 1985; 200 at Amboromalandy Lake, July 1987). Feeds in a group, forming a "car-pet" of outspread wings over the water: each takes a few steps, stops, lowers head, and quickly spreads wings over its head, thus creating a shady area in which to fish. Maintains this posture for some seconds before repeating the procedure a little farther on. Feeding is exclusively di-urnal, but "shading" technique is also used with overcast skies or at dusk. Be-fore nightfall, Black herons gather at roosts that sometimes number several hundred (500 at Bemamba, Oct. 1985), sometimes with other heron species, such as Dimorphic egret.

VOICE: Silent outside nesting sites.

HABITAT: Frequents fresh, more rarely brackish, shallow waters of lakes, ponds, and rivers; also rice paddies or any other flooded area. Observed at elevations from sea level to 1,500 m.

DIET: Chiefly small fish; also crusta-ceans and insects.

NESTING: Nests in colonies, most often monospecific, more rarely with other her-ons, such as Great egret, Dimorphic egret, Squacco heron, and Malagasy pond heron. Colonies can be very large, with 5,000 pairs reported in single col-ony, 1940–50, near Antananarivo. Fol-lowing disturbances, however, large, excessively exposed colonies have dis-persed, and it is now rare to find more than 40–50 pairs in a colony. Nest of in-terlaced branches is built in a tree or shrub, occasionally in reeds, always in

immediate vicinity of water. Clutch numbers 2–4 gray-blue to dark blue eggs.
Chicks are covered in dark-gray down.
Nesting has been observed Nov.–June
(Dec. at Maroantsetra, Nov.–June at Antananarivo); it is later than that of other
herons, peaking in Feb.

DISTRIBUTION AND STATUS: Limited to Africa and Madagascar. In Madagascar, distributed throughout country:
rare in s, fairly common in e and on High
Plateau, common in w. Without doubt
this is the species of heron most affected
by disruptions of human origin. Numbers
have declined considerably over past 30
years, especially on High Plateau, where
it is now rare to encounter groups of
more than 30.

30. *Dimorphic Egret*

Egretta dimorpha Hartert, 1924
Malagasy: Vanofotsy, Langorofotsy,
Vanomainty
French: Aigrette dimorphe

DESCRIPTION: Length 55–65 cm.
Adult. Sexes similar. Polymorphic species. Plumage has two common morphs,
one entirely white, the other black; individuals may show any intermediate stage.
White Morph. Plumage entirely white,
with 2 long tapering feathers on the head
sweeping down over the neck and long
plumes on front of neck and upper chest.
Mantle and scapular feathers are exceptionally long, with fine, separate barbs.
Slender, long black bill, yellow lores,
light-yellow iris. Black tarsi, yellow to orange-yellow toes.
Black Morph. Plumage entirely black, except for white throat and white patch of
varying size on lesser wing coverts. Yellow lower mandible, sooty upper mandible, yellowish lores, yellow iris.
Immature. Similar to adult, except for or-

namental feathers of underparts and
upperparts.

IDENTIFICATION: Medium-sized
egret with slender, streamlined silhouette,
rather flimsy black bill, black tarsi, and
yellow toes. White morph is distinguished
from Great egret by considerably smaller
size, black, smaller bill, and yellow toes
set off by black tarsi. Differs from Cattle
egret by larger size, more streamlined silhouette, absence of ocher tinge in plumage, and black bill and tarsi. Dark morph
is distinguished from Black heron by
larger size, white throat, white patch on
lesser wing coverts (visible in flight) and
yellowish lower mandible. In flight its
rather short wings and its legs reaching
beyond the tail are noticeable. Wingbeats
are more rapid than those of Great egret
but slower than those of Cattle egret.

BEHAVIOR: Aquatic species often encountered alone or in pairs, more rarely
in small groups (except in areas where
food is abundant). Quest for food is pursued during daylight. Slow gait in shallow
water is smartly accelerated to seize prey.
Sometimes it walks in place on muddy or
silted bottom and catches small creatures
thus disturbed. During heat of day and at
nightfall, individuals congregate on trees
near their feeding ground, sometimes in
company of other species, such as Gray
heron, Great egret, or Humblot's heron.

VOICE: Generally silent outside nesting
sites.

HABITAT: Frequents all sorts of fresh,
brackish, or saltwater habitats: ponds,
lakes, rivers, estuaries, mangroves, mud
or sand flats along the seacoast, and often
coral islets, even well away from the
coast. Observed at elevations from sea
level to 1,600 m.

DIET: Fish, crabs, snails, shellfish; also
insects.

NESTING: Nests in mixed colonies that also accommodate Black-crowned night-heron, Squacco heron, Malagasy pond heron, Cattle egret, and Great egret. The colonies may contain several hundred nests (400 pairs of Dimorphic egrets, 30 of Black-crowned night-herons, 500 of Squacco herons, 30 of Malagasy pond herons and 30 of Great egrets at Antananarivo, Dec. 1981). Nest of interlaced branches and twigs is located in trees or shrubs, more rarely on the ground, always near water. Clutch numbers 2–3 green-blue eggs. Both parents incubate. Chick is covered in white or black down, depending on morph. Individuals in black or gray morph are seldom outside coastal zones, where they represent about a quarter of population. Pairs may consist of partners in different morphs.

DISTRIBUTION AND STATUS: Distributed in Madagascar, Aldabra, Cosmoledo, Astove, and Pemba. Taxonomy on species is poorly defined and varies among authorities. Some authors treat Dimorphic egret *Egretta dimorpha* as a simple subspecies of the Little egret *E. garzetta dimorpha*. It ranges over all Madagascar, where it is common, indeed locally very common. Black morph is rather common along seashore, less so at freshwater sites, and rare in interior, except in the region of Fianarantsoa, where it is quite common. Like other herons nesting in colonies, suffers disruptions and depredations by villagers.

31. *Great Egret*

Casmerodius albus (Linnaeus, 1758)
Malagasy: Vanofotsy, Langorofotsy, Kilandry be, Langaraka, Langorona
French: Grande Aigrettte

DESCRIPTION: Length 90–100 cm, wingspan 150–65 cm.

Adult. Sexes similar. Plumage varies seasonally.
Breeding Plumage. Pure white all over. Black bill with yellow base, pearly emerald-green lores and orbital zone, pale yellow iris. Scapulars exceptionally long, with fine separate barbs. Black tarsi and toes. *Nonbreeding Plumage.* Differs by yellow bill, olive-green lores and orbital zone, and absence of ornamental feathers. *Immature.* Similar to adult in nonbreeding plumage.

IDENTIFICATION: Large heron with very slender silhouette, long neck, entirely white plumage, bill black in breeding period and yellow in nonbreeding period, and black tarsi and toes. Distinguished from Dimorphic egret in white morph by its much larger size, commensurately longer neck, more powerful bill, and black toes. In flight its wings appear rather narrow and its legs extend well past its tail. Slow wingbeats.

BEHAVIOR: Aquatic species encountered alone, also in sometimes very large groups (1,000 on shore of a lake near Bemamba Lake, Nov. 1985). Waits motionless for prey to come within striking distance or walks slowly, sometimes in deep water, neck near surface. Seizes prey with quick stab, often immersing head and part of neck. Feeding is chiefly diurnal. Shortly before sunset, Great egrets congregate in roosts on large trees alongside lakes or rivers or in mangroves, often in company with Reed cormorants, Black herons, Dimorphic egrets, Gray herons, Humblot's herons, and African spoonbills.

VOICE: Generally silent outside nesting sites. Sometimes, generally in flight, utters guttural calls sounding like *kro-ak, kro-ak*, much more solemn in character than call of Dimorphic egret.

HABITAT: Wide variety of wetlands (ponds, lakes, rivers, marshes, estuaries, mud flats, seashore, and coral islets, sometimes well offshore). Observed at elevations from sea level to 1,700 m.

DIET: Chiefly fish but also batrachians, reptiles, and numerous terrestrial and aquatic insects.

NESTING: Nests in mixed colonies also accommodating Black-crowned night-herons, Squacco herons, Malagasy pond herons, Cattle egrets, and Dimorphic egrets. Nest is almost always high in a tree, otherwise on a bush or shrub, usually near water. Nest is a platform consisting of branches lined with softer vegetal material in the middle. Both parents incubate. Chick is covered in white down. Nesting has been observed Sept.–May, peaking in Dec. (Dec.–Mar. at Maroantsetra, Sept.–May at Antananarivo, Dec. at Ihotry Lake).

DISTRIBUTION AND STATUS: Distributed over 5 continents. Represented in Madagascar by subspecies *C. a. melanorhynchos* (Wagler, 1827), common to Africa. Very common throughout Madagascar, except in s, where it is rarer. Suffers depredations by local populations. Large colonies too frequently disturbed and raided are abandoned in exchange for smaller, less obvious, or inaccessible ones (nesting in trees of rocky islet 15 km off Maroantsetra). Some impressive colonies still exist at Antananarivo, such as those at Parc de Tzimbazaza (40 pairs, Dec. 1982) and at Alarobia Lake (50 pairs in Mar. 1983).

32. *Purple Heron*

Ardea purpurea Linnaeus, 1766
Malagasy: Langorovoanga, Vagna, Vanomena, Kehambe, Langorofalafa
French: Héron pourpré

DESCRIPTION: Length 79 cm. *Adult.* Sexes similar. Black forehead, nape, and crown, with 2 long black plumes sweeping along the neck. Rufous sides of head and neck. One black line is drawn from bill along sides of head to nape, another from bill down sides of neck. White chin, throat, and front of neck. Lower part of front of neck broadly streaked with black. Rather slender orange-brown bill, green-yellow lores, yellow iris. Upperparts: gray mantle tinged with rufous, long, plumed scapulars ranging from gray at base to fawn at tip, dark gray back. Underparts: mottled dark brown and black chest, brown-gray flanks, black belly. Brown tarsi and toes. Wings gray, except for black primary remiges and russet underwing coverts. Slate gray tail. *Immature.* Differs from adult by absence of ornamental head feathers, mantle plumes, and scapulars. Upperparts brown with tan-edged feathers, underparts uniformly tan-brown.

IDENTIFICATION: Medium-sized heron with streamlined silhouette and slender neck and bill. Distinguished from all other heron species by rufous neck, dark gray upperparts, and russet and black underparts. In flight its silhouette is less hunched than that of other large herons, and its legs extend well beyond its tail.

BEHAVIOR: Aquatic species generally found alone, sometimes in pairs, in thick marshy vegetation of lakes, ponds, or riverbanks. Feeds by remaining immobile in shallow water or on floating vegetation for long periods, waiting for prey to come within striking distance. Sometimes walks slowly in water, bill almost touching surface. Seizes prey with whiplike uncoiling of neck. Feeds alone mainly at dusk. Several may gather during diurnal and nocturnal resting periods, generally in areas protected by aquatic vegetation.

VOICE: Utters harsh, rather nasal call, *kwah-ahk*, resembling that of Gray heron but more piercing.

HABITAT: Prefers freshwater lakes and rivers offering dense aquatic vegetation (reeds), but also frequents bodies of water in woodlands and rice paddies. Very occasionally encountered in estuaries and mangroves. Observed at elevations from sea level to 1,800 m.

DIET: Chiefly fish, also amphibians and reptiles, even small birds.

NESTING: Nests in small monospecific colonies of 3–7 pairs, rarely more, established in aquatic vegetation. Sometimes nests in isolation. More rarely, a few nests occupy a tree. Nest consists of reeds or branches. Clutch numbers 3 green-blue eggs. Both parents incubate. Chick is covered in down, dark gray on top and white below. Nesting has been observed June–Dec.

DISTRIBUTION AND STATUS: Distributed in Europe, Africa, and Asia. Represented in Madagascar by endemic subspecies *A. p. madagascariensis* (Van Oort, 1910). Range covers all Madagascar; common throughout, except in s, where it is rare. Chooses remote or inaccessible nesting sites, and its nests seem therefore to have been raided less than those of other herons.

33. *Gray Heron*

Ardea cinerea Linnaeus, 1758
Malagasy: Vano, Vanokasira, Langoromavo
French: Héron cendré

DESCRIPTION: Length 90–98 cm, wingspan 175–90 cm.
Adult. Sexes similar, female smaller on average. Head white all over, except for 2 lateral black stripes that start behind eyes, join on nape, and end in crest of 2 long, tapering feathers. Whitish neck with 2 black lines in front. Yellow to orange-yellow bill (may be bright orange to vermillion in breeding period). Yellowish lores, greenish skin around eyes, pale yellow iris. Upperparts ash gray with lanceolate scapulars. Underparts white, except for gray flanks and black sides of chest and belly. Light brown tarsi and toes (orange to red during breeding period). Wings blue-gray, except for dark gray remiges and primary coverts and white mark on lesser coverts. Gray tail.
Immature. Differs from adult by less contrasted plumage and absence of ornamental feathers. Crown and nape dark gray, front of neck flecked with dark brown, flanks brown-gray, upperparts gray-brown. Brownish bill and legs.

IDENTIFICATION: Large heron with rather slender silhouette and black-and-white plumage. Size intermediate between Purple heron and Humblot's heron. Flight slow and cumbersome. Distinguished from Humblot's heron by smaller size, lighter build, much lighter and contrasted plumage, and white mark at lesser coverts. Distinguished from Purple heron by larger size, slightly stockier silhouette, and light plumage with no brown tints. Hunched silhouette in flight (neck curved and legs extended). Conspicuous contrast, from above, between blackish remiges and gray coverts and, from below, between white underparts and dark underside of wings.

BEHAVIOR: Aquatic species frequenting both fresh and saltwater. Usually feeds alone or in small, loose-knit groups, with peak activity at dawn and dusk. May also feed at night. Fishes in shallow water, waiting immobile for prey to come within striking distance or walking slowly. May take up wait-and-watch position on anything that provides a slightly raised platform, and is sometimes seen in water-logged or flooded grassy areas. Seizes prey with whiplike uncoiling of neck. Usually roosts in groups, sometimes alone, on a tree, mudbank, sandbank, cliff, or rock near feeding grounds or nesting site.

VOICE: Often utters harsh, raucous call, a loud, nasal *krreh-ehk*, as it takes flight or in flight.

HABITAT: Fresh and saltwater (lake-shores, riverbanks, seashores, coral islets, mangroves, mud flats, rice paddies, or flooded areas). Observed at elevations from sea level to 1,500 m.

DIET: Chiefly fish, amphibians, crabs, and mollusks, also reptiles and insects.

NESTING: Nests in colonies that can accommodate several dozen pairs, much more rarely as a solitary pair. Colonies may be monospecific or multispecific. In mixed colonies, associates most commonly with Reed cormorant, Dimorphic egret, and Humblot's heron (Belo-sur-Tsiribihina, Nov. 1985). Nest, usually placed at end of a branch in a tree's crown, consists of interlaced branches and is often lined with grasses in the middle. More rarely, nests are on bushes or on the ground in rocky hollows. Clutch generally numbers 3 blue or blue-gray eggs. Both parents incubate. Chick is covered in down, brown-gray on top and white below. Nesting has been observed during rainy season, starting in Nov., but some pairs occasionally nest outside that period.

DISTRIBUTION AND STATUS: Distributed in Europe, Africa, and Asia. Represented in Madagascar by subspecies *A. c. firasa* (Hartert, 1917), common to Aldabra and Comoros. Distributed throughout Madagascar, where it is common everywhere but High Plateau, where it is uncommon (Alarobia Lake, Sept.

1988; Ivato Lake, Oct. 1988). Like all colonially nesting herons, Gray heron is subject to depredations by villagers, who remove eggs and young.

34. *Black-headed Heron*

Ardea melanocephala
Vigors and Children, 1826
French: Héron à tête noire
No Map

DESCRIPTION: Length 92 cm.
Adult. Sexes similar. Black head, with 1–3 plumes on nape. White chin, throat, and front of upper neck. Sides and back of neck black, front of lower neck mottled white on black. Upper mandible black, lower yellow. Yellowish to greenish lores, yellow iris. Upperparts dark gray, with plumes on scapulars and back lighter gray at tips. Gray underparts, black tarsi and toes. Wings gray, except for dark gray primary and secondary remiges and white underwing coverts. Dark gray tail. A rare melanic morph has uniformly black chin, throat, and underparts.
Immature. Differs from adult by brown-gray crown and neck and by white, tan-tinged underparts.

IDENTIFICATION: Large heron with slender silhouette and highly contrasted black-and-white plumage. Distinguished from Gray heron by marked contrast between black of head and neck and white of chin and throat, and by gray underparts. Differs from Goliath heron and Purple heron by total absence of rufous or brown hue. Flight displays contrast between black remiges and white underwing coverts.

HABITAT: In its original range, species frequents lakes, rivers, estuaries, seashores, and grasslands.

DISTRIBUTION AND STATUS: African species local to sub-Saharan region, sighted only once in Madagascar.

35. Humblot's Heron

Ardea humbloti Milne-Edwards and Grandidier, 1885
Malagasy: Vano, Vorompasika, Voronomby
French: Héron de Humblot

DESCRIPTION: Length 100 cm. *Adult.* Sexes similar. Black crown adorned with 2 long, tapered feathers sweeping nape. Black mask and chin. Rest of head, throat, and neck gray. Very stout bill varies in color from ivory (outside nesting period) to orange, with claret base (during nesting period). Greenish to claret lores, yellow to pale-yellow iris. Gray upperparts and underparts, brown-gray tarsi and toes. Wings gray, except for black remiges. Underside of wings uniformly gray. Gray tail.
Immature. Differs from adult by absence of black face-mask and by gray chin.

IDENTIFICATION: Very large, powerful heron, with uniform dark gray plumage and black cap. Readily distinguishable from Gray heron by larger size, total absence of white, and longer, much stouter bill. Stocky silhouette and uniform plumage in flight. Flight slow and cumbersome.

BEHAVIOR: Rather inactive aquatic species. Found alone, but may also associate with such other herons as Dimorphic egret or Great egret. Fishes in shallow water, either waiting immobile for prey to come within striking distance or walking slowly. Uncoils neck in swift strike to seize large prey. Frequently returns to water's edge or sandbank to swallow what is often substantial prey. Almost always rests alone, usually on a quiet, inaccessible bank, sandbank, or mudbank (rarely sits in treetop). Outside breeding period, shows animosity to Gray heron and other members of genus during quest for food.

VOICE: Outside nesting sites, utters loud, harsh, nasal, dissonant *krah-ahk* when taking flight or in flight.

HABITAT: Frequents fresh, brackish, or salt waters of lakes, rivers, coral islets, mangroves, estuaries, seashores, or more rarely rice paddies. Observed at elevations from sea level to 1,500 m.

DIET: Chiefly large fish and crustaceans.

NESTING: Nests in mixed colonies that often accommodate a larger number of Gray herons, but also nests in isolation. Nest of intertwined branches built in treetop or rock hollow. Clutch numbers 3 blue eggs. Both parents incubate. Nesting has been observed in Nov.

DISTRIBUTION AND STATUS: Endemic to Madagascar, with some sightings in Aldabra and Comoros (Moheli and perhaps Anjouan). In Madagascar it is distributed in w and n, where it is fairly common (Betsiboka River between Ambato Boeni and Mahajanga, Bemamba, and Masama lakes, marsh at Belo-sur-Tsiribihina, lakes and marshes of Soalala, Port-Bergé, and Antsohihy), and in s, where it is uncommon (Mandrare River). Few sightings recorded on High Plateau near and at Antananarivo (Nov., Dec. 1986), at Alaotra Lake (Dec. 1983), and on e coast at Maroantsetra (Nov. 1982) and Antalaha (Oct. 1988). These sightings usually involved immature individuals.

36. *Goliath Heron*

Ardea goliath Cretzchmar, 1827
French: Héron Goliath
No Map

DESCRIPTION: Length 140 cm.
Adult. Sexes similar. Rufous crown,
cheeks, and back of neck. Crown feathers
are more brightly colored and form a
short crest. White chin and throat. Sides
of neck pale rufous and front speckled
with black. Very stout and long black bill.
Yellow-green lores, yellow iris. Upperparts slate gray with lanceolate mantle
and scapular feathers. Underparts dark
rufous, except for white chest, speckled
with black above and showing lanceolate
white feathers below. Black tarsi and toes,
slate gray wing, rufous underwing coverts. Slate gray tail.
Immature. Differs from adult by paler,
more subdued plumage and by gray upperparts mixed with brown.

IDENTIFICATION: Largest heron in
the world. Its size and its rufous, gray,
black, and white coloring make it easy to
identify. Distinguished from Purple
heron by being almost twice as big and by
its rufous crown and very stout black bill.

HABITAT: In its original range, frequents fresh, brackish, and salt waters of
lakes, rivers, estuaries, and seashore.

DISTRIBUTION AND STATUS: Distributed in sub-Saharan Africa and Asia.
Sighted in Madagascar only once, in w.

Scopidae – Hamerkop

Family represented by only 1 species,
Hamerkop, distributed in sub-Saharan
Africa and Madagascar. Unique silhouette, appearance, and habits. It falls ana-
tomically between herons and storks, but
its lineage is unknown. Brown plumage,
with rather short legs and neck for a
wader, and a large crest pointing back
from the head in line with the bill. Its bill
is curved, deep but narrow, with mandibles cutting from halfway to the tip.
Upper half of tibiotarsus is bare. Unlike
all other waders, the Hamerkop builds a
very large, enclosed nest consisting of
branches and miscellaneous materials
with a small, circular entrance.

37. *Hamerkop*

Scopus umbretta Gmelin, 1789
Malagasy: Takatra, Takatsy
French: Ombrette

DESCRIPTION: Length 50–60 cm,
wingspan 90–94 cm.
Adult. Male slightly larger than female.
Plumage entirely dull brown, slightly
paler on chin and throat. Prominent crest
gives head an anvil-like shape. Black,
vertically flattened, rather stout bill seems
slender from front. Dark brown iris,
black tarsi and toes.
Immature. Similar to adult.

IDENTIFICATION: Unique species,
easy to identify. Distinguished from herons and storks by heavy build and shorter
legs, uniformly brown color, and characteristic shape of head. In flight wide
wings show and legs do not extend past
short tail. Vigorous wingbeats; supple
flight recalls nocturnal birds of prey.
Fond of soaring.

BEHAVIOR: Generally seen alone or in pairs, more rarely in small groups of 3 or 4. Activity, strictly diurnal, intensifies at day's end. Spends heat of day perched in tree or by lake or river edge. Stalks prey by walking slowly in shallow water and striking forward with bill. Often deposits prey on solid ground before eating it. May probe mud for invertebrates. Often seen near villages, even a few meters from peasants in rice paddies; enjoys a "bad reputation" in Madagascar, which prompts natives to respect its life and nest.

VOICE: Silent when alone, but very vocal when several meet. Most common call, uttered in flight or at rest, is a sort of loud, nasal, repetitive *wek wek wek wek,* often taken up in turn by those present.

HABITAT: All sorts of wetlands. Commonly found in rice fields, where it feeds in irrigation ditches, alongside clear, shallow, sluggish rivers, lakes, including those in woodland settings, ponds, and temporary water holes. Observed at elevations from sea level to 1,700 m.

DIET: Chiefly amphibians (tadpoles, frogs), fish (*Tilapia* spp.), crustaceans, worms, sometimes insects and small mammals *(Rattus rattus).*

NESTING: Nest, built on lower forks of tree (5–10 m above ground), is an enormous spherical structure (1.5 m diameter) consisting of branches, tufts of grass, and sometimes odds and ends found around villages (rags, paper, pieces of plastic bags). Nest is usually used from year to year, but sometimes a new one is built near the first. A pair may thus have 2–3 nests near each other though only 1 serves regularly for nesting. Clutch numbers 2 white eggs. Chicks are covered with gray down. Nesting has been observed July–Sept.

DISTRIBUTION AND STATUS: Distributed in sub-Saharan Africa and Madagascar. In Madagascar, represented by subspecies *S. u. bannermanni* (Grant, 1914), common to central, e, and s Africa. Distributed throughout Madagascar, where it is common on High Plateau and w coast, much less common on e coast, and rare in s (Betioky, Toliara).

Ciconiidae – Storks

Large waders with long bill differing from herons by stockier bodies and legs. The bill is longer than the head and generally straight, but the form varies among genera. The nostrils are closer to base than middle of bill. Powerful toes are webbed at the base, with thick, sharp claws. Storks are characteristically non-vocal but are given to clacking their bills. Some species are sedentary, but most are migrants. Of the 17 species belonging to this cosmopolitan family, 2 nest in Madagascar.

38. *Yellow-billed Stork*

Mycteria ibis (Linnaeus, 1766)
Malagasy: Mefo, Voronomby
French: Tantale africain

DESCRIPTION: Length 95–105 cm, wingspan 150–65 cm.
Adult. Male slightly larger than female. Plumage varies seasonally.
Nonbreeding Plumage. White head with red facial skin. Bill bright yellow, long and stout at base, slightly curved. Brown iris. Rest of body white, except for black tail and primary and secondary remiges. Pink tarsi and toes.
Breeding Plumage. White of upperparts and especially wings tinged with pink, bright red facial skin spreads to middle of head, and coloring of legs turns brighter.
Immature. Brown-gray plumage all over. Light gray bill, very little facial skin. Brown wings, black primary and secondary remiges and tail. Brownish legs.

IDENTIFICATION: White-and-black stork that cannot be confused with any other species. In flight shows characteristic black-and-white wings and black tail, neck is extended, and legs reach well past tail.

BEHAVIOR: Gregarious; frequents wetlands. Seen in small groups of up to 30, often in company of African spoonbill. Hunts by walking in shallow water and immersing bill, often completely, closing it quickly when it feels prey. Short active periods. Usually observed on sandbanks near feeding grounds, resting on tarsi. Flies very gracefully and uses thermal updrafts to soar during its long journeys.

VOICE: Silent outside breeding season.

HABITAT: Large rivers with sandy banks, shallow lakes, coastal lagoons. Observed normally at elevations from sea level to 150 m and occasionally up to 1,500 m.

DIET: Amphibians (frogs), small fish (*Tilapia* spp.), crustaceans (crabs), and aquatic insects.

NESTING: No proven nesting in Madagascar. Sighting of young barely able to fly at Kinkony in Oct., however, suggests that species nests there.

DISTRIBUTION AND STATUS: Distributed in sub-Saharan Africa and Madagascar. In Madagascar, species is local to w coast along Betsiboka River, where it is common, and Bemamba and Kinkony lakes, where it has been observed in small numbers. Formerly also sighted around Antananarivo and at Alaotra Lake.

39. *African Openbill Stork*

Anastomus lamelligerus Temminck, 1823
Malagasy: Famakiakora, Mojoa, Mijoha, Fipaikakora, Vorombemainty
French: Cigogne à bec-ouvert africaine

DESCRIPTION: Length 85 cm.
Adult. Sexes similar. Uniformly brown plumage. Bill light brown, lighter at base,

long and stout, especially at base. Bill always open because lower mandible is curved. Brown iris, dark brown tarsi and toes. In breeding period feathers of mantle and chest are long, stiff, and iridescent, shot through with green and violet. *Immature.* Differs from adult by dull brown plumage, white-flecked on back of neck, shorter bill, and absence of intermandibular gap.

IDENTIFICATION: Large brown stork with light-hued "open" bill. In flight the long, wide wings are very digited, legs reach well past tail, and neck is extended.

BEHAVIOR: Gregarious; seen in groups numbering up to several dozen. Feeds individually in shallow waters. Often immerses head completely, probing bottom with bill. Neither crushes nor carries prey in intermandibular gap but brings it to dry land in tip of bill before eating it. Roosts in groups in big trees near feeding grounds and often spreads wings facing sun. Often soars.

VOICE: Normally silent; may utter brief hoarse, croaking calls when disturbed in roost.

HABITAT: Shallow freshwater lakes and nearby rice paddies, as well as, occasionally, seashores and mangroves. Observed at elevations from sea level to 150 m, and sometimes to 1,500 m.

DIET: Chiefly mollusks, particularly snails but also bivalves.

NESTING: Nests in small monospecific colonies installed in trees near water, more rarely on ground among aquatic vegetation. Nest of twigs and plants characteristic of lacustrine environments accommodates 2–3 dull white eggs. Both parents incubate. Nesting has been observed during rainy season.

DISTRIBUTION AND STATUS: Distributed in sub-Saharan Africa and Madagascar. Represented in Madagascar by endemic subspecies *A. l. madagascariensis* (Milne Edwards, 1880). Distributed in w between Mahajanga and Morombe, where it is rather common. Occasional sightings on Ihotry Lake. Reported in the past at Alaotra Lake, from where it seems to have disappeared, and at Antananarivo in 1973. Range and population have shrunk in recent years because of destruction of rookeries by villagers.

Threskiornithidae – Ibises, Spoonbill

Cosmopolitan family of fairly large, stocky waders with rather short tarsi, longish toes, moderately long neck, and long bill. They are often gregarious and nest in colonies or in isolation. The family is represented by 17 species belonging to 2 subfamilies, the subfamily Threskiornithinae, or Ibises, with thin, decurved bills, and the subfamily Plataleinae, or Spoonbills, with spoon-shaped bills. Four species nest in Madagascar: 1 spoonbill and 3 ibises, including a woodland ibis belonging to an endemic monospecific genus.

40. *Sacred Ibis*

Threskiornis aethiopicus (Latham, 1790)
Malagasy: Voronosy, Voronondry
French: Ibis sacré

DESCRIPTION: Length 75–80 cm, wingspan 112–24 cm.
Adult. Male slightly larger than female. Black, bare-skinned head and neck. Black, rather long, curved, and very thick bill, light gray iris. White upperparts and underparts, black tarsi and toes. Wings white, except for black tip of primary and secondary remiges and black ornamental plumes. White tail.
Immature. Distinguished from adult by feathered head and neck, black head and back of neck, white throat and front of neck, thinner bill, and absence of ornamental feathers.

IDENTIFICATION: Cannot be confused with any other species. At rest, characterized by stocky silhouette, white body, black head, neck and ornamental feathers, and long, black, curved bill. In flight, shows wide white wings marked with black at end of primary and secondary remiges, neck and legs extended.

BEHAVIOR: Less gregarious than Glossy ibis. Sometimes found feeding alone, more often in pairs or small groups, probing the mud or silt with its long bill. Gregarious nature more evident when roosting, when several dozen may be observed settled on an islet or in a tree near feeding grounds. Returning to night quarters, Sacred ibises often fly rather low in V-formation, alternately beating their wings and gliding.

VOICE: Generally silent outside nesting sites, but sometimes utters raucous call in flight.

HABITAT: Wetlands such as freshwater or even brackish lakes, river mouths, seashores, or mangroves. Observed at elevations from sea level to 150 m.

DIET: Rather varied, chiefly invertebrates: insects, crustaceans, snails, spiders, worms. Also small vertebrates: frogs, reptiles, young birds.

NESTING: Usually nests in mixed heron colonies. Nest of small branches is built in a tree. Clutch numbers 2 dull white eggs. Both parents incubate. Chicks are covered in white down, but their head and neck are dark brown. Nesting has been observed at start of rainy season (Nov.–Dec.).

DISTRIBUTION AND STATUS: Distributed in sub-Saharan Africa, Iraq, Aldabra, and Madagascar. Represented in Madagascar by endemic subspecies *T. a. bernieri* (Bonaparte, 1855). Distributed in w, where it is uncommon. Probably also subject to the nest raiding with which all colonially nesting species must contend.

41. *Glossy Ibis*

Plegadis falcinellus (Linnaeus, 1766)
Malagasy: Famakisifotra
French: Ibis falcinelle

DESCRIPTION: Length 55–65 cm,
wingspan 80–95 cm.
Adult. Sexes similar. Plumage varies
seasonally.
Breeding Plumage. Chestnut head, neck,
upper back, small wing coverts, and
shoulders. Dark olive-brown bill, bluish
black lores edged with white, dark chestnut iris. Upperparts dark green with
bronze or purple sheen, underparts
brown. Olive-brown legs.
Nonbreeding Plumage. Differs by more
somber, less shiny plumage. Head, throat,
and neck dark brown flecked with white.
Immature. Similar to adult in nonbreeding plumage.

IDENTIFICATION: Ibis with long, decurved bill and dark plumage with metallic sheen that cannot be mistaken for any
other species. Slender silhouette. Walks
like a heron. In flight shows rounded
wings, extends neck and legs, and alternates rapid wingbeats with glides. Easily
distinguishable from Eurasian curlew by
longer legs and neck.

BEHAVIOR: Very gregarious. Often seen
searching for food in small groups of up
to 20 or 30. Walks with stately gait in
shallow water, poking at mud with bill
from time to time in search of food. To
hunt, may use eyes or proceed by touch.
Roosting groups are larger and often join
other species, especially herons. Roosts
may be relatively far from feeding
grounds.

VOICE: Silent outside nesting sites.

HABITAT: Shallow fresh or brackish
water of lakes, rivers, deltas, estuaries,
rice paddies, and other flooded cultivated
ground. Roosts are established in large
trees in reed beds. Observed at elevations
from sea level to 1,500 m.

DIET: Chiefly invertebrates (snails,
worms, insects, insect larvae, leeches,
crustaceans), as well as small vertebrates
(tadpoles, frogs, fish, reptiles).

NESTING: Nests in mixed colonies, often in company of herons. Nest, in trees
or in aquatic vegetation, consists of twigs
or reed stalks, respectively. Clutch numbers 2–3 dark blue-green eggs. Both
parents incubate. Nesting has been observed in rainy season (Nov.–Dec.).

DISTRIBUTION AND STATUS: Cosmopolitan species distributed in Europe,
Asia, N and S America, Africa, Oceania,
and Madagascar. Represented in Madagascar by nominate subspecies *P. f. falcinellus*, common to Europe, Asia, N and S
America, and Africa. In Madagascar species appears sedentary and is distributed
throughout the country, except in s.
Fairly common in w between Port-Bergé
and Morondava, rare in other regions, although once common on High Plateau in
vicinity of Antananarivo and at Alaotra
Lake. Dwindling numbers noted throughout Madagascar: its decline has probably
been the most rapid of any species since
1950. Hunting and nest raiding are
mainly responsible.

42. *Madagascar Crested Ibis*

Lophotibis cristata (Boddaert, 1793)
Malagasy: Akohon'ala, Akohovohitra,
Akoholahiala, Lampirana
French: Ibis huppé de Madagascar

DESCRIPTION: Length 50 cm.
Adult. Sexes similar.
  Nominate subspecies *L. c. cristata.*
  Forehead and crown metallic green,
rest of head bare red skin. Nape and back
of neck covered with long, fine, metallic
green and white feathers. Chestnut chin,

throat, and front of neck. Pale brown bill, chestnut iris. Rufous upperparts and underparts, red tarsi and toes, white wings, rufous tail.

Subspecies *L. c. urschi* (Lavauden, 1929).

Differs from nominate subspecies by more consistent rufous overall hue and by metallic-green nape feathers less mixed with white.

IDENTIFICATION: Cannot be mistaken for any other species. Madagascar crested ibis and Helmeted guineafowl are largest terrestrial forest birds. Large, long-legged, russet bird with elegant shape, long neck, and long, decurved bill. In flight shows wide white wings contrasting with somber hue of rest of body.

BEHAVIOR: Woodland species; shy, often found in pairs or family group, rarely alone. Walks rather briskly in underbrush, with frequent stops to explore forest litter, moss, or loose earth with long bill. When surprised, flies away noisily and settles close by on high branch of a tree. Has become extremely wary because of persecution. Pair habitually spends night on same roost, usually a tree's first major branches.

VOICE: Fairly vocal species, unlike other ibises frequenting Madagascar. Call is a flat, monotonous *goo-goo-goo*, usually uttered at nightfall from perch, sometimes in broad daylight from ground.

HABITAT: All types of original island forest. In e it seeks out swampy ground and small forest streams. Adapts to slightly degraded areas on fringe of original forest, dense shaded areas like vanilla or oil-palm plantations. In w and s it frequents only original forest. Observed at elevations from sea level to 2,000 m.

DIET: Invertebrates and small vertebrates (insects, larvae, worms, spiders, snails, frogs, reptiles).

NESTING: Nests in isolation. Fairly large (70 cm diameter) nest of interlaced branches is built on first major forks of trees (7–15 m high in e forests), usually shielded from sun. Clutch numbers 3, sometimes 2, dull, mottled white eggs (average size: 41 mm × 58 mm). Both parents incubate. Chick is covered in white down. Nesting has been observed Sept.–Jan.

DISTRIBUTION AND STATUS: Endemic to Madagascar, distributed throughout island, except for extreme sw, which it appears not to frequent. Subspecies *L. c. cristata* is local to humid e and n forest. Subspecies *L. c. urschi* lives in dry w and s forests. Species, victim of intensive trapping, shows dwindling numbers throughout range.

43. *African Spoonbill*

Platalea alba Scopoli, 1786
Malagasy: Sotrovava, Sotrobevava, Sotromolotro, Sotrosogny, Vangadrano
French: Spatule africaine

DESCRIPTION: Length 90 cm. *Adult.* Male slightly larger than female. Entirely white plumage with slightly bristling cream-colored feathers on nape and upper neck. Head partly bare, with red facial skin covering forehead, eye, chin, and throat. Pale gray iris. Long bill ends in spatula, mandibles gray edged with rosy red. Long red legs. *Immature.* Distinguished from adult by feathered face, less prominent crest on nape, dark brown tip of primary remiges and black underwing feathers. Yellow bill, black legs.

IDENTIFICATION: Graceful bird with white plumage all over, red face, and characteristic spoon-shaped bill. Neck and legs are extended in flight.

BEHAVIOR: Very gregarious. Feeds in small groups of 10–15, walking in shallow water, leaning forward, and making sideways movements with bill to catch small fish. May be seen roosting in groups of up to 30, very rarely in large numbers (120 observed at Bemamba, Nov. 1985), on a sandbank, lakeshore, or riverbank. Sometimes associates with such other waterbirds as Greater flamingo, Lesser flamingo, or Yellow-billed stork. Like flamingos, it rests with head under wing, on one leg.

VOICE: Generally silent species that sometimes utters a kind of *mark mark* in flight.

HABITAT: Shallows of lakes, rivers, deltas, estuaries, and coastal lagoons. Normally observed at elevations from sea level to 150 m, rarely to 1,500 m.

DIET: Chiefly aquatic invertebrates.

NESTING: Nests in colonies, usually mixed. Nest is built in trees or bushes or among aquatic vegetation. Clutch numbers 3 dull white to pale rufous eggs, variously speckled with brown. Both parents incubate. Chick is covered in white down. Nesting has been observed in Feb.

DISTRIBUTION AND STATUS: Distributed in sub-Saharan Africa and Madagascar. Appears sedentary in Madagascar. Encountered on w coast, particularly around Kinkony, Bemamba, and Ihotry lakes and large rivers (Betsiboka), where it is common. Once well known at Alaotra Lake, numbers there have dwindled considerably, and it is sighted only occasionally at Antananarivo (Feb., Aug., Sept. 1987, Oct. 1988). Species is seriously threatened by destruction of nesting colonies.

Phoenicopteridae – Flamingos

Flamingos have extremely long legs and necks and webbed feet. Their bill is angled and equipped on its inner surface with notched lamellae that act as filters for retaining food while the bird pumps out water scooped up from muddy shallows. Their plumage is white, tinged to varying degrees with scarlet, with black remiges. Very gregarious, they nest in colonies and mold nests in the mud, with a hollow at the top for eggs. The chicks are nidifugous. The family comprises only 5 species distributed in Asia, N and S America, southern Europe, Africa, and Madagascar. It is represented in Madagascar by 2 species, but only 1 seems to nest there.

44. *Greater Flamingo*
Phoenicopterus ruber Linnaeus, 1758
Malagasy: Samaky, Gagao
French: Flamant rose

DESCRIPTION: Length 125–50 cm, wingspan 140–65 cm.
Adult. Male slightly larger than female, with longer legs. Pale pink head, neck, body, and tail. Shade of pink varies by individual and depends on diet. Scarlet lesser and median coverts, axillaries, and underwing feathers. Black-tipped pink bill, pink lores. Eyes surrounded by pink flesh. Yellow iris, pink tarsi, toes, and webs.
Immature. Seems brownish. Neck and legs shorter than adult's. Gray head and neck, brown upper back and scapulars. Wing coverts white or pink, flecked with brown. Dark brown remiges, rest of body and tail dirty white. Lead gray bill, lores, eye ring, and legs, brown iris. Plumage gradually turns white, then pink. Individuals turn fully pink only after 3–4 years.

IDENTIFICATION: In Madagascar, can be confused only with Lesser flamingo, from which it is distinguishable by larger size, paler shade of pink, black-tipped pink bill, and more violent contrast between scarlet over- and underwing coverts, and pink back and belly. Immature Greater flamingos differ from immature Lesser flamingos by larger size and browner coloring. In flight shows narrow, pointed wings, with disproportionately long legs and neck extended. Flight is swift, with powerful wingbeats, neck undulating in time with wingbeats.

BEHAVIOR: Gregarious but wary. Often associates with Lesser flamingo and congregates in groups of several dozen or a hundred individuals, much more rarely several thousand. Feeds in groups, walking in shallow water, repeatedly immersing head and contacting muddy bottom with bill to suck in food particles. May sometimes use webbed toes to swim in deep water in search of food. When resting, flamingos form dense groups in middle of water, often on one leg with bill tucked under wing. If danger threatens they first walk away, then take flight en masse after a short takeoff run. In flight they tend to fall into ragged single file or diagonal versions of a V-formation.

VOICE: Vocal species. On feeding grounds utters, in chorus, a continuing nasal *kuk kuk ke-kuk kuk*. Alarm call is a sort of *gaaaaah* or *kaaaaah*. In flight utters repetitive *hook-ahook*.

HABITAT: Shallow salt or brackish waters (coastal lagoons, salt marshes, deltas, brackish lakes). Observed at sea level.

DIET: Chiefly organic detritus extracted from mud, as well as small crustaceans, larvae, diptera, and other insects extracted or captured by filtering system.

NESTING: Rarely recorded in Madagascar; breeding period and locations vary a great deal. Nests in large colonies on flat islets of soft earth. Species requires undisturbed nesting sites. Slightest disturbance (including such human intervention as entering or overflying colony) may cause total abandonment of colony. Nest, built on ground level, is conical. Measures 20–45 cm high, 50–80 cm at base, and 25–40 cm at slightly concave top. Single egg is chalky white. Both parents incubate. Chick is covered in grayish down. Nesting has been observed May–June.

DISTRIBUTION AND STATUS: Widely distributed throughout the world, in Africa, Europe, Asia, N and S America, and Madagascar. Known only since 1929 in Madagascar, where it is represented by subspecies *P. r. roseus* (Pallas), common to Europe, Africa, and Asia. Encountered on w coast s of Port Bergé and on s coast to w of Tolagnaro. Some sightings at Nosy Be, Antsiranana, and Iharaná. Groups of varying size observed at almost all lakes of this area: 2,500 at Bemamba Lake, June 1982; 3,000 at Erombo Lake, Sept. 1982; 15,000 at Ihotry Lake, Aug. 1983; 400 at Kinkony Lake, Sept. 1983; 300 at Tsimanampetsotsa Lake, Mar. 1987. Nesting at Tsimanampetsotsa was confirmed by local residents, and nest building was noted at Ihotry. Species is well represented in Madagascar but is target of constant trapping at feeding grounds. Potential nesting sites where perfect peace and quiet are ensured are rare if not nonexistent. Future of species in Madagascar depends on presence, unknown to villagers, of one or more colonies, or on possibility of exchange with African populations.

45. *Lesser Flamingo*

Phoeniconaias minor
(Geoffroy Saint-Hilaire, 1798)
Malagasy: Samaky
French: Petit Flamant

DESCRIPTION: Length 80–100 cm,
wingspan 95–100 cm.
Adult. Male slightly larger than female.
Plumage pink overall. Chest and tail are
of more intense pink. Intensity of hue
varies by individual. Black primary and
secondary remiges. Primary remiges often covered with long scapulars, of which
some are pink at center. Underside of
wings pink, axillaries very bright pink.
Upperside of wings pink, lesser and median wing coverts bright pink. Black-
tipped dark red bill. Red or orange-red
iris, fleshy reddish pink lores and eye
ring. Bright pink legs.
Immature. Gray-brown overall. Dark
brown primary and secondary remiges.
Gray bill, sooty iris, gray legs. Plumage
gradually turns white, then pink. Birds
become fully pink only after 3–4 years.

IDENTIFICATION: In Madagas-
car, species can be confused only with
Greater flamingo, from which it is distinguishable by smaller size, by generally
brighter pink coloring, and especially by
dark red bill, lores, and eye ring, which
may appear black at a distance. Immature
Lesser flamingo resembles its Greater
flamingo counterpart somewhat but is
smaller and less brown. In flight, shows
more compact shape, thicker neck, and
shorter legs. Brightly colored scapulars
are sometimes visible.

BEHAVIOR: In many respects similar
to Greater flamingo but has more no-
madic bent, moving frequently from one
feeding ground to another for no apparent reason. Deep-water feeder, seeks
food while swimming, head completely
submerged. Moves between feeding

grounds in late evening or at night. Flies
in groups, often in V-formation. Direct
flying speed averages 50–60 kph, which
suggests that Lesser flamingos sighted in
Madagascar may come from Africa.

VOICE: Related to that of Greater flamingo but pitched higher. Most common
call is a sort of sharp *kwirik*. When walking in groups, also utter a sort of subdued
bleating sound. Calls are frequently
heard during nocturnal flights.

HABITAT: Same habitats as Greater flamingo, but includes deeper waters. Observed at sea level.

DIET: Rather different from that of
Greater flamingo. Chiefly microscopic algae (blue algae and diatoms) trapped by
filtering system, sometimes tiny invertebrates. Food preferences preclude competition with Greater flamingo.

NESTING: Never authoritatively recorded in Madagascar.

DISTRIBUTION AND STATUS: Distributed chiefly in sub-Saharan Africa,
also more modestly in Persian Gulf, nw
of India and Madagascar. Main breeding
site consists of lakes of the Great Rift
Valley of Ethiopia, Kenya, and Tanzania.
An area of secondary importance is located in South Africa. These 2 sites,
populated by roughly 2–4.5 million individuals, are only 2,000 km from the w
coast of Madagascar. Malagasy individuals probably come from Africa, therefore,
no nesting having thus far been reported
in Madagascar. In Madagascar the species is found in w from Port-Bergé and in
s to w of Tolagnaro, where it is fairly
common, and in n as far as Antsiranana,
where it is fairly rare. Groups of up to
1,000 birds have been observed, often in
the company of larger contingents of
Greater flamingos, at the lakes referred
to in connection with Greater flamingos
(1,000 at Bemamba Lake, June 1982; 300

at Erombo Lake, July 1982). The less
common of the 2 species of flamingo frequenting Madagascar, it is, like the
Greater, threatened by trapping at its
feeding grounds.

Anseriformes

Anatidae – Ducks, Teals, Pochard

Aquatic web-footed birds with short tarsi adapted for swimming, plump bodies, rather short wings and tail, and bill equipped with notched lamellae on the inner surface to filter and trap food scooped out of the water. They are gregarious but do not nest in colonies. Hatchlings are nidifugous. Most species are widely distributed, moving or migrating as availability of food dictates. All representatives of the family undergo simultaneous molting of remiges, which prevents them from flying for a brief period. This molting generally occurs after nesting. The family is cosmopolitan and is represented by more than 140 species. Of the 10 species nesting in Madagascar, 3 are endemic.

46. *Fulvous Whistling Duck*

Dendrocygna bicolor (Vieillot, 1816)
Malagasy: Tahia, Tsoea
French: Dendrocygne fauve

DESCRIPTION: Length 50 cm.
Adult. Sexes similar. Tawny head, darker on forehead, crown, and nape. Dark brown stripe from back of head down neck to back. Rest of neck very light tan. Black base of neck feathers sometimes show, creating speckled appearance. Slate gray bill, brown iris. Upperparts: brown mantle, brown scapulars with rufous trim, yellowish white uppertail coverts, and dark brown rump. Underparts tawny with long feathers whose yellow-white edges overhang the flanks. Slate gray legs, brown wings and tail.
Immature. Differs from adult by paler underparts.

IDENTIFICATION: Surface-feeding species with upright, slender silhouette, long neck, long legs. Body rides high on surface when waterborne. In flight, absence of wing bar and extension of legs past tail are noticeable. These are field marks common to both Whistling duck species. At rest, Fulvous whistling duck is distinguishable from White-faced Whistling Duck by black bar on back of neck and nape, whitish throat speckled with black, and white patches on flanks. In flight, distinguishable by white bar on tail.

BEHAVIOR: Shy, but very gregarious outside nesting season. Found in groups of dozens to hundreds, often associated with larger groups of White-faced whistling duck. Sometimes large monospecific gatherings may be observed (1,500 at Bemamba Lake, June 1982). Feeds chiefly by day, peaking at dawn and at dusk. Also visits rice paddies at night. Searches for food either by wading in slightly inundated areas or by swimming and immersing head, rarely by diving. Rarely rests on water, preferring banks, floating vegetation, or rocks.

VOICE: Bisyllabic hooting call, *tsoo-ii,* uttered frequently, under almost all circumstances.

HABITAT: Freshwater lakes, major rivers, deltas, inundated areas, and rice paddies. Observed at elevations from sea level to 1,500 m.

DIET: Seeds of aquatic plants and rice.

NESTING: Nest, built on ground amid vegetation on fringes of watery area, consists of interlaced plants and is lined with a layer of down. Clutch numbers 6–10 white eggs. Incubation is performed chiefly by male. Nesting has been observed Dec.–Apr.

DISTRIBUTION AND STATUS: Species distributed in sub-Saharan Africa, Asia, N and S America, and Madagascar. Formerly common throughout Madagascar. Now rare in e, locally common in w and n (Sahaka Lake, Maromandia and Bealanana marshes)—where large gatherings can still be encountered on major lakes (as many as 2,000 at Ihotry Lake, Sept. 1983)—and rather rare on High Plateau (vicinity of Antananarivo; 31 at Alarobia Lake, Nov. 1988). Species has declined greatly at Alaotra Lake, like all aquatic birds of that area. Species decline is due to hunting (shooting and trapping), and only inaccessible lakes of w coast still harbor substantial populations.

47. *White-faced Whistling Duck*
Dendrocygna viduata (Linnaeus, 1766)
Malagasy: Tsiriry, Vivy
French: Dendrocygne veuf

DESCRIPTION: Length 50 cm.
Adult. Sexes similar. Face white to behind eyes, rest of face and nape black. White chin, white throat sometimes separated from chin by black band. Neck black above, chestnut below. Long black bill with bluish gray transverse band toward tip. Brown iris. Upperparts olive brown with ocher bars across back. Caramel scapulars edged with yellow ocher. Underparts: chestnut chest, black belly, black flanks and sides of belly with fine ocher stripes. Blue-gray tarsi and toes. Black wings, chestnut lesser wing coverts, black tail.
Immature. Differs from adult by its duller hues. White face, nonexistent at first, develops gradually. At 4 months, young bird is difficult to distinguish from adult.

IDENTIFICATION: Surface feeder identical in general appearance to Fulvous whistling duck, from which it is distinguished by black-and-white head, chestnut chest, and black belly. Distinguished in flight by absence of white on tail and by dark wings, except for chestnut upper- and underwing coverts. Its almost constant cries in flight are an excellent field mark.

BEHAVIOR: Resembles that of Fulvous whistling duck. Gregarious outside breeding period. Resting groups of both species of Whistling duck are often seen. In flight, groups are monospecific. When disturbed, White-faced whistling duck takes flight whistling and circles overhead for a long time before alighting again nearby on water.

VOICE: Very vocal species, utters rather shrill, trisyllabic call *wee-wee-oo* under almost all circumstances, repeated after pause.

HABITAT: Freshwater lakes, rivers, rice paddies, rocky islands near seacoast. Observed at elevations from sea level to 1,500 m.

DIET: Seeds of aquatic plants and rice.

NESTING: Nests individually. Nest, built on the ground near water, consists of interlaced plants and is lined with down. Clutch numbers 8–13 smooth white eggs. Incubation is performed chiefly by male. Nesting has been observed Nov.–June.

DISTRIBUTION AND STATUS: Distributed in sub-Saharan Africa, S America, and Madagascar. Common throughout Madagascar, very common in some locations, such as certain w lakes and rivers. Together with Red-billed teal, most frequently encountered waterfowl species.

48. *Knob-billed Duck*

Sarkidiornis melanotos (Pennant, 1769)
Malagasy: Tsivongo, Ongongo, Arosy
French: Canard à bosse

DESCRIPTION: Length 48–55 cm.
Adult. Sexes differ. Plumage of male varies seasonally.
Male Breeding Plumage. Head and neck creamy white (sometimes orange-tinged) sprinkled with black. Sprinkling is much denser on crown and back of neck (varies greatly by individual). Black bill with large semicircular slate gray comb on upper mandible. Dark brown iris. Upperparts iridescent blue, green, and purple on black ground, light gray uppertail coverts. Underparts: white chest and belly, gray flanks. Undertail coverts white, except for orange spots on the sides. Dark gray tarsi, toes, and webs. Iridescent black wings and tail.
Male Nonbreeding Plumage. Smaller comb, no orange tinge on neck.
Female. Differs from male in nonbreeding plumage by much smaller size, gray bill with no comb, duller upperparts, white rump.
Immature. Differs from female by having much more spotted head and neck and orange-tinged white underparts.

IDENTIFICATION: Large black-and-white surface feeder (largest in Madagascar). In flight, barless black wings contrast with white of underparts. Flight is powerful, with rather slow wingbeats. Comb of male is evident both at rest and in flight.

BEHAVIOR: Gregarious outside breeding period. Seen in small groups (55 at Soalala, July 1987), often associated with other ducks (Fulvous whistling duck, White-faced whistling duck, Meller's duck, Red-billed teal) resting on muddy or vegetation-covered banks of a lake or sandbanks of a river. Also perches alone in trees or on stumps overhanging water. Feeds by grazing, wading in shallows, or swimming in waters invaded by floating vegetation. Takes flight immediately if disturbed. Generally flies in groups, forming Vs or lines.

VOICE: Generally silent. Sometimes emits a soft, wheezing hiss in flight.

HABITAT: Wetlands of all kinds: lakes, major rivers, flooded areas, rice paddies. Observed at elevations from sea level to 1,500 m.

DIET: Seeds of aquatic plants, rice, also aquatic insects.

NESTING: Pairs nest in isolation (in Africa species forms harems, with several females laying eggs in one nest). Nest, unlined with down, is built in tree or cliff hollow or on the ground, always near water. Clutch numbers 4–8 shiny white eggs. Female incubates. Duckling is covered in sooty down on crown, wings, and back, yellowish on rest of body.

DISTRIBUTION AND STATUS: Distributed in sub-Saharan Africa, Asia, S America, and Madagascar. Found throughout Madagascar. Especially fond of wetlands of w and n, where it is present throughout in small numbers and abundant in some locations (Bemamba Lake, Soalala lakes and marsh, Betsiboka River). Seen in small numbers at some lakes around Antananarivo. Has become rare at Alaotra Lake and in e. Decline of species is due to hunting pressure (shooting and trapping).

49. *African Pygmy Goose*

Nettapus auritus (Boddaert, 1783)
Malagasy: Soafify, Vorontsara, Vorombila, Tsaravanga
French: Anserelle naine

DESCRIPTION: Length 33 cm.
Adult. Sexes differ.
Male. White forehead, cheeks, chin, throat, and front of neck. Greenish black crown, nape, and back of neck. Large oval emerald green patch outlined in black behind eyes and on side of neck. Very bright orange-yellow bill with black nail. Brown iris. Dark green upperparts and wings. Underparts: cinnamon chest and flanks, white belly, black undertail coverts. Dark gray tarsi, toes, and webs. Dark green wings with white bar created by lesser and median wing coverts and secondary remiges.
Female. Differs from male by slightly smaller size, duller plumage, absence of emerald green patches on head and neck, white parts of head, and grayish white neck. Bill less bright; no black nail.
Immature. Similar to female.

IDENTIFICATION: One of world's smallest ducks, smallest in Madagascar. Sitting position shows off head ornamented with 2 big emerald green patches, thick, short, bright orange bill, dark green upperparts, and cinnamon chest and flanks. Female and immature have much more subdued plumage. In flight, white bar contrasts with dark green tail, wings, back, and rump.

BEHAVIOR: Sometimes found in pairs but more often in small groups of 10–40, occasionally more (120 seen on a pond at Morondava, Oct. 1983). Not shy, it is unobtrusive and camouflages itself in floating vegetation. Rarely observed on the ground. When alarmed it takes flight rapidly and skims over the water in zigzags before settling a short distance away. Swims as it feeds, occasionally dives.

VOICE: Generally silent. Male sometimes emits soft whistle, *pee-wee*, on taking wing.

HABITAT: Freshwater covered with floating vegetation (*Nymphaea* spp.—Nymphaeaceae), lakes, sluggish rivers, water holes (whether temporary or perennial), brackish lakes with islets of vegetation. Observed at elevations from sea level to 1,500 m.

DIET: Chiefly seeds of aquatic plants, also plants and aquatic insects.

NESTING: Nest, lined with white down, is built in tree hollow or in herbaceous vegetation on a bank. Clutch numbers 5–9 mottled white eggs. Female probably incubates. Hatchling covered in white down below, black above, has white face with black spots around eyes. Nesting has been observed Dec.–Apr.

DISTRIBUTION AND STATUS: Limited to sub-Saharan Africa and Madagascar. Distributed throughout Madagascar except for High Plateau. Common in w, particularly at Bemamba Lake, in vicinity of Morondava and at lakes of Soalala, and in n (Sahaka Lake, Antsohihy, and Maromandia marshes), uncommon in e, rare in s and at Alaotra Lake. Numbers have declined considerably through hunting and trapping.

50. *Bernier's Teal*

Anas bernieri (Hartlaub, 1860)
Malagasy: Mireha
French: Sarcelle de Bernier

DESCRIPTION: Length 42–45 cm. *Adult.* Male slightly larger than female. Tan head with brown cap, light brown neck, reddish bill, brown iris. Upperparts: feathers of mantle and back brown edged with tan. Underparts: tan-ocher chest, belly and undertail coverts dotted with brown. Reddish legs. Wings: primary and secondary remiges tan-ocher with metallic green bar framed in white.

Tail feathers brown edged with tan. *Immature.* No data.

IDENTIFICATION: Medium-sized surface feeder characterized by mottled plumage, two-tone head coloring, and, in flight, metallic green bar set in 2 large white fields. Sitting, it is distinguished from Hottentot teal by larger size, and from Red-billed teal by less contrasting head coloration. In flight cannot be mistaken for any other species.

BEHAVIOR: Rather gregarious; groups number up to 40, but in July and Aug. found only in pairs. Seems not to associate with other ducks. Feeds in early morning or evening by wading in shallows. Rests on sandy banks during day.

VOICE: Few data. Call said to be bisyllabic and to resemble that of White-faced whistling duck.

HABITAT: Marshes and shallow alluvium-rich lakes, river mouths, and mangroves. Observed at sea level.

DIET: No data.

NESTING: No specific data. Nesting may begin in Sept.

DISTRIBUTION AND STATUS: Little-known species endemic to Madagascar, with distribution between Morombe and Ambilobe. Rare species but well represented in sector containing Bemamba Lake and mouth of Tsiribihina.

51. *Meller's Duck*

Anas melleri Sclater, 1864
Malagasy: Angaka, Akaka, Akaky mainty, Rahaka
French: Canard de Meller

DESCRIPTION: Length 55 cm. *Adult.* Male slightly larger than female. Brown head, chin, and throat. Bill blue-gray, except for black part of lower

mandible. Brown iris. Upperparts and underparts brown streaked with fawn. Orange-yellow legs. Upper side of wings brown streaked with fawn with a blue and black iridescent bar finely edged in white. Underside of wings white. Tail feathers brown edged with fawn.
Immature. Differs from adult by more subdued hues of plumage.

IDENTIFICATION: Large, heavily built surface feeder with slender neck, uniformly brown plumage, long blue-gray bill, and wings marked with an iridescent blue bar. Can be mistaken only for certain barnyard hybrids traceable to Mallard duck *(Anas platyrhynchos)*. In flight shows stocky silhouette, rather long neck, and characteristic prominent blue bar and white underside of wings. Flight is swift and powerful.

BEHAVIOR: Unobtrusive; found in pairs within loose-knit groups of 4–12, or in small numbers within multispecies feeding flocks of ducks (White-faced whistling duck and Red-billed teal). Rarely joins other species in flight.

VOICE: Little known. Harsh call, *kahaka*, sometimes uttered on taking wing.

HABITAT: Freshwater lakes, rivers (may be fast-flowing), streams, and woodland ponds. Observed at elevations from sea level to 2,000 m.

DIET: Little known; aquatic seeds and plants.

NESTING: Nest, built on bank in tuft of herbaceous vegetation, consists of interlaced dry grasses and is lined with down. Clutch numbers 5–10 yellowish green eggs (average size: 52.7 mm × 38.5 mm). Nesting has been observed Sept.–Apr.

DISTRIBUTION AND STATUS: Species endemic to Madagascar, introduced into Mauritius. Distributed in e and on High Plateau, where it is uncommon (Andasibe, Ranomafana, Alaotra Lake, Andringitra, Antananarivo). Some sightings in w (Port Bergé, Bemamba Lake, Kinkony Lake, July 1987). Net decline in numbers noted over past 20 years through hunting and poaching.

52. *Red-billed Teal*

Anas erythrorhyncha Gmelin, 1789
Malagasy: Menasogny, Sadakely, Fotsielatra, Menamolotra
French: Canard à bec rouge

DESCRIPTION: Length 45 cm.
Adult. Sexes similar. Pale gray head with dark brown cap from bill to nape, encompassing eyes. Pale gray chin and throat. Brown back of neck, carmine bill with black nostrils. Brown iris. Upperparts: brown back, feathers of mantle and scapulars brown edged with fawn. Underparts: chest and belly feathers and undertail coverts tan edged with white, feathers of flanks light brown edged with white. Grayish tarsi, toes, and webs. Wings brown, except for tan secondary remiges and tips of greater wing coverts separated by narrow black line. Brown tail.
Immature. Differs from adult by more subdued plumage and rufous bill.

IDENTIFICATION: Medium-sized surface feeder characterized by mottled plumage, two-tone head coloring, and red bill. Conspicuous white bar in flight. Distinguished from Hottentot teal by larger size, red bill, and entirely white bar and from Bernier's teal by red bill, greater contrast in coloring of head, and entirely white bar.

BEHAVIOR: Very gregarious species often found in groups, sometimes associated with other ducks, especially White-faced whistling duck. Large congregations (up to several hundred individuals) have been observed both in such roosts as sandy islets, riversides, and lakeshores and in the middle of bodies of water. Pairs or groups feed together in floating vegetation or on banks rich in aquatic plants; seem to feed at night in rice paddies.

VOICE: Generally silent, but male may utter a soft *weezz* and female a loud *kah-ahk*.

HABITAT: Watery environments of all kinds: lakes, rivers (may be fast flowing), flooded areas. Observed at elevations from sea level to 2,000 m.

DIET: Aquatic plants, seeds, fruits, rhizomes—certainly of rice—and aquatic invertebrates.

NESTING: Only report pointing to nesting of this species in Madagascar refers to observation of 2 young birds unable to fly at Manakara, June 1987 and of 1 adult accompanied by 4 downy chicks near Itasy Lake, March 1988.

DISTRIBUTION AND STATUS: Distributed in sub-Saharan Africa and Madagascar. Range encompasses island. Much more common in w and s and on High Plateau than in e, where it is uncommon. With White-faced whistling duck, the most common species in Madagascar.

53. *Hottentot Teal*

Anas hottentota Eyton, 1838
Malagasy: Kazazaka, Kizazaka
French: Sarcelle hottentote

DESCRIPTION: Length 35 cm.
Adult. Sexes differ slightly.
Male. Fawn head dotted with black behind eyes; dark brown cap extending from bill to nape, encompassing eyes and continuing to back of neck. Fawn chin, throat, and upper neck. Blue bill with sooty nail, brown iris. Upperparts: feathers of mantle and scapulars dark brown edged with fawn. Dark brown back. Underparts fawn, dotted with black on chest, belly, and flanks. Paler undertail coverts. Blue-gray legs. Wings: upper side dark brown with metallic white-and-green bar, underside black and white. Fawn tail.
Female. Differs from male by duller blue bill, less well defined fawn underparts, less dotted belly, and duller green bar.
Immature. Similar to female but more subdued.

IDENTIFICATION: Small surface feeder with contrasting head, gray-blue bill, and characteristic mottling of upperparts and dotting of underparts. In flight, green-and-white bar catches the eye. Distinguished from Bernier's teal and Red-billed Teal by smaller size, color of bill, and bar. Head distinguishes it from Red-billed teal, which has more striking contrast, and from Bernier's teal, which has uniform head.

BEHAVIOR: Rather unsociable duck usually found in pairs, more seldom in small groups, sometimes associated with other ducks, such as Red-billed teal. Feeds in shallow or vegetation-rich waters, in morning and at dusk. During the day joins others of same species to rest on dry land in company of Red-billed teal or White-faced whistling duck. Rather unobtrusive duck whose mottled plumage blends with floating vegetation. When alarmed, it takes flight quickly and alights again nearby, landing behind an obstacle. No large gatherings observed in Madagascar.

VOICE: Hissing sound emitted in flight.

HABITAT: Freshwater partly covered by vegetation (lakes, ponds, river mouths). Observed at elevations from sea level to 1,500 m.

DIET: Seeds and other parts of aquatic plants; small aquatic invertebrates.

NESTING: Cup-shaped nest of aquatic plants is built near water. Clutch numbers 6–8 light brown eggs. Nesting has been observed June–Apr.

DISTRIBUTION AND STATUS: Distributed in Africa and Madagascar. Range encompasses Madagascar. Common in w, uncommon in e and n, rather rare in s and on High Plateau.

54. Madagascar Pochard

Aythya innotata (Salvadori, 1894)
Malagasy: Fotsy maso, Onjo
French: Fuligule de Madagascar

DESCRIPTION: Length 45 cm.
Adult. Sexes differ. Plumage varies seasonally.
Male Breeding Plumage. Chestnut head and neck, dark chestnut chin and throat. Dark gray bill, white iris. Upperparts dark brown. Underparts: dark chestnut chest and upper half of belly, rest of belly and underwing coverts white, shading to brown on flanks. Dark gray legs. Dark brown wings with broad white wing bar. Dark brown tail.
Male Nonbreeding Plumage. Darker and more subdued.
Female. Darker and more subdued. Contrast between brown and white parts of belly less clear-cut. Dark gray bill, brown iris.
Immature. Similar to female. Iris of young male gradually whitens.
IDENTIFICATION: With White-backed duck, only diving duck of Madagascar. Characterized by dark brown coloring and white underwing coverts; differs from all surface feeders by heavier build and short neck. Distinguished from White-backed duck by larger size, by darker col-

oring, and, in flight, by sooty back and broad white wing bar.

BEHAVIOR: Diving species usually found alone, occasionally in pairs. Does not associate with other ducks and is always very secretive. This shy species flies little and habitually stays near islets of aquatic vegetation, venturing into open water only in total absence of danger. Feeds by diving in shallow waters.

VOICE: Unknown.

HABITAT: Shallow bodies of water with many islets of vegetation. Observed at elevations of 750–1,500 m.

DIET: Very few data. Invertebrates and aquatic plant seeds.

NESTING: Few data. Nest, lined with down, is built in tuft of vegetation on a bank. Clutch numbers 2 brown-gray eggs (average size: 55 mm × 40 mm). Incubation takes 26–28 days. Nesting has been observed Mar.–Apr.

DISTRIBUTION AND STATUS: Endemic to Madagascar and strictly local to Alaotra Lake region. A few isolated data exist outside this region, however, particularly at Antananarivo's Ambohibao and Itasy lakes. The Madagascar Pochard is certainly one of the island's rarest and most threatened bird species. Its progressive decline since 1930 at Alaotra Lake, where it used to be common, has accelerated substantially, primarily due to trapping and hunting, introduction of exotic fish species that have reduced aquatic flora, and steady transformation of Alaotra Lake area into rice paddies.

55. White-backed Duck

Thalassornis leuconotus Eyton, 1838
Malagasy: Beloha, Maheriloha, Danamona, Salapiko, Bedoka
French: Erismature à dos blanc

DESCRIPTION: Length 35–44 cm. *Adult.* Sexes similar, male slightly larger than female. Crown, nape, and back of neck sooty, sprinkled with fawn. Sooty chin and throat, fawn cheek and front of neck. White spot at commissure of mandibles, black-and-yellow bill, brown iris. Upperparts fawn striped with black, except for white back. Underparts tan, marbled with black on flanks. Gray legs. Wings and tail fawn with black stripes. *Immature.* Generally darker and more subdued than adult. White spot of commissure in less marked.

IDENTIFICATION: Small diver with brownish plumage, body low in water when swimming. Neck rather long. Large head marked with large white spot at commissure of bill. In flight shows short wings, absence of wing markings, and white back. Legs extend past tail.

BEHAVIOR: Secretive and shy, found in groups of 2–8, seldom in larger flocks. Feeds by diving. When alarmed, it flees by submerging or takes wing after labored take-off run on water. Flight is swift and direct.

VOICE: Unknown.

HABITAT: Lakes with islets of vegetation and undisturbed areas of open water. Observed at elevations from sea level to 1,000 m.

DIET: Nest is a floating structure of heaped aquatic plants. Clutch numbers 6 ocher-brown eggs. Nesting has been observed Apr.–July.

DISTRIBUTION AND STATUS: Distributed in Africa and Madagascar. Represented in Madagacar by endemic subspecies *T. l. insularis* (Richmond, 1897). Located throughout the island except for High Plateau. Formerly quite common, now rather rare throughout range, except for at lakes and marshes of Soalala, where it is fairly common. Hunting and trapping are chiefly to blame for population decline.

Falconiformes

Accipitridae – Cuckoo-Falcon, Hawks, Kite, Fish-Eagle, Serpent-Eagle, Harrier-Hawk, Harrier, Goshawk, Sparrowhawks, Buzzard

Cosmopolitan family containing most diurnal birds of prey, which vary considerably in size, shape, plumage, habits, and habitat. In Madagascar, family is represented by 11 nesting species, including 7 endemics. Two species have limited distribution (to Madagascar and the Comoros and to Madagascar and Réunion, respectively). Most of the endemic species are forest birds. In comparison with the African continent, forest habitats have been well colonized by representatives of the family. Degraded habitats and savanna of more recent date have proved less appealing, however. No migratory species has been reported to winter in Madagascar.

56. *Madagascar Cuckoo-Falcon*

Aviceda madagascariensis (Smith, 1834)
Malagasy: Bobaka
French: Baza malgache

DESCRIPTION: Length 40–45 cm. *Adult.* Sexes similar. Dark brown-gray head, brown bill and iris. Upperparts dark brown, except for rump and whitish uppertail coverts. Underparts: whitish chest marked with brown on sides, whitish belly with brownish band across it, whitish undertail coverts. Brownish tarsi and toes. Brown wings. Tail brown above, gray with 3 dark brown bands below.

IDENTIFICATION: Medium-sized raptor. Brownish above, except for whitish area on rump, whitish below with brownish ventral band. Small head with bulging eyes. Distinguished from Madagascar buzzard by smaller size, slimmer silhouette, small flat head, large eyes, brownish ventral band, and tail marked with 3 dark bands. Pattern of underparts is the opposite of that of the Madagascar buzzard. Characteristic in flight are short, stiff wings carried forward, slightly indented and rather long tail, and head carried above plane of wings, well detached from body. Flight consists of vigorous wing-beats and periods of gliding.

BEHAVIOR: Secretive, solitary forest species generally found below the canopy. Never soars, unlike Madagascar buzzard, but uses breaks in the forest. Spends much time concealed, in wait for its prey, which it usually catches in thick foliage. Sometimes observed active at dusk.

VOICE: Probably a quiet species; voice unknown.

HABITAT: All types of forest on the island, secondary forest growth, and, less commonly, tree plantations (coconut and other palms). Most often encountered at edge of forest or around clearings. Observed at elevations from sea level to 1,600 m.

DIET: Small reptiles (*Phelsuma* spp., *Gecko* spp., *Chamaeleo* spp.) and large insects taken in foliage.

NESTING: Few data. Nesting has been observed Nov.–Dec.

DISTRIBUTION AND STATUS: Endemic to Madagascar with distribution throughout all forest zones. Fairly common in w, n, and e. Uncommon in s and on High Plateau (Tsimbazaza Park and Alarobia Lake at Antananarivo, forest of Manjakatompo).

57. *Bat Hawk*

Machaeramphus alcinus
Westerman, 1851
Malagasy: Hila
French: Milan des Chauves-Souris

DESCRIPTION: Length 45 cm.
Adult. Sexes similar. Head entirely brown, except for throat, which is marked with white in degrees varying by individual. Black bill, blue-gray cere, yellow iris. Upperparts and underparts dark brown, except for whitish stripes on uppertail coverts. Light gray tarsi and toes. Dark brown wings, black tail with whitish stripes.
Immature. Differs from adult by brown hue of all its plumage, marked with white on chest and belly.

IDENTIFICATION: Medium-sized dark brown raptor with whitish throat and yellow bulging eyes. Flight silhouette suggests large falcon, but size readily distinguishes it from Sooty falcon and Eleonora's falcon. Long, pointed wings, and long, fairly narrow tail.

BEHAVIOR: Secretive, essentially crepuscular, spends daylight hours in thick foliage of large trees. At nightfall, pursues prey silently, in swift, flapping, pirouetting flight. Take prey on the wing. Probably also hunts under full moon.

VOICE: Quiet species whose piercing call, *kwik-kwik-kwik-kwik,* recalls that of falcons.

HABITAT: Clear spaces near wooded (even very sparsely) areas. Much more commonly observed near villages, which provide bats with daytime shelter. Observed at elevations from sea level to 1,500 m.

DIET: Bats (*Tadarida* sp.) and insects (Coleoptera, Lepidoptera). In Africa, swallows and swifts are regular prey, but this habit has not been reported in Madagascar.

NESTING: No confirmed evidence of nesting in Madagascar, but it is more than probable.

DISTRIBUTION AND STATUS: Distributed in Africa, Asia, Oceania, and Madagascar. In Madagascar it is represented by subspecies *M. a. anderssoni* (Gurney, 1865), common to Africa. Sighted at a few places in Madagascar: Maroantsetra and Manakara in the e, Morombe, Manja, Antsalova, and Ampijoroa in the w, and Ambohitantely on the High Plateau. Sudden winter appearance of individuals in sw (Manja) points to migratory movement. Determination of status is made more difficult by combination of secretiveness and rarity.

58. *Black Kite*

Milvus migrans (Boddaert, 1783)
Malagasy: Papango, Tsimalaho
French: Milan noir

DESCRIPTION: Length 55–60 cm, wingspan 160–80 cm.
Adult. Brown head with thin dark brown stripes. Yellow bill and cere, orange iris. Dark brown upperparts, russet underparts. Yellow tarsi and toes. Wings brown, except for dark brown remiges. Russet tail.
Immature. Differs from adult by generally more subdued hue, creamy streaks on belly, black bill, and brownish iris.

IDENTIFICATION: Medium-sized, uniformly brown raptor. In flight, field marks are long angled wings and forked tail. Easily distinguished from all other raptors of Madagascar by lack of white in plumage and forked tail.

BEHAVIOR: Very gregarious, opportunistic species. It is common to see 10 or so individuals soaring together or to observe large (300) congregations around urban refuse dumps, slaughterhouses, or just burned areas. Rests in groups in large trees, sandbanks of rivers, or beaches. In roosts it gathers on large trees.

VOICE: Fairly vocal species whose call is a mewing sort of *kew kew-yew-yew-yooo* . . . uttered both in flight and at rest.

HABITAT: Undemanding species; frequents all types of biotopes, with a preference for wetlands (rivers, lakes), seashore, towns, and villages, and forest degraded by slashing and burning. Shuns dense forest habitats. Observed at elevations from sea level to 1,800 m.

DIET: Very varied; sick or dead fish, carrion, rats, chicks, also insects and larvae.

NESTING: Few data. Gregarious, nests in loose-knit colonies. Nest of branches, lined with leaves, built in large trees. Clutch numbers 3 white eggs marked with more or less dark brown. Nesting has been observed in Sept.

DISTRIBUTION AND STATUS: Distributed in Europe, Africa, Asia, Oceania, and Madagascar. Represented in Madagascar by subspecies *M. m. parasitus* (Daudin, 1800), common to tropical and s Africa. Distributed over entire island, very common in w and n and on High Plateau, common in e and s.

59. *Madagascar Fish-Eagle*

Haliaeetus vociferoides (Desmurs, 1845)
Malagasy: Ankoay
French: Pygargue de Madagascar

DESCRIPTION: Length 70–80 cm, wingspan 200 cm.
Adult. Sexes similar. Front and back of

head and nape light tan. White cheeks, whitish sides of neck, chin, and throat. Sooty bill and blue-gray cere. Dark brown iris. Upperparts and underparts brown, except for broad fawn fringes on chest. Brown wings with fine lighter brown edges, except for solid brown primary and secondary remiges. White tail. *Immature.* Differs from adult by more subdued plumage. Head light brown, except for whitish cheeks, light brown chest, and smudged white-gray tail marked with darker terminal band. *Juvenile.* Differs from immature by tawny-brown head with tan cheeks. Underparts and wings marked with fawn at apex, chest tawny brown. End of primary remiges fawn, primary and secondary remiges gray below, tail whitish gray with gray terminal band.

IDENTIFICATION: Very large raptor, biggest in Madagascar. At rest, field marks are stocky silhouette and small head; points of wings cover end of tail. In flight, distinguished from other raptors by uniform dark color, wide, rectangular, digited wings, and short, squared tail.

BEHAVIOR: Generally found alone or in pairs. Does little flying, sometimes soars for extended periods using thermals. Spends much of the day immobile, perched in full view on large tree, post, or dead tree reaching over water. Leaves observation posts during heat of day in favor of leafy, shadier spots from which to continue surveillance. Hunts by stealth and eats prey on a perch or on the ground, close to point of capture.

VOICE: Very vocal species whose shrill, clear, very loud *ko ko koy-koy-koy-koy-koy* resembles call of gull. Call is generally uttered at rest, rarely in flight. Adopts characteristic attitude during call: head is tipped back and bill points at the sky. Often utters call before daybreak.

HABITAT: Aquatic habitats near wooded areas and rocky shore. Favorite biotopes are rocky islands near coast, mangroves, large rivers, and lakes to 90 km inland. Observed at elevations from sea level to 1,200 m (Lake Maudit in Montagne d'Ambre National Park).

DIET: Chiefly surface fish (*Tilapia* sp., *Fistularia* sp., *Strongylura* sp., *Tylosurus* sp.), also crabs. Unsuccessful attacks on Humblot's heron and African spoonbill have been recorded.

NESTING: Few data. Builds nest high up on a rock, cliff, mangrove, or large tree by the water (*Tamarindus indica*—Leguminosae; *Adansonia* sp.—Bombacaceae). Substantial (120 cm diameter) nest made of big branches, central part (70 cm × 50 cm) carpeted with fresh leaves. One observed nest contained 1 white egg (size 68 mm × 54 mm) and a 2-day-old chick with white down. Usually only 1 young bird is raised. Nesting has been observed in Aug.–Sept. but seems to occur May–Sept.

DISTRIBUTION AND STATUS: Endemic to Madagascar, distributed over w coast between Antsiranana and Belo-sur-Mer. Tendency to wander has been noted in immatures observed as far as 200 km s of the above area. Formerly known as common species, Madagascar fish-eagle is now considered one of world's rarest birds of prey. Current population estimated at 50 breeding pairs. Recent decline in numbers is due to direct assaults (hunting, trapping, nest raiding) and to alteration of its favorite biotopes through deforestation.

60. *Madagascar Serpent-Eagle*

Eutriorchis astur Sharpe, 1875
Malagasy: Firasabe, Fandrasalambo
French: Aigle serpentaire de Madagascar

DESCRIPTION: Length 66 cm.
Adult. Dark brown head. Black bill, very small gray cere, yellow iris. Upperparts dark brown with very conspicuous rufous-brown bars, underparts whitish with conspicuous brown bars. Yellow tarsi and toes. Brown wing, tail marked with 6 dark bands.
Immature. Differs from adult by white edging of feathers on back, shoulders, and top of head. Stripes on underparts are much more spaced.

IDENTIFICATION: Large brown raptor with striped underparts. With Madagascar harrier-hawk and Henst's goshawk, largest raptor of the eastern forest. Distinguished from immature Madagascar harrier-hawk by broadly striped belly and chest (Madagascar harrier-hawk has white chest). Distinguished from adult Henst's goshawk by larger size and dark brown upperparts (appears black in Henst's goshawk) and tarsi, which have small and jointed rather than large and overlapping scales. Differs from immature Henst's goshawk by belly stripes (Henst's goshawk has belly flecked with brown spots). In flight, short wings and long tail make it resemble Henst's goshawk, from which it differs by its larger size.

BEHAVIOR: Unknown.

VOICE: Unknown.

HABITAT: All captured individuals have come from e rain forest, from sea level to about 1,000 m elevation. Species seems strictly local to undisturbed forest.

DIET: Stomach contents in captured birds indicate species feeds partly on chameleons. Reported by local populations to feed on small mammals and chickens, but possible confusion with Henst's goshawk renders these data suspect.

NESTING: Unknown.

DISTRIBUTION AND STATUS: Endemic to Madagascar, known by 10 specimens captured 1875–1935 (Maroantsetra, Analamazaotra, Sihanaka forest, Rogez) but not sighted since last capture. Because vast tracts of rain forest remain intact on e coast, hope for survival of species remains. Impossible to estimate existing population. One of the 4 endemic species that have been observed or collected fewer than 3 times in the past 50 years.

61. *Madagascar Harrier-Hawk*

Polyboroides radiatus (Scopoli, 1786)
Malagasy: Fihiaka
French: Polyboroide rayé

DESCRIPTION: Length 68 cm.
Adult. Sexes similar. Sooty gray head. Facial skin yellow and/or pink, depending on individual and degree of excitement. Pink or yellow cere, black bill, dark brown iris. Upperparts uniform sooty gray. Underparts: chest sooty gray, belly and undertail coverts white with fine black bars. Pink legs, black claws. Sooty gray wings with black primary remiges. Black tail marked with white median band.
Immature. Brownish head with dark brown headband. Feathers of upperparts brown edged with white. Underparts white with rufous markings.

IDENTIFICATION: Largest raptor of island after Madagascar fish-eagle. At rest, distinguished from all other raptors by its slender silhouette, very long legs, and gray coloring of adult. Field marks for immature bird are whitish head, dark body, and very long legs. In flight, wings are wide, rounded, and digited, and tail is long, black, and marked with white band. Elegant flight with slow, sweeping wingbeats alternating with periods of soaring.

BEHAVIOR: Relatively secretive, seen only alone or in pairs. Can remain immobile for long spells in thick foliage of a tree at edge of forest but is commonly seen soaring high above canopy. Feeding habits vary by region and biotope. May be observed on the ground, walking about in quest of insects hiding under stones or zebu dung, or inspecting termite mounds or dead fallen branches. In wooded areas it searches base of leaves of certain trees (*Ravenala madagascariensis*—Strelitziaceae) and crevices of others.

VOICE: Rather vocal, often uttering a long, shrill *pee-ee-ee-ee*, generally in flight.

HABITAT: Various original forest types, as well as degraded woodlands. Observed at elevations from sea level to 2,000 m.

DIET: Very varied; insects (ants, termites, crickets, cockroaches, larvae) and vertebrates (young birds, eggs, batrachians, reptiles). Behavior of certain species of lemur *(Lemur fulvus, L. coronatus, Propithecus diadema, Hapalemur griseus)* at approach of Madagascar harrier-hawk suggests that it may prey on these primates.

NESTING: Few data. Nest of branches is built in main fork of a large tree. Clutch numbers 2 whitish eggs spotted with brown. Nesting has been observed July–Nov.

DISTRIBUTION AND STATUS: Endemic to Madagascar, distributed in all woodland areas. Fairly common throughout its range.

62. *Réunion Harrier*

Circus maillardi Verreaux, 1863
Malagasy: Fanindry, Kipanga
French: Busard de Maillard

DESCRIPTION: Length 54–59 cm. *Adult.* Sexes differ. Female larger than male.
Male. Head, chin, and throat white with black streaks going down to chest. Yellow cere, black bill, light yellow iris. Upperparts black, except for whitish overtail coverts. Underparts white, except for chest streaked with black. Yellow legs. Upper side of wings black, except for light gray secondary remiges. Underside of wings white, except for dark brown primary remiges and light gray secondary remiges. Tail gray with brown bars.
Female. Head brown, except for discreet lighter supercilium. Chin and throat whitish, streaked with white. Black bill, yellow iris. Upperparts brown, except for white uppertail coverts. Underparts light brown, uppertail coverts and thighs fawn. Yellow legs. Wings brown, with gray wing bar. Brown tail, marked with 4–6 darker bands.
Immature. Differs from female by uppertail coverts tinged with brown and by whitish underparts flecked with brown, except for fawn undertail coverts and thighs.

IDENTIFICATION: Raptor with slender silhouette and long legs and tail. Cannot be confused with any other species. In flight, shows long wings and long, forkless tail. Male is characterized by highly contrasted plumage (appears black and white from distance), female by white rump.

BEHAVIOR: Usually observed alone or in pairs, flying over clearings, zigzagging level with the vegetation while scanning it for prey, which it takes by plunging on victim. Spends long intervals resting on ground or perch.

VOICE: Silent outside nesting sites.

HABITAT: Vegetation-covered lakeshores, marshes, rice paddies, and grassy areas. Observed at elevations from sea level to 1,800 m.

DIET: Chiefly small vertebrates: batrachians, reptiles, rodents, birds.

NESTING: Few data. Nests on the ground amid vegetation. Nest consists of green plants. Clutch numbers 3–5 white eggs.

DISTRIBUTION AND STATUS: Range covers Madagascar, Réunion, and Comoros. Thinly distributed throughout Madagascar (Anivorano, Ankazobe, Massif de l'Isalo, Massif de l'Itremo, Maroantsetra, Alaotra Lake, Antananarivo, Antsirabe, Maevatanana, Amboromalandy Lake, Horombe Plateau, Masama Lake, Ihotry Lake). Distribution and status of Réunion harrier in Madagascar are yet to be defined.

63. Henst's Goshawk

Accipiter henstii (Schlegel, 1873)
Malagasy: Rehila, Rehito, Firasabe
French: Autour de Henst

DESCRIPTION: Length 52–62 cm. *Adult.* Sexes similar. Female larger than male. Head dark brown with a slight white supercilium, chin and throat white with brown bars. Yellow cere, black bill, yellow iris. Upperparts brown, underparts white with emphatic brown bars. Yellow legs. Black wings. Tail brown marked with 5–6 black bands above, solid brown-gray below.
Immature. Differs from adult by tan underparts marked with large brown spots and brown upperparts.

IDENTIFICATION: Distinguished from Madagascar serpent-eagle by smaller size, small head, and tarsi, which have large scutella of overlapping rather than jointed type. Distinguished from other *Accipiter* by larger size and overall somber

coloration. In flight, adult's light-colored underparts and rump are field marks.

BEHAVIOR: Secretive and usually solitary forest raptor. Spends long intervals perched waiting for prey, rarely soars above canopy. Gliding flight interspersed with a few rapid wingbeats.

VOICE: While perched, utters loud, shrill *kuh-ee kuh-ee kuh-ee kuh-ee.*

HABITAT: Undisturbed rain and dry forests and slightly degraded woodlands. Observed at elevations from sea level to 1,800 m.

DIET: Few data; chicks and barnyard birds as well as forest birds (Meller's duck, White-breasted mesite, Helmeted guineafowl). Probably also catches lemurs.

NESTING: Few data. Nest of interlaced branches, 80 cm by 120 cm diameter, is built on main fork of large tree. Nesting has been observed Oct.–Nov.

DISTRIBUTION AND STATUS: Endemic to Madagascar, distributed in e (Marojejy, Maroantsetra, Analamazaotra, Andringitra, Ranomafana) and in w (Ihotry Lake, Morondava forest, Bemamba Lake, Bemaraha, Analamera). Seems not to frequent s. Fairly rare throughout its range.

64. Madagascar Sparrowhawk

Accipiter madagascariensis Smith, 1834
Malagasy: Firasa, Tsipara, Pera
French: Epervier de Madagascar

DESCRIPTION: Length 34–40 cm. *Adult.* Sexes differ. Female larger than male.
Male. Head almost black. Yellow cere, black bill, yellow iris. Upperparts dark brown lightly tinged with blue. Underparts and underside of wings whitish with

dark brown to rufous-brown stripes. White undertail coverts. Yellow legs. Wings dark brown, lightly tinged with blue. Tail dark brown with 7–8 light bands.

Female. Differs from male by considerably larger size, dark gray upperparts, and wide, dark brown bars on underparts. *Immature.* Differs from adults by brown upperparts and vertical brown stripes on underparts.

IDENTIFICATION: Sparrowhawk with powerful silhouette, intermediate in size between Henst's goshawk and Frances's sparrowhawk. Distinguished from Henst's goshawk by smaller size and, for female, by brown coloring and less closely spaced stripes. Distinguished from Frances's sparrowhawk by very somber coloring in both sexes and by dark brown rather than rufous-brown stripes.

BEHAVIOR: Solitary species often found perched on first branches of a tree, watching prey in thick undergrowth. Swift flight with frequent wingbeats interspersed with brief glides.

VOICE: Similar to that of Frances's sparrowhawk.

HABITAT: Undisturbed or slightly degraded rain and dry forest, thorn scrub. Observed at elevations from sea level to 1,500 m.

DIET: Insects, batrachians, reptiles, birds.

NESTING: Nest of interlaced branches, roughly 50 cm diameter, built in tree. Clutch numbers 3 smooth white eggs lightly marked with brown. Nesting has been observed in Nov.

DISTRIBUTION AND STATUS: Endemic to Madagascar, distributed thinly in e (Anjanaharibe sud, Maroantsetra, Andasibe), n (Montagne d'Ambre), w (Antsalova, Morondava), and s (Tsima-nampetsotsa Lake, Berenty), very thinly on High Plateau (Antananarivo).

65. Frances's Sparrowhawk

Accipiter francesii Smith, 1834
Malagasy: Firasa, Fandraokibo, Tsiparahorovana, Tsipera, Perakibo
French: Epervier de Frances

DESCRIPTION: Length 30–35 cm. *Adult.* Sexes differ. Female larger than male.

Male. Top of head and cheeks dark blue-gray. White throat. Gray cere, black bill, yellow iris. Upperparts dark blue-gray, underparts white, marked to varying degrees with fine rufous stripes on belly. White undertail coverts. Gray legs. Wings dark blue-gray above, white below. Dark blue-gray tail.

Female. Differs from male by larger size, rather dark tan-rufous upperparts, and dirty white underparts striped with rather wide rufous marks. *Immature.* Similar to female.

IDENTIFICATION: Small sparrowhawk with slender silhouette. The male, blue-gray on top and white below, cannot be confused with any other species. Female is distinguished from male Madagascar sparrowhawk by wider, lighter stripes on belly. Distinguished from female and immature Madagascar sparrowhawk by considerably smaller size and horizontal stripes on underparts. In flight, wide, short wings are a field mark. Distinguishing species from Madagascar sparrowhawk may be difficult, but smaller size and less stocky silhouette are always evident.

BEHAVIOR: Close to that of Madagascar sparrowhawk.

VOICE: When perched, sometimes utters piercing, monosyllabic *kee, kee, kee.*

HABITAT: Various original forest types, degraded woodlands, and such artificial woodland areas as parks, large gardens, and plantations of coconut palms, coffee, cacao, sisal, or fruit trees. Observed at elevations from sea level to 2,000 m.

DIET: Insects, batrachians, reptiles, birds.

NESTING: Nest of small branches, 35 cm diameter, built in first major fork of tree. Eggs laid in shallow hollow carpeted with fresh leaves, 15 cm diameter. Clutch numbers 3–4 white eggs (37 mm × 29 mm). Nesting has been observed Oct.–Dec.

DISTRIBUTION AND STATUS: Distributed in Madagascar and Comoros. In Madagascar it is represented by the nominate subspecies *A. f. francesii*. Fairly common throughout island, except in s, where it is rarer. Most common *Accipiter*.

66. *Madagascar Buzzard*

Buteo brachypterus Hartlaub, 1860
Malagasy: Hindry, Bobaka, Bemanana, Beririna, Bevorotse
French: Buse de Madagascar

DESCRIPTION: Length 48–51 cm. *Adult.* Sexes similar. Plumage varies individually. Generally gray head more or less tinged with brown (may be striped). Yellow cere, black bill, pale yellow iris. Upperparts brown or rufous-brown. Rump usually white, sometimes brown. Underparts: brown or gray chest, white belly. Breeches and undertail coverts brown or white with brown stripes. Yellow legs. Wings brown or rufous-brown.

Tail brown on top, gray below, and marked with 6–8 brown bands. *Immature.* Differs from adult by orange-brown iris.

IDENTIFICATION: Medium-sized raptor with brownish plumage, except for partly white underparts. Only other similar species is Madagascar cuckoo-falcon, from which it differs by stockier silhouette, more massive head, and short tail. Pattern of underparts, with its brown chest, is the opposite that of the Madagascar cuckoo-falcon. In flight, wide wings and wide, rounded tail are field marks.

BEHAVIOR: Forest raptor often seen alone, sitting in full view in large or dead tree or at any other observation point. Often soars over forest, alone or in pairs.

VOICE: Utters piercing, plaintive mew, *pee-oooooo . . .* , often in flight, sometimes perched.

HABITAT: Various original forest types and degraded woodlands, as well as elevated rocky areas. Observed at elevations from sea level to 2,300 m.

DIET: Small vertebrates, reptiles, batrachians.

NESTING: Few data. Nest may be built in large tree, wedged in large fork or on epiphytic fern. Clutch numbers 2 white eggs. Nesting has been observed Oct.–Dec.

DISTRIBUTION AND STATUS: Endemic to Madagascar, distributed throughout island and fairly common except on High Plateau, where it is rare (Ambohitantely, Antananarivo, Manjakatompo).

Falconidae – Falcons

Diurnal birds of prey having a single indentation on the maxilla and a corre-
sponding notch on the lower mandible.
Unlike other diurnal raptors, falcons do
not build nests but lay their eggs in hollows of rocks or old trees or sometimes
use the nests of other species. Falcons are
generally found in pairs or family groups,
though some species may be gregarious
during migration or at winter quarters.
They are a cosmopolitan family represented by 61 species. Three species nest
in Madagascar: 1 endemic, 1 common to
Madagascar and Aldabra, and 1 that is
widely distributed. Two Palearctic species winter in Madagascar.

67. *Madagascar Kestrel*

Falco newtoni (Gurney, 1863)
Malagasy: Hitikitike, Hitsikitsike
French: Faucon de Newton

DESCRIPTION: Length 30 cm. Polymorphic species.
Adult. Sexes differ.
Male, White Morph. Blue-gray head with
thin black mustache. Yellow ceres, black
bill, dark brown iris. Upperparts bright
rufous lightly flecked with black. Underparts white, barely marked with black
spots. Yellow legs. Wings bright rufous
lightly flecked with black. Tail gray with
5–7 dark bands.
Female, White Morph. Differs from male
by tan head, brown tail, and much more
heavily flecked upperparts and underparts.
Rufous Morph. Distinguished by dark rufous belly and chest.
Immature. Similar to female.

IDENTIFICATION: Smallest falcon of
Madagascar. Its mahogany rufous coloring is a quick and unfailing field mark. In
flight, small size sets it apart from other
falcons. Hovers. May be mistaken in
flight for Broad-billed roller, which has
similar color pattern, but Madagascar
kestrel has less choppy flight, less sweeping wing beats, much less angled wings.

BEHAVIOR: Not shy, easily spotted
alone or in pairs, infrequently in small
groups of up to 5. Active, spends much of
day hunting. Surveys scene by hovering
or keeping look-out in full view from
elevated vantage point. Seizes prey on
ground, less frequently on the wing, and
eats it at observation post or on nearby
ledge.

VOICE: Frequently utters loud, shrill,
rapid-fire *kitty-kitty-kitty-kitty*.

HABITAT: Widespread ubiquitous species, found in all environments except
dense forest. Observed at elevations from
sea level to 2,000 m.

DIET: Chiefly insects (Orthoptera, Coleoptera), also small vertebrates.

NESTING: Nests in crevices in cliffs,
under roofs of houses, in ruins, in hollow
trees, or less frequently in old nests of
other species (Pied crow). Clutch numbers 4 rufous eggs (average size: 35.8 mm
× 28.8 mm). Nesting has been observed
Sept.–Jan.

DISTRIBUTION AND STATUS: Distributed in Madagascar and Aldabra.
Represented in Madagascar by nominate subspecies *F. n. newtoni*. Abundant
throughout range. Most common bird of
prey of Madagascar.

68. *Banded Kestrel*

Falco zoniventris (Peters, 1854)
Malagasy: Hitsikitsik'ala
French: Faucon à ventre rayé

DESCRIPTION: Length 35 cm.
Adult. Sexes similar. Gray head, no mustache. Yellow cere, stout black bill, pale yellow iris. Yellow bare skin around eyes. Upperparts and wings blue-gray with dark brown bars. Underparts: striped chest, belly and undertail coverts clearly barred with brown. Yellow legs. Blue-gray tail has 6–8 dark bands.
Immature. Overall brown coloration replaces adult gray coloration; darker iris and less bare skin around eyes than adult.

IDENTIFICATION: At rest, striped belly is reminiscent of sparrowhawks, but Banded kestrel differs by its large head and very stout bill. Distinguished from other falcons by its compact silhouette, striped upperparts, and light-colored eyes surrounded by an expanse of yellow skin. In flight, long wings barred above and below and long tail barred with dark bands are field marks.

BEHAVIOR: Solitary, not shy. Often seen in full view at rest in lower reaches of an isolated tree, immobile for long periods. Rarely flies: if disturbed, it flies as far as next convenient perch. Hunts within a radius not exceeding 150 m around its observation post. Seizes immobile prey (on ground, tree trunks, and branches and amid foliage) and returns to its perch to eat it.

VOICE: Generally quiet; in flight utters loud, shrill, staccato call reminiscent of Madagascar kestrel's call.

HABITAT: All types of original forest and degraded woodlands. Favors forest edge and clearings, whether natural or artificial. Observed at elevations from sea level to 2,000 m.

DIET: Small prey: invertebrates, insects (Orthoptera, Coleoptera), small vertebrates, reptiles (*Phelsuma* spp., *Chamaeleo* spp.).

NESTING: Few data. Eggs are laid in old nests, especially of Sickle-billed vanga, or in a tree cavity. Clutch numbers 3 yellowish eggs (average size: 42.8 mm × 33.7 mm). Nesting has been observed Sept.–Dec.

DISTRIBUTION AND STATUS: Only falcon endemic to Madagascar. Distributed all over island except for High Plateau (1 immature sighted at Antananarivo, Sept. 1988). Fairly rare in nw, n, and e (Sambirano, Marojejy, Ankarana, Maroantsetra, Andasibe); fairly common in w (Ankarafantsika, Bemamba Lake, Morondava, Morombe, Zombitse) and in s (Ihotry Lake, Toliara, Betioky).

69. *Eleonora's Falcon*

Falco eleonorae Gené, 1839
Malagasy: Firasambalala
French: Faucon d'Eléonore

DESCRIPTION: Length 33–38 cm. Polymorphic species.
Adult. Sexes similar. Black bill, dark brown iris. Cere and legs yellow in male, gray-blue in female.
Light Morph. Head brown-black, except for lower part of cheek, which has a brown-black mustache, and white chin and throat. Upperparts bluish black to dark brown, underparts rufous flecked with black. Rufous undertail coverts. Wings bluish black to dark brown. Dark gray tail.
Dark Morph. Plumage is sooty brown all over.
Immature, Light Morph. Differs from adult in light morph by brownish upperparts and less rufous underparts and more flecked with brown.
Immature, Dark Morph. Similar to adult in dark morph.

IDENTIFICATION: Falcon with long, sharply angled wings. Adult in light morph differs from all other falcons by its rufous undertail coverts. Distinguished from Peregrine falcon by slimmer silhouette and longer, finer black mustache. In flight, Eleonora's falcon has streamlined silhouette, and from below, wings show white area at base of remiges that contrasts with rest of dark wings (in immature as well as adults in both morphs).

BEHAVIOR: Gregarious, often forming groups of up to 25, sometimes associating with Sooty falcon. Feeding is diurnal but becomes intense at twilight and early at night when an artificial light source attracts insects. Seizes and decorticates prey on the wing.

VOICE: Silent at winter quarters.

HABITAT: Mainly areas where water is present (rice paddies, watercourses, lakes), also rain forest and sparsely wooded terrain. Observed at elevations from sea level to 1,500 m.

DIET: Insects (Odonates, Orthoptera, Coleoptera) at its winter quarters.

DISTRIBUTION AND STATUS: Migratory species nesting in colonies in Mediterranean basin and on Atlantic coast of Morocco. Madagascar provides almost exclusive winter quarters (small population winters in E Africa). Present late Oct.–late Apr., distributed mainly in e and on High Plateau.

70. *Sooty Falcon*

Falco concolor Temminck, 1825
Malagasy: Firasambalala, Tomaimavo, Fandrasambary
French: Faucon concolore

DESCRIPTION: Length 31–33 cm. *Adult.* Sexes similar. Sooty gray head with paler throat. Yellow cere, black bill, dark brown iris. Upperparts and under-

parts uniformly sooty gray. Yellow legs. Wings sooty gray, except for black primary remiges. Sooty gray tail. *Immature.* Large dark mustache, top of head brown, nape light brown. Upperparts brown-gray (feathers edged with narrow creamy border), underparts light flecked with brown, especially on chest.

IDENTIFICATION: Falcon of streamlined silhouette, with long, pointed, and sharply angled wings. Easily identifiable by uniform sooty gray plumage. Immature bird differs from immature Eleonora's falcon in light morph by wide mustache and more conspicuously striped chest and from immature Peregrine falcon by gray coloration of upperparts.

BEHAVIOR: Crepuscular; less gregarious than Eleonora's falcon, with which it is sometimes seen hunting. Hunting has been recorded at night. Observed in groups of 2–23 (23 resting in baobabs at Morondava, Jan. 1989), most often 3–5. Remains in full view in tree overlooking its hunting territory. Seizes and decorticates prey on the wing.

VOICE: Generally silent at winter quarters. Call reminiscent of Peregrine falcon's call.

HABITAT: Areas where water is present (lakes, rivers, rice paddies) and sparsely wooded terrain. Often seen at edge of forest and above canopy. Observed at elevations from sea level to 1,500 m.

DIET: Insects (Diptera, Orthoptera, Coleoptera), rarely birds, at winter quarters.

DISTRIBUTION AND STATUS: Migratory species nesting in ne Africa, Red Sea coast, and Middle East and wintering almost exclusively in Madagascar. First birds arrive late Oct., and last depart early May. Fairly abundant throughout island.

NOTE: Some authors consider this species as polymorphic and describe a dark morph, the existence of which has been questioned in recent publications.

71. *Peregrine Falcon*

Falco peregrinus Tunstall, 1771
Malagasy: Voromahery
French: Faucon pèlerin

DESCRIPTION: Length 36–46 cm, wingspan 75–105 cm.
Adult. Female larger and paler than male. Head black, except for white cheek, chin, and throat. Black mustache well marked. Yellow cere, black bill, dark brown iris. Upperparts dark gray. Underparts white with thin black stripes. Yellow tarsi and toes, black claws. Dark gray wings, gray tail barred with 4–6 dark bands.
Immature. Distinguished from adult by brown upperparts, creamy white underparts with brown stripes. Brown mustache.

IDENTIFICATION: Falcon with contrasting plumage. Adult is distinguished from Eleonora's and Sooty falcons by stockier silhouette, proportionally shorter wings, sharp contrast in the head (black and white), large mustache, and thin bars on the belly, which lacks rufous markings. Immature differs from Eleonora's and Sooty falcons by larger mustache and by shorter wings that do not extend beyond the tail. In flight, distinguished from all other falcons by stocky, powerful silhouette and short, stubby tail.

BEHAVIOR: Secretive raptor found alone, less frequently in pairs. Most active in morning and late afternoon, spending rest of day immobile on perch. Usually seizes prey on the wing, but can also take chicks in villages and is occasionally observed near houses. Dismembers and eats prey on ledge (tree, rock) near location of kill.

VOICE: Rather quiet outside breeding period. Near nest, male utters piercing, strident, repetitive *kyeh-kyeh-kyeh-kyeh-kyeh* and female makes a sort of loud yapping.

HABITAT: Nesting is associated with rocky terrain: inland or coastal cliffs. However, dispersion of immature and nonbreeding adults produces sightings in biotopes as varied as degraded woodlands, riversides, and lakeshores. Observed at elevations from sea level to 2,000 m.

DIET: Almost exclusively birds, generally small; also chickens.

NESTING: First observed in Madagascar on High Plateau near Antsirabe in 1983. Clutch numbers 4 creamy rufous eggs slightly mottled with brown, laid directly on rock surface of steep cliff ledge. Parents participate unequally in incubation. Nesting has been observed July–Aug.

DISTRIBUTION AND STATUS: Range encompasses 5 continents. Represented in Madagascar by subspecies *F. p. radama* (Hartlaub, 1861), which also occurs in the Comoros. Rather patchy distribution, but encountered throughout island (Antsiranana, Ankarana, Marojejy, Maroantsetra, Manakara, Andringitra, Antsirabe, Antananarivo, Mitsinjo, Bemamba Lake, Berenty, Anakao).

Galliformes

Phasianidae – Partridge, Quails

Terrestrial birds with short, rounded wings that perch in trees only when greatly disturbed. They nest in bushes and under tufts of grass, and most species have fairly large clutches. The chicks are nidifugous. The largest species are sedentary, but the smallest (quail) tend to migrate. Their diet consists of vegetal matter often associated with insects and larvae. They are generally gregarious and have distinctive calls. The family is represented by almost 200 species. One species belonging to an endemic monospecific genus nests in Madagascar and is sedentary. Also found are 2 migratory species from Africa.

72. *Madagascar Partridge*

Margaroperdix madagascarensis
(Scopoli, 1786)
Malagasy: Traotrao, Tsipoy, Kipoy
French: Caille de Madagascar

DESCRIPTION: Length 24–26 cm.
Adult. Sexes differ. Male slightly larger than female.
Male. Forehead and crown brown, slightly spotted with black and having a white median band. Black lores, white mustache and supercilia, black chin and throat, black bill. Dark brown iris. Upperparts: rufous-brown mantle with black and white flecks (rachis of feathers is white). Back and uppertail coverts brown with tan stripes. Underparts: side of neck and chest gray. Center of chest rufous. Black belly marked with large white ocelli. Flanks, thighs, and undertail coverts rufous-brown flecked with white. Gray tarsi and toes. Wings same color as upperparts, except for brown primary

remiges and black-barred brown secondary remiges. Short tail, same color as upperparts.

Female. Light brown head with small black scales. Tan chin and throat. Black bill, dark brown iris. Upperparts tan-brown streaked with black. Underparts tan with black stripes. Gray tarsi and toes. Wings same color as upperparts, except for light brown primary remiges. Tail same color as upperparts.

Juvenile. Differs from female by more subdued hue of plumage.

IDENTIFICATION: Terrestrial, distinguished from Common quail, Harlequin quail, and Madagascar buttonquail by larger size. Male field marks are black-and-white mask, black throat, buff chest, and black belly ocellated with white. Female has much more subdued plumage: tan-brown with dark brown stripes. In flight shows short, round wings.

BEHAVIOR: Secretive and rather shy, lives alone, in pairs, or in family groups. Feeds while walking about slowly. If startled, draws itself up and runs swiftly or takes flight briefly. Flight is direct—swift, powerful wingbeats alternating with glides.

VOICE: Fairly silent; sometimes utters muffled calls as well as a rapid succession of trilled notes on taking flight.

HABITAT: Grassy, bushy, or cleared terrain, forest clearings and edges, dry fields. Observed at elevations from sea level to 2,700 m.

DIET: Chiefly seeds, also berries and insects.

NESTING: Nest is a simple hollow fashioned in ground where a tuft of grass or bush afford protection. Clutch numbers 14–20 rufous-brown eggs mottled with dark brown. Chicks are nidifugous. Nesting has been observed Mar.–June on High Plateau.

DISTRIBUTION AND STATUS: Endemic to Madagascar, introduced to Réunion in 18th century. Distributed throughout Madagascar, except for extreme s. Formerly common, especially on High Plateau, but has declined considerably to become uncommon in most of range, its numbers reduced by local hunting and trapping.

73. *Common Quail*

Coturnix coturnix (Linnaeus, 1758)
Malagasy: Papelika
French: Caille des blés

DESCRIPTION: Length 18 cm.
Adult. Sexes differ.
Male. Forehead, crown, and nape brown, marked with yellow median band. Large yellowish supercilium extends to sides of neck. Light brown cheeks with thin brown mustache. Dark brown chin and center of throat, rest of throat pale rufous crossed by brown jugular band connecting with mustache on either side. Sooty bill, light brown iris. Upperparts brown with dark brown and yellowish flecks, underparts pale rufous flecked with yellow on chest and flanks. Pale brown tarsi and toes. Brown primary remiges. Tail brown with dark brown bars.
Female. Differs from male by absence of jugular and median band on head, by brown spots on upper chest, and by generally less rufous hue of plumage.
Juvenile. Differs from female by more black spots on underparts, especially flanks.

IDENTIFICATION: Medium-sized terrestrial bird with plump silhouette and uniform brownish plumage. Male distinguished from male Harlequin quail by absence of white on throat and chest and by light colored underparts. Differs from female Madagascar buttonquail by clear supercilium, brown chest free of rufous and gray, and larger size. Female distinguished from female Harlequin quail by lighter underparts and absence of brown pectoral band and from male Madagascar buttonquail by more somber hue of upperparts, black bill, darker eyes, and larger size. Flight is direct—swift, powerful wingbeats alternating with glides.

BEHAVIOR: Terrestrial, difficult to observe, moves secretively in the grasslands where it feeds. If disturbed, runs for safety or, rarely, takes flight only to alight again after a few meters and continues to seek safety on foot.

VOICE: Fairly vocal. Loud, accented *weet poo weet*—3 distinct syllables following rapidly on one another, constantly repeated—provides excellent means of location and identification. On taking wing, bird utters a brief *preepree*.

HABITAT: Dry grasslands. Observed at elevations from sea level to 2,000 m.

DIET: Chiefly seeds.

NESTING: Never observed in Madagascar.

DISTRIBUTION AND STATUS: Distributed in Europe, Asia, and Africa. Represented in Madagascar by subspecies *C. c. africana* (Temminck and Schlegel, 1849), limited to sub-Saharan Africa. Found at several locations in n and w Madagascar, but most often near Antananarivo and Ankazobe, around Alaotra and Tritriva lakes, and in the Andringitra. Rare in s, where it was seen at Berenty (Aug. 1987). May breed in Madagascar.

74. *Harlequin Quail*

Coturnix delegorguei Delegorgue, 1847
Malagasy: Kibonaomby
French: Caille arlequine

DESCRIPTION: Length 18 cm.
Adult. Sexes differ.
Male. Forehead and front of head dark brown. Crown and nape dark brown marked with thin white median band. White supercilium and thin line under eye. Dark brown mustache and cheeks. Black bill, brown iris. Upperparts graybrown flecked with fawn and showing fine tan bars. Underparts: dark brown center of chest and upper belly. Rufous sides of chest, flanks, belly, and undertail coverts. Chestnut tarsi and toes. Wings same color as upperparts, except for brown-gray primary remiges. Short graybrown tail.

Female. Gray-brown head marked with whitish median band and diffuse light supercilium, whitish chin and throat. Black bill, brown iris. Upperparts brown spotted dark brown and yellowish. Underparts light, except for dark brown pectoral band, with dark brown marks on flanks and sides of chest. Chestnut tarsi and toes. Wings same color as upperparts. Brown-gray primary remiges. Graybrown tail.

Juvenile. Plumage similar to that of female, but overall hue is more subdued.

IDENTIFICATION: Medium-sized terrestrial species, plump silhouette. Male distinguished from Common quail and female Madagascar buttonquail by highly contrasted black-and-white head and by black and rufous undersides. Female similar in many respects to female Common quail but differs by dark brown collar and more profusely black-flecked chest. Distinguished from male Madagascar buttonquail by larger size, generally brownish hue of plumage, rufous underparts, and dark eyes.

BEHAVIOR: Terrestrial, difficult to observe, found in pairs or groups of 5–10. Moves secretively in grasslands where it feeds. Like Common quail, it takes wing suddenly when faced with danger and flies a few meters before landing and fleeing further on foot.

VOICE: Male utters loud *weet weet-weet weet weet-weet weet*. Alarm call uttered on taking wing is a sort of clipped *pit*.

HABITAT: Frequents dry grasslands and croplands (cassava, dry rice-fields). Observed at elevations from sea level to 200 m. Generally, species frequents drier, lower-altitude biotopes than those favored by Common quail.

DIET: Chiefly seeds, also insects and green shoots.

NESTING: Never observed in Madagascar.

DISTRIBUTION AND STATUS: Migratory visitor from Africa. Distributed over much of sub-Saharan Africa, s Arabia, and Madagascar. Represented in Madagascar and Africa by nominate subspecies *C. d. delegorguei*. Has been sighted at many locations on island: in n at Antsiranana, Nov. and Jan., and Ambanja, Feb.; in w at Mahajanga, Sept.; and in sw at Ihotry Lake, June, July, and Dec. A regular migratory movement seems to bring Harlequin quail to Madagascar Nov.–Feb. In Africa, species is known for sudden movements, appearing in large numbers and disappearing as suddenly for no apparent reason. Sightings in June–July should perhaps be attributed to such unexplained migrations. Remains rather infrequent visitor to Madagascar.

Numididae – Guineafowl

Family close to Phasianidae. Guineafowls are characterized by powerful tarsi adapted for running, bare head except, in some cases, for a plumed crest (helmeted in genus *Numida*), short bill, and stocky body. They are very gregarious except in breeding period. The family, represented by 7 species, is primarily African. The species found in Madagascar was probably introduced.

75. *Helmeted Guineafowl*
Numida meleagris (Linnaeus, 1758)
Malagasy: Akanga, Vitro, Vitro-ala
French: Pintade mitrée

DESCRIPTION: Length 58–65 cm. wingspan 95–100 cm.
Adult. Sexes similar. Bare head, chin, throat, and neck. Blue head with triangular red helmet. Red lores and wattles hanging from sides of head. Neck blue with small, sooty gray feathers, sparse and bristling on back of neck. Pale brown bill, dark brown iris. Upperparts, underparts, wings, and tail sooty gray with white dots. Black tarsi and toes.
Immature. Differs from adult by generally more subdued plumage, faint grayish coloring of bare parts of head and less developed helmet.

IDENTIFICATION: Large terrestrial species with plump silhouette, rather short neck, brightly colored helmeted head, stout, short bill, strong legs, very characteristic sooty plumage dotted with white. Only guineafowl in Madagascar, it cannot be confused with any other species. In flight, wings appear short and round, and powerful wingbeats alternate with glides. Species is often domesticated. Individuals seen near villages frequently show partial albinism, often on wings and belly, and head and helmet are much duller.

BEHAVIOR: Terrestrial, gregarious, wary. Found in groups of 5–30, sometimes in much bigger flocks of up to 150 birds. Feeds on the ground, walking about deliberately, raising head frequently to inspect surroundings. When alarmed, members of group stay together, fleeing by running swiftly or suddenly taking wing to perch atop a large nearby tree. Noisy take-off. At nightfall, group forms roost in large tree .

VOICE: Vocal, produces loud cackling of clipped, jangling, dissonant calls, a sort of rapid-fire *kekekekekeke,* most often heard in roost before nightfall.

HABITAT: Frequents woodlands and grasslands, croplands, any cleared terrain (lakeshores, riversides) adjacent to wooded tract. Observed at elevations from sea level to 1,500 m.

DIET: Varied; chiefly seeds, also invertebrates (insects, worms, snails).

NESTING: Nests on ground protected by tuft of herbaceous or arboreal vegetation. Nest is simple hollow fashioned in the ground and holds 6–14 smooth, creamy yellow eggs with large pores. Nidifugous chicks have brown-, tan-, and rufous-striped down. Nesting has been observed Nov.–Mar., peaking in Dec.

DISTRIBUTION AND STATUS: Distributed principally in sub-Saharan Africa and locally in N Africa and Middle East. Introduced into numerous parts of the world as a domestic species and has sometimes returned to wild state (Comoros). Represented in Madagascar by subspecies *N. m. mitrata* (Pallas, 1767), common to se Africa. Malagasy population probably springs from birds introduced by humans from nearby coast of Mozambique. Range includes all of Madagascar except for High Plateau. Abundantly distributed in n, w, and s, thinly in e. Numbers currently declining steeply, especially near populated areas, where species is under severe pressure from hunting and trapping.

PLATE 1

Preceding page:

De. Wandering albatross *Diomedea exulans*

3. Southern giant petrel *Macronectes giganteus:* (*i*) immature (both giant petrels)

2. Black-browed albatross *Diomedea melanophrys*

Mh. Northern giant petrel *Macronectes halli*

Dc. Yellow-nosed albatross *Diomedea chlororhynchos*

Pf. Sooty albatross *Phoebetria fusca*

Pa. White-chinned petrel *Procellaria aequinoctialis*

Dca. Shy albatross *Diomedea cauta*

21. Brown booby *Sula leucogaster*

Sd. Masked booby *Sula dactylatra:* (*a*) immature, (*b*) adult

20. Red-footed booby *Sula sula:* (*a*) dark morph with white head and tail, (*b*) white morph

16f. Greater frigatebird *Fregata minor:* female

17f. Lesser frigatebird *Fregata ariel:* female

Opposite page:

4. Cape petrel *Daption capense*

5. Antarctic prion *Pachyptila desolata*

Pm. Great-winged petrel *Pterodroma macroptera*

Par. Herald petrel *Pterodroma arminjoniana*

Pl. Audubon's shearwater *Puffinus lherminieri*

Bf. Jouanin's petrel *Bulweria fallax*

Pat. Mascarene petrel *Pterodroma aterrima*

Pmo. Soft-plumaged petrel *Pterodroma mollis*

Pb. Barau's petrel *Pterodroma baraui*

7. Wedge-tailed shearwater *Puffinus pacificus*

Pc. Flesh-footed petrel *Puffinus carneipes*

8. Wilson's storm petrel *Oceanites oceanicus*

Fg. White-bellied storm petrel *Fregetta grallaria*

Om. Matsudaira's storm petrel *Oceanodroma matsudairae*

9. Black-bellied storm petrel *Fregetta tropica*

14. Red-tailed tropicbird *Phaethon rubricauda*

15. White-tailed tropicbird *Phaethon lepturus*

13. Red-billed tropicbird *Phaethon aetherus*

PLATE 2

12. Alaotra little grebe *Tachybaptus rufolavatus*

11. Madagascar little grebe *Tachybaptus pelzelnii*

10. Little grebe *Tachybaptus ruficollis*: (*a*) breeding, (*b*) nonbreeding

18. Reed cormorant *Phalacrocorax africanus*: (*a*) adult breeding,
    (*b*) adult nonbreeding, (*c*) immature

19. Darter *Anhinga melanogaster*: (*a*) male, (*b*) female, immature

22. Pink-backed pelican *Pelecanus rufescens*

PLATE 3

12

11

10b

12

11

10a

18b

18a

19a

18

19

18c

19b

22

22

23. Little bittern *Ixobrychus minutus*: (*a*) adult, (*b*) immature

· 28. Green-backed heron *Butorides striatus*: (*a*) adult, (*b*) immature

24. Black-crowned night-heron *Nycticorax nycticorax*: (*a*) adult, (*b*) immature

· 27. Cattle egret *Bubulcus ibis*: (*a*) adult breeding, (*b*) adult nonbreeding, immature

25. Squacco heron *Ardeola ralloides*: (*a*) adult breeding, (*b*) immature

26. Malagasy pond heron *Ardeola idae*: (*a*) adult breeding, (*b*) immature

PLATE 4

23a

23b

24a

24b

25a

25b

26a

26b

27a

27b

28a

28b

. 33. Gray heron *Ardea cinerea*
. 35. Humblot's heron *Ardea humbloti*: (*a*) adult, (*b*) immature
32. Purple heron *Ardea purpurea*: (*a*) adult, (*b*) immature
34. Black-headed heron *Ardea melanocephala*
36. Goliath heron *Ardea goliath*
31. Great egret *Casmerodius albus*: (*a*) breeding, (*b*) nonbreeding
30. Dimorphic egret *Egretta dimorpha*: (*a*) light morph, (*b*) intermediate morph, (*c*) dark morph
29. Black heron *Egretta ardesiaca*

PLATE 5

37. Hamerkop *Scopus umbretta*

41. Glossy ibis *Plegadis falcinellus*: (*a*) adult breeding, (*b*) adult nonbreeding, (*c*) immature

42. Madagascar crested ibis *Lophotibis cristata*: (*a*) eastern subspecies, (*b*) western subspecies

40. Sacred ibis *Threskiornis aethiopicus*: (*a*) adult breeding, (*b*) immature or nonbreeding

39. African openbill stork *Anastomus lamelligerus*

38. Yellow-billed stork *Mycteria ibis*

43. African spoonbill *Platalea alba*

44. Greater flamingo *Phoenicopterus ruber*: (*a*) adult, (*b*) immature

45. Lesser flamingo *Phoeniconaias minor*: (*a*) adult, (*b*) immature

PLATE 6

39. African openbill stork *Anastomus lamelligerus*

37. Hamerkop *Scopus umbretta*

38. Yellow-billed stork *Mycteria ibis*

41. Glossy ibis *Plegadis falcinellus*

40. Sacred ibis *Threskiornis aethiopicus*

42. Madagascar crested ibis *Lophotibis cristata*

45. Lesser flamingo *Phoeniconaias minor*

44. Greater flamingo *Phoenicopterus ruber*

43. African spoonbill *Platalea alba*: (*a*) adult, (*b*) immature

33. Gray heron *Ardea cinerea*

32. Purple heron *Ardea purpurea*

35. Humblot's heron *Ardea humbloti*

31. Great egret *Casmerodius albus*

25. Squacco heron *Ardeola ralloides*

28. Green-backed heron *Butorides striatus*

26. Malagasy pond heron *Ardeola idae*

27. Cattle egret *Bubulcus ibis*

24. Black-crowned night-heron *Nycticorax nycticorax*

29. Black heron *Egretta ardesiaca*

30. Dimorphic egret *Egretta dimorpha*: (*a*) light morph, (*b*) dark morph

PLATE 7

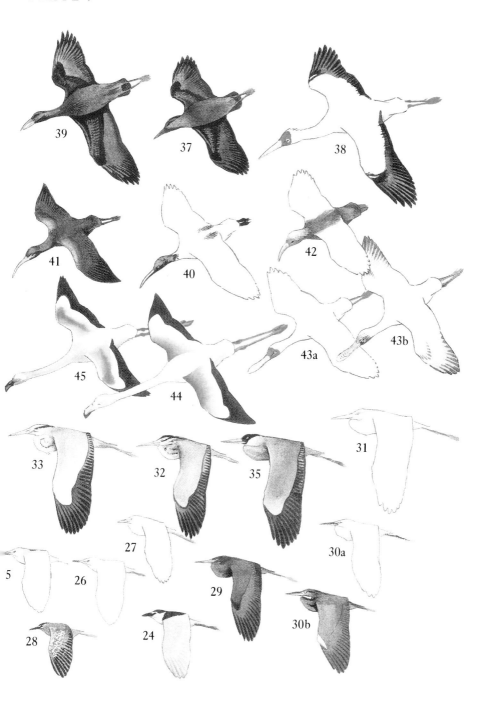

- 48. Knob-billed duck *Sarkidiornis melanotos*: (*a*) male, (*b*) female
51. Meller's duck *Anas melleri*
52. Red-billed teal *Anas erythrorhyncha*
47. White-faced whistling duck *Dendrocygna viduata*
53. Hottentot teal *Anas hottentota*
50. Bernier's teal *Anas bernieri*
- 46. Fulvous whistling duck *Dendrocygna bicolor*
- 49. African pygmy goose *Nettapus auritus*: (*a*) male, (*b*) female
54. Madagascar pochard *Aythya innotata*: (*a*) male, (*b*) female
55. White-backed duck *Thalassornis leuconotus*

PLATE 8

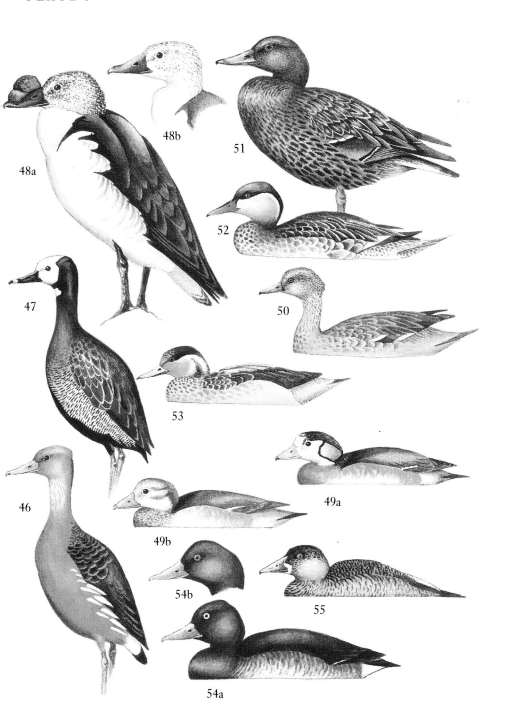

48b

51

48a

52

47

50

53

49a

46

49b

54b

55

54a

59. Madagascar fish-eagle *Haliaeetus vociferoides*: (*a*) adult, (*b*) juvenile

58. Black kite *Milvus migrans*: (*a*) adult, (*b*) immature

57. Bat hawk *Machaeramphus alcinus*: (*a*) adult, (*b*) immature

62. Réunion harrier *Circus maillardi*: (*a*) male, (*b*) female and immature

56. Madagascar cuckoo-falcon *Aviceda madagascariensis*

66. Madagascar buzzard *Buteo brachypterus*: (*a*) light plumage, (*b*) dark plumage

PLATE 9

60. Madagascar serpent-eagle *Eutriorchis astur*: (*a*) adult, (*b*) immature

63. Henst's goshawk *Accipiter henstii*: (*a*) male, (*b*) immature (female represented)

‣ 65. Frances's sparrowhawk *Accipiter francesii*: (*a*) male, (*b*) female and immature

64. Madagascar sparrowhawk *Accipiter madagascariensis*: (*a*) male, (*b*) female, (*c*) immature

PLATE 10

60a

60b

63a

63b

64c

64b

65b

64a

65a

61. Madagascar harrier-hawk *Polyboroides radiatus*: (*a*) adult with pink face, (*b*) adult with yellow face, (*c*) immature
68. Banded kestrel *Falco zoniventris*: (*a*) adult, (*b*) immature
70. Sooty falcon *Falco concolor*: (*a*) adult, (*b*) immature
71. Peregrine falcon *Falco peregrinus*: (*a*) adult, (*b*) immature
69. Eleonora's falcon *Falco eleonorae*: (*a*) adult light morph, (*b*) adult dark morph, (*c*) immature
67. Madagascar kestrel *Falco newtoni*: (*a*) male light morph, (*b*) female light morph, (*c*) male dark morph, (*d*) female dark morph

PLATE 11

59. Madagascar fish-eagle *Haliaeetus vociferoides*: (*a*) adult, (*b*) immature
61. Madagascar harrier-hawk *Polyboroides radiatus*: (*a*) adult (*b*) immature
58. Black kite *Milvus migrans*
62. Réunion harrier *Circus maillardi*: (*a*) male, (*b*) female, (*c*) immature
56. Madagascar cuckoo-falcon *Aviceda madagascariensis*: (*a,b*) extreme variants
57. Bat hawk *Machaeramphus alcinus*: (*a*) adult, (*b*) immature
66. Madagascar buzzard *Buteo brachypterus*: (*a,b*) extreme variants

PLATE 12

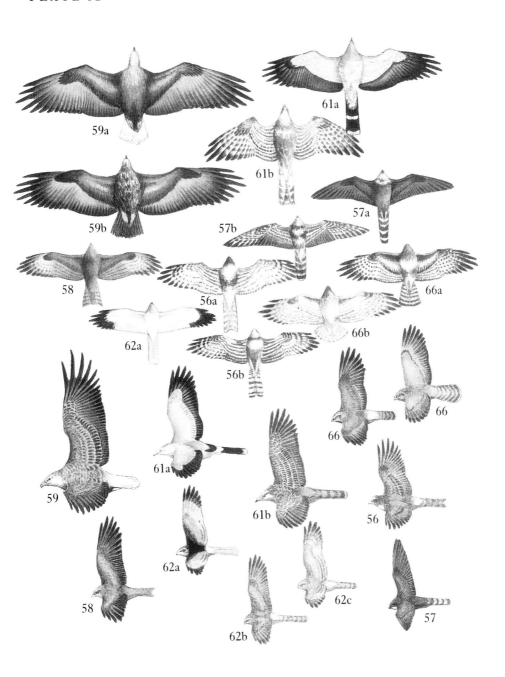

59a

61a

61b

59b

57a

57b

58

56a

66a

62a

66b

56b

59

66

61a

66

61b

56

58

62a

62b

62c

57

71. Peregrine falcon *Falco peregrinus*

68. Banded kestrel *Falco zoniventris*

67. Madagascar kestrel *Falco newtoni*: (*a,b*) male, (*c*) female

69. Eleonora's falcon *Falco eleonorae*: (*a*) adult light morph, (*b*) adult dark morph, (*c*) immature

70. Sooty falcon *Falco concolor*

63. Henst's goshawk *Accipiter henstii*

65. Frances's sparrowhawk *Accipiter francesii*

PLATE 13

71

68

67a

69a

67b

69c

71

69b

70

67c

71

70

67

69

70

65

63

65

75. Helmeted guineafowl *Numida meleagris*: (*a*) adult breeding, (*b*) immature
72. Madagascar partridge *Margaroperdix madagascarensis*: (*a*) male, (*b*) female and immature
79. Madagascar buttonquail *Turnix nigricollis*: (*a*) male, (*b*) female
74. Harlequin quail *Coturnix delegorguei*: (*a*) male, (*b*) female
73. Common quail *Coturnix coturnix*: (*a*) male, (*b*) female

PLATE 14

76. White-breasted mesite *Mesitornis variegata*

77. Brown mesite *Mesitornis unicolor*: (*a*) typical, (*b*) atypical

78. Subdesert mesite *Monias benschi*: (*a*) male, (*b*) female

82. Madagascar wood rail *Canirallus kioloides*

81. White-throated rail *Dryolimnas cuvieri*

85. Madagascar flufftail *Sarothrura insularis*: (*a*) male, (*b*) female

86. Slender-billed flufftail *Sarothrura watersi*: (*a*) male, (*b*) female

PLATE 15

89. Purple swamphen *Porphyrio porphyrio*

90. Red-knobbed coot *Fulica cristata*: (*a*) adult, (*b*) immature

87. Common moorhen *Gallinula chloropus*: (*a*) adult, (*b*) juvenile

83. Baillon's crake *Porzana pusilla*: (*a*) adult, (*b*) juvenile

80. Madagascar rail *Rallus madagascariensis*

88. Allen's gallinule *Porphyrula alleni*: (*a*) adult, (*b*) juvenile

84. Sakalava rail *Amaurornis olivieri*

116. Madagascar snipe *Gallinago macrodactyla*

91. Madagascar jacana *Actophilornis albinucha*: (*a*) adult, (*b*) immature

92. Greater painted snipe *Rostratula benghalensis*: (*a*) male, (*b*) female

PLATE 16

106. Bar-tailed godwit *Limosa lapponica*

105. Black-tailed godwit *Limosa limosa*

108. Eurasian curlew *Numenius arquata*

107. Whimbrel *Numenius phaeopus*

94. Eurasian avocet *Recurvirostra avosetta*

93. Black-winged stilt *Himantopus himantopus*

95. Crab plover *Dromas ardeola*: (*a*) adult, (*b*) immature

110. Common greenshank *Tringa nebularia*

PLATE 17

98. Black-bellied plover *Pluvialis squatarola*

97. Pacific golden plover *Pluvialis fulva*

115. Ruddy turnstone *Arenaria interpres*: (*a*) adult breeding, (*b*) adult nonbreeding

103. Greater sand plover *Charadrius leschenaultii*

99. Common ringed plover *Charadrius hiaticula*: (*a*) adult, (*b*) immature

102. Three-banded plover *Charadrius tricollaris*

101. Kittlitz's plover *Charadrius pecuarius*: (*a*) adult, (*b*) immature

104. White-fronted plover *Charadrius marginatus*

100. Madagascar plover *Charadrius thoracicus*: (*a*) adult, (*b*) immature

PLATE 18

119. Curlew sandpiper *Calidris ferruginea*: (*a*) adult breeding, (*b*) adult nonbreeding
118. Little stint *Calidris minuta*
117. Sanderling *Calidris alba*
113. Terek sandpiper *Xenus cinereus*
111. Green sandpiper *Tringa ochropus*
120. Ruff *Philomachus pugnax*
112. Wood sandpiper *Tringa glareola*
114. Common sandpiper *Actitis hypoleucos*

PLATE 19

129. Caspian tern *Sterna caspia*: (*a*) adult breeding, (*b*) adult nonbreeding

128. Gull-billed tern *Sterna nilotica*

135. Greater-crested tern *Sterna bergii*: (*a*) adult breeding, (*b*) adult nonbreeding

133. Sooty tern *Sterna fuscata*: (*a*) adult, (*b*) immature

132. Bridled tern *Sterna anaethetus*: (*a*) adult, (*b*) immature

136. Lesser-crested tern *Sterna bengalensis*: (*a*) adult breeding, (*b*) adult nonbreeding

139. White tern *Gygis alba*: (*a*) adult, (*b*) immature

137. Brown noddy *Anous stolidus*

134. Saunders's tern *Sterna saundersi*: (*a*) adult, (*b*) immature

131. Roseate tern *Sterna dougallii*: (*a,b*) adult breeding, (*c*) immature, (*d*) adult nonbreeding

138. Lesser noddy *Anous tenuirostris*

130. Common tern *Sterna hirundo*

Sa. Arctic tern *Sterna paradisaea*

96. Madagascar pratincole *Glareola ocularis*

Ss. Black-naped tern *Sterna sumatrana*

125. Whiskered tern *Chlidonias hybridus*: (*a*) adult breeding, (*b*) adult nonbreeding

126. White-winged tern *Chlidonias leucopterus*

127. Black tern *Chlidonias niger*

PLATE 20

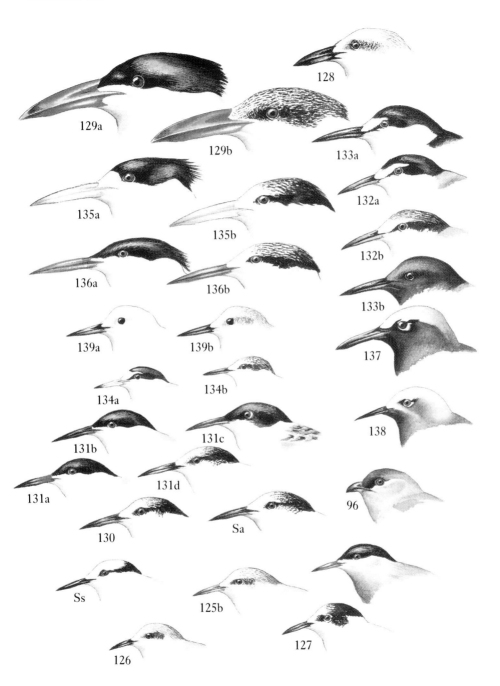

129. Caspian tern *Sterna caspia*

123. Kelp gull *Larus dominicanus*: (*a*) adult, (*b*) immature

121. Subantarctic skua *Catharacta antarctica*

124. Gray-headed gull *Larus cirrocephalus*: (*a*) adult, (*b*) immature

136. Lesser-crested tern *Sterna bengalensis*

135. Greater-crested tern *Sterna bergii*

137. Brown noddy *Anous stolidus*

138. Lesser noddy *Anous tenuirostris*

133. Sooty tern *Sterna fuscata*: (*a*) adult, (*b*) immature

132. Bridled tern *Sterna anaethetus*

PLATE 21

96. Madagascar pratincole *Glareola ocularis*

125. Whiskered tern *Chlidonias hybridus*: (*a*) adult breeding, (*b*) adult nonbreeding

127. Black tern *Chlidonias niger*

126. White-winged tern *Chlidonias leucopterus*

139. White tern *Gygis alba*

131. Roseate tern *Sterna dougallii*: (*a*) adult breeding, (*b*) adult nonbreeding,
(*c*) immature

130. Common tern *Sterna hirundo*

Ss. Black-naped tern *Sterna sumatrana*

Sa. Arctic tern *Sterna paradisaea*

134. Saunders's tern *Sterna saundersi*: (*a*) adult, (*b*) immature

PLATE 22

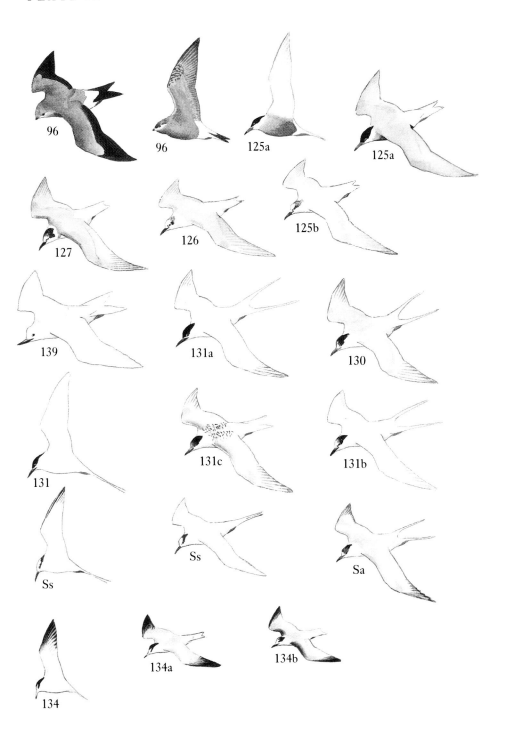

96

96

125a

125a

127

126

125b

139

131a

130

131

131c

131b

Ss

Ss

Sa

134

134a

134b

140. Madagascar sandgrouse *Pterocles personatus*: (*a*) male, (*b*) female

144. Madagascar green pigeon *Treron australis*

145. Madagascar blue pigeon *Alectronenas madagascariensis*

142. Madagascar turtledove *Streptopelia picturata*

143. Namaqua dove *Oena capensis*: (*a*) male, (*b*) female

148. Gray-headed lovebird *Agapornis cana*: (*a*) male, (*b*) female,
(*c*) male subspecies *A. c. ablectanea*

PLATE 23

140b

140

140a

140

144

145

142

144

144

145

142

145

143b

143a

148a

148b

143

143

148c

146. Greater vasa parrot *Coracopsis vasa*

147. Lesser vasa parrot *Coracopsis nigra*

161. Madagascar coucal *Centropus toulou*: (*a*) adult, (*b*) immature

150. Madagascar lesser cuckoo *Cuculus rochii*: (*a*) adult, (*b*) immature

149. Thick-billed cuckoo *Cuculus audeberti*

160. Blue coua *Coua caerulea*

158. Crested coua *Coua cristata*: (*a*) *C. c. cristata* subspecies,
(*b*) *C. c. dumonti* subspecies, (*c*) *C. c. pyropyga* subspecies

159. Verreaux's coua *Coua verreauxi*

PLATE 24

151. Snail-eating coua *Coua delalandei*

156. Running coua *Coua cursor*

152. Giant coua *Coua gigas*

157. Red-capped coua *Coua ruficeps*: (*a*) *olivaceiceps* subspecies,
    (*b*) nominate subspecies

153. Coquerel's coua *Coua coquereli*

154. Red-breasted coua *Coua serriana*

155. Red-fronted coua *Coua reynaudii*

PLATE 25

151

156

152

157a

153

157b

154

155

166. Madagascar long-eared owl *Asio madagascariensis*

167. Marsh owl *Asio capensis*

163. Common barn owl *Tyto alba*

162. Madagascar red owl *Tyto soumagnei*

165. White-browed owl *Ninox superciliaris*

164. Malagasy scops-owl *Otus rutilus* (three variants)

PLATE 26

173. Alpine swift *Apus melba*
174. African black swift *Apus barbatus*
171. Malagasy spine-tailed swift *Zoonavena grandidieri*
172. African palm swift *Cypsiurus parvus*
192. Sand martin/Bank swallow *Riparia riparia*
191. Brown-throated sand martin *Riparia paludicola*
194. Swallow/Barn swallow *Hirundo rustica*
193. Mascarene martin *Phedina borbonica*

PLATE 27

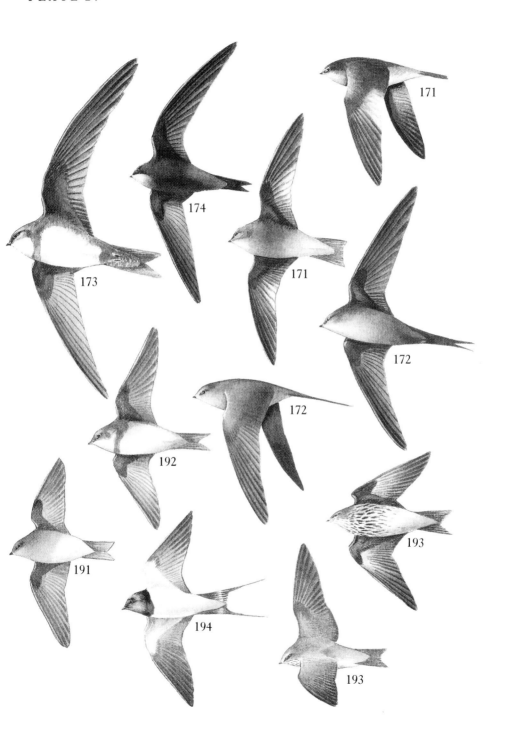

⌄175. Malagasy kingfisher *Corythornis vintsioides*: (*a*) adult, (*b*) immature

176. Madagascar pygmy kingfisher *Ispidina madagascariensis*

178. Broad-billed roller *Eurystomus glaucurus*

⌄177. Madagascar bee-eater *Merops superciliosus*: (*a*) adult, (*b*) immature

67. Madagascar kestrel *Falco newtoni* (for comparison)

PLATE 28

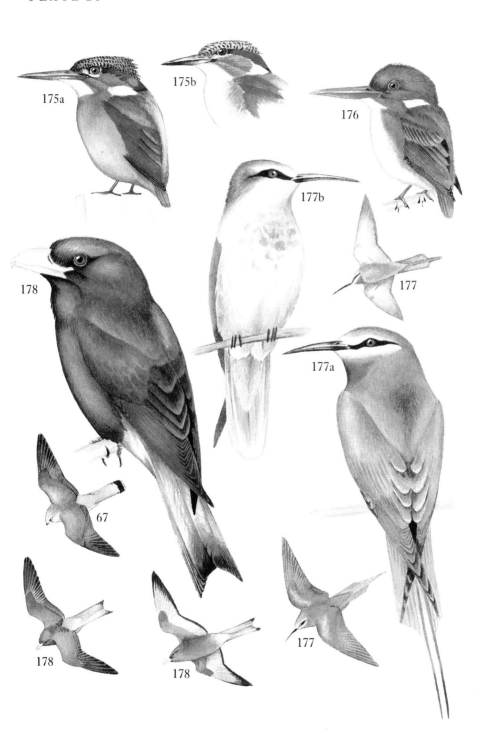

175a

175b

176

177b

177

178

177a

67

178

178

177

180. Scaly ground-roller *Brachypteracias squamiger*

179. Short-legged ground-roller *Brachypteracias leptosomus*

181. Pitta-like ground-roller *Atelornis pittoides*

183. Long-tailed ground-roller *Uratelornis chimaera*

182. Rufous-headed ground-roller *Atelornis crossleyi*

PLATE 29

247. Pied crow *Corvus albus*

184. Cuckoo-roller *Leptosomus discolor*: (*a*) male, (*b*) female

249. Common myna *Acridotheres tristis*

185. Hoopoe *Upupa epops*

168. Madagascar nightjar *Caprimulgus madagascariensis*

169. Collared nightjar *Caprimulgus enarratus*

PLATE 30

186. Velvet asity *Philepitta castanea*: (*a*) male breeding (note that skin may appear fluorescent), (*b*) female, (*c*) male molting

187. Schlegel's asity *Philepitta schlegeli*: (*a*) male breeding, (*b*) male nonbreeding and female

188. Sunbird-asity *Neodrepanis coruscans*: (*a*) male breeding,
(*b*) male nonbreeding
and female

189. Yellow-bellied sunbird-asity *Neodrepanis hypoxantha*: (*a*) male,
(*b*) female

⌣ 229. Long-billed green sunbird *Nectarinia notata*: (*a*) male breeding,
(*b*) male nonbreeding and female

⌣ 228. Souimanga sunbird *Nectarinia souimanga*: (*a*) male breeding,
(*b*) male nonbreeding and female

213. Gray emutail *Dromaeocercus seebohmi*

212. Brown emutail *Dromaeocercus brunneus*

PLATE 31

186a

186b

186c

187a

187b

188a

188b

229a

229b

228b

189a

189b

228a

213

212

199. Appert's greenbul *Phyllastrephus apperti*

201. Gray-crowned greenbul *Phyllastrephus cinereiceps*

200. Dusky greenbul *Phyllastrephus tenebrosus*: (*a*) adult, (*b*) juvenile

226. Yellow-browed oxylabes *Crossleyia xanthophrys*

197. Long-billed greenbul *Phyllastrephus madagascariensis*: (*a*) male, (*b*) female, (*c*) western subspecies

198. Spectacled greenbul *Phyllastrephus zosterops*: (*a*) eastern subspecies, (*b*) western subspecies

225. White-throated oxylabes *Oxylabes madagascariensis*

227. Crossley's babbler *Mystacornis crossleyi*: (*a*) male, (*b*) female

PLATE 32

203. Madagascar magpie-robin *Copsychus albospecularis*: (*a*) nominate subspecies male, (*b*) nominate subspecies female, (*c*) *C. a. inexpectatus* subspecies male, (*d*) *C. a. inexpectatus* subspecies female, (*e*) *C. a. pica* subspecies male, (*f*) *C. a. pica* subspecies female

207. Benson's rock-thrush *Pseudocossyphus bensoni*: male

205. Forest rock-thrush *Pseudocossyphus sharpei*: (*a*) nominate subspecies male, (*b*) *P. s. erythronotus* subspecies male, (*c*) nominate subspecies female, (*d*) *P. s. erythronotus* subspecies female

206. Littoral rock-thrush *Pseudocossyphus imerinus*: female

PLATE 33

203c

203a

203e

203b

203f

203d

205b

207

205a

205d

206

205c

➤ 224. Madagascar paradise flycatcher *Terpsiphone mutata*: (*a,d*) two male variants light morph, (*b*) rufous morph male breeding, (*c*) female and immature, (*e*) rufous morph male nonbreeding

➤ 204. Stonechat *Saxicola torquata*: (*a*) male, (*b*) female

223. Ward's flycatcher *Pseudobias wardi*

➤ 216. Common newtonia *Newtonia brunneicauda*

➤ 217. Archbold's newtonia *Newtonia archboldi*: (*a*) adult, (*b*) juvenile

215. Dark newtonia *Newtonia amphichroa*

218. Red-tailed newtonia *Newtonia fanovanae*

PLATE 34

195. Madagascar wagtail *Motacilla flaviventris*

190. Madagascar bush lark *Mirafra hova*

211. Madagascar cisticola *Cisticola cherina*: (*a,b*) color variants

208. Madagascar swamp-warbler *Acrocephalus newtoni*

209. Madagascar brush-warbler *Nesillas typica*: color variants (*a*) east, (*b*) south

210. Thamnornis warbler *Thamnornis chloropetoides*

PLATE 35

195

190

211a

208

211b

209a

210

209b

219. Common jery *Neomixis tenella*: (*a*) *N. t. tenella* subspecies, (*b*) *N. t. orientalis* subspecies, (*c*) *N. t. debilis* subspecies, (*d*) *N. t. decaryi* subspecies

221. Stripe-throated jery *Neomixis striatigula*: (*a*) *N. s. striatigula*, (*b*) *N. s. pallidor*

214. Rand's warbler *Randia pseudozosterops*

220. Green jery *Neomixis viridis*

222. Wedge-tailed jery *Hartertula flavoviridis*

230. Madagascar white-eye *Zosterops maderaspatana*

PLATE 36

239. White-headed vanga *Leptopterus viridis*: (*a*) male, (*b*) female, (*c*) immature

232. Red-tailed vanga *Calicalicus madagascariensis*: (*a*) male, (*b*) female

244. Nuthatch vanga *Hypositta corallirostris*: (*a*) male, (*b*) female

216. Common newtonia *Newtonia brunneicauda* (for comparison)

240. Chabert's vanga *Leptopterus chabert*

241. Blue vanga *Cyanolanius madagascarinus*: (*a*) adult, (*b*) immature

PLATE 37

239c

239b

232a

239a

232b

244a

244b

216

241a

240

241b

235. Lafresnaye's vanga *Xenopirostris xenopirostris*: (*a*) male, (*b*) female

236. Van Dam's vanga *Xenopirostris damii*: (*a*) male, (*b*) female

237. Pollen's vanga *Xenopirostris polleni*: (*a*) male, (*b*) female

245. Tylas vanga *Tylas eduardi*: (*a*) male eastern subspecies,
(*b*) female eastern subspecies, (*c*) male western subspecies

196. Ashy cuckoo-shrike *Coracina cineria*: (*a*) eastern, (*b*) western

202. Madagascar bulbul *Hypsipetes madagascariensis*

PLATE 38

243. Helmet vanga *Euryceros prevostii*: (*a*) adult, (*b*) immature

⌣ 238. Sickle-billed vanga *Falculea palliata*

242. Bernier's vanga *Oriolia bernieri*: (*a*) male, (*b*) female

⌣ 234. Hook-billed vanga *Vanga curvirostris*: (*a*) nominate subspecies, (*b*) subspecies *V. c. cetera*

233. Rufous vanga *Schetba rufa*: (*a*) male, (*b*) female

PLATE 39

248. Madagascar starling *Hartlaubius auratus*: (*a*) male, (*b*) female and juvenile

246. Crested drongo *Dicrurus forficatus*

253. Madagascar red fody *Foudia madagascariensis*: (*a*) male breeding, (*b*) male nonbreeding, female, and juvenile

255. Madagascar mannikin *Lonchura nana*

256. Common waxbill *Estrilda astrild*

254. Forest fody *Foudia omissa*: (*a*) male breeding, (*b*) male nonbreeding, female, and juvenile

252. Sakalava weaver *Ploceus sakalava*: (*a*) male breeding, (*b*) male nonbreeding and female

251. Nelicourvi weaver *Ploceus nelicourvi*: (*a*) male breeding, (*b*) male nonbreeding and female

PLATE 40

248b

246

248a

253a

255

256

253b

254b

254a

251b

251a

252a

252b

Gruiformes

Mesitornithidae – Mesites

Endemic family numbering only 3 species, 2 in the genus *Mesitornis* and 1 constituting the genus *Monias*. In certain anatomical respects the 2 genera are close to the Rails (Rallidae). They are considered primitive forms of the rail, but far enough removed to comprise a separate family. Mesites are characterized by sparse plumage and short, round wings. Though able to fly, they are almost exclusively terrestrial. One of the 3 species are sexually dimorphic, and only *Monias* behaves gregariously. Mesites boast a broad vocal repertoire in which resonant and harmonious sounds predominate. Their nest is a rather flimsy structure built low off the ground and accessible without flying via a system of branches or creepers.

76. *White-breasted Mesite*

Mesitornis variegata
(Geoffroy Saint-Hilaire, 1838)
Malagasy: Tolohon'ala, Arefy,
Pangalatrovy
French: Mésite variée

DESCRIPTION: Length 31 cm.
Adult. Sexes similar. Rufous-brown cap and eye stripe, rest of head white, except for brown mustache. White chin and throat. Black bill, brown iris. Upperparts chestnut, except for gray mantle. Underparts: white chest tinged with rufous-brown and dotted with black. Brown belly and flanks show thin tan stripes. Yellow-brown tarsi and toes. Wings chestnut tinged with green, except for solid chestnut remiges. Tail chestnut.
Immature. Similar to adult.

IDENTIFICATION: Terrestrial species with brownish plumage above, whitish with black dots below, head marked with eye stripe and thin, rufous-brown mustache. Long tail, short, straight bill. Characteristic silhouette: short-legged, horizontal, with head, back, and tail on same plane. Tail is broad but always held tight. White-breasted mesite cannot be confused with any other species in its range.

BEHAVIOR: Strictly terrestrial forest species, secretive and active, found in groups of 2–4. Feeds in litter of dead leaves of underbrush, vigorously probing down to the ground with bill. This activity often creates noise reminiscent of Madagascar buttonquail, which scratches ground with feet. Walks with body held horizontal, head rocking forward and backward slightly but with no discernible motion of tail. Sometimes runs a few meters to cross open space. In case of sudden danger, it runs away on a zigzag course, only flying a few meters under special circumstances. Frequently freezes in place on completion of run, to confuse pursuer. At rest, lies in shade on carpet of dead leaves. Several individuals may spend night perched on low horizontal branch.

VOICE: Fairly vocal. Melodic song, sort of *wee-hoo-hoo-hoo-hoo weeweeweehoo weewee-hoo-hoo-hoo-hoo*, uttered both at early morning and during the day, is sometimes taken up by another individual. When surprised or alarmed, may a emit drawn-out hiss, *sheesh*, followed by several short, clipped *tsik*. While feeding, all members of the group utter a soft, thin *seesee . . .* with bills closed.

HABITAT: Large tracts of closed deciduous dry forest growing on sandy soil, underbrush of which is covered with dead leaves and free of herbaceous strata or has sparse or discontinuous herbaceous cover. Observed at elevations from sea level to 150 m.

DIET: Little known; seeds and small insects.

NESTING: Very few data. The nest, a simple platform of interwoven twigs, is built close to ground on a bush or tangle of creepers. Clutch numbers 1–2 creamy white eggs with rusty spots (average size: 33 mm × 26 mm). Nidifugous chick has rufous down. Nesting has been observed in Oct. and May.

DISTRIBUTION AND STATUS: Locally distributed species belonging to family endemic to Madagascar. Known only from 4 locations in w deciduous dry forest: Kirindy forest n of Morondava, Ankarafantsika, Ankarana, where it was recently rediscovered after having been unrecorded for more than 50 years (last capture, 1930), and Analamera, where it was first sighted in May 1987. This rare species is threatened by restricted range but also by degradation of original deciduous dry forest by slashing and burning and by invasion of forest by dogs and rats *(Rattus rattus)*, especially near villages.

77. Brown Mesite

Mesitornis unicolor (Desmurs, 1845)
Malagasy: Roatelo, Vorona atambo
French: Mésite unicolore

DESCRIPTION: Length 30 cm. *Adult.* Sexes similar. Chin and throat whitish tinged with rufous, neck pale rufous, white stripe well behind eye (varies by individual), rest of head pinkish gray. Black bill, dark brown iris. Upperparts chestnut. Underparts: pale rufous chest, chestnut belly and flanks with greenish tinge, chestnut undertail coverts. Yellow-gray tarsi and light green-yellow toes. Chestnut wings, brown remiges, brown tail.

Immature. Differs from adult by generally more subdued plumage.

IDENTIFICATION: Terrestrial species with uniformly chestnut plumage, except for gray head marked with white stripe (not always visible), whitish throat, short, straight bill. Silhouette generally similar to that of White-breasted mesite: short-legged, horizontal, with head, back, and tail on same plane and tail wide but always held tight. Brown mesite is only representative of family in its range and is easily distinguishable from other terrestrial species, notably Madagascar wood rail, by its smaller body, stretched-out silhouette, long tail, shorter legs, and uniform plumage.

BEHAVIOR: Strictly terrestrial forest species, very secretive and fearful. Habits little known. Active, feeds on forest floor, turning dead leaves over with bill. This activity may be pursued in family groups of 2–3, silently, head drawn in, tail twitching up and down slightly in time with its regular footsteps. Flies, but seldom, to escape sudden danger or to cross natural obstacle.

VOICE: Fairly vocal. On the ground during day, especially in morning, Sept.–Feb., loud song may be heard over considerable distances, consisting of series of 3–4 *ooh-coo* or *yew-chew* preceded by separate, soft *ooh* or *oogh* audible only at close range. This *ooh . . . oohcoo-oohcoo-oohcoo-oohcoo* may be repeated up to 5 times in 30 seconds, followed by a silence of up to 10 minutes. The song prompts response from another individual. Disturbed or alarmed, Brown mesite may utter hissing sort of *shwee-yew, shwee-yew,* or clipped call sounding like *trak, tsak,* or *tsik.*

HABITAT: Undisturbed evergreen forest. Lives in dark parts of forest where sun penetrates only a few spots and undergrowth consists of sparsely developed herbaceous stratum and substantial litter of dead leaves. Seems to like steep slopes. Observed at elevations from sea level to 900 m.

DIET: Very little known; seeds and small insects.

NESTING: Very few data. Rather loose structure built 1–1.5 m off the ground, on bush usually accessible without flying. Nest is a slightly concave platform of interwoven twigs, reminiscent of doves' nest. Clutch numbers 1 mottled white egg in form of short ellipse, dull shell marked with large gray-brown spots at larger pole. Only 1 parent broods. Nidifugous chicks have chestnut down. Nesting has been observed Nov.–Dec.

DISTRIBUTION AND STATUS: Rare species belongs to family endemic to Madagascar. Distributed in e from Andapa to northern Tolagnaro (Strict Nature Reserve 12 of Marojejy, Masoala peninsula, Sihanaka forest, Andasibe, Ranomafana, Bemangidy). Secretive, rarely sighted; status of species very difficult to ascertain. Protected by taboo, which prevents productive gathering of information from local citizens. Near villages, invasion of forest by dogs and rats *(Rattus rattus)* may threaten species.

78. *Subdesert Mesite*

Monias benschi
Oustalet and Grandidier, 1903
Malagasy: Naka
French: Monias de Bensch

DESCRIPTION: Length 32 cm.
Adult. Sexes differ.
Male. Green-brown cap and eye stripe, rest of head white, except for brownish, diffuse, thin mustache. White chin and throat. Bill red with black tip, iris chestnut. Upperparts solid green-brown. Underparts: white chest mottled with large

black spots, more numerous on sides. White belly. Greenish flanks and under-tail coverts. Red tarsi and toes. Green-brown wings, dark brown tail.

Female. Differs from male by bold rufous markings on white chin, throat, and chest. *Immature.* Differs from adult by more subdued plumage and shorter tail. Rust-brown head with lighter supercilium. Sooty bill. Whitish brown chest and upper belly, with appearance only of dark spots. Flesh-colored feet. Grayish wings.

IDENTIFICATION: Terrestrial species with brownish plumage above, white spotted with black below (or liberally tinged with rufous in female), head marked with broad eye stripe and thin green-brown mustache, long, layered tail, long (35 mm), and decurved red bill. Slimmer silhouette and longer legs than representatives of genus *Mesitornis*. Head much more prominent, held above plane of back. Only representative of family in its range; cannot be mistaken for any other species.

BEHAVIOR: Terrestrial forest species, gregarious and active, found in groups of 3–6, sometimes as many as 10, very rarely alone or in pairs. Sex ratio of groups varies greatly. Group is cohesive in moving from place to place. Subdesert mesite sometimes walks deliberately, head moving forward and backward and tail twitching downward, sometimes rapidly, constantly changing direction. Stops for long intervals to probe bare patches of soil with bill. Same individual may return to same place several times in space of minutes. If alarmed, group remains close, all members running swiftly. To escape sudden danger, one bird may decide to fly a few meters to perch on low horizontal branch and may occupy new spot for several minutes. Group may spend night perched together on low horizontal branch (3 m from ground).

VOICE: Vocal species whose melodic, resonant song, emitted in early morning, is a long (up to 35, even 45 seconds), rhythmic succession of accented notes, a sort of *tsitsitsi tsee tsee tsee,* its pattern often repeated and sometimes ending with a low-pitched *irr* that may be produced by another individual. Location can often be pinpointed by characteristic alarm call, a clipped *nak nak* repeated at quick intervals by various individuals in group.

HABITAT: Undisturbed or slightly degraded subarid thickets, with sandy soil, undergrowth free or nearly free of herbaceous cover, and generous litter of dead leaves. Same habitat as Long-tailed ground-roller. Observed at elevations of 10–100 m.

DIET: Chiefly invertebrates (Coleoptera, Homoptera), also small fruits and seeds.

NESTING: Nest is simple, shallow platform of interwoven twigs, built on horizontal branch 1–1.5 m above ground, accessible without flying. Clutch numbers 1–2 whitish eggs speckled to varying degrees with light brown and gray (average size: 28.1 mm × 35.1 mm). Nesting has been observed Nov.–Dec.

DISTRIBUTION AND STATUS: Uncommon, very local species of family endemic to Madagascar. Distributed in sw along narrow coastal strip about 200 km long between Mangoky River to n and Fiherenana to s, and bordered at e by mountains. Threatened by narrowness of range, destruction of habitat, and invasion of woodlands by dogs and rats *(Rattus rattus).*

Turnicidae – Buttonquail

Small terrestrial birds with short rounded
wings, short tail, short and slight bill, and
short, heavy tarsi with only 3 toes (no
hind toe). The female is larger than the
male and has more colorful plumage.
The family is represented by 15 species
and numerous subspecies distributed in
the temperate and tropical regions of the
Old World. Only 1 endemic species nests
in Madagascar.

79. *Madagascar Buttonquail*

Turnix nigricollis (Gmelin, 1789)
Malagasy: Kibo, Kibobo
French: Turnix de Madagascar

DESCRIPTION: Length 14–16 cm.
Adult. Sexes differ. Female slightly larger
and more brightly colored than male.
Male. Brown head dotted with tan.
Lighter supercilium. Tan chin and throat.
Light gray bill, pale yellow iris. Upperparts brown marked with tan and dark
brown. Underparts: chest and flanks
tan with brown stripes. Light tan belly
and rufous-brown undertail coverts.
Light gray tarsi and toes, white claws.
Brown wing marked with tan. Brown-gray
primary remiges. Tail same color as
upperparts.
Female. Gray head flecked with white.
Substantial white mustache. Black chin
and throat. Bill and iris as in male. Upperparts gray mixed with rufous-brown
and brown. Underparts: middle of chest
black, sides gray with bright rufous extending to flanks. White belly tinged with
rufous, undertail coverts russet. Tarsi and
toes as in male. Brown wings marked
with rufous and white. Uniformly gray-
brown primary remiges. Tail same color
as upperparts.

IDENTIFICATION: Small terrestrial
species with plump silhouette, short-
legged, very suggestive of quail. Sexual
dimorphism favors female, according her
colorful plumage. Female is easily identified by black throat and chest, and bright
rufous spots on sides of chest and flanks.
Male is difficult to identify but differs
from Common and Harlequin quails by
smaller size, light underparts with brown
stripes, pale yellow eye, and light hue
of bill.

BEHAVIOR: Terrestrial species with behavior close to that of quail, usually seen
in pairs or small groups of 3–5. Walks
about indefatigably, stopping frequently
to scratch ground busily in search of food
after having noisily cleared it of dead
leaves. Small, circular bare areas about
10 cm in diameter on forest floor betray
its recent passage. Runs for safety when
disturbed. When flushed, flies 3–10 m,
then abruptly drops back to ground and
continues fleeing on foot. Seems active
throughout day, even at hottest times.

VOICE: Rapid *bub bub bub* . . . heard at
close quarters.

HABITAT: Grassland savanna, undisturbed forest or degraded woodlands, not
too dense, dry croplands (cassava, sisal),
scrub. Observed at elevations from sea
level to 1,900 m.

DIET: Seeds, insects.

NESTING: Nest is small hollow fashioned in ground, lined with leaves and
grasses and protected by tuft of grass or
bush sometimes covered by a grassy
dome. Clutch numbers 4–5 light tan eggs
with dark brown and gray spots. Only
male incubates. Nidifugous chick has
brown down adorned with 2 white stripes
on back and 3 on head. Nesting has been
observed Sept.–Feb.

DISTRIBUTION AND STATUS: Endemic to Madagascar, also distributed on

Réunion, where it was probably introduced. Distributed throughout Madagascar, abundantly in n, w, and s, rather thinly in e and on High Plateau.

Rallidae – Rails, Crake, Flufftails, Moorhen, Gallinule, Swamphen, Coot

Rather furtive birds generally associated with wetlands but also encountered on bodies of water, in woodlands, and even in dry environments. They have rounded wings, short tails, and generally long toes. Some species are widely distributed, while others are very local, and they are generally sedentary, although small species of the genus *Porzana* perform long migrations. The family is cosmopolitan and represented by more than 130 species. Eleven species nest in Madagascar, 5 of them endemic and 1 of them limited to Madagascar and Aldabra.

80. *Madagascar Rail*

Rallus madagascariensis Verreaux, 1833
Malagasy: Kiky, Tsikea, Kitsiakely, Voronondrika
French: Râle de Madagascar

DESCRIPTION: Length 25 cm.
Adult. Sexes similar. Gray forehead, front of head, lores, cheeks, chin and throat. Rest of head and neck maroon flecked with black. Bill mauve, except for black ridge of upper mandible and dark ivory tip of bill. Brick red iris. Upperparts brown olive-green, except for maroon mantle flecked with black. Underparts: maroon chest with sooty flecks, burgundy belly and flanks, white undertail coverts. Brown-gray tarsi and toes. Green-brown wings with sooty flecks, brown remiges with sooty bars, brownish tail.
Immature. Differs from adult by generally more subdued plumage, brownish bill, and brown eyes.

IDENTIFICATION: Medium-sized rail with slender silhouette and long legs. Long (40 mm), decurved bill. Characterized by gray and maroon head, brown-green upperparts flecked with black, and burgundy underparts, except for white undertail coverts. Distinguished from White-throated rail by considerably smaller size, gray head and throat, long, decurved bill, and uniformly colored belly and flanks. Distinguished from Madagascar wood rail by gray throat, long, decurved bill, and white undertail coverts.

BEHAVIOR: Secretive and shy, found alone or in pairs. Moves about slowly in dense aquatic vegetation, searching for food and probing the mud with long bill.

VOICE: Little known. Utters loud, bisyllabic call.

HABITAT: Dense herbaceous vegetation of marshes and wet woodlands, preferably at high elevations. Observed at elevations from sea level to 1,800 m.

DIET: Chiefly invertebrates.

NESTING: Few data. Nest built on the ground in aquatic vegetation. Reddish white eggs spotted with brown. Nesting has been observed Aug.–Oct.

DISTRIBUTION AND STATUS: Endemic to Madagascar, distributed in e and in e part of High Plateau, where it is rather rare.

81. White-throated Rail

Dryolimnas cuvieri (Pucheran, 1845)
Malagasy: Agoly, Kitsiabe, Tsikoza, Drovika
French: Râle de Cuvier

DESCRIPTION: Length 30–32 cm. *Adult.* Sexes similar. Maroon-brown head and back and sides of neck. White chin, throat, and front of neck. Dark red bill with black tip, reddish iris. Upper-parts solid olive green except for black streaks on back. Underparts: maroon-brown chest, olive green belly, flanks and undertail coverts with tawny stripes. Olive green tarsi and toes. Wings olive green above, brown with white bars below, except for sooty remiges. Dark olive green tail.
Immature. Differs from adult by light brown head and underparts, black bill, brown iris, and sepia tarsi and toes.

IDENTIFICATION: Medium-sized rail characterized by brown head and chest, white throat, striped belly and undertail coverts, and straight bill of average length. Distinguished from Madagascar rail by larger size, white throat, and straight bill. Distinguished from Madagascar wood rail by larger size, slimmer silhouette, white throat, brown head and chest, and longer bill.

VOICE: Vocal species whose characteristic call constitutes an excellent means of location and identification. Usually uttered toward evening, sometimes in the middle of the night, it is a loud, piercing whistle, *dwee-ee dwee-ee dwee dwee dwee,* rising in intensity with each syllable. Call often becomes duet. Brief muffled grunts may be heard while bird is feeding.

HABITAT: Woodland watercourses, wetlands, including rice paddies, mangroves, and coral-islet beaches. Observed at elevations from sea level to 1,800 m.

DIET: Chiefly invertebrates.

NESTING: Bowl-shaped nest of interwoven leaves and grasses is built on ground in densest part of clump of aquatic vegetation. Clutch numbers 3–6 brown eggs with dark brown spots. Chicks are covered in black down. Nesting has been observed Nov.–Mar.

DISTRIBUTION AND STATUS: Distributed in Madagascar and Aldabra. Represented in Madagascar by endemic nominate subspecies *D. c. cuvieri*. Abundant throughout range.

82. *Madagascar Wood Rail*

Canirallus kioloides (Pucheran, 1845)
Malagasy: Tsikoza-ala, Tsikoza vohitra, Vorotrandraka, Drovikala
French: Râle à front gris

DESCRIPTION: Length 28 cm. Nominate subspecies *C. k. kioloides*. *Adult*. Sexes similar. Gray forehead, front of head and eye ring. Olive-green crown, nape, and back of neck. Thick rufous-brown mustache. Pure white chin and throat sometimes edged with black dots. Rufous-brown sides of neck. Blue-gray bill with black base, brown iris. Upperparts olive-green, tinged with rufous-brown on back. Underparts: rufous-brown chest and flanks. Belly and undertail coverts dark brown with thin tan stripes. Chestnut-colored, powerful tarsi and toes. Wings: rufous-brown above, except for sooty primary remiges mottled with white patches on inside half of remiges (patches are invisible when wing is folded). Underside of wings sooty all over, marked with white patches. Tail rufous brown.

Subspecies *C. k. berliozi* (Salomonsen, 1934).
Adult. Differs from nominate subspecies by slightly larger size, but especially by gray of head, which extends from forehead to crown, and by lighter shades of gray and olive-green of upperparts. *Immature*. Differs from adults by generally duller plumage and by less extensive patch of gray on head and undertail coverts marked with yellow spots.

IDENTIFICATION: Forest rail distinguished from White-throated rail (only species with which it can be confused) by smaller size, stockier silhouette, generally russet coloring of upperparts, gray head, much shorter (almost by half) bill, and dark undertail coverts.

BEHAVIOR: Generally seen in pairs, less frequently alone. Secretive, hardly noticeable when feeding. Covers ground swiftly in underbrush, stops suddenly, probes litter, moves on, sometimes returns several times to area just inspected. Head and tail bob and twitch as it moves. Runs away when disturbed, takes wing only in extreme danger.

VOICE: Rather vocal species whose calls constitute an excellent means of location and identification. Sonorous call consists of series of loud, piercing whistles. While feeding, bird constantly emits muffled, throaty chortles reminiscent of contact calls of Brown lemur *(Lemur fulvus)*, very brief, sharp, metallic notes, as well as a staccato *nak nak nak nak . . .* repeated several times and sometimes speeded up at the finish so as to produce a rattle-like effect.

HABITAT: Undisturbed rain forest, slightly degraded, contiguous second growth offering fairly sparse herbaceous stratum, and banks of ponds and woodland watercourses. Observed at elevations from sea level to 1,450 m. Recently observed in dry deciduous forest established on a karstic substratum.

DIET: Few data; insects, amphibians, seeds.

NESTING: Bowl-shaped nest of grasses and leaves is built 2–3 m above ground in bush or tangle of creepers. Clutch numbers 2 pinkish white eggs with gray and rufous spots (average size: 42 mm × 32 mm). Nidifugous chick has sooty down that is unvariegated on upperparts, spotted with brown everywhere else. Breeding has been observed in Nov.

DISTRIBUTION AND STATUS: Endemic to Madagascar. Nominate subspecies *C. k. kioloides* is distributed in e and on High Plateau. Subspecies *C. k. berliozi* is local to Sambirano, where it is fairly common. Species was recently (July 1987) observed in Tsingy de Bemaraha (Strict Nature Reserve 9), but which subspecies was involved is not yet known.

83. *Baillon's Crake*

Porzana pusilla (Pallas, 1776)
Malagasy: Birindrano
French: Marouette de Baillon

DESCRIPTION: Length 17 cm.
Adult. Sexes similar. Head blue-gray, except for chestnut front of head, crown, nape and back of neck. Yellow-green bill, red iris. Upperparts chestnut flecked with black and white. Underparts: blue-gray chest and upper belly, barred black-and-white flanks, lower belly, and undertail coverts. Olive-green tarsi and toes. Wings chestnut, except for brown remiges. Chestnut tail.
Immature. Differs from adult by paler upperparts and crown and by whitish rest of head and underparts, except for flanks and undertail coverts barred with white and light brown. Ivory bill, brown iris, and brownish legs.

IDENTIFICATION: Small aquatic rail, easily identified by blue-gray and chestnut, spotted plumage and by partially black-and-white barred underparts. Distinguished from Slender-billed flufftail by larger size, partially blue-gray head, blue-gray chest, and boldly barred flanks. Immature differs from Slender-billed flufftail by black-and-white flecked upperparts and chestnut tail.

BEHAVIOR: Furtive and secretive, normally found alone, or in pairs during breeding season. Feeds as it walks on floating aquatic vegetation, passing alongside reed beds or stands of *Cyperus* spp. (Cyperaceae). Active in early morning, toward evening, and at twilight. Flies to pass over obstacle or flee immediate danger.

VOICE: Quiet species; utters sharp, trilled call, mostly at night. Alarm call is a brief *veek*.

HABITAT: Marshes, shores of freshwater or brackish lakes offering islets of reeds or *Cyperus* spp., and banks with dense aquatic vegetation. Observed at elevations from sea level to 1,500 m.

DIET: Insects, aquatic plant seeds.

NESTING: Few data. Bowl-shaped nest of interwoven leaves of grassy plants built in tuft of wetland vegetation near or on water. Clutch numbers 5–6 fawn eggs spotted with brown. Both parents incubate.

DISTRIBUTION AND STATUS: Distributed in Europe, Africa, Asia, and Oceania. Represented in Madagascar by subspecies *P. p. obscura* (Neumann, 1897), common to e and s Africa. Patchily distributed throughout Madagascar (Alaotra Lake, Antananarivo, Ihotry Lake).

84. *Sakalava Rail*

Amaurornis olivieri
(Grandidier and Berlioz, 1929)
French: Râle d'Olivier

DESCRIPTION: Length 19 cm.
Adult. Sexes similar. Head black all over, except for white chin and traces of white on throat in some individuals. Bright yellow, straight, rather short bill, red iris. Upperparts dark gray tinged with brown and green. Underparts uniformly sooty. Pinkish red tarsi and toes. Wings same

color as upperparts, except for black primary remiges. Short black tail.

IDENTIFICATION: Small rail with black plumage and yellow bill; cannot be confused with any other species.

BEHAVIOR: Few data. Has been observed moving on floating lake vegetation near reedbeds.

VOICE: Unknown.

HABITAT: Marshes offering at once stretches of open water, patches of floating vegetation (*Nymphaea* sp.—Nymphaeaceae), and reedbeds (*Phragmites* sp.—Gramineae).

DIET: Unknown.

NESTING: Very few data. Nest built near water in mass of vegetation (*Typha* sp.—Typhaecea), about 50 cm above ground, contains 2 creamy-white eggs marked with chestnut. Nesting has been observed in Mar.

DISTRIBUTION AND STATUS: Endemic to Madagascar. The few data come from sites in w between Mahajanga and Morombe: Ambararatabe, Kinkony Lake, Antsalova, Bemamba Lake, along the Tsiribihina, and Nosy Ambositra.

85. *Madagascar Flufftail*

Sarothrura insularis (Sharpe, 1870)
Malagasy: Biry biry, Tsobeboka, Pangalatrovy, Biny
French: Râle insulaire

DESCRIPTION: Length 14 cm.
Adult. Sexes differ.
Male. Head, nape, neck, chin and throat bright rufous all over. Black bill, brown iris. Upperparts black, flecked with white and tan. Underparts: chest bright rufous, belly, flanks and undertail coverts black streaked with white. Light brown tarsi and toes. Wings same color as upper-

parts, except for brown primary remiges. Bright rufous, fluffy tail.
Female. Top of head fawn, heavily streaked black. Cheek fawn finely spotted with black. Chin and throat light tan. Black bill, brown iris. Upperparts finely flecked black and light brown. Underparts: fawn chest, finely spotted with black, rufous sides heavily streaked with black, belly tan, and undertail coverts streaked with black. Wings same color as upperparts, except for brown primary remiges. Fluffy brown tail with black bars.

IDENTIFICATION: Very small rail with plump silhouette and short, fluffy tail. Male easily identified by bicolor plumage (rufous head and chest, black wings and belly). Female distinguished from male and female Slender-billed flufftail by black flecks over almost all her plumage. Similar in size to Slender-billed flufftail, but with shorter bill, tarsi, and toes.

BEHAVIOR: Terrestrial, furtive species, lives alone or in pairs and is very difficult to observe. Encounters are always very brief. If surprised, it vanishes into vegetation or flies a few meters before running away.

VOICE: Vocal, its presence is often signaled only by highly characteristic call, a powerful, resonant *bee bee bee bee beeree beeree beeree beeree bee bee bee*, rapidly strung together in diminishing volume (the first and last monosyllabic notes are often separate).

HABITAT: Local to grasslands of edges and clearings of undisturbed or degraded rain forest as well as marshes. Observed at elevations from sea level to 2,300 m.

DIET: Few data; insects, seeds.

NESTING: Few data. Spherical nest built on ground in dense vegetation is woven from leaves of grassy plants and lined with more delicate plant matter.

Clutch numbers 3–4 relatively round white eggs (average size: 26 mm × 20 mm). Only female incubates. Chicks have sooty down. Breeding has been observed in Oct.

DISTRIBUTION AND STATUS: Endemic to Madagascar, distributed in e and on High Plateau. Abundant throughout range.

86. Slender-billed Flufftail

Sarothrura watersi (Bartlett, 1879)
Malagasy: Manganahitra
French: Râle de Waters

DESCRIPTION: Length 14–17 cm.
Adult. Sexes differ.
Male. Head rufous-brown, darker on crown. Chin and throat white with rufous tinge. Dark brown bill. Upperparts olive green–brown streaked with dark brown, except for rufous upper back. Brown iris, black bill. Underparts: rufous-brown chest and flanks, pink-gray belly and undertail coverts, light brown tarsi and toes. Wings same color as upperparts, except for uniformly dark brown–gray primary remiges. Tail slightly fluffed, rufous-brown tipped with black.
Female. Light brown head, except for whitish chin and throat, and thin light tan streaks on crown. Dark brown bill. Upperparts brown with lightly marked whitish streaks on uppertail coverts. Underparts: tan chest, brown flanks, brown-gray belly, brown-gray undertail coverts with white stripes. Tarsi and toes identical to those of male. Brownish wings. Slightly fluffed brownish tail.

IDENTIFICATION: Very small rail with rather plump silhouette and short fluffed tail. Male and female distinguished from female Madagascar flufftail by almost evenly colored upper- and underparts. Bill and especially tarsi and toes are much longer than those of Madagascar flufftail, in keeping with its aquatic habits. In flight, legs are long and hang down, as in Baillon's crake.

BEHAVIOR: Aquatic species difficult to observe. Takes wing only in sudden danger, when it flies a short distance before running and vanishing into aquatic vegetation.

VOICE: Muffled, solemn call uttered in daytime, over long intervals without break, GOO goo GOO goo . . . , with every other syllable accentuated. Issues from dense vegetation.

HABITAT: Elevated wetlands (Cyperus spp.—Cyperaceae) and adjacent dense, grassy terrain or even croplands (rice paddies) near rain forest. Observed at elevations of 950–1,800 m.

DIET: Unknown.

NESTING: No data. Examination of 1 male and 1 female capable of breeding, captured near Andapa in Sept., has provided only specific data relating to reproduction of species. Male's call has been heard in Nov.

DISTRIBUTION AND STATUS: Endemic to Madagascar, rare, known only from 5 locations: "Southeast Betsileo" (no further details), "near Andapa," Antananarivo (doubtful observation), Analamazaotra, and Ranomafana, where species was first encountered in 1987. One of 4 endemic species observed fewer than 2 times in the past 50 years.

87. Common Moorhen

Gallinula chloropus (Linnaeus, 1758)
Malagasy: Akohondrano
French: Poule d'eau commune

DESCRIPTION: Length 32 cm.
Adult. Sexes similar. Sooty gray head and neck. Vermilion bill with yellow tip, ver-

milion forehead shield, brown iris. Upperparts dark brown tinged with green. Underparts sooty, except for white line on flanks and orange-tinged undertail coverts. Yellow-green tarsi and toes. Dark brown wings, gray tail.
Juvenile. Light brown head. Black bill. Upperparts brown, underparts light brown, except for whitish undertail coverts.

IDENTIFICATION: Large rail with dark brown plumage marked with lateral white line on flanks, red beak with red forehead shield, and orangy undertail coverts. Distinguished from Allen's gallinule by larger size, red forehead shield, chestnut tinge of underparts, white lateral line, orangy undertail coverts, and yellow-green legs.

BEHAVIOR: Rather secretive, not shy, found alone or in pairs along edges of vegetation in wetlands. Feeds on foot or swimming, frequently immersing head. Laborious take-off run precedes flight. Legs often left hanging in first moments of flight.

VOICE: Rather vocal, utters variety of brief, muffled calls, as well as a characteristic alarm call—a brief, piercing *pree-ee.*

HABITAT: Marshes offering stretches of open water, lakes, and rivers with luxuriant banks. Observed at elevations from sea level to 2,300 m.

DIET: Invertebrates, aquatic plant seeds.

NESTING: Nest, made of leaves of aquatic plants, built in tuft of vegetation, above water or floating. Clutch numbers 5 tan eggs with chestnut and gray spots. Both parents incubate. Chick has black down. Nesting has been observed Oct.–Mar.

DISTRIBUTION AND STATUS: Distributed in Europe, Africa, Asia, and Oceania. Represented in Madagascar by subspecies *G. c. pyrrhorhoa* (Newton, 1861), also occurring in Réunion, Comoros, and Mauritius. Abundantly distributed throughout Madagascar.

88. *Allen's Gallinule*

Porphyrula alleni Thomson, 1842
Malagasy: Aretakely, Andevolahintalevana, Talevana
French: Poule d'Allen

DESCRIPTION: Length 25 cm.
Adult. Sexes similar. Dark blue head, neck, chin, and throat. Vermilion bill, sky blue forehead shield, red iris. Upperparts dark green, underparts dark blue, except for white undertail coverts. Red tarsi and toes. Dark green wings and tail.
Juvenile. Light brown head and upperparts. Tan underparts. Light brown bill and legs.

IDENTIFICATION: Medium-sized rail with somber plumage, red bill topped by sky-blue forehead shield, and red legs. Distinguished from Purple swamphen by considerably smaller size, sky-blue forehead shield, and thinner bill. Distinguished from Common moorhen by smaller size, sky-blue forehead shield, white undertail coverts, absence of white marking on flanks, and red legs.

BEHAVIOR: Secretive, found alone, in pairs, or in family groups in wetland vegetation. Feeds as it walks deliberately among water plants or on floating vegetation. Often flies short distance to move from one island of vegetation to another. Legs remain hanging during flight. Active chiefly in morning and at dusk.

VOICE: Vocal species with extended but unharmonious vocal register. Utters brief, piercing calls, sometimes stringing together repeated utterances of what sounds like *kills.*

HABITAT: Marshes, freshwater lakes, and river mouths having substantial islands of aquatic vegetation. Observed at elevations from sea level to 800 m.

DIET: Insects, aquatic plant seeds.

NESTING: Deep, bowl-shaped nest of interwoven leaves of aquatic plants is built in tuft of vegetation just above waterline. Clutch numbers 4 tan eggs spotted with chestnut. Both parents incubate. Chick has black down. Nesting has been observed in Jan.

DISTRIBUTION AND STATUS: Distributed in Africa and Madagascar. Uncommon but distributed throughout Madagascar except for High Plateau, where it is absent, and s, where it is rare.

89. *Purple Swamphen*

Porphyrio porphyrio (Linnaeus, 1758)
Malagasy: Vatry, Talecana, Talevanabe
French: Poule sultane

DESCRIPTION: Length 46 cm.
Adult. Sexes similar. Blue head, neck, and throat, with violet tinge on crown, nape, and back of neck. Vermilion bill and forehead shield, red iris. Upperparts blue tinged with bronze green. Underparts blue with violet sheen, except for white undertail coverts. Vermilion tarsi and toes. Bronze green–blue wings, except for midnight blue remiges. Midnight blue tail.
Immature. Differs from adult by more subdued plumage, especially paler underparts, by less stout bill, and by less developed forehead shield.

IDENTIFICATION: Very large rail, biggest in Madagascar, with dark blue plumage, very large red bill topped by red forehead shield, and long red legs. Distinguished from Allen's gallinule, which has same color pattern, by considerably larger size, stouter bill, and more developed red forehead shield.

BEHAVIOR: Usually found in pairs or in small loose-knit groups of 4–10. Active chiefly in morning and at dusk. Feeds as it walks deliberately along islands of aquatic vegetation, in shallows, or on floating vegetation. Frequently seen swimming to cross open water.

VOICE: Vocal species with varied repertory of dissonant calls. Most common is a loud, trumpetlike *poohoo-ey.*

HABITAT: Marshes and freshwater or brackish lakes having islands of reeds or *Cyperus* spp. (Cyperaceae) and substantial aquatic vegetation. Observed at elevations from sea level to 800 m.

DIET: Invertebrates, small vertebrates, and aquatic plant seeds.

NESTING: Nest of interwoven aquatic plants is built in tuft of vegetation above waterline or floating. Clutch numbers 3–5 slightly shiny, light brown eggs spotted red and gray. Both parents incubate. Nesting has been observed in Jan.

DISTRIBUTION AND STATUS: Distributed in Europe, Africa, Asia, and Oceania. Represented in Madagascar by subspecies *P. p. madagascariensis* (Latham, 1801), also distributed in Africa. Rather abundantly distributed throughout island, except for High Plateau, where it is absent, and s, where it is rare. Heavily hunted locally.

90. *Red-knobbed Coot*

Fulica cristata Gmelin, 1789
Malagasy: Sarako, Vantsiano, Tsohia, Otrika, Akoharano, Vorondrano
French: Foulque à crêtes

DESCRIPTION: Length 35–41 cm.
Adult. Sexes similar. Black head and neck. White forehead shield sometimes tinged with pink, topped by 2 more or less developed red tubercules. White bill,

red iris. Sooty gray upperparts, gray underparts. Slate gray tarsi and toes. Wings sooty gray above, gray below. Sooty gray tail.

Immature. Head dark brown edged with white on front of neck and whitish on cheeks and throat. Much smaller forehead shield. Grayish bill, brown iris. Brown-gray upperparts, pale gray underparts. Dark gray legs. Wings and tail as in adult.

IDENTIFICATION: Large aquatic bird with rounded back, black plumage, and white forehead shield. Cannot be confused with any other species. From a distance, the red tubercules ornamenting head may hardly be visible, especially since their size and coloring vary greatly. In flight, wings are short and rounded, neck is extended, and legs point to rear. Rapid, shallow wingbeats. Immature distinguished from juvenile Common moorhen by larger size, more somber upperparts, and uniformly gray underparts.

BEHAVIOR: Aquatic, fairly gregarious outside breeding season, commonly found in small groups of 10–12 or in loose-knit groups of 20–330 (at Tsimanampetsotsa, 90, Mar. 1987; 330, Dec. 1988). To feed, dives briefly or immerses head in shallows. Also seen feeding on shore. Awkward walker. Prefers to flee danger by swimming, since taking wing is a laborious process involving run of some 20 m on water. In breeding season becomes aggressive toward own species, as well as other water birds.

VOICE: Limited vocal register; utters loud, solemn *hoo hoo hoo hoo* and a loud trumpetlike sound call.

HABITAT: Shallow freshwater or brackish lakes. Observed at elevations from sea level to 1,500 m.

DIET: Chiefly aquatic plants, including Water hyacinth *(Eichhornia crassipes)*, also aquatic invertebrates.

NESTING: Nests on bodies of water fringed with vegetation. Nest of dead stalks and leaves is built on water. Clutch numbers 1–7 pale gray eggs with dark brown spots. Nidifugous chicks. Breeding has been observed Dec.–May.

DISTRIBUTION AND STATUS: Distributed in e and s Africa and Madagascar, as well as specific localities in Spain and N Africa. In Madagascar, common on lakes of s (Anony), sw (Timanampetsotsa and Ihotry), w (Bemamba, Masama, Kinkony); uncommon in e (Alaotra Lake); much rarer on High Plateau (lakes of Antananarivo).

Charadriiformes

Jacanidae – Jacana

Tropical aquatic birds with extremely long toes and claws, which enable them to walk and run on aquatic vegetation. The family is represented by 8 species comprising 6 genera. One species is endemic to Madagascar and belongs to a genus common to Africa.

91. *Madagascar Jacana*

Actophilornis albinucha
(Geoffroy Saint-Hilaire, 1832)
Malagasy: Piritry, Fandionga, Tsikai
French: Jacana malgache

DESCRIPTION: Length 30 cm.
Adult. Sexes similar. Female slightly larger than male. White crown, pearl gray forehead shield extending halfway up crown, black cheeks, white chin. Black throat and front of neck. Nape, back, and sides of neck white marked with 2 golden spots on each side of base of neck. Pearl gray, straight bill, brown iris. Upperparts rufous, rump and uppertail coverts sometimes white. Underparts rufous. Pearl gray tarsi. Extremely long toes with very thin, very long claws. Wings rufous, except for black primary remiges. Short rufous tail.
Immature. Forehead shield very small, may be absent. Crown, nape, and back of neck black, ending in 2 golden spots on each side of black area. White chin, cheeks, throat, and sides and front of neck. Upperparts brown-green, except for russet rump and undertail coverts. Underparts whitish, flanks russet. Wings same color as upperparts, except for black primary remiges.

IDENTIFICATION: Slender silhouette, long neck and legs, rufous plumage, except for black-and-white head and neck. Only representative of family in Madagascar. Cannot be confused with any other species.

BEHAVIOR: Aquatic species usually found alone or in pairs, more rarely in groups (75 on Ankerika Lake, Nov. 1985). Not shy, walks deliberately on floating vegetation, thanks to extraordinary length of toes. In danger will fly short distance, legs pointing to rear, alight again, and continue to seek safety by running.

VOICE: Vocal, utters sharp, nervous *kreeeeee*, repeated in diminishing volume, particularly during frequent quarrels with other jacanas. Call reminiscent of Madagascar little grebe's call.

HABITAT: Aquatic settings offering floating vegetation (*Nymphaea* spp.— Nymphaeaceae), lakes, ponds (even if small), more rarely banks of sluggish rivers. Observed at elevations from sea level to 750 m.

DIET: Insects, larvae, aquatic plant seeds.

NESTING: Floating nest consisting of pile of aquatic plants. Clutch numbers 4 green-brown eggs with dark brown spots. Breeding observed Dec.–June.

DISTRIBUTION AND STATUS: Endemic to Madagascar. Abundant in n and w (Anivorano, Maromandia, Port-Bergé, Tsaramandroso, Soalala lakes, Antsalova, Morondava, and Ihotry Lake), rare in e, has been seen at Maroantsetra, Toamasina, and Alaotra Lake, where it was formerly abundant.

Rostratulidae – Painted Snipe

Family represented by 2 species, 1 distributed in Africa, Asia, Australia, and Madagascar, the other in S America. Its eyes are placed well forward, providing good binocular vision. Female has brighter plumage than male, who assumes duties of nest building, incubation, and rearing of nidifugous young.

92. *Greater Painted Snipe*

Rostratula benghalensis (Linnaeus, 1758)
Malagasy: Tatoka, Katobary, Voadivy
French: Rhynchée peinte

DESCRIPTION: Length 23–26 cm.
Adult. Sexes differ.
Male. Brown head marked with fawn median band and white eye ring extending behind eyes. Light brown cheeks, whitish chin and throat, dark brown neck. Long (40 mm) bill decurved at end, brown with dark brown or chestnut tip. Brown iris. Upperparts dark brown, except for brown mantle and scapulars edged with tan, forming a V. Underparts white, except for brown chest, darker on lower portion. White line along sides of neck separates head and neck from rest of body. Coloring of tarsi and toes varies: may be light green, green-blue, or green-brown. Brown wings marked with dark brown bars and large tan ocelli. Primary remiges brown-gray thinly striped with dark brown and marked with large fawn ocelli on outer half. Gray tail subtly barred with brown and marked with small fawn ocelli.
Female. Head differs from male by rufous cheeks, throat, nape, and neck. Upperparts green-brown subtly barred with black, except for rufous upper part of

mantle and white or broadly tan-edged scapulars, with 2 lines joining in V above. Underparts white, except for rufous and dark brown lower portion of chest. White line on sides of neck. Green-brown wings with subtle dark brown stripes; primary remiges identical to those of male. Underside of wings is gray subtly striped with brown. Tail same as that of male. *Immature.* Differs from male by less contrasting underparts, light brown throat and chest running to tan, and absence of color change between chest and belly.

IDENTIFICATION: Contrasting plumage (brown on top, brown or rufous chest, and white underside), slightly decurved bill, and relatively long legs. Easily distinguished from Madagascar snipe by smaller size, shorter bill, white underparts, and round, wide white wings marked with numerous fawn ocelli. Behavior and general impression are reminiscent of rails. Distinguished from Madagascar rail by slightly larger size, bulkier silhouette, rufous head and neck, white eye ring, white underparts, and tan V marking upperparts. In flight, wide, round wings and slow, full wingbeats are field marks.

BEHAVIOR: Aquatic, secretive, largely crepuscular, solitary, found in pairs only when breeding. Spends daylight hidden in dense, low-growing marshland vegetation, emerging at dawn, dusk, and night to feed. Uses bill to probe muddy areas near its refuge, also more distant waterlogged grasslands. While feeding it may be seen swimming to cross smooth watercourse or irrigation canal. When disturbed, it will fly some tens of meters, letting legs hang like a rail, then land amid vegetation and seek further safety by running.

VOICE: Vocal during breeding period. Female utters loud *cot cot cot cot . . .* , sometimes heard at night but usually 2–3

hours after sunset or just before daybreak. Some phrases of call are reminiscent of doves cooing.

HABITAT: Marshes offering islands of rather low dense vegetation and stretches of open water, coastal marshlands, brackish lakes, rice paddies. Observed at elevations from sea level to 1,500 m.

DIET: Seeds (including rice), aquatic invertebrates (insects, mollusks, crustaceans, worms).

NESTING: Female is polyandrous, mating with several males and laying several clutches in nests built by males. Shallow, bowl-shaped nest of leaves and leafstalks is built on ground near water, in dense tuft of grass. Clutch numbers 4 slightly shiny light tan eggs with distinctive brown and black spots. Only male broods. Nesting has been observed June–July.

DISTRIBUTION AND STATUS: Distributed in Africa, Oceania, Asia, and Madagascar. Represented in Madagascar by nominate subspecies *R. b. benghalensis*, common to Africa and Asia. Rather patchily distributed throughout e (Andapa, Maroantsetra, Analamazaotra, Ivohibe), w (Soalala, Ampijoroa, Antsalova, Ihotry Lake), and n (Ambanja). Rather frequently encountered on High Plateau (Antananarivo, Ambatolampy). Appears absent from s. Crepuscular habits and secretiveness make status difficult to assess.

Recurvirostridae – Stilt, Avocet

Shore birds with long, thin bills, straight in representatives of the genus *Himantopus* (stilt) and curved upward in those of the genus *Recurvirostra* (avocet), and long or very long legs with first toe absent or much reduced. The family is cosmopolitan and generally recognized as including 13 species. Only 1 stilt nests in Madagascar, and 1 avocet occasionally visits Malagasy coasts.

93. *Black-winged Stilt*

Himantopus himantopus (Linnaeus, 1758)
Malagasy: Tsakaranta, Tafaly, Takapaly
French: Echasse à manteau noir

DESCRIPTION: Length 35–40 cm, wingspan 70 cm.
Adult. Sexes differ. Plumage varies seasonally.
Male Breeding Plumage. Sooty crown, nape, and back of neck. Black bill, dark red iris. Upperparts black, except for white upper portion of mantle, back, rump, and uppertail coverts. Underparts white. Red tarsi and toes. Wings black, except for white axillaries. White tail.
Female Breeding Plumage. Differs from male in breeding plumage by entirely white crown, nape, and back of neck.
Adult Nonbreeding Plumage. Differs from male in breeding plumage by white-edged black crown, nape, and back of neck.
Juvenile. Crown and nape brown edged with tan. Back of neck light gray, rest of head, and neck white. Black bill, light brown iris. Upperparts light brown edged with tan, except for white back, rump, and uppertail coverts. Underparts white.

Dull red tarsi and toes. Wings light brown, edged with tan. Dark brown remiges. Light gray tail.

IDENTIFICATION: Large but slightly built black-and-white shorebird with very slender silhouette, very long, red legs, and straight, thin black bill. At rest, cannot be confused with any other species. In flight, characterized by white or grayish crown, black wings above and beneath, and white rump and uppertail coverts contrasting with black of rest of upperparts and large portion of wings. Long red legs extend well behind tail. Flight is fairly slow, but wingbeats are full and frequent. In flight, distinguished from Eurasian avocet and Crab plover by black wings, black upperparts marked with big V on the back, legs that are much longer than tail.

BEHAVIOR: Rather gregarious, found alone, in pairs or in small loose-knit groups on feeding grounds, or in denser flocks of 200–300 in roosts on silt islets or quiet shores. Daytime feeder, walks in shallows with long, sedate steps. Adopts horizontal position, head pointing forward toward water surface to seize prey, for which head may be completely immersed. Very suspicious during breeding period, takes wing at slightest danger, sounding alarm over and over above intruder.

VOICE: Quiet outside nesting sites. Often utters loud, harsh alarm call, a slurred, discontinuous *kite kite kite....*

HABITAT: Freshwater and brackish lakes, rivers and estuaries with level, sandy or muddy shores, or other types of wetlands (rice paddies). Observed at elevations from sea level to 750 m.

DIET: Invertebrates, chiefly aquatic insects and crustaceans.

NESTING: Nest is simple hollow in ground built up with twigs or piled conically with vegetation if located in wet-lands. Clutch numbers 2 yellow-brown eggs boldly spotted with dark brown and gray. Both parents incubate. Chick has yellow-gray down with black spots. Nesting has been observed Mar.–Apr.

DISTRIBUTION AND STATUS: Distributed over 5 continents. Represented in Madagascar by nominate subspecies *H. h. himantopus*, common to Europe and Africa. Fairly common in e, n, and s, common in w but absent from High Plateau. Observation of huge congregations (500–600 at Ihotry Lake, Apr. 1982) in nonbreeding plumage during breeding season suggests that individuals of African origin may swell local population.

94. *Eurasian Avocet*

Recurvirostra avosetta Linnaeus, 1758
French: Avocette à tête noire
No Map

DESCRIPTION: Length 42–45 cm, wingspan 80 cm.
Adult. Sexes similar. Plumage varies seasonally.
Breeding Plumage. Black forehead, front and top of head, including eyes, and back of neck. Rest of head and neck, chin, and throat white. Black bill, brown iris. Upperparts white, except scapulars black.

Underparts white. Gray-blue tarsi, toes, and webs. White wing, except for black lesser and middle upper wing coverts. White-based black primary remiges. White tail.
Nonbreeding Plumage. Differs by brownish to gray-brown upperparts.
Juvenile. Differs from adult in breeding plumage by brownish upperparts edged with light tan and by white upperparts spotted with brown and tan.

IDENTIFICATION: Very large shorebird with black-and-white plumage, very long black legs, and long, very upwardly curved bill. In flight, characterized by wings that are black-and-white above, white below, white upperparts with black markings, and legs extending beyond tail. Distinguished in flight from Black-winged stilt by black head, black-and-white wings, and white mantle and from Crab plover by black head, long, thin bill, white secondary remiges, and black lesser and middle wing coverts.

DISTRIBUTION AND STATUS: Migratory, breeding in Europe, Africa, and Asia. Infrequent visitor to Madagascar, rarely mentioned in older literature and only sighted once recently: 1 individual accompanying a group of Black-winged stilts in saltwater shallows at Morombe, Apr. 1961.

Dromadidae – Crab Plover

Monospecific family of the w Indian Ocean. The Crab plover has highly developed eyes, in keeping with its nocturnal habits, a powerful, laterally flattened bill, a highly developed first toe, and webbed front toes. Gregarious, it nests in colonies, laying 1 white egg in a cavity prepared at the end of a 1–2-m-long tunnel dug in a sandy spot close to the sea. Visits the w coast of Madagascar regularly.

95. *Crab Plover*

Dromas ardeola Paykull, 1805
Malagasy: Tsarakaranta, Firatsa, Tsakaranta
French: Drome ardéole

DESCRIPTION: Length 33–36 cm, wingspan 75–78 cm.
Adult. Sexes similar. Plumage varies seasonally.
Breeding Plumage. White head. Small sooty spot in front of eyes. White chin, throat, nape, and neck. Black, very stout bill indented on ridge of lower mandible, often paler at base. Dark brown iris. Upperparts: black mantle and back, white rump and uppertail coverts. Underparts white. Blue-gray tarsi and toes. White wings, except for black greater wing coverts and black outer half of primary remiges. Underside of wings white, except for dark gray end of primary remiges. Light gray tail.
Nonbreeding Plumage. Differs by gray cap and back of neck.
Immature. Differs from adult by less contrasting plumage: cap and nape light gray speckled with brown, mantle dark gray, wing coverts and tail gray.

IDENTIFICATION: Large, powerful shorebird with black-and white plumage, massive head, very stout, short, straight bill, and long legs. In flight, neck is extended and appears long, legs extend beyond tail, and black of greater wing coverts and primary remiges contrast with white of rest of wings. Differs in flight from Black-winged stilt by black-and-white wings, black back, and short, stout bill and from Eurasian avocet by black trailing edge of wings, white head, and short, stout bill.

BEHAVIOR: Gregarious coastal shorebird, active chiefly at dusk and at night. Commonly found in groups of 5–30, sometimes in much larger groups at resting sites, especially at high tide (500 at Androka in Mar. 1964, 150 at Belo-sur-Tsiribihina, Nov. 1985). Feeds in groups, walking rather slowly. Seizes prey in mud and silt of intertidal zone at low tide, more rarely in shallows. Rests on bent tarsi.

VOICE: Rather vocal, utters various loud, raucous calls in course of feeding, also powerful whistles, *kyoo keeh keeh* or *keeh kyoo keeh*. These calls and whistles are often uttered at night.

HABITAT: Coasts offering mud flats or sandbanks, estuaries, mangroves, and coral islands. Observed at sea level.
DIET: Chiefly crabs.

NESTING: No nesting observed in Madagascar.

DISTRIBUTION AND STATUS: Distribution limited to w Indian Ocean, for which few nesting sites are known. This partly migratory species is found in large numbers along coasts of India, Arabia, e

Africa and Madagascar. In Madagascar, species is common all over w coast from extreme n of island (Antsiranana) to extreme s (Androka). Seen in all seasons.

Glareolidae – Pratincole

Birds reminiscent of terns in flight and plovers on the ground, with short, powerful bill, long, pointed wings, forked tail, and short legs with first toe present. Pratincoles feed on insects seized on the wing. The family comprises 16 species spread over Europe, Asia, Africa, and Madagascar. Represented in Madagascar by a single endemic, migratory species.

96. *Madagascar Pratincole*

Glareola ocularis Verreaux, 1833
Malagasy: Viko-viko, Vorombato
French: Glaréole malgache

DESCRIPTION: Length 25 cm.
Adult. Sexes similar. Dark brown forehead, front and top of head. Light brown chin, throat, cheeks, and nape. Broad white stripe under and behind eye. Short hooked bill, black except for red base. Dark brown iris. Upperparts light brown, except for white uppertail coverts. Underparts: light brown chest, pale rufous upper belly, white lower belly and undertail coverts. Dark gray tarsi and toes. Wings light brown, except for dark brown primary remiges. Rufous-brown underwing coverts. Forked white tail ending in broad oblique black band, except for entirely white external tail feathers.
Immature. Differs from adult by upperparts edged with tan, chest streaked with rufous, and absence of white mark near eyes.

IDENTIFICATION: Only pratincole on Madagascar. At rest, differs from terns by longer-legged silhouette and more marked neck. Flight silhouette with long, pointed brown wings recalls that of tern. Conspicuously forked black-and-white

tail. Energetic flight, propelled by powerful wingbeats.

BEHAVIOR: Gregarious, found in
groups of 10–50 at rest in grasslands,
sand spits, or rocky coastal islets. Some
flocks number up to 150, hunting in
flight, especially in late afternoon (Maroantsetra, Nov.–Dec. 1982).

VOICE: Fairly vocal, usually utters its
piercing succession of *veet ee veet—veet
ee veet—veet ee veet* while feeding on
the wing.

HABITAT: Surroundings of lakes and
rivers, short grasslands, sandspits in rivers or estuaries, and rocky islets in watercourses or near seacoast. Observed at
elevations from sea level to 1,500 m.

DIET: Insects (Neuroptera, Hymenoptera, Coleoptera).

NESTING: Very few data. Nest, on
rocks in the sea near the coast, consists of
slight rocky hollow, sometimes lined with
sheaths of Coleoptera. Several pairs nest
near one another. Clutch numbers 2 tan
eggs reticulated with more-or-less dark
brown (average size: 35 mm × 28 mm).
Nesting has been observed in early Nov.

DISTRIBUTION AND STATUS: Migratory, endemic to Madagascar. Madagascar pratincole leaves Madagascar
during austral winter (May–Aug.) for E
Africa, especially Kenya and Tanzania. In
Madagascar its range extends n (Sambirano, Iharanä), w (Soalala, Kinkony Lake,
and Manja—sw limit of observation),
which it seems only to transit, e, which
may constitute its breeding range (Maroantsetra, Mananara-nord, Toamasina,
Ampasimanolotra, Andasibe, Mangoro
River near Moramanga, Ranomafana),
and on High Plateau (Ambohitantely).
Nesting has been observed in Nosy Mangabe. Fairly common species whose migratory habits are still little known.

Charadriidae – Plovers

Small and medium-sized shorebirds with
large, round head, big eyes, short, thick
neck always shorter than head, and long
wings and tarsi. Most species have 3
short toes, with the first toe generally
missing or very reduced. They frequent
open terrain near rivers, lakes, and the
sea. The family is cosmopolitan, represented by some 60 species. Four species
nest in Madagascar, 1 of them endemic;
3 species are regular winter visitors; and
2 occasionally visit the island during the
boreal winter.

97. *Pacific Golden Plover*
Pluvialis fulva (Gmelin, 1789)
French: Pluvier doré du Pacifique
No Map

DESCRIPTION: Length 23–26 cm,
wingspan 60–70 cm.
Adult. Sexes similar. Plumage varies
seasonally.
Nonbreeding Plumage. Brown crown
speckled with tan, whitish supercilium
tinged with tan. Rest of head and sides of
neck light gray faintly marked with fuzzy
brown spots. Black bill, brown iris. Upperparts gray-brown spotted with tan, except for light brown back, rump, and
uppertail coverts. Underparts grayish,
tinged with tan on upper chest. Sooty
legs. Gray-brown wings with sooty remiges and end of greater wing coverts
faintly marked with white. Underside of
wings light brown with lighter remiges.
Gray-brown tail streaked with brown.

IDENTIFICATION: Large plover,
brownish above and whitish below, whose
silhouette somewhat resembles that of a
sandpiper. Distinguished from Black-

bellied plover by smaller size, slimmer silhouette, thinner neck and bill, somber crown, generally browner hue of plumage, and light, solid-colored underparts. In flight, wings are shorter and faintly marked with narrow whitish bar, light brown below without black spot.

DISTRIBUTION AND STATUS: Migratory, breeds in n Asia, in Alaska, and winters in part on coasts of SE Asia, India, and Sri Lanka. Exceptional visitor to Madagascar (sighted once: 2 at Ihotry Lake, Nov. 1961), more common in E Africa, and observed regularly in Seychelles during boreal winter and even occasionally in boreal summer.

NOTE: Recent taxonomic works consider *P. fulva* a full species, although in the past it was considered a subspecies of *P. dominica* (Müller, 1776). Old records of that species, especially those from E Africa and Madagascar, were described initially under *P. apricarius*.

98. *Black-bellied Plover*

Pluvialis squatarola (Linnaeus, 1758)
French: Pluvier argenté
No Map

DESCRIPTION: Length 27–30 cm, wingspan 70–80 cm.
Adult. Sexes similar. Plumage varies seasonally.
Nonbreeding Plumage. Head and neck brownish gray touched with white, except for grayish forehead, whitish eyebrow and white chin. Black bill, dark brown iris. Upperparts brown-gray flecked with white and dusky brown, except for white undertail coverts very faintly barred with black. Underparts white, except for brown-gray chest touched with white. Sooty-gray tarsi and toes. Brown-gray wings flecked with white and dusky brown, marked with a white wing bar

created by white base of black primary remiges and white tip of greater wing coverts. White underwing coverts, black axillaries. White tail with several black bars.

IDENTIFICATION: Large grayish and white plover with chunky body and long wings and legs. Distinguished from Pacific golden plover by more massive and longer-legged silhouette, stouter bill, and generally gray plumage. In flight, easily identifiable by long wings with long white wing bar and white uppertail coverts. Wings whitish below, with conspicuous black patch at axillaries.

BEHAVIOR: Gregarious coastal species found in loose groups of 3–12, sometimes as many as 80.

VOICE: Silent on wintering sites.

HABITAT: Mainly coastal: mud flats, mangroves, estuaries, more seldom fresh water or meadowlands near the coast. Has been observed at sea level.

DIET: Crustaceans, mollusks, insects.

DISTRIBUTION AND STATUS: Migratory, breeds in arctic areas of Europe, Asia, and N America. Winters partly on African and Malagasy coasts. Common in Madagascar on all coasts during boreal winter, remains in small numbers during boreal summer.

99. *Common Ringed Plover*

Charadrius hiaticula Linnaeus, 1758
French: Grand Gravelot
No Map

DESCRIPTION: Length 19 cm.
Adult. Sexes similar. Plumage varies seasonally.
Nonbreeding Plumage. Dark gray-brown crown and nape. Broad gray-brown eye stripe spreading from forehead to

nape. White front of head and subtle supercilium behind eyes. White chin and throat, with white stretching into a collar on neck. Sooty bill with orangy-gray base, dark brown iris. Upperparts gray-brown with white sides and uppertail coverts. Underparts white with dark gray breastband. Orangy tarsi and toes. Gray-brown wing with more somber, dark brown primary and secondary remiges. White wing bar formed by tip of greater upperwing coverts and base of primary and secondary remiges. White underwing coverts and axillaries. Tail white, except for gray-brown central tail feathers.

IDENTIFICATION: Medium-sized plover with powerful silhouette, plumage dark brown on upper side and white below, and orangy legs. In flight, long wings and tail, white wing bar, and white sides of tail and uppertail coverts are field marks, contrasting with somber upperparts. Distinguished from Madagascar plover by larger size, darker upper parts, unbroken white collar, and orangy legs. In flight, differs by conspicuous white wing bar. Distinguished from Three-banded plover by single breastband and eye stripe. In flight, differs by conspicuous white wing bar.

BEHAVIOR: Found in small groups of 3–5, seldom more, often in company of Ruddy turnstones.

VOICE: Quiet at wintering sites, call is brief, gentle, simple connected *tweep-tweep*.

HABITAT: Coastal mud flats, beaches, estuaries, mangroves, and lakes near coast. Observed near sea level.

DIET: Invertebrates (mollusks, crustaceans, insects).

DISTRIBUTION AND STATUS: Migratory, breeds in Europe, Asia, and N America. Winters partly in Africa and on coasts of Madagascar, where it is represented by subspecies *C. h. tundrae* (Lowe, 1915). Common along entire Madagascar coastline and on large w and sw lakes (Kinkony, Bemamba, Ihotry, Tsimanampetsotsa) during boreal autumn and winter.

100. *Madagascar Plover*

Charadrius thoracicus (Richmond, 1896)
French: Gravelot de Madagascar

DESCRIPTION: Length 13 cm.
Adult. Sexes similar. Plumage varies seasonally.
Breeding Plumage. White forehead, cheeks, chin, and throat. Black eye bar from base of bill along sides of neck. Front of head black, joining the black eye stripe at eye level. Tan-brown crown and nape surrounded by white band. Black bill, brown iris. Upperparts brown-gray, except for brown rump and uppertail coverts. Underparts: white chest barred with black band to sides of neck. Orangy white lower chest, belly, and flanks. Undertail coverts less tinged with orange. Rather dark blue-gray tarsi and toes. Light brown wings, except for dark brown secondary remiges and dark brown primary remiges marked with white on base half, forming a faint wing bar. Underside of wing white, except for gray remiges. Light brown tail with brown central tail feathers.
Nonbreeding Plumage. Differs from adult in breeding plumage by absence of black on front of head, light brown crown and cheeks, fuzzy brown-gray breastband, and upperparts slightly tinged with orange.
Immature. Rather similar to adult in nonbreeding plumage. Differs from it by fuzzy whitish supercilium, light brown eye stripe, and lighter and less scaly upperparts.

IDENTIFICATION: Small, rather squat plover with square head, brown crown surrounded by white band, black in front, isolating the white forehead, and thick white supercilium that extends to back of neck. In flight, inconspicuous wing bar. Distinguished from Kittlitz's plover by black breastband, white band surrounding brown crown, underparts tinged orange to level of belly. In flight, can be distinguished with difficulty by less scaly appearance of upperparts and less conspicuous white wing bar. Distinguished from Common ringed plover by smaller size, paler overall hue of upperparts, and orangy tinge of underparts. In flight, differs by less conspicuous white wing bar. Distinguished from Three-banded plover by slightly smaller size, black eye and forehead bands, and orangy tinge of underparts.

BEHAVIOR: Found alone or in pairs, less frequently in small groups (8 at Anakao, Aug. 1985, 14 at Tsimanampetsotsa, Mar. 1987). Often associated with Kittlitz's plover or White-fronted plover on feeding grounds (18 with 4 White-fronted plovers at Tsimanampetsotsa Lake, Mar. 1987). Forms homogeneous groups to roost (33 at Morombe in Nov. 1961 within groups including other shorebirds: Common ringed plover, White-fronted plover, Greater sand plover, Curlew sandpiper). Roosts are established on sand spits facing sea or a lake, or dunes covered with creeping vegetation.

VOICE: Quiet, few data. Cries, *peet peerts* . . . and *tweet tweet tweet* . . . is rather similar to that of Kittlitz's plover, but more raucous. Alarm call is a sort of *twee* or *tweets*.

HABITAT: Coastal meadowlands with short vegetation, dry and clear surroundings of bodies of fresh or brackish water, less frequently mangroves and muddy lakeshores, more seldom sandy ocean beaches. Observed at sea level.

DIET: Invertebrates (insects).

NESTING: Nest is a sandy hollow prepared on dry meadowland near coast or salt lake. Clutch numbers 2 tan, dullish eggs elaborately spotted and vermiculated with brown and dark brown (average size: 32.0 mm × 23.1 mm). Both parents incubate. Upon leaving nest, brooder partially or completely covers eggs with sand or dry vegetation. Chick has whitish down with black spots and no tan markings whatsoever. Nesting has been observed Aug.–Apr.

DISTRIBUTION AND STATUS: Endemic to Madagascar, rather rare, distributed in w and sw between Antsalova and Tsimanampetsotsa. Principal observations conducted at Bemamba Lake, Morondava, Morombe, Toliara, Anakao, and Tsimanampetsotsa Lake. Infrequently reported on e coast, near Manakara, 1985, and once reported near Antananarivo, Jan. 1971.

101. *Kittlitz's Plover*

Charadrius pecuarius Temminck, 1823
Malagasy: Viky-viky
French: Pluvier de Kittlitz

DESCRIPTION: Length 13 cm.
Adult. Sexes differ slightly in breeding period. Plumage varies seasonally.
Male Breeding Plumage. Chestnut crown fringed with tan. Black front of head connects with black eye stripe beginning at base of bill and continuing to sides of neck. White forehead. White supercilium continuing to back of neck. White chin and throat. Black bill, dark brown iris. Upperparts dark brown-gray fringed with tan, except for black rump and central uppertail coverts and white outer uppertail coverts. Underparts tinged orange, except for white lower belly and undertail coverts. Sooty green tarsi and toes. Dark

brown-gray wings edged with tan, except
for sooty lesser wing coverts, dark brown
primary remiges marked with white on
the basal internal part, dark brown secondary remiges, and white underwing
coverts and axillaries. Tail: dark brown
central tail feathers narrowly edged with
white, dark brown-gray lateral tail feathers tipped with white, and almost entirely
white external tail feathers.
Female Breeding Plumage. Differs from
male in breeding plumage by blurred
bands of front of head and eye stripes
and by underparts less richly colored with
orange tinge.
Adult Nonbreeding Plumage. Differs from
adult in breeding plumage by absence of
black on front of head, very fuzzy brown-
on-black eye patch, gray-brown crown,
brown-gray streaks on sides of neck and
upper chest, brown-gray chest sometimes
tinged with rust, and olive-green legs.
Immature. Differs from adult in nonbreeding plumage by less clear delimita-
tion of head colors and by gray-brown
crown, upperparts, and wings edged
with tan.

IDENTIFICATION: Small plover with
brown crown and head marked with black
band isolating white forehead and with
heavy white supercilium continuing to
back of neck. In flight, wing has scaly appearance with an inconspicuous white
bar, tail is somber and narrowly edged
with white. Distinguished from Madagascar plover by barless chest. In flight can
be distinguished from Madagascar plover
with difficulty by scalier appearance of
upperparts. Distinguished from White-
fronted plover by smaller size, less developed white area on forehead, clearly
marked eye stripe continuing to sides of
neck, somber upper side, and orangy
underside.

BEHAVIOR: Fairly gregarious, sometimes found in pairs but more frequently

in monospecific groups numbering 3–35.
Readily associates with other species of
shorebird, such as Common ringed plover, Madagascar plover, or Curlew sandpiper. Roosts, established on sand spits or
dunes, can number up to 150 birds.

VOICE: Rather quiet, utters brief, shrill
peewee on taking wing. Also utters plaintive *twee-pee* at rest and piercing, trilled
tritritritrit . . . in flight, reminiscent of
Madagascar plover.

HABITAT: Coastal mud flats, mangroves, sandy shores of rivers, estuaries,
and lakes, but particularly favors short
grasslands, which may be far from water.
Observed at elevations from sea level to
1,400 m.

DIET: Terrestrial and aquatic invertebrates (insects, spiders, mollusks,
crustaceans).

NESTING: Nest is a hollow prepared in
sand on a bank or beach, in short grasslands or on completely open terrain.
Clutch numbers 2 creamy-yellow eggs
richly vermiculated with black (average
size: 32.0 mm × 22.0 mm). Both parents
incubate. Upon leaving nest, brooder
partially or completely covers eggs with
sand. Chick has light tan down mottled
with black above and white below. Nesting has been observed June–Nov. and
occasionally outside that period.

DISTRIBUTION AND STATUS: Distributed in Africa and Madagascar. Present year-round throughout range. It is
seasonal on High Plateau (30 at Antananarivo, Nov.–Dec. 1988). Common in s,
w, and e.

102. *Three-banded Plover*
Charadrius tricollaris Vieillot, 1818
French: Gravelot à triple collier

DESCRIPTION: Length 17 cm.
Adult. Sexes similar. Sooty crown sepa-

rated from slate-gray rest of head by white patch extending from front of head over eyes to nape. Slate-gray chin and throat. Bright red bill with black tip. Pale yellow-brown iris, bright red eye ring. Upperparts brown, except for white nucal collar. Underparts white with 2 black bands on the chest. Tarsi and toes red. Wing brown, except for dark brown greater primary coverts, white-trimmed greater upperwing coverts, dark brown primary remiges, and brown secondary remiges narrowly trimmed with white. Tail white, except for central tail feathers brown trimmed with white.
Immature. Differs from adult by brown upperparts edged with tan, very slight head contrast, incomplete brown patch separating throat from chest, and blurred, grayish band separating chest from belly.

IDENTIFICATION: Medium-sized plover with stocky silhouette, long wings and legs, and boldly contrasted plumage on head and chest. Double breastband, white patch around head, and red orbital ring are field marks. In flight, displays faint wing bar and tail edged and tipped with white. Distinguished from Madagascar and Kittlitz's plovers by larger size, double breastband, sooty face and throat, red orbital ring, and black-tipped red bill.

BEHAVIOR: Usually found alone or in pairs, very rarely associated with other species. Feeds at rather leisurely pace on inundated or muddy terrain that may be open or have islands of herbaceous vegetation.

VOICE: Fairly vocal, at rest utters fluty, shrill, plaintive *teewit teewit teewit . . . .*

HABITAT: Muddy shores of freshwater or brackish portions of rivers, lakes, ponds, pools, rice paddies, occasionally mangroves and coastal mud flats. Observed at elevations from sea level to 1,800 m.

DIET: Terrestrial and aquatic invertebrates (insects, mollusks, crustaceans).

NESTING: Nest is simple hollow in ground, located in fairly open, stony terrain, often strewn with tufts of grass. Clutch numbers 2 dull, creamy white eggs, richly vermiculated and spotted with brown and gray (average size: 30.7 mm × 22.6 mm). Chick has black-spotted grayish down. Nesting has been observed July–Sept.

DISTRIBUTION AND STATUS: Distributed in Africa and Madagascar. Represented in Madagascar by endemic subspecies *C. t. bifrontatus* (Cabanis, 1882). Common in w and n, rare in e and on High Plateau.

103. *Greater Sand Plover*

Charadrius leschenaultii Lesson, 1826
French: Gravelot de Leschenault

DESCRIPTION: Length 23 cm.
Adult. Sexes similar in nonbreeding plumage. White forehead and supercilium. Brown-gray crown, nape, and area behind eyes. White chin and throat. Black bill, dark brown iris. Upperparts uniform pale brown-gray, except for white sides of uppertail coverts. Underparts white, except for brown-gray chest. Olive-gray to yellow-gray tarsi, sooty toes. Wings pale brown-gray, except for white-tipped greater wing coverts, dark brown and white base portions of primary remiges, and dark brown secondary remiges. Tail: dark brown-gray tail feathers edged and tipped with white, except for almost entirely white external tail feathers and dark brown-gray central tail feathers narrowly edged with white.

IDENTIFICATION: Large plover with stocky silhouette. Long-legged, horizontal posture, generally light-colored plumage: pale brown-gray above and white below. In flight, white wing bar and partially white uppertail coverts and sides of tail are field marks.

BEHAVIOR: Found in groups of 5–50, sometimes more numerous (maximum 200) at roosts.

VOICE: Rather quiet, sometimes utters brief, shrill, liquid *tree-ee*.

HABITAT: Coastal mud flats, sandy beaches, mangroves, freshwater or brackish lakes, and short grasslands near the coast. Observed near sea level.

DIET: Insects, crustaceans.

DISTRIBUTION AND STATUS: Migratory, breeds in Asia. Winters partly on coasts of Africa and Madagascar. Common on all Malagasy coasts and big lakes of w during boreal winter. Few individuals stay for boreal spring.

104. *White-fronted Plover*

Charadrius marginatus Vieillot, 1818
Malagasy: Viky-viky, Fandia fasika, Mondrita, Vivitra
French: Pluvier pâtre

DESCRIPTION: Length 18 cm.
Adult. Sexes differ. Plumage varies seasonally.
Male Breeding Plumage. White forehead, black front of head, pale gray crown and nape. Black eye stripe from base of bill to behind eyes. White supercilium. Partly pale brown-gray cheeks. White chin, throat and back of neck. Black bill and dark brown iris. Upperparts uniformly pale gray-brown, except for white sides of uppertail coverts, underparts white, marked with rusty tan on sides of chest. Sooty tarsi and toes. Pale gray-brown wings, except for brown greater primary coverts, white tip of greater upperwing coverts, dark brown primary remiges, white in their basal internal half, and dark

brown secondary remiges. Tail white with brown central tail feathers.
Male Nonbreeding Plumage. Differs from male in breeding plumage by brown front of head and less pronounced rusty tan on sides of chest.
Female. Differs from male in nonbreeding plumage by absence of black band separating white forehead from pale gray-brown crown.
Immature. Differs from female by absence of black eye stripe.

IDENTIFICATION: Medium-sized plover with pale plumage above and white below, broad white forehead, faint, dark eye stripe. In flight, white wing bar, somber remiges contrasting with upper side of wings and body, and white-edged tail are field marks. Distinguished from Kittlitz's and Madagascar plovers by larger size, light plumage, broad white forehead with faint eye stripe, and white underparts with faint rufous markings on sides of chest. In flight distinguished from them by light upper side and white wing bar. Distinguished from Greater sand plover by broad white forehead, black front of head, fine black eye stripe, and thinner bill.

BEHAVIOR: Rather gregarious, found in pairs or small monospecific flocks, or associated with other shorebirds, especially Kittlitz's plover or Madagascar plover. Gathers in much larger groups at roosting sites (200 on w coast). Feeds on beaches or any other sandy terrain near water, running swiftly to catch prey.

VOICE: Rather quiet, utters brief, soft *wee* or *wearit* in flight.

HABITAT: Sand beaches, dunes, coastal lagoons, sandbanks and sandy shores of lakes and rivers, which it sometimes follows upstream to sites well inland. Observed at elevations from sea level to 1,500 m.

DIET: Insects, mollusks, crustaceans.

NESTING: Clutch numbers 1–2 creamy tan eggs, spotted and vermiculated with brown and gray, laid directly on sand, often on slight prominence. Eggs are not covered with sand by departing brooder, but same effect is often partially achieved by wind. Chick has rufous-tinged white down with black spots. Nesting has been observed Mar.–Oct.

DISTRIBUTION AND STATUS: Distributed in Africa and Madagascar. Represented in Madagascar by subspecies *C. m. tenellus* (Hartlaub, 1861), common to e Africa. Common on all Malagasy coasts, rather rare in the interior. Madagascar's most common nesting shorebird.

Scolopacidae – Godwits, Curlews, Sandpipers, Turnstone, Snipe, Ruff

Small to large shorebirds with rather long necks and legs, long, slender bills, small and occasionally absent hind toes, long wings, and short tails. The family is cosmopolitan and numbers more than 80 species. An endemic species nests in Madagascar, 8 species commonly winter there, and 6 species are occasional visitors during the boreal winter.

105. *Black-tailed Godwit*
Limosa limosa (Linnaeus, 1758)
French: Barge à queue noire

DESCRIPTION: Length 40 cm.
Adult. Sexes similar.
Nonbreeding Plumage. Light brown-gray head and neck, paler on chin, throat, and front of neck. Conspicuous light supercilium. Bill: pinkish gray basal half, sooty apical half. Dark brown iris. Upperparts brown, except for white lower back and uppertail coverts. Underparts white, except for light gray chest. Black tarsi and toes. Wing gray, except for black primary remiges and large white wing bar. Tail white with large black band at tip.

IDENTIFICATION: Large, light brown-gray shorebird with slender silhouette, very long legs, and long, straight bill. Distinguished from Bar-tailed godwit by more brown-gray plumage, tail ending in black band, longer and straighter bill, and longer legs. In flight, white tail with black bar at extremity, large white wing bar, and legs extending to well past tail are good field marks.

DISTRIBUTION AND STATUS: Migratory, breeds in Europe and Asia and winters partly in Africa. Infrequent migrator in Madagascar, usually sighted singly on w coast during boreal winter.

106. *Bar-tailed Godwit*

Limosa lapponica (Linnaeus, 1758)
French: Barge rousse

DESCRIPTION: Length 42 cm
Adult. Sexes similar.
Nonbreeding Plumage. Grayish head and neck with fine brownish stripes. Light gray cheeks, chin and throat. Conspicuous light supercilium. Bill: pinkish gray basal half, sooty apical half. Dark brown iris. Upperparts grayish brown edged with light gray, except for white uppertail coverts. Underparts white, except for faint brown flecks on chest. Black legs. Wings same color as upperparts, except for black primary remiges. White tail, barred with several black bands.

IDENTIFICATION: Large grayish brown shorebird with rather slender silhouette, long legs, rather long, turned-up bill. Distinguished from Black-tailed Godwit by less slender silhouette, shorter legs, and shorter, slightly turned-up bill. In flight, shows barred tail and no wing bar, and legs barely extend beyond tail.

BEHAVIOR: Fairly gregarious, found in groups of 3–35, rarely more.

VOICE: Silent in wintering sites.

HABITAT: Coastal mud flats, estuaries, mangroves. Observed at sea level.

DIET: Chiefly invertebrates.

DISTRIBUTION AND STATUS: Migratory, breeds in n Europe, Asia, and N America. Winters in part on coasts of Africa and Madagascar. Common on all Malagasy coasts. Rarely sighted outside boreal winter.

107. *Whimbrel*

Numenius phaeopus (Linnaeus, 1758)
Malagasy: Mantazazana, Kiokoika
French: Courlis corlieu

DESCRIPTION: Length 40–42 cm.
Adult. Sexes similar. Grayish head striped with brown, except for dark brown cap marked with median stripe and whitish supercilium. Brown bill with roseate base on lower mandible, dark iris. Upperparts brown edged with pale tan, except for white lower back, rump and uppertail coverts. Underparts: brownish chest marked with dark stripes, barred flanks, and white belly. Gray tarsi and toes. Wings same color as upperparts with dark brown primary remiges and white underwing coverts, barred with brown. Brown tail with dark brown bars.

IDENTIFICATION: Large, bulky shorebird with brownish plumage, long, curved bill, and rather long legs. Can be confused only with Eurasian curlew, from which it differs by smaller size, more short-legged silhouette, much shorter bill and light stripes on head. Movements and flight are more rapid than those of Eurasian curlew.

BEHAVIOR: Gregarious, found in groups of 3–25 on feeding grounds, sometimes more at roosting sites (500 on a sw mud flat in Oct.). Often seen perching in mangroves.

VOICE: Vocal at wintering sites. Frequently utters sequence of characteristic loud, piping *cur lew cur lew*, usually on taking wing but also at rest.

HABITAT: Coastal mud flats, sandy shores, coral islets, estuaries, mangroves, freshwater areas near coast. Goes inland short distances by following major rivers. Observed from sea level to 750 m.

DIET: Chiefly invertebrates.

DISTRIBUTION AND STATUS: Migratory, breeds in n Europe, Asia, and N America. Winters partly on coasts of Africa and Madagascar. Very common on all Malagasy coasts during boreal winter and remains in fairly large numbers during boreal summer. One of most common wintering shorebirds, along with Curlew sandpiper and Ruddy turnstone.

108. *Eurasian Curlew*

Numenius arquata (Linnaeus, 1758)
Malagasy: Mantazazana, Koikoika
French: Courlis cendré

DESCRIPTION: Length 50–60 cm. *Adult.* Sexes similar. Head and neck gray-brown finely striped with dark brown. Whitish throat. Dark brown bill with roseate base on lower mandible. Dark brown iris. Upperparts gray-brown with dark brown stripes, except for whitish lower back and rump and whitish uppertail coverts with brown bars. Underparts: light brown chest striped with brown, barred flanks, and white belly. Grayish tarsi and toes. Wings gray-brown with dark brown stripes, except for dark brown primary remiges and white underwing coverts with brown bars. Light brown tail with conspicuously dark brown bars.

IDENTIFICATION: Very large, stout shorebird with relatively even brownish plumage, very long, curved bill, and long legs. Distinguished from Whimbrel by larger size, stouter body, longer-legged silhouette, and longer and more curved bill. Slower movements, more powerful flight with slower wingbeats.

BEHAVIOR: Gregarious, found in groups of 3–20, sometimes alone, associated with such other shorebird species as Whimbrel.

VOICE: Fairly vocal in wintering sites, utters characteristic sequence of piping, loud *cur lew cur lew* similar to that of Whimbrel.

HABITAT: Coastal mud flats, sandy shores, estuaries, mangroves. Observed at sea level.

DIET: Chiefly invertebrates.

DISTRIBUTION AND STATUS: Migratory, breeds in Europe and Asia, winters partly on coasts of Africa. Infrequent winter visitor in Madagascar, found on w coast during boreal winter.

109. *Marsh Sandpiper*

Tringa stagatilis (Bechstein, 1803)
French: Chevalier stagnatile

DESCRIPTION: Length 23 cm. *Adult.* Sexes similar. *Nonbreeding Plumage.* Top of head, nape, and back of neck sooty gray edged with white and streaked with dark brown. Grayish area behind eyes; rest of head, chin, and throat white. Black bill with dark greenish base, dark brown iris. Upperparts light gray edged with white and spotted with dark brown, except for white lower back, rump, and uppertail coverts. Underparts white, sides of chest faintly striped with brown-gray. Olive-green or yellow-green tarsi and toes. Gray wings faintly spotted brown, with sooty primary remiges, gray-brown secondary remiges, and white underwing coverts and axillaries. Tail, except for gray central feathers, white with dark brown bars.

IDENTIFICATION: Medium-sized sandpiper with slim, streamlined silhouette and generally light coloring—gray above and white below—long legs, and very slender, long black bill. In flight, characterized by white back and rump contrasting with dark remiges, absence of wing bar, and legs extending well behind tail. Distinguished from Common greenshank by considerably smaller size, much slimmer and longer-legged silhouette, very thin, straight black bill, and white sides of neck and cheeks. In flight, the contrast is greater between dark remiges and gray upperwing coverts, and legs extend farther beyond tail.

VOICE: Rather quiet, sometimes utters brief, shrill *teeweet*, as well as succession of loud, piercing tones *tweetweetweetweetwee-tyootyoo* . . . .

DIET: Small aquatic invertebrates.

DISTRIBUTION AND STATUS: Migratory, breeds in Europe and Asia, winters in part in Africa. Uncommon winter visitor in Madagascar, where lone individuals or small groups (3–8) have been spotted on bodies of freshwater along the w coast (lakes around Belo-sur-Tsiribihina, Jan. 1989) during boreal winter.

110. *Common Greenshank*

Tringa nebularia (Gunnerus, 1767)
French: Chevalier aboyeur
No Map

DESCRIPTION: Length 30 cm.
Adult. Sexes similar.
Nonbreeding Plumage. Top and sides of head, nape, neck, and throat white with dark gray stripes. White forehead and chin. Dark gray bill, dark brown iris. Upperparts gray faintly striped with black, except for white back, rump, and uppertail coverts. Underparts white, faintly striped with dark brown on upper chest. Olive-green to yellowish green tarsi and toes. Gray-brown wings edged with white and spotted with brown, except for sooty primary remiges, gray-brown secondary remiges, and white underwing coverts and axillaries faintly speckled with brown-gray. White tail with dark brown bars.

IDENTIFICATION: Large, robust sandpiper with gray plumage above and white below. Long, powerful, turned-up dark bill and long, stout, greenish legs. In flight shows somber, even-colored wings that set off large white triangle of upperparts, and legs extending beyond tail. Distinguished from Marsh sandpiper by considerably larger size, powerful build, and stout, turned-up bill. In flight, differs from Marsh sandpiper by solid-colored upper side of wings and shorter extension of legs past tail.

BEHAVIOR: Rather gregarious, found in small, loose-knit groups of 3–80, sometimes in larger flocks numbering as many as 300.

VOICE: Vocal, in flight or on taking wing utters clear, emphatic, loud whistle, *teeyoo teeyoo teeyoo,* usually bi- or trisyllabic.

HABITAT: Shallow waters (mud flats, pools, rivers, rice paddies, estuaries, mangroves). Observed sea level to 1,400 m.

DIET: Chiefly invertebrates, also small vertebrates (amphibians, fish).

DISTRIBUTION AND STATUS: Migratory, breeds in n Europe and Asia. Winters partly in Africa and in Madagascar. Common on all Malagasy coasts during boreal winter, and some individuals remain during boreal spring and summer. Observed seasonally in interior (80 in Antananarivo, Nov.–Dec. 1988).

111. *Green Sandpiper*

Tringa ochropus Linnaeus, 1758
French: Chevalier cul-blanc
No Map

DESCRIPTION: Length 22 cm.
Adult. Sexes similar.
Nonbreeding Plumage. Top of head, nape, and back of neck olive-brown with whitish specks. White supercilium. White sides of head and neck striped with olive-brown. White chin and throat. Black bill with greenish base, dark brown iris. Upperparts dark olive-brown, marked with fuzzy white dots. White rump and uppertail coverts. Underparts white with olive-brown stripes on chest. Sooty gray to olive-green tarsi and toes. Wings brown, except for sooty brown remiges. White tail with 3–4 black bars on central tail feathers.

IDENTIFICATION: Small sandpiper with rather slender silhouette and very somber plumage marked with fuzzy spots above, white beneath. White supercilium contrasts with dark cap. Fairly short, straight bill. In flight, no wing bar, conspicuous white rump, and dark undersides of wings. Can be confused with Wood sandpiper, from which it differs by slightly stouter build, darker overall hue of upperparts, longer wings, and shorter, darker legs. In flight, Green sandpiper is black-brown above and tail is marked with larger bars, legs extend barely beyond tail, and, most important, dark underside of wings contrast with white underparts. Distinguished from Marsh sandpiper by bulkier silhouette, shorter, thicker bill, much shorter legs, and dark back.

VOICE: Fairly silent in wintering sites.

DIET: Invertebrates.

DISTRIBUTION AND STATUS: Migratory, breeds in n of Europe and Asia. Winters in part in Africa. Recorded in 1932; not seen in Madagascar since then.

112. *Wood Sandpiper*

Tringa glareola Linnaeus, 1758
French: Chevalier sylvain
No Map

DESCRIPTION: Length 20 cm.
Adult. Sexes similar.
Nonbreeding Plumage. Greenish gray-brown crown, dotted with white. Gray-brown eye stripe. Brownish streaks on neck and sides of head. White supercilium, chin, and throat. Black bill with olive-green base, dark brown iris. Upperparts gray-brown dotted with white and dark brown, except for white rump and uppertail coverts. Underparts white with fine, dark brown streaks on chest and bars on flanks. Olive-green or yellow-green tarsi and toes. Wings: brown upperwing coverts dotted with white, dark brown remiges edged with white at base of secondary remiges, and white underwing coverts and axillaries faintly dotted with brown. White tail barred with dark brown, more intensely at center.

IDENTIFICATION: Small sandpiper with slim, streamlined silhouette, somber plumage punctuated with white above, and white below, and rather short, straight bill. In flight, no wing bar, conspicuous white rump and light underside of wings. Distinguished from Green sandpiper by slimmer silhouette, shorter wings, longer, greenish or yellowish legs, overall lighter hue of plumage, and marked contrast between supercilium and crown. In flight, Wood sandpiper shows lighter coloring above, tail has thinner bars, legs extend farther beyond tail, and, most important, there is no contrast between light underside of wings and white underparts. Distinguished from Marsh sandpiper by less slender silhouette, shorter, thicker bill, shorter legs, and dark back.

BEHAVIOR: Generally found alone or in pairs, associated with other shorebirds (Curlew sandpiper, Common greenshank).

VOICE: Frequently utters characteristic brief, shrill *teehee teehee* . . . .

HABITAT: Freshwater or slightly brackish lakes near coast. Observed near sea level.

DIET: Chiefly insects, also mollusks and crustaceans.

DISTRIBUTION AND STATUS: Migratory, breeds in n of Europe and Asia. Winters in part in Africa and Madagascar. Fairly rare in Madagascar, where it is most often sighted on lakes near the w coast (Morombe, Bevoay Lake, Kinkony Lake) during boreal autumn and winter.

113. *Terek Sandpiper*

Xenus cinereus (Güldenstädt, 1775)
French: Bargette de Terek
No Map

DESCRIPTION: Length 23 cm.
Adult. Sexes similar.
Nonbreeding Plumage. Head and neck brown-gray, except for white forehead, inconspicuous supercilium and patch under eyes. White chin and throat. Black bill with orange-yellow base, dark brown iris. Upperparts brown-gray. Underparts white, except for light brown-gray sides of chest. Orange tarsi and toes. Wings: brown-gray, except for white-tipped primary remiges other than four outside ones, gray-brown secondary remiges

broadly tipped with white, and white underwing coverts and axillaries. Light brown-gray tail.

IDENTIFICATION: Small, squat, short-legged sandpiper with long, turned-up bill, orange legs, and generally pale-hued plumage: light brown-gray above, white below. In flight, contrast between broad white trailing edges and rest of upper wing, and white underside of wings, are field marks. Squat silhouette and horizontal posture are reminiscent of Common sandpiper, with which it shares habit of twitching its tail. Easily distinguished from Common sandpiper by larger size, long, turned-up bill, and orange legs; in flight, by more conspicuous wing bar and gray tail.

BEHAVIOR: Very active, with quick, darting movements and energetic twitching of tail. Found in small monospecific groups of 3–8, sometimes accompanied by Ruddy turnstones.

VOICE: Rather vocal, utters soft, piping *tewdewdew* . . . similar to Common greenshank's call.

HABITAT: Sand, mudbanks along coast, much more rarely freshwater mud flats near coast. Observed at sea level.

DIET: Invertebrates (small insects, crustaceans, mollusks).

DISTRIBUTION AND STATUS: Migratory, breeds in n Europe and Asia. Winters in part on coasts of Africa and Madagascar. Fairly common on Malagasy coasts during boreal winter.

114. *Common Sandpiper*

Actitis hypoleucos (Linnaeus, 1758)
French: Chevalier guignette
No Map

DESCRIPTION: Length 20 cm.
Adult. Sexes similar.

Nonbreeding Plumage. Olive-brown head and neck finely streaked with sooty gray on crown and back of neck. White supercilium, brown eye stripe. White chin and throat. Green-gray bill, lighter at base, dark brown iris. Upperparts solid olive brownish, except for black tip of uppertail coverts. Underparts white with brown-striped upper chest. Yellow-green tarsi and toes. Wings: solid olive-brown coverts, except for white-tipped greater coverts. Dark brown primary remiges with white spot in the middle, dark brown secondaries with white bars in the middle and faint white tips. Partially white underwing coverts and white axillaries. White tail barred with brown, except for olive-brown central tail feathers.

IDENTIFICATION: Sandpiper with stocky silhouette, short legs, short, straight bill, and uniform brown-gray plumage above and white below, with brown-gray chest. In flight, shows characteristic pattern: white wing bar, dark rump and back, and white and barred sides of tail. Easily distinguished from Terek sandpiper by smaller size, short, straight bill, yellow-green legs, and in flight by faint wing bar and white sides of tail.

BEHAVIOR: Usually found alone or in pairs. Movements, accompanied by bobbing of head and tail, are less rapid than those of Terek sandpiper. Flight usually involves skimming over water, alternating shallow wingbeats with short glides.

VOICE: From time to time, on taking wing, utters shrill, rather thin *tsee see see . . .* or *chew chew chew chew . . . .*

HABITAT: All types of areas where water is present (seaside mud flats, sandy beaches, coral islets, mangroves, estuaries, wooded, muddy, rocky, or grassy banks of lakes, rivers, and streams, as well as rice paddies). Observed at elevations from sea level to 2,200 m.

DIET: Invertebrates (insects, mollusks, crustaceans).

DISTRIBUTION AND STATUS: Migratory, breeds in Europe and Asia. Winters partly in Africa and Madagascar. Common throughout range during boreal winter.

115. *Ruddy Turnstone*

Arenaria interpres (Linnaeus, 1758)
French: Tournepierre à collier
No Map

DESCRIPTION: Length 22–24 cm. *Adult.* Sexes similar. Plumage varies seasonally.
Breeding Plumage. White crown and nape streaked with black (more streaks in female). White forehead marked with black stripe extending to eyes and going down cheeks. White cheeks marked with black band connecting chest with nape. White chin and throat. Black bill, dark brown iris. Upperparts black with rufous-brown stripes, except for white lower back and rump and black uppertail coverts. Underparts white, except for black breastband. Orange tarsi and toes. Wings: dark brown greater wing coverts marked with white at tip, white median and lesser wing coverts. Solid dark brown remiges, except for white base of inside primary remiges and secondary remiges. Black tail with white base and white terminal band. Central tail feathers have black base.
Nonbreeding Plumage. Dark brownish head. White chin and throat. Upperparts dark brown edged with light brown. Underparts white, except for dark brown breastband. Orange-yellow tarsi and toes. Dark brown lesser and median wing coverts.

IDENTIFICATION: Short-legged shorebird with short, slightly turned-up bill and showy breeding plumage pattern of black, brown, rufous, and white, which changes to nonbreeding brown above and white below. In flight, field marks are double white wing markings (invisible at rest), light coloration of head, white rump contrasting with black uppertail coverts, and black-and-white tail. Cannot be confused with any other species.

BEHAVIOR: Gregarious coastal species found in large groups often numbering 30–150, or in smaller numbers associated with other shorebirds (Terek sandpiper).

VOICE: Quiet species in wintering sites. On taking wing sometimes utters brief, high-pitched but not very loud *kitty tea*.

HABITAT: Frequents coastal environments: mud flats, sandy or rocky shores, coral islets, mangroves, and estuaries. Much rarer in freshwater habitats close to coast. Observed at sea level.

DIET: Invertebrates (mollusks, crustaceans).

DISTRIBUTION AND STATUS: Migratory, breeds in n Europe, Asia, and N America, winters in part on coasts of Africa and Madagascar. Very common on all Malagasy coasts during boreal winter, and remains in fairly large numbers during boreal summer. More abundant on w than e coast. Most common wintering shorebird, along with Curlew sandpiper and Whimbrel.

116. *Madagascar Snipe*

Gallinago macrodactyla Bonaparte, 1839
Malagasy: Agoly, Aretaky, Hotrika, Ravarava, Harakaraka, Kitananata, Kekakeka
French: Bécassine malgache

DESCRIPTION: Length 26 cm.
Adult. Sexes similar. Black crown marked with 3 fawn bands: 1 median and 2 lat-

eral. Black lores, cheeks sprinkled with brown. Tan-white chin and throat. Bill very long (11 cm), straight and dark yellow, except for black apical third. Brown iris. Upperparts brown streaked with tan. Underparts: tan chest speckled with brown, tan-white belly, whitish flanks and undertail coverts heavily barred with brown. Brown tarsi and toes. Wings same color as upperparts, except for dark brown primary remiges. Short tail with bright rufous and black bars.
Juvenile. Similar to adult.

IDENTIFICATION: Shorebird with brownish plumage, dark striped head, slender silhouette, very long, straight bill. Distinguished from male Greater painted snipe by straight, much longer bill, striped head, and barred flanks and undertail coverts.

BEHAVIOR: Fairly gregarious outside nesting season, frequently found feeding in small groups of 4–8. Feeds in muddy or slightly inundated areas, amid vegetation. Probes mud thoroughly with its very long bill at each step. In case of danger it freezes before taking wing with rapid wingbeats, only to alight again quickly and conceal itself in vegetation. Flight is very swift and wingbeats are shallow.

VOICE: On taking flight, utters characteristic harsh, nasal *kik kik kik kik*. During breeding season, while flying, makes a series of a dozen short, melodic notes that crescendo (6 notes) and then decrescendo (6 notes).

HABITAT: Wetlands with dense vegetation and muddy areas (marshy shores of lakes and watercourses, sometimes rice paddies). Observed at elevations from sea level to 2,700 m.

DIET: Invertebrates, seeds, plants.

NESTING: Few data. Nest is simple hollow prepared in dense tuft of grass in or adjacent to marsh. Clutch numbers 2 olive-brown eggs with dark brown and grayish spots, especially at larger pole (average size: 49.2 mm × 33.8 mm). Nidifugous chicks have mottled tan, black, and rufous down. Nesting has been observed July–Jan.

DISTRIBUTION AND STATUS: Endemic to Madagascar, distributed in n and e (Bealanana, Andapa, Tsaratanana, Andasibe, Alaotra Lake, Ile Sainte-Marie, Ranomafana, Ivohibe, Manakara, Vondrozo, Andringitra) and on High Plateau (Antananarivo, Itasy Lake, Fianarantsoa). Species is uncommon, rather secretive, and threatened by habitat transformation (development of rice-growing areas) and pressure from hunting.

117. *Sanderling*

Calidris alba (Pallas, 1764)
French: Bécasseau sanderling
No Map

DESCRIPTION: Length 20 cm.
Adult. Sexes similar.
Nonbreeding Plumage. Pale gray crown and cheeks, white forehead, supercilium, chin, and throat. Black bill, dark brown iris. Upperparts pale gray, except for sooty central uppertail coverts. Underparts white, except for gray sides of chest. Black tarsi and toes. Wings: gray greater upperwing coverts, black median and lesser upperwing coverts. Black primary remiges with white base, secondary remiges black in apical half, white in basal half. White underwing coverts and axillaries. Tail gray, except for black median tail feathers.

IDENTIFICATION: Medium-sized sandpiper with plump silhouette, rather short legs, and short, straight, black bill. Light plumage: gray above, white below, marked with black at lesser upperwing

coverts. In flight shows characteristic contrast between wing marked with large white bar and black remiges and lesser coverts. Underside of wings is white edged with black. Cannot be confused with any other species, especially given its characteristic behavior and habitat.

BEHAVIOR: Gregarious coastal species found on beaches in groups of 5–40, sometimes as many as 300 at rest on rocks or a sandbank. Feeds in compact flocks in tidal zone, staying out of reach of each incoming wave and running back after it.

VOICE: Silent in wintering sites.

HABITAT: Frequents sandy areas exposed to waves almost exclusively. Observed at sea level.

DIET: Chiefly invertebrates.

DISTRIBUTION AND STATUS: Migratory, breeds in arctic zones of Europe, Asia, and N America. Winters in part on coasts of Africa and Madagascar. Common on all Malagasy coasts during boreal winter, very few staying for boreal summer.

118. *Little Stint*

Calidris minuta (Leisler, 1812)
French: Bécasseau minute
No Map

DESCRIPTION: Length 13 cm.
Adult. Sexes similar.
Nonbreeding Plumage. White forehead, supercilium, chin, and throat. White cheeks finely striped with gray. Gray-brown crown edged with gray. Gray nape and back of neck. Black bill, dark brown iris. Upperparts light brown-gray, except for dark gray-brown lower back, rump, and uppertail coverts. Underparts white, sides of chest tinged with gray. Black tarsi and toes. Wings: gray-brown, except for

brown primary remiges, brown secondary remiges with white base and white edge at ends, white-tipped brown-gray greater upperwing coverts, and white underwing coverts and axillaries. Brown-gray tail, except for dark brown central tail feathers.

IDENTIFICATION: Very small sandpiper with stocky silhouette, brown-gray plumage above and white below, white supercilium in contrast with dark crown and grayish cheeks, and short, straight black bill. In flight, wings are marked with faint white bar and gray tail is marked with brown in the middle.

BEHAVIOR: Generally found alone or associated with other shorebirds (Curlew sandpiper, Kittlitz's plover). Constantly active.

VOICE: Quiet in wintering sites.

HABITAT: Brackish coastal lakes, more rarely muddy shoreline. Observed at sea level.

DIET: Invertebrates.

DISTRIBUTION AND STATUS: Migratory, breeds in n Europe and Asia. Winters in part in Africa. Uncommon winter visitor in Madagascar, where it has been observed on lakes or ponds, usually brackish, near w coast in boreal autumn and winter (Andranobe, Ihotry, Kinkony lakes).

119. *Curlew Sandpiper*

Calidris ferrugine (Pontoppidan, 1763)
French: Bécasseau cocorli
No Map

DESCRIPTION: Length 18 cm.
Adult. Sexes similar.
Nonbreeding Plumage. Forehead, crown, cheeks, eye stripe, sides and back of neck gray-brown finely streaked with black.

White chin, throat, and supercilium. Black bill, dark brown iris. Upperparts brown-gray faintly marked with black and edged with white, except for white uppertail coverts. Underparts whitish with front of neck and chest streaked with brown-gray. Black tarsi and toes. Wings: gray except for white-based black primary remiges, black secondary remiges and primary coverts, and white greater wing coverts with white ends. Tail grayish, except for brown central tail feathers.

IDENTIFICATION: Medium-sized grayish and white sandpiper with rather slender silhouette, fairly long neck and legs, long, thin, black decurved bill, and white supercilium contrasting with dark crown and gray eye stripe. In flight, conspicuous white wing bar, white uppertail coverts, and white underside of wings are field marks.

BEHAVIOR: Gregarious coastal species found in often large groups of 30–300, sometimes more numerous in roosting sites.

VOICE: Utters soft, trilled *dweerrreet.*

HABITAT: Coastal mud flats, mangroves, estuaries, bodies of freshwater near coast with open, muddy banks. Observed at elevations from sea level to 1,400 m.

DIET: Invertebrates (mollusks, insects), occasionally plants and seeds.

DISTRIBUTION AND STATUS: Migratory, breeds in n Asia and winters in part on coasts of Africa and Madagascar. Very common during boreal winter on all Malagasy coasts and seasonally on the High Plateau (70 at Antananarivo, Nov.– Dec. 1988), and not rare during boreal summer. Most common wintering shorebird, along with Whimbrel and Ruddy turnstone.

120. Ruff

Philomachus pugnax (Linnaeus, 1758)
French: Combattant
No Map

DESCRIPTION: Length 26–30 cm (male), 20–24 cm (female).
Adult. Sexes differ.
Female Nonbreeding Plumage. Gray-brown front and top of head, marked with median black spots. Uniform gray-brown sides of head and neck. Whitish forehead, chin and throat. Brownish bill, dark brown iris. Upperparts gray-brown, edged with pale gray or light brown and slightly dotted with black on mantle and scapulars. White uppertail coverts. Underparts white, except for pale gray-brown chest and flanks. Tarsi and toes vary somewhat in color but are usually greenish. Wings: greater wing coverts dark brown ending in white, small and median coverts gray-brown edged with gray or pale brown. Dark brown primary and secondary remiges, latter finely tipped with white. White underwing coverts and axillaries. Dark gray-brown tail.
Male Nonbreeding Plumage. Generally similar but may retain white parts of neck or head from breeding plumage. Coloration of bill and legs highly variable.

IDENTIFICATION: Large shorebird with rather short, straight, stout bill, long legs, dull gray-brown plumage, scaly appearance above. Powerful body, rather small head. In flight, body and wings appear somber above, with inconspicuous white wing bar and 2 white oval spots (formed by uppertail coverts) set off by dark tail; wings are light below, and legs extend beyond tail.

VOICE: Silent in wintering sites.

DISTRIBUTION AND STATUS: Migratory, breeds in Europe and Asia, winters in part in Africa. Rare visitor in Madagascar, observed alone or associated with other shorebirds (Curlew sandpiper, Kittlitz's plover, Common ringed plover) in Nov.–Dec. on w coast (Ihotry Lake, Morombe).

Stercorariidae – Skua, Jaeger

Migratory seabirds having a stout bill
with hooked tip. The base of the upper
mandible and the nostrils are covered
with a horny sheath. The neck is short
and thick, the tarsi and toes scutellated,
the claws powerful and sharp, the wings
long and pointed. Flight is powerful and
agile. Skua and Jaeger are carrion eaters
and kleptoparasites but can also catch
some prey. The family is represented by 7
species that breed in high latitudes and
are widespread in all oceans outside the
breeding season. Two species have been
observed along Malagasy coasts.

parasite. Scouts in leisurely flight, then
suddenly swoops to seize live bird, claim
carrion, or force other seabird to disgorge
its prey.

VOICE: Appears silent in wintering sites.

HABITAT: Observed along coasts.

DIET: Birds, fish, marine invertebrates,
carrion, refuse.

DISTRIBUTION AND STATUS: Migratory, breeds on many islets of subantarctic zone. Observed regularly in
Madagascar along e coast (Tolagnaro,
Farafangana, Manakara, Toamasina, Maroantsetra). Individual banded on Marion
Island (46°54′E–37°45′E) was recap-
tured at Tolagnaro, Mar. 1987.

121. *Subantarctic Skua*

Catharacta antarctica (Lesson, 1831)
Malagasy: Sombe, Vorondreky
French: Grand Labbe subantarctique
No Map

DESCRIPTION: Length 63–65 cm.
Adult. Sexes similar. Dark brown head,
touches of black and faint yellowish white
flecks on neck. Black bill, light brown
iris. Upperparts dark brown with touches
of black. Underparts dark grayish brown,
sometimes with yellowish spots on chest.
Black tarsi, toes, and webs. Wings dark
brown, except for large white band on
lower and upper surfaces of primary
remiges. Sooty brown tail.
Immature. Differs from adult by more
uniform upperparts and more rufous-
brown underparts.

IDENTIFICATION: Big seabird with
somber plumage, with large fields of
white on wings (invisible when wings are
folded). Cannot be confused with any
other species in Madagascar.

BEHAVIOR: Generally solitary in wintering sites. Predator, carrion eater, and

122. *Parastic Jaeger*

Stercorarius parasiticus (Linnaeus, 1758)
French: Labbe parasite
No Map

DESCRIPTION: Length 42 cm.
Adult. Sexes similar. Polymorphic
species.

Nonbreeding Plumage.
Light Morph. Brownish forehead and front and top of head. Light brown sides of head and nape. White chin and throat streaked yellowish. Black bill, whitish cere, dark brown iris. Upperparts brown, darker on lower back and rump. Underparts generally white with brown-gray areas on belly and flanks and a more-or-less complete tan-gray breastband of variable width. Sooty tarsi and toes. Wings: rust-brown above, blackish brown below; white base of primary remiges and outside edge of 4 last primary remiges. Blackish brown tail with black terminal band above. Whitish tan external tail feathers below. Long (8–14 cm) blackish brown central tail feathers.
Dark Morph. Dark brown plumage all over with black crown, yellowish or olive-brown cheeks and collar. White of wings remains as in light morph.
Intermediate Morphs. Brownish with whitish throat and cheeks streaked brownish, and variable or nonexistent white area on underparts.

IDENTIFICATION: Medium-sized seabird, excellent glider having slender silhouette, with long wings marked with white on primary remiges and tail, and with the 2 central tail feathers elongated.

DISTRIBUTION AND STATUS: Migratory, breeds in n of N Hemisphere. Winter range includes all oceans. Exceptional visitor in Madagascar: sighted only once.

Laridae – Gulls

Generally marine birds, large or medium-sized, plumper and taller than terns, having bills that are shorter than their heads and thin in the smaller species, stout and slightly curved in the larger. Tarsi and toes are short, the 3 front toes are webbed and the first toe is rudimentary. The tail is generally straight. Gulls are highly opportunistic feeders. They are generally vocal and gregarious. The family is cosmopolitan and is represented by 46 species, 2 of which nest in Madagascar.

123. *Kelp Gull*

Larus dominicanus Lichtenstein, 1823
Malagasy: Kolokoloky, Betehoky
French: Goéland dominicain
No Map

DESCRIPTION: Length 58 cm.
Adult. Sexes similar. White head, neck, chin, and throat. Yellow bill, red gonys, straw yellow iris. Red orbital ring. Upperparts black, except for white rump and uppertail coverts. Underparts white. Greenish yellow tarsi, toes, and web. Wings black, except for round white spot on end of primary remiges, and white tips of secondary remiges. White tail.
Immature. Pale gray-brown head dotted with white, lighter on forehead. Darker gray nape and cheeks, pale gray-brown chin and throat. Sooty bill, dark brown iris. Upperparts brown dotted with black, except for light brown-gray rump and uppertail coverts barred with brown. Underparts brown mottled with white, darker on belly, except for light brown-gray undertail coverts barred with brown. Sooty tarsi, toes, and webs. Wings brownish, with grayish edges. Dark brown primary and secondary remiges,

latter tipped with white. Light brown-gray tail with dark brown bars and a much more extensive terminal band.

IDENTIFICATION: Large, massively built black-and-white gull with large angular head, thick neck, stout yellow bill, and powerful legs. In flight, field marks are long, wide, black wings with white trailing edges and white head and tail contrasting with black upperparts.

BEHAVIOR: Found alone or in pairs, infrequently in small groups of 3–8 (13 at Tsimanampetsotsa Lake, Mar. 1987), sometimes in company of other species in roosting sites (Caspian tern). Often observed walking slowly on beaches or lakeshores, or swimming on the calm surface of a body of water, or flying low over shore. Visits tern colonies and frequently seizes eggs or chicks despite nesters' hostility.

VOICE: Fairly quiet, utters raucous, rather low-pitched, resonant *coy coy coy* . . . as well as loud, dissonant *kok kok kok* . . . .

HABITAT: Sandy beaches, coral islets, open, flat shores of saltwater lakes (Tsimanampetsotsa, Anony), and certain ports (Tolagnaro).

DIET: Varied; includes crustaceans taken on seashore, eggs and chicks taken from nests, dead fish, and birds.

NESTING: Few precise data. Usually nests in isolation. Nesting has been observed Oct.–Jan.

DISTRIBUTION AND STATUS: Widely distributed s of Tropic of Capricorn, in Africa, S America, Oceania, and Madagascar. Range in Madagascar covers sw and s coasts from Toliara to Tolagnaro, where it is fairly common. Sighted once at Manakara and Maroantsetra.

124. *Gray-headed Gull*

Larus cirrocephalus Vieillot, 1818
Malagasy: Varevaka, Goakarano
French: Goéland à tête grise

DESCRIPTION: Length 40 cm.
Adult. Sexes similar. Light gray head, chin, and throat, paler on forehead, which is delimited by narrow, dark gray line. White nape and neck. Red bill, pale yellow iris. Red orbital ring. Upperparts white, except for ashy gray back and upper rump. Underparts white. Dark red tarsi, toes, and web. Ashy gray wings. The 2 primary remiges are white at base, black at end, and marked with white subapical patch; the rest are gray with black tips. Secondary remiges gray with white tips, underwing coverts and axillaries gray. White tail.
Immature. Differs from adult by whitish head with brownish markings on the back, grayish back of neck, dull yellow bill with black tip, brownish mantle, back, and upperwing coverts, and dull yellow legs.

IDENTIFICATION: Medium-sized gull with slender silhouette, long, narrow wings, and gray-and-white plumage, characterized by gray hood, long, fine, red bill, and light eye. In flight, shows largely gray upperparts setting off white rump and tail, and gray wings with black-and-white primary remiges marked, at ends, with white ocelli.

BEHAVIOR: Fairly gregarious, seen in pairs or small groups of 3–8 flying over water or at rest on sandy shore or island of vegetation near water. Feeds in small groups, swimming and taking its prey on the surface with quick stabs of bill.

VOICE: Rather quiet, utters kind of harsh, loud, dissonant chuckle: *kree-yeah.*

HABITAT: Large bodies of fresh or brackish water. Observed at elevations from sea level to 1,500 m.

DIET: Aquatic invertebrates and small fish, also eggs and nestlings of various species.

NESTING: Nests in colonies. Nest, thinly lined with grass and twigs, is built on the ground near water, sometimes on emergent mass of vegetation. Clutch numbers 2–3 green-brown eggs spotted with brown and gray (average size: 53.9 mm × 37.9 mm). Chick has light brown down. Nesting has been observed June–Dec.

DISTRIBUTION AND STATUS: Distributed in S America, sub-Saharan Africa, and Madagascar. Represented in Madagascar by subspecies *L. c. poliocephalus* (Swainson, 1925), common to Africa. Uncommon in Madagascar, confined to large lakes: in e, Alaotra Lake, where species breeds, on High Plateau, Itasy Lake, and environs of Antananarivo; in w, lakes of Antsalova and Masoarivo region and Kinkony Lake; and in s, Ihotry Lake.

Sternidae – Terns, Noddies

Medium-sized birds slimmer than the gulls, having narrow, pointed wings, a long, pointed bill, a more or less forked tail, and webbed toes. Most species are migratory and marine, and some nest inland and winter by the sea. Most feed on fish and crustaceans caught by diving after hovering. The family is cosmopolitan, and 42 species are generally recognized. Eight species nest in Madagascar, and 7 others are occasionally observed along its coasts.

125. *Whiskered Tern*
Chlidonias hybridus (Pallas, 1811)
Malagasy: Samby
French: Guifette moustac

DESCRIPTION: Length 26 cm.
Adult. Sexes similar. Plumage varies seasonally.
Breeding Plumage. Black forehead, front and top of head (including eyes), and nape. White cheeks, whitish chin, gray throat. Red bill, dark brown iris. Upperparts bluish gray. Underparts dark gray, except for white undertail coverts. Red tarsi, toes, and webs. Gray upper side of wings. Gray primary remiges tipped with black. White underside of wings. Gray tail edged with white.
Nonbreeding Plumage. Differs from adult in breeding plumage by white forehead and front of head, crown speckled with black, black back of head, nape, and stripe behind eyes, dull, dark red bill, light gray upperparts, white underparts, dark red legs.
Immature. Differs from adult in nonbreeding plumage by ocher-brown upperparts edged with black, except for gray

rump and uppertail coverts, brown median upperwing coverts, and black bill.

IDENTIFICATION: Small, elegant, slender freshwater tern with black cap and long wings, characterized by solid light gray body and top of wings and slightly indented tail. In breeding plumage cannot be confused with any other species in its habitat. In nonbreeding plumage can be mistaken for White-winged tern in nonbreeding plumage, from which it is distinguished by larger size, white cheeks, and gray rump, uppertail coverts, and tail. Differs from Black tern in nonbreeding plumage by larger size, light top of head, and white cheeks and sides of neck.

BEHAVIOR: Found in small groups of 3–15 skimming over water partly covered with floating vegetation. Flight is graceful, direct, easy, and punctuated with dives to seize prey at surface of water. Wingbeats are deep and incisive. Large numbers may be seen assembled during boreal winter (1,000 in nonbreeding plumage on flat, open shore of Ihotry Lake, Aug. 1982).

VOICE: Quiet outside nesting sites, where it utters a harsh, grating *craze craze*... alternating with a shrill *keek keek*....

HABITAT: Shallow freshwater or brackish ponds and lakes offering a certain amount of floating vegetation (*Nymphaea* sp.—Nymphaeaceae). Seen on inundated rice paddies. Observed at elevations from sea level to 1,500 m.

DIET: Aquatic insects, also batrachians and fish.

NESTING: Nests in colonies on floating vegetation or a pile of plant debris in shallows or wetlands. Nest consists of grasses. Clutch numbers 3 creamy brown eggs mottled with chestnut. Both parents

incubate. Semi-nidifugous chick is covered in orangy fawn down. Nesting has been observed Oct.–Nov.

DISTRIBUTION AND STATUS: Distributed in Europe, Asia, Oceania, Africa, and Madagascar. Represented in Madagascar by subspecies *C. h. sclateri* (Mathews and Iredale, 1921), common to e and s Africa. Local to some sites, where it is fairly common (Alaotra Lake, Mandroseza and Ivato lakes near Antananarivo, Mitsinjo and Kinkony lakes, lakes and marshes of Soalala and Antsalova regions, and Ihotry Lake). Large congregations seen in w suggest possible migration between Madagascar and Africa.

126. White-winged Tern

Chlidonias leucopterus (Temminck, 1815)
French: Guifette leucoptère
No Map

DESCRIPTION: Length 23 cm.
Adult. Sexes similar.
Nonbreeding Plumage. White forehead and front of head, sooty crown and back of head. Sooty patch behind eyes. White chin, throat and neck. Black bill, dark brown iris. Upperparts light gray, except for white rump and uppertail coverts, underparts white. Orange-red tarsi, toes and webs. Wings: light gray above, whitish below. Primary remiges have dark gray tips. White tail.

IDENTIFICATION: Small, elegant, slender freshwater tern with light plumage above and below, sooty back of head, and slightly indented tail. Distinguished from Whiskered tern in nonbreeding plumage by smaller size, black patch behind eyes, white rump and tail contrasting with rest of upperparts, and gray wings. Bill is thinner and darker, legs orange-red. Distinguished from Black tern in nonbreeding plumage by white crown, rump, and tail, absence of patch on white chest, shorter bill, and orange-red legs.

BEHAVIOR: Generally found in small groups of 2–12. Catches insects on the wing, low over water. Unlike other terns, it can be seen hunting over grassy terrain quite far from water.

VOICE: Sometimes utters brief, loud, throaty *kech*.

HABITAT: Shallow freshwater or brackish ponds and lakes and surrounding grasslands. Observed at elevations from sea level to 750 m.

DIET: Chiefly insects, also fish.

DISTRIBUTION AND STATUS: Migratory, breeds in Europe and Asia, winters in part in Africa. Rather rare in Madagascar but sighted several times during boreal winter and spring at Alaotra Lake.

127. *Black Tern*

Chlidonias niger (Linnaeus, 1758)
French: Guifette noire
No Map

DESCRIPTION: Length 23 cm.
Adult. Sexes similar.
Nonbreeding Plumage. White forehead, chin, throat, and neckband, rest of head black. Black bill, dark brown iris. Upperparts gray, underparts white, except for dark gray sides of chest. Sooty tarsi, toes, and web. Gray wings with dark gray-tipped primary remiges. Gray tail.

IDENTIFICATION: Small, elegant, slender freshwater tern with solid gray plumage, head largely black, and tail slightly indented. Distinguished from Whiskered tern in nonbreeding plumage by smaller size, dark crown, and dark gray sides of chest. Distinguished from

White-winged tern in nonbreeding plumage by dark crown, longer bill, and black legs.

DISTRIBUTION AND STATUS: Migratory, breeds in Europe, Asia, and N America, winters in part on coasts of w and s Africa. Exceptional visitor: sighted only once in Madagascar.

128. *Gull-billed Tern*

Sterna nilotica Gmelin, 1789
French: Sterne hansel
No Map

DESCRIPTION: Length 39 cm, wingspan 94 cm.
Adult. Sexes similar.
Nonbreeding Plumage. Head white, except for short, thick black stripe behind eyes. Black bill and dark brown iris. Upperparts pale gray, underparts white. Black tarsi, toes, and web. White wings, primary remiges tipped with sooty gray. White tail.

IDENTIFICATION: Bulky silhouette with fairly wide, not very pointed wings, slightly indented tail, and almost entirely white plumage. Black patch behind eyes and stout black bill are field marks. Distinguished from immature White tern by larger size, stouter bill, white crown, pale gray upperparts, and barely indented tail.

DISTRIBUTION AND STATUS: Migratory, breeds in Europe, Asia, N and S America, and Oceania, winters in part in Africa. Exceptional visitor: sighted only once in Madagascar.

129. *Caspian Tern*

Sterna caspia Pallas, 1770
Malagasy: Trobaky, Samby, Varevaka
French: Sterne caspienne

DESCRIPTION: Length 48–59 cm, wingspan 127–40 cm.
Adult. Sexes similar. Plumage varies seasonally.
Breeding Plumage. Black cap, raised to form slight crest on nape. Red bill tinged brownish before tip, dark brown iris. Upperparts light gray, except for white rump. Underparts white. Black tarsi, toes, and web. Wings: pale gray above, white below, with primary remiges slate gray above and sooty gray below. Forked, gray-tinted white tail.
Nonbreeding Plumage. Differs by white forehead and cap sprinkled with white.
Immature. More or less complete cap sprinkled with white. Dull orange-yellow bill. Upperparts scaly in appearance, gray with brown spots, especially at scapulars. Gray-tinted white rump. Underparts white. Sooty tarsi, toes, and web. Upper side of wings marked with brown at level of coverts, almost black primary remiges, dark gray secondary remiges, gray tertiary remiges with brown tips. White tail marked with brown and gray bars at end.

IDENTIFICATION: Very large tern with black cap and stout, bright red bill. Imposing, rather long-legged silhouette at rest. Ends of wings extend beyond end of tail. Flight is powerful but graceful, with deep wingbeats similar to a gull's. Sooty ends of wings are distinctive. In Madagascar, cannot be confused with any other species.

BEHAVIOR: Gregarious, found in small groups of 3–12. Fishing is often done alone or in pairs. Prey is caught by diving in manner typical of terns, but bird will also, more rarely, fish by skimming surface of water. Roosts are established on sandy, muddy, or open shores and can accommodate up to 200 (Ihotry Lake, Aug. 1982; 70 at Belo-sur-Tsiribihina, Dec. 1988).

VOICE: Rather vocal, most common call is slow, low-pitched, raucous, and very loud croaking *kra-ah kra-ah* or *kre-eh kre-eh*, uttered on the ground or in flight. Brief *ra-ra-ra* sounds alarm, and staccato *krek-krek-krek-krek-krek* expresses anger.

HABITAT: Saltwater environments, such as coastal areas and lagoons, as well as fresh or brackish waters of rivers and lakes. Observed at elevations from sea level to 1,500 m.

DIET: Chiefly fish, sometimes young birds or eggs.

NESTING: Nests in isolation or in small colonies near coasts, on beaches or sandy islets, or on open shores of large lakes and rivers. Nest is simple hollow fashioned in sand. Clutch generally numbers 2 creamy white eggs with light gray and dark brown spots. Both parents incubate. Chick has brown-spotted grayish down. Nesting has been observed June–Aug.

DISTRIBUTION AND STATUS: Distributed on 5 continents. Population in Madagascar appears sedentary. Common on all Malagasy coasts, except for e coast, where it is rather rare, on large lakes of w coast, and along major w rivers, along which it sometimes works its way inland for several hundred km. Very infrequently recorded on High Plateau (Antananarivo).

130. *Common Tern*

Sterna hirundo Linnaeus, 1758
French: Sterne pierregarin
No Map

DESCRIPTION: Length 32–38 cm, wingspan 79–81 cm.
Adult. Sexes similar.
Nonbreeding Plumage. Head white, except for black crown, nape, and area behind eyes. Black bill, dark brown iris. Upper-

parts pale gray, except for white rump and uppertail coverts. Underparts white. Red-brown tarsi, toes, and webs. Gray wings with darker ends of primary remiges. White tail.

IDENTIFICATION: Medium-sized, short-legged tern with indented tail that does not extend beyond ends of wings. Distinguished from Roseate tern by shorter tail, darker upperparts and wings, and white underparts.

BEHAVIOR: Coastal, gregarious species that fishes in manner typical of terns.

VOICE: Vocal, utters harsh, shrill *kiirrrrrr-kiiirrrrr* or *keh-ehk-ehk-ehrrrrrrr*.

HABITAT: Coastal species.

DIET: Invertebrates and fish.

DISTRIBUTION AND STATUS: Breeds chiefly in Europe, N America, and Asia, winters in part along coasts of Africa. Infrequent visitor. Sighted several times along n and w coasts of Madagascar Dec.–Jan.

131. *Roseate Tern*

Sterna dougallii Montagu, 1813
Malagasy: Kirinina
French: Sterne de Dougall

DESCRIPTION: Length 35–43 cm, wingspan 78 cm.
Adult. Sexes similar. Plumage varies seasonally.
Breeding Plumage. Black forehead, cap (including eyes), and nape. Rest of head, chin, and throat white tinged with pink. Vermilion bill with black point, dark brown iris. Upperparts light gray, except for white rump and uppertail coverts. Underparts white tinged with pink. Vermilion tarsi, toes, and web. Light gray wings. Light gray tail, except for elongated white external tail feathers.
Nonbreeding Plumage. Differs from breeding plumage by white forehead and front of head, white crown speckled with black, black bill, brown-gray mantle, absence of pink tint on underparts, and non-elongated external tail feathers.
Immature. Differs from adult in nonbreeding plumage by white crown and nape speckled with brown and upperparts marked with brown scales.

IDENTIFICATION: Medium-sized, short-legged tern with deeply indented tail that extends well past ends of wings. Distinguished from Common tern by very long external tail feathers, lighter upperparts, and pink-tinged underparts.

BEHAVIOR: Coastal, gregarious species that fishes in manner typical of terns. Usually found in monospecific flocks of 15–300, also associated with other species (Sooty tern) in roosting sites. Roosts are established on rocky islet or sand spits.

VOICE: Vocal in nesting sites, utters shrill, oft-repeated, bisyllabic *dree-vik*. Sounds alarm with low-pitched, grating *krah-ah dree-vik*.

HABITAT: Coastal species, observed at sea level.

DIET: Small fish.

NESTING: Nests in monospecific colonies accommodating up to 4,000 pairs (Nosy Manitra) or sometimes in mixed colonies (500 Roseate tern pairs with 50 Sooty tern pairs on Barren Islands, June 1982). Colonies are established on sandy islets, generally covered with creeping vegetation (*Convolvulus* sp.—Convolvulaceae). Clutch numbers 1–2 light brown eggs with dark brown spots (average size: 42.0 mm × 30.0 mm), laid in simple hollow fashioned in sand. Both parents incubate. Chick has tan down. Nesting has been observed Apr.–Sept.

DISTRIBUTION AND STATUS: Cosmopolitan species distributed on coasts of 5 continents. Distributed on all coasts of Madagascar, common in areas surrounding islands near Antsiranana, Maintirano, Morombe, Toliara, Toamasina, and Maroantsetra. Colonies suffer depredations by local citizens. Nesting sites near coast tend to be abandoned in favor of sites farther offshore.

132. *Bridled Tern*

Sterna anaethetus Scopoli, 1786
Malagasy: Samby, Mavolambosy
French: Sterne bridée

DESCRIPTION: Length 35–38 cm, wingspan 76 cm.
Adult. Sexes similar. Small white frontal area extending as subtle supercilium to behind eyes and separated from white cheek by black stripe joining base of bill to eyes. Black cap and nape, gray back of neck. Black bill, dark brown iris. Upperparts brown-gray, underparts white lightly tinged with gray. Black tarsi, toes, and web. Wings dark brown above with white leading edge to lesser wing coverts, white below with sooty primary and secondary remiges. Tail sooty above with elongated white external tail feathers, white below.
Immature. White forehead, pepper-and-salt cap, gray nape. Subtle white supercilium extending to behind eyes, gray patch from in front of eyes to well behind them. White cheeks, chin, and throat. Black bill, dark brown iris. Upperparts brown-gray dotted with white and fawn, especially on scapulars. Underparts gray-tinted white, with gray sides of chest and flanks. Black tarsi, toes, and web. Wings dark brown-gray above, marked with fawn on coverts. Leading edge of wings white to lesser wing coverts. Underside of wings as in adult. Tail brownish gray above, white below.

IDENTIFICATION: Tern with contrasting plumage (dark gray above, white below), forked tail, and slender silhouette. Distinguished from Sooty tern by smaller size and less black upperparts, especially mantle. Gray back of neck, subtle white supercilium, and smaller white area on forehead are evident at close range. Flight is supple and graceful, with faster wingbeats than Sooty tern.

BEHAVIOR: Gregarious at nesting sites, fishing grounds, and roosts. Feeds by skimming water to catch prey. Occasionally rests on water. Habits are less pelagic than those of Sooty tern.

VOICE: Harsh, nasal *krah* . . . .

HABITAT: Oceanic and coastal species.

DIET: Small fish.

NESTING: Few data. Nests in colonies. Nest is simple hollow sheltered by bush or rocky overhang. Clutch numbers single reddish white egg with brown spots. Nesting has been observed July–Sept.

DISTRIBUTION AND STATUS: Distributed in intertropical zones of Atlantic, Pacific, and Indian oceans. Represented in Madagascar by subspecies *S. a. antarctica* (Lesson, 1831), which also breeds on Seychelles and Mauritius. Some nesting colonies are recorded on w and sw coasts near Morondava and Toliara. Uncommon in Madagascar. Observed around nesting colonies when breeding, and seen at other times near the coast.

133. *Sooty Tern*

Sterna fuscata Linnaeus, 1766
Malagasy: Varevaka
French: Sterne fuligineuse

DESCRIPTION: Length 43–45 cm, wingspan 86–94 cm.

Adult. Sexes similar. Large white area on forehead separated from white cheeks by black stripe joining base of bill to eyes. Black cap and nape, white chin and throat. Black bill, brown iris. Upperparts sooty brown, underparts white, except for slightly gray-tinted flanks. Black tarsi, toes, and web. Wings sooty brown above, except for white leading edge, white below, except for brownish primary and secondary remiges. Tail sooty brown above, whitish below, deeply indented, the 2 white external tail feathers elongated.

Immature. Head entirely dull sooty brown. Dark brown chin and throat. Black bill. Upperparts dark brown speckled with white, especially scapulars. Underparts mainly sooty, shading to gray on belly and lightening further on undertail coverts. Tail shorter than in adult, without elongated external tail feathers, black above with gray tip and external feathers, white below.

IDENTIFICATION: Tern with boldly contrasting plumage (black above, white below), deeply indented tail, and slender silhouette. Flight is supple and powerful. Can be confused only with Bridled tern, from which it differs by larger size, darker hue of upperparts, and black back of neck.

BEHAVIOR: Most pelagic tern in Madagascar. Gregarious both at nesting sites and fishing grounds, where flocks of 10–50 may be seen skimming over water, less frequently sitting on it. Does not dive to catch its prey like most terns, but seizes it by skimming surface. Often associates with other seabirds, such as Roseate tern or Brown noddy.

VOICE: Rather vocal, utters nasal, trisyllabic *wah-kee-wahk*.

HABITAT: Chiefly oceanic species occasionally found near coasts, comes to land only to nest.

DIET: Small fish.

NESTING: Nests in colonies, sometimes associated with other seabirds, such as Roseate tern or Brown noddy, on sandy islets, generally covered with creeping plants (*Convolvulus* sp.—Convolvulaceae). Clutch numbers single tan egg with brown spots (average size: 52.0 mm × 36.0 mm), laid on ground. Both parents incubate. Chick has brown-gray down. Nesting has been observed May–Sept.

DISTRIBUTION AND STATUS: Distributed in tropical and subtropical zones of Atlantic, Pacific, and Indian oceans. Represented in Indian Ocean by subspecies *S. f. nubilosa* (Milon, 1948), which breeds in large numbers in the Seychelles and the Glorieuses. In Madagascar some colonies have been recorded on islets off e coast s of Toamasina, the w coast near Maintirano, s of Toliara and w of Antsiranana. Sightings generally occur near colonies at breeding time and seen at other times near the coast. Colonies suffer depredations by local citizens and are moving to islets ever farther offshore.

134. *Saunders's Tern*

Sterna saundersi Hume, 1877
French: Sterne de Saunders
No Map

DESCRIPTION: Length 20–28 cm, wingspan 50–55 cm.
Adult. Sexes similar.
Nonbreeding Plumage. Head white, except for sooty top, back, and eye stripe. Black bill, brown iris. Upperparts light gray, underparts white. Brownish tarsi, toes, and web. Wings light gray above and primary remiges dark gray, white below. White tail.
Immature. Differs from adult in nonbreeding plumage by white forehead with brownish tinge, white crown with brown-

ish specks, scaly appearance of gray
and brown upperparts, gray wings with
brown spots above, and grayish tail with
brown tip.

IDENTIFICATION: Small tern, smallest
of Madagascar, characterized by black
bill, white forehead, black cap, and relatively short tail with shallow fork. At rest,
silhouette is short-legged with ends of
wings extending beyond tail. Flight consists of hurried, energetic wingbeats.

BEHAVIOR: Coastal tern, less gregarious than other terns, always very active.
Fishes in small groups and catches prey
in manner typical of terns.

VOICE: Highly vocal, almost ceaselessly
uttering harsh, shrill *witt . . . witt . . .
witt . . . .* Call is a good field mark.

HABITAT: Coastal species, fishes in
tidepools formed at low tide.

DIET: Small fish, crustaceans, small marine mollusks.

DISTRIBUTION AND STATUS: Distributed s of Red Sea, in Persian Gulf
and in Indian Ocean to Madagascar. In
Madagascar this infrequent visitor has
been observed in small flocks of about 30
on w coast, Nov.–Mar. (15 at Toliara,
Dec. 1988).

135. *Greater-crested Tern*

Sterna bergii Lichtenstein, 1823
Malagasy: Samby
French: Sterne huppée

DESCRIPTION: Length 43–48 cm,
wingspan 99–109 cm.
Adult. Sexes similar. Plumage varies
seasonally.
Breeding Plumage. White head with black
cap with raised feathers in back and separated from base of bill by narrow white
band. Yellow bill and dark brown iris.

Upperparts light gray with lighter rump,
underparts white. Black tarsi, toes, and
web. Wings light gray above, edged with
white, with black-edged gray primary
remiges. Underside of wings white with
primary remiges dark gray at tips. Light
gray tail.
Nonbreeding Plumage. Differs by dull coloration of bill, white forehead and front
part of cap, and white flecks on rest of
cap and nape.
Immature. Head similar to that of adult in
nonbreeding plumage, bill generally
darker, often with black point. Upperparts grayish with brown spots, lighter
rump. Underparts and underside of
wings as in adult. Upper side of wings
dark brown at primary remiges and primary coverts, dark brown secondary
remiges edged and tipped with white,
brown-gray greater and median coverts
edged with white. Gray tail (darker than
rump), generally darker tip and external
tail feathers.

IDENTIFICATION: Large tern with
black cap and stout yellow bill, intermediate in size between Caspian tern and
Lesser-crested tern. Flight is powerful,
and long, narrow wings are field mark.
Immature is distinguished from immature
Caspian and Lesser-crested terns by yellowish bill and especially by great contrast
between dark upperparts and wings and
white underparts.

BEHAVIOR: Gregarious, feeds in manner typical of terns. Fish in small groups,
but several hundred can assemble in
roosts. Sometimes associates with Lesser-
crested tern.

VOICE: Raucous, low-pitched *kreh-kreh.*

HABITAT: Coastal species, frequents
shallows, sometimes estuaries. Rests on
sandy or muddy shores, on rocky out-
crops in open sea, in estuaries, or in middle of mangroves.

DIET: Chiefly fish.

NESTING: Few data. Nests in colonies on sandy islets. Clutch numbers one or two tan eggs with dark brown spots, laid in simple hollow fashioned in sand. Chick has light tan down. Nesting has been observed Apr.–July.

DISTRIBUTION AND STATUS: Distributed in intertropical zones of Pacific and Indian oceans. In Madagascar, species frequents all coasts and breeds on sandy islets of nw and e. After Lesser-crested tern, Madagascar's most common coastal seabird.

136. *Lesser-crested Tern*

Sterna bengalensis Lesson, 1831
Malagasy: Samby
French: Sterne voyageuse

DESCRIPTION: Length 38–43 cm, wingspan 89–94 cm.
Adult. Sexes similar. Plumage varies seasonally.
Breeding Plumage. White head with black cap extending from root of bill to nape. Rather stout, bright orange bill, dark brown iris. Upperparts gray, underparts white. Black tarsi, toes, and web. Upper side of wings gray edged with white, primary remiges darker with sooty tips. Underside of wings white. Pale gray tail.
Nonbreeding Adult. Differs by duller bill, white forehead, and almost entirely white cap with black remaining evident only on nape.
Immature. Head similar to that of adult in nonbreeding plumage, except for dull yellow bill usually tinged with gray. Upperparts slightly speckled with brown, underparts white. Wings gray above edged with white, except for brown primary remiges and brown-edged lesser coverts and secondary remiges. Under-

side of wings white. Light gray tail with brown tip.

IDENTIFICATION: Rather large tern with black cap (greatly faded in nonbreeding plumage), rather stout orange or orangy yellow bill. Distinguished from Greater-crested tern by smaller size and orange bill. Immature distinguished from immature Greater-crested tern by lighter upperparts. Supple flight, powerful but graceful.

BEHAVIOR: Very gregarious, feeds in small groups in manner typical of terns, skimming sea surface and plunging after sudden stop. More numerous roosting flocks may number several hundred, even thousands (2,000 in Antongil Bay, Jan. 1982). Sometimes associates with Greater-crested tern or Sooty tern.

VOICE: Rather vocal, utters harsh, raucous call, piercing shrieks and cackles: *krr-ep* or *kek-kerek*.

HABITAT: Coastal species, frequents shallow waters. Rests on sand- or mudbanks, rocky islets in open sea, estuaries, and mangroves.

DIET: Chiefly small fish.

NESTING: No proof of nesting in Madagascar.

DISTRIBUTION AND STATUS: Distributed in Mediterranean basin and intertropical zone of Indian and Pacific oceans. Present year-round on all coasts of Madagascar. Most common coastal seabird.

137. *Brown Noddy*

Anous stolidus (Linnaeus, 1758)
French: Noddi brun

DESCRIPTION: Length 40–45 cm, wingspan 79–86 cm.
Adult. Sexes similar. Light gray forehead,

rest of head brown-gray. Narrow and incomplete white orbital ring. Black bill, dark brown iris. Brown upperparts, underparts, and wings. Black tarsi, toes, and web. Brown tail with elongated external rectrices.
Immature. Differs from adult by gray of forehead, which appears only gradually.

IDENTIFICATION: Characterized by brown plumage all over, except for gray forehead, long stout bill, wide, long, indented tail. Can be confused with Lesser noddy, from which it differs by larger size, stouter silhouette, and partly brown head (gray forehead). Flight is more ponderous and wingbeats slower.

BEHAVIOR: Gregarious pelagic species that comes to land only at nesting time but can be observed near coasts at other times. Does not dive like terns.

VOICE: Rather vocal, utters raucous *krah krah krah* both on fishing grounds and in nesting sites.

HABITAT: Oceanic species.

DIET: Fish, invertebrates.

NESTING: Few data. Nests in colonies on rocky islets, more rarely on cliffs or sandy islets. Nest is simple platform of coral debris and shells, or hole in rock. Clutch numbers 1 pink-gray egg sprinkled with sepia and brown spots (average size: 54.0 mm × 35.0 mm). Nesting has been observed Apr.–May.

DISTRIBUTION AND STATUS: Distributed in tropical and subtropical zone of Atlantic, Pacific, and Indian oceans. Represented in Madagascar by subspecies *A. s. pileatus* (Scopoli, 1786), occurring in Indian Ocean. Can be observed on all coasts but is more common near nesting areas. Recorded nesting sites are located near Toamasina, Antsiranana, Nosy Be, and Morondava. As with all seabirds, prosperity of colonies is threatened by depredations of local citizens.

138. *Lesser Noddy*

Anous tenuirostris (Temminck, 1823)
French: Noddi à bec grêle
No Map

DESCRIPTION: Length 30–34 cm, wingspan 58–63 cm.
Adult. Sexes similar. Head light gray all over, gray nape. Slender black bill, light brown iris. Upperparts brown, except for brown-gray back. Underparts brown, except for brown-gray chest and belly. Sooty tarsi, toes, and web. Brown wings. Brown tail with elongated external remiges.
Immature. Similar to adult.

IDENTIFICATION: Light head, brown plumage, slender black bill, long, indented tail. Can be confused only with Brown noddy, from which it differs by smaller size and entirely gray head, which appears white at a distance. Flight is lighter, wingbeats faster.

BEHAVIOR: Similar to that of Brown noddy. Usually found in small groups (up to 12 birds) within larger flocks of Brown noddies.

DIET: Surface fish and invertebrates.

HABITAT: Oceanic species.

NESTING: No evidence in Madagascar.

DISTRIBUTION AND STATUS: Distributed in tropical and subtropical zone of Indian Ocean. Breeds in large numbers on Mauritius and Seychelles. Fairly regular visitor in Madagascar, seen in small numbers on w coast.

139. *White Tern*

Gygis alba (Sparrman, 1786)
French: Gygis blanc
No Map

DESCRIPTION: Length 30 cm, wingspan 78 cm.

Adult. Sexes similar. Plumage entirely white. Black bill, dark brown iris, black orbital ring. Blue-gray legs.
Immature. Differs from adult by black mark behind eyes, gray back of head, brown-gray back and scapulars, some remiges edged with black.

IDENTIFICATION: Very characteristic tern with entirely white plumage and black, fairly stout, turned-up bill. Adult cannot be confused with any other seabird.

HABITAT: Oceanic species.

DIET: Fish.

DISTRIBUTION AND STATUS: Distributed in tropical zone of Atlantic, Pacific, and Indian oceans. Breeding site closest to Madagascar is Seychelles. Rather rare visitor to nw and ne coasts of Madagascar.

Columbiformes

Pteroclididae – Sandgrouse

Sandgrouse have short bills, very short tarsi feathered to base of toes, and long, wide wings. Some species are migratory. The family is represented by 16 species, most of which are distributed in arid and subarid regions of the Old World. One species is endemic to Madagascar.

140. *Madagascar Sandgrouse*

Pterocles personatus Gould, 1843
Malagasy: Katakatra, Hatrakatrake, Katrakatraka
French: Ganga masqué

DESCRIPTION: Length 35 cm.
Adult. Sexes differ.
Male. Russet-tan head and neck, except for light tan cheeks and throat and black mask encompassing forehead, chin, and root of bill. Light gray, black-tipped bill, dark brown iris. Upperparts light brown, subtly tinted brown on rump and upper-tail coverts. Underparts tan with bold brown stripes, except for rusty tan chest. Short, stout, gray tarsi. Wings tan marked with 3 brown bands on greater upperwing coverts. Dark brown primary remiges and underside of wing. Tail tan with fine brown stripes.
Female. Head finely striped with brown, except for solid light tan cheeks and front of neck. Upperparts tan tinged with brown. Underparts tan with brown stripes, except for solid light tan upper chest. Tan wings tinged with brown. Dark brown primary remiges. Tan tail, tinged with brown.
Immature. Differs from female only by generally duller hue of plumage and smaller size.

IDENTIFICATION: Reminiscent of terrestrial pigeon with stout, cylindrical body, small, round head, short, conical bill, and very short tarsi, which give it a ground-hugging horizontal silhouette. Only sandgrouse of Madagascar, easily identified by rufous-tan plumage, black mask, and wing marks that are brown in male and brown-tinged tan in female. Flight silhouette is stocky, with wings broad where they join body and pointed at ends. Dark underside of wings contrasts sharply with light underparts. From above, contrast between dark primary remiges and light rest of wing is striking. Flight is swift, with powerful, fast, uninterrupted wingbeats.

BEHAVIOR: Terrestrial, gregarious species found in groups of 3–7 pairs, sometimes more. Feeds on ground during day. Walks, little and slowly, in dry terrain where vegetation does not hamper visibility or progress. Noisy flocks on their way to feeding grounds or water are frequent sight, morning and evening. Large flocks gather on sandbanks of rivers or lakes, drinking or resting during heat of day (300–400 on a sandbank of Befandriana River, Nov. 1983). Easily alarmed, it freezes when disturbed, then departs slowly with rolling gait or suddenly takes wing.

VOICE: Highly vocal. Call, useful field mark and locator, is uttered in flight almost constantly low-pitched, resonant *katakatakata* . . . . Taken up every 3–4 seconds by different members of group. Always uttered when group takes wing.

HABITAT: Open, sparsely covered terrain of w and s (grassland savanna, open shores, surroundings of lakes and rivers, and level, bare, rocky, or pebbly areas). Observed at elevations from sea level to 700 m.

DIET: Seeds.

NESTING: Nest, established in uncovered, flat, often pebbly spot with sparse grassy or bushy vegetation, consists of simple hollow in the ground, its sides thinly lined with dry grasses and small twigs. Clutch numbers 3 shiny light green-brown eggs flecked with brown-gray (average size: 45.5 mm × 33.0 mm). Both parents incubate. Chicks are nidifugous. Nesting has been observed May–Oct.

DISTRIBUTION AND STATUS: Endemic to Madagascar, distributed in Western Region, patchily distributed in n (Antsiranana, Antsohihy), common in w and s.

Columbidae – Pigeons, Doves

Medium-sized arboreal and terrestrial birds with plump, stocky silhouette, small head, rather short neck and legs, and short bill. They can be solitary or gregarious. Their flight is powerful, and some species are migratory. The family of nearly 300 species is cosmopolitan. The Feral pigeon excluded, 4 species nest in Madagascar: 2 frugivorous pigeons of the subfamily Treroninae, 1 endemic and the other confined to Madagascar and the Comoros; and 2 of the subfamily Columbinae, 1 confined to Madagascar, Aldabra, the Seychelles, and the Comoros.

141. *Rock Dove / Feral Pigeon*

Columba livia Gmelin, 1789
Malagasy: Voromailala
French: Pigeon biset
No Map

DESCRIPTION: Length 30 cm.

DISTRIBUTION AND STATUS: Introduced species not found in wild. Observer may be led astray by variations in plumage resulting from cross-breeding. Distributed throughout populated areas of Madagascar but has not, as in New Zealand and Réunion, established itself in its original biotope, cliffs. In Madagascar, confined to towns and villages, where it is often raised as food but also for recreation.

142. *Madagascar Turtledove*

Streptopelia picturata (Temminck, 1813)
Malagasy: Domohina, Dehoke, Deho, Pakatovo
French: Tourterelle peinte

DESCRIPTION: Length 28 cm.
Adult. Sexes similar. Blue-gray head, chin, and throat. Gray nape tinged with mauve. Front of neck maroon, back and sides of neck mauve-gray with sooty spots (bases of feathers) and deep mauve iridescent dots. Bill gray at tip, red at base. Fine red orbital ring. Iris brown at center, surrounded by red. Upperparts brown-mauve, except for brown-gray back and uppertail coverts. Underparts deep maroon, except for paler belly and white undertail coverts. Reddish tarsi and toes. Wings rufous-brown, except for brown remiges finely edged with rufous on outer rim, and uniformly brown below. Tail gray-brown all over, except for sooty external tail feathers with white tips. *Immature.* Differs from adult by overall dull gray-brown hue and rufous edge of most feathers of underparts.

IDENTIFICATION: Largest Columbidae of terrestrial habits in Madagascar. Size similar to that of Madagascar blue pigeon and smaller than that of Madagascar green pigeon. In flight, field marks are absence of wing bar, wings rather dark above and uniform lighter shade below, white undertail coverts, and dark, white-tipped tail. Fluttering, very rapid flight. Often snaps wings a few times on taking flight.

BEHAVIOR: Cautious, generally found alone or in pairs, in small groups when food is plentiful. Chiefly a ground feeder, it walks in woodlands free of dense undergrowth or on roads, trails, or natural breaks in wooded or cultivated areas. Perches in dense foliage to rest and sing.

VOICE: Vocal, often utters its bisyllabic, repetitive song, a solemn, muted, melodic *day-oo*, louder than that of Namaqua dove.

HABITAT: Varied original forest types, degraded woodlands, croplands, and wooded areas of towns and villages. Observed at elevations from sea level to 2,000 m.

DIET: Chiefly seeds, sometimes fallen fruit and small invertebrates (insects).

NESTING: Nest, built low off the ground, 1.5–5 m high, on fork of a tree or bush, is flat, loose structure of interlaced twigs. Clutch numbers 2 white eggs (average size: 31.0 mm × 23.0 mm). Nesting has been observed July–Feb.

DISTRIBUTION AND STATUS: Species distributed in Madagascar, Comoros, Aldabra, and Seychelles. Introduced into Mauritius, Seychelles, and Réunion. Represented in Madagascar by nominate endemic subspecies *S. p. picturata,* abundantly distributed throughout Madagascar, except High Plateau. Sometimes raised in captivity and hunted locally.

143. *Namaqua Dove*

Oena capensis (Linnaeus, 1766)
Malagasy: Katoto, Tsakatoto, Tsikoloto, Dehofona, Tsiazotenonina
French: Tourterelle à masque de fer

DESCRIPTION: Length 28 cm.
Adult. Sexes differ.
Male. Black forehead, face, chin, and throat, rest of head and nape light blue-gray. Bill orange at base and red-orange at tip, iris dark brown. Upperparts: gray-brown mantle and back, gray rump marked with white bar framed by two dark brown bars, and brown-gray uppertail coverts tipped with dark brown. Underparts: central part of chest black, sides of chest light gray. White belly and flanks. Black undertail coverts. Dark red tarsi and toes. Wings: light brown-gray wing coverts marked with two purple iridescent patches, gray-brown secondary remiges, primary remiges brown in external half, rufous in internal half, except for brown

tip. Underside of wings rufous, except for brown primary remiges. Tail dark brown, except for silvery gray base.
Female. Differs from male by white forehead, face, chin, and throat. Rest of head, nape, and neck light gray. Gray chest.
Immature. Plumage appears dappled above, showing black, white, and fawn markings.

IDENTIFICATION: Smallest Columbidae of Madagascar. Easily identified by slender silhouette and long, graduated tail. Rufous underside of wings shows in flight. Flight is very swift.

BEHAVIOR: Found alone, in pairs or in small groups of 3–7, sometimes larger flocks (up to 20) when food is locally plentiful. Feeds on ground, walking in open terrain. At rest or to sing it perches at different heights, but almost always in a tree at the end of a branch. Sings even during heat of day.

VOICE: Vocal, produces melodic, muted, bisyllabic *da-ay hoo,* in which first syllable is long and second shorter but more emphatic.

HABITAT: Frequents open, sparsely wooded, or cleared terrain, often in form of sandy areas, such as trails, roads, surroundings of houses, and croplands. Observed at elevations from sea level to 1,500 m.

DIET: Small seeds.

NESTING: Nest, built 1.5–5 m off ground on a horizontal tree fork or bush, is a flat structure of interlaced twigs. Clutch numbers 2 yellowish white eggs (average size: 20.1 mm × 14.9 mm). Both parents incubate. Nesting has been observed Sept.–Mar.

DISTRIBUTION AND STATUS: Distributed in sub-Saharan Africa, Arabia, and Madagascar. Represented in Madagascar by endemic subspecies *O. c. aliena*

(Bangs, 1918). Distributed chiefly in s, w, and n, where it is very common. Range is spreading on High Plateau and in e (regular sightings at Antananarivo, Manakara, Toamasina, Maroantsetra, Ambatondrazaka), where it is still infrequently observed.

144. *Madagascar Green Pigeon*

Treron australis (Linnaeus, 1771)
Malagasy: Fonimaitso, Voronadabo, Finengo
French: Pigeon vert de Madagascar

DESCRIPTION: Length 32 cm.
Adult. Sexes similar.
Nominate subspecies *T. a. australis.*
Yellow-green head, nape, chin, and throat. Small, pale gray bill, pink cere, navy blue iris surrounded by a dark red field. Upperparts olive-green, except for yellow-green mantle. Underparts: yellow-green chest, yellow-green upper belly and flanks tinged with gray; lower belly gray-green mixed with yellow, rufous undertail coverts with broad, dirty white borders. Yellow tarsi and toes. Wings: gray-green upperwing coverts, maroon lesser wing coverts, pale yellow wing bar. Primary remiges black, secondary remiges black, finely edged with pale yellow on external half. Wings gray below. Short, dark gray tail with light gray terminal band.
Subspecies *T. a. xenia* (Salomonsen, 1934).
Differs by paler plumage and generally grayer hue.

IDENTIFICATION: Largest Columbidae of Madagascar, easily identifiable by green coloring. In flight, characterized from above by yellow wing bar enhanced by black remiges and from below by uniform greenish color. Typical very swift flight of pigeons.

BEHAVIOR: Arboreal, fairly gregarious outside breeding season, seen in pairs or small groups of 3–8, also larger groups, on trees bearing varieties of fruit on which it feeds (25 in a *Ficus* sp.—Moraceae, at Ampijoroa in Feb. 1987, 15 in a *Ficus* sp. at Manongarivo in June 1987, with about 10 Madagascar starlings). Frequents treetops almost exclusively, and often rests in thick foliage, where it is difficult to detect.

VOICE: Fairly vocal. Song is soft and melodic, a trill followed by a few whistled notes.

HABITAT: Undisturbed rain forest, deciduous dry forest, subarid thicket, second growth, also degraded woodlands and wooded surroundings of towns and villages (plantations, parks). Observed at elevations from sea level to 1,000 m.

DIET: Fruit eaten from trees or sometimes bushes.

NESTING: Nest, built on horizontal fork of a tree in forest or plantation, is loose, flat structure, a sort of platform of interlaced twigs. Clutch numbers 2 white eggs (average size: 32.0 mm × 24.0 mm). Nesting has been observed Oct.–Dec.

DISTRIBUTION AND STATUS: Distributed in Madagascar and Comoros (Moheli). Represented in Madagascar by 2 endemic subspecies. Nominate subspecies *T. a. australis*, widely distributed, is found in e, n, and w as far as Besalampy (s limit), where it is common. Subspecies *T. a. xenia* is distributed w from Besalampy (n limit) to extreme s, where it is uncommon (Ihotry Lake, Tsimanampetsotsa Lake, Itampolo). Hunting is causing local decline of species.

NOTE: This species forms a superspecies with the African green pigeon (*T. calva*).

145. *Madagascar Blue Pigeon*

Alectroenas madagascariensis (Linnaeus, 1766)
Malagasy: Finengo, Finengo manga, Finengo menamaso, Finengo mainty, Finengo menavody
French: Pigeon bleu de Madagascar

DESCRIPTION: Length 28 cm. *Adult.* Sexes similar. Head black except for wide oval area of bare red skin around eyes. Silvery blue-gray chin, throat, and nape. Greenish bill with yellowish tip. Green-yellow iris with red external ring. Upperparts midnight blue except for silvery blue-gray upper mantle. Underparts midnight blue except for silvery blue-gray chest and blood red undertail coverts. Red, partly feathered tarsi, red toes. Wings midnight blue above, brown-gray below with gray primary remiges. Tail blood red except for midnight blue external tail feathers with blood red tips. *Immature.* Differs from adult by absence of gray tinge on chest and nape and by smaller area of bare skin around eyes.

IDENTIFICATION: Only blue pigeon of Madagascar. Same size as Madagascar turtledove, smaller than Madagascar green pigeon. In flight, field marks are absence of wing bar, wings that are dark above and light below, and red tail. Flapping, very swift flight.

BEHAVIOR: Arboreal, fairly gregarious, usually found in pairs or small groups of 3–12, sometimes more when food is plentiful. Madagascar blue pigeon frequents treetops and returns regularly to same perch, generally bare, dead branches emerging from canopy at clearing or forest edge.

VOICE: Little known. Cooing call.

HABITAT: Undisturbed rain forest, degraded forest, surroundings of towns and villages (plantations, parks). Observed at elevations from sea level to 2,000 m.

DIET: Fruit picked from trees or bushes.

NESTING: Nest is loosely built platform of interlaced twigs on horizontal fork of tree, 6–20 m above ground, in forest or plantation. Clutch numbers 1 white egg (average size: 33.0 mm × 24.0 mm). Nesting has been observed Oct.–Dec.

DISTRIBUTION AND STATUS: Endemic to Madagascar, distributed in e, n, and nw (Montagne d'Ambre, Sambirano, and Tsaratanana, Nosy Be, Bora), where it is common, and on High Plateau (Ambohitantely and Manajakatompo). Seasonal incursions into the W Domain have been noted. As with Madagascar green pigeon, local populations may be thinned by hunting.

NOTE: The genus *Alectroenas* is distributed only in Madagascar, Comoros, Aldabra, and Seychelles, where it is represented by 3 species. Another species formerly occurred on Mauritius.

Psittaciformes

Psittacidae – Parrots, Lovebird

Arboreal birds with stout, decurved bill, articulated upper mandible hinged with the frontal bone, 2 toes pointed forward and 2 backward, and strong, sharp claws. They are fairly gregarious and feed on fruit, seeds, and other vegetal matter. The family is widely distributed in the intertropical zone of African, American, and Australasian continents, and 234 species are generally recognized. Three species nest in Madagascar: an endemic lovebird and 2 parrots, of which 1 is confined to Madagascar and the Comoros and 1 to Madagascar, the Comoros, and the Seychelles.

146. *Greater Vasa Parrot*

Coracopsis vasa (Shaw, 1811)
Malagasy: Boloky, Boeza be, Sihotsy, Sihotse be, Vazambe, Vaza, Loakiho, Matsiaka
French: Grand Perroquet Vasa

DESCRIPTION: Length 50 cm.
Adult. Sexes similar.

Nominate subspecies *C. v. vasa.*

Plumage dark brown all over except for lighter underparts, light gray undertail coverts, gray-brown wing coverts and gray outer edge of primary remiges. Pale brown bill (dark gray outside breeding season), dark brown iris. Rather extensive roseate-gray area of bare skin around eyes sometimes reaches to root of bill. Roseate-brown tarsi and toes. The head is bare and takes on an orange coloration in certain individuals during breeding season.

Subspecies *C. v. drouhardi* (Lavauden, 1929).

Differs from *C. v. vasa* by slightly

smaller size and lighter plumage especially on underparts. Some individuals show characteristics intermediate between these 2.

Immature. Differs from adult by generally duller and more brownish hue of plumage, dusky bill, and smaller or absent area of bare skin around eyes.

IDENTIFICATION: Large, dark brown parrot with rather long tail and light colored, very stout bill. Powerful flight with vigorous, sustained wingbeats. Distinguished from Lesser vasa parrot by larger size, lighter coloration of underparts, particularly undertail coverts, shorter tail faintly marked with dark median band, much stouter bill, and more bare skin around eyes. In flight, silhouette is plumper, and lighter wing coverts contrast with dusky remiges. Often difficult to distinguish from Lesser vasa parrot in natural surroundings in spite of these field marks.

BEHAVIOR: Gregarious and vocal, congregates in groups of 3–8, seldom more. Feeds during day but is also active on full moonlit nights. Punctuates activity with calls. Looks for food in treetops and bushes, as well as on the ground on river sandbanks, grassland savanna, or cropland. Usually roosts in larger flocks, which can number several hundred birds in a large tree (200 at Tsimanampetsotsa Lake, Mar. 1987).

VOICE: Vocal species whose calls are less varied and less melodic than those of Lesser vasa parrot. Most common call, emitted from perch or in flight, is a bisyllabic, low-pitched *pee-oh*, with second syllable lower than the first. In flight also utters loud, dissonant, raucous sort of *kra-ach, krach* . . . .

HABITAT: Any of Madagascar's original forest types at appropriate altitudes, second growth, savanna, wooded surround-ings of towns and villages, and croplands (rice, maize, millet, sisal). Observed at elevations from sea level to 1,000 m.

DIET: Fruits, berries, seeds.

NESTING: Few data available. Nests in hollow of tree or branch, several meters above ground. Chamber where eggs are laid may be at the end of a tunnel as much as 2 m deep. Clutch numbers 2–3 white eggs. Nesting has been observed Oct.–Jan.

DISTRIBUTION AND STATUS: Distributed in Madagascar and Comoros. Found throughout Madagascar. Represented by 2 endemic subspecies. Nominate subspecies *C. v. vasa* is distributed in e, subspecies *C. v. drouhardi* in w and s. Fairly common throughout range. Often hunted as food or captured as pet.

147. *Lesser Vasa Parrot*

Coracopsis nigra (Linnaeus, 1758)
Malagasy: Koakio, Boezantsikoira, Sihotsy, Boeza kely, Koakiho, Vasatsihotsy
French: Petit Perroquet noir

DESCRIPTION: Length 35 cm.
Adult. Sexes similar.
  Nominate subspecies *C. n. nigra.*
  Plumage dark brown all over except for slightly grayer undertail coverts and gray outer edge of primary remiges. Plumage has an iridescent green sheen during breeding season. Pale bill (dusky outside breeding season), dark brown iris. Small roseate-gray area of bare skin around eyes does not reach root of bill. Roseate-brown tarsi and toes. Subspecies *C. n. libs* (Bangs, 1927).
  Differs from *C. n. nigra* by slightly smaller size and lighter plumage.
Immature. Differs from adult by duller and browner overall coloration of plum-

age, roseate-gray bill, and absence or very small dimensions of bare-skinned area around eyes.

IDENTIFICATION: Entirely dark brown parrot with long, slightly rounded tail and stout, light colored bill. Flight is graceful, direct, powerful wingbeats alternating with periods of gliding. Distinguished from Greater vasa parrot by smaller size, dark undertail coverts, and plain dark brown tail. In flight, silhouette is slender, light undersides of fairly long wings contrasting with dark underparts.

BEHAVIOR: Close to that of Greater vasa parrot. Gregarious, forms noisy groups of 3–15 birds. Diurnal, with peaks of activity in early morning and late afternoon, when loose-knit, constantly calling flocks of several dozen birds may be seen flying about. Also active on full moonlit nights, again calling incessantly. Feeds on fruit in treetops, sometimes picking it while hanging upside down from a branch. Holds hard fruits in feet to be opened. Large flocks can be seen where food is abundant (50 birds feeding on the ground at rice-threshing location on Bemamba Lake in June 1982). Wary but not shy.

VOICE: Vocal, with varied and more melodic repertory than Greater vasa parrot. Most frequent call, uttered indefatigably from perch or on long flights, is a fluty, shrill, trisyllabic *wee too twee*, of which the second note is lower than the other two. Also utters harsh, dissonantly croaked *ka-ach kach*.

HABITAT: More of a forest species than Greater vasa parrot, adapts to various original forest types, also frequents second growth and wooded surroundings of towns and villages. Sometimes found in mangroves. Observed at elevations from sea level to 2,000 m.

DIET: Chiefly fruits, berries, flowers, and seeds.

NESTING: Few data available. Nests in hollows of branches or tree trunks, generally well above ground (at least 15 m). As with Greater vasa parrot, egg chamber may be at end of a tunnel more than 1 m deep. Clutch numbers 2–3 white eggs. Nesting has been observed Nov.–Dec.

DISTRIBUTION AND STATUS: Distributed in Madagascar, Comoros, and Seychelles. Found throughout Madagascar. Represented by 2 endemic subspecies: nominate subspecies *C. n. nigra* in e and subspecies *C. n. libs* in w and s. Common throughout range. Often hunted as food or captured as pet.

148. *Gray-headed Lovebird*

Agapornis cana (Gmelin, 1788)
Malagasy: Sarivazo, Karaoka, Kariaka, Sarengy, Kariga, Kitrehoka, Fodindriaka
French: Inséparable à tête grise

DESCRIPTION: Length 14–16 cm.
Adult. Nominate subspecies *A. c. cana.*
Sexes differ.
Male. Light gray head, neck, throat, and upper chest. Pale gray, almost white bill, brown iris. Upperparts green, brighter green on rump. Underparts yellow-green except for light gray upper chest. Gray tarsi and toes. Green wings with black-fringed remiges on outer half. Black underwing coverts. Green tail with bright-green external tail feathers barred black at tips.
Female. Differs by uniform green tint of plumage, slightly darker on head, neck, throat, and upper chest, and by green underwing coverts.
  Subspecies *A. c. ablactanea* (Bangs, 1918).
  Differs from *A. c. cana* by darker green

of upperparts, more consistent gray of head and chest (male) and by less yellow-tinged underparts (female).
Immature. Similar to female, except for yellowish bill marked with black at base of upper mandible.

IDENTIFICATION: Small green-and-gray lovebird with plump silhouette, big round head, short pointed wings, and short tail. Flight is direct with uninterrupted, very rapid wingbeats. Only lovebird of Madagascar. Cannot be confused with any other species.

BEHAVIOR: Fairly noisy, gregarious, congregating in flocks of 5–30 birds, sometimes more where food is abundant. Feeds on the ground in compact, close-knit groups. If alarmed, flock takes wing to perch on stalks of grasses or in bushes or trees near feeding ground, to which it returns as soon as danger is past. Not shy, may be seen in surroundings of villages and in rice-threshing areas in company of Madagascar red fody, Sakalava weaver, or Madagascar mannikin. Often roosts in flocks in bare or dead trees.

VOICE: Brief, shrill, metallic *plee plee* . . .

is often uttered by all members of a flock, in flight or roosting.

HABITAT: Sparsely wooded terrain, grassland savanna, subarid thicket, edges of forest, clearings, croplands, even in immediate proximity to towns and villages. Observed at elevations from sea level to 1,500 m.

DIET: Seeds (chiefly of grasses).

NESTING: Few data available. Nests in hole in tree on carpet of leaf fragments or wood shavings. Clutch numbers 3 white eggs. Both parents incubate. Nesting has been observed Nov.–Dec.

DISTRIBUTION AND STATUS: Endemic to Madagascar, introduced at turn of century to Comoros (well distributed), Seychelles, Mauritius (failed to acclimatize), Rodrigues, and Zanzibar. In Madagascar it is distributed throughout island. *A. c. cana* is distributed throughout range except in s, where it is replaced by *A. c. ablactanea*. Common throughout range, except in e, where it is uncommon, and on High Plateau, where it is rare (sighting of 4 birds near Lake Itasy, Mar. 1988). Commonly caught and sold caged.

Cuculiformes

Cuculidae – Cuckoos, Couas, Coucal

A rather heterogeneous family whose representatives have bills that vary in stoutness but are always elongated, with the nostrils near the base, generally long tails, and a reversible first toe. Some species build no nest but lay their eggs in the nests of other species, who then raise the cuckoo chick. The family is fairly cosmopolitan and numbers more than 140 species spread over 4 subfamilies. In Madagascar it is represented by 2 parasitic species, 1 of them endemic, of the subfamily Cuculinae, 9 species of the endemic subfamily Couinae—the couas—and 1 sedentary species of the subfamily Centropinae, distributed in Madagascar and Aldabra. The couas are characterized by short, round wings, thin plumage, a long, stiff tail, and fleshy skin around the eyes. Coua chicks have a species-specific buccal pattern on the inside of the bill that is evident only when the bill is opened widely. A tenth species of coua is considered extinct.

149. *Thick-billed Cuckoo*

Cuculus audeberti (Schlegel, 1879)
French: Coucou d'Audebert

DESCRIPTION: Length 36 cm.
Adult. Sexes similar. Black head, nape, and neck. Upper mandible black, lower mandible yellow. Dark brown iris, yellow eye ring. Upperparts black, underparts white with undertail coverts barred with black. Yellow tarsi and toes. Wings black with light gray tips on primary remiges and edges on secondary remiges. Black tail with white tip.
Immature. Differs from adult by black-

and-white head and upperparts and by white tips of all wing and tail feathers.

IDENTIFICATION: Stout cuckoo, black above, white below, with short wings and tail and stout bill. Easily distinguished from Madagascar lesser cuckoo by larger size, black head and upperparts, white underparts except for black-barred undertail coverts, and short, black, white-tipped tail.

BEHAVIOR: Strictly forest species, secretive, and very little known.

VOICE: No reports from Madagascar.

HABITAT: Undisturbed rain forest. Observed at elevations from sea level to 900 m.

DIET: No data in Madagascar.

NESTING: No data in Madagascar. In e Africa, species parasitizes Retz's red-billed shrike (*Prionops retzii*, family Laniidae, subfamily Prionopinae). Given the taxonomic similarity between the Prionopinae and the Vangidae, it can be assumed that the Thick-billed cuckoo parasitizes a vanga.

DISTRIBUTION AND STATUS: Distributed in tropical and s Africa and in Madagascar. Represented in Madagascar by nominate endemic subspecies *C. a. audeberti*. Rare species in Madagascar. Five mentions are recorded, the most recent dating from 1922. Has been collected in e near Maroantsetra, at Mananara, in Sihanaka forest, and near Rogez (Andekaleka).

150. *Madagascar Lesser Cuckoo*

Cuculus rochii Hartlaub, 1862
Malagasy: Kakafotra, Taotaonkafa, Taotaokafo
French: Coucou de Madagascar

DESCRIPTION: Length 28 cm.
Adult. Sexes similar. Entirely gray head and neck, slightly lighter chin and throat. Bill black except for yellow base and commissures. Brown iris, yellow eye ring. Upperparts gray, underparts white barred with dark brown, except for entirely white undertail coverts. Straw yellow tarsi and toes. Dark gray wings, dark gray tail with white spots on external retrices.
Immature. Differs from adult by brown head, upperparts, and wing coverts and by white underparts barred with brown.

IDENTIFICATION: Small cuckoo with elongated silhouette, gray above, heavily barred white below, with long wings and tail. Flight is direct with rapid, rather shallow wingbeats alternating with short gliding periods. Easily distinguished from Thick-billed cuckoo by smaller size, plumage paler above and barred below, and solid-colored undertail coverts and spotted tail. In flight, distinguished from Frances's sparrowhawk by smaller size, long wings, heavily barred underparts, and long, white-spotted tail.

BEHAVIOR: Solitary, secretive, and shy, seldom observed in the open. It is much more commonly heard singing, sometimes 10–20 minutes without stopping, from a perch in thick foliage. Captures prey on leaves and branches of trees, occasionally on ground. Outside breeding season sometimes joins multispecies feeding flocks; example: 1 Madagascar lesser cuckoo, 2 Ashy cuckoo-shrikes, 4 Long-billed greenbuls, 5 Madagascar bulbuls, 3 Common newtonias, 6 Common jeries, 2 Madagascar paradise flycatchers, 5 Madagascar white-eyes, 3 Blue vangas, and 4 Crested drongos in Bora forest, June 1987.

VOICE: Very vocal with highly characteristic song uttered all day, and often at night, for long uninterrupted sessions. Song is tri- or quadrisyllabic, a resonant and accented *kew kew koo* or *kew kew kew koo*, with first 3 syllables on same note

and last one lower. Song is heard
Aug.–Apr., peaking Sept.–Dec.

HABITAT: Any area that is even sparsely
wooded. Observed at elevations from sea
level to 1,800 m.

DIET: Chiefly insects, especially
caterpillars.

NESTING: Parasitic; usual host is
Madagascar cisticola, or occasionally
Common jery or Madagascar paradise
flycatcher. Clutch numbers 1 creamy
white egg mottled with brown (average
size: 18.0 mm × 13.0 mm). Breeding has
been observed Sept.–Apr.

DISTRIBUTION AND STATUS: Migratory, endemic to Madagascar. Leaves
Madagascar during austral winter (May–
Aug.) for E Africa. Distributed throughout Madagascar, common in all regions
except s, where it is seen only occasionally. Few observations of individuals staying in Madagascar outside breeding
season.

151. *Snail-eating Coua*

Coua delalandei (Temminck, 1827)
Malagasy: Famakiakora
French: Coua de Delalande

DESCRIPTION: Length 57 cm.
Adult. Dark blue head, large area of bare
skin around eyes, wider below and in
front of eye, surrounded by a border of
black feathers. Short, thick eyebrows.
White chin and throat. Black bill (42 mm
long, 20 mm high). Upperparts blue with
violet sheen. Underparts: white chest, rufous-brown belly and flanks, bright rufous-brown undertail coverts. Powerful,
sooty tarsi and toes. Wings blue with violet sheen. Long (300 mm) blue tail with
violet sheen and 4 central tail feathers
tipped with white (15 mm).

IDENTIFICATION: Largest of the
couas, it is characterized by boldly contrasting plumage—blue above, white and
rufous below—large, stout bill, and stout
tarsi. Cannot be confused with any other
species.

BEHAVIOR: Very few data. Terrestrial, feeds on large snails whose shells it
breaks with its bill against a stone. Said to
be shy.

VOICE: Unknown.

HABITAT: Primary rain forest, near sea
level.

DIET: Few data. Large forest snails.

NESTING: Unknown.

DISTRIBUTION AND STATUS: Endemic to Madagascar, considered extinct.
Known by 13 specimens kept in mu-
seums throughout the world. The only
labels specifying collection site read "Ile
Sainte-Marie." The hypothesis that species frequents forest of Pointe-à-Larrée,
across from Ile Sainte-Marie, and the
expanse of forest between Fito and Maroantsetra, has no factual basis. Deforestation would be the principal cause
of this local species's demise, but hunting and the introduction of rats *(Rattus
rattus)* would have also contributed to its
extinction.

152. *Giant Coua*

Coua gigas (Boddaert, 1783)
Malagasy: Lejabe, Eoke, Gory be
French: Coua géant

DESCRIPTION: Length 62 cm.
Adult. Sexes similar. Bronze green crown
and neck. Bare skin around eyes: ultramarine blue below and behind eye, pearly
light blue above, and marked with a
pearly pink spot behind eye. Black line,
very thick below, surrounds this area.

Pale tan chin and throat. Black bill, dark brown iris. Upperparts bronze green, darker at uppertail coverts. Underparts: upper chest tan, rest of chest and upper belly orangy rufous, rest of belly and undertail coverts black. Black tarsi and toes. Bronze green wings, black tail with metallic blue sheen, tipped with white, except for entirely metallic black central tail feathers.

Immature. Differs from adult by generally duller hue, less bright coloration of chest and belly, brownish crown, dull blue area around eyes, flesh-colored bill, and fawn apical spot on wings and on scapular feathers.

IDENTIFICATION: Large terrestrial coua, biggest of W Domain, powerful and streamlined, with very long tail and stout bill. Field marks include greenish upperparts, partially orangy rufous underparts, and extensive blue area around eyes with pink spot and emphasized with heavy black line. Distinguished from Coquerel's coua by considerably larger size, massive impression, and stout bill. Distinguished from Red-capped coua by considerably larger size and extensive blue area around eyes, marked with pink spot. Distinguished from Running coua by considerably larger size and much more somber general hue of plumage.

BEHAVIOR: Terrestrial, found alone, in pairs, or in family groups. Moves slowly, deliberately, head raised and tail held almost horizontal. Feeds unhurriedly in carpet of dead leaves of forest floor. Silhouette changes when utters call: draws itself up, stretches its neck slightly, and raises its tail. Fairly secretive but not shy. Often observed for several minutes at a few meters distance while feeding, or for a few moments when it pauses in the middle of a forest trail. If flushed, runs away swiftly, body leaning forward in horizontal posture. Seldom flies, and then only short distances. Sometimes rests on low stump or branch and always takes advantage of sunny spots on forest floor in early morning, in course of which it adopts an attitude common to all couas on such occasions: it ruffles its feathers, wings drooping to the ground and trembling slightly.

VOICE: Vocal, with characteristic call generally uttered on the ground, sometimes in lower reaches of a tree, a sort of sonorous, guttural *ayoo-ew*, often preceded by a sort of deep, muted *wok wok wok*... audible only over a short distance. Also clear, resonant *kookookookookoo-gogo* or *kookoogogo*, of which the last 2 syllables are pitched lower, and short, muted grunts, often several in succession.

HABITAT: Deciduous forest, subarid thorn scrub, gallery forests. Prefers forests with large trees, because they furnish clear floor without too much grassy vegetation and bushes. Tends to avoid second growth, where the grassy and bushy undergrowth is generally too luxuriant and slows its progress. Observed at elevations from sea level to 800 m.

DIET: Insects (Lepidoptera), occasionally seeds.

NESTING: Bowl-shaped nest of twigs and small branches, pieces of bark, and large leaves. Receptacle is lined with leaf petioles. Built in a tree 3–10 m above ground. Clutch numbers 3 dull white eggs (average size: 43.5 mm × 32.3 mm). Nesting has been observed Nov.–Dec.

DISTRIBUTION AND STATUS: Endemic to Madagascar, distributed thinly in s, rather abundantly in w, ranging n to the Betsiboka River. Like other terrestrial couas, Giant coua is a victim of trapping and hunting.

153. *Coquerel's Coua*

Coua coquereli Grandidier, 1867
Malagasy: Akoke, Gory, Fandikalalana,
Aliotsy, Leja
French: Coua de Coquerel

DESCRIPTION: Length 42 cm.
Adult. Sexes similar. Olive green crown
and neck. Bare skin around eyes: ultramarine blue below and behind eye, pearly
sky blue above, with pearly violet-pink
spot behind eye. This area is surrounded
by a black line, thicker below. Pale tan
chin and throat. Black bill, dark brown
iris. Upperparts olive green. Underparts:
upper chest tan-brown, rest of chest,
flanks, and upper belly rufous, rest of
belly and undertail coverts black. Black
tarsi and toes. Olive green wings. Black
tail with metallic sheen, white-tipped except for entirely metallic-black central tail
feathers.
Immature. Differs from adult by generally
duller hue, more subdued coloration of
chest and belly, brownish crown, dull
blue area around eyes, flesh-colored bill,
and fawn apical spot on wings and on
scapular feathers.

IDENTIFICATION: Large terrestrial
coua with slender, elegant silhouette,
olive green above, partly rufous below,
and blue bare skin around eyes marked
with pink spot and emphasized with black
line. Distinguished from Giant coua by
considerably smaller size, slimmer build,
and thinner bill. Distinguished from
Red-capped coua by slightly stockier silhouette, olive green crown, more richly
colored underparts, black belly and undertail coverts, and pink spot on bare skin
around eyes. Distinguished from Running coua by slightly stockier silhouette,
darker upperparts, rufous chest and part
of belly, and black undertail coverts.

BEHAVIOR: Similar to that of Giant
coua. Terrestrial, secretive, forest species. Found alone or in pairs. Moves
slowly on forest floor, often carrying tail
above line of back while collecting food
on ground. If alarmed, runs swiftly to escape danger.

VOICE: Vocal, utters loud, clear *kewkew-
kewkew*, sometimes taken up by other individuals. Muted grunts also recorded.
On the ground or perched, utters higher-
pitched *ayoo-ew* than Giant coua.

DIET: Insects (Orthoptera, Lepidoptera,
Hemiptera), spiders, and occasionally
berries.

HABITAT: Deciduous dry forest and
humid forest of nw, whose undergrowth
includes limited herbaceous stratum.
Seldom encountered in second growth,
and only when it is contiguous with preferred habitats. Observed from sea level
to 800 m.

NESTING: Nest is a solidly constructed
bowl-shaped structure of twigs, small
branches, leaf petioles, and pieces of bark
built in a dense bush 2 m above ground.
Receptacle is lined with leaf petioles.
Clutch numbers 2 dull white eggs (average size: 33.5 mm × 25.2 mm). Nesting
has been observed Nov.–Jan.

DISTRIBUTION AND STATUS: Endemic to Madagascar, distributed in w
with Morombe and Sakaraha as s limit,
and n to Antsiranana (forests of Ankarana
and Analamera). It also occurs in the
Sambirano. Fairly common, but less well
represented in s part of range. Like other
terrestrial couas, Coquerel's coua suffers
effects of trapping and hunting.

154. *Red-breasted Coua*

Coua serriana Pucheran, 1845
Malagasy: Koa
French: Coua de Serre

DESCRIPTION: Length 42 cm.
Adult. Sexes similar. Grayish head and neck. Ultramarine bare skin around the eyes, sky blue above. Black chin and throat. Black bill, brown iris. Upperparts dark green-brown. Underparts dark brown except for chestnut chest. Black tarsi and toes. Dark green-brown wings. Shiny midnight blue tail.
Immature. Differs from adult by overall dull olive brown hue, dark brown head, dull chestnut chest, and black tail. Feathers of upperparts and wings marked by russet apical patch and sooty subapical patch. Bare skin around eyes is feathered or slightly denuded dull blue. Flesh-colored bill with sooty tip.

IDENTIFICATION: Large coua with rather stocky silhouette and very somber plumage except for chestnut chest and blue area around eyes. Easily distinguished from Red-fronted coua by slightly larger size, black head, black and chestnut underparts, and darker upperparts.

BEHAVIOR: The most terrestrial coua, secretive and rather shy, found alone, in pairs, or in family groups. Often seen on roads. Walks deliberately on forest floor, pausing regularly as it feeds. Sometimes darts to capture flying prey. At rest, remains perfectly immobile on the ground or, more often, perched on a horizontal branch, stump, or fallen trunk, at least 80 cm off the ground. If alarmed, draws itself up, then withdraws at a run or rapid walk, body held horizontal, to melt perfectly into plant cover. Seldom flies. In the morning or after rain it seeks sunny spots to warm or dry itself, ruffles its feathers, lets its wings droop to the ground, and fans its tail widely.

VOICE: Rather vocal, repeats loud *koo ha* from ground or very low branch several times; call is often taken up by others. Typical call, a sort of *tee oooo*, bisyllabic,

melodic, and rather high-pitched, is emitted from ground and sometimes followed by muted grunts.

HABITAT: Undisturbed rain forest from sea level to 1,000 m.

DIET: Chiefly berries, fruits, and insects.

NESTING: Bowl-shaped nest of intertwined branches is built low (2–4 m above ground) in an epiphytic fern (*Asplenium nidus*—Aspleniaceae) or a Pandanus (*Pandanus* sp.—Pandanaceae). Clutch numbers 2 white eggs. Nesting has been observed in Dec.

DISTRIBUTION AND STATUS: Endemic to Madagascar, distributed in e from Zahamena (s limit) to Sambava (n limit), where it is fairly common, even common locally in vicinity of Maroantsetra. Also occurs in the Sambirano.

155. *Red-fronted Coua*

Coua reynaudii Pucheran, 1845
Malagasy: Koa, Taitohaka, Fandikalalana
French: Coua de Reynaud

DESCRIPTION: Length 40 cm.
Adult. Sexes similar. Bright rufous forehead, front of head, and crown. Bare skin around eyes ultramarine blue, pearly sky blue behind, surrounded by black stripe. Chin and throat gray. Back of head and neck dark olive green. Underparts: darker gray on belly and undertail coverts. Black tarsi and toes. Dark olive green wings. Olive green tail with metallic blue sheen.
Immature. Differs from adult by generally duller plumage, especially that of cap, dull rufous underparts, upperwing coverts edged with rufous, and no metallic sheen on tail.

IDENTIFICATION: Medium-sized coua with short-legged silhouette, olive green above and gray below, and rufous head.

Easily distinguished from Red-breasted coua by smaller size, shorter legs, green hue of upperparts, gray with no rufous on underparts, and bright rufous crown. Distinguished from Coquerel's coua by smaller size, shorter legs, rufous head, dark gray belly, and blue skin around eyes with no pink spot.

BEHAVIOR: Terrestrial, secretive, furtive, and rather shy, seen alone, in pairs, or in family groups. To feed, walks on ground in dense tangles of underbrush, climbing on creepers, low branches, or fallen tree trunks, sometimes to height of 7–8 m. Explores floor of densest, most impenetrable areas of forest, edges of forests, clearings, and deadwood. If alarmed, runs away at great speed, its body, head, and tail held horizontal, and almost immediately vanishes into dense vegetation. Roosts, on occasion, on low branches up to 2–3 m above ground. If flushed, takes wing for a rather short, awkward glide, during which its short wings can be observed, and then dashes for safety on foot.

VOICE: Fairly vocal, utters rather brief, raucous, plaintive *koo-ah* decreasing in volume, repeated several times at intervals of a few dozen seconds and often taken up by others.

HABITAT: Densest parts of undisturbed rain forest, luxuriant second growth. Observed at elevations from sea level to 2,500 m. Seems more common at higher elevations.

DIET: Chiefly insects (Coleoptera, Orthoptera, Lepidoptera), but also fruits and seeds.

NESTING: Few data. Nest of dry stalks, palm fibers, and large leaves is built 5–7 m up in base of first leaves of Pandanus (*Pandanus* sp.—Pandanaceae) or on arborescent fern (*Asplenium nidus*—Aspleniaceae). Clutch numbers 2 chalky, dull white eggs (average size: 36.0 mm × 28.1 mm). Nesting has been observed Sept.–Jan., peaking Oct.–Dec.

DISTRIBUTION AND STATUS: Endemic to Madagascar, distributed in e from Tolagnaro to Sambava and in nw in Tsaratanana and Sambirano forests. Fairly common throughout range.

156. *Running Coua*

Coua cursor Grandidier, 1867
Malagasy: Aliotse, Kadibake
French: Coua coureur

DESCRIPTION: Length 40 cm. *Adult.* Sexes similar. Green-gray crown and back of neck. Skin around eyes ultramarine blue below, sky blue above and behind eyes, marked with roseate-red spot behind eyes and surrounded by black line, thicker below. Whitish chin and throat, tan sides of neck. Black bill, dark brown iris. Upperparts green-gray, darker on uppertail coverts. Underparts: chest maroon except for tan upper portion, white belly. Black tarsi and toes. Green-gray wings. Gray-green tail tipped with white, except for monocolored central tail feathers. *Immature.* Differs from adult by duller overall plumage, less vivid hue of skin around eyes, flesh-colored bill, and fawn apical spot on feathers of wings and upperparts.

IDENTIFICATION: Medium-sized coua with slender silhouette, fairly long legged, with plumage pale green above and light below, and blue skin around eyes marked with red spot behind eyes. Easily distinguished from Giant coua by considerably smaller size, slim silhouette, much lighter upperparts, and nonrufous underparts. Distinguished from Red-capped coua (subspecies *C. r. olivaceiceps*) by tan sides of neck and upper chest and by red spot of skin around eyes surrounded by finer black line.

BEHAVIOR: Terrestrial and secretive, behavior very similar to that of Coquerel's coua.

VOICE: Fairly vocal, utters loud, clear *kewkewkewkookoor*, as well as muted grunts. A call made from the ground, *ayreeyoo*, has also been recorded.

HABITAT: Subarid thorn scrub and dry woodlands free of grassy vegetation. Will also frequent second growth adjacent to biotopes of origin, provided trees and bushes are not too widely spaced. Observed at elevations from sea level to 200 m.

DIET: Insects.

NESTING: Bowl-shaped nest made of twigs and bits of bark. Receptacle lined with leafstalks. Nest built in bush, 2 m above ground. Clutch numbers 2 whitish eggs (average size: 34.4 mm × 22.6 mm). Nesting has been observed in Nov.

DISTRIBUTION AND STATUS: Endemic to Madagascar, thinly distributed in S Domain (Morombe marks n limit).

157. *Red-capped Coua*

Coua ruficeps Gray, 1846
Malagasy: Aliotse, Akoky, Gory, Beloha
French: Coua à tête rousse

DESCRIPTION: Length 42 cm.
Adult. Sexes similar.
  Nominate subspecies *C. r. ruficeps*.
  Front and top of head bright rufous. Skin around eyes ultramarine blue delimited by heavy black line below. Whitish chin and throat, maroon neck. Black bill, dark brown iris. Upperparts light brown except for rust brown uppertail coverts. Underparts rufous-tan except for maroon chest. Black tarsi and toes. Light brown

wings, dark brown tail tipped with white on external tail feathers.
  Subspecies *C. r. olivaceiceps* (Sharpe, 1875).
  Differs from *C. r. ruficeps* by light brown-green crown, tan-gray belly and undertail coverts, and paler upperparts, wings, and tail.
Immature. Differs from adult by generally duller plumage, light brown crown, less extensive and less vividly colored skin around eyes, flesh-colored bill, and fawn apical spot on feathers of upperparts and wings.

IDENTIFICATION: Large coua with slender, long-legged silhouette, light brown above, partially maroon below, with evenly colored skin around eyes accentuated by heavy black line. Distinguished from Coquerel's coua by slimmer silhouette, emphasized by longer neck, small head, and long legs, bright rufous head, maroon chest, and solid blue skin around eyes. Distinguished from Running coua by larger size and solid blue skin around eyes surrounded by much heavier black line.

BEHAVIOR: Terrestrial, found alone, in pairs, or in family groups. Movements are rather deliberate, body held horizontal and tail in line with back. If disturbed or surprised, draws itself up, stretches neck, raises tail, and walks away. If alarmed, runs away in a succession of swift bounds or takes wing for heavy glide of a few meters. Often ends dash for safety by finding refuge just above ground in bush or tree branches. May take advantage of terrain to escape danger, for example by hiding behind termite mound. At daybreak can often be seen atop a bush, in a clearing, at the edge of a wooded area, or on a forest trail, warming itself, feathers ruffled and wings drooping.

VOICE: Vocal, utters loud *hug yew yew yew kuh kuh*, with last 2 syllables pitched lower. Song is more rapid than that of other couas of same area. Brief grunts and series of muted grunts have also been noted. A loud call, sort of *coy coy coy coy coy* similar to that of Crested coua but lower pitched, has been noted at dusk.

HABITAT: Dry deciduous forest, sub-arid thorn scrub, second growth following degradation of original settings. Sometimes encountered in woodland savanna where grassy cover is not too dense. Only terrestrial coua to frequent degraded forest habitats and lightly wooded terrain with even moderate grass cover and to show itself in open terrain. Observed at elevations from sea level to 850 m.

DIET: Chiefly insects, occasionally fruits and berries.

NESTING: Shallow bowl-shaped nest of thin branches, old pieces of bark, and creepers is built 2–10 m above ground in tree. Receptacle is lined with finer material. Clutch numbers 2 white eggs tinged with dull blue (average size: 34.8 mm × 27.8 mm). Nesting has been observed Nov.–Dec.

DISTRIBUTION AND STATUS: Endemic to Madagascar, distributed in w and s. *C. r. ruficeps* is distributed in w and s from Mahajanga to vicinity of Morondava. Common throughout range and particularly abundant in forest of Ankarafantsika and Kinkony Lake. *C. r. olivaceiceps* is distributed in s from Morondava to Anony Lake, where it is common. Like other terrestrial couas, Red-capped coua is target of trapping and hunting.

158. *Crested Coua*

Coua cristata (Linnaeus, 1766)
Malagasy: Tivoka, Abosanga, Tokambolo, Tsikokofotsy, Tsiloko
French: Coua huppé

DESCRIPTION: Length 40–44 cm.
Adult. Sexes similar.
    Nominate subspecies *C. c. cristata* (Sclater, 1924).
    Pearl gray crested head, neck, chin, and throat. Violet skin around eyes, pearly sky-blue behind eye and surrounded by black line, the top part of which is more pronounced. Black bill, dark brown iris. Upperparts green-gray, darker on rump and uppertail coverts. Underparts white except for orangy fawn lower chest and maroon upper chest. Black tarsi and toes. Green-gray wings, midnight blue tail with purple-violet metallic sheen, broadly tipped with white on external tail feathers.
    Subspecies *C. c. dumonti* (Dumont, 1932).
    Differs from C. c. cristata by larger size, generally paler plumage, longer crest, faintly rufous-tinged undertail coverts, and more extensive white apical part of external tail feathers.
    Subspecies *C. c. pyropyga* (Milne Edwards and Grandidier, 1881).
    Differs from 2 preceding subspecies by larger size, paler plumage, and especially bright rufous tinge of undertail coverts.
    Subspecies *C. c. maxima* (Milon, 1950).
    Larger and darker than all other subspecies.
Immature. Differs from adult by very limited area of skin around eyes reduced to dull blue trace behind eyes, flesh-colored bill, gray chin, throat, and chest, and feathers of upperparts and wings marked by russet apical spot.

IDENTIFICATION: Large arboreal coua with powerful but streamlined silhouette, gray head with crest and marked by sky blue skin around eyes, green-gray upperparts and light underparts with gray throat and orangy fawn chest, and long midnight blue tail having external tail feathers marked with white on their apical quarter. In flight, field marks are short, round wings and long midnight blue tail tipped with white. Can be confused only with Verreaux's coua, from which it differs by larger size, gray chin and throat, orangy fawn chest, and rufous undertail coverts.

BEHAVIOR: Arboreal species seen alone, in pairs, or in family groups. Feeds in trees, searching dense foliage or inspecting branches. Moves by walking, running, and hopping on branches. Its explorations often lead to top of tree, from where it changes trees with long, elegant gliding flight. Sometimes seen on the ground, hopping and searching carpet of dead leaves. If excited, stretches neck, raises crest almost vertically from forehead, and slowly wags tail. If disturbed, hides in foliage and climbs to upper branches before taking wing for short, gliding flight. In early morning can often be seen perched atop bush or tree, basking in sunshine, feathers ruffled and wings drooping.

VOICE: Vocal, its call is loud and clear *coy coy coy coy* . . . , the syllables well separated and decreasing in volume. Call is immediately taken up by others nearby. Such choruses are especially common an hour before sunset and sometimes at night. Also utters series of muted grunts.

HABITAT: Original forest types, also second growth. Observed at elevations from sea level to 900 m.

DIET: Chiefly insects (Orthoptera, Lepidoptera, Hemiptera, Coleoptera), also mollusks, small vertebrates (*Chamaeleo* sp.), berries, fruits.

NESTING: Shallow bowl-shaped nest of twigs and rootlets is built 4–15 m above ground in tree. Clutch numbers 2 dull white eggs (average size: 34.7 mm × 26.5 mm). Nesting has been observed Nov.–Dec.

DISTRIBUTION AND STATUS: Endemic to Madagascar, distributed throughout territory at appropriate altitudes. *C. c. cristata* is uncommon in e, common in n and w to Mahajanga. *C. c. dumonti* is common w from Mahajanga to Morondava. *C. c. pyropyga* is very common in w and s between Morondava and Toliara and uncommon in s to Amboasary. *C. c. maxima* is very rare, known only by specimen collected near Tolagnaro. Crested coua has widest range of couas, most common and best adapted to degraded forest.

159. *Verreaux's Coua*

Coua verreauxi Grandidier, 1867
Malagasy: Tivoka, Arefy
French: Coua de Verreaux

DESCRIPTION: Length 38 cm. *Adult.* Sexes similar. Green-gray head with light gray crest darkening at apical quarter. Ultramarine skin around eyes, rearmost portion pearly sky blue. White chin and throat. Black bill, dark brown iris. Upperparts light green-gray, underparts white. Black tarsi and toes. Green-gray wings. Dark blue tail with metallic sheen, white markings on apical third of external tail feathers.

IDENTIFICATION: Small arboreal coua with solid green-gray plumage above, white below, gray crested head, small blue area of skin around eyes and long, dark blue tail broadly tipped with white. In flight, field marks are short, round wings and long, dark, white-tipped tail. Easily distinguished from Crested coua by noticeably smaller size, uniformly white underparts, small area of skin around eyes not accentuated with black, and thinner bill.

BEHAVIOR: Little known. Arboreal and active, found alone, in pairs, or in family groups, behaves similarly to Crested coua, in whose company it is sometimes encountered. Feeds in bushes and vegetation of subarid thorn scrub, occasionally descending to ground to take prey. Spends long intervals motionless in uppermost part of shrub or tree. Flight, like that of Crested coua, begins with swift wingbeats, then changes to gliding period at end of which it alights on new perch, sometimes only to continue journey using same procedure.

VOICE: Fairly vocal. One of its calls, *coy coy coy* repeated 3–4 times, suggests briefer, shriller version of that of Crested coua. Loud, dissonant *quark quark* followed by soft *coo coo* also reported. At dusk, loud *trew-ee trew-ee trew-ee* followed by solemn, less audible *crow crow crow* is uttered from dense foliage of bush or tree and often taken up by others.

HABITAT: Subarid thorn scrub of bushes and small trees (*Alluaudia dumosa, A. procera*—Didiereaceae, and *Euphorbia tirucali, E. stenoclada*—Euphorbiaceae) growing on sandy or calcareous soil and adjoining degraded areas. Observed at elevations from sea level to 100 m.

DIET: Few data. Chiefly insects, also fruit of *Cassia meridionalis*—Cesalpiniaceae.

NESTING: No data.

DISTRIBUTION AND STATUS: Endemic to Madagascar, located in s between Fiherenana River and Mandrare River (which forms n and e boundary of range). Fairly common between Onilahy and Menarandra rivers. Observations e of the Menarandra (Cap Sainte-Marie, Beloha, Tsiombe, Berenty) are recent.

160. *Blue Coua*

Coua caerulea (Linnaeus, 1766)
Malagasy: Taitso, Mariha, Taitso mainty, Taitso manga
French: Coua bleu

DESCRIPTION: Length 50 cm.
Adult. Sexes similar. Dark blue head. Ultramarine skin around eyes, sky blue or pearly turquoise behind eyes. Black bill, dark brown iris. Dark blue upperparts and underparts. Black tarsi and toes. Dark blue wings with violet metallic sheen on remiges. Dark blue tail with violet metallic sheen.
Immature. Differs from adult by absence of bare skin around eyes, by dark brown back of belly, back, and rump, and by absence of violet sheen on remiges.

IDENTIFICATION: Large arboreal coua with bulky silhouette, short wings, long, broad tail, entirely dark blue plumage, and pearly sky-blue skin around eyes. Cannot be confused with any other species.

BEHAVIOR: Strictly arboreal, not shy, found alone, in pairs, or in family groups. Slowly and carefully inspects foliage, base of palms, and epiphytic ferns as it feeds. Moves by walking or hopping on horizontal branches, adopting varied postures, now vertical, then horizontal, tail raised well above line of back, and goes from tree to tree in short glides. To cross open spaces (rivers, clearings, roads), undertakes long, rather heavy gliding flights from top of tree, during which characteristic dark silhouette, short wings, and long, broad tail are evident. Arrival is often announced with typical brief, trilled call. Often seen sunning on a branch after rain, feathers ruffled, wings drooping, and tail low and spread out.

VOICE: Vocal, with varied but unmelodious repertory. Most common call is brief, accented, trilled, rather shrill *brrree-ee* increasing in volume, characteristic enough to permit bird's location and immediate identification. Also utters, usually in late afternoon, loud series of spaced *coy coy coy coy* decreasing in intensity, reminiscent of Crested coua and Red-breasted coua but louder and lower pitched. This call is delivered with wide-open bill and slightly trembling wings and tail. Also reported is brief, muted contact call resembling grunt of Brown lemur *(Lemur fulvus)*: *kroo kroo* or *krong krong.*

HABITAT: Undisturbed evergreen rain forest, adjacent second growth when trees are not too widely spaced, also dense tree plantations (cloves). Observed at elevations from sea level to 1,800 m. Very locally, in forests of Bora, Analamera, and Ankarana, occupies deciduous dry forest.

DIET: Insects (Hemiptera, Orthoptera, Lepidoptera, Coleoptera, Diptera), small reptiles (*Chamaeleo* spp., *Brookesia* spp., *Phelsuma* spp.), also fruits and occasionally gums.

NESTING: Few data. Domed nest, built 3.5–10 m above ground in dense foliage of tree or other vegetation, consists of interlaced dry vegetal matter. Clutch numbers 1 small white egg. Nesting has been observed July–Nov.

DISTRIBUTION AND STATUS: Endemic to Madagascar, distributed in e from Sambava to Tolagnaro and in nw in Tsaratanana and Sambirano forests, also locally in vicinity of Antsohihy (Bora forest) and in n in Ankarana and Analamera forests. No sightings from Montagne d'Ambre. Common throughout range.

161. *Madagascar Coucal*

Centropus toulou (Müller, 1776)
Malagasy: Toloho, Kotohake, Monjo
French: Coucal malgache

DESCRIPTION: Length 45–50 cm.
Adult. Sexes similar. Plumage varies seasonally.
Breeding Plumage. Shiny black head, neck, chin, and throat. Black bill and red iris. Upperparts black except for bright rufous back. Underparts black. Black tarsi and toes. Bright rufous wings, shiny black tail.
Nonbreeding Plumage. Head, neck, chin, and throat heavily striped with tan. Roseate-brown bill, red iris. Upperparts: heavy tan stripes on black mantle, rufous back, black rump, and uppertail coverts. Underparts black except for heavy tan striping of chest. Black tarsi and toes. Rufous wings, black tail.
Immature. Similar to adult in nonbreeding plumage.

IDENTIFICATION: Large black bird with long, graduated, shiny black tail and bright rufous wings. Outside breeding season, black is heavily striped with tan. Flight silhouette is characteristic, with long tail and short, round wings. Cannot be confused with any other species.

BEHAVIOR: Vigilant, feeds in dense undergrowth. Adept at moving about in tangled vegetation, sometimes almost crawling. Moves effortlessly on branches, hops rather heavily on ground, where it is often seen. Seldom flies, preferring to move in familiar network of bushes. Laborious flight consists of vigorous but ineffective wingbeats followed by long glide that brings it to new thicket. During nesting season its presence prompts aggressive reaction from passerines (Madagascar paradise flycatcher, Madagascar red fody, Madagascar mannikin), whose nests it frequently raids. If alarmed, withdraws into densest foliage, accompanying flight with a threatening hiss. If plant cover is insufficient, will fly to denser growth. Generally partly concealed when spotted, except in early morning or after rain, when it perches atop bush or other fairly low vantage point and suns itself, ruffling feathers, letting wings droop slightly away from body, and spreading tail.

VOICE: Highly vocal, usually utters sonorous but muffled *toogoo toogoo toogoo . . .* decreasing in volume, usually in early morning and late afternoon, sometimes at night. Final elements of call follow each other more slowly and trail off. Two or 3 birds in separate locations may utter this call, timing their responses so as to create an echo effect. Frequently emits, for purposes of intimidation, an eerie, sudden, guttural, hissing *Choogooo . . .* which it holds for a few seconds.

HABITAT: Any habitat that provides dense vegetation or underbrush: different types of original forest, second growth, mangroves, reedbeds, rice paddies, cropland, town and village gardens. Observed at elevations from sea level to 1,800 m.

DIET: Invertebrates: large insects (Coleoptera, Orthoptera, Hemiptera), spiders, also such small vertebrates as lizards, chameleons, chicks, and eggs.

NESTING: Voluminous domed, spherical nest, woven from dry grasses, is built low off ground (1–4 m) in dense bush, shrub, or tree with dense foliage. Clutch numbers 3 smooth white eggs (average size: 30.4 mm × 21.1 mm). Both parents incubate. Nesting has been observed Sept.–Mar.

DISTRIBUTION AND STATUS: Distributed in Madagascar and Aldabra. Represented in Madagascar by endemic nominate subspecies *C. t. toulou*, common throughout island.

Strigiformes

Tytonidae – Red Owl, Barn Owl

Nocturnal birds of prey with large for-ward-facing eyes, soft and supple plum-age, and silent flight, distinguished from other nocturnal birds of prey by the un-broken outline of their unique facial mask (2 upper curves joining on forehead), the pectinated internal edge of the middle toe claw, and the absence of feathers on tarsi to base of toes (feathers scattered on the lower part of the toes). The family is rep-resented by 12 species, some of which are widely distributed. Two species, 1 en-demic, nest in Madagascar.

162. *Madagascar Red Owl*

Tyto soumagnei (Grandidier, 1878)
French: Effraie de Soumagne

DESCRIPTION: Length 30 cm.
Adult. Sexes similar. Orangy head, crown sprinkled with sooty dots. Facial disk tinged orangy white, more pronounced toward top, and fringed with orange. Yel-lowish white bill. Orangy upperparts, un-derparts, and wings, sprinkled with black dots; lighter chest. Feathered tarsi and light brown toes. Orangy and faintly barred short tail, extending past points of wings by 2 cm.
Immature. Unknown.

IDENTIFICATION: Small owl, smaller by one-third than Common barn owl. Madagascar red owl is easily distin-guished from all other nocturnal birds by wide facial disk and overall orangy hue.

BEHAVIOR: Very few data. Strictly noc-turnal forest species, living alone or in pairs.

VOICE: Reported to emit a *wok wok wok*, as well as a brief, resonant call of alarm.

HABITAT: Strictly evergreen undisturbed rain forest. Observed or collected at elevations of 900–1,200 m.

DIET: Batrachians.

NESTING: Unknown.

DISTRIBUTION AND STATUS: Endemic to Madagascar, very rare, with only 1 sighting in past half-century, near Andasibe. Old records are based on birds collected at Analamazoatra and Fito in Sihanaka forest. One of 4 endemic species observed or collected fewer than 3 times in past 50 years.

163. Common Barn Owl

Tyto alba (Scopoli, 1769)
Malagasy: Tararaka, Vorondolo, Hekoheko
French: Chouette effraie

DESCRIPTION: Length 32–36 cm, wingspan 90 cm.
Adult. Sexes similar. Gray head finely dotted with white. White facial disk edged with tan and marked with brown on internal sides of eyes. Ivory bill, dark brown iris. Gray upperparts speckled with brown and white. Underparts: tan-white chest speckled with brown, white belly speckled with brown, white undertail coverts. Feathered tarsi and yellowish toes. Wings orangy gray and tan above, white below, remiges barred with orangy tan and gray above, white with brown stripes below. Orangy tan and brown-gray bars on tail. Points of wings extend about 3 cm past tail.

IDENTIFICATION: Easily identifiable by white underparts, gray-and-tan upperparts, and heart-shaped facial disk. Cannot be confused with any other species.

BEHAVIOR: Nocturnal, but commonly seen at dusk, rarely during day. Flies low to hunt, making sudden swoops and turns. Spends day perched upright in a dark, quiet place (tree hollow, building, belfry, cliff).

VOICE: Vocal, utters shrill, plaintive, quavering call in flight; hisses and snores when at rest.

HABITAT: Any open or moderately wooded environment, grassland savanna, shores of lakes and large rivers, rice paddies and other croplands, as well as towns and villages. Observed at elevations from sea level to 1,800 m.

DIET: Chiefly small mammals: rodents *(Rattus rattus)*, insectivores (Tenrecidae, Chiroptera), primates *(Microcebus murinus)*, also birds (Madagascar bee-eater, Madagascar bulbul, Madagascar red fody) and insects.

NESTING: Nests in hollow trees, rocky crevices, belfries, or uninhabited parts of houses. No structured nest. Clutch numbers 4–7 dull white eggs (average size: 40.5 mm × 31.1 mm). Only female broods. Nesting has been observed Apr.–July.

DISTRIBUTION AND STATUS: Cosmopolitan species distributed on 5 continents. Represented in Madagascar by subspecies *T. a. affinis* (Sclater, 1924), common to sub-Saharan Africa and Comoros. Distributed throughout Madagascar. Most widely and plentifully distributed nocturnal bird of prey on island. All evidence suggests species is increasing its numbers as it profits from degradation of great expanses of forest and spread of human population, even though the Common barn owl, more than other nocturnal birds of prey, is often persecuted as a bird of ill omen by villagers.

Strigidae – Owls

Nocturnal birds of prey characterized by a less pronounced facial disk than Tytonidae, generally incomplete and interrupted on forehead. They often have ear tufts and tarsi feathered to base of toes. Family is cosmopolitan and represented by more than 130 species. Four species nest in Madagascar, 2 endemic and 1 limited to Madagascar and the Comoros.

164. *Malagasy Scops-Owl*

Otus rutilus (Pucheran, 1849)
Malagasy: Kotoroka, Fitaliha, Torotoroka
French: Petit duc de Madagascar

DESCRIPTION: Length 22–24 cm, wingspan 53 cm.
Adult. Sexes similar. Plumage varies greatly among individuals. Gray to rufous-brown face, always with lighter area between bill and eyes. Brown to rufous-brown crown, finely flecked with dark brown. Earlike tufts. Black bill, yellow iris. Upperparts brown-gray to rufous-brown and finely flecked with dark brown. Underparts same but always lighter. White line on scapulars, created by succession of large white dots. Feathered tarsi, pink-gray toes, and black claws. Wings same color as upperparts, with primary remiges barred whitish on external half. Tail same color as upperparts.

IDENTIFICATION: Small nocturnal bird of prey (smallest of Madagascar), characterized by coloration varying from gray to rufous, earlike tufts, and yellow eyes.

BEHAVIOR: Forest species, strictly nocturnal, generally recognized and localized by call. Spends daylight hours concealed in thick foliage.

VOICE: Vocal, utters call at nightfall, sometimes all night: *hoo hoo hoo hoo hoo hoo hoo* or *broo broo broo*, 5–7 notes delivered at same pitch, but last 2 softer. This muffled, monotonous, slightly quavering call is uttered from perch, with owl usually concealed.

HABITAT: Various original forest types, as well as second growth and any wooded area, even artificially planted, and frequently encountered in villages. Observed at elevations from sea level to 1,800 m.

DIET: Chiefly insects.

NESTING: Few data. Nests in hollow trees, occasionally in abandoned nest. Clutch numbers 4–5 eggs. Nesting has been observed Nov.–Dec.

DISTRIBUTION AND STATUS: Distributed in Madagascar and Comoros. Represented in Madagascar by endemic nominate subspecies *O. r. rutilus*, common in all woodlands of Madagascar except those of High Plateau, where it is rare (Ambohitantely, Antananarivo).

165. *White-browed Owl*

Ninox superciliaris (Vieillot, 1823)
Malagasy: Tovotovoka, Vorondolo
French: Ninox à sourcils

DESCRIPTION: Length 30 cm.
Adult. Sexes similar. Brown crown sprinkled with white dots. Tan-gray face with white supercilia meeting on forehead. Light brown chin and throat. Whitish bill with numerous long vibrissae, brown iris. Upperparts uniform brown, sometimes marked with white dots on mantle. Underparts tan-white, boldly marked with brown bars that blur in middle, especially

on belly. Pure white undertail coverts. Tan feathered tarsi, yellow-white toes, brown claws. Upperside of wings brown with big white spots on upperwing coverts and primary remiges, underside brown-gray and spotted, with white underwing coverts. Brown tail.

IDENTIFICATION: Intermediate in size between Madagascar scops-owl and Madagascar long-eared owl. Field marks are plump silhouette, white supercilia, dark iris, and boldly barred underparts and, in flight, boldly spotted dark wings.

BEHAVIOR: Strictly nocturnal, often seen watching for prey on branch over-looking open space (road, trail, natural or artificial clearing). Generally located by its call, uttered frequently at night.

VOICE: Vocal. Characteristic call is a series of *kiang kiang . . .* , first 5 notes building in volume and pitch to a series of 15 intense notes. Overall effect is pow-erful, loud, and dissonant. Call is always preceded by a muffled bisyllabic *ho-o-o hoo.* Several individuals often heard call-ing to each other.

HABITAT: Subarid thorn scrub, de-ciduous dry forest, evergreen rain forest, also clearings, open terrain with few trees, even surroundings of villages. Ob-served at elevations from sea level to 800 m.

DIET: Chiefly insects.

NESTING: Few data. Nest, built on ground, holds 3–5 shiny white eggs. Nesting has been observed Oct.–Dec.

DISTRIBUTION AND STATUS: En-demic to Madagascar, distributed in s (Amboasary, Beza Mahafaly), w (Saka-raha, Morondava, Antsalova), and n (An-karana), where it is fairly common, also in E Region (Isalo, Marojejy, Pointe-à-Larrée, Mananara, Masoala Peninsula), where it is uncommon.

166. *Madagascar Long-eared Owl*

Asio madagascariensis (Smith, 1834)
Malagasy: Hanka, Ankana, Hakagna
French: Hibou de Madagascar

DESCRIPTION: *Male.* Length 40 cm. *Female.* Length 50 cm. *Adult.* Sexes similar. Female larger than male. Dark brown head flecked with tan. Tan face, dark brown around eyes with darker peripheral border. Long earlike tufts. Stout sooty bill with lighter point, orange iris. Upperparts variable, gener-ally dark brown mixed with tan, more in-tensely so on mantle. Underparts tan flecked with brown, except for solid tan undertail coverts. Stout, feathered tarsi and toes, sooty claws. Wings same color above as upperparts, outer half of remiges barred with tan and brown. Underside of wings tan, remiges barred with brown-gray and gray. Tail barred with dark and light brown.

IDENTIFICATION: Large owl charac-terized by brown plumage above and tan below and by earlike tufts. Cannot be confused with any other species.

BEHAVIOR: Few data. Strictly nocturnal forest species, very secretive. Spends day concealed in thick foliage.

VOICE: Sometimes utters, in isolation, loud, characteristic, lilting *han kan, han kan . . . .*

HABITAT: Evergreen rain forest, de-ciduous dry forest, and gallery forests of south, also secondary woodlands. Ob-served at elevations from sea level to 1,800 m.

DIET: Unknown.

NESTING: Very few data. Chick has en-tirely white down except for black mask. Earlike tufts are fully visible. Nesting has been observed Aug.–Oct.

DISTRIBUTION AND STATUS: Endemic to Madagascar, distributed in E Region, where it has been seen at numerous locations (Andapa, Maroantsetra, Sihanaka forest, Andasibe, Ranomafana, and forests of Sambirano and Montagne d'Ambre), on High Plateau (Tsimbazaza park at Antananarivo), and in W Region at Morondava and Berenty. Rare and secretive forest species. It is persecuted by villagers, who regard it, like all nocturnal birds of prey, as a bird of ill omen.

167. Marsh Owl

Asio capensis (Smith, 1834)
Malagasy: Vorondolo
French: Hibou du Cap

DESCRIPTION: Length 37–40 cm. *Adult.* Sexes similar. Light brown crown, tan-gray face except for dark brown eye patch. Small brown earlike tufts. Fairly stout dark gray bill, dark brown iris. Upperparts gray-brown. Underparts: gray-brown chest, white belly and undertail coverts with light brown stripes. Feathered tarsi, slightly feathered slate gray toes, slate gray claws. Upper side of wings brown, boldly barred with fawn on primary remiges. Underside brown with fawn bars. Brown tail barred with tan.

IDENTIFICATION: Large owl with stocky silhouette, uniformly dark upperparts, light underparts, dark eyes set off by light facial disk, and small earlike tufts. In flight, long, wide wings are solid brown except for barred primary remiges.

Distinguished from Common barn owl by larger size, much longer and less round wings, and somber upperparts.

BEHAVIOR: Crepuscular and nocturnal, hunts alone or in pairs. Sometimes 3–4 hunt a few hundred meters apart. Flies close to the ground. Flight is supple, slow, and follows zigzag course, powerful wingbeats interspersed with fast, frequent swerves—very similar to that of Réunion harrier. Often seen at rest on ground before nightfall.

VOICE: Call, heard as *kah-ah* uttered in flight or on the ground, is reminiscent of frog's croak.

HABITAT: Flat grasslands, preferably damp (lakeshores, marshes, rice paddies, croplands). Regularly encountered in towns. Observed at elevations from sea level to 1,500 m.

DIET: Insects (large Coleoptera), rodents (*Rattus rattus*), occasionally terrestrial birds (Madagascar buttonquail).

NESTING: Few data. Nest is simple hollow concealed in stand of vegetation of wetlands. Clutch numbers 2–4 white eggs. Chick has fawn-brown down with eyes contoured in black. Nesting has been observed Apr.–June.

DISTRIBUTION AND STATUS: Distributed in Africa and Madagascar. Represented in Madagascar by endemic subspecies *A. c. hova* (Stresemann, 1922), uncommon, with irregular distribution over entire island (Antananarivo and vicinity, Antsirabe, Alaotra Lake, Iharanä, and Ihotry and Tsimanampetsotsa lakes).

Caprimulgiformes

Caprimulgidae – Nightjars

Nocturnal insectivores with soft sandy or earth-colored plumage resembling that of the nocturnal birds of prey. They seize their prey on the wing at dusk and at night. They have a very short, very widely cleft bill equipped with long vibrissae, large eyes, short legs, and long, pointed wings. Nightjars spend the daylight hours on the ground or perched on a tree branch. The family is cosmopolitan and represented by 75 species. Two nest in Madagascar, 1 endemic and 1 limited to Madagascar and Aldabra.

168. *Madagascar Nightjar*

Caprimulgus madagascariensis
Sganzin, 1840
Malagasy: Tataro, Ofaka, Langopaka, Lopaka, Goapaka, Matoriandro, Tatarovorona, Tatarofatrama
French: Engoulevent de Madagascar

DESCRIPTION: Length 21 cm. *Adult.* Sexes similar. Dull gray head with brown cap. Brown cheeks, chin, and throat with tan line stretching from throat to ear. Gray nape and neck. Short, wide sooty bill with rather short vibrissae. Brown iris. Upperparts brown-gray flecked with black. Underparts: dark brown chest marked with small lighter spots. Light brown belly and undertail coverts with fine brown stripes. Brown scapulars marked with tan. Very short gray legs. Wings brown above, light brown barred with dark brown below. Dark brown primary remiges with white bar in the middle of first 4. Tail same color as upperparts, with apical one-third of 4 external tail feathers white.

IDENTIFICATION: Characterized by generally grayish hue and by broad white patch on wings, visible even when at rest. Distinguished from Collared nightjar by smaller size, coloration, and wing patch.

BEHAVIOR: Crepuscular and nocturnal, seen over open terrain from nightfall. Seizes prey in fluttering flight. Spends daylight hours concealed on leaf litter.

VOICE: Vocal. Song, highly distinctive and delivered at night from perch in full view, has been compared to sound that would be made by a ping-pong ball bouncing on a glass surface: a tight series of crisp notes. These are preceded by a brief, muted *cop cop cop* and cooing that cannot be heard from afar.

HABITAT: All habitats except for dense forests. Particularly fond of open or lightly wooded terrain (partially or totally degraded woodlands, plantations, croplands, urban areas). Commonly seen at rest on roads or trails at dusk. Observed at elevations from sea level to 1,800 m.

DIET: Insects.

NESTING: Nest is slight hollow fashioned in carpet of dead leaves in clearing or open forest. Clutch numbers 2 white eggs spotted brown-gray. Chick is partly nidifugous. Nesting has been observed Oct.–Nov.

DISTRIBUTION AND STATUS: Distributed in Madagascar and Aldabra. Represented in Madagascar by endemic nominate subspecies *C. m. madagascariensis*, common throughout island.

169. *Collared Nightjar*

Caprimulgus enarratus Gray, 1871
Malagasy: Matoriandro, Tataroala
French: Engoulevent à collier

DESCRIPTION: Length 24 cm, wingspan 40 cm.

Adult. Sexes similar. Dull brown crown with rufous and black scales, brown cheeks, tan chin and throat. Narrow tan collar and wide, bright rufous collar. Short (1 cm), wide, pink-gray bill with black point and long black vibrissae. Brown iris. Upperparts brown with black scales. Underparts variable in color: chest scaly in appearance, predominantly rufous-brown with black spots, tan belly and undertail coverts finely striped with brown. Very short pink-gray legs. Upper side of wings and scapulars have brown, black, and tan scales. Brown primary remiges with tan bars on external border. Underside of wings entirely gray-brown. Long brown black-barred tail, with white tips on 4 external tail feathers.

IDENTIFICATION: Forest nightjar with disproportionately large head and scaly-appearing plumage with wide, bright rufous collar. Distinguished from Madagascar nightjar by larger size, rufous collar, and absence of white wing patch.

BEHAVIOR: Very little known, strictly forest species. Spends daylight hours on ground, concealed among roots or on carpet of dead leaves.

VOICE: Unknown.

HABITAT: Undisturbed rain forest of e, occasionally adjacent second growth and some deciduous dry forests. Observed at elevations from sea level to 1,800 m.

DIET: Insects.

NESTING: Very few data. Clutch numbers 2 mottled brown eggs laid on forest floor. Nesting has been observed Oct.–Nov.

DISTRIBUTION AND STATUS: Endemic to Madagascar, distributed in e (Andapa, Maroantsetra, Analamazaotra, Ranomafana) and in n and nw (Montagne d'Ambre, Ankarana, Tsaratanana, Sambirano). Secretive, rather rare species.

Apodiformes

Apodidae – Swifts

Swifts have extremely short tarsi and all 4 toes pointing forward, so that they can neither perch nor move on the ground. They are airborne almost constantly and feed on insects caught on the wing. The wings of swifts are long and pointed, while their tail is generally short and often forked. They are gregarious, and several species are migratory but faithful to their nesting sites. The family is cosmopolitan, and 84 species are generally recognized. Four nest in Madagascar: 3 that are widely distributed, and a fourth local to Madagascar and the Comoros. A fifth species nests in the Mascarenes and has been sighted in Madagascar.

170. *Mascarene Swiftlet*

Collocalia francica (Gmelin, 1788)
French: Salangane des Mascareignes
No Map

DESCRIPTION: Length 10.5 cm.
Adult. Sexes similar. Dark brown head, pale brown chin and throat. Upperparts dark brown except for dirty white upper-tail coverts. Underparts: pale brown chest, lighter belly and undertail coverts. Dark brown wings, black-brown tail.

IDENTIFICATION: Very small swift with highly characteristic silhouette: long, narrow wings and very short, slightly indented tail. Plumage dark above, with whitish marks on rump, and pale brown below.

DISTRIBUTION AND STATUS: Breeds on Mascarenes and on many Asian islands. Accidental migrant to Madagascar, where it has only been sighted once.

171. *Malagasy Spine-tailed Swift*

Zoonavena grandidieri (Verreaux, 1867)
Malagasy: Fangalamoty, Tsidisidina, Manaviandro
French: Martinet de Grandidier

DESCRIPTION: Length 12 cm.
Adult. Sexes similar. Gray-brown head, whitish chin and throat. Upperparts gray-brown, paler on rump. Underparts grayish except for brownish belly. Wings brown with whitish secondary remiges. Brown tail.

IDENTIFICATION: Small swift having rather long, narrow wings marked with a light wing bar, a short, square tail, and brown plumage above with paler rump, light below with brownish chest. Easily distinguished from other swifts by considerably smaller size, square tail, and light wing bar. Flight is fairly fast but slower than that of other swifts, slightly fluttering, seldom holding straight line for long.

BEHAVIOR: Not very gregarious, found in pairs or in small, loose-knit groups of 3–15. Hunts just above canopy, around and over stands of trees, generally in restricted space.

VOICE: Rather silent, occasionally utters shrill, brief *zree* while hunting, sometimes several times in succession.

HABITAT: Hunts over various original forest types, second growth, and savanna, around stands of trees (preferably big, tall trees), in clearings, and over pools, lakes, rivers, and all wetlands. Observed at elevations from sea level to 1,000 m.

DIET: Insects.

NESTING: Very few data. Nest, an agglomeration of stems and other plant materials, is built in a crevice, rocky hollow, hollow tree, or well. Nesting suspected Apr.–Jan.

DISTRIBUTION AND STATUS: Distributed in Madagascar and Comoros. Represented in Madagascar by endemic subspecies *A. g. grandidieri*. Appears sedentary. Distributed throughout Madagascar except in High Plateau. Common in e, less common in w and s.

172. *African Palm Swift*

Cypsiurus parvus (Lichtenstein, 1823)
Malagasy: Fangalamoty, Tsidisidina, Manaviandro
French: Martinet des palmes

DESCRIPTION: Length 17 cm.
Adult. Sexes similar. Brown head, whitish chin and throat. Upperparts and underparts brown except for lighter chest. Brown wings and tail.

IDENTIFICATION: Medium-sized swift with delicate, slender silhouette, long, narrow wings, very long and deeply indented tail (often held tight in flight, masking indentation), brown plumage, and light throat. Cannot be confused with any other species.

BEHAVIOR: Fairly gregarious, found in small monospecific groups of 2–8, growing in numbers as twilight approaches. Roosts in palms, clinging to base or underside of leaves.

VOICE: Rather vocal, utters very shrill, fairly brief *zrezrezeh* . . . mostly at roosts and nesting sites, also while hunting.

HABITAT: Closely associated with presence of palms, preferably tall and near water (lakes, rivers, rice paddies) at low elevations. Observed at elevations from sea level to 800 m.

DIET: Insects.

NESTING: Few data. Nest, made of feathers bonded with saliva, is attached to base of lower surface of palm leaf. Clutch numbers 2–3 white eggs. Nesting has been observed Sept.–Oct.

DISTRIBUTION AND STATUS: Distributed in sub-Saharan Africa, Comoros, and Madagascar. Represented in Madagascar by endemic subspecies *C. p. gracilis* (Sharpe, 1871), common on all coastal plains except in s, where it is rarer.

173. *Alpine Swift*

Apus melba (Linnaeus, 1758)
Malagasy: Fangalamoty, Tsidisidina, Poadranofotsy
French: Martinet à ventre blanc

DESCRIPTION: Length 20 cm, wingspan 52 cm.
Adult. Sexes similar. Gray-brown head, white chin and throat. Upperparts gray-brown, underparts white except for gray-brown breastband, flanks, and undertail coverts. Brown wings and tail.
Immature. Differs from adult by whitish fringed remiges.

IDENTIFICATION: Large swift with long, narrow, strongly arched wings, indented tail, brown plumage above and white below, and brown breastband. Cannot be confused with any other species.

BEHAVIOR: Very gregarious, found in loose-knit or dense monospecific flocks of a few dozen to several hundred. Sometimes associated with African black swift. Congregates in denser, larger flocks as dusk approaches. Roosts are established in walls or rocky cavities, where birds cling overnight. Calls during frantic flights in vicinity of roosts.

VOICE: Vocal around roosts. Call is a trilled, shrill, whistling *keerrreeteerreerr.*

HABITAT: Any biotope where food is abundant. Hunts over forests, savanna, mountains, marshes, rice paddies, cotton fields. Observed at elevations from sea level to 1,800 m.

DIET: Insects.

NESTING: Never observed in Madagascar. Suspected in various rocky sites.

DISTRIBUTION AND STATUS: Distributed in Europe, Africa, and Asia. Represented in Madagascar by endemic subspecies *A. m. willsi* (Hartert, 1896), which seems to be sedentary. It is very similar, however, to the African subspecies, hindering determination of migratory movements. Seen throughout Madagascar, but moves en masse in response to weather conditions that cause considerable variation in food available (such as cyclonic rains). Entire regions will be abandoned when food becomes scarce, population moving to better-supplied areas. On such occasions, flocks of several hundred swifts may be seen, their great flying ability enabling them to cover long distances rapidly. Nesting sites could be located in rocky terrain of Ankazobe, Isalo, or Andringitra regions.

174. *African Black Swift*

Apus barbatus (Sclater, 1865)
Malagasy: Fangalamoty, Tsidisidina
French: Martinet noir africain

DESCRIPTION: Length 17 cm, wingspan 40 cm.
Adult. Sexes similar. Black head, whitish chin and throat. Rather shiny black upperparts and underparts. Black wings and tail.

IDENTIFICATION: Medium-sized swift with long, narrow wings, indented tail, and entirely black plumage except for whitish throat. Typical fast flight of swifts. Distinguished from African palm swift and Malagasy spine-tailed swift by larger size, uniform, somber plumage, and slightly forked tail.

BEHAVIOR: Gregarious, found in monospecific flocks varying in size from several dozen to 1,000–2,000, sometimes associated with Alpine swift. Sizable congregations often seen at dusk.

VOICE: Whole flocks utter loud, shrill *sreeee, sreeee . . . .*

HABITAT: Any biotope where food is abundant. Hunts over forests, savanna, mountains, marshes, rice paddies, and cotton fields. Observed at elevations from sea level to 1,800 m.

DIET: Insects.

NESTING: Few data. Nest of grassy stems, plant fibers, and feathers bonded with saliva is built in crevice or cavity of cliff or rocky island. Clutch numbers 2 white eggs. Nesting has been observed Nov.–Mar.

DISTRIBUTION AND STATUS: Distributed in sub-Saharan Africa and represented in Madagascar by endemic subspecies *A. b. balstoni* (Bartlett, 1879). Its sedentariness on the island is disputed by population decline noted Apr.–July in sw, Apr.–Sept. on High Plateau, and by observation of large flocks coming from nw over Mozambique Channel near Antsiranana and from sw over the sea by Cap Sainte-Marie in Mar. However, no capture of the Malagasy subspecies has been effected in Africa to confirm such a hypothetical migration. Seen throughout Madagascar; like Alpine swift, moves en masse in response to weather conditions and may temporarily disappear from given region. Several thousand birds may then be seen congregating. Nesting has been observed on rocky islands s of Morombe and Maroantsetra and in rock faces of High Plateau.

Coraciiformes

Alcedinidae – Kingfishers

Generally sedentary birds, with long, stout, pointed bill, short wings, and short legs, with the third and fourth toes fused for their entire length and the second and third toes fused at the base. Kingfishers generally feed on small fish that they catch by diving; some also eat other vertebrates, and others are insectivores that frequent habitats far from water. All representatives of the family nest in burrows. The family is cosmopolitan and represented by more than 90 species. Two species nest in Madagascar, one endemic and the other confined to Madagascar and the Comoros.

175. *Malagasy Kingfisher*

Corythornis vintsioides
Eydoux and Gervais, 1836
Malagasy: Vintsy, Litotsy, Vintsirano
French: Martin-pêcheur malachite

DESCRIPTION: Length 15 cm.
Adult. Sexes similar. Light blue crown with fairly long erectile feathers. Electric-blue stripe behind eyes and along nape and back of neck. Rest of head bright orange. White chin and throat. Sides of neck orange and marked with bold white stripe extending to back of neck. Black bill, red commissures, dark brown iris. Upperparts electric blue. Underparts: sides of chest, flanks, and undertail coverts bright orange, rest of chest and belly paler orange. Red tarsi and toes. Ultramarine blue wings, black primary remiges, electric blue tail.
Immature. Differs from adult by generally duller and paler overall plumage and by whitish underparts with faint orangy tinge.

IDENTIFICATION: Small kingfisher, electric blue above and orange below, with sides of neck marked with a broad white stripe, compact silhouette, and long black bill. Flight typical of kingfishers: very fast, direct, and skimming. Cannot be confused with any other species.

BEHAVIOR: Aquatic, solitary, not shy, seen watching for prey on a branch, rock, raised bank, or any other high point near water. Seizes prey at surface following short, swift flight, then returns to perch to eat it. If excited, motions animatedly with head, and sometimes raises ornamental feathers on cap slightly. Quarrels are frequent and lead to chases during which the 2 birds utter chirping calls.

VOICE: Quiet, with limited vocal range. Utters very shrill *treeeeeee* on taking wing or while quarreling.

HABITAT: Any biotopes near fresh, brackish, or saltwater: lakes, ponds (even in forests), pools, rivers, streams, rice paddies, estuaries, mangroves, and seashores. Observed at elevations from sea level to 1,800 m.

DIET: Invertebrates (insects and crustaceans) and small vertebrates (frogs and fish).

NESTING: Nest is established at end of tunnel 40 cm long and 5 cm in diameter dug in rising ground very near water or in bank of watercourse. Chamber is bare or thinly lined with fish bones and scales. Clutch numbers 5–6 shiny white eggs (average size: 20.0 mm × 16.2 mm). Both parents incubate. Nesting has been observed Oct.–Mar.

DISTRIBUTION AND STATUS: Distributed in Comoros and Madagascar. In Madagascar, represented by nominate endemic subspecies *A. v. vintsioides*. Distributed throughout island, where it is common, except for s, where it is rather rare.

NOTE: This species forms a superspecies with the Malachite kingfisher *(Corythornis cristata)*.

176. *Madagascar Pygmy Kingfisher*

Ispidina madagascariensis (Linnaeus, 1766)
Malagasy: Vintsiala, Vintsimena
French: Martin-chasseur malgache

DESCRIPTION: Length 14 cm. *Adult.* Sexes similar. Head entirely bright rufous with violet or mauve sheen. White chin, throat, and stripe on side of neck. Long (25 mm), bright orange-red bill, dark brown iris. Upperparts bright rufous with violet sheen. Underparts white except for orangy rufous flanks. Bright orange tarsi and toes. Bright rufous wings except for dark gray primary and secondary remiges, the external half of the latter edged with rufous. Very short, bright rufous tail with violet shimmer.

IDENTIFICATION: Small kingfisher, orange-red above and white below, with stocky silhouette and long, stout, bright orange-red bill. Rapid, direct flight typical of kingfishers. Cannot be confused with any other species.

BEHAVIOR: Strictly forest species, secretive, usually found alone. To feed, waits in ambush on low branch in dense undergrowth, body twitching. Seizes prey on ground after lightning sally, following which bird carries it back to perch to eat it.

VOICE: Rather quiet. Utters brief high-pitched call, sort of *treet treet*. When flushed, utters very shrill *treeeeeee* on taking wing.

HABITAT: Dense undergrowth of evergreen rain forest and deciduous dry forest. Observed at elevations from sea level to 1,800 m.

DIET: Invertebrates, insects (Orthoptera, Coleoptera, Hymenoptera), spiders, and small vertebrates (frogs, lizards, chameleons).

NESTING: Nest is established at end of tunnel 30–35 cm long and 5 cm diameter, dug into a bank or mound. Embankments of forest trails are often used. Chamber is unlined. Clutch numbers 4 shiny white eggs (average size: 20.4 mm × 17.3 mm). Both parents incubate. Nesting has been observed Oct.–Jan., peaking Nov.–Dec.

DISTRIBUTION AND STATUS: Endemic to Madagascar. Represented by 2 subspecies: nominate subspecies *I. m. madagascariensis* is widely distributed in e, n, and nw, where it is fairly common (Montagne d'Ambre, Analamera, Ankarana, Tsaratanana, Sambirano), on High Plateau (Ambohitantely), and in w down to Morondava (Bora, Ampijoroa, Morondava), where it is uncommon. Subspecies *I. m. diluata* is rare and local to Sakaraha forest. One isolated observation (subspecies not pinpointed) in gallery forest of Mandrare near Amboasary suggests species also frequents some s locales.

Meropidae – Bee-Eater

Bee-eaters have a long, laterally compressed, pointed, and slightly decurved bill, short tarsi, partly fused front toes, brightly colored plumage, and a more or less forked tail. They feed on insects on the wing. Gregarious, they nest in colonies and dig burrows in steep slopes. Several species are migratory. The family is represented by 24 species distributed mainly in Old World tropics. One widely distributed species nests in Madagascar.

177. *Madagascar Bee-Eater*

Merops superciliosus Linnaeus, 1766
Malagasy: Kirikioka, Tsikiriokirioke, Kiriokirioke, Kirioke
French: Guêpier de Madagascar

DESCRIPTION: Length 27–33 cm. *Adult.* Sexes similar. Green-brown forehead and front and top of head. Thin, pale yellow supercilium and black eye stripe. Pale yellow chin and cheeks. Pale rufous throat. Long (36 mm) black bill, reddish iris. Upperparts emerald green, underparts light green except for rufous flanks. Brownish tarsi and toes. Wings emerald green, except for black internal half of remiges. Emerald green tail with 2 elongated tapering central tail feathers. *Immature.* Differs from adult by much drabber plumage and absence of tapering tail feathers.

IDENTIFICATION: Only bee-eater of Madagascar. Easily identifiable at rest by slender silhouette, short legs, generally green plumage, long bill, and tail elongated by 2 narrow feathers. In flight, wings are narrow and pointed, and wingbeats alternate with glides.

BEHAVIOR: Gregarious year-round, found in flocks of 5–100. Perches in ambush to hunt, sometimes close to ground (fencepost, termite mound, telegraph pole, tree), swooping on prey and performing sudden twist to seize it from below. Returns to perch to eat it, breaking hard-shelled species by striking them against a nearby surface. Loose flocks are commonly seen flying over canopy or slashed-and-burned clearings. More than 100 will congregate to roost in a large tree.

VOICE: Vocal, almost constantly uttering rapid succession of melodically warbled *tweep, tweep* . . . in flight. Call constitutes good field mark and locator.

HABITAT: All habitats, from sea level to elevation of 1,700 m.

DIET: Insects (Hymenoptera, Coleoptera, Lepidoptera, Homoptera).

NESTING: Nests in dense colonies of 10–100 pairs. Nest is cavity fashioned at end of tunnel 1–2 m long, dug in riverbank, natural or roadside embankment, or ravine. Nest gives off unpleasant odor. Clutch numbers 2–3 white eggs. Nesting has been observed Sept.–Dec.

DISTRIBUTION AND STATUS: Distributed in Asia, Africa, and Madagascar. Represented in Madagascar by nominate subspecies *M. s. superciliosus*, common to E Africa and Comoros. Common throughout island and present year-round but may carry out migratory movements to Africa.

Coraciidae – Roller

Rollers are medium-sized birds that have a stout, curved bill with more or less evident terminal hook, brightly colored plumage with some blue in the wings, a notched tail, and a reversible first toe. They feed exclusively on large insects. They nest in tree holes and their eggs are white. Most species are sedentary. The family is represented by 11 species spread over Europe, Africa, Asia, Oceania, and Madagascar. One species, common to Africa, nests in Madagascar and migrates to Africa during the austral winter.

178. *Broad-billed Roller*

Eurystomus glaucurus (Müller, 1776)
Malagasy: Vorombaratra, Harakaraka, Vorona-kahaka, Tsararahaka, Arakaraka, Gadragadra
French: Rollier malgache

DESCRIPTION: Length 32 cm.
Adult. Sexes similar. Rufous head, lilac chin and throat. Bright yellow bill, light brown iris. Upperparts rufous except for sky blue rump and uppertail coverts. Underparts lilac except for blue lower belly and blue undertail coverts. Greenish tarsi and toes. Wings rufous above except for navy blue remiges. Underside of wings: rufous underwing coverts and axillaries, light blue remiges tipped with navy blue. Sky blue tail tipped with navy blue. *Immature.* Differs from adult by generally drabber plumage, dull yellow bill spotted with brown, chestnut throat and chest, and blue belly mixed with brown.

IDENTIFICATION: Stocky silhouette, long wings and tail, large head, very wide bill. Characteristic at rest are rufous head and upperparts, lilac underparts, and bright yellow bill. In flight, field marks above are rufous and blue wings, rufous mantle and back, sky blue rump and tail; below, rufous and sky blue wings, lilac chest and belly, and sky blue undertail coverts and tail. Flight is easy, swift, and graceful, with deep, supple wingbeats. Only roller of Madagascar; can be confused only with Madagascar kestrel. Distinguished by its more halting flight, deeper wingbeats, and more angled wings.

BEHAVIOR: Found alone or in pairs. When hunting, perches in ambush on large dead or bare trees overlooking broad, open terrain (edge of forest, degraded area). Swoops from perch in a long glide at end of which it halts abruptly to seize prey on the wing, returning to perch to eat it. Quarrelsome, does not hesitate to chase birds of its own or other species (Madagascar kestrel, Madagascar buzzard) from its territory, harassing and scolding. Broad-billed Rollers may congregate to hunt together when food is plentiful (7 in company of 3 Madagascar pratincoles in Oct. 1982 at Maroantsetra, 8 in Dec. 1986 at Sakaraha). Remains faithful year after year to its breeding site, returning to it punctually.

VOICE: Highly vocal, uttering loud, harsh, dissonant *crak crak crak . . .* or *sararakasararaka . . .* , which may be taken up by several others, in flight or at rest.

HABITAT: Any wooded area bordering open terrain (edge of forest, clearings, wooded shore of river, lake, or pond, savanna, gallery forest of s), even sparsely wooded degraded terrain. Prefers to be near tall trees that serve as both ambushes and nesting sites. Observed at elevations from sea level to 1,500 m.

DIET: Chiefly large insects (Hemiptera, Coleoptera).

NESTING: Nests in hole in trunk or main branch of a large tree. Clutch numbers 3 shiny, relatively round white eggs (average size: 33.5 mm × 28.5 mm). Nesting has been observed Oct.–Dec., peaking Nov.

DISTRIBUTION AND STATUS: Distributed in sub-Saharan Africa and Madagascar. Represented in Madagascar by nominate endemic subspecies *E. g. glaucurus*, which breeds in Madagascar but migrates to e Africa during austral winter (May–Sept.). Common throughout island, except on High Plateau, where it is rare.

Brachypteraciidae – Ground-Rollers

Endemic family represented by 5 forest, terrestrial, and diurnal species classified into 3 genera. All species have a large head, stout bill, short wings, long tail, and rather long, sturdy tarsi. Their vocal repertory is limited to brief, guttural calls. They nest at the bottom of a burrow, and their eggs are white and spherical. Four species are confined to e rain forests, and the fifth is local to sw subarid thorn scrub.

179. *Short-legged Ground-Roller*

Brachypteracias leptosomus (Lesson, 1833)
Malagasy: Fandikalalana, Famakiakora, Fangadiovy
French: Rollier terrestre leptosome

DESCRIPTION: Length 38 cm. *Adult.* Sexes similar. Front of head brown. Purplish blue crown, nape, and back of neck. Large, conspicuous white supercilium. Cheeks and sides of neck dotted with white, chin and throat slightly marked with brown. Stout black bill, brown iris. Upperparts bronze green. Underparts white heavily barred with brown, except for broad white breastband and undertail coverts. Yellowish legs. Green-brown wings marked with white apical spot on each feather, except for black primary remiges marked with central white patch and bronze green secondary remiges. Brown tail ending with black terminal bar, except for white-tipped external tail feathers. *Immature.* Differs from adult by brown head with small white dot on apex of each feather, rufous coloration of underparts, and indistinct breastband.

IDENTIFICATION: Largest ground roller. Plump appearance accentuated by habit of sinking head and keeping legs almost invisible when perched. Easily identifiable by conspicuous white supercilium, ruffled throat feathers, white breastband, and white wing markings. In flight, which is noisy, direct, and never long, white tips of external tail feathers show clearly.

BEHAVIOR: Secretive, difficult to spot. Least terrestrial ground roller of rain forest. Found alone or, as breeding season approaches, in pairs. Often perched at a height of 4–5 m, sometimes as much as 15 m, with predilection for horizontal branches, on which it can remain motionless for long periods. Forages among carpet of dead leaves or moss. When alarmed, freezes in place or flies to a low perch a few meters away.

VOICE: Utters brief, low-pitched *coo-oo* from its perch, repeating it several times at intervals of some seconds.

HABITAT: Undisturbed rain forest, particularly dark, humid spots offering underbrush moderately covered with herbaceous, mossy vegetation and a thick litter of dead leaves. Observed at elevations from sea level to 1,200 m.

DIET: Few data. Chiefly invertebrates (insects and snails), also small vertebrates (chameleons, small snakes).

NESTING: Few data. Digs 1-m long tunnel in a slope and fashions receptacle at end. Nesting has been observed in Dec.

DISTRIBUTION AND STATUS: Belongs to family endemic to Madagascar, distributed in e from s of Iharaña (n limit) to Andohahela (s limit). Secretive and rather rare throughout range, which includes Andapa, Maroantsetra, Mananara, Zahamena, Analamazaotra, Ranomafana, Midongy.

180. *Scaly Ground-Roller*

Brachypteracias squamiger
Lafresnaye, 1838
Malagasy: Fagadiovy
French: Rollier terrestre écailleux

DESCRIPTION: Length 27–31 cm.
Adult. Sexes similar. Feathers of fore-head and sides of head tan marked with black central spot, which produces scaly appearance. Heavy black stripe behind eyes. Wide black mustache. Pink skin around eye (more or less extensive, depending on individual and season). Scaly chin and throat. Rather stout black bill, brown iris. Upperparts bronze green except for wide rufous collar. Underparts: chest and upper belly scaly, rest of belly and undertail coverts white. Pink tarsi and toes, white claws. Bronze green wings marked with white at outer ends of wing coverts. Tail: except for 2 bronze green median tail feathers, feathers are bronze green at base, then mottled with rufous and marked with a black bar before ending in a sky blue bar.
Immature. Differs from adult by rufous upperparts, dull red underparts, and faint black mustache.

IDENTIFICATION: Medium-sized ter-restrial roller with rather plump silhou-ette. Characterized by scaly appearance of plumage and by black mustache. Posture is vertical when standing but hori-zontal when moving rapidly.

BEHAVIOR: Terrestrial, but often seen perching 3–4 m above ground. Favors horizontal perches. Generally found alone or, during breeding season, in pairs. Feeds on ground, remaining mo-tionless, then running 1–2 m, and prob-ing ground energetically with bill. Flies when in danger or when emerging from nest. Flight is short, direct, and noisy. When alarmed, flees either by running or by hopping. Tail is generally held tight;

only when bird is excited is tail raised vertically and fanned.

VOICE: Fairly quiet. Most common calls are brief, muffled *ko-uh*, uttered while feeding, and, when excited, a brief, trilled *frrret* or hissing *kwish-sh*, decreasing in volume. Song is a soft, deliberate *coorrr-coorrr-coorrr . . .* lasting about 30 seconds, uttered from raised area on ground or from low branch.

HABITAT: Undisturbed evergreen rain forest. Favors relatively dark under-growth, that offers fairly low herbaceous vegetation and carpet of dead leaves and branches. Generally frequents drier envi-ronments than Short-legged ground-roller. Observed at elevations from sea level to 950 m.

DIET: Invertebrates, chiefly earthworms, but also snails, centipedes, spiders, ants, and Coleoptera, and more rarely small vertebrates (frogs).

NESTING: Few data. Digs tunnel roughly 1 m long and 7 cm diameter. At end, lines 20 cm × 15 cm cavity with dead leaves to hold eggs. Digs tunnel in forest, in a bank or slope, and sometimes conceals entrance with vegetation. Both parents feed young.

DISTRIBUTION AND STATUS: Be-longs to family endemic to Madagascar, distributed in n and center of e rain for-est (Marojejy, Maroantsetra, Masoala peninsula, Mananara, Sihanaka forest, Andasibe). Rather rare throughout range.

181. *Pitta-like Ground-Roller*

Aterlornis pittoides (Lafresnaye, 1834)
Malagasy: Sakoka, Tsakoka, Fangadiovy
French: Rollier terrestre pittoide

DESCRIPTION: Length 26 cm.
Adult. Sexes similar. Head entirely dark blue except for narrow white supercilium.

White chin and throat. Wide dark blue necklace separating throat from chest and meeting mustache. Fairly stout black bill, dark brown iris. Upperparts: rufous nape and neck, bronze green back and mantle. Underparts orangy except for whitish undertail coverts. Fairly long pinkish gray legs. Bronze green wings with brown primary remiges. Brown tail.
Immature. Differs from adult by light blue crown, white supercilium tinged with fawn, dull olive brown mantle and throat sprinkled with dark spots.

IDENTIFICATION: Medium-sized ground roller with rather slender silhouette. Characterized by white throat contrasting strongly with dark upperparts, blue necklace and head, rufous nape, and orangy underparts.

BEHAVIOR: Terrestrial, sometimes flies short distances, especially to and from nest. Spends long intervals motionless on ground watching for insects, which it catches after a quick sally. Upon stopping, adopts vertical posture, tail lowered, and blends perfectly into forest floor. Runs in horizontal position, tail in line with body. Flees only in extreme danger, often preferring to freeze in place. Secretive, easily observed only during breeding period.

VOICE: Vocal when breeding, uttering muffled *kooK-kooK-kooK* . . . on rising note at all hours of day, generally from stump or horizontal branch of tree, sometimes fairly high above ground (up to 5 m). Several birds, sometimes closer than 200 m, may call at once. Alarm call is heard as *Trrrrt.*

HABITAT: Undisturbed evergreen rain forest with sparse herbaceous stratum, rich litter of dead leaves, and much fallen deadwood. Observed at elevations from sea level to 2,000 m.

DIET: Few data; insects (Coleoptera, Lepidoptera) and small chameleons.

NESTING: Digs tunnel 0.5–1 m long by 9 cm diameter in loose soil of embankment. Nesting chamber is fashioned at end of tunnel. Clutch numbers 3 shiny, smooth, relatively round white eggs (average size: 22 mm × 27 mm). Female, fed by male, broods. Both parents feed young. Parents arrive at nest on wing and fly or walk into it after alighting on nearby branch. Nesting has been observed Oct.–Feb.

DISTRIBUTION AND STATUS: Belongs to family endemic to Madagascar. Observed in n (Montagne d'Ambre) and nw (Sambirano) and ne (Andapa, Maroantsetra), e center (Sihanaka forest, Andasibe), se (Ranomafana, Andringitra, Vondrozo, Midongy) and on High Plateau (Ambohitantely). Most common and most widely distributed ground-roller.

182. *Rufous-headed Ground-Roller*

Atelornis crossleyi Sharpe, 1875
Malagasy: Vorontotra, Voromboka
French: Rollier terrestre de Crossley

DESCRIPTION: Length 26 cm.
Adult. Sexes similar. Head entirely bright rufous. Wide black collar with fine white streaks. Chin and rest of throat rufous. Black bill with conspicuous vibrissae, brown iris. Dark green upperparts and tail. Underparts tan-brown tinged with rufous, except for entirely rufous chest and dark green undertail coverts. Dark brown legs. Wings dark green with white patch on shoulder and white bar on primary remiges.
Immature. Differs from adult by more purplish cap and poorly defined collar.

IDENTIFICATION: Small ground roller. Field marks are plump appearance, rufous head, finely white-streaked black throat, and white wing bar.

BEHAVIOR: Few data. Difficult to see, usually staying in shadows of low vegetation of undisturbed forest. Flies little, generally to escape danger. Moves by alternating fast runs for a few meters with intervals at rest during which it remains motionless. For fast movement adopts horizontal position.

VOICE: Few data. Vocal during breeding period, when call is a solemn *koohoo* similar to that of Pitta-like ground-roller.

HABITAT: Undisturbed rain forest offering dark undergrowth, moderate herbaceous vegetation, and many dead branches and roots. Frequents thicker, more tangled growth than Pitta-like ground-roller. Observed at elevations from sea level to 1,500 m.

DIET: Few data. Chiefly insects (small Lepidoptera).

NESTING: Few data. Digs tunnel 50 cm long at end of which it fashions nesting chamber. Clutch numbers 2 eggs. Nesting has been observed in Dec.

DISTRIBUTION AND STATUS: Belongs to family endemic to Madagascar, distributed in e (Marojejy, Tsaratanana, Sihanaka forest, Andasibe, Ranomafana, Andringitra). Fairly rare throughout range.

183. *Long-tailed Ground-Roller*

Uratelornis chimaera Rothschild, 1895
Malagasy: Bokitsy, Tolohoranto
French: Rollier terrestre à longue queue

DESCRIPTION: Length 47 cm (tail 25–30 cm).
Adult. Sexes differ; male's tail longer than female's. Crown all tan-brown flecked with brown, giving finely streaked appearance. Brown patch extends from bill to well behind eyes, framed above by light tan supercilium above and below by broad white band. Stout black bill, brown iris. Tan-brown upperparts more or less flecked with brown. Underparts white except for brown collar that bars upper chest and widens as it goes up sides of neck. Roseate-white legs. Tan-brown wings flecked with brown except for sky blue greater primary coverts and lesser and median underwing coverts. Tail marked with some 20 dark brown bands. Sky blue external tail feathers.

IDENTIFICATION: Terrestrial, with distinctive silhouette, plump body held vertically, and long, narrow, horizontal or slightly raised tail. Characterized by tan-brown plumage flecked with brown above, white below, black band on eyes under light tan supercilium, and brown collar running up sides of neck. Cannot be confused with any other species.

BEHAVIOR: Found alone or in pairs. Seldom flies except to change calling post. Faced with danger, prefers to seek safety by running, with horizontal silhouette, a few dozen meters, then freezing. Run generally ends with a few bounds. If danger is not pressing it may also hop away. Often perches, usually on horizontal branches, either to escape pursuit or to call. Spends most of day motionless under low, dense bush. Feeds in undergrowth, probing leaf litter with bill.

VOICE: Fairly vocal, utters muffled *boof boof boof . . .* reminiscent of Madagascar coucal. Emits call from perch in very early morning, but also during day and at night when moon is full. At height of singing season, during austral summer, callers may answer each other. Call is loud and distinctive, often helpful in locating species.

HABITAT: Undisturbed or slightly degraded subarid thorn thicket, on sandy soil offering thin herbaceous layer and substantial litter of dead leaves. Shares same habitat with Subdesert mesite. Observed at elevations from sea level to 80 m.

DIET: Insects (Coleoptera, Orthoptera, Dictyoptera, Lepidoptera), caterpillars, larvae, worms.

NESTING: Digs slightly sloping tunnel about 1.2 m long by 7 cm diameter. Cavity 20 cm diameter and 11 cm high, lightly lined with dry leaves and rootlets, is fashioned at end. Clutch numbers 3–4 shiny, spherical white eggs. Nesting has been observed Oct.–Nov.

DISTRIBUTION AND STATUS: Belongs to family endemic to Madagascar. Distributed in sw along a narrow coastal strip about 200 km long between Mangoky River to n and Fiherenana River to s, and bounded by mountains to e. Well represented throughout range, particularly at Ihotry Lake, where it is fairly common. Threatened by deforestation, trapping, dogs, and increasing rat *(Rattus rattus)* populations.

Leptosomatidae – Cuckoo-Roller

Monospecific family distributed in Madagascar and the Comoros. The Cuckoo-roller is characterized by sexual dimorphism, colorful plumage, a slender silhouette, and a limited but fairly melodic vocal repertory.

184. *Cuckoo-Roller*

Leptosomus discolor (Hermann, 1783)
Malagasy: Vorondreo, Kirombo, Dreodreo, Reoreo
French: Courol

DESCRIPTION: Length 50 cm.
Adult. Sexes differ.
Male. Gray head, except for black crown and nape with metallic green sheen, with black stripe extending from commissure of mandibles over eyes to nape and black patch from eyes to crown. Gray chin, throat, and neck. Black bill, brown iris. Upperparts metallic green with violet or purple sheen. Underparts white, except for gray chest. Brown tarsi and toes. Wings same color above as upperparts, with midnight blue primary and secondary remiges. Underside of wings white with apical two-thirds of primary remiges midnight blue. Tail dark green with metallic violet or purple sheen.
Female. Head, chin, nape, and neck brown with dark brown bars. Tan throat marked with large brown spots. Black bill, brown iris. Upperparts brown, with chestnut markings on mantle. Underparts white, more or less tinged with tan and marked with large brown spots. Upper side of wings brown edged with chestnut, remiges black with slight green sheen. Underside of wings whitish spotted

with brown except for apical two-thirds of brown-gray primary remiges. Dark brown tail.

Immature. Differs from female by generally drabber plumage.

IDENTIFICATION: Large bird with distinctive, rather heavy silhouette and massive head with eyes that seem set very far back. Plumage of male shows sharp contrast, white-gray below and metallic green above, with black eye patch on black-capped gray head. Female is more uniform but easily recognizable by white plumage with big brown spots below and light brown head heavily barred with dark brown. In flight, field marks are dark plumage above, light below, except for dark primary remiges and tail. Flight itself is characteristic: slow, undulating, and swerving, with supple, deep wingbeats rising well above the horizontal plane and descending low against the body. Cannot be confused with any other species.

BEHAVIOR: Usually seen in pairs or groups of 3–8, seldom encountered alone. Frequents upper stratum of forest, feeds on branches and in foliage. Remains motionless for long spells, hidden in dense treetop vegetation, and moves about by flying over canopy. Commonly seen flying in circles, sometimes very high, calling continually.

VOICE: Highly vocal, with loud, distinctive call of 3 identical liquid notes uttered in diminishing volume, *dree-oo dree-oo*

dree-oo, repeated at regular intervals of approximately 3–6 seconds and sometimes continuing for several minutes without stopping. This call, uttered usually in flight but also at rest, can be heard even at night. Also makes a sort of *vree-oo* or *gree-oo hoohoohoo*.

HABITAT: Most original forest types, also degraded terrain containing large trees, plantations (coffee, cacao), and parks. Observed at elevations from sea level to 2,000 m.

DIET: Invertebrates—large insects (Orthoptera, Coleoptera, Hemiptera), furry caterpillars—and small vertebrates (*Chamaeleo* spp., *Uroplatus* sp.).

NESTING: Nests in holes of trunks or main branches of large trees. Hole is strewn with wood and insect debris. Clutch numbers 4–5 smooth whitish eggs slightly tinged with green (average size: 45.2 mm × 38.4 mm). Only female broods. Chick has long, white down. Unpleasant odor emanates from nest while young are being reared. Nesting has been observed Nov.–Dec.

DISTRIBUTION AND STATUS: Monospecific family distributed solely in Madagascar and Comoros. Represented in Madagascar by nominate subspecies *L. d. discolor.* Common in n, e, and w, less common in s, where it is found most frequently in gallery forests of major rivers, and common in relict forests of High Plateau (Ambohitantely and Manjakatompo), and occasionally at Antananarivo.

Upupidae – Hoopoe

Monospecific Old World family represented by numerous subspecies. The Hoopoe is characterized by its long, delicate, curved, pointed bill and rather long wings. Toes show a slight tendency to fuse at plantar surfaces, and the first toe is as long as the others. The Hoopoe is chiefly insectivorous and nests in natural cavities. It is represented by a subspecies endemic to Madagascar.

185. *Hoopoe*

Upupa epops Linnaeus, 1758
Malagasy: Takodara, Barao, Tsakodara, Drao
French: Huppe fasciée

DESCRIPTION: Length 32 cm.
Adult. Sexes differ; female is slightly smaller and drabber than male. Orange head surmounted by long black-tipped feathers forming an erectile crest. Orange neck, pale orange chin and throat. Dark brown bill with light base, brown iris. Upperparts: orange mantle, orangy brown back prominently barred with white and black, rump and upperwing coverts barred with black and white. Underparts: orangy chest, white belly and flanks tinged with orange, whitish undertail coverts. Brown-gray tarsi and toes. Black wings barred with white, with black primary remiges crossed by white bar. Black tail marked with broad white band in the middle.
Immature. Differs from female by duller plumage and brownish head and upperparts.

IDENTIFICATION: Characterized by orangy head surmounted by fan-shaped erectile crest, long, thin decurved bill, and boldly black-and-white striped upperparts and wings. Striking coloration of rounded wings in flight. Distinctive flight, rather slow, unsure, fluttering, and undulating, full and rapid wingbeats alternating with moments during which wings are kept closed. Cannot be confused with any other species.

BEHAVIOR: Not shy but vigilant and not gregarious, usually found in pairs or, less often, alone. Feeds on ground, scurrying about and stopping a few seconds to probe ground with bill or inspect cracks between stones. When alarmed, takes wing to perch short distance away on unobstructed horizontal branch.

VOICE: Vocal, repeats soft but trilled and rather resonant *rrrooooo* at short, regular intervals. Also utters repeated low-pitched, raucous, hissing *chrrshhh.* Its call in Madagascar differs greatly from that in Europe and Asia.

HABITAT: Dry open terrain, sparse dry forests with light underbrush, subarid thorn scrub, open lakeshores, croplands, plantations (palm groves), and surroundings of villages. Observed at elevations from sea level to 1,500 m.

DIET: Invertebrates (insects, caterpillars).

NESTING: Few data. Builds nest in tree hole. Clutch numbers 2 whitish eggs. Nesting has been observed Oct.–Dec.

DISTRIBUTION AND STATUS: Cosmopolitan species distributed in Europe, Asia, and Africa. Represented in Madagascar by endemic subspecies *U. e. marginata* (Canabis and Heine, 1860), distributed throughout Madagascar except for e, where it appears rarely to take advantage of deforestation. Common in n (s limit Antalaha), w, and s, rarer on High Plateau (Antananarivo, Ambalavao).

Passeriformes

Philepittidae – Asities and Sunbird-Asities

Endemic family represented by 4 species classified into 2 genera, *Philepitta* and *Neodrepanis*. All representatives of the family inhabit forests and are sexually dimorphic, and all have seasonally varying plumage. The males have a colored caruncle over the eyes that expands during the nesting period. All 4 species build hanging globular nests. The 2 Asities are medium-sized, have plump silhouettes and short tails, and are principally frugivorous. The 2 Sunbird-Asities are small, have plump silhouettes, short tails, and long, thin decurved bills, and feed on insects that they find in flowers.

186. *Velvet Asity*

Philepitta castanea (Müller, 1776)
Malagasy: Asity, Asitilahimanga, Soisoy
French: Philépitte veloutée

DESCRIPTION: Length 16 cm.
Adult. Sexes differ. Plumage varies seasonally.
Male Breeding Plumage. Head velvety black all over. Bluish black, slightly curved bill, dark brown iris. Large pearly blue or green caruncle over and in front of eyes, forming an excrescence on forehead. Velvety black upperparts and underparts. Yellow brown tarsi and toes. Velvety black wings with dark brown remiges and golden yellow shoulder patch. Black tail.
Male Nonbreeding Plumage. Black forehead, crown, nape, and neck, marked with small yellow scales. Rest of head, chin, and throat velvety black. Vestige of caruncle forms narrow strip of bare blue skin over eyes, sometimes totally absent.

Black bill, brown iris. Yellow and black scaly upperparts, underparts and wings. Dark brown primary remiges, more-or-less faded golden yellow shoulder patch. Black tail.
Female. Olive green crown. Small area of bare skin around eyes. Subtle yellow supercilium, more conspicuous in front of eyes. Yellow mustache. Scaly yellow-and-green chin and throat. Black bill, dark brown iris. Upperparts olive green, underparts olive green with yellow scales, except for yellow undertail coverts. Yellow-brown tarsi and toes. Olive green wings have brown-gray primary remiges with narrow yellow edge on external half (visible when wing is folded). Olive green–gray tail.
Immature. Similar to female.

IDENTIFICATION: Chunky passerine with plump silhouette accentuated by short tail. Male in breeding or nonbreeding plumage cannot be confused with any other species. Female is recognized by olive green plumage above, scaly below. Distinguished from Schlegel's asity by larger size, generally darker hue, scaly belly, and longer, slightly curved bill.

BEHAVIOR: Forest species, rather inactive, secretive but not shy, generally seen alone or in pairs, low above ground in bushy stratum of forest. Sometimes mixes with multispecies feeding flocks. Spends long intervals motionless in dense shrubbery.

VOICE: High-pitched, sweet, melodious whistle, not very loud.

HABITAT: Understory of rain forest. Observed at elevations from sea level to 1,800 m.

DIET: Chiefly fruit.

NESTING: Nest, spherical structure of moss, palm fibers, and leaves, some 20 cm diameter, hangs from low branch. Opening placed 5 cm below dome. Interior is lined with dead leaves. Clutch numbers 3 smooth white eggs. Both parents feed young. Nesting has been observed Aug.–Jan.

DISTRIBUTION AND STATUS: Belongs to family endemic to Madagascar. Distributed in nw (Sambirano, Tsaratanana) and in e from Sambava to Tolagnaro. Seems absent from Montagne d'Ambre. Fairly common throughout range. Range overlaps with that of Schlegel's asity in Sambirano. Most common of 4 representatives of family.

187. *Schlegel's Asity*

Philepitta schlegeli Pollen, 1866
French: Philépitte de Schlegel

DESCRIPTION: Length 13 cm.
Adult. Sexes differ. Plumage varies seasonally.
Male Breeding Plumage. Velvety black head. Yellow chin and throat. Very large quadrilobed caruncle, pearly light green below and in front of eyes, blue above eyes, turquoise behind eyes. Short, wide black bill, brown iris. Upperparts olive green, except for yellow top of mantle. Underparts entirely bright yellow, except for green-tinged flanks. Sooty tarsi and toes. Olive green wings have dark brown primary remiges with yellow-green outer edges (visible when wing is folded). Very short, olive green tail.
Male Nonbreeding Plumage. Crown and cheeks olive green flecked with yellow. Greenish yellow chin and throat. Vestige of caruncle forms narrow strip of bluish skin over eyes; sometimes totally absent. Black bill, brown iris. Upperparts: olive green back more-or-less tinged with yellow and marked with large black spots, yellow mantle similarly spotted, rest of upperparts olive green. Underparts: chest, flanks, and part of belly olive green

with large yellow scales, rest of belly and undertail coverts yellow. Sooty tarsi and toes. Wings and tail unchanged.

Female. Head as that of nonbreeding male but with area of bare skin over eyes. Upperparts olive green with yellow-flecked mantle. Underparts, tail, and wings as in male in nonbreeding plumage.

Immature. Similar to female.

IDENTIFICATION: Small, stocky passerine with plump silhouette accentuated by extremely short tail. Male cannot be confused with any other species. Female is recognized by extensive areas of spotted plumage; distinguished from female Velvet asity by smaller size, generally lighter hue, yellow belly and undertail coverts, and shorter, straighter bill.

BEHAVIOR: Rather inactive forest species, not shy, seen alone or in pairs in bushy stratum of forest. Spends long periods motionless, seldom making itself visible. Sometimes joins multispecies feeding flocks, e.g., as observed in Bora forest in June 1987: 4 Schlegel's asities, 6 Crested drongos, 4 Long-billed greenbuls, 2 Madagascar paradise flycatchers, 2 Common newtonias, 3 Ashy cuckoo-shrikes, 3 Blue vangas, 2 Chabert's vangas, 4 White-headed vangas, and 1 Hook-billed vanga.

VOICE: Fairly vocal, utters distinctive high-pitched, not very loud whistle. Song, delivered by male from generally concealed perch, is heard as *tseetseetsee* . . . lasting 3–4 seconds, first rising then falling in volume.

HABITAT: Bushy stratum of deciduous dry forests, especially those on calcareous substratum, as well as nw rain forests. Observed at elevations from sea level to 800 m.

DIET: Unknown.

NESTING: No data. Males in breeding plumage are seen Nov.–June.

DISTRIBUTION AND STATUS: Belongs to family endemic to Madagascar, mostly local to nw (Sambirano and Bora forests), where it is common, and some calcareous areas of w (Tsiandro, Namoroka, Anaborano), where it is rather rare. Also observed in Ankarafantsika and Ankazoabo forests. Range overlaps that of Velvety asity in Sambirano.

188. *Sunbird-Asity*

Neodrepanis coruscans Sharpe, 1875
Malagasy: Soinala, Takobodimozinga, Zafindrasity
French: Philépitte faux-souimanga caronculée

DESCRIPTION: Length 10–11 cm.
Adult. Sexes differ. Plumage varies seasonally.

Male Breeding Plumage. Metallic dark blue head, yellow chin and throat. Large caruncle over and behind eyes is pearly sky-blue except for ultramarine lower part and turquoise eye ring. Long (25–27 mm), markedly curved black bill, with ultramarine blue base of upper mandible and light green-blue base of lower mandible, makes up quarter of bird's length. Upperparts metallic dark blue, underparts yellow with brighter yellow flanks and undertail coverts and dark gray dots on chest. Gray tarsi and toes. Metallic dark blue wings except for gray-yellow greater upperwing coverts, yellow secondary remiges, and brown-gray primary remiges with yellow outer border. Very short, metallic dark blue tail hardly extends past ends of wings.

Male Nonbreeding Plumage. Greenish head, green-gray chin and throat. Black bill, dark brown iris. Upperparts green-gray, underparts light green-gray except for bright yellow flanks and undertail coverts. Gray tarsi and toes. Wings green-

gray except for brown-gray remiges with yellow outer edge. Greenish gray tail.
Female Breeding Plumage. Similar to male in nonbreeding plumage.
Female Nonbreeding Plumage. Differs from female in breeding plumage by yellowish flanks and undertail coverts.

IDENTIFICATION: Very small passerine with long, markedly curved bill and very short tail. Distinguished from Souimanga sunbird and Madagascar long-billed green sunbird by smaller size, rounder silhouette, much more sharply curved bill, and very short tail and from Yellow-bellied sunbird-asity by larger size, black-dotted chest, and much more sharply curved bill.

BEHAVIOR: More active than Velvet asity, found alone or in pairs in bushy rain forest vegetation. Favors plants in full flower (*Impatiens humblotiana*—Balsaminaceae; *Hedychium coronarium*—Zingiberaceae) on which insects concentrate. While feeding, may associate with other species, e.g., Souimanga and Madagascar green sunbirds or Madagascar white-eye.

VOICE: Little known. Shrill *tseeee* uttered in flight.

HABITAT: Dense bushy vegetation of undisturbed rain forest, also adjacent second growth. Observed at elevations from sea level to 1,700 m.

DIET: Insects and spiders.

NESTING: Nest resembles that of Velvet asity. Spherical structure covered with moss outside, dead leaves inside, generally suspended from end of branch. Both parents feed young. Nesting has been observed Sept.–Jan.

DISTRIBUTION AND STATUS: Belongs to family endemic to Madagascar, distributed in nw (Tsaratanana—but seems absent from Montagne d'Ambre) and all e forests. Fairly common through-

out range. Ranges of Sunbird-asity and Yellow-bellied sunbird-asity probably overlap in Sihanaka forest.

189. *Yellow-bellied Sunbird-Asity*

Neodrepanis hypoxantha
Salomonsen, 1933
French: Philépitte faux-souimanga de Salomonsen

DESCRIPTION: Length 9–10 cm.
Adult. Sexes differ. Plumage varies seasonally.
Male Breeding Plumage. Metallic dark blue head, bright yellow chin and throat. Large caruncle over and behind eyes. Fairly long (18–21 mm), slightly curved bill. Upperparts metallic dark blue, underparts golden yellow. Dark tarsi. Wings dark blue except for gray-yellow greater upperwing coverts, yellow secondary remiges, and brown-gray primary remiges with yellow outer edges. Very short metallic blue tail barely extends past ends of wings.
Male Nonbreeding Plumage. Differs from male in breeding plumage by less metallic sheen on head and upperparts and by dull yellow underparts.
Female Breeding Plumage. Greenish crown, bright yellow cheeks, chin, and throat. Bill same as that of male. Upperparts greenish, underparts bright yellow. Dark tarsi. Wings green-gray except for brown-gray remiges with yellow outer edges. Very short greenish gray tail.
Female Nonbreeding Plumage. Differs from female in breeding plumage by generally duller plumage.

IDENTIFICATION: Smaller than Sunbird-asity, with shorter, much less curved bill and solid yellow underparts.

BEHAVIOR: Close to that of Sunbird-asity. Flight is swift and direct. Sometimes observed within multispecies feeding flocks, e.g., at 1,800 m in Andringitra in May 1987: 1 Yellow-bellied sunbird-asity, 1 Long-billed greenbul, 2 Madagascar bulbuls, 2 Madagascar brush warblers, 4 Common newtonias, 2 Common jeries, 3 Souimanga sunbirds, and 1 Tylas vanga.

VOICE: Shrill *tseeee* uttered in flight.

HABITAT: Canopy of high undisturbed rain forest. Observed at elevations of 1,050–2,000 m.

DIET: Very few data. Known to include insects (termites).

NESTING: Few data. Nesting has been observed Nov., Jan.

DISTRIBUTION AND STATUS: Rare, belongs to family endemic to Madagascar and is known from a dozen specimens collected at higher elevations (near Antananarivo, near Fianarantsoa, and in Sihanaka forest) and from recent sightings at Andasibe (1973), in the Andringitra (1987), and Marojejy (1988). Ranges of Yellow-bellied sunbird-asity and Sunbird-asity probably overlap in Sihanaka forest.

Alaudidae – Lark

Terrestrial passerines with generally sandy or earth-colored plumage, generally short, stout bill, long claw on the first toe, and long tarsi whose rear sides are covered with well-separated, rounded scales. Larks are ground-nesters. Some species sing on the ground, though more often on a branch, and most sing in flight. Most larks are sedentary, though some do migrate. The family comprises more than 80 species distributed throughout the tropics and in other warm regions, as well as some species from the temperate regions of the N Hemisphere. In Madagascar the family is represented by 1 endemic sedentary species.

190. *Madagascar Bush Lark*
Mirafra hova Hartlaub, 1860
Malagasy: Sorohitra, Jorioke, Soritsy, Boria, Borisa
French: Alouette malgache

DESCRIPTION: Length 13 cm.
Adult. Sexes similar. Light brown head streaked with dark brown. Light tan chin and supercilium, light brown chin dotted with brown. Fleshy bill, brown iris. Upperparts tan-brown streaked with dark brown, underparts tan streaked with dark brown on chest. Fleshy tarsi and toes. Upper side of wings same color as upperparts except for subtle tan edge of primary remiges and tan outer edge of secondary remiges. Underside of wings gray-brown and undertail coverts rufous-tan. Tail: brown tail feathers edged with tan on outer side; inner tail feathers entirely tan.

IDENTIFICATION: Only lark of Madagascar. Recognized by non-contrasting tan-brown plumage streaked with brown, except for solid tan supercilium, belly, and flanks. Short, rather stout bill. Cannot be confused with any other species.

BEHAVIOR: Fairly gregarious outside breeding period, found in pairs or groups of 3–6. Runs on ground to feed, often flitting to a different spot nearby. Sings while hovering.

VOICE: Vocal; harmonious song of liquid notes is usually delivered in flight.

HABITAT: Any open (grassland savanna) or moderately wooded (woodland savanna) terrain. Frequently seen on trails, roads, dry surroundings of lakes, and major rivers. Observed at elevations from sea level to 2,500 m.

DIET: Seeds and insects (Orthoptera).

NESTING: Bowl-shaped nest of fine interlaced grasses is built on ground in tuft of grasses, depression in ground, or sand. Clutch numbers 2 whitish eggs spotted with brown and gray (average size: 20.6 mm × 15.0 mm). Nesting has been observed almost year-round.

DISTRIBUTION AND STATUS: Endemic to Madagascar, widely distributed over entire island. Very common in n, w, and s, and on High Plateau, common in e. One of few species adapted to grassland savanna of High Plateau.

Hirundinidae – Swallows

Highly aerial insectivorous passerines that seize their prey on the wing, having a short, flattened, and widely cleft bill and angular wings. They perch like other passerines, and several species are migratory. The family is fairly cosmopolitan, and nearly 80 species are recognized. Of the 2 species that nest in Madagascar, 1 is limited to Madagascar and the Mascarenes, while 1 is widely distributed. Two migratory species occasionally visit the island during the boreal winter.

191. *Brown-throated Sand Martin*
Riparia paludicola (Vieillot, 1817)
Malagasy: Tsidisidina
French: Hirondelle paludicole

DESCRIPTION: Length 12 cm. *Adult.* Sexes similar. Brown head, pale gray chin and throat. Black bill, light brown iris. Upperparts brown, underparts whitish, except for light brown chest. Black tarsi and toes. Brown wings and tail.

IDENTIFICATION: Small swallow with short, slightly notched tail and entirely brown plumage except for whitish belly and undertail coverts. In flight, wings are brown below. Flight is swift, periods of gliding alternating with rapid wingbeats. Distinguished from Mascarene martin by smaller size, much slimmer silhouette, and absence of streaking on underparts. Differs from Malagasy spine-tailed swift by shorter wings, slightly notched tail, lighter chest, white belly, and absence of clear marking on remiges.

BEHAVIOR: Fairly gregarious, found in small groups of 2–8, rarely more, hunting insects just above water surface. Often perches by water on bush or dead branch. Larger congregations may be observed at roosts established near water in reed beds, or in colonies, even outside breeding season.

VOICE: Rather quiet, with small repertory. Weak *tre-eh* uttered in flight.

HABITAT: Wetlands with good nesting sites (sandy or earthy banks), marshes, rivers, streams, rice paddies, edges of undisturbed and second-growth rain forests. Observed at elevations from sea level to 2,400 m.

DIET: Chiefly small insects.

NESTING: Nests alone or in colonies. Nest is established at end of tunnel 40 cm long dug in a bank, side of ravine, or embankment of road or trail. Receptacle is lined with dry grasses. Clutch numbers 4 smooth, slightly shiny white eggs (average size: 17.0 mm × 12.3 mm). Both parents incubate. Nesting has been observed Nov.–Apr., peaking Nov.–Feb.

DISTRIBUTION AND STATUS: Distributed in Africa and Asia. Represented in Madagascar by endemic subspecies *R. p. cowani* (Sharpe, 1882). Distributed in e and nw (Tsaratanana) and on High Plateau, where it is common, except at elevations below 500 m, where it is rarer.

192. *Sand Martin / Bank Swallow*

Riparia riparia (Linnaeus, 1758)
French: Hirondelle de rivages
No Map

DESCRIPTION: Length 12 cm.
Adult. Sexes similar. Brown head, white chin and throat. Black bill, dark brown iris. Upperparts brown, underparts white except for brown breastband. Black tarsi and toes. Brown wings and tail.
Immature. Differs by rusty white fringes on upperparts.

IDENTIFICATION: Small swallow with brown plumage above, white below, with dark breastband and solid brown, slightly notched tail. In flight, underside of wing is brown. Easily distinguished from Alpine swift by considerably smaller size and white flanks and undertail coverts.

DISTRIBUTION AND STATUS: Migratory, breeds in Europe and Asia and winters partly in sub-Saharan Africa. Rare visitor to Madagascar, observed only a few times at Ihotry Lake, Manakara, and Maroantsetra during boreal winter.

193. *Mascarene Martin*

Phedina borbonica Gmelin, 1789
Malagasy: Tsidisidina, Firinga, Vikiviky, Poadranofotsy
French: Hirondelle des Mascareignes

DESCRIPTION: Length 14 cm.
Adult. Sexes similar. Gray-brown head and neck, whitish chin and throat streaked with brown. Dark brown bill and iris. Upperparts gray-brown. Underparts: chest and upper belly whitish, heavily streaked with brown, rest of belly and undertail coverts white. Black tarsi and toes. Brown wings and tail.

IDENTIFICATION: Swallow with chunky silhouette, short, wide, triangular wings, slightly notched tail, brown plumage above, whitish and heavily streaked below. In flight, wing is brown below, marked with lighter area at base of remiges. Flight is rather slow, wingbeats alternating with gliding periods. Distinguished from Brown-throated sand martin by larger size, more massive silhouette, and streaked underparts.

BEHAVIOR: Fairly gregarious, found in small groups of 3–12, rarey in large groups (300 at Maroantsetra, Dec. 1982). Feeds on wing, catching prey over forest

canopy and rice paddies or rivers. Often
rests near water, on small bare or dead
branches or electric wires. Larger flocks
may be seen in nocturnal roosts established in rocky crevices or abandoned
buildings.

VOICE: Vocal, utters piercing *trizzz* or
melodious warbling in flight, shrill *cheep
cheep tree-ew* near nest.

HABITAT: Frequents undisturbed forests and second growth, mangroves, tree
plantations, marshes, lakes, rivers. Observed at elevations from sea level to
2,200 m.

DIET: Small insects.

NESTING: Nest, bowl of interlaced
twigs and dry grasses, is built in rocky
crevice, cave, or little-used building or
under eaves. Several nests are often seen
in a favorable site. Clutch numbers 3–4
roseate-white eggs with light brown spots
tending to cluster on larger pole (average
size: 22.0 mm × 16.0 mm). Nesting has
been observed Sept.–Dec.

DISTRIBUTION AND STATUS: Distributed over Réunion, Mauritius, and
Madagascar. Represented in Madagascar
by endemic subspecies *P. b. madagascariensis* (Hartlaub, 1860), which is un-
doubtedly migratory in view of observations made in e and s Africa during
austral winter. Internal migratory movements have been observed, but their details are not known. Common species,
found throughout island.

194. *Swallow / Barn Swallow*

Hirundo rustica Linnaeus, 1758
French: Hirondelle de cheminées
No Map

DESCRIPTION: Length 19 cm.
Adult. Sexes similar. Head and neck metallic midnight blue except for reddish
forehead, chin, and throat. Black bill,
dark brown iris. Upperparts metallic
midnight blue. Underparts white except
for midnight blue breastband. Black tarsi
and toes. Metallic midnight blue wings,
sooty remiges. Midnight blue tail marked
with blurred light bar. Very long, narrow
external tail feathers.
Immature. Differs by duller hue without
metallic sheen and absence of long external tail feathers.

IDENTIFICATION: Swallow with slender silhouette, very somber above, light
below, with reddish throat, dark breastband, and deeply forked tail. In flight,
wing is white below, except for dark
remiges. Cannot be confused with any
other species.

DISTRIBUTION AND STATUS: Migratory, breeds in Europe and Asia, winters partly in sub-Saharan Africa. Rare
migrant in Madagascar, observed during
boreal winter, alone or in small groups of
3–7, in w and ne (Maroantsetra).

Motacillidae – Wagtail

Passerines that are generally good fliers but live chiefly on the ground, bobbing their long tails when walking or running. Wagtails feed on insects and build bowl-shaped nests. They are characterized by a slender silhouette and the scales on their tarsi, of which the anterior surface is scu-tellated while the posterior surface shows only one patch on each side. The family is cosmopolitan and numbers some 50 species. In Madagascar it is represented by 1 endemic species.

195. *Madagascar Wagtail*

Motacilla flaviventris Hartlaub, 1860
Malagasy: Triotrio, Kitriotrio, Pila
French: Bergeronnette malgache

DESCRIPTION: Length 19 cm.
Adult. Sexes differ. Female often paler than male.
Male. Front and top of head and nape are mouse gray. White supercilium starts at forehead. Black eye patch and mus-tache start at base of bill. Light gray cheeks, white chin and throat. Black bill, dark brown iris. Upperparts: mouse gray mantle and back, green-gray rump, dark brown uppertail coverts. Underparts: white chest marked by broad black V starting at sides of neck. Bright yellow belly and flanks, yellow undertail coverts. Black tarsi and toes. Wings mouse gray except for dark brown primary and sec-ondary remiges with white markings on basal half. Tail brown-gray, except for 2 white external tail feathers.

IDENTIFICATION: Recognized by slender, long-legged silhouette, con-trasted plumage with gray above and yel-low below, and long black tail edged with white. Only wagtail of Madagascar; can-not be confused with any other species.

BEHAVIOR: Readily accepts human presence, largely terrestrial, not shy, usu-ally found in pairs. When feeding, walks or runs on ground bobbing its tail; will suddenly flutter to catch prey a few me-ters away.

VOICE: Vocal. Song is a bisyllabic, me-lodious, slightly trilled *tree treeoo*, fre-quently delivered from ground or perch or in flight, usually repeated several times and sometimes followed by a melodic phrase.

HABITAT: Any area with open space, preferably wetlands or terrain situated near fresh, brackish, or saltwater. Often observed on beaches, lakeshores, floating vegetation, and rocks or islets of rivers and brooks, or in clearings, mountain ter-rain, towns, and villages. Observed at ele-vations from sea level to 2,600 m.

DIET: Insects, spiders.

NESTING: Nest is usually built low above ground (0.5–6.5 m) in dense fo-liage of low bush, fork of tree, or rock crevice, or under roof, but almost always near water (brook, river, rice paddy, sea-shore). Bowl-shaped, capacious nest con-sists of intertwined leafstalks, twigs and moss. Interior is lined with softer forms of same materials. Clutch numbers 2, sometimes 3–4 smooth, slightly shiny tan-white eggs boldly spotted with grayish brown and sepia, especially at larger pole. Nesting has been observed Aug.–Nov.

DISTRIBUTION AND STATUS: En-demic to Madagascar, distributed through-out island. Common in e and on High Plateau, less common in n and w, rare in extreme s. Internal migratory movements have been observed, but their details are unknown (not present on High Plateau during austral winter).

Campephagidae – Cuckoo-Shrike

Arboreal passerines having broad, flat bills and loose, soft plumage with stiff feathers on rump. Cuckoo-shrikes are solitary or gregarious and build bowl-shaped nests. They feed on insects. The family is represented by more than 70 species spread over the Old World tropics. One species that also occurs in the Comoros nests in Madagascar.

196. Ashy (Madagascar) Cuckoo-Shrike

Coracina cinerea (Müller, 1776)
Malagasy: Kikiomavo, Tsirikititio, Voromaregny, Mokasavomavoloha, Vorondavenona
French: Echenilleur malgache

DESCRIPTION: Length 24 cm.
Adult. Sexes differ.
  Nominate subspecies *C. c. cinerea* (Sclater, 1924).
Male. Black head, chin, throat, nape, and neck. Black bill, dark brown iris. Upperparts uniformly dark gray; underparts light gray, lighter on upper chest. Black tarsi, gray toes. Wings dark gray above, light gray below. Tail gray with 2 black external tail feathers.
Female. Differs from male by gray head, chin, throat, nape, and neck and by light gray upperparts.
  Subspecies *C. c. pallida* (Delacour, 1931).
Male. Paler than male of nominate subspecies, from which it differs by gray head (same color as that of female of nominate species), whitish area separating gray throat from light gray under-

parts, white undertail coverts, and light underside of wing.
Female. Differs from female of nominate subspecies by generally paler coloration.
Immature. Differs from females of respective subspecies by brown-edged feathers of upperwing coverts.

IDENTIFICATION: Only cuckoo-shrike of Madagascar. Robust species with color pattern reminiscent of certain Vangidae. Female distinguished from female White-headed vanga by larger size, gray upperparts and tail, and black bill.

BEHAVIOR: Gregarious, sometimes found alone or in pairs but more often found in mobile multispecies feeding flocks. Examples in a rain forest: *(a)* 1 pair of Ashy cuckoo-shrikes, 1 pair of White-headed vangas, 1 pair and 1 female of Bernier's vangas, 2 adult and 1 immature Helmet vangas, 1 Hook-billed vanga, and 2 Pollen's vangas; *(b)* 1 male Ashy cuckoo-shrike, 5 Common newtonias, 2 Madagascar paradise flycatchers, 20 Spectacled greenbuls, 7 Souimanga sunbirds, 1 Red-tailed vanga, 1 White-headed vanga, and 1 pair of Nelicourvi weavers. Example in a dry deciduous forest: 1 male Ashy cuckoo-shrike, 6 Common newtonias, 1 pair of Madagascar paradise flycatchers, 1 Long-billed greenbul, 2 Souimanga sunbirds, 1 Common jery, and 2 Crested drongos. Almost always stays near treetops. Feeds in foliage or on branches. Prey is often struck against perch.

VOICE: Fairly vocal. Distinctive song is an excellent field mark: brief, emphatic, separately articulated *kiap kiap kiap kiap* followed by series of fluted notes decreasing in volume, heard as *Cheekeekeekee kee .. kee ... kee*. Entire song is sometimes repeated several times from perch. Final fluted, trailing notes often come as bird takes wing.

HABITAT: Various original forest types
and sometimes adjacent degraded terrain.
Observed at elevations from sea level to
2,300 m.

DIET: Invertebrates: Coleoptera, cica-
das, mantises, spiders, centipedes, larvae,
caterpillars.

NESTING: Few data. Nest, built high
above ground, is a shallow bowl made up
largely of mosses and lichens. Clutch
numbers 1 roseate-white egg spotted with
red. Nesting has been observed
Nov.–Mar.

DISTRIBUTION AND STATUS: Distributed in Madagascar and Comoros.
Represented in Madagascar by 2 endemic
subspecies: *C. c. cinerea* in e and nw and
on High Plateau (Ambohitantely) and *C.
c. pallida* in w and s. Ashy cuckoo-shrike
is common throughout range.

Pycnonotidae – Greenbuls, Bulbul

Heterogeneous family of frugivorous or
insectivorous passerines, generally gregarious and normally frequenting forest
habitats, rather short-legged, with varying
forms of bill. The family numbers nearly
120 species spread through Africa, Asia,
and Madagascar. Of the 6 species that
nest in Madagascar, 5 are endemic.

NOTE: The position of the Pycnototidae
of Madagascar of the genus *Phyllastrephus*
is challenged by some taxonomists who
maintain that the Malagasy species differ
too much from the African species to be
placed in the same genus. They advocate
the use of the original endemic genus
Berniera for the Malagasy species.

197. Long-billed Greenbul

Phyllastrephus madagascariensis
(Gmelin, 1789)
Malagasy: Tekitekiala, Droadroaka,
Tetraka, Toaiky
French: Bulbul de Madagascar

DESCRIPTION: Length 20 cm (male),
17.5 cm (female).
Adult. Sexes differ; male larger than
female.

Nominate subspecies *P. m. madagascariensis* (Sclater, 1924).

Front and top of head, nape, and
cheeks dark green. Bright yellow chin
and throat. Long (male 23 mm, female 18
mm) bill. Brown upper mandible with
terminal hook. Concave roseate lower
mandible. Chestnut iris. Upperparts dark
green. Underparts: yellow center of chest
and belly, olive green sides of chest,
flanks, and undertail coverts. Dark green

wings with brown primary remiges. Dark green tail.

Subspecies *P. m. inceleber* (Bangs and Peters, 1926).

Differs by generally paler plumage.

IDENTIFICATION: Bulbul with long, slender silhouette, often adopts vertical position at rest. Distinguished from Spectacled greenbul by noticeably larger size, longer bill, and much paler yellow underparts.

BEHAVIOR: Gregarious forest species found in groups of 3–10, associated with Spectacled greenbul or as members of multispecies feeding flocks. Noisy and bold. Feeds in bushy layer of forest, nimbly climbing up and down even vertical trunks and branches. Carefully inspects tangles of plants and epiphytic vegetation for prey. Flies infrequently, and only short distances.

VOICE: Vocal, utters harsh, loud *cherrr cherrr* while feeding, also whistling *truh truh truh . . . .* Sings loud but decrescendo *chee tee tee tee* from perch at all hours of day, often repeating song after few seconds.

HABITAT: Lower and middle reaches of evergreen rain forest and deciduous dry forest, seldom adjacent degraded terrain. Observed at elevations from sea level to 1,800 m.

DIET: Chiefly insects (Coleoptera, Lepidoptera) and caterpillars.

NESTING: No detailed data. Breeding period is thought to be Sept.–Feb.

DISTRIBUTION AND STATUS: Endemic to Madagascar, represented by 2 subspecies. *P. m. madagascariensis* distributed in e from Andapa to Tolagnaro. *P. m. inceleber* distributed in n (Montagne d'Ambre and Sambirano) and in sw to Toliara. Common in all but sw part of range, where it is rarer.

198. *Spectacled Greenbul*

Phyllastrephus zosterops (Sharpe, 1875)
Malagasy: Tetraka, Farifotra
French: Bulbul zosterops

DESCRIPTION: Length of *P. z. zosterops* 16 cm; of *P. z. fulvescens* 16.5 cm.
Adult. Sexes similar.

Nominate subspecies *P. z. zosterops* (Delacour, 1932).

Front and top of head, nape, and cheeks dark green. Bright yellow chin, throat, lores, and eye ring, except behind eyes. Bill (14 mm): brown upper mandible, light brown lower mandible. Chestnut iris. Upperparts dark green, underparts bright yellow except for green-yellow flanks. Flesh-colored tarsi and toes. Wings dark green with yellow outer half of primary remiges. Dark green tail.

Subspecies *P. z. fulvescens* (Delacour, 1931).

Differs from nominate subspecies by generally paler and less contrasting plumage.

Three other geographically very local subspecies that are impossible to distinguish from the nominate subspecies are recognized: *P. z. maroantsetra* (Salomonsen, 1934), *P. z. andapae* (Salomonsen, 1934), and *P. z. ankafanae* (Salomonsen, 1934).

IDENTIFICATION: Differs from Long-billed greenbul by noticeably smaller size, much shorter bill, and bright yellow eye ring.

BEHAVIOR: Forest species with behavior similar to that of Long-billed greenbul: gregarious, found in groups of 4–20, or as members of multispecies feeding flocks, most often composed of Long-billed greenbuls and White-throated oxylabes, sometimes Common newtonias, Madagascar white-eyes, Ashy cuckooshrikes, Red-tailed vangas, or White-headed vangas. Active and bold. Feeds in low vegetation, creepers, ferns, as well as trunks and branches, which it climbs easily even if they are vertical, though it does so less readily than Long-billed Greenbul. Flies little, and only short distances.

VOICE: Rather quiet, utters brief, nasal calls while feeding.

HABITAT: Lower stratum of undisturbed rain forest and adjacent second growth. Observed at elevations from sea level to 1,800 m.

DIET: Chiefly insects (Coleoptera).

NESTING: Hemispherical nest, built low above ground, consists of interlaced mosses or other soft components. Clutch numbers 3–4 roseate-white eggs with chestnut spots. Nesting has been observed Sept.–Dec.

DISTRIBUTION AND STATUS: Species endemic to Madagascar, distributed in E Region from Montagne d'Ambre to Tolagnaro. Nominate subspecies *P. z. zosterops* has widest distribution; other subspecies are very local. *P. z. fulvescens* is local to forest of Montagne d'Ambre, *P. z. andapae* to high forest near Andapa, *P. z. maroantsetrae* to vicinity of Maroantsetra, and *P. z. ankafanae* to high forest near Fianarantsoa. Validity of last 3 localized subspecies named is often challenged. Common throughout range.

199. *Appert's Greenbul*

Phyllastrephus apperti Colstom, 1972
French: Bulbul d'Appert

DESCRIPTION: Length 15 cm.
Adult. Front and top of head and nape dark gray. Whitish lores, faint supercilium extending behind eyes. White chin and throat. Bill: dark upper mandible,

light lower mandible. Dark brown iris. Upperparts olive green–gray, underparts yellow. Pale red tarsi and toes. Olive green–gray wings and tail.

IDENTIFICATION: Terrestrial bulbul, greenish gray above, yellow below, with gray head. Distinguished from Thamnornis warbler by gray head, yellow underparts, and less graduated, solid-colored tail.

BEHAVIOR: Gregarious, found in groups of 2–8 in dense underbrush of dry forest. Sometimes associates with flocks of Long-billed greenbuls. Feeds on leaf litter and low branches, seldom climbing more than 1 m above ground. Only passerine of such terrestrial habits in region. When disturbed, perches in low bush.

VOICE: Vocal, often utters shrill, reedy *tsee* or *tseetsee* from inside bush, also high-pitched, secretive alarm call, *tsirr*.

HABITAT: Dense underbrush of undisturbed dry forest. Observed at elevation of about 500 m.

DIET: Unknown.

NESTING: Unknown.

DISTRIBUTION AND STATUS: Endemic to Madagascar, recently discovered, rather rare and very localized. Known only from 2 forests, one located 40 km s of Ankazoabo (Vohibasia forest), the other 12 km ne of Sakaraha (Zombitse forest).

200. *Dusky Greenbul*

Phyllastrephus tenebrosus
(Stresemann, 1925)
French: Bulbul fuligineux

DESCRIPTION: Length 14.5 cm.
Adult. Front and top of head and nape

dark brown. Yellow lores and eye ring, except behind eyes. Bright yellow chin and throat. Bill (13 mm): dark upper mandible, lighter lower mandible. Upperparts very dark brown-green. Underparts: dark green flanks and undertail coverts, yellow belly. Brown tarsi and toes. Dark green wings with dark brown inner half of primary remiges. Fairly short dark brown tail.

IDENTIFICATION: Bulbul of about same size as Spectacled greenbul but with stockier silhouette. Distinguished from Spectacled greenbul by much darker underparts and by yellow throat and belly that contrast much more with rest of dark underparts. Longer tail, sturdier, longer, and darker legs, slightly shorter, stouter-looking bill.

BEHAVIOR: Secretive forest species frequenting undergrowth and low branches of forest. Four observations of lone individual recorded, 3 of these with other species: *(a)* 2 White-throated oxylabes; *(b)* 1 White-throated oxylabe and 1 Madagascar paradise flycatcher; *(c)* 7 Spectacled greenbuls, 2 Madagascar paradise flycatchers, 1 Nelicourvi weaver, and 1 Sunbird-asity.

VOICE: Unknown.

HABITAT: Few data. Observed in lower story of undisturbed evergreen rain forest at elevations of 500 and 950 m.

DIET: Unknown.

NESTING: Unknown.

DISTRIBUTION AND STATUS: Endemic to Madagascar, rare species known from 8 museum specimens (1 collected at Andasibe in 1929 and 7 collected in Sihanaka forest in 1930), and from about 10 recent (since 1974) sightings at Andasibe and Maroantsetra.

201. *Gray-crowned Greenbul*

Phyllastrephus cinereiceps (Sharpe, 1881)
Malagasy: Farifotramavoloha, Farifotra
French: Bulbul à tête grise

DESCRIPTION: Length 14 cm. *Adult.* Sexes similar. Front and top of head and nape gray. Light gray cheeks, dirty white chin and throat. Fairly short (12 mm) brown bill, light on basal two-thirds of lower mandible. Dark brown iris. Upperparts dark green. Underparts: bright yellow center of chest and belly, yellow-green sides of chest, flanks, and undertail coverts. Light tarsi and toes. Wings dark green except for brown primary remiges, outer half edged with green. Brown-green tail.

IDENTIFICATION: Bulbul with slender silhouette, easily identified by gray head, green upperparts, and yellow underparts.

BEHAVIOR: Active forest-dweller found alone, in pairs, or associated with such species as Spectacled greenbul, White-throated oxylabe, or Madagascar paradise flycatcher. Feeds in dense forest undergrowth, frequently on trunks and large vertical branches, which it climbs as nimbly as Long-billed greenbul.

VOICE: Generally quiet, repeats very shrill reedy *tseeet* while feeding.

HABITAT: Fairly dense underbrush of lower story of undisturbed rain forest. Observed at elevations of 600–2,000 m.

DIET: Chiefly small insects.

NESTING: Few data. Bowl-shaped nest, built on fork of small horizontal branch 1.5 m above ground, consists exclusively of interlaced soft mosses. Clutch numbers 3 eggs. Nesting has been observed in Nov.

DISTRIBUTION AND STATUS: Endemic to Madagascar, known only from few locales in E Region (Tsaratanana,

Marojejy, Fito in Sihanaka forest, Fanovana, Ranomafana). Rare except at Ranomafana, where it is fairly common.

202. *Madagascar (Black) Bulbul*

Hypsipetes madagascariensis (Müller, 1776)
Malagasy: Tsikorovana, Tsikoreva, Horovana
French: Bulbul noir

DESCRIPTION: Length 24 cm.
Adult. Sexes similar. Black forehead, front and top of head and nape. Feathers more or less ruffled on forehead and front of head. Dark gray cheeks, chin and throat. Orange bill, dark red iris. Upperparts dark gray. Underparts gray, paler on flanks and belly than on chest. Straw yellow tarsi and toes. Wings gray except for gray-brown primary and secondary remiges, dark gray-brown underside. Dark gray-brown tail.

IDENTIFICATION: Largest bulbul of Madagascar, with slender silhouette and uncontrasted dull gray plumage, often ruffled black crown, orange bill. Cannot be confused with any other species.

BEHAVIOR: Gregarious when not nesting, found in rowdy bands of 5–15, seldom more, or as members of multispecies feeding flocks. Feeds in treetops, fruiting bushes, seldom on ground. Very active, moving about frequently with straight, easy flight.

VOICE: Highly vocal. Most commonly heard phrase of varied but unmelodic repertory is brief, nasal, bisyllabic, slightly trilled *tireet,* which, repeated several times and taken up by other birds, may be elaborated into *tireet teetee tireet.* Another characteristic call is plaintive, nasal, monotonous *eeeeee* or *eee-ew.*

HABITAT: Various original forest types, as well as degraded, even sparsely wooded, terrain, orchards, surroundings of villages and city parks. Observed at elevations from sea level to 2,500 m.

DIET: Berries, fruits, and insects (Coleoptera).

NESTING: Hemispherical nest with open-mesh bottom (eggs visible from below), built low off ground, usually at end of branch, consists of plant matter (small twigs, grasses, mosses, vegetal fragments). Clutch numbers 3 roseate-white eggs densely speckled with red, especially on larger pole (average size: 25.7 mm × 18.7 mm). Nesting has been observed Sept.–Jan.

DISTRIBUTION AND STATUS: Distributed in Asia, Comoros, Aldabra, and Madagascar. Represented in Madagascar by endemic nominate subspecies *H. m. madagascariensis* (Sclater, 1924). Very common throughout island. A forest species that has adapted well to deforestation.

NOTE: Four very close species are found on Comoros, Réunion, Mauritius, and Seychelles.

Turdidae – Magpie-Robin, Stonechat, Rock-Thrushes

Heterogeneous family of small or medium-sized passerines frequenting varied habitats, having a fairly long, rather thin, and slightly curved bill, and with rather sturdy legs in the arboreal species and slimmer legs in the terrestrial species. Turdidae build bowl-shaped nests, and most species are good singers. Their diet is varied, consisting of invertebrates and often berries and fruits. The family is cosmopolitan and numbers more than 300 species. Of the 5 species found in Madagascar, 4 are endemic.

203. *Madagascar Magpie-Robin*

Copsychus albospecularis (Eydoux and Gervais, 1836)
Malagasy: Fatsimboay, Atodiana, Pida, Pidaehy, Fitatra'ala, Fitatsy, Fitatra, Fitadahy (male) + Fitavavy (female)
French: Dyal malgache

DESCRIPTION: Length 18 cm.
Adult. Sexes differ.
Nominate subspecies *C. a. albospecularis.*
Male. Jet black head, chin, throat, and neck. Black bill, dark brown iris. Upperparts jet black, underparts black. Dark gray tarsi and toes. Wings black except for white median and lesser upperwing coverts. Jet black tail.
Female. Chestnut head, except for light brown skin around eyes. Chestnut chin, gray throat and neck. Black bill, dark brown iris. Upperparts chestnut, underparts light gray, except for rufous flanks and undertail coverts. Dark gray tarsi and toes. Chestnut wings, except for white median and lesser underwing coverts.

Brown tail, except for chestnut central tail feathers.
Subspecies *C. a. inexpectatus* (Richmond, 1897).
Male. Differs from male of nominate subspecies by white belly and undertail coverts.
Female. Differs from female of nominate subspecies by lighter underparts.
Subspecies *C. a. pica* (Pelzeln, 1858).
Male. Differs from male of nominate subspecies by white belly, undertail coverts, secondary remiges (outer half), external tail feathers, apical half of second tail feathers, and apical third of third tail feathers.
Female. Differs from female of nominate subspecies by much lighter hue of underparts and white inner secondary remiges in their outer half.
Immature. Male differs from adult male by drab black plumage, whitish throat, and yellow commissures of bill. Female differs from adult female by top of head, mantle, and scapulars marked with small brown spots and by fawn-edged underparts.

IDENTIFICATION: Medium-sized member of the Turdidae with slender silhouette. Male is characterized by jet black or black-and-white plumage, with white wing bar shared by all subspecies. Female has much more subdued plumage, brownish above, gray and rufous below, with varying degrees of lightness according to subspecies and conspicuous wing bar varying in size by subspecies.

BEHAVIOR: Not shy but rather furtive, often staying in shadows of underbrush. Seen alone or in pairs. Feeds on forest floor among tangled plants of underbrush, sometimes with mobile multispecies feeding flocks. Hops nervously on ground while feeding, raising tail to vertical position when excited. Male often perches, with no attempt at concealment, for extended intervals to sing indefatigably. Males are aggressive toward other males, and frantic pursuits in undergrowth are frequently observed.

VOICE: Very vocal, sings melodiously. Male delivers long, linked phrases of high-pitched, resonant, melodic trills. Alarm call, uttered by both sexes, is heard as shrill, harsh, resonant *tree tree tree . . . .*

HABITAT: Various original forest types, second growth, woodland savanna, mangroves, arboricultural areas (coffee, cacao, and banana plantations), and wooded surroundings of towns and villages. Observed at elevations from sea level to 1,800 m.

DIET: Chiefly insects, less frequently berries and fruits.

NESTING: Bowl-shaped nest of interlaced mosses, grasses, and leafstalks, with softer lining, is built in hole of tree, bamboo, epiphytic fern, stump, or rock, 0.8–8 m above ground. Clutch generally numbers 3 (sometimes 2 or 4) smooth, shiny blue-green eggs mottled with brown and violet-gray (average size: 21.0 mm × 16.0 mm). Female broods. Nesting has been observed Sept.–Jan.

DISTRIBUTION AND STATUS: Endemic to Madagascar, common throughout island. *C. a. albospecularis* is local to n and ne. *C. a. inextectatus* is distributed from e center to se. *C. a. pica* is more widely distributed, being found in se, w, and n.

NOTE: Individuals with characters intermediate between the subspecies *C. a. albospecularis* and *C. a. inexpectatus* and between *C. a. inexpectatus* and *C. a. pica* are found locally.

204. *Stonechat*

Saxicola torquata (Linnaeus, 1766)
Malagasy: Fitatra, Fitadroranga
French: Traquet pâtre

DESCRIPTION: Length of *S. t. sibilla* 14 cm.
Adult. Sexes differ.
   Subspecies *S. t. sibilla* (Sclater, 1924).
Male. Black head, chin, and throat. Black neck with white on sides. Black bill, dark brown iris. Upperparts black edged with brown, except for whitish uppertail coverts. Underparts white marked with wide, bright orange–rufous bib. Black tarsi and toes. Wings: dark brown edged with rusty brown, except for white greater and median upperwing coverts. Brown-edged black primary and secondary remiges with white base of inner secondaries. Dark brown tail.
Female. Differs from male by less contrasting plumage and by brown head and upperparts edged with light brown, yellowish sides of neck spotted with brown, whitish underparts tinged with orange, and smaller white wing patch.
Immature. Dark brown head and upperparts speckled with whitish and rust marks. Yellowish tan underparts spotted with black. Brown wings with wide light brown edges. Small wing bar in male, none in female.
   Subspecies *S. t. ankaratrae* (Salomonsen, 1934).
   Differs from *S. t. sibilla* by larger size.
   Subspecies *S. t. tsaratananae* (Milon, 1951).
   Differs from *S. t. sibilla* by darker upperparts and by largely black chest with tips of feathers marked with orangy rufous.

IDENTIFICATION: Small member of the Turdidae with plump silhouette, upright posture, and large black head isolated by white at sides of neck. Characterized by highly contrasting plumage, black above and white below, with rufous on chest, and by white wing bar. In flight, which is generally low and jerky, field marks are white wing bar and uppertail coverts contrasting with sooty rest of upperparts.

BEHAVIOR: Active, vigilant, seen alone or in pairs. Waits upright in ambush on bush, isolated branch, or electric wire overlooking grassy terrain or fairly open new growth. While waiting, nervously twitches wings and tail. Catches prey on wing by means of aerial acrobatics near its ambush site, more rarely on ground.

VOICE: Fairly vocal, utters repetitive brief, clipped, metallic *tek trek* . . . or shrill *weetik* from perch. Song, delivered in flight, is a brief, high, clear, liquid trill.

HABITAT: Any open terrain offering scattered bushes and shrubs (forest edges, clearings, and second-growth formations of original forests, savanna, open areas near lakes and rivers, and highland scrub). Observed at elevations from sea level to 2,400 m.

DIET: Insects.

NESTING: Nest, built on ground among grasses, or some centimeters above ground in dense tuft of grass or thick shrubbery, is a bowl of moss and grass lined with softer material. Clutch numbers 3 greenish blue eggs speckled with chestnut, more heavily at larger pole (average size: 18.4 mm × 14.5 mm). Female broods. Nesting has been observed July–Dec., peaking Oct.

DISTRIBUTION AND STATUS: Distributed in Europe, Africa, and Asia. In Madagascar the species is distributed throughout island and common in n, e, and w but rather rare in s, where it is confined to river and lake surroundings.

S. t. sibilla is widely distributed all over the territory but is replaced locally by *S. t. ankaratrae*, local to mountainous areas near Ankaratra and areas s and sw of Antananarivo, where it is fairly common, and by *S. t. tsaratananae*, local to Tsaratanana highlands, where it is common.

205. *Forest Rock-Thrush*

Pseudocossyphus sharpei (Gray, 1871)
Malagasy: Androbaka, Tsinoly, Olioly
French: Merle de roche de forêt

DESCRIPTION: Length 16 cm.
Adult. Sexes differ.
   Nominate subspecies *P. s. sharpei* (Delacour, 1932).
Male. Slate gray–blue head, chin, throat and neck. Black bill, dark brown iris. Upperparts slate gray–blue except for rufous-brown rump and uppertail coverts. Underparts bright orangy rufous except for slate gray–blue chest. Roseate-gray tarsi and toes. Rufous-brown wings with dark brown remiges. Tail rufous tipped with black bar, except for solid dark brown central tail feathers.
Female. Light brown head and neck, light tan chin, throat, lores, and skin around eyes. Black bill, dark brown iris. Upperparts brown except for rufous-brown rump and uppertail coverts. Underparts: tan chest and undertail coverts marked with diffuse brown spots, light brown belly marked with diffuse dark brown spots, brown flanks. Roseate-gray tarsi and toes. Brown wings with dark brown remiges. Rufous tail tipped with sooty bar, except for solid dark brown central tail feathers.
   Subspecies *P. s. erythronotus* (Lavauden, 1929).
   Slightly larger than nominate subspecies.

Male. Differs from male *P. s. sharpei* by brighter and lighter gray-blue of head, bright orange-rufous throat and chest, rufous-brown underparts, and limited dark terminal bar on tail.

Female. Differs from female *P. s. sharpei* only by slightly lighter hue of plumage.

Subspecies *P. s. salomonseni* (Salomonsen, 1934).

Differs from *P. s. sharpei* by larger size.

IDENTIFICATION: Medium-sized member of the Turdidae, with rather slender silhouette, slate gray–blue above, with orangy belly and rufous tail. Male cannot be confused with any other species. Female is easily distinguished from female of Madagascar magpie-robin by smaller size, brown underparts speckled with darker spots, rufous tail, and absence of wing bar.

BEHAVIOR: Sedate, secretive, but not shy forest species usually found alone or in pairs in darkest parts of underbrush. Stays motionless for long spells on low branch, stump, stone, or ground, even at approach of intruder. Flies short distances to seize prey on ground.

VOICE: Vocal, male delivers various melodious whistles, including a sort of rising *teedew teedew*.

HABITAT: Dense undergrowth of undisturbed rain forest, more rarely adjacent second-growth terrain. Observed at elevations of 500–2,200 m.

DIET: Insects, berries, fruits.

NESTING: Few data. Nest, built low (2 m) above ground in rocky crevice or bush, consists of interlaced plant parts. Nesting has been observed Oct.–Feb.

DISTRIBUTION AND STATUS: Endemic to Madagascar, distributed in e, n, and High Plateau. *P. s. sharpei* is the most widely distributed, found from Sambava to Tolagnaro, where it is fairly common at elevations of over 800 m. *P. s. erythronotus* is local to forest of Montagne d'Ambre, where it is common at elevations of 1,000–1,300 m. Subspecies *P. s. salomonseni* is distributed in relict forests of High Plateau near Antananarivo (Ambohitantely, Manjakatompo) and Fianarantsoa, where it is uncommon.

206. *Littoral Rock-Thrush*

Pseudocossyphus imerinus (Hartlaub, 1860)
Malagasy: Tsibotrotsy
French: Merle de roche du sub-désert

DESCRIPTION: Length 16 cm.
Adult. Sexes differ.
Male. Gray-blue head, neck, chin, and throat. Black bill, dark brown iris. Upperparts gray-blue, underparts orange except for gray-blue chest. Black tarsi and toes. Gray-blue wings with dark gray remiges. Dark gray tail.
Female. Gray head with pale gray supercilium and lores. Pale gray chin and throat. Black bill, dark brown iris. Upperparts gray except for rufous-brown uppertail coverts. Underparts pale gray with darker smudges on chest. Black tarsi and toes. Gray wings with gray-brown remiges. Gray-brown tail.

IDENTIFICATION: Medium-sized member of the Turdidae with rather slender silhouette, gray-blue and bright orange plumage, and dark gray tail. Much drabber female has uniform gray plumage with rufous markings and darker uppertail coverts, wings, and tail. Cannot be confused with any other species.

BEHAVIOR: Rather sedate and not shy, found alone or in pairs. Stays motionless for long intervals, sitting on bush or low branch. Feeds on ground, hopping about. If disturbed, takes wing to fly easily and directly to higher perch, adopting a characteristic posture to observe intruder, body upright, neck and head extended, and bill pointing upward.

VOICE: Vocal, delivers soft, melodious, gentle song from unconcealed perch.

HABITAT: Subarid scrub on sandy soil along coast or on coastal dunes, consisting of medium-sized shrubs and sparse Euphorbes (*Euphorbia stenoclada*—Euphorbiaceae). Observed near sea level (maximum elevation 190 m at Cap Sainte-Marie).

DIET: Berries, fruits, insects.

NESTING: Few data. Bowl-shaped nest consists of interlaced twigs, lined with softer material. Clutch numbers 2 greenblue eggs. Nesting has been observed Oct.–Feb.

DISTRIBUTION AND STATUS: Endemic to Madagascar, local to s coastal strip from Morombe to Anony Lake. Common, except n of Toliara, where it is rather rare.

207. *Benson's Rock-Thrush*

Pseudocossyphus bensoni (Farkas, 1971)
Malagasy: Singetringetry (male) +
Tomo (female)
French: Merle de roche de Benson

DESCRIPTION: Length: 16 cm.
Adult. Sexes differ.
Male. Light ash gray head, chin, and throat. Dusky brown bill, dark brown iris. Upperparts light ash gray, except for bright orange rump and uppertail coverts. Underparts orange, except for ash gray chest. Pale yellowish tarsi and toes. Wings dark gray above, orangy below on coverts and axillaries. Tail: 2 dark brown central tail feathers, bright orange outer tail feathers edged with black on inner apical half and tipped with black.
Female. Brownish head, chin, and throat. Upperparts brownish. Underparts pale

gray. Tail pale orange, except for dark brown 2 central tail feathers.
Immature Male. Differs from adult male by gray head speckled with light gray and by narrow light gray median band on orangy belly.
Immature Female. Differs from adult female by entirely gray plumage speckled with light gray, except for rufousbrown tail.

IDENTIFICATION: Medium-sized member of the Turdidae having rather slender silhouette with ash gray plumage above, orange and ash gray below (male), and orange tail. Plumage of female is much more subdued, brownish above and gray-brown below. Cannot be confused with any other species.

BEHAVIOR: Rupicolous, little known, found alone or in pairs in sunny, rocky terrain. Occasionally shelters in bushes or trees (*Uapaca bojeri*—Uapacaceae) during heat of day. Feeds as it hops about on rocks, more rarely in rocky vegetation. Occasionally seizes prey in swift, acrobatic flight. If disturbed, seeks refuge atop rocks. Flight is swift and straight, close to ground or rocks.

VOICE: Vocal. Male frequently sings from rock or in dense shrubbery during hottest time of day. Song is melodious, sweet, and fairly resonant.

HABITAT: Rocky settings offering bushy or limited rocky arborescent vegetation (cliffs, rocky terrain, gorges). Observed at elevations of 700–1,000 m on breeding sites.

DIET: Insects.

NESTING: Few data. Deep bowl-shaped nest, built in cliff hollow, consists of interlaced fine roots and leafstalks. Nesting has been observed in Dec.

DISTRIBUTION AND STATUS: Endemic to Madagascar, recently discovered, has received little investigation.

Local to Isalo massif, where it is common. In austral winter, disperses to Mangoky and Sakaraha region (Zombitse forest).

NOTE: Species was initially described under genus *Monticola*. Presented here under genus *Pseudocossyphus* because distinction of 2 genera is not justified for Madagascar's 3 species of rock-thrush. Taxonomic review of the 3 species should establish most appropriate genus.

Sylvidae – Warblers, Cisticola, Emutails, Newtonias, Jeries

Rather heterogeneous family of passerines whose representatives are smaller than those of the family Turdidae. They frequent forests, marshes, savannas, and steppes, and build closed or bowl-shaped nests. Most species give voice to various types of song, and almost all are insectivores. A few species also eat fruit. The family numbers more than 300 species distributed in the Old World. In Madagascar it is represented by 15 species, of which 13 are endemic while the other 2 belong to the region.

208. *Madagascar Swamp-Warbler*

Acrocephalus newtoni (Hartlaub, 1863)
Malagasy: Vorombatra
French: Rousserole de Newton

DESCRIPTION: Length 18 cm.
Adult. Sexes similar. Gray-brown head and neck, except for barely marked pale supercilium. Solid gray-white chin, gray-white throat with brown-gray stripes. Bill: black upper mandible, roseate-gray lower mandible. Chestnut iris. Upperparts brown. Underparts: gray-white chest with brown-gray stripes, tan-tinged white belly, light brown-gray flanks. Dark gray tarsi and toes. Brown wings with dark brown remiges. Brown tail.

IDENTIFICATION: Large warbler with slender silhouette, long bill, brown plumage above and whitish below, throat and chest streaked with brown, and long, graduated tail. Only member of genus in Madagascar. Distinguished from Madagascar brush-warbler by slightly larger size, stockier silhouette, longer bill, and, especially, streaked underparts.

BEHAVIOR: Marsh-dwelling, generally solitary, bold, but furtive and difficult to observe. Sometimes perches atop reed before plunging back into dense vegetation beneath. Flies little and only for short distances, preferring to move within reedbed from one vertical stalk to another. Flies low and awkwardly, with tail spread.

VOICE: Vocal. Song, excellent means of location and identification, is a sometimes prolonged succession of liquid, resonant, melodious low and high notes, curiously articulated and punctuated with low, throaty notes, sung mostly within vegetation.

HABITAT: Aquatic vegetation of ponds, lakes, rivers, also mangroves. Observed at elevations from sea level to 2,000 m.

DIET: Chiefly insects.

NESTING: Nest, suspended from several vertical reed stalks or built inside a dense bush, 0.5–1 m above water, consists of interlaced dry grasses, dry pieces of bark, and down. Interior is lined with finer bits of same material and some feathers. Clutch numbers 3 slightly shiny white eggs with bluish tinge, mottled and vermiculated with gray and olive brown, more densely at larger pole (average size: 19.8 mm × 14.6 mm). Nesting has been observed May–Jan., peaking Nov.–Dec.

DISTRIBUTION AND STATUS: Endemic to Madagascar, distributed throughout island, where it is generally common.

209. Madagascar Brush-Warbler

Nesillas typica (Hartlaub, 1866)
Malagasy: Poretaka, Aretika, Lava-Salaka
French: Fauvette de Madagascar

DESCRIPTION: Length 17–18 cm.
Adult. Sexes similar.

Nominate subspecies *N. t. typica* (Hartlaub, 1877).
Adult. Pale olive head marked with short, pale supercilium. Pale green-gray chin and throat. Bill: black upper mandible, grayish pink lower mandible with black tip. Chestnut iris. Upperparts solid brown-gray. Underparts grayish white, tinged with green-gray on chest, flanks, and undertail coverts. Roseate-gray tarsi and toes. Gray–olive green wings with darker remiges. Gray-brown tail.
Immature. Similar to adult.
Subspecies *N. t. lantzii* (Grandidier, 1867).
Differs from *N. t. typica* by much paler hue of plumage, entirely pale gray above and whitish below.
Subspecies *N. t. obscura* (Delacour, 1931).
Differs from *N. t. typica* by much darker hue of plumage, entirely dark brown except for whitish supercilium, chin, throat, and belly, and by longer bill.

IDENTIFICATION: Large warbler with slender silhouette, long, graduated tail, very short wings, subdued plumage—brown-gray above, paler below—and head marked by inconspicuous short, light supercilium. Distinguished from Madagascar swamp-warbler by more delicate silhouette and even-colored underparts with no markings. Easily distinguished from Brown emutail by considerably larger size, plumage that is never rufous-brown, light supercilium, long, graduated tail, and longer bill.

BEHAVIOR: Very active, furtive but not shy, found alone or in pairs. Keeps to interior of low, bushy vegetation and dense shrubbery, in which it moves constantly and easily, uttering characteristic call. While feeding, occasionally walks and hops on ground and climbs to low heights, repeatedly raising tail nervously.

VOICE: Vocal, can be readily located and identified by call, a succession of metallic, clipped, shrill, rapid-fire notes heard as *trick trick trick* . . . , trailing off at end and emitted from thick of vegetation. Its song is a succession of melodic whistled notes.

HABITAT: Low vegetation of various original forest types, savanna, second growth, even if very degraded, tree plantations, parks, and gardens. Observed at elevations from sea level to 2,700 m.

DIET: Insects.

NESTING: Nest, built only 0.2–0.6 m above ground in dense tuft of grass or bush, consists of interlaced dry grasses and is lined with softer material. Clutch numbers 2 smooth, slightly shiny white eggs tinged with varying shades of pink and variably spotted with gray and chestnut (average size: 20.1 mm × 15.5 mm). Nesting has been observed Aug.–Feb., peaking Oct.–Dec.

DISTRIBUTION AND STATUS: Distributed in Madagascar and Comoros. In Madagascar, this common species is represented by 3 endemic subspecies distributed throughout island: in e, n, and nw and on High Plateau by *N. t. typica*, in w by *N. t. obscura*, and in s by *N. t. lantzii*.

NOTE: Coloration of plumage varies considerably throughout range. Those variations, linked to geographic and altitudinal factors, were once reflected in descriptions of 5 subspecies, now reclassified into the 3 listed above. Thus *N. t. ellisi* (Schlegel and Pollen, 1868), localized to Montagne d'Ambre and Sambirano, and *N. t. monticola* (Hartert and Lavauden, 1931), local to Tsaratanana, have been incorporated into *N. t. typica*.

210. *Thamnornis Warbler*

Thamnornis chloropetoides
(Grandidier, 1867)
Malagasy: Aritiky
French: Thamnornis

DESCRIPTION: Length 15 cm. *Adult.* Sexes similar. Brown-gray head, except for white chin, throat, sides of neck, and supercilium. Light brown bill, brown iris. Upperparts gray-green, underparts white with yellowish tinge, except for yellow-green flanks and undertail coverts. Flesh-colored tarsi and toes. Wings gray-green, except for primary remiges edged with yellow-green on outer half. Yellow-green graduated tail, tipped with white on 3 external feathers.

IDENTIFICATION: Medium-sized warbler with slight contrast between green plumage above and green-white below. Distinguished from Appert's greenbul by bolder light supercilium, very graduated tail, and white-tipped external tail feathers.

BEHAVIOR: Gregarious outside nesting season, generally found in groups of 4–10. Readily associates with such species as Common newtonia, Archbold's newtonia, Common jery, Sakalava weaver, Madagascar magpie-robin, or Red-tailed vanga. Feeds on branches and small trunks of underbrush, also frequently on leaf litter.

VOICE: Rather vocal. Characteristic song, heard from high perch or inside of bush, is composed of 2 fragments with variable delivery times. Second is almost always longer. The fragments also differ as to timbre, first being a sort of buzzing, vibrating *geerrr* produced with bill wide open, followed immediately by whistled *dewdewdewdew* . . . . Complete song can be heard only during breeding period.

HABITAT: Dense underbrush of undisturbed subarid scrub and adjacent second growth. As likely to be found in subarid with sandy soil as in those growing on rocky hillsides, but seems to shun gallery forests. Observed at elevations from sea level to 500 m.

DIET: Almost exclusively insects and caterpillars.

NESTING: Nest, built in deep shrubbery close to ground (0.25 m), consists of dry leaves and pieces of bark, its interior lined with tender leafstalks. Nest is attached by spiders' webs to small vertical branches. Clutch numbers 3 shiny reddish white eggs boldly spotted with brown or maroon and diffuse red-gray spots, especially at larger pole (average size: 18.6 mm × 14.7 mm). Nesting has been observed Nov.–Dec.

DISTRIBUTION AND STATUS: Endemic to Madagascar, distributed in S Domain and locally at the limit between W and S domains near Ankazoabo. Fairly common throughout range.

211. *Madagascar Cisticola*

Cisticola cherina (Smith, 1843)
Malagasy: Tsintsina, Tinty, Abido, Tintina
French: Cisticole de Madagascar

DESCRIPTION: Length 12 cm.
Adult. Sexes similar. Fawn-brown cap with dark brown stripes. Rest of head fawn-brown, except for white lores prolonged as subtle supercilium. White chin and throat. Bill: black upper mandible, yellow lower mandible. Light brown iris. Upperparts fawn-brown streaked with brown, except for solid light brown rump. Underparts white, tinged with fawn on flanks. Pink tarsi and toes. Wings fawn-brown, with dark brown remiges edged

with fawn-brown. Brown graduated tail marked with black subterminal bar and tipped with white, except for solid brown central tail feathers.
Immature. Differs from adult by more boldly dark brown–striped head and upperparts and by underparts strongly tinged with brown.

IDENTIFICATION: Small member of the Sylvidae having fawn-brown plumage with dark stripes above, white below, graduated tail tipped with white, and long legs. Its flight is fluttering and unsteady, with nervous, rapid wingbeats. Only species of its genus in Madagascar; cannot be confused with any other species.

BEHAVIOR: Found alone, in pairs, or in small groups of 3–5. Very active but often difficult to observe unobstructed. Lives among grassy tufts or low, thick bushes, darting in and out and nimbly climbing along stalks. From time to time it exhibits bounding flight, punctuating each dip with a brief, shrill, metallic call, then disappears again into vegetation.

VOICE: Vocal, utters characteristic brief, shrill, metallic *tint tint tint . . .* in flight.

HABITAT: Any open grassy terrain: savanna, clearings, degraded woodlands, cereal croplands (especially rice paddies), wetlands covered or surrounded by tall grasses, grassy roadside embankments. Observed at elevations from sea level to 2,000 m.

DIET: Chiefly insects.

NESTING: Nest has pyramidal shape with side opening just below top. Built in dense tuft of grass or bush, only 0.1–0.5 m above ground, it consists of dry grasses reinforced with spiders' webs. Clutch numbers 3–5 matte greenish white eggs speckled with chestnut, especially at larger pole (average size: 15.0 mm × 11.3 mm). One of species parasitized by Madagascar lesser cuckoo.

DISTRIBUTION AND STATUS: Distributed in Madagascar, Glorieuses, Cosmoledo, and Astove. Common throughout Madagascar.

212. *Brown Emutail*

Dromaeocercus brunneus Sharpe, 1877
Malagasy: Serika
French: Dromaeocerque brun

DESCRIPTION: Length 15 cm.
Adult. Sexes similar. Brown head, rufous-tinged white chin and throat. Dark brown bill, brown iris. Upperparts brown. Underparts: rufous-brown chest and belly, brown flanks. Brown tarsi and toes. Brown wings with darker primary remiges. Long, graduated dark brown tail with widely spaced barbs.

IDENTIFICATION: Warbler with slender silhouette, brown plumage, and graduated, downy tail. Distinguished from Gray emutail by smaller size, uniformly brown plumage, and less full tail. Distinguished from Madagascar brushwarbler by smaller size, rusty underparts, light chin and throat, and downy tail.

BEHAVIOR: Solitary, hard to observe, lives almost constantly concealed in depths of low vegetation, in which it moves about rapidly. Flies little and always for short distances, usually skimming ground. Behavior is reminiscent of that of Madagascar brush-warbler but is even more furtive. Only sign of its presence is song issuing from within vegetation, more rarely from visible perch.

VOICE: Vocal, warbles loud whistles, high-pitched, melodious *tok-tok-tockatok-tockatok tia-tia teek-teek.*

HABITAT: Grassy terrain or very dense bushes of rain forest. Observed at elevations of 500–1,500 m.

DIET: Small insects.

NESTING: Few data. Nest is built 30 cm above ground in low vegetation. Clutch numbers 2 eggs.

DISTRIBUTION AND STATUS: Endemic to Madagascar, little known, distributed in E Region. Fairly common in Sihanaka forest and at Ranomafana, observed on several occasions at Andasibe and more commonly at Andapa, at Maroantsetra, and in Tsaratanana.

213. *Gray Emutail*

Dromaeocercus seebohmi Sharpe, 1879
Malagasy: Serika, Tanimbary
French: Dromaeocerque de Seebohm

DESCRIPTION: Length 16.5 cm.
Adult. Sexes similar. Brown head streaked with dark brown. White chin and throat finely streaked with chestnut brown. Bill: black upper mandible, gray lower mandible. Brown iris. Upperparts brown-gray streaked with black, except for rufous-brown upperrtail coverts. Underparts: brown-gray chest and flanks streaked with dark brown. Whitish belly, tan-brown undertail coverts. Pink tarsi and toes. Wings same as upperparts, except for dark gray primary remiges finely edged with light brown. Long, graduated tail has widely spaced brown barbs with dark brown rachis.

IDENTIFICATION: Warbler with slender silhouette, light, streaked plumage, graduated tail with widely spaced barbs, short wings reaching to base of tail. Distinguished from Brown emutail by larger size, lighter, streaked plumage, and fuller tail. Distinguished from Madagascar brush-warbler by black-striped plumage and tail with widely spaced barbs.

BEHAVIOR: Solitary, lives almost permanently concealed in depths of low vegetation. Flies little, for short distances and always skimming over vegetation. Moves about in grasses by nimbly climbing stalks. Behavior is reminiscent of that of Madagascar brush-warbler but is even more furtive. As with Brown emutail, only sign of presence is song.

VOICE: Vocal. High-pitched, melodic song issues from low bushes, briefly and only once before bird vanishes into vegetation again. The song is a sort of *teo teo teo . . .* , loud, the syllable repeated 12 times and preceded by a harsh *chairr.*

HABITAT: Marshy meadows and dense grassy or bushy areas on fringe of rain forest, near stagnant water. Observed at elevations of 900–2,600 m.

DIET: Small insects.

NESTING: Capacious, bowl-shaped nest, built in a large tuft of grass on a marsh, consists of large entwined bits of grass, lined with similar but softer material. Clutch numbers 2 eggs. Nesting has been observed in Nov.

DISTRIBUTION AND STATUS: Little-known endemic species, distributed in n, at Tsaratanana (2,600 m); in e, at Andapa, Didy (1,500 m), Andasibe (900 m), Ranomafana (1,200 m), Andringitra, and on High Plateau (Ankaratra), where it is uncommon.

214. *Rand's Warbler*

Randia pseudozosterops
Delacour and Berlioz, 1931
French: Fauvette de Rand

DESCRIPTION: Length 12 cm.
Adult. Sexes similar. Gray head, except for whitish lores continuing as supercilium over and behind eyes, and whitish cheeks and chin. Yellowish brown bill, brown iris. Upperparts gray, underparts

whitish gray tinged with pale brown on flanks, belly, and undertail coverts. Brownish gray wings have remiges with narrow light gray edges. Brown-gray tail.

IDENTIFICATION: Small warbler with subdued plumage, gray above and white below, partly gray head marked with white supercilium, and long, thin bill. Distinguished from Stripe-throated jery and Common jery by larger size, slimmer silhouette, gray upperparts, all-gray throat, and white supercilium.

BEHAVIOR: Strictly forest species, restricted to canopy, which makes observation difficult. Found alone or in pairs, often in multispecies feeding flocks, but also frequently associated with Stripe-throated jery—in early morning the 2 species commonly sing together from treetops.

VOICE: Rather vocal, sings *chop chop chop* energetically repeated 8–15 times from fully visible, very high perch, or *chih chih chih* repeated 6–10 times increasing in volume.

HABITAT: Tops of tall trees in undisturbed rain forest. Observed at elevations of 800–1,500 m.

DIET: Unknown.

NESTING: Unknown.

DISTRIBUTION AND STATUS: Endemic to Madagascar, distributed in e (Andapa, Maroantsetra, Zahamena, Andasibe, Ranomafana, Ivohibe), where it is fairly common but hard to observe.

215. *Dark Newtonia*

Newtonia amphichroa Reichenow, 1891
French: Newtonie sombre

DESCRIPTION: Length 12 cm.
Adult. Sexes similar. Brown head and neck,

tan chin and throat. Dusky brown bill with many vibrissae, light yellow iris. Upperparts brown, underparts tan, darker on flanks and undertail coverts. Black tarsi and toes. Brown wings and tail.

IDENTIFICATION: Small, plump passerine with plumage brown above, tan below, and light eye. Distinguished from Common newtonia by brown crown and more evenly tan underparts.

BEHAVIOR: Forest species with behavior very close to that of Common newtonia, except that Dark newtonia feeds in middle and lower levels of forest, including underbrush.

VOICE: Vocal. Its resonant and harmonious song, a tireless succession of shrill *tweedy tew, tweedy tew* emanates from within bushes, close to ground. The song is an excellent means of distinguishing it from Common newtonia.

HABITAT: Undisturbed rain forest and adjacent second growth. Observed at elevations of 500–1,800 m.

DIET: Insects.

NESTING: Suspected Aug.–Nov.

DISTRIBUTION AND STATUS: Endemic to Madagascar, distributed in e (Montagne d'Ambre, Marojejy, Maroantsetra, Sihanaka forest, Analamazaotra, Ranomafana), where it is uncommon, except for Montagne d'Ambre, where it is as common as Common newtonia.

216. Common Newtonia

Newtonia brunneicauda (Newton, 1863)
Malagasy: Tretretre, Katekateky
French: Newtonie commune

DESCRIPTION: Length 12 cm.
Adult. Sexes similar.
Nominate subspecies *N. b. brunneicauda* (Sclater, 1924).
Gray head and neck. Whitish chin and

pale tan throat. Black bill, pale yellow iris. Upperparts gray, underparts white tinged with rosy tan on chest and flanks. Lead gray tarsi and toes. Gray wings with dark green-gray remiges. Dark gray tail.
Immature. Little known. Differs by white stripe on rachis of cap feathers, by fawn edges of upperwing coverts, and by gray-brown iris.
Subspecies *N. b. monticola* (Salomonsen, 1934).
Differs from *N. b. brunneicauda* by darker gray of head and upperparts, and by deeper tinge of rosy tan on underparts.

IDENTIFICATION: Small, plump passerine with stocky silhouette, gray above and on head, white tinged with rosy tan below, dark gray tail, and pale yellow eyes. Distinguished from Dark newtonia by paler upperparts and by white undertail coverts, and from Red-tailed newtonia by entirely gray upperparts and dark gray tail. Distinguished from female and immature Red-tailed vanga by smaller size, smaller bill, light eye, gray tail, and absence of light eye ring.

BEHAVIOR: Rather bold, active, found alone, in pairs, or more rarely in groups of 3–5, but often associated with mobile multispecies feeding flocks. Example of flock observed at Maroantsetra at 500 m elevation: 2 Common newtonias, 2 Madagascar paradise flycatchers, 30 Madagascar white-eyes, 5 Souimanga sunbirds, 1 Madagascar long-billed green sunbird, 1 pair of Ashy cuckoo-shrikes, 2 Crested drongos, 5 Madagascar bulbuls, 3 Red-tailed vangas, and 2 Nuthatch-vangas. Most commonly observed with Common jery, Stripe-throated jery, Madagascar white-eye, and Souimanga sunbird. Searches for food by minutely inspecting foliage and branches of middle and upper levels of forest; occasionally seizes prey on wing.

VOICE: Vocal, often emits surprisingly powerful song of succession of rapid-fire, resonant, staccato notes heard as *kiappak-iappakiap*, sometimes followed by series of more whistled, melodic *tugidugi-dugidu.* . . . Delivers song from perch, usually concealed. Alarm call is succession of harsh, loud *shir shir shir.*

HABITAT: Middle and upper levels of undisturbed rain forest, deciduous dry forest, mangroves, subarid scrub. Also found in degraded woodlands adjacent to original forests. Observed at elevations from sea level to 2,200 m.

DIET: Chiefly insects.

NESTING: Unknown. Thought to occur July–Mar.

DISTRIBUTION AND STATUS: Endemic to Madagascar, distributed throughout island, represented principally by *N. b. brunneicauda*, which is common throughout range. *N. b. monticola* is local to highland forests of Ankaratra range, where it is common.

217. *Archbold's Newtonia*

Newtonia archboldi
Delacour and Berlioz, 1931
French: Newtonie d'Archbold

DESCRIPTION: Length 12 cm. *Adult.* Sexes similar. Gray forehead, rufous front of head, brown crown and neck. Gray chin and throat. Black bill, pale yellow iris. Upperparts gray-brown, underparts whitish, except for cinnamon upper belly and flanks. Black tarsi and toes. Gray-brown wings have darker remiges with pale edges. Dark gray-brown tail. *Immature.* Differs from adult by limited rufous area of front of head and by rufous edges of upperwing coverts.

IDENTIFICATION: Small passerine with plump silhouette, rather long legs, and massive head, brown above and white below, with gray throat and russet chest, rufous front of head, and pale eyes. Distinguished from Common newtonia by brown not gray upperparts, deeply rufous-tinged chest, gray forehead, and rufous front of head.

BEHAVIOR: Similar to that of Common newtonia. Searches for food actively, hopping among branches and carefully inspecting branches and foliage.

VOICE: Vocal, with much more melodic repertory than Common newtonia. Song is rather long succession of 3 groups of melodious notes, the first trisyllabic, the second bisyllabic, and the third monosyllabic, a sort of *Teekeetee toodee tee*, delivered from concealed perch.

HABITAT: Subarid scrub. Observed at elevations from sea level to 100 m.

DIET: Insects.

NESTING: Unknown.

DISTRIBUTION AND STATUS: Endemic to Madagascar, localized in s (Ihotry Lake, n of Toliara, Tsimanampetsotsa Lake, Beza-Mahafaly, Hatokaliotsy, Berenty), where it is uncommon. Observed in sympatry with Common newtonia in all sites listed.

218. *Red-tailed Newtonia*

Newtonia fanovanae Gyldenstolpe, 1933
French: Newtonie de Fanovana

DESCRIPTION: Length 12 cm. *Adult.* Gray front and top of head and nape. Narrow bill with pale lower mandible. Upperparts dull brown except for gray mantle and upper back. Underparts white except for creamy fawn chest. Dull brown wings, rufous tail. *Immature.* Unknown.

IDENTIFICATION: Small passerine, brown above, white below, with plump silhouette, gray head, and rufous tail. Generally resembles Common newtonia and Dark newtonia; differs from both chiefly by its rufous tail. Easily distinguished from female Red-tailed vanga by smaller size, much slimmer silhouette, slighter bill, and absence of eye ring.

BEHAVIOR: Unknown.

VOICE: Unknown.

HABITAT: Only known specimen was captured in rain forest at elevation of about 800 m. Presumably frequents canopy.

DIET: Unknown.

NESTING: Unknown.

DISTRIBUTION AND STATUS: Endemic to Madagascar, known from lone specimen collected at Fanovana, Dec. 1931, and preserved at Stockholm Museum. Assuming this taxon's validity— i.e., that it is not an aberrant form of another species of newtonia (*N. brunneicauda* or *N. amphichroa*)—late date of discovery is certainly proof of limited range, perhaps allied to occupation of upper level of forest. One of 4 endemic species observed or collected fewer than 3 times in the past 50 years.

219. Common Jery

Neomixis tenella (Hartlaub, 1866)
Malagasy: Jijy, Tsisy, Zezea, Kimitsy
French: Petite Eroesse

DESCRIPTION: Length 10 cm. *Adult.* Sexes similar.
   Nominate subspecies *N. t. tenella.*
   Olive yellow front and top of head, and cheeks. Yellow lores continue as supercilium. Gray nape and back of neck. Bright yellow chin and throat faintly streaked with green. Bill: brown upper mandible, roseate lower mandible. Light brown iris. Upperparts green-yellow, underparts grayish white, except for yellow chest faintly streaked with green. Yellow tarsi and toes. Green-yellow wings. Grayish remiges have outer half edged with green-yellow. Yellow-green tail.
   Immature. Differs from adult by generally more subdued plumage, yellow underparts with faint breastbands, yellow mandibular commissures, and brown iris.
   Subspecies *N. t. orientalis* (Delacour, 1931).
   Differs from *N. t. tenella* by darker plumage more tinged with green above and gray below and by larger gray nape-collar.
   Subspecies *N. t. debilis* (Delacour, 1931).
   Differs from *N. t. tenella* by greenish gray tinge of upperparts, which considerably lessens contrast with gray nape-collar, and by underparts extensively tinged with gray.
   Subspecies *N. t. decaryi* (Delacour, 1931).
   Differs from *N. t. tenella* by generally duller plumage and by grayish green upperparts.

IDENTIFICATION: Very small, plump passerine with short, thin bill, green-yellow plumage above marked with gray nape-collar, and white below with faintly streaked yellow chest. Distinguished from Green jery by generally yellow rather than green head and upperparts and gray nape-collar, and from Stripe-throated jery by smaller size, short, light-colored bill, less-streaked underparts, and yellow front of head.

BEHAVIOR: Gregarious, forest species, bold, found in groups of 2–15, often within multispecies feeding flocks. Particularly apt to associate with Stripe-throated jery, Green jery, Common newtonia, Madagascar white-eye, Souimanga sunbird, and vangas. Example of flock observed at Mitsinjo, Apr. 1982: 7 Common jeries, 5 Common newtonias, 1 pair of Madagascar paradise flycatchers, 1 Long-billed greenbul, 2 Souimanga sunbirds, 2 Crested drongos, 1 pair of Ashy cuckoo-shrikes, and 1 pair of Rufous vangas. Hunts actively in forest canopy, constantly on the move and frequently hanging upside down to look inside flowers, in process coloring head and throat with pollen.

VOICE: Vocal, utters characteristic thin, high-pitched, sibilant *seeseeseesee* almost continuously as it searches for food.

HABITAT: Various original forest types, savanna, mangroves, degraded woodlands, tree plantations (coffee, cacao, cloves), parks, and gardens. Observed at elevations from sea level to 1,800 m.

DIET: Chiefly insects.

NESTING: Few data. Nest has oval, globular shape with side entrance near top. It is a flimsy structure of vegetal down lined with moss, suspended from leaves of tree with dense foliage. Clutch numbers 2 smooth, rather shiny white eggs speckled, especially at larger pole, with reddish brown and grayish spots (average size: 13.0 mm × 10.4 mm). Nesting has been observed in Dec.

DISTRIBUTION AND STATUS: Endemic to Madagascar and common throughout. Boundaries of ranges of 4 subspecies are hard to define. *N. t. tenella* is distributed in n, nw, and ne. *N. t. orientalis* is distributed in e center and se. *N. t. debilis* is distributed in s. *N. t. decaryi* is distributed in w center and on High Plateau.

220. *Green Jery*

Neomixis viridis Salomonsen, 1934
French: Eroesse verte

DESCRIPTION: Length 10.5 cm.
Adult. Sexes similar.

Nominate subspecies *N. v. viridis.*

Greenish head and neck with lighter cheeks finely streaked with gray. Pale yellow cheeks and throat. Pale yellow chin and throat. Bill: black upper mandible, whitish lower mandible with gray tip. Light brown iris. Upperparts olive green, underparts grayish white. Pale yellow tarsi and toes. Dark green-gray wings and tail. *Immature.* Differs from adult by light orange-brown bill marked with brown on upper ridge, by yellow mandibular commissures, and by dark brown iris.

Subspecies *N. v. delacouri* (Salomonsen, 1934).

Differs from nominate subspecies by generally drabber plumage.

IDENTIFICATION: Very small, plump passerine with rather short, thin bill, green plumage above, whitish below. Distinguished from Common jery by darker, greener hue of head and upperparts and solid whitish underparts.

BEHAVIOR: Discreet species, sometimes associated with multispecies feeding flocks.

VOICE: Song, emitted from a concealed perch, is a series of 8–12 sharp notes uttered in staccato fashion so as to form a single monotonous whistle, a sort of *tchee tchee tee tee tee tee . . . .*

HABITAT: Upper level of undisturbed rain forest, with predilection for medium and higher elevations. Observed at elevations of 100–2,050 m.

DIET: Insects.

NESTING: Few data. Nests at least in Sept.

DISTRIBUTION AND STATUS: Endemic to Madagascar, little known, distributed in e from Sambava to Tolagnaro, where it is uncommon. Range of distribution between the 2 subspecies is not precise—*N. v. viridis* is local to s part and *N. v. delacouri* to n part.

221. *Stripe-throated Jery*

Neomixis striatigula Sharpe, 1881
Malagasy: Kimitsy, Kimimitsy
French: Grande Eroesse

DESCRIPTION: Length 12 cm.
Adult. Sexes similar.

Nominate subspecies *N. s. striatigula.* *Adult.* Dark green front and top of head, gray nape, green-yellow cheeks and supercilium to over eyes, yellow chin. Paler yellow throat streaked with gray. Black bill, light brown iris. Upperparts yellowish olive-green except for gray upper back. Underparts whitish except for yellowish chest streaked with gray. Brown tarsi and toes. Olive green wings have yellowish edges on outer half. Dark olive green tail.

Subspecies *N. s. sclateri* (Delacour, 1931).

Differs from *N. s. striatigula* by darker upperparts, more marked stripes on chest, and greenish gray sides of chest.

Subspecies *N. s. pallidior* (Salomonsen, 1934).

Differs from *N. s. striatigula* by generally paler plumage.

IDENTIFICATION: Small, plump passerine with long, thin bill, yellow-green plumage above, whitish below, except for streaked yellow chest. Distinguished from Common jery and Green jery by larger size, black, longer bill, streaked yellow chest, and dark front of head contrasting with yellow supercilium and cheeks.

BEHAVIOR: Discreet species often observed in early morning hours singing from treetop, sometimes with Rand's warbler.

VOICE: Vocal. Song, a succession of high-pitched, melodious notes delivered in distinctive crescendo heard as *twee tweetewtewtweetsee tsee tseekeekee* constitutes excellent field mark.

HABITAT: Undisturbed rain forest and adjacent second growth at elevations of 800–1,800 m; subarid thorn scrub and adjacent second growth and mangroves at elevations from sea level to 800 m.

DIET: Insects.

NESTING: Few data. Oval, globular nest has side entrance near top. Hangs from end of branch and consists of vegetal down, dry grasses, and leaves held together by spiders' webs. Clutch numbers 3–5 smooth, fairly shiny whitish eggs with bluish tinge and dark brown spots (average size: 15.3 mm × 11.3 mm). Nesting has been observed Nov.–Dec.

DISTRIBUTION AND STATUS: Endemic to Madagascar, distributed in e, center, and s. *N. s. striatigula* is distributed in center, between Fianarantsoa and Ihosy, where it is uncommon. *N. s. sclateri* is distributed in e, from Sambava to Tolagnaro, where it is fairly common. *N. t. pallidior* is distributed in s, where it is common, with Morombe as n limit.

222. *Wedge-tailed Jery*

Hartertula flavoviridis (Hartert, 1924)
French: Eroesse à queue étagée

DESCRIPTION: Length 12 cm.
Adult. Sexes similar. Olive green head, pale at supercilium, gray cheek. Bright yellow chin and throat. Bill: sooty upper mandible, pale blue-gray lower mandible.

Brown iris. Upperparts and wings olive green. Underparts: bright yellow chest, yellow belly, yellowish flanks, and olive green undertail coverts. Light yellowish gray tarsi and toes. Olive green graduated tail.

Immature. Similar to adult.

IDENTIFICATION: Small passerine, larger than Stripe-throated jery, with much slimmer silhouette, long, thin bill, olive green plumage on head and upperparts, bright yellow below, and characteristic long, graduated green tail. Easily distinguished from Spectacled greenbul by smaller size, bright yellow chest, absence of yellow eye ring, thinner, shorter bill, and graduated tail. Distinguished from Yellow-browed oxylabes by smaller size, more vividly colored underparts, more discreet supercilium, and long, graduated tail.

BEHAVIOR: Gregarious, rather secretive, behaves similarly to Spectacled greenbul, with which it often associates. Found in monospecific groups of 3–7 or amid mobile multispecifies feeding flocks (Spectacled greenbul, Long-billed greenbul). Flock observed at Ranomafana, Apr. 1988: 3 Wedge-tailed jeries, 3 Long-billed greenbuls, 3 Spectacled greenbuls, 2 Gray-crowned greenbuls, 1 Ward's flycatcher, 2 White-throated oxylabes, 3 Yellow-browed oxylabes, and 2 Nelicourvi weavers. Active, constantly hopping from branch to branch and occasionally hanging upside down.

VOICE: Vocal, constantly uttering, as it moves, shrill, rather reedy, nasal, rapid *tsee zeezeezeezeezeezeezee zee zee,* with intervals between the last notes. Phrase is sometimes preceded by shrill, detached *tsit tsit.*

HABITAT: Dense lower stratum of undisturbed rain forest, favoring elevations of 500–900 m. Observed at elevations from sea level to 2,300 m.

DIET: Chiefly insects.

NESTING: Globular nest, with entrance in top third, hangs low above ground (1.5 m) and consists of interlaced grasses and thin vegetal material. Clutch numbers 2 eggs. Nesting has been observed Jan.

DISTRIBUTION AND STATUS: Endemic to Madagascar, distributed in e (Tsaratanana, Zahamena, Sihanaka forest, Andasibe, Ranomafana), where it is uncommon.

Monarchidae – Flycatchers

Small, insectivorous passerines having a
bill widened at the base and surrounded
by vibrissae and generally seizing their
prey on the wing. They build bowl-shaped
nests. Some species produce trills or
fairly resonant notes, but most are not
highly vocal. Flycatchers are generally
sedentary, though some rare species migrate. The family is represented by more
than 250 species distributed in the temperate and tropical regions of the Old
World. Two species are found in Madagascar, 1 endemic and 1 limited to Madagascar and the Comoros.

223. *Ward's Flycatcher*

Pseudobias wardi Sharpe, 1870
Malagasy: Serikalambo, Vorona masiaka,
Vorombarika
French: Gobe-mouche de Ward

DESCRIPTION: Length 15 cm.
Adult. Sexes similar. Jet black head and
neck. White chin and throat. Blue-gray
bill with black tip, brown iris. Jet black
upperparts. Underparts white except for
wide jet-black breastband. Black tarsi and
toes. Black wings except for white-edged
wing coverts and secondary remiges.
Black tail.

IDENTIFICATION: Medium-sized flycatcher with fairly slender silhouette,
black head and upperparts, white underparts crossed by black breastband, and
wing marked by white bar. Easily distinguished from Chabert's vanga by black
breastband and white wing bar. Distinguished from male Madagascar paradise
flycatcher in white morph by absence of
elongated tail feathers, white throat, black
breastband, and black upperparts.

BEHAVIOR: Found alone or in pairs, but
usually within multispecies feeding flocks.
Flock observed at 700 m elevation at
Ranomafana in Aug. 1985: 3 Ward's flycatchers, 1 Pollen's vanga, 1 pair of
White-headed vangas, 2 Blue vangas, 1
pair of Ashy cuckoo-shrikes, and 4 Long-
billed greenbuls. Very active, feeds in
middle and upper levels of forest. Favors
canopy and major branches. Spots prey
from ambush and captures it on wing after short flight. Changes perch frequently,
especially after failed strike.

VOICE: Vocal. Nasal, high-pitched call,
a sort of *tree tree tree teeeee,* is delivered
from unconcealed perch.

HABITAT: Middle and upper levels of
undisturbed rain forest, preferably at elevations above 300 m, more rarely adjacent to degraded tracts. Observed at
elevations from sea level to 1,800 m.

DIET: Chiefly insects.

NESTING: Few data. Nesting has been
observed in Nov.

DISTRIBUTION AND STATUS: En-
demic to Madagascar, rather patchily distributed in e (Tsaratanana, Marojejy,
Maroantsetra, Zahamena, Andasibe,
Ranomafana, Tolagnaro).

224. *Madagascar Paradise Flycatcher*

Terpsiphone mutata (Linnaeus, 1766)
Malagasy: Siketry, Singetry
French: Gobe-mouche de paradis de
Madagascar

DESCRIPTION: Length 18 cm (up to 30
cm, including central tail feathers). Polymorphic species.
Male. Exhibits 2 morphs, each of which
varies appreciably.
White Morph. Jet black head, neck, chin,

and throat. Ultramarine fleshy ring around eyes. Ultramarine bill with black tip, brown iris. Upperparts black, white, or white mixed with varying amounts of black. Underparts white. Blue-gray tarsi and toes. Wings, black except for median and lesser upperwing coverts fringed with white and secondary remiges edged with white. Tail: black tail feathers are edged with white on inner half; very elongated white central tail feathers.

Rufous Morph. Jet black head and nape, bright rufous neck, chin, and throat. Ultramarine fleshy ring around eyes. Ultramarine bill with black tip, brown iris. Bright rufous upperparts and underparts. Blue-gray tarsi and toes. Wings black, except for median and lesser upperwing coverts fringed with white and secondary remiges edged with white. Tail rufous, except for very elongated white tail feathers.

Female. Black head and nape. Ultramarine eye ring smaller than that of male. Rufous neck, chin, and throat. Ultramarine bill with black tip, brown iris. Rufous upperparts and underparts. Blue-gray tarsi and toes. Wings rufous, except for rufous-edged black primary and secondary remiges. Rufous tail.

Immature. Differs from female by more subdued plumage, brownish bill with yellow commissures, and pale gray tarsi and toes.

IDENTIFICATION: Fairly large flycatcher with slender silhouette, very long tail (male), highly contrasting plumage, black head, and blue eye ring. Cannot be confused with any other species.

BEHAVIOR: Forest species, very active, found in pairs or within multispecies feeding flocks. Strong preference for lower and middle levels of forest. Hunts in manner typical of flycatchers, watching prey and then seizing it on wing after short, often acrobatic, flight and bearing it back to perch to eat it. Males are quarrelsome and can frequently be seen chasing each other through undergrowth. Flight is fairly swift and very elegant. In both male and female, excitement causes bird to erect feathers on front of head and to fan tail.

VOICE: Vocal. Frequently uttered call and song provide excellent means of location and identification. Call is harsh *retret retret retretret* lasting 1–3 seconds and repeated at short, regular intervals, often followed by crescendo of bubbling, high-pitched, melodious notes.

HABITAT: Various original forest types, also savanna, mangroves, degraded woodlands, tree plantations, parks, and gardens. Observed at elevations from sea level to 2,300 m.

DIET: Chiefly insects.

NESTING: Deep bowl-shaped nest, built 1–6 m above ground, often at intersection of 2 slender branches, consists of finely interlaced twigs and grasses reinforced with moss and lined with softer material. Clutch numbers 3 smooth, slightly shiny, uneven white eggs mottled with reddish brown and gray, especially at larger pole (average size: 18.2 mm × 13.8 mm). Both parents incubate. Nesting has been observed Sept.–Jan.

DISTRIBUTION AND STATUS: Distributed in Madagascar and Comoros. Represented in Comoros by 4 subspecies: *T. m. comoroensis, T. m. voeltzkowiana, T. m. vulpina,* and *T. m. pretosia.* Represented in Madagascar by nominate subspecies *T. m. mutata,* distributed all over island, where it is common.

NOTE: Some taxonomists distinguish 2 subspecies: *T. m. mutata,* distributed in e and on High Plateau, and *T. m. singetra,* occupying s, w, and n of island. This differentiation is based on the fact that white-morph males have both black-backed and white-backed forms. White-morph males in e are predominantly white-backed, while white-morph males of s, w, and n are predominantly black-backed.

Timaliidae – Oxylabes, Babblers

Fairly heterogeneous family resembling the family Turdidae but differing in several anatomical details. These passerines have a generally rather long bill, often dentated at the tip, short, rounded wings with 10 primary remiges, and a tail of variable length. They feed on insects and berries. The family numbers nearly 250 species and some 50 genera spread throughout the tropical and subtropical regions of the Old World. Three endemic monospecific genera are found in Madagascar.

225. *White-throated Oxylabes*

Oxylabes madagascariensis (Brisson, 1760)
Malagasy: Farifitra mena, Sirontsirona
French: Oxylabe à gorge blanche

DESCRIPTION: Length 16.5–18 cm. *Adult.* Sexes differ: female slightly smaller than male. Front and top of head and cheeks chestnut. White lores extend to behind eyes. White chin and throat. Bill: black upper mandible, pale gray lower mandible. Chestnut iris. Brown upperparts, chestnut underparts. Dark gray tarsi and toes. Brown wings with chestnut remiges, brown tail.
Immature. Differs from adult by dirty brown cap, olive-tinged upperparts, yellowish chin and throat, and yellowish-tinged underparts.

IDENTIFICATION: Easily identifiable by stocky silhouette, rather long, robust legs, short wings, rather stout bill, and entirely brown plumage, except for chestnut cap, white throat, and white stripe in front of and behind eyes. Cannot be confused with any other species.

BEHAVIOR: Strictly forest species, fairly secretive but not shy, gregarious, found in monospecific groups of 3–8 or associated with such species as Spectacled greenbul, Dusky greenbul, Long-billed greenbul, or Nelicourvi weaver within multispecies feeding flocks. Moves about swiftly amid dense underbrush and on ground, climbing vegetation nimbly in search of food.

VOICE: Rather vocal, has melodious song of a few whistled notes composed of varied motifs in constant crescendo and delivered in staccato fashion 10–12 times, a repeated *tsoo teeoo*.

HABITAT: Stays close to floor of undisturbed rain forest, rarely seen in adjacent secondary growth. Observed at elevations from sea level to 1,800 m.

DIET: Chiefly insects.

NESTING: Few data. Nest is built 1.5–2.5 m above ground. Clutch numbers 2 reddish eggs, but usually only 1 chick is raised.

DISTRIBUTION AND STATUS: Endemic to Madagascar. Distributed in e, nw (Tsaratanana and Sambirano), and n (Montagne d'Ambre), where it is common.

226. *Yellow-browed Oxylabes*

Crossleyia xanthophrys (Sharpe, 1875)
Malagasy: Foditany
French: Oxylabe à sourcils jaunes

DESCRIPTION: Length 15 cm. *Adult.* Sexes similar. Front and top of head, eye patch, and nape dark green. Bright yellow lores and supercilium extending back to sides of neck. Bright yellow chin and throat. Short yellowish brown bill, brown iris. Upperparts dark olive green. Underparts: bright yellow chest and belly more or less tinged with green, olive green flanks and undertail coverts. Yellowish brown tarsi and toes. Dark green wings with green-brown remiges. Dark green-brown tail. *Immature.* Differs from adult by duller plumage.

IDENTIFICATION: Easily identifiable by green plumage above, yellow below, long, pronounced, yellow supercilium, and almost exclusively terrestrial habits.

BEHAVIOR: Strictly terrestrial forest species, habits somewhat reminiscent of White-throated oxylabes. Found in pairs or small groups of 3–5 in undergrowth of rain forest. Active, scurries about on ground, probing leaf litter with bill. Threads its way deftly through dense vegetation. Rarely flies, taking wing only to negotiate excessively steep slopes or to escape immediate danger, and then only for a short distance.

VOICE: Rather vocal, with frequent and characteristic high, thin, rather soft chirping *seet* uttered as it moves about.

HABITAT: Lower stratum of rain forest. Observed at elevations of 600–2,300 m.

DIET: Insects.

NESTING: Few data. Bowl-like nest, built by both sexes at ground level on leaf litter, consists of interwoven grasses and delicate moss. Clutch numbers 3 eggs. Nesting has been observed Sept.–Dec.

DISTRIBUTION AND STATUS: Endemic to Madagascar. Fairly rare, distributed only in e in Sihanaka forest and at Ranomafana, where it has been observed several times, and in Tsaratanana and Andasibe, where it has been seen on rare occasions.

227. *Crossley's Babbler*

Mystacornis crossleyi (Grandidier, 1870)
Malagasy: Talapiotany, Soratrala,
Sohohitrala
French: Mystacornis

DESCRIPTION: Length 16 cm.
Adult. Sexes differ.
Male. Front and top of head slate gray
tinged with brown on neck. Wide black
eye stripe from base of bill to behind eyes
as far as neck, marked with white spot
over eyes. Heavy white mustache reaching back to neck. Black chin and throat.
Long (20 mm) bill has blue edges on
black upper mandible, black tip on blue
lower mandible. Chestnut iris. Upperparts green-rufous-brown. Underparts:
gray chest, light gray belly, pale rufous-
brown flanks and undertail coverts. Pink
tarsi and toes. Rufous-brown wings with
brighter rufous remiges. Rufous-brown
tail.
Female. Front and top of head and neck
brown. Narrow black eye stripe extending
back to neck, surmounted by light gray
band marked with white spot over eyes.
Heavy white mustache extending back to
neck. Whitish chin and throat. Bill and
iris as in male. Upperparts green-rufous-
brown, lighter than in male. Underparts:
whitish, except for pale rufous-brown
sides of chest, flanks, and undertail coverts. Tarsi and toes, wings, and tail as
in male.
Immature. Differs from female by chestnut head marked with black eye stripe,
chestnut neck, rufous upperparts, and
light chestnut throat and underparts, except for white center of chest and belly.

IDENTIFICATION: Easily identifiable
by plumage rufous-brown above, whitish
below, contrasting with black throat (male
only), and by head marked with black eye
stripe and white mustache. Rather stocky
silhouette, very short wings, rather long,
well-developed legs, and elongated bill.

BEHAVIOR: Strictly terrestrial forest
species, furtive but not shy, found alone
or in pairs. Walks or runs about on floor
of underbrush, hunting for prey in litter
of dead leaves. Male is highly territorial
and quarrelsome, acts aggressively toward
other males. Flies rarely, only to flee danger or out of excitement during displays
or during altercation between males.

VOICE: Noisy. Highly distinctive song
provides excellent means of location and
identification. Main section is resonant,
sweet, high-pitched, uninflected, prolonged whistling heard as melancholic
tweeeeeee. At close range a short, high-
pitched, swelling *wee wee* is heard preceding the long plaintive tone, and song ends
with harsh *tsishrrr.*

HABITAT: Dark undergrowth of undisturbed rain forest. Observed at elevations
from sea level to 1,800 m.

DIET: Exclusively insects.

NESTING: Nest, built no higher than 1
m above ground in small tree or fern,
consists of haphazardly intertwined twigs.
Clutch numbers 3 white eggs mottled
with chestnut. Both parents incubate.
Nesting has been observed Sept.–Nov.

DISTRIBUTION AND STATUS: Endemic to Madagascar, distributed in e,
where it is fairly common.

Nectariniidae – Sunbirds

Small passerines having a long, more-or-less decurved, finely pointed bill and a long, tubular, bifid tongue. The males are generally richly colored, the females more rarely so. Sunbirds feed on insects and flower nectar. They are fairly vocal but generally not loud. They build spherical or oval nests of delicate bits of plants with a side entrance near the top. The family numbers 112 species spread through the tropical and subtropical regions of the Old World. Two species nest in Madagascar, 1 also distributed in Aldabra, the Glorieuses, and the Comoros, and 1 also distrbuted only in the Comoros.

228. Souimanga Sunbird

Nectarinia souimanga (Gmelin, 1788)
Malagasy: Soy, Soisoy, Soikely, Sianga, Sobitiky, Antsoy
French: Souimanga malgache

DESCRIPTION: Length 10–11 cm. *Adult.* Sexes differ. Plumage of male varies seasonally.

Nominate subspecies *N. s. souimanga*. *Male Breeding Plumage.* Metallic green head, chin, and throat. Long (18–20 mm) black, curved bill, dark brown iris. Upperparts gray-brown, except for metallic green mantle with purple sheen. Underparts: metallic blue chest, except for narrow, dull red band on lower portion, bright yellow sides of chest, dark brown upper belly, and bright yellow rest of belly, flanks, and undertail coverts. Black tarsi and toes. Dull gray-brown wings with metallic green lesser wing coverts. Metallic green tail.
Male Nonbreeding Plumage. Dull green-gray head, dull green-yellow chin and throat. Upperparts entirely gray-brown. Underparts green-yellow, except for bright yellow central part of belly. Black tarsi and toes. Dull gray-brown wings, except for persistent metallic green patch on lesser wing coverts. Dull brown tail.
Female. Green-gray head. Short, faint, yellow supercilium. Green-gray chin and throat dotted with dark gray (base of dark feathers). Black bill, brown iris. Upperparts solid green. Underparts: green-gray chest dotted with dark gray (base of dark feathers). Gray-green flanks, yellow belly, pale yellow undertail coverts. Green-gray wings, except for dark brown primary and secondary remiges. Dark brown tail.

Subspecies *N. s. apolis* (Hartert, 1920). Differs from *N. s. souimanga* only by generally paler plumage.

IDENTIFICATION: Small sunbird with slender silhouette. Male in breeding plumage cannot be confused with any other species. Male in nonbreeding plumage is recognized by metallic green elbow patch. Female is distinguished from female of Long-billed green sunbird by smaller size and green-gray head, upperparts, and chest.

BEHAVIOR: Very active species, gregarious outside breeding season, found in groups of 2–6 or more around trees or shrubs in full flower. Commonly found within forest multispecies feeding flocks, most often with Madagascar white-eye, Long-billed green sunbird, Common jery, or Common newtonia. Feeds from inflorescences of trees or shrubs, hovering by flowers or perching on them. Moves frequently from one spot to another with swift and direct flight.

VOICE: Highly vocal, with varied repertory. Utters constant characteristic brief *pit*, repeating it up to 4 times. Also a mewing, plaintive, diminishing *teeeeeee* and a resonant, staccato *teeteeteetee*. The 3 elements may be combined.

HABITAT: All woodlands, undisturbed and second-growth forests, mangroves, parks and gardens of towns and villages. Observed at elevations from sea level to 2,300 m.

DIET: Chiefly insects, also spiders and nectar.

NESTING: Nest is usually built at end of branch in tree or shrub, 0.8–5.0 m above ground, usually about 1.5 m, sometimes lower in thick grass. It has an oval, globular shape and a side entrance near top indicated by awning. Nest consists of moss and delicate interlaced plant matter and has thick, sturdy walls. Clutch numbers 2 smooth, slightly shiny whitish eggs sometimes mottled with blurred brown spots, especially at larger pole (average size: 14.9 mm × 11.0 mm). Female broods. Nesting has been observed Sept.–Jan.

DISTRIBUTION AND STATUS: Distributed in Madagascar, Glorieuses, Comoros (Mayotte), and Aldabra. Represented in Madagascar by *N. s. souimanga*, over entire territory except s. *N. s. apolis* is endemic to Madagascar and is local to subarid area of s. Common throughout Madagascar.

229. *Long-billed Green Sunbird*

Nectarinia notata (Müller, 1776)
Malagasy: Soy, Sohimanga, Soimangavola
French: Souimanga angaladian

DESCRIPTION: Length 14 cm.
Adult. Sexes differ. Plumage of male varies seasonally.
Male Breeding Plumage. Metallic green head, chin, and throat, black lores. Long (30 mm), curved black bill, dark brown iris. Upperparts metallic green with blue sheen, except for metallic blue uppertail coverts. Underparts: metallic green upper chest, metallic blue breastband with violet

sheen, velvet black belly and undertail coverts. Black tarsi and toes. Midnight blue wings except for metallic green lesser wing coverts. Midnight blue tail.
Male Nonbreeding Plumage. Similar to female, with sparse metallic green feathers.
Female. Brown-gray head, yellow-gray chin and throat dotted with brown (base of dark feathers). Black bill and dark brown iris. Upperparts brown-gray, underparts yellow-gray dotted with dark brown, except for solid pale yellow ventral portion. Black tarsi and toes. Dark gray-brown wings, black tail.
Immature. Differs from female by shorter bill and solid dark gray chin, throat, and chest.

IDENTIFICATION: Large, rather robust sunbird. Male in breeding plumage cannot be confused with any other species. Male in nonbreeding plumage and female are distinguished from female Souimanga sunbird by larger size, longer bill, and brown-gray hue of head and upperparts.

BEHAVIOR: Similar to that of Souimanga sunbird. Fairly gregarious outside breeding period. Found in pairs or small groups of 3–5 or within multispecies feeding flocks. Prefers to associate with Souimanga sunbird, Madagascar white-eye, or Common newtonia. Always active, moves about frequently with swift flight. Hovers or settles on inflorescences of trees or shrubs (often seen in groves of flowering bananas) in search of food, but also clings to twigs, branches, and trunks. Often observed in treetops, on dead or bare branch, always easily visible.

VOICE: Vocal. Harmonious, high-pitched, resonant *twee twee twee twee twee twee* is sung repeatedly from visible perch. First 2 *twee*s rise in volume and last 2 diminish, those in the middle remaining unchanged.

HABITAT: All wooded settings, undisturbed and second-growth forest, mangroves, parks and gardens of towns and villages. Observed at elevations from sea level to 1,800 m.

DIET: Chiefly insects, caterpillars, spiders, and nectar.

NESTING: Nest, built 2–10 m above ground in foliage of tree or shrub and usually suspended near end of branch, has oval, globular shape with side entrance pointing upward. It is made of dry grasses, moss, and vegetal lining, sometimes held together with spider webs. Clutch numbers 2 shiny, dark olive green eggs (average size: 19.4 mm × 14.1 mm). Nesting has been observed Sept.–Dec.

DISTRIBUTION AND STATUS: Distributed in Madagascar and Comoros (Grande Comore and Mohéli). Represented in Madagascar by endemic nominate subspecies *N. m. notata*, distributed throughout island and common in e and on High Plateau, fairly common in w, and rare in s.

Zosteropidae – White-Eye

Small, short-billed passerines with plumage tending to olive or yellow with an olive cast, and having a circle of small white feathers around the eyes. White-eyes feed on fruits, insects, and nectar and have a partly tubular tongue. Their wings have only 9 primary remiges. The family is distributed in Africa, Asia, Australia, and Indian Ocean islands, and 84 species are generally recognized. A single species also distributed in Aldabra, the Comoros, Europa, and Cosmoledo is found in Madagascar.

230. *Madagascar White-Eye*

Zosterops maderaspatana (Linnaeus, 1766)
Malagasy: Fotsy maso, Ramanjerika, Jerina, Sobery, Vorompotsy maso, Vorontsaramaso
French: Zosterops malgache

DESCRIPTION: Length 11–12 cm. *Adult.* Sexes similar. Yellow forehead, chin, and throat. Front and top of head, nape, and cheeks yellow-green. Black lores. Ring of white feathers around eyes, less abundant or absent in front of eyes. Black bill, light brown iris. Upperparts olive green, underparts light gray except for yellow undertail coverts. Dark gray tarsi and toes. Olive green wings except for sooty primary remiges, with narrow green edges on outer half. Sooty tail.

IDENTIFICATION: Only white-eye of Madagascar. Field marks are ring of white feathers around eyes, green upperparts, whitish underparts, and yellow throat.

BEHAVIOR: Active, bold, gregarious, usually found in rather loose monospecific flocks numbering up to 40 birds or within multispecies feeding flocks of which it almost always constitutes the majority. Most often associates with Common newtonia, Souimanga and Long-billed green sunbirds, and Common jery. Flock observed at 200 m elevation at Maroantsetra in Mar. 1982: 30 Madagascar white-eyes, 2 Ashy cuckooshrikes, 5 Madagascar bulbuls, 2 Common newtonias, 2 Madagascar paradise flycatchers, 5 Souimanga sunbirds, 1 Long-billed green sunbird, 3 Red-tailed vangas, 2 Nuthatch vangas, and 2 Crested drongos. Frequents treetops and tops of shrubs, especially those flowering or fruiting. Readily hangs upside down to feed.

VOICE: Vocal. While searching for food almost constantly utters characteristic soft *tsit tsit*. Sings harmoniously from unconcealed perch.

HABITAT: Any woodland setting, undisturbed and second-growth forest, scrub, mangroves, parks and gardens of towns and villages. Observed at elevations from sea level to 2,300 m.

DIET: Insects, small fruits, and nectar.

NESTING: Deep bowl-shaped nest, built in fork of tree or leafy bush 3–8 m above ground, consists of mosses and plant fibers outside, delicate plant fibers inside. Clutch numbers 2–3 smooth, shiny, unvariegated pale blue-green eggs (average size: 15.4 mm × 12.0 mm). Nesting has been observed Sept.–Mar., peaking Oct.–Nov.

DISTRIBUTION AND STATUS: Distributed in Madagascar, Aldabra, Comoros, Glorieuses, and Europa. Represented in Madagascar by nominate subspecies *Z. m. maderaspatana*, common to Glorieuses. Distributed and common throughout island.

NOTE: Gray-backed white-eye (*Zosterops hovarum*) (Tristram, 1887), collected in Madagascar and described on basis of single specimen, is not a valid taxon. Specimen represents an aberrant form with gray coloration of upperparts that has since been found on 2 other birds on Cosmoledo Atoll.

Oriolidae – Oriole

Rather large passerines with fairly long, stout, slightly curved bills, generally red or pink, with yellow or green and black plumage. Orioles frequent tall trees and forest habitats. Some species are sedentary, while others migrate. The family numbers 25 species spread through Europe, Africa, Asia, and Oceania. A single migratory species has been observed on rare occasions in Madagascar.

Immature. Differs from female by having head and flanks less tinged with yellow and by brown bill and iris.

IDENTIFICATION: Large black-and-yellow passerine with stout red bill. Female and immature have subdued plumage, greenish above and whitish streaked with black below. Cannot be confused with any other species.

DISTRIBUTION AND STATUS: Migratory, breeds in Europe, North Africa, and Asia. Nominate subspecies *O. o. oriolus*, of European origin, winters in e Africa. Rare visitor to Madagascar mentioned in a few scattered old references and observed only once recently.

231. *European Golden Oriole*
Oriolus oriolus (Linnaeus, 1758)
French: Loriot d'Europe
No Map

DESCRIPTION: Length 24 cm.
Adult. Sexes differ.
Male. Golden yellow head except for black lores. Red bill and iris. Golden yellow upperparts and underparts. Slate gray tarsi and toes. Black wings. Black tail with golden yellow tip.
Female. Yellow-green head. Pale gray chin and throat, streaked with black. Reddish bill and iris. Upperparts yellow-green except for yellowish rump and uppertail coverts. Underparts pale gray, streaked with black. Gray-brown wings. Brown-gray tail with yellowish tip.

Vangidae – Vangas

Family represented by 14 species in 12 genera, 13 species of which are endemic to Madagascar and 1 also found in the Comoros. The forms of bill shown by these 14 species reflect a spectacular range of evolutionary adaptations. All vangas are forest species, and they often constitute the mainstay of multispecies feeding flocks. Only 2 form monospecific groups. All feed on invertebrates and small vertebrates and build deep bowl-shaped nests. Their vocal repertory is elaborate and melodic.

232. Red-tailed Vanga

Calicalicus madagascariensis (Linnaeus, 1766)
Malagasy: Totokarasoka
French: Vangae à queue rousse

DESCRIPTION: Length 13.5–14 cm.
Adult. Sexes differ.
Male. Front and top of head and nape slate gray. Narrow white streak extending from forehead to over eyes. White mustache, black lores, chin, and throat. Black bill, dark brown iris. Upperparts gray tinged with green, except for rufous rump and uppertail coverts. Underparts whitish, except for tan sides of chest and flanks and rufous thighs. Gray tarsi and toes. Green-gray wings, except for rufous upperwing coverts and white underwing coverts. Tail rufous, except for gray apical half of 2 gray central tail feathers.
Female. Gray front and top of head and nape. Tan lores, cheeks, and thin supercilium. Light tan eye ring. White chin and throat. Black bill, dark brown iris. Upperparts gray tinged with green, except for rufous uppertail coverts. Un-

derparts tan except for white undertail coverts. Gray tarsi and toes. Gray wings tinged with green, except for brown-gray primary remiges and tan underwing coverts. Tail as in male.
Immature. Differs from female only by gray top of head and nape flecked with tan.

IDENTIFICATION: Smallest vanga after Nuthatch vanga. Male is easily identifiable by contrasting plumage, gray and rufous above, white below, gray, black, and white head, and rufous tail. Female and immature have much more subdued plumage, gray above and tan below. They can be confused only with Common newtonia, from which they differ by light tan eye ring, dark brown iris, stouter bill, and rufous uppertail coverts and tail.

BEHAVIOR: Active forest species, found in pairs (during breeding season) and within multispecies feeding flocks that sometimes include other vangas but often also include such small forest passerines as Common jery, Stripe-throated jery, and Sakalava weaver or such larger species as Crested drongo and Ashy cuckoo-shrike. Flock observed at 200 m elevation at Maroantsetra in Mar. 1982: 1 female Red-tailed vanga, 1 White-headed vanga, 1 Ashy cuckoo-shrike, 5 Long-billed greenbuls, 5 Spectacled greenbuls, 5 Common newtonias, 2 Madagascar paradise flycatchers, 7 Souimanga sunbirds, and 2 Nelicourvi weavers. Red-tailed vanga frequents all levels of forest; small branches are its favorite hunting ground. In e, tends to gravitate to upper level of forest, whereas in w forests sometimes feeds among fallen leaves on floor.

VOICE: Vocal. Male calls often, sometimes while searching for food, which provides good means of locating species or entire flock that bird has joined. Most characteristic calls are heard as incessant *cheep cheep rew* (last note audible only from nearby) and, for the female, *tsit tsit geshleep*, often repeated several times. Male sings resonant, melodic trilled phrases from treetops.

HABITAT: Various original forest types, including adjacent second growth, except for subarid scrub. Observed at elevations from sea level to 2,000 m.

DIET: Small and medium-sized insects (Orthoptera, Coleoptera), caterpillars, and small vertebrates (*Chamaeleo* spp.).

NESTING: Few data. Nest, built high above ground (near treetop) on branch, consists of interwoven leafstalks reinforced with spider webs, without any special interior lining. External appearance of nest is reminiscent of that of Chabert's vanga. Clutch numbers 2 green-blue eggs with small, widely scattered chestnut and reddish-gray spots increasing in density at larger pole (average size: 18.1 mm × 14.5 mm). Both parents incubate. Nesting has been observed in Dec.

DISTRIBUTION AND STATUS: Endemic to Madagascar, distributed in e and w, where it is common, and absent from s. Most widely distributed and common vanga after Chabert's vanga and White-headed vanga.

233. *Rufous Vanga*

Schetba rufa (Linnaeus, 1766)
Malagasy: Siketriala, Poapoabava
French: Artamie rousse

DESCRIPTION: Length 20 cm.
Adult. Sexes differ.
Nominate subspecies *S. r. rufa.*
Male. Black head, nape, neck, chin, and throat with blue sheen. Wide blue-tinged gray bill, dark red iris. Upperparts rufous, underparts white, except for black chest. Rufous wings have dark brown primary remiges edged with brown on outer side

and white underwing coverts. Rufous tail. *Female.* Front and top of head and nape black. White cheeks, chin, and throat. Wide blue-tinged gray bill, dark red iris. Upperparts rufous, except a gray nape-collar. Underparts: light gray chest and flanks. White belly and undertail coverts. Blue-gray tarsi and toes. Rufous wings with gray-brown inner half of primary remiges and rufous outer half. White underwing coverts. Rufous tail. *Immature.* Resembles female, but black of head and rufous of upperparts and wings are dull brown. Black bill with white tip, brown iris. Chest tinged with brown, tail dull rufous.
Subspecies *S. r. occidentalis* (Delacour, 1931).
Differs from *S. r. rufa* by generally paler plumage and smaller bill.

IDENTIFICATION: Medium-sized vanga with stocky silhouette, rufous upperparts, white underparts, and black head. Cannot be confused with any other species.

BEHAVIOR: Strictly forest species, seldom encountered alone, occasionally in pairs or family groups of 4–8, most often within multispecies feeding flocks usually composed of vangas. Sometimes joins such forest species as Ashy cuckoo-shrike, Common jery, Stripe-throated jery, Madagascar paradise flycatcher, Common newtonia, or Madagascar magpie-robin. Inactive, spends long intervals watching for prey on low branch. Surveys immediate surroundings and seizes prey on branches, trunks, sometimes among dead leaves of forest floor, rarely on wing. Of all vangas, this species is most inclined to feed on ground. Flies rarely, and then only for short distances. Over longer distances, flight appears slow and uncertain.

VOICE: Vocal, with harmonious and varied repertory. Song is sweet, rather resembling that of Helmet vanga, a tumbling sequence of piping, slightly trilled notes decreasing in volume, heard as *tew chudew chudew dewdewdewdewdewdew dew dew dew*, repeated several times and often punctuated with clacking of bill from another individual. Such clacking, rapid and resonant, also occurs without singing. Song can be taken up in an antiphonal duet by 2 birds. Alarm call is harsh, loud *kerekerekerekeh*, sometimes with clacking.

HABITAT: Low and middle levels of undisturbed rain forest from sea level to 1,800 m elevation and undisturbed or slightly degraded dry forest as far as areas of transition to subarid scrub from sea level to 900 m. Has not been observed in savanna or mangroves.

DIET: Medium-sized insects (Orthoptera), sometimes small lizards (*Ligodactylus* sp., *Phelsuma* spp.).

NESTING: No firm data. Designation of Oct.–Dec. as breeding period for both subspecies rests on observation of fledglings Nov.–Jan.

DISTRIBUTION AND STATUS: Endemic to Madagascar. *S. r. rufa* is distributed e from Andapa to Tolagnaro; it is fairly common in the n half and uncommon in the s half. *S. r. occidentalis* ranges w from Ankarafantsika, where it is common, as far as Sakaraha.

234. *Hook-billed Vanga*

Vanga curvirostris (Linnaeus, 1766)
Malagasy: Vangasoratra, Tsilovanga, Fifiokala, Bekapoaky
French: Vanga écorcheur

DESCRIPTION: Length 25–29 cm.
Adult. Sexes similar.
Nominate subspecies *V. c. curvirostris*.
Head entirely white, except for black top and back of head. White nape, neck,

chin, and throat. Black bill (25–30 mm) ending in hook with white point, dark brown iris. Upperparts black, underparts white, except for light gray flanks. Long, stout gray-blue tarsi and toes. Wings: black primary remiges, narrowly edged with white on outer side and more widely on inside. Black secondary remiges with wide white borders on both sides. Large white upperwing coverts. Rest of wings black. Underside of wing: white coverts, dark gray and white remiges. Tail: gray basal half, black apical half, except for white terminal band.
Immature. Similar to adult, but white of head and undersides is replaced by gray, upperparts and wings are spotted with light brown, and primary and secondary remiges are brown-gray.
Subspecies *V. c. cetera* (Bangs, 1928).
Differs from *V. c. curvirostris* by longer (27–30 mm) and thinner bill, by black of head restricted to back of head, and by wider nape-collar.

IDENTIFICATION: Large black-and-white vanga, size intermediate between White-headed vanga and Sickle-billed vanga. Easily distinguished from them by partly black head, white wing bars, bicolored gray-and-black tail ending with white bar, and straight, stout black bill.

BEHAVIOR: Usually solitary, sometimes in pairs or individually on periphery of multispecies feeding flocks of vangas or other forest species. Flies little. Spends long intervals motionless, watching for prey, or slowly inspects branches in search of food. Catches prey on branches of all sizes, from treetops to just off or even on ground. Often target of aggressive reaction by small birds, whose nests it very likely raids.

VOICE: Vocal. Utters characteristic shrill, monotonous *te-ew*, drawn out for about 2 seconds and repeated at regular short intervals in early morning. Bird is difficult to locate because it often sings concealed in foliage of high treetops. Two individuals often respond to each other, and song then rises 1 note higher with each response. Resonant, fluted, diminishing *twee twee twee tew tew* is often uttered on taking wing, resembling song of Ashy cuckoo-shrike. Calls of alarm and displeasure are harsh, loud, dissonant *huh huh huh huh*. Also given to clacking bill, especially between sections of song.

HABITAT: Various original forest types, savanna if not too open, mangroves, riverside woodlands, tree plantations (coffee, clove, mango), and surroundings of villages. Observed at elevations from sea level to 1,800 m.

DIET: Small reptiles (*Chamaeleo* spp., *Phelsuma* spp.), amphibians, insects (Orthoptera, Coleoptera, Diptera, Hemiptera), occasionally nestlings.

NESTING: Nest is large structure made of interwoven moss, stalks, and rootlets reinforced by spider webs and cocoons. Interior lined with rootlets and dry leaves. Built low above ground in first fork of tree or squeezed into cracks of split trunks. Clutch numbers 2–3 more-or-less pink-tinged white eggs mottled with pink-brown and lilac, more densely at large pole (average size: 28.5 mm × 20.9 mm). Both parents incubate. Nesting has been observed Sept.–Nov.

DISTRIBUTION AND STATUS: Endemic to Madagascar. *V. c. curvirostris* is widely distributed in e from Sambava to Tolagnaro, in n, including Montagne d'Ambre, Sambirano, and Tsaratanana, and in w to Morombe. Fairly common throughout that area. *V. c. cetera* is uncommon and local to subarid thorn scrub. Hook-billed vanga is one of the vangas not strictly bound to undisturbed forest.

235. Lafresnaye's Vanga

Xenopirostris xenopirostris
(Lafresnaye, 1850)
Malagasy: Tsilovanga
French: Vanga de Lafresnaye

DESCRIPTION: Length 24 cm.
Adult. Sexes differ.
Male. Head black, except for white throat and front and sides of neck. Stout, laterally compressed bill with median intermandibular gap, gray except for pale brown apical half of lower mandible. Brown iris. Gray upperparts, white underparts. Gray tarsi and toes. Gray wings with sooty gray primary remiges. Gray tail.
Female. Differs from male by white head with black crown, nape, and back of neck.
Immature. Differs from female by brown marks on scapulars and upperparts.

IDENTIFICATION: Large vanga, gray above, white below, with head entirely (male) or largely (female) black, has light, stout, laterally compressed bill with intermandibular gap. Cannot be confused with any other species in its range.

BEHAVIOR: Strictly forest species, not gregarious, usually found alone or in pairs, occasionally in small groups of up to 8. Searches for food on dead branches or trunks, vigorously stripping off bark to extract prey, which it strikes against branch before eating. Inspects deadwood from bottom up, spending much time to remove bark, often working with head pointing down. Noise accompanying this activity sometimes helps to locate bird. Flight is powerful, slightly uneven over long distances. Loud and distinctive whirring of wings, identical to that of Sickle-billed vanga, is audible as far as 20 m away.

VOICE: Vocal. Characteristic whistled call is short, resonant, pure, swelling *tsee-*

yew, usually uttered from easily viewed singing post, more rarely in flight. Voiced at regular intervals, call evokes response from distant members of same species. Also has nasal sequence heard as *ksay ksay ksay ksay*, delivered with bill wide open, as well as *weez ksay ksay*.

HABITAT: Frequents subarid thorn scrub exclusively, with strong preference for areas with plentiful deadwood. Observed at elevations from sea level to 100 m.

DIET: Insects and small reptiles.

NESTING: Few data. Nest, built in fork of tree 5 m above ground, consists of plant matter reinforced on outside with spider webs. Interior is lined with leaf-stalks and long rootlets. Clutch numbers 2 dull, oval reddish-white eggs sprinkled with reddish-gray spots (average size: 25.1 mm × 18.3 mm). Nesting has been observed Nov.–Dec.

DISTRIBUTION AND STATUS: Endemic to Madagascar, local to subarid s (Ihotry Lake, Toliara, Anakao, Tsimanampetsotsa Lake, Beza-Mahafely, Berenty, Andohahela), where it is fairly common.

236. *Van Dam's Vanga*

Xenopirostris damii Schlegel, 1866
French: Vanga de Van Dam

DESCRIPTION: Length 23 cm.
Adult. Sexes differ.
Male. Head and back of neck black with blue sheen. Chin, throat, and rest of neck white. Stout, sooty gray, laterally compressed bill without intermandibular gap. Brown iris. Upperparts gray except for dark gray mantle, underparts white. Dark gray tarsi and toes. Gray wings with sooty gray primary remiges. Gray tail.
Female. White forehead, lores, cheeks, chin, and throat. Front and top of head,

nape, and back of neck black with blue sheen. Rest of plumage similar to that of male.
Immature. Differs from female by generally lighter plumage with brown markings on scapulars and upperparts.

IDENTIFICATION: Large vanga, gray above, white below, with entirely (male) or largely (female) black head and stout, laterally compressed black bill. Cannot be confused with any other species in its range.

BEHAVIOR: Few data. Strictly forest species, usually found alone or in pairs, sometimes in family groups of 4–8 and also with Rufous vanga. Strips bark off dead branches as it feeds. Flight produces loud whirring.

VOICE: Vocal. Short, resonant, pure whistling very similar to that of Lafresnaye's vanga. Two individuals produce an antiphonal duet.

HABITAT: Frequents undisturbed deciduous dry forest exclusively. Observed at elevation of 150 m.

DIET: Few data. Certainly includes insects (Coleoptera).

NESTING: No data.

DISTRIBUTION AND STATUS: Endemic to Madagascar, with very small range. After collection of a few rare specimens in 1864 in Ambazoana valley near bay of Ampasindava, species was rediscovered only in 1928 in Ankarafantsika and in 1987 in forest of Analamera. Because of its limited range, Van Dam's Vanga is Madagascar's rarest and most threatened vanga.

237. *Pollen's Vanga*

Xenopirostris polleni (Schlegel, 1868)
Malagasy: Vangamaintiloha, Vanga
French: Vanga de Pollen

DESCRIPTION: Length 23.5 cm.
Adult. Sexes similar. Head black, except
for white, orange-tinged sides of neck.
Stout, laterally compressed gray bill without intermandibular gap. Brown iris. Upperparts gray tinged with olive green, underparts orangy, except for white, orange-
tinged upper chest. Gray tarsi and toes.
Dark gray wings. Dark gray, green-tinged
tail.

IDENTIFICATION: Large vanga, gray
above, orangy below, with black head and
throat and stout, laterally compressed bill.
In its range, can be confused only with
slightly smaller Tylas vanga, from which
it differs chiefly by much stouter bill and
more powerful tarsi and toes.

BEHAVIOR: Few data. Forest species,
seen alone, in pairs, or in family groups
of 3–4, but most often within multispecies feeding flocks. Flock observed at
elevation of 500 m at Maroantsetra: 1
Pollen's vanga, 2 Red-tailed vangas, 4
White-headed vangas, 6 Chabert's vangas, 3 Blue vangas, and 2 Tylas vangas.
At 900 m at Ranomafana, Nov. 1986: 3
Pollen's vangas, 3 Red-tailed vangas, 2
Ward's flycatchers, 5 Common jeries, and
5 Madagascar white-eyes.

VOICE: Vocal. Short, resonant, pure
whistling very similar to that of Lafresnaye's vanga, which often helps locate
it. Two individuals produce an antiphonal duet.

HABITAT: Middle and upper levels of
undisturbed rain forest. Observed at elevations from sea level to 1,000 m.

DIET: Invertebrates (caterpillars, insects,
spiders).

NESTING: Few data. Clutch numbers
2 eggs. Nesting has been observed
Oct.–Dec.

DISTRIBUTION AND STATUS: Endemic to Madagascar, distributed in e

(Marojejy, Maroantsetra, Sihanaka forest,
Andasibe, Ranomafana, Tolagnaro),
where it is rather rare, except in Sihanaka forest and Ranomafana, where it is
uncommon.

238. *Sickle-billed Vanga*

Falculea palliata
(Geoffroy Saint-Hilaire, 1835)
Malagasy: Voronjaza, Tseatseake,
Tsiatsiaka
French: Falculie mantelée

DESCRIPTION: Length 32 cm.
Adult. Sexes similar. Entirely white head,
neck, chin, and throat. Very long (to 70
mm), highly curved, light gray bill, dark
brown iris. Upperparts black with blue
sheen, underparts white. Sturdy pale blue
tarsi and toes. Black wings with white underwing coverts. Black tail.
Immature. Differs from adult by much
less developed bill and by tan marks on
upperparts and upperwing coverts.

IDENTIFICATION: Very large vanga
(family's largest representative), with
boldly contrasting black-and-white plumage and long, thin, curved bill. Cannot be
confused with any other species.

BEHAVIOR: Frequents forest and savanna, noisy, bold, very gregarious.
Groups often number a dozen, rarely
more than 20 (32 in Feb. 1982 at Ampijoroa, 28 with 6 Crested drongos in May
1987 in Ankarana). Nightly roosts number up to 40 birds, sometimes more. Less
gregarious during breeding season, but
several dozen pairs may still be seen
banding together, especially to intimidate
an enemy. White-headed vangas and
Crested drongos are often seen with
flocks of Sickle-billed vangas. Favors
large branches, living or dead, as sources
of food, which it seeks by hopping about,
probing rotten sections of wood, and

peeling bark and searching cracks and hollows with its long bill. Bill is too slight to strip bark from branches. Holds large prey with feet and dismembers it with bill. Flight is straight, rather cumbersome, and loud (audible from nearby), like that of Helmet vanga or Lafresnaye's vanga.

VOICE: Highly vocal. Characteristic prolonged, plaintive *wa-ahh* resembling wail of newborn baby is repeated several times, and all members of flock often join in remarkable choruses of this call. Also frequently uttered is loud, full *gay gay gay* or *gaya gaya gaya*. Alarm call is heard as *kekekekeh* . . . .

HABITAT: Dry and thorn forests, savanna even if sparsely wooded, wooded surroundings of villages, local patches of rain forest, mangroves. Particularly fond of baobabs. Observed at elevations from sea level to 900 m.

DIET: Insects (Coleoptera, Orthoptera), spiders, snails, small arboreal lizards, such as *Phelsuma* spp. Suspected of raiding other species' nests.

NESTING: Large (30–40 cm diameter) nest, built high in fork of tree (*Adansonia grandidieri, A. madagascariensis*—Bombacaceae) or resting on large branch and held in place by smaller ones, is made of thorny or smooth twigs; interior is lined with more delicate material. Clutch numbers 4 creamy white, slightly shiny eggs heavily mottled with gray to violet-gray or maroon, especially at larger pole (average size: 30.0 × 20.9 mm). Both parents incubate. Nesting has been observed Nov.–Dec.

DISTRIBUTION AND STATUS: Endemic to Madagascar, distributed in n and ne, including Sambirano (Antsiranana, Iharanä, and as far as 40 km n of Sambava), and in w and s. Fairly common throughout range.

239. *White-headed Vanga*

Leptopterus viridis (Müller, 1776)
Malagasy: Vanga, Voromasiaka, Tsakeky, Tretreky
French: Artamie à tête blanche

DESCRIPTION: Length 20 cm.
Adult. Sexes differ.
 Nominate subspecies *L. v. viridis.*
Male. White head. Stout, conical blue-gray bill, dark brown iris. Upperparts entirely black with green sheen, except for small white area on rump. Underparts white. Blue-gray tarsi and toes. Wings black with green sheen, except for black primary remiges. Underside of wing black, except for white underwing coverts. Black tail with green sheen.
Female. Gray head with lighter chin and throat. Bill and iris as in male. Upperparts black with green sheen, except for small gray area on rump. Underparts: chest light gray, belly, flanks, and undertail coverts white tinged with tan. Bluish-gray tarsi and toes. Wings and tail as in male.
Immature. Fairly similar to female, but feathers of scapulars and uppertail coverts are gray edged with brown at apex.
 Subspecies *L. v. annae* (Sclater, 1924).
 Differs from *L. v. viridis* by longer, less massive bill.

IDENTIFICATION: Medium-sized vanga, male having boldly contrasted bicolored plumage: white below, black above, white head. Plumage of female shows less contrast, partly gray below, black above with gray head; could be confused with female Ashy cuckoo-shrike, from which it differs by stockier silhouette, darker upperparts, and lighter, longer bill.

BEHAVIOR: Frequents forest or savanna, fairly gregarious, sometimes found alone or in pairs, or within multispecies feeding flocks of vangas or other forest species. A few White-headed vangas may be seen in flocks of Sickle-billed vangas, both during day and in nocturnal roost. Example of multispecific flock observed at Maroantsetra at elevation of 500 m in Jan.: 2 White-headed vangas, 6 Chabert's vangas, 1 Blue vanga, 1 Bernier's vanga, 1 Helmet vanga, 2 Nuthatch vanga, and 2 Tylas vangas. Searches for food on branches of all sizes, even if almost vertical. Probes under peeling bark, occasionally removing fragments. Often hangs upside down. Holds large prey with one foot and dismembers them with bill. Rarely observed on ground. Flight is rather cumbersome and direct, producing characteristic whirring, though less than Sickle-billed Vanga.

VOICE: Vocal, sings fluted, harmonious *yippie-hoo yippie-hoo yippie-hoo*. Alarm call is harsh, bisyllabic *tshree-yeh*, uttered several times in succession.

HABITAT: Middle and upper level of 3 main forest types, also savanna, mangroves, and adjacent second-growth forests. Observed at elevations from sea level to 2,000 m.

DIET: Insects, spiders, also small reptiles (*Chamaeleo* spp.) and nestlings.

NESTING: Hemispherical nest, built high above ground in fork, is made of plant fibers and interwoven twigs. Interior is lined with more delicate materials. Clutch numbers 3 white, slightly shiny eggs speckled with chestnut, gray, and brown (average size: 26.4 mm × 19.5 mm). Nesting has been observed Oct.–Dec.

DISTRIBUTION AND STATUS: Endemic to Madagascar. *L. v. viridis* is distributed in n in Montagne d'Ambre and Tsaratanana and in e from Sambava to Tolagnaro, where it is fairly common. *L. v. annae* is distributed in w, s of Sambirano, where it is fairly common, and in s,

where it is rarer. White-headed vanga is among those vangas not strictly bound to undisturbed forest.

240. *Chabert's Vanga*

Leptopterus chabert (Müller, 1776)
Malagasy: Pasasatra, Tsa-Tsak, Tsaramaso, Sarigaga, Razangoaka, Soroanja, Fotsy tretreka
French: Artamie de Chabert

DESCRIPTION: Length 14 cm.
Adult. Sexes similar.
   Nominate subspecies *L. c. chabert*.
   Head black with blue sheen, except for white chin, throat, and sides of neck. Pale gray conical bill tinged with blue, brown iris. Eyes surrounded by fleshy ring, sky blue above and ultramarine below. Upperparts black with blue sheen, underparts white. Black tarsi and toes. Wings and tail black with blue sheen.
   Subspecies *L. c. schistocercus* (Neumann, 1908).
   Differs from *L. c. chabert* by shorter bill and white, black-tipped external tail feathers.
Immature. Black parts mottled with white.

IDENTIFICATION: Smallest black-and-white vanga. Recognized by bold contrast of plumage, white below, black above, with black head and blue orbital ring. Distinguished from Ward's flycatcher by pure white chest.

BEHAVIOR: This and Sickle-billed vanga are the most gregarious vangas. Rarely found alone or in pairs outside breeding season. Generally lives in flocks of 6–25, rarely more (32 at Farafangana in Jan. 1987), and sometimes joins multispecies vanga flocks. Actively searches for food on small branches of canopy, frequently hanging upside down, and catches much prey on wing by making vertical sallies from perch. Of all vangas, Chabert's vanga is most given to catching prey on wing. Fond of flying, has easy, slightly undulating flight. Frequently glides from one treetop to another.

VOICE: Fairly vocal. Frequently utters shrill *tleetlee dzewdzewdzew* or a rapid series of *teedy teedeedeedee deedy* or *tiah tiah tiah tiah tiah*. Clacks bill if irritated.

HABITAT: All 3 principal original forest types, also mangroves, second growth, tree plantations (eucalyptus, coffee, cacao, mango), and wooded village surroundings. Observed at elevations from sea level to 1,800 m.

DIET: Small and medium-sized insects (Coleoptera, Diptera) and small berries. Only vanga, together with Blue vanga, whose diet is partly vegetal.

NESTING: Hemispherical nest, built high in a tree in forest, generally near end of horizontal branch, with vertical walls stuck against branches or wedged into small fork, consists of lichens and vegetal fibers bound by spider webs. Light gray in color, its external appearance is smooth and compact. Clutch numbers 3 dull bluish green eggs stippled with small violet-gray to olive-brown specks (average size: 20.0 mm × 16.2 mm). Both parents incubate. To defend nest, will attack, among others, Crested drongo, Hook-billed vanga, Sickle-billed vanga, Madagascar kestrel, and Madagascar harrier-hawk. Nesting has been observed Aug.–Mar.

DISTRIBUTION AND STATUS: Endemic to Madagascar, distributed throughout island. Common throughout range, except High Plateau, where it is rare. *L. c. schistocercus* is limited to subarid s. Most common vanga and best adapted to degraded woodland habitats.

241. *Blue Vanga*

Cyanolanius madagascarinus
(Linnaeus, 1766)
Malagasy: Pasasatrala, Raisasatra, Sarahesa, Vorontsara-elatra
French: Artamie azurée

DESCRIPTION: Length 16 cm.
Adult. Sexes similar.
Front and top of head and nape ultramarine. Black lores and eye ring. Black chin, white throat, fairly wide, ultramarine bill with black tip. Pale sky blue iris. Upperparts shiny ultramarine, underparts white. Black tarsi and toes. Ultramarine wings except for black primary remiges with blue-edged outer half. Tail: entirely black external tail feathers, ultramarine central tail feathers with black tips, remaining tail feathers with ultramarine outer half and black inner half.
Immature. Differs from adult by less vivid blue (gray-blue) head and upperparts and by black bill and brown iris.

IDENTIFICATION: Rather small vanga with contrasting ultramarine and white plumage. Cannot be confused with any other species.

BEHAVIOR: Strictly forest species. Found in pairs during breeding season, but at other times may frequently be seen in small groups of 2–6 or within multispecies feeding flocks. Readily associates with other vanga species and also such smaller non-vanga species as Common newtonia or Madagascar white-eye. Flock observed at sea level at Maroantsetra in Mar. 1982: 2 Blue vangas, 2 Red-tailed vangas, 2 White-headed vangas, 2 Ashy cuckoo-shrikes, 10 Madagascar bulbuls, 2 Common newtonias, 2 Madagascar paradise flycatchers, 6 Souimanga sunbirds, 6 Long-billed green sunbirds, 40 Madagascar white-eyes, and 2 Crested drongos. At 500 m elevation at Maroantsetra in Jan. 1982: 1 Blue vanga, 2

White-headed vangas, 6 Chabert's vangas, 1 Bernier's vanga, 2 Helmet vangas,
and 2 Tylas vangas. Active, hunts in
branches of leafy parts of trees. Readily
hangs upside down to inspect undersides
of branches, almost vertically on trunks
or large branches. Glides to new trees if
they are far away. Often holds prey with
foot and dismembers it with bill. Seldom
catches prey on wing.

VOICE: Vocal. Utters harsh *chrr* or
Chreddayday and *teea teea teea tea tea*.
Similar to call of Chabert's vanga.

HABITAT: Middle and upper levels of
evergreen rain forest and of deciduous
dry forest, adjacent second growth, mangroves. Observed at elevations from sea
level to 1,800 m.

DIET: Insects (Coleoptera, Orthoptera),
occasionally berries. Only vanga, together
with Chabert's vanga, whose diet is partly
vegetal.

NESTING: Few data. Nest, built 12 m
high in leafy tree at end of branch near
treetop, consists of interlaced bits of plant
matter (twigs and leafstalks). Nesting has
been observed in Dec.

DISTRIBUTION AND STATUS: Only
vanga found outside Madagascar. Represented in the Comoros on Mohéli and
Grande Comore by endemic subspecies
C. m. comorensis (Shelley, 1894). Represented in Madagascar by endemic nominate subspecies *C. m. madagascarinus*,
distributed throughout island except in
subarid s. Common in e from extreme n
(Montagne d'Ambre) to extreme s at Tolagnaro. Also found in nw (Sambirano).
Evenly distributed in w to terrain forming
transition to subarid s, but rarer than in e.

242. *Bernier's Vanga*

Oriolia bernieri
Geoffroy Saint-Hilaire, 1838
Malagasy: Taporo
French: Oriolie de Bernier

DESCRIPTION: Length 23 cm.
Adult. Sexes differ.
Male. Head entirely black with blue
sheen. Stout, conical, light gray bill, grayish white iris. Upperparts and underparts
black with blue sheen. Light gray tarsi
and toes. Black wings with blue sheen,
except for dark brown primary remiges.
Black tail with blue sheen.
Female. Tan-rufous head with fine black
stripes. Stout, conical, light gray bill,
grayish white iris. Upperparts rufous with
fine black stripes. Underparts rufous with
black stripes. Light gray tarsi and toes.
Upper side of wings like upperparts, with
uniformly rufous primary remiges. Basal
half or third of primary remiges is often
more brightly colored. Underside of
wings uniformly rufous, except for finely
black-striped rufous underwing coverts.
Rufous tail.
Immature. Similar to female.

IDENTIFICATION: Large vanga with
slender silhouette and conical, light-
colored bill. Male is recognized by entirely black plumage and female by rufous
plumage finely striped with black. This
species and Red-tailed vanga are only
vangas to show such considerable sexual
chromatic differences. Cannot be confused with any other species.

BEHAVIOR: Strictly forest species,
found in isolated pairs or in multispecies
feeding flocks made up principally of
vangas. Flock observed at Maroantsetra,
Jan. 1982: 1 male Bernier's vanga, 2
White-headed vangas, 6 Chabert's vangas, 1 Blue vanga, 2 Nuthatch vangas,
and 2 Tylas vangas. Bernier's vanga is always present in small numbers in such

flocks, whereas other species are always better represented. Roams forest at different heights in search of vegetal debris that attracts its prey. Particularly fond of leaves of Pandanus (*Pandanus* spp.—Pandanaceae), Ravenala (*Ravenala madagascariensis*—Strelitziaceae), and palms, which it inspects minutely. Sometimes grips almost vertical trunks like a woodpecker. Makes short, swift, frequent flights during which its wings produce a whirring sound.

VOICE: Male utters loud, resonant, monosyllabic *chew* from visible perch while slowly bobbing tail.

HABITAT: Various levels of undisturbed rain forest. Observed at elevations from sea level to 900 m.

DIET: Invertebrates (Coleoptera, Orthoptera, spiders).

NESTING: Unknown.

DISTRIBUTION AND STATUS: Endemic to Madagascar, distributed in ne (Marojejy, Maroantsetra) and e center (Sihanaka forest, Zahamena). Rather rare throughout range.

243. *Helmet Vanga*

Euryceros prevostii (Lesson, 1830)
Malagasy: Siketribe
French: Eurycère de Prévost

DESCRIPTION: Length 28–30.5 cm. *Adult.* Sexes similar. Bulbous hooked, pearly light blue bill (51 mm long, 30 mm high) has black commissures, sharp black point, upper ridge higher than top of head. Light yellow iris. Upperparts rufous, underparts black with delicate, diffuse light brown stripes on belly, flanks, and undertail coverts. Robust gray-blue tarsi and toes. Rufous wings with black remiges. Rather long, wide tail is black, except for 2 rufous central tail feathers.

Immature. Chestnut head. Bill same size as adult's, black except for yellow tip and commissures. Brown iris. Upperparts chestnut. Underparts: chestnut chest, gray belly and undertail coverts. Gray tarsi and toes. Wings chestnut, except for black primary and rufous secondary remiges. Tail black, except for 2 rufous central tail feathers.

IDENTIFICATION: Very large vanga with bicolored black-and-rufous plumage, big, bright, light blue bulbous hooked bill. Cannot be confused with any other species.

BEHAVIOR: Strictly forest species, found alone, in pairs, or in multispecies feeding flocks composed principally of vangas. Flock observed at 500 m elevation at Maroantsetra, Feb. 1982: 5 Helmet vangas (2 adults, 3 immatures), 1 Hook-billed vanga, 2 White-headed vangas, 3 Bernier's vangas, 2 Tylas vangas, and 1 Ashy cuckoo-shrike. Explores lower levels of forest to treetops. Moves about frequently and rapidly with forceful flight; whirring of wings can be heard at 25 m. Seizes prey on wing as well as on branches or trunks. May also spend long spells immobile and unnoticed on horizontal branch near trunk, 2.5–6 m above ground.

VOICE: Vocal. Sings early in morning, often before sunrise. Rather soft, harmonious song recalls that of Rufous vanga. It consists of 8 whistled, trilled notes, diminishing in volume and sometimes repeated 5–6 times: *Tree tree tree tree tree . . . .* Alarm call is harsh, rowdy *treh treh treh . . .* or loud, nasal *hink hink . . . .*

HABITAT: Undisturbed rain forest exclusively. Observed at elevations of 200–1,800 m, but usually stays between 400 and 900 m.

DIET: Insects (Orthoptera, Hemiptera, Coleoptera).

NESTING: Few data. Nest, built in fork of tree low (2.5 m) above ground or at base of leaves of tree fern (*Cyathea* spp.—Cyatheaceae), consists of moss and woven plant fibers. Clutch numbers 2–3 pink-white eggs mottled with carmine red, especially at larger pole. Nesting has been observed Oct.–Nov.

DISTRIBUTION AND STATUS: Endemic to Madagascar, local to ne (Marojejy, Maroantsetra) and e center (Zahamena), where it is uncommon, and to Analamazaotra, where it is known only by 1 specimen taken in 1935.

244. Nuthatch Vanga

Hypositta corallirostris (Newton, 1863)
Malagasy: Sakodidy, Voronakodidina
French: Vanga-Sittelle

DESCRIPTION: Length 13–14 cm.
Adult. Sexes differ.
Male. Black forehead, lores, and chin. Rest of head and throat gray-blue. Bright red bill with black hook. Dark brown iris. Gray-blue upperparts, underparts, tarsi, and toes. Elongated (20 mm) claw of first toe. Wings gray-blue, except for sooty gray primary remiges. Tail gray-blue above, sooty below.
Female. Differs from male by brown-green head, duller red bill, dull gray-blue upperparts, wings, and tail, and brown-green underparts.
Immature. Similar to female.

IDENTIFICATION: Smallest vanga. Uniformly gray-blue plumage and bright red bill distinguish it easily from all other species.

BEHAVIOR: Strictly forest species, secretive, active, found most often in groups of 2–3 or within multispecies feeding flocks. Flocks observed at Maroantsetra: *(a)* Elevation of 500 m in Jan. 1982—2 Nuthatch vangas, 2 White-

headed vangas, 6 Chabert's vangas, 2 Blue vangas, 1 Bernier's vanga, 1 Helmet vanga, and 2 Tylas vangas; *(b)* elevation of 200 m in Mar.—2 Nuthatch vangas, 3 Red-tailed vangas, 2 Ashy cuckoo-shrikes, 5 Madagascar bulbuls, 2 Common newtonias, 2 Madagascar paradise flycatchers, 5 Souimanga sunbirds, 1 Long-billed green sunbird, 30 Madagascar white-eyes, and 2 Crested drongos. Climbs along trunks and large branches in search of food. Frequents upper half of trunks with deep bark. Having worked its way to top of one trunk, flies to lower section of another trunk to continue examination. Does not work from top down. Flight is swift and always limited to short distances.

VOICE: Unknown.

HABITAT: Middle and upper levels of undisturbed rain forest. Observed at elevations from sea level to 1,800 m.

DIET: Small insects.

NESTING: Very few data. Nesting probably occurs Aug.–Sept.

DISTRIBUTION AND STATUS: Endemic to Madagascar, distributed in e from Marojejy forest to Tolagnaro. Fairly common in n part of range (Marojejy, Maroantsetra, Sihanaka forest, Andasibe) and rather rare in s part (Vondrozo, Andohahela).

245. Tylas Vanga

Tylas eduardi Hartlaub, 1862
Malagasy: Mokazavona, Kinkimavo
French: Tylas

DESCRIPTION: Length of *T. e. eduardi* 21 cm; of *T. e. albigularis* 20 cm.
Adult. Sexes differ slightly.
Nominate subspecies *T. e. eduardi.*
Male. Black head, nape, and chin. Black bill, brown iris. Upperparts gray-green.

Underparts orangy, except for white band on upper chest extending up sides of neck. Black tarsi and toes. Gray-green wings with dark brown primary remiges and white lesser underwing coverts. Green-brown tail.
Female. Differs from male by dark gray forehead and front of head and whitish chin.

Subspecies *T. e. albigularis* (Hartlaub, 1877). Sooty gray forehead and front of head. Black crown, checks, and nape. White chin, throat, and sides of neck. Sooty bill. Upperparts gray tinged with green. Underparts: light tan chest and undertail coverts. Dirty white belly and flanks. Black tarsi and toes. Gray wings with sooty primary remiges. Gray tail.

IDENTIFICATION: Medium-sized vanga with slender silhouette, gray-green above, orangy below, black head and throat, and thin bill. Very similar to Pollen's vanga, which has same color pattern. Differs from Pollen's vanga by smaller size, smaller tarsi and toes, and especially thin black bill.

BEHAVIOR: Strictly forest species, sometimes found alone or in pairs but usually observed within multispecies feeding flock composed chiefly of vangas. Flock observed at 900 m at Andasibe, May 1982: 2 Tylas vangas, 6 Red-tailed vangas, 4 White-headed vangas, 3 Blue vangas, 1 Nuthatch vanga, and 1 Ashy cuckoo-shrike. In w, Tylas vanga has been observed in a multispecies feeding flock composed of Long-billed greenbuls, Ashy cuckoo-shrikes, and Rufous vangas, as well as in a monospecific flock of Blue vangas. Hunts from ambush, often seizes prey on wing. Also minutely inspects leaves, small branches, and epiphytic plants.

VOICE: Fairly vocal, repeats harmonious *weeta weet yew-ew*, several times at regular intervals from fixed post; also repeats brief, energetic *chop* several times.

HABITAT: *T. e. eduardi* frequents middle and upper levels of primary rain forest, occasionally adjacent second growth. Observed at elevations from sea level to 1,800 m. *T. e. albigularis*, for which only few data are available, has been observed in deciduous, almost leafless dry forest, and a few times in mangroves. Observed at elevations from sea level to approximately 900 m.

DIET: Medium-sized insects.

NESTING: Few data. Bowl-shaped nest, built in fork of tree only 4 m above ground, is made of moss and interwoven rootlets. Clutch numbers 2 eggs. Nesting has been observed Nov.–Jan. Data on *T. e. albigularis* are scant; thought to breed Aug.–Sept.

DISTRIBUTION AND STATUS: Endemic to Madagascar. *T. e. eduardi* is distributed in E Region from Andapa to Tolagnaro, where it is fairly common. *T. e. albigularis* is known only from Morondava, Morombe (mangroves), and Ankazoabo, where it is rare.

NOTE: Claim to membership of *T. eduardi* in the Vangidae remains in doubt because it lacks certain morphological features, such as hook at end of bill, typical of this endemic family.

Dicruridae – Drongo

Medium-sized passerines with black plumage, a stout, short, rather curved bill containing numerous vibrissae, and generally a forked tail. They are solitary, frequent savannas and woodlands, and feed on insects. Drongos have a highly varied vocal range and act aggressively toward other species. The family is distributed in Africa, India, and Australia; 20 species are recognized. One species nests in Madagascar; it is common to Anjouan, in the Comoros.

246. *Crested Drongo*

Dicrurus forficatus (Linnaeus, 1766)
Malagasy: Railovy, Relovy, Lova, Railomba
French: Drongo malgache

DESCRIPTION: Length 26 cm. *Adult.* Sexes similar. Head entirely black with bluish sheen. Black, stout, broad-based bill. Tuft of 3 feathers at base of bill. Dark red iris. Upperparts and underparts black with bluish sheen. Wings black except for dark brown primary remiges. Black tail.
Immature. Differs from adult by generally dark brown plumage and more precisely by dark brown and white mottling of crown, nape, and neck, absence or small size of frontal tuft, white tinge of upperparts and underparts, white scales on brown upper- and underwing coverts, and shorter, less forked tail.

IDENTIFICATION: Only representative of family, cannot be confused with any other species. Recognized by black plumage all over, tuft of erect feathers on forehead, and long, notched tail with diverging external tail feathers.

BEHAVIOR: Generally found alone, less frequently in pairs. Also associates with multispecies feeding flocks. Flock observed at Maroantsetra in Mar. 1982: 2 Crested drongos, 2 Ashy cuckoo-shrikes, 10 Madagascar bulbuls, 2 Common newtonias, 2 Madagascar paradise flycatchers, 5 Souimanga sunbirds, 6 Long-billed green sunbirds, 40 Madagascar white-eyes, 2 Red-tailed vangas, 2 White-headed vangas, and 2 Blue vangas. In w forest at Mitsinjo in Apr. 1982: 2 Crested drongos, 1 Ashy cuckoo-shrike, 1 Long-billed greenbul, 6 Common newtonias, 1 Common jery, 1 pair of Madagascar paradise flycatchers, and 6 Souimanga sunbirds. Bellicose enough to attack and pursue such large birds as Madagascar fish-eagle, or harass zebus, dogs, or humans near its nest. Hunts from ambush, making sallies from exposed perch to seize prey on wing and returning to observation post. Capable of aerial acrobatics to catch an insect. Flight is not sustained and rarely undertaken for long distances.

VOICE: Highly vocal. Sings from fixed post. Usually delivers jumble of shrill, nasal, rapid-fire notes strung together without harmony. Sometimes utters monotonous, trisyllabic whistled *twee to-ee*, but often imitates calls of other birds. Individuals living near villages sometimes imitate domestic animals, meowing like cats or clucking like hens.

HABITAT: Any terrain that is even sparsely wooded, with particular fondness for wooded areas dominating open space (forest edges, clearings). Observed at elevations from sea level to 1,800 m, but rarely over 1,000 m.

DIET: Insects.

NESTING: Nest is light bowl woven of plant fibers, often built fairly high at end of branch. Clutch numbers 2–4 white eggs mottled with brown and gray. Nesting has been observed Sept.–Dec.

DISTRIBUTION AND STATUS: Distributed in Madagascar and Anjouan, Comoros. Represented in Madagascar by nominate endemic subspecies *D. f. forficatus*. Distributed throughout woodlands, where it is common, except for High Plateau (Ambohitantely), where it is rather rare.

Corvidae – Crow

The largest passerines, with black or black-and-white plumage, a generally stout bill, with nostrils hidden under long vibrissae, most crows adapt readily to areas occupied by people. They utter various raucous sounds, are omnivorous, and build rather large nests out of branches. The family is cosmopolitan, and about 100 species are recognized. A single species common to Africa is found in Madagascar.

247. *Pied Crow*

Corvus albus Müller, 1776
Malagasy: Goaka, Gaga, Gagnake
French: Corbeau pie

DESCRIPTION: Length 45–52 cm. *Adult.* Sexes similar. Shiny black head, nape, chin, and throat. Stout black bill with feathered basal half of upper mandible. Dark brown iris. Upperparts shiny black, except for white back of neck and upper mantle. Underparts shiny black, except for sides and lower portion of chest and upper belly. Powerful black tarsi and toes. Black wings and tail. *Immature.* Differs from adult by drab plumage and black tips on some feathers of white areas.

IDENTIFICATION: Very large black-and-white passerine. Only crow of Madagascar; cannot be confused with any other species.

BEHAVIOR: Fairly gregarious outside breeding period, adapts warily but opportunistically to areas inhabited by people. Found in pairs or loose groups of 3–50, sometimes more in places where food is abundant or in trees chosen as roosts during heat of day or for the night (up to

1,000 at Antsiranana, Sept. 1985). Feeds mainly on ground, walking slowly or hopping ponderously. Often seen with Common myna among grazing zebus. Flight is rather heavy and powerful; often soars in groups, taking advantage of thermals.

VOICE: Vocal. Utters loud, resonant, raucous, dissonant caw heard as *ha-arr ha-arr ha-arr* or *ka-arr ka-arr ka-arr* from unconcealed perch or in flight. Leans back when cawing at rest. May utter an assortment of peculiar sounds.

HABITAT: Slightly wooded open biotopes, savanna, degraded forest, riversides, beaches, surroundings of towns and villages. Observed at elevations from sea level to 2,000 m.

DIET: Very varied. Invertebrates (insects, caterpillars, spiders, worms), small vertebrates (batrachians, reptiles, nestlings, eggs, small mammals), carrion, items of vegetal origin (seeds, fruits).

NESTING: Capacious nest, almost always built high in isolated tree, is woven of small branches and twigs; interior is lined with more delicate material. Clutch numbers 4–6 light green eggs mottled with olive green, pale violet-gray, and dark brown. Female broods. Nesting has been observed Aug.–Dec., peaking Oct.

DISTRIBUTION AND STATUS: Distributed in sub-Saharan Africa, Madagascar, Comoros, Aldabra, Glorieuses. Common throughout Madagascar, except for High Plateau, where it is uncommon.

Sturnidae – Starling, Myna

Medium-sized passerines with a somewhat long, slightly curved bill and rather chunky tarsi and toes. The plumage of most species has a certain amount of metallic sheen. They are generally very gregarious, especially within their roosts. Their diet is varied, though it consists chiefly of fruits. The family is represented by 108 species spread across the Old World, and some species have been introduced in various places. Two species nest in Madagascar, 1 an endemic forest species and 1 introduced.

248. *Madagascar Starling*
Hartlaubius auratus (Müller, 1776)
Malagasy: Vorontainaomby
French: Etourneau de Madagascar

DESCRIPTION: Length 18–20 cm.
Adult. Sexes differ.
Male. Uniformly brown head. Black bill, dark brown iris. Upperparts dark brown, lighter than head. Underparts: brown chest and flanks, lighter belly, white undertail coverts. Black tarsi and toes. Dark brown wings with green sheen, except for midnight blue primary remiges with white outer half. Underside of wings dusky brown, except for white underwing coverts. Black tail with blue sheen, except for 2 white external remiges.
Female. Entirely brown head. Black bill, dark brown iris. Upperparts uniformly dark brown. Underparts: light brown chest, gray-brown flanks, and undertail coverts, brown-gray belly. Black tarsi and toes. Brown wings have green-and-blue sheen on secondary remiges, and primary remiges with midnight blue and white outer half. Underside of wings brown-gray, except for white underwing coverts.

Dusky brown tail with blue or green sheen.

IDENTIFICATION: Smaller of 2 Sturnidae in Madagascar. Recognized by slender silhouette, long, thin black bill, long legs. Distinguished from Madagascar bulbul by brown upperparts, white external tail feathers, white-and-blue primary remiges, and white underside of wings. Flight is straight but not buoyant, periods of wingbeats alternating with glides.

BEHAVIOR: Gregarious, normally found in small flocks of 4–22 (12 eating fruit of *Ficus* sp.—Moraceae in company of 25 Madagascar green pigeons at Manongarivo in June 1987), sometimes as members of multispecifies feeding flocks. Favors treetops and forest edges; often settles on dead trees next to open area, clearing, or river.

VOICE: Not very vocal, sings harmonious, piping, high-pitched, trisyllabic *chee chreetee* for several minutes without stopping from visible perch.

HABITAT: Undisturbed evergreen rain forest, secondary growth, or any woodlands, even if sparse, near villages and rice paddies, deciduous dry forest, subarid thorn scrub. Observed at elevations from sea level to 1,800 m.

DIET: Chiefly fruits and berries, occasionally insects.

NESTING: Few data. Nest is built in tree hollow. Sky blue eggs are mottled with chestnut. Nesting has been observed Sept.–Nov.

DISTRIBUTION AND STATUS: Endemic to Madagascar, distributed throughout island. Fairly common in e, from Andapa to Tolagnaro, n (Ankarana, Montagne d'Ambre), and nw (Sambirano, Tsaratanana), rather rare in w, particularly s of Tsiandro, rare in s (Ihotry and Tsimanampetsotsa lakes), rather rare on High Plateau (Ambohitantely).

249. *Common Myna*

Acridotheres tristis (Linnaeus, 1766)
Malagasy: Martaina, Ramaro
French: Martin triste

DESCRIPTION: Length 24 cm. *Adult.* Sexes similar. Black head, chin, and throat. Broad, lozenge-shaped area of bare yellow skin around eyes. Orange-yellow iris. Upperparts burgundy-brown. Underparts: upper part of chest dark brown, lower part tan-rufous. Rufous-brown flanks, tan belly, white undertail coverts. Yellow tarsi and toes. Wings burgundy-brown, except for black primary remiges with broad white markings at base. Black tail with white tip, except for uniform central tail feathers.

IDENTIFICATION: Larger of 2 Sturnidae in Madagascar. Recognized by stocky silhouette, yellow bill, broad bare yellow area around eyes, white wing markings, black-and-white underside of wings, and white tip of tail.

BEHAVIOR: Very gregarious outside breeding season, found in flocks of 10–80, sometimes more when food is locally plentiful. Hundreds congregate extremely noisily at nightfall to roost, usually in large tree in or near village. Opportunistic and unspecialized, species adapts readily if warily to environments occupied by people. Commonly observed hopping about on ground among livestock, feeding with Cattle egrets and Pied crows. Often perches on backs of zebus. Also found on trees fruiting or in seed. Travels in loose, noisy bands.

VOICE: Highly vocal. Most frequently voiced song is fluted, resonant, fairly harmonious *teeyoo teeyoo teeyoo* or *tweeyoo*

tweeyoo tweeyoo rapidly enunciated 6–12 times from perch or ground. Various piercing, harsh calls are also uttered in roost in early morning or evening. Also imitates, almost perfectly, such species as Madagascar bulbul, Lesser vasa parrot, and Crested drongo, as well as wide range of sounds heard around human settlements.

HABITAT: Sparsely wooded degraded terrain, croplands, pasture, surroundings of towns and villages. Observed at elevations from sea level to 1,700 m.

DIET: Eclectic; insects, small vertebrates (reptiles, amphibians, nestlings, eggs), fruits, and seeds.

NESTING: Nest is haphazard collection of miscellaneous materials (twigs, feathers, paper) placed in natural (tree hollow) or artificial (gutter, roof) cavity 3–10 m above ground and almost always difficult of access. Clutch numbers 3–4 shiny turquoise eggs (average size: 32.5 mm × 23.0 mm). Both parents incubate. Nesting has been observed Nov.–Dec.

DISTRIBUTION AND STATUS: Original range is in Asia. During past 2 centuries, has been introduced in numerous places, including South Africa, Madagascar, Comoros, Mauritius, Réunion, Seychelles, Tahiti, and New Zealand. Represented in Madagascar by nominate subspecies *A. t. tristis,* originating in India and SE Asia. Introduced in second half of 19th century to control proliferating locusts. Birds released at Toamasina came from Réunion, where species had first been introduced around 1750, then again 8 years later after it failed to establish itself. Individuals released then were imported from India. Range, limited in 1879 to e coastal strip between Toamasina and Pointe-à-Larrée, has since expanded considerably. Now found in n and nw (Antsiranana, Nosy Be, Ambanja, Iharanä), e from Sambava to Tolagnaro. It has also entered subarid thorn scrub (Amboasary, Tsiombe, Cap Sainte-Marie, Itampolo) and is gradually advancing to High Plateau. Already present at Moramanga, Fianarantsoa, Ambalavao, and Antananarivo, where a small colony of 25 birds became established in Aug. 1988. Common throughout range, which is expanding as continuous forest cover (a natural barrier to species) shrinks.

Ploceidae – Sparrow, Weavers, Fodies

Small or medium-sized passerines. They are generally granivorous and have a short, stout bill, but some forest species are insectivorous and have a more slender bill. Many species are colonial. Nests vary in size and structure, and some species are parasites. The family is represented by 145 species spread through the temperate and tropical regions of the Old World, principally Africa and Asia. In Madagascar it is represented by 5 species: 4 endemic, and 1, of recent appearance, possibly introduced.

250. *House Sparrow*

Passer domesticus (Linnaeus, 1758)
French: Moineau domestique

DESCRIPTION: Length 14–15 cm.
Adult. Sexes differ.
Male. Gray forehead and front and top of head. Rufous nape, back of neck, and stripe behind eye. Short white supercilium, white cheeks. Black lores, chin, and throat. Black bill, dark brown iris. Upperparts brown streaked with black, except for brownish-gray rump and upperwing coverts. Underparts grayish, except for black upper chest. Light brown

tarsi and toes. Wings chestnut, marked with brown, except for white median coverts and brown remiges. Brown tail.
Female. Gray-brown head with paler cheeks and supercilium. Whitish chin and throat. Light brown bill, dark brown iris. Upperparts gray-brown with sooty streaks, underparts pale gray-brown. Wings as in male, with less contrast. Brown tail.
Immature. Differs from female by brown-speckled crown and rump and generally paler upper- and underparts.

IDENTIFICATION: Small granivorous, gregarious passerine, russet above and whitish below, with stout bill. Male cannot be confused with any other species. Female is distinguished from female Madagascar red fody by larger size and chestnut upperparts.

BEHAVIOR: Gregarious, adapts readily to environments populated by people.

VOICE: Vocal. Chirps and utters high-pitched, brief *chissip* or *cheep* from perch.

DIET: Chiefly seeds, but will vary with opportunity.

NESTING: Nest of dry grasses is built in cavity (roof, building, street lamp). Nesting has been observed in Nov.

DISTRIBUTION AND STATUS: From group of some 20 birds confined to port of Toamasina in 1984, population grew to about 100 by 1986, now established in port and along seafront. Introduction may have been deliberate, but accidental arrival on board freighter from, perhaps, Réunion, seems more probable. Very common on Réunion, where its introduction around 1860 certainly involved individuals of 2 distinct geographic origins: nominate subspecies *P. d. domesticus* of Europe and subspecies *P. d. indicus* of Asia.

251. *Nelicourvi Weaver*

Ploceus nelicourvi (Scopoli, 1786)
Malagasy: Fodisaina, Fodifetsy
French: Tisserin nelicourvi

DESCRIPTION: Length 14.5 cm.
Adult. Sexes differ.
Male. Black forehead, front and top of head, and cheeks. Golden yellow nape, neck, chin, and throat. Stout, conical black bill, dark brown iris. Upperparts yellow-green, underparts dark gray, except for green breastband and rufous-brown undertail coverts. Gray tarsi and toes. Wings yellow-green, except for sooty gray remiges edged with yellow-green on outer half. Tail: dark brown tail feathers edged with yellow-green on outer half.
Female. Yellow forehead, front of head, supercilium, and cheeks. Green crown and eye patch. Yellow chin, throat, and nape-collar. Upperparts, underparts, wings, and tail as in male.
Immature. Differs from female by green, not yellow, forehead, front of head, nape-collar, and throat and by generally drabber plumage.

IDENTIFICATION: Stocky passerine with contrasting yellow-and-black plumage (male). Female has more subdued plumage, with green-and-yellow head and yellow supercilium and nape-collar.

BEHAVIOR: Forest species, ungregarious, usually found alone or in pairs but often also in small numbers—rarely more than 2 or 3—within multispecies feeding flocks, especially with Long-billed greenbul. Feeds among branches, from treetops to low forest vegetation.

VOICE: Nasal *tiang tiang tiang.*

HABITAT: Undisturbed rain forest and adjacent second growth. Observed at elevations from sea level to 1,800 m.

DIET: Insects—Coleoptera and Orthoptera.

NESTING: Nests in isolation. Spectacular nest is unique: suspended from branch 2–7 m over natural (river) or artificial (road) thoroughfare by a braided vegetal peduncle 15–30 cm long, and woven of grasses and palm fibers, it is oval in shape with a side opening near the top, extended by a vertical access tunnel 12–20 cm long. Clutch generally numbers 3 (sometimes 2 or 4) oval, fairly shiny, pale greenish-blue eggs (average size: 21.0 mm × 15.5 mm). Nesting has been observed Sept.–Jan.

DISTRIBUTION AND STATUS: Endemic to Madagascar, distributed in e, from Sambava to Tolagnaro, as well as in n and nw in Montagne d'Ambre, Sambirano, and Tsaratanana. Fairly common throughout range.

252. *Sakalava Weaver*

Ploceus sakalava (Hartlaub, 1861)
Malagasy: Fodisahy, Fodibeotse, Zaky, Draky, Tsiaka
French: Tisserin sakalave

DESCRIPTION: Length of *P. s. sakalava* 15–15.5 cm; of *P. s. minor* 13 cm.
Adult. Sexes differ. Plumage varies seasonally.
  Nominate subspecies *P. s. sakalava.*
Male Breeding Plumage. Front and top of head, nape, chin, and throat bright yellow. Red bare skin around eyes. Pale blue, very stout, conical bill, light brown iris. Upperparts solid gray-brown, except for mantle flecked with light tan. Underparts light gray, and undertail coverts dirty white. Pink tarsi and toes. Gray-brown wings have brown primary remiges with very fine tan edges and brown secondary remiges with tan borders. Underside of

wings gray, except for white underwing coverts. Gray-brown tail.

Male Nonbreeding Plumage. Similar to female, but with bare skin around eyes.

Female. Front and top of head and nape tan-brown. Light tan supercilium and mustache. Light gray chin and throat. Very stout, pale blue-gray conical bill. Light brown iris. Upperparts solid gray-brown, except for mantle flecked with dark brown. Underparts white-gray. Pink tarsi and toes. Wings and tail as in male in breeding plumage.

Immature. Similar to female.

Subspecies *P. s. minor* (Delacour and Berlioz, 1931).

Differs from nominate subspecies only by smaller size and slightly smaller bill.

IDENTIFICATION: Granivorous passerine with yellow head (male). Female is distinguished from female Madagascar red fody by much heavier build, stouter bill, and generally grayer plumage.

BEHAVIOR: Very gregarious, often in areas occupied by people, found in flocks of up to 250. Feeds on ground as well as in trees, may be seen feeding in rice paddies with Madagascar red fody.

VOICE: Fairly vocal, not melodious. From singing post in full view near nesting colony, male utters droning *dji dji dji dji* . . . with wings quivering. Also utters brief *treeyoo* in flight.

HABITAT: Open terrain (degraded areas, surroundings of villages, croplands), moderately wooded areas (savanna, subarid thorn scrub) and, more rarely, dense woodlands (deciduous dry forest). Observed at elevations from sea level to 700 m.

DIET: Largely grass seeds but also insects, caterpillars, and spiders, especially while feeding young.

NESTING: Nests in colonies of 10–120 nests in a tree or stand of trees, usually situated in heart of village. Sometimes attached to structure of large nest (Pied crow, Madagascar buzzard, Black kite). Spherical, rather loosely constructed nest, built 2–20 m above ground, with side opening extended by long, vertical tunnel, is woven of dry plants. Clutch numbers 3–4 green-blue eggs (average size: 20.5 mm × 15.1 mm). Nesting has been observed Nov.–Apr.

DISTRIBUTION AND STATUS: Endemic to Madagascar, distributed in n, w, and s. Nominate subspecies *P. s. sakalava* is distributed in n and w (Antsiranana, Iharanä, Mahajanga, Maintirano, Morondava), where it is common. Subspecies *P. s. minor* is distributed in subarid s, where it is common (Morombe, Toliara, Ejeda, Amboasary, Andohahela).

253. *Madagascar Red Fody*

Foudia madagascariensis (Linnaeus, 1766)
Malagasy: Fody, Fodimena, Fodilahimena
French: Foudi de Madagascar

DESCRIPTION: Length 13.5–14 cm.
Adult. Sexes differ. Plumage varies seasonally.

Male Breeding Plumage. Head vermilion, except for black lores and triangular patch behind eyes. Vermilion chin and throat. Stout, conical black bill, brown iris. Upperparts vermilion streaked with black, except for solid red rump and uppertail coverts. Underparts red, lighter at belly and undertail coverts. Pink tarsi and toes. Dark gray-brown wings have outer side of each feather edged with light brown. Dark gray-brown tail. Some individuals may have orangy yellow coloration instead of vermilion.

Male Nonbreeding Plumage. Similar to female.

Female. Green-brown forehead, front and top of head, and nape, delicately streaked

with black. Solid green-brown cheeks, lores, chin, and throat, green-yellow supercilium. Pale brown bill, brown iris. Upperparts green-brown streaked with black, except for uniformly green-brown rump and uppertail coverts. Underparts: greenish chest and flanks, green-gray belly, yellowish undertail coverts. Pink-gray tarsi and toes. Wings and tail as in male in breeding plumage.
Immature. Similar to female.

IDENTIFICATION: Small granivorous passerine. Male in breeding plumage, entirely bright red, except for brown wings and tail, is easily distinguished from Forest fody by slightly smaller size, less stout bill, and especially all-red upperparts and underparts and brownish hue of wings and tail. Confusion is possible between male Madagascar red fody in intermediate plumage, which may present red chest and gray belly, and male Forest fody in breeding or intermediate plumage. Female has brownish plumage and is difficult to distinguish from female Forest fody; differs by slightly smaller size, generally brown hue of plumage, less stout bill, and more pronounced light-colored supercilium.

BEHAVIOR: Gregarious, found alone or in pairs at breeding time, in flocks at other times. Flocks may number several hundred individuals in areas where food is plentiful, or in roosts established in trees or bamboo stands in parks, in mangroves, or in reedbeds.

VOICE: Fairly vocal. Male usually delivers song from unconcealed, generally rather low perch at end of reed or branch. Song is drawn-out, trilled, high-pitched, rather metallic *cheet cheet cheet . . .*, which may rise to very high pitch and end with harmonious trilled diminuendo. Alarm call is sort of shrill *tik tik*.

HABITAT: Any natural open or degraded terrain, savanna, surroundings of well-watered terrain, croplands (especially rice paddies), parks and gardens of towns and villages. Observed at elevations from sea level to 2,300 m.

DIET: Primarily seeds (especially of grasses), also insects, caterpillars, and spiders, especially during breeding season, and occasionally nectar of certain flowers.

NESTING: Nest is established 1–3 m above ground in a tree or shrub. Spherical nest, woven of grass leaves, is loose structure with side opening near top extended by short, wide, access tunnel. Clutch numbers 3–4 slightly shiny, pale green-blue, oval eggs (average size: 18.0 mm × 12.8 mm). Nesting has been observed Dec.–May.

DISTRIBUTION AND STATUS: Endemic to Madagascar, introduced into neighboring islands: Réunion (origin uncertain), Comoros (origin uncertain), Mauritius, Seychelles, Amirantes, Rodrigues, Chagos. In Madagascar it is distributed throughout the island and is very common. Most commonly encountered species in Madagascar.

NOTE: Existence of specimens whose morphology is intermediate between *F. madagascariensis* and *F. omissa* suggests that hybridization is occurring between those species.

254. *Forest Fody*
Foudi omissa Rothschild, 1912
Malagasy: Fodiala
French: Foudi de Forêt

DESCRIPTION: Length 14.5 cm.
Adult. Sexes differ. Plumage varies seasonally.
Male Breeding Plumage. Head vermilion,

except for black lores and triangular
patch behind eyes. Vermilion chin and
throat. Bill: stout, conical black upper mandible, pale brown lower mandible. Brown
iris. Upperparts olive green striped with
black, except for orangy red uppertail
coverts. Underparts: vermilion chest,
belly and flanks light gray tinged with
green, pale yellow undertail coverts.
Pink tarsi and toes. Wings: olive green
streaked with black; outer half of dark
brown primary remiges has olive green
edges. Dark brown tail.
Male Nonbreeding Plumage. Similar to
female.
Female. Olive green forehead, front and
top of head, and nape streaked with
black. Olive green cheeks and lores,
green-yellow supercilium. Yellow-green
chin and cheeks. Pale brown bill, brown
iris. Upperparts olive green streaked with
black, except for solid olive green rump
and uppertail coverts. Underparts: greenish chest and flanks, green-gray belly,
yellowish undertail coverts. Pink-gray
tarsi and toes. Wings and tail as in male
in breeding plumage.
Immature. Similar to female.

IDENTIFICATION: Small granivorous
passerine. Male in breeding plumage,
greenish with bright red head, chest, and
undertail coverts, is easily distinguished
from male Madagascar red fody by
slightly larger size, stouter bill, light
belly, flanks, and undertail coverts, and
especially largely green upperparts. Female has greenish plumage and is difficult
to distinguish from female Madagascar
red fody; differs by slightly larger size,
generally greenish hue of plumage,

stouter bill and less pronounced light
supercilium.

BEHAVIOR: Forest species, secretive,
little known, found alone or in pairs at
breeding time, in flocks of 4–15 at other
times. May also be seen in multispecies
feeding flocks. Frequents middle and upper levels of forest. Along line where
edge of forest meets open terrain, Forest
fody may be seen with Madagascar red
fody.

VOICE: Little known. Similar to voice of
Madagascar red fody.

HABITAT: Undisturbed rain forest. Observed at elevations from sea level to
2,000 m.

DIET: Seeds.

NESTING: Unknown.

DISTRIBUTION AND STATUS: Endemic to Madagascar, distributed in e
from Sambava to Tolagnaro, in n and nw
in Montagne d'Ambre and Tsaratanana
and on High Plateau (Manjakatompo).
Uncommon throughout range.

NOTE: Some authors do not consider
F. omissa a valid taxon but classify it with
F. eminentissima (Bonaparte) distributed
in Comoros and Aldabra. Existence of
specimens morphologically intermediate
between *F. madagascariensis* and *F. omissa*
suggests that the 2 are hybridizing. Existence of non-hybridized individuals
would depend on keeping large tracts of
forest intact. Breaking up such tracts will
encourage *F. madagascariensis* to enter
and lead to disappearance of *F. omissa* by
hybridization.

Estrildidae – Mannikin, Waxbill

Small granivorous, ground-feeding passerines with short, rounded wings, quite close to the family Ploceidae but generally smaller and having only 9 primary remiges (instead of the Ploceidae's 10). Some species do not build a nest but parasitize other species. The family is represented by 130 species distributed mainly in Africa but also in Asia and Oceania. An endemic species is distributed in Madagascar and a second species, of recent appearance, was probably introduced.

255. *Madagascar Mannikin*

Lonchura nana (Pucheran, 1845)
Malagasy: Tsiporitika, Tsikirity, Tsipiritiky, Tsipiritse
French: Mannikin de Madagascar

DESCRIPTION: Length 9 cm.
Adult. Sexes similar. Brown forehead, front and top of head, and nape. Gray-brown cheeks. Black lores and central part of throat. Stout, short, conical bill with dark brown upper mandible, grayish roseate lower mandible. Dark brown iris. Upperparts gray-brown, except for yellow-green uppertail coverts finely striped with dark brown. Underparts tan, except for finely brown-striped tan undertail coverts. Pink tarsi and toes. Dark brown wings with tan underwing coverts. Dark brown tail.
Immature. Differs from adult by uniformly dull brown plumage, absence of black bib, absence of stripes of upper- and undertail coverts, and entirely black bill.

IDENTIFICATION: Very small brown-and-tan granivorous passerine, recog-

nized by black bib and stout, conical bill. Smallest species of Madagascar, cannot be confused with any other.

BEHAVIOR: Gregarious species usually found in flocks of 4–50. Principally a ground feeder. Bold, often observed near human dwellings. At rest, flock perches side-by-side on horizontal branch.

VOICE: Rather quiet. Utters soft, thin, harmonious succession of *tsee tsee*. Also, in flight, brief, high-pitched *tseet*.

HABITAT: Any open terrain (degraded forests, grasslands, rice paddies, parks in towns and villages). Observed at elevations from sea level to 2,000 m.

DIET: Seeds, chiefly of grasses.

NESTING: Oval, almost entirely closed nest built in tree, shrub, or dense, short vegetation 1–4 m above ground, woven of dry plant fibers. Interior lined with softer material and feathers. Sometimes uses nest of Madagascar red fody or Sakalava weaver. Clutch numbers 4–7 smooth white eggs (average size: 14 mm × 11 mm). Nesting has been observed Oct.–June.

DISTRIBUTION AND STATUS: Endemic to Madagascar, common throughout island.

256. *Common Waxbill*

Estrilda astrild (Linnaeus, 1758)
French: Astrild à bec de corail
No Map

DESCRIPTION: Length 10 cm.
Adult. Sexes similar. Front and top of head and nape brown, with fine sooty markings. Dirty white chin, throat, and cheeks. Wide, bright red lozenge-shaped area around eyes. Short, bright red conical bill, brown iris. Upperparts brown with fine sooty markings. Underparts: dirty white chest and sides of neck. Light

brown flanks with fine sooty markings. Pink patch on belly. Dark brown undertail coverts. Black tarsi and toes. Wings and tail same color as upperparts. *Immature.* Differs from adult by fewer markings on plumage, absence of pink patch on belly, and black bill.

IDENTIFICATION: Very small granivorous passerine with largely brownish plumage, recognized by red bill and eye ring, pink patch on belly, and long, narrow tail.

BEHAVIOR: Gregarious, behavior resembles that of Madagascar mannikin. Observed flock numbered 15 Common waxbills with about 30 Madagascar mannikins.

VOICE: Brief, nasal *tzeep* uttered in flight.

DIET: Seeds.

NESTING: No proof of nesting in Madagascar.

DISTRIBUTION AND STATUS: Distributed in sub-Saharan Africa, introduced into various parts of the world (Portugal, Tahiti, Seychelles, Mauritius, Réunion). In Madagascar this species, recorded recently, was observed in 1983 at Nosy Be. Specimens spotted were certainly introduced and may breed in the wild. No sighting since 1983.

Distribution Maps

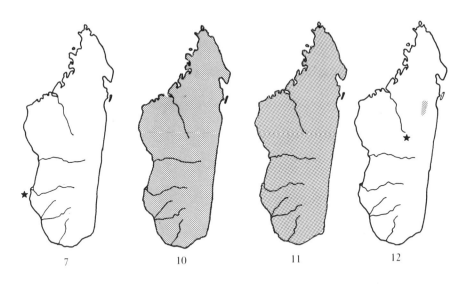

7   10   11   12

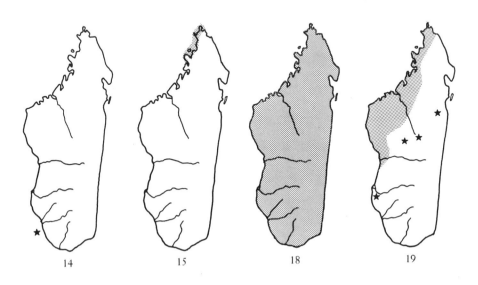

14   15   18   19

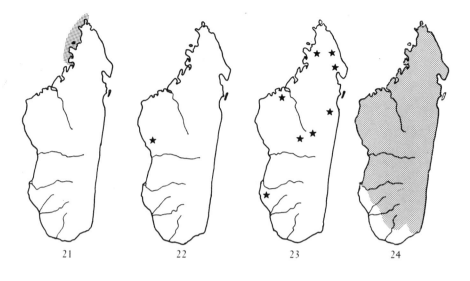

21   22   23   24

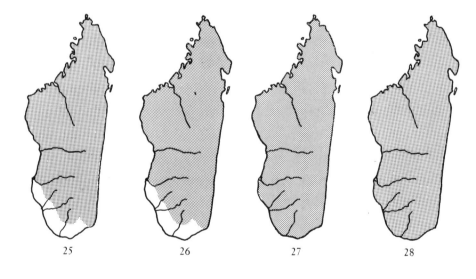

25   26   27   28

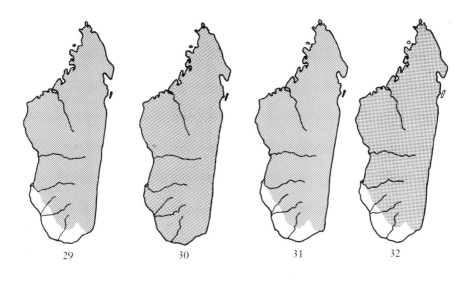

29 30 31 32

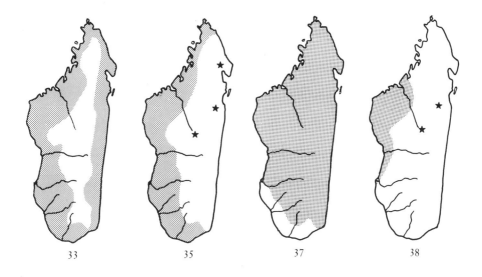

33 35 37 38

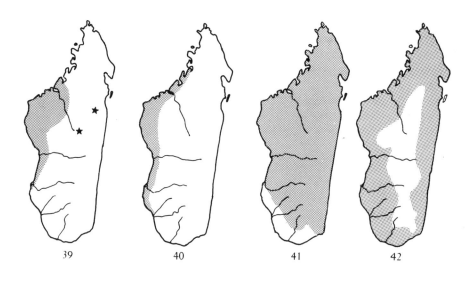

39   40   41   42

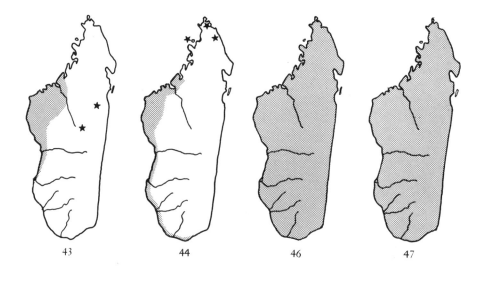

43   44   46   47

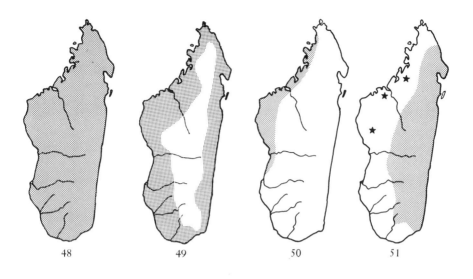

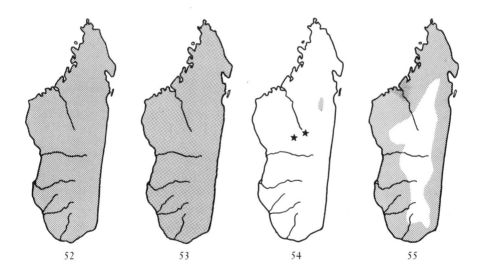

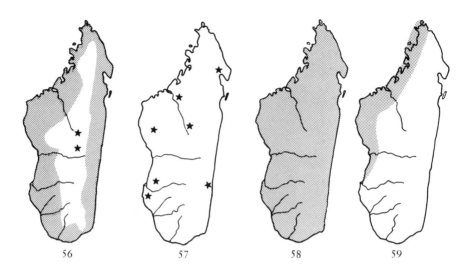

56   57   58   59

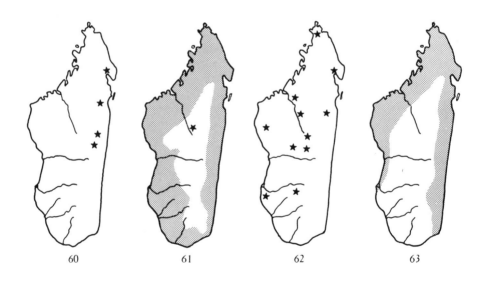

60   61   62   63

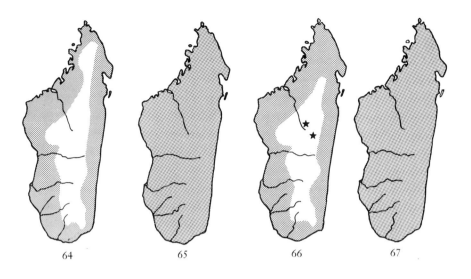

64   65   66   67

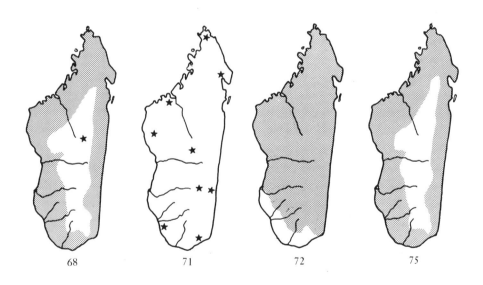

68   71   72   75

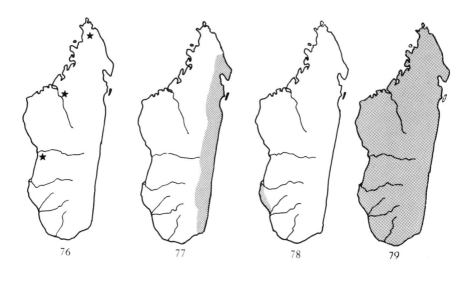

76   77   78   79

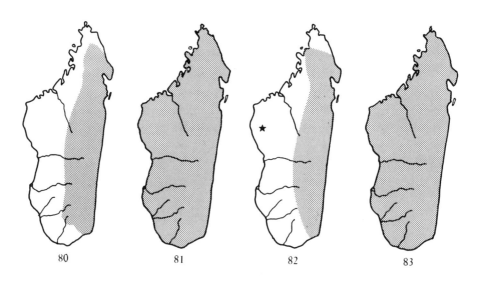

80   81   82   83

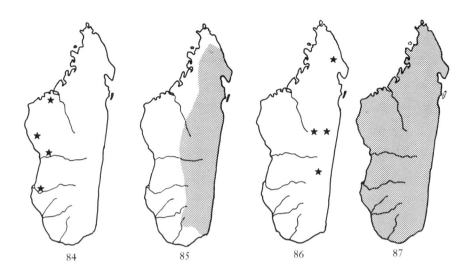

84   85   86   87

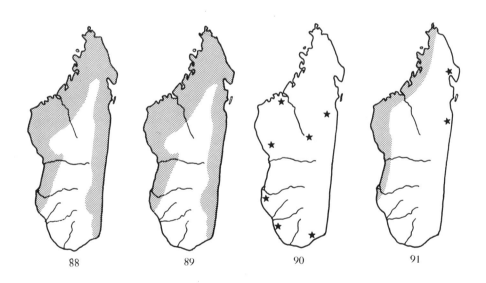

88   89   90   91

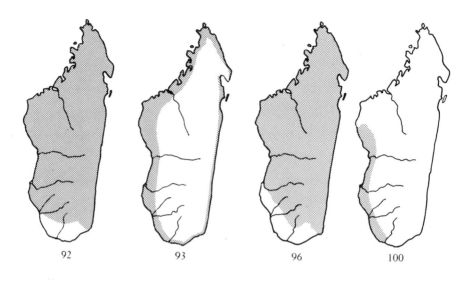

92   93   96   100

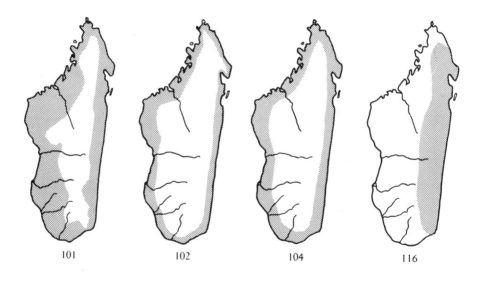

101   102   104   116

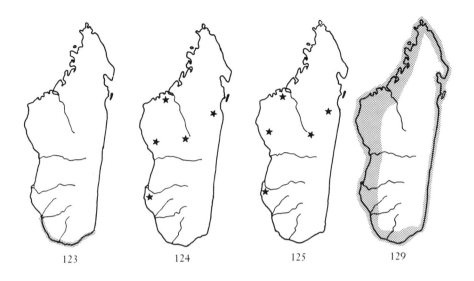

123   124   125   129

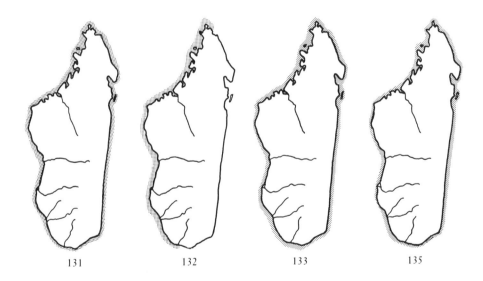

131   132   133   135

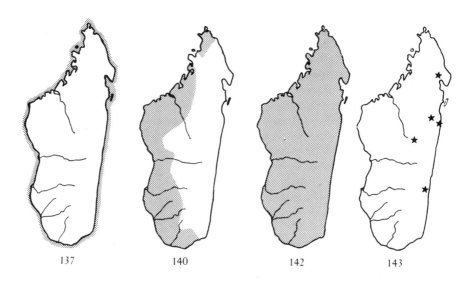

137   140   142   143

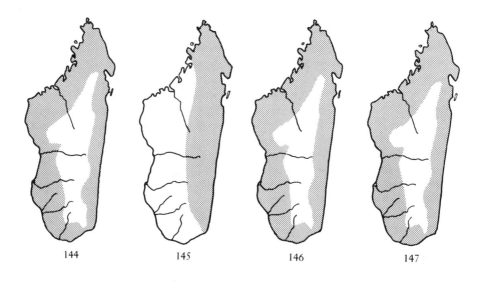

144   145   146   147

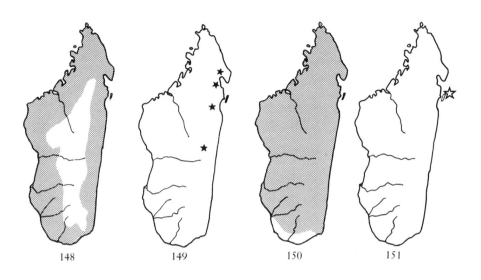

148   149   150   151

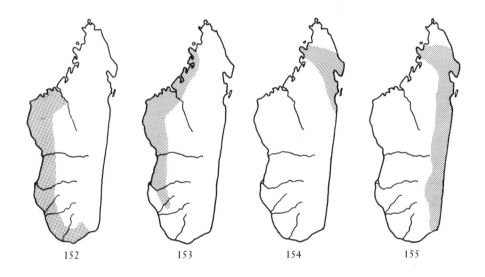

152   153   154   155

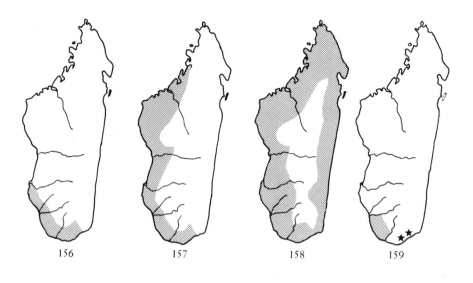

156   157   158   159

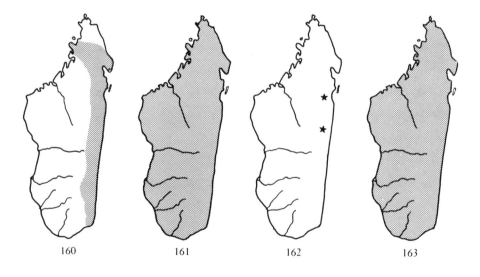

160   161   162   163

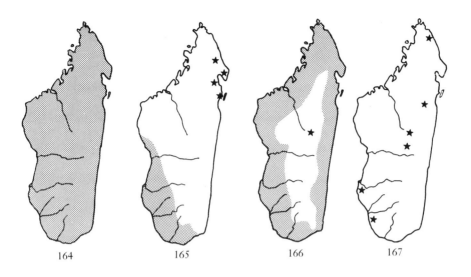

164 165 166 167

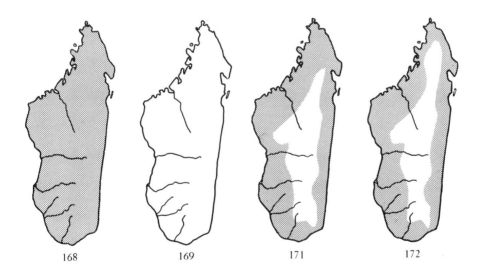

168 169 171 172

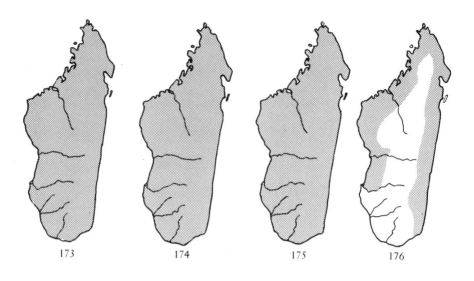

173   174   175   176

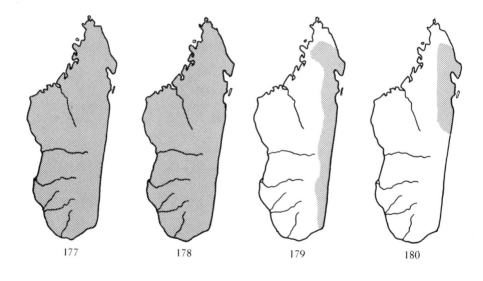

177   178   179   180

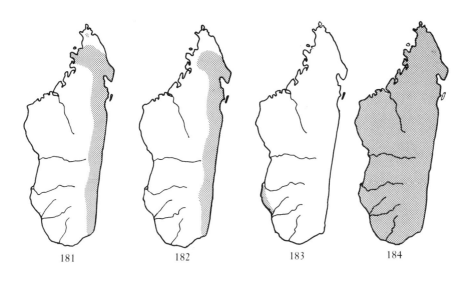

181   182   183   184

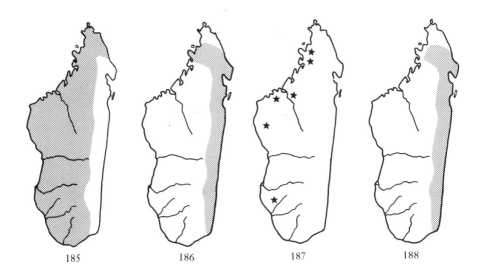

185   186   187   188

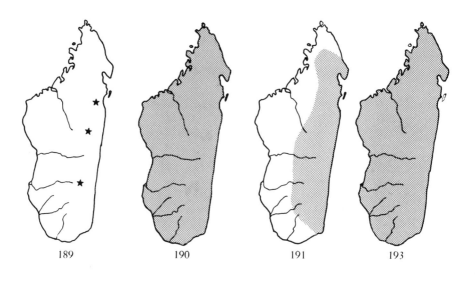

189   190   191   193

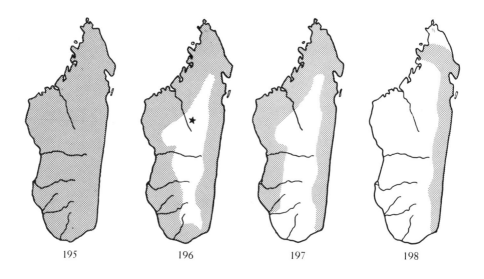

195   196   197   198

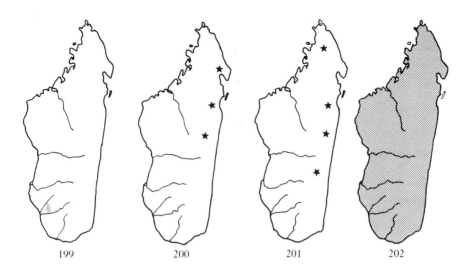

199 200 201 202

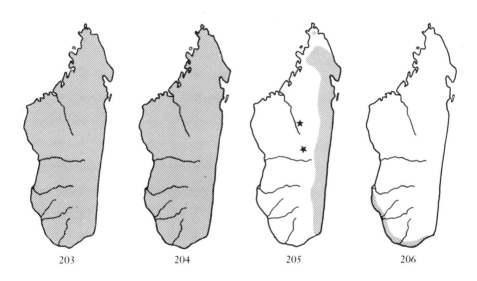

203 204 205 206

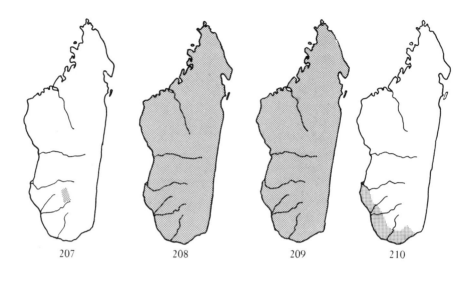

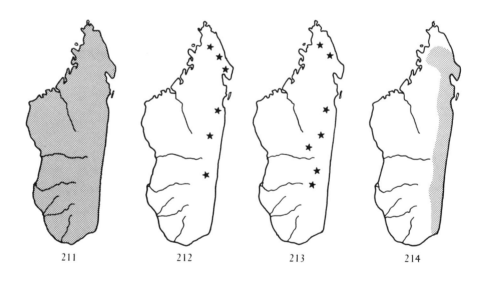

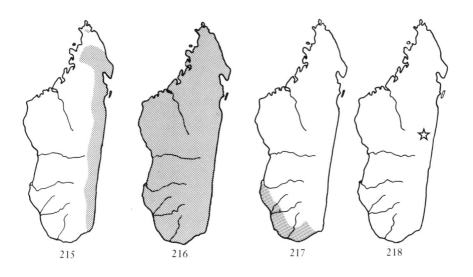

215   216   217   218

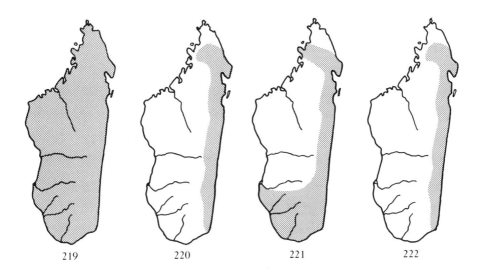

219   220   221   222

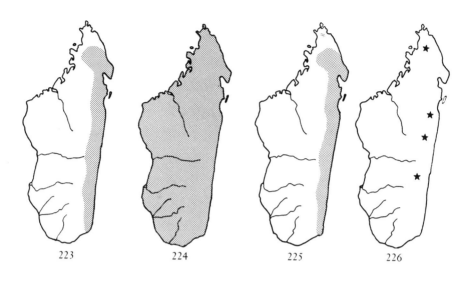

223   224   225   226

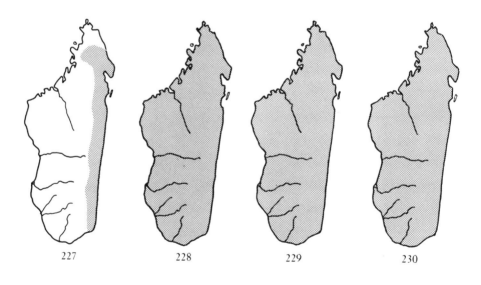

227   228   229   230

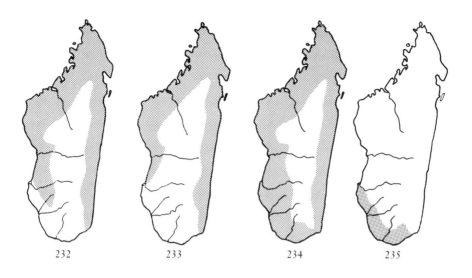

232   233   234   235

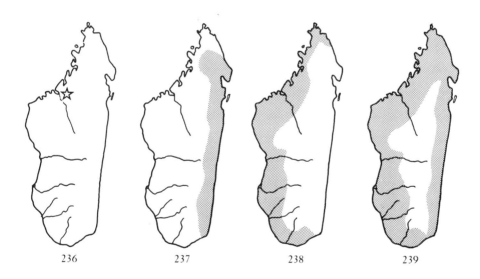

236   237   238   239

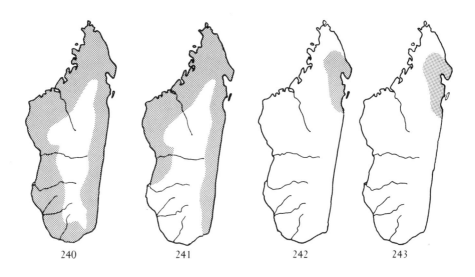

240   241   242   243

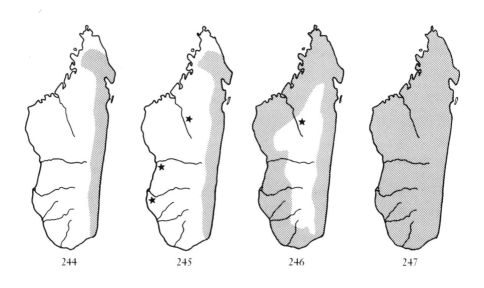

244   245   246   247

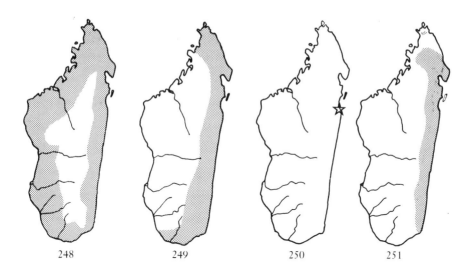

248   249   250   251

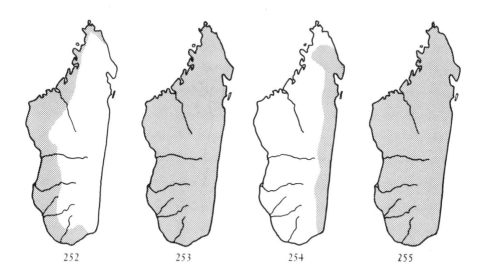

252   253   254   255

Alphabetical and Etymological Key
to Malagasy Names

Numbers are keyed to the species identification number.

Abosanga (high crest) 158
Adibo 211
Agoly 81, 116
Akaka 51
Akaky mainty 51
Akanga (imitation of cry) 75
Akoharano (water hen) 90
Akoholahiala 42
Akohon'ala (forest cock) 42
Akohondrano (water hen) 87
Akohovohitra (cock of the hills) 42
Akoke or Akoky (imitation of cry) 153, 157
Aliotse or Aliotsy (zigzagger) 153, 156, 157
Ambaramaty 28
Andevolahin-talevana ("Purple swamphen's" slave) 88
Andevondangoro (the heron's slave) 25
Androbaka 205
Angaka (imitation of cry) 51
Ankana (imitation of cry) 166
Ankoay (imitation of cry) 59
Antsoy 228
Arakaraka (imitation of cry) 178
Arefy (imitation of cry) 76, 159
Aretaky (imitation of cry) 116
Aretakely (imitation of cry) 88
Aretika (imitation of cry) 209
Aritiky (imitation of cry) 210
Arosy 48
Asitilahimanga 186
Asity (imitation of cry) 186
Atodiana 203
Barao (imitation of cry) 185
Bedoka (big head) 55
Bekapoaky (which hits wood with bill) 234
Beloha (big head) 55, 157
Bemanana (the easy life) 66
Beririna (which grows up in winter) 66
Bevorotse 66
Biny 85
Birindrano (water "Madagascar flufftail") 83

Biry biry (imitation of cry) 85
Bobaka (plenty) 56, 66
Boeza be (big parrot) 146
Boeza kely (little parrot) 147
Boezantsikotra (little parrot) 147
Bokitsy (imitation of cry) 183
Boloky (imitation of cry) 146
Bomomandry 16, 17
Boria (imitation of cry) 190
Borisa (imitation of cry) 190
Danamona 55
Deho (imitation of cry) 142
Dehofona 143
Dehoke (imitation of cry) 142
Doaka (imitation of cry) 24
Domohina (imitation of cry) 142
Draky (imitation of cry) 252
Drao (ruffled) 185
Dreodreo (imitation of cry) 184
Droadroaka (imitation of cry) 197
Drovika (imitation of cry) 81
Drovikala ("White-throated rail" of the forest) 82
Eoke (imitation of cry) 152
Famakiakora (shell-breaker) 39, 151, 179
Famakisifotra (snail-breaker) 41
Fanaliandro (always on the move) 10
Fandikalalana (road-runner) 153, 155, 179
Fandionga (tail-bobber) 91
Fandia fasika (sand-walker) 104
Fandraokibo (which catches buttonquails) 65
Fandrasalambo (the African bush pig companion) 60
Fangalamotamboay (who keeps the crocodile's eyes clean) 18
Fangadiovy (which digs for tubers *Dioscorea* sp) 179, 180, 181
Fangalamoty 171, 172, 173, 174
Fanindry (which flattens) 62
Farifotra (furtive) 198, 201
Farifotra mena (red bulbul) 225
Farifotramavoloha (sooty-headed bulbul) 201
Fatsimboay 203
Fifiokala (which whistles in the forest) 234
Finengo 144, 145
Finengo mainty (dark pigeon) 145
Finengo manga (blue pigeon) 145
Finengo menamaso (red-eyed pigeon) 145
Finengo menavody (pigeon with red undertail coverts) 145
Fiandrivoditatratra (those who stay close to the canal) 23, 25, 26
Fihiaka (imitation of cry) 61

Fipaikakora (shell-breaker) 39
Firasa (carver) 64, 65
Firasabe (tall carver) 60, 63
Firasambalala (which attacks grasshoppers) 69, 70
Firatsa 95
Firinga (imitation of cry) 193
Fitadahy (male pied bird) 203
Fitadroranga (pied bird of the clearings—or meadows) 204
Fitaliha 164
Fitatra (pied bird) 203, 204
Fitatra'ala (pied forest bird) 203
Fitatsy (pied bird) 203
Fitavavy (female pied bird) 203
Fodiala (forest fody) 254
Fodibeotse 252
Fodifetsy (clever fody) 251
Fodilahimena (red male fody) 253
Fodimena (red fody) 253
Fodindriaka 148
Fodisahy (bold fody) 252
Fodisaina (flag fody) 251
Foditany (earth fody) 226
Fody 253
Fonimaitso (green bird) 144, 148
Fotsielatra (white wing) 52
Fotsy maso (white eye) 54, 230
Fotsy tretreka (white throat) 240
Gadragadra (imitation of cry) 178
Gaga (imitation of cry) 247
Gagao (imitation of cry) 44
Gagnake (imitation of cry) 247
Gisandrano (water goose) 22
Goadrano (imitation of cry) 24
Goaka (imitation of cry) 24, 247
Goakarano (water crow) 124
Goapaka 168
Godrano (imitation of cry) 23
Gory (imitation of cry) 153, 157
Gory be (large "Coquerel's coua") 152
Hakagna (imitation of cry) 166
Hanka (imitation of cry) 166
Harakaraka (imitation of cry) 116, 178
Hatrakatrake (imitation of cry) 140
Heko-heko 163
Hila (imitation of cry) 57
Hindry (imitation of cry) 66
Hitikitike (which beats its wings in place) 67

Hitsikitsike (which beats its wings in place) 67
Hitsikitsik'ala (forest "Madagascar kestrel") 66
Horovana (imitation of cry) 202
Hotrika (wing noise) 116
Jerina (imitation of cry) 230
Jijy (imitation of cry) 219
Jorioke (imitation of cry) 190
Kadibake 156
Kafotsy (white bird) 15
Kakafotra (imitation of cry) 150
Karaoka (imitation of cry) 148
Kariaka (imitation of cry) 148
Kariga (imitation of cry) 148
Katakatra (imitation of cry) 140
Katekateky (imitation of cry) 216
Katobary 92
Katoto (imitation of cry) 143
Katrakatraka (imitation of cry) 140
Kazazaka (imitation of cry) 53
Kehambe (large size) 32
Keho (imitation of cry) 28
Kekakeka (imitation of cry) 116
Kibo (imitation of cry) 79
Kibobo (imitation of cry) 79
Kibonaomby (large buttonquail) 74
Kiborano (water buttonquail) 10, 11, 12
Kikimavo (imitation of cry + sooty) 196
Kiky (imitation of cry) 80
Kilandry 27
Kilandry be (large "Cattle egret") 31
Kimimitsy 221
Kimitsy (imitation of cry) 219, 221
Kinkimavo (imitation of cry + sooty) 245
Kipanga 62
Kipoy (imitation of cry) 72
Kirikioka (imitation of cry) 177
Kirinina (imitation of cry) 131
Kirioke (imitation of cry) 177
Kiriokirioke (imitation of cry) 177
Kirombo (imitation of cry) 184
Kisanjy (imitation of cry) 28
Kitanatana (imitation of cry) 116
Kitrehoka (imitation of cry) 148
Kitriotrio (imitation of cry) 195
Kitsiabe (imitation of cry) 81
Kitsiakely 80
Kizazaka (imitation of cry) 53

Koa (imitation of cry) 154, 155
Koaka (imitation of cry) 24
Koakiho (imitation of cry) 147
Koakio (imitation of cry) 147
Koaky (imitation of cry) 28
Koikoika (imitation of cry) 107
Kolokoloky (imitation of cry) 123
Kontomboay (crocodile's servant) 18
Kotohake 161
Kotoroka (imitation of cry) 164
Lampirana 42
Langaraka (imitation of cry) 31
Langopaka 168
Langorofalafa 32
Langorofotsy (white heron) 30, 31
Langoromavo (sooty heron) 33
Langorona (long neck) 31
Langorovoanga (heron with striped neck) 32
Lava-Salaka (long tail) 209
Leja (lazy) 153
Lejabe (big lazy one) 152
Litotsy 175
Loakiho 146
Lombokoma (which hides to eat) 29
Lopaka (which lies flat on the ground) 168
Lova 246
Maheriloha (dense head) 55
Manaramboalavo 18
Manarana (diver) 19
Manaranomby (big diver) 19
Manaviandro (day-bat) 171, 172
Manganahitra 86
Mantazazana 107, 108
Mariha (imitation of cry) 160
Martaina 249
Matoriandro (which sleeps during the day) 168, 169
Matsiaka 146
Mavolambosy (sooty back) 132
Mefo 38
Menamolotra (red bill) 52
Menasogny (red bill) 52
Mijoha (which remains standing) 39
Mireha (imitation of cry) 50
Mojoa 39
Mokazavona 245
Mokasavomavoloha (sooty-headed "Tylas vanga") 196
Mondrita 104

Monjo (weak) 161

Mpiandravoditra (those who stay next to the canal) 23

Mpiandri voditatatra (heron's slave) 25, 26

Naka (imitation of cry) 78

Ngovo 21

Ofaka 168

Olioly (imitation of cry) 205

Ombikomana 29

Ongongo (hump) 48

Onjo (tailless) 54

Otrika (imitation of cry) 90

Pakatovo (unmarried) 142

Pangalatrovy (which digs for tubers *Dioscorea* sp) 85

Papango 58

Papelika (imitation of cry) 73

Pasasatra (imitation of cry) 240

Pasasatrala (forest "Chabert's vanga") 241

Pera 64

Perakibo (which picks up buttonquails) 65

Pida 203

Pidaehy 203

Pila 195

Piritry (imitation of cry) 91

Poadranofotsy (which arrives when the water is rising) 173, 193

Poapoabava (which clacks its bill) 233

Poretaka (imitation of cry) 209

Rafanopoka (which covers "something") 29

Ragniboay (crocodile's friend) 19

Rahaka 51

Rahoaka (imitation of cry) 24

Railomba 246

Railovy 246

Rainibao 27

Raisasatra 241

Ramangarana (which dives) 18

Ramanjerika (imitation of cry) 230

Ramaro (makes enough noise for several—used for tame birds) 249

Ravarava (imitation of cry) 116

Razamboay (crocodile's ancestor) 18

Razangoaka (crow's parent) 240

Rehila (imitation of cry) 63

Rehito (imitation of cry) 63

Relovy 246

Reoreo (imitation of cry) 184

Roatelo (two-three, or never three) 77

Sadakely (small bicolored one) 52

Sakaizamboay (crocodile's friend) 18

Sakodidy (which turns around the trunk) 244
Sakoka (prudent or imitation of cry) 181
Salapiko 55
Salobokomana (which covers itself to eat) 29
Samaka (which spreads its knees) 45
Samaky (which spreads its knees) 44, 45
Samby (which settles on boats) 125, 129, 132, 135, 136
Sarahesa 241
Sarako 90
Sarengy 148
Sarivazo (pretty parrot) 148
Sarigaga (pretty crow) 240
Serika 212
Serikalambo (emutail of the wild boar) 223
Serikatanimbary (emutail of the rice paddies) 212
Sianga (blue sunbird) 228
Sihotse be 146
Sihotsy 146, 147
Siketriala (forest flycatcher) 233
Siketribe (big flycatcher) 243
Siketry (imitation of cry) 224
Singetringetry (female) 207
Singetry (imitation of cry) 224
Sirontsirona 225
Soafify (beautiful face) 49
Sobery (little green one) 230
Sobitiky (small sunbird) 228
Sohimanga (blue sunbird) 229
Sohohitrala (prober of dead leaves) 227
Soikely (small sunbird) 228
Soimangavola (silvery blue sunbird) 229
Soinala (forest sunbird) 188
Soisoy (imitation of cry) 186, 228
Sombe 121
Soratrala (color of dead leaves) 227
Soritsy (imitation of cry) 190
Soroanja 240
Sorohitra (savior-legend) 190
Sotrobevava (funny bill) 43
Sotromolotro (spoonlip) 43
Sotrosogny (spoonlip) 43
Sotrovava (spoonbill) 43
Soy (imitation of cry, small) 228, 229
Tafaly (taboo, not to be eaten) 93
Tahia (imitation of cry) 46
Taitso (imitation of cry) 160
Taitso mainty (imitation of cry + somber) 160

Taitso manga (imitation of cry + blue) 160
Taitohaka (imitation of cry) 155
Takatra (imitation of cry) 37
Takatsy 37
Takobodimozinga (small in all likelihood) 188
Takodara (imitation of cry) 185
Talapiotany (which whistles on the ground) 227
Talevana (which floats) 88, 89
Talevanabe (great floater) 89
Tambakoratsy (color of badly dried tobacco) 28
Taotaokafo (imitation of cry) 150
Taotaonfaka (imitation of cry) 150
Taporo 242
Tararaka (imitation of cry) 163
Tataro (imitation of cry) 168
Tataroala (forest nightjar) 169
Tatarofatrama 168
Tatarovorona (bird that does "tataro") 168
Tatoka 92
Tekitekiala (imitation of cry) 197
Tetraka (imitation of cry) 197, 198
Tintina (imitation of cry, very lightly) 211
Tinty (imitation of cry, very lightly) 211
Tivoka (imitation of cry) 158, 159
Toaiky 197
Tokambolo (one single color) 158
Toloho (imitation of cry) 161
Tolohon'ala (forest coucal) 75
Tolohoranto (sand coucal) 183
Tomaimavo (gray color) 70
Tomo (male) 207
Torotoroka (imitation of cry) 164
Totokarasoka (imitation of cry) 232
Tovotovoka (imitation of cry) 165
Traotrao (imitation of cry) 72
Tretreky (imitation of cry) 239
Tretretre (imitation of cry) 216
Triotrio (imitation of cry) 195
Trobaky 129
Tsa-Tsak (imitation of cry) 240
Tsakaranta 93, 95
Tsakatoto (imitation of cry) 143
Tsakekey (imitation of cry) 239
Tsakodara (imitation of cry) 185
Tsakoka (imitation of cry, which stays hidden) 181
Tsarakaranta 95
Tsaramaso (beautiful eye) 240

Tsararahaka (imitation of cry) 178
Tsaravanga (pretty color) 49
Tseatseake (imitation of cry) 238
Tsiaka (imitation of cry) 252
Tsiatsiaka (imitation of cry) 238
Tsiazotenonina (whose name may not be spoken) 143
Tsibotrotsy 206
Tsidisidina (imitation of cry) 171, 172, 173, 174, 191, 193
Tsikai (light) 91
Tsikea 80
Tsikiriokirioke (imitation of cry) 177
Tsikirity (imitation of cry) 255
Tsikokofotsy 158
Tsikoloto 143
Tsikoreva (imitation of cry) 202
Tsikorovana (imitation of cry) 202
Tsikoza 81
Tsikoza-ala 82
Tsikoza vohitra 82
Tsiloko 158
Tsilovanga 234, 235
Tsimalaho 58
Tsinoly (imitation of cry) 205
Tsintsina (imitation of cry) 211
Tsipara 64
Tsiparahorovana (which attacks "Madagascar bulbuls") 65
Tsipera 65
Tsipiritiky (imitation of cry) 255
Tsipiritse (imitation of cry) 255
Tsiporitika (imitation of cry) 255
Tsipoy (which shakes itself in the dust) 72
Tsirikititio 196
Tsiriry (imitation of cry) 10, 11, 47
Tsisy (imitation of cry) 219
Tsivongo (hump) 48
Tsobeboka 85
Tsoea (imitation of cry) 46
Tsohia (imitation of cry) 90
Vadimboay (crocodile's companion) 18, 19
Vagna 32
Vanga (pied bird) 237, 239
Vangadrano 43
Vangamaintiloha (black-headed pied bird) 237
Vangasoratra (pied bird) 234
Vano 33, 35
Vanofotsy (white heron) 30, 31
Vanokasira 33

Vanomainty (dark heron) 30

Vanomena (red heron) 32

Vantsiano 90

Varevaka (imitation of cry) 124, 129, 133

Vasatsihotsy 147

Vatry (imitation of cry) 89

Vaza (bill) 146

Vazambe (big bill) 146

Vikiviky (imitation of cry) 193

Viko-viko (imitation of cry) 96

Viky-viky (imitation of cry) 101, 104

Vintsiala (forest kingfisher) 176

Vintsimena (red kingfisher) 176

Vintsirano (water kingfisher) 175

Vintsy 175

Vitro (imitation of cry) 75

Vitro-ala 75

Vivitra 104

Vivy (imitation of cry) 10, 11, 12, 47

Voadivy 92

Voromahery (strong bird) 71

Voromailala (clever bird) 141

Voromalemy (gentle, silent bird) 23

Voromaregny (deaf bird) 196

Voromasiaka (wicked bird) 239

Voromaty (dead bird) 28

Vorombararata (bird of the reeds) 208

Vorombarika (bird of the lemurs) 223

Vorombato (stone bird) 96

Vorombatra (thunder bird) 178

Vorombemainty (big black bird) 39

Vorombilo (pretty bird) 49

Voromboka (leprous bird) 182

Vorompamono (killer or nasty bird) 3

Vorompano (sea-turtle bird) 14

Vorompantsika 28

Vorompasika (beach heron) 35

Vorompotsy (white bird) 27

Vorompotsy maso (white-eyed bird) 230

Vorona atambo (odd bird) 77

Vorona-kahaka (imitation of cry) 178

Voronakodidina (bird that turns around the trunk) 244

Vorona lava ambozona (long-necked bird) 19

Vorona masiaka (wicked bird) 223

Voronadabo (ficus bird) 144

Vorondavenona (sooty bird) 196

Vorondolo (bird of the dead, or of evil spirits) 163, 165, 167

Vorondrano (water bird) 18, 90
Vorondreky (sea bird) 121
Voronjaza (baby bird) 238
Voronomby (strong bird) 35, 38
Voronodrika (which bobs its tail) 80
Voronondry (sheep bird) 40
Voronosy (goat bird) 40
Vorontainaomby (bird the color of zebu-dung) 248
Vorontotra 182
Vorontsara (beautiful bird) 49
Vorontsara-elatra (bird with pretty wings) 241
Vorontsaramaso (bird with beautiful eyes) 230
Vorotomany (weeping bird) 7
Vorotrandraka (bird of the tenrec) 82
Zafimbano (heron's grandchild) 23
Zafindrasity (asity's grandchild) 188
Zaky (imitation of cry) 252
Zezea (imitation of cry) 21

Index of English Names

Italicized numbers refer to the main description.

Albatross, *75*
Albatross, black-browed, *75–76*, pl. 1
  shy, 47, 48, pl. 1
  sooty, 47, 48, pl. 1
  wandering, 47, 48, pl. 1
  yellow-nosed, 47, 48, pl. 1
Asity, Schlegel's, 35, *249–50*, pl. 31
  velvet, 17, *248–49*, 251, pl. 31
Avocet, Eurasian, 166, *167*, 168, pl. 17

Babbler, Crossley's, 18, *284*, pl. 32
Bee-eater, Madagascar, 13, 14, 226, *238–39*,
  pl. 28
Bittern, little, *97–98*, pl. 4
Boobies, *94*
Booby, brown, 51, 89, *94–95*, pl. 1
  masked, *51*, pl. 1
  red-footed, 13, 51, *94*, 95, pl. 1
Bulbul, Madagascar, 11, 213, 226, 252, *262*,
  274, 288, 298, 303, 307, pl. 38
Bulbuls, *259*
Buttonquail, Madagascar, 12, 145, 146, 150,
  153–54, 229, pl. 14
Buzzard, Madagascar, 37, 132, *139*, 240, 310,
  pl. 9, 12

Cisticola, Madagascar, *271–72*, pl. 35
Coot, red-knobbed, 37, *161–62*, pl. 16
Cormorant, reed, *91–92*, 93, 106, 109, pl. 3
Coua, blue, *222–23*, pl. 24
  Coquerel's, 35, 215, *216*, 218, 219, pl. 25
  crested, *220–21*, 222, 223, pl. 24
  giant, 35, 36, *214–15*, 216, 218, pl. 25
  red-breasted, 16, 20, *216–17*, 218, 223,
    pl. 25
  red-capped, 35, 36, 215, 216, 218, *219–20*,
    pl. 25
  red-fronted, 16, *217–18*, pl. 25
  running, 24, 25, 35, 36, 215, 216,
    218–19, pl. 25
  snail-eating, 10, 11, 16, *214*, pl. 25
  Verreaux's, 24, 25, 35, *221–22*, pl. 24
Couas, *212*
Coucal, Madagascar, *223–24*, 244, pl. 24
Crake, Baillon's, *157*, 159, pl. 16
Crow, pied, 140, *304–5*, 306, 310, pl. 30
Cuckoo, Madagascar lesser, 11, *213–14*, 272,
  pl. 24
  thick-billed, 16, *212–13*, pl. 24

Cuckoo-falcon, Madagascar, 37, *131–32*, 139,
  pl. 9, 12
Cuckoo-shrike, ashy, 213, 250, *257–58*, 259,
  274, 276, 280, 288, 290, 291, 293, 296,
  298, 300, 302, 303, pl. 38
Curlew, Eurasian, 116, 178, *179*, pl. 17

Darter, 37, 91, *92–93*, pl. 3
Dove, Namaqua, 204, *205–6*, pl. 23
  rock, 12, *204*
Doves, 204
Drongo, crested, 213, 250, 257, 274, 276,
  288, 290, 295, 298, 301, *303–4*, 307, pl. 40
Duck, fulvous whistling, *122–23*, 124, pl. 8
  knob-billed, *124–25*, pl. 8
  Mallard, 127
  Meller's, 12, 23, 35, 37, 38, 124, *126–27*,
    137, pl. 8
  white-backed, 23, 82, *129–30*, pl. 8
  white-faced whistling, 37, 82, *123–24*, 126,
    127, 128, pl. 8
Ducks, *122*

Egret, cattle, 99, 100, 101, *102–3*, 105, 106,
  107, 306, pl. 4, 7
  dimorphic, 100, 101, 102, 104, *105–6*, 107,
    109, 110, pl. 5, 7
  great, 37, 91, 92, 102, 104, 105, *106–7*,
    110, pl. 5, 7
Egrets, *97*
Emutail, brown, 17, 34, *269*, 272, 273, pl. 31
  gray, 17, 34, *272–73*, pl. 31

Falcon, Eleonora's, 12, 37, 132, *141–42*, 143,
  pl. 11, 13
  Peregrine, 142, *143*, pl. 11, 13
  sooty, 12, 37, 132, *142–43*, pl. 11, 13
Falcons, *140*
Fish-eagle, Madagascar, 22, 24, 33, 35,
  133–34, 135, pl. 9, 12
Flamingo, greater, 36, *118–19*, 120, pl. 6, 7
  lesser, 13, 118, 119, *120–21*, pl. 6, 7
Flamingos, *118*
Flufftail, Madagascar, *158–59*, pl. 15
  slender-billed, 11, 15, 16, 34, 157, 158,
    159, pl. 15
Flycatcher, Madagascar paradise, 213, 214,
  223, 250, 257, 261, 274, *280–82*, 288,
  291, 298, 303, pl. 34

Flycatcher, (*continued*)
    Ward's, 18, 279, *280*, 295, 297, pl. 34
Fody, forest, 19, *311–12*, pl. 40
    Madagascar red, 12, 19, 211, 223, 226,
        310–11, 312, 313, pl. 40
Frigatebird, greater, 13, *89–90*, pl. 1
    lesser, 13, 38, 89, *90*, pl. 1
Frigatebirds, *89*

Gallinule, Allen's, *160–61*, pl. 16
Geese, *122*
Godwit, bar-tailed, 177, *178*, pl. 17
    black-tailed, *177–78*, pl. 17
Godwits, *177*
Goose, African pygmy, 36, 82, *125–26*, pl. 8
Goshawk, Henst's, 34, 36, 135, *137*, 138, pl.
    10, 13
Grebe, Alaotra little, 7, 11, 15, 37, 82, 83,
    84–85, pl. 3
    little, 23, *82–83*, 84, 85, pl. 3
    Madagascar little, 23, 33, 36, 82, *83–84*,
        164, pl. 3
Grebes, *82*
Greenbul, Appert's, 11, 22, *260*, 270, pl. 32
    dusky, 11, 17, *260–61*, 283, pl. 32
    gray-crowned, 17, 34, *261–62*, 279, pl. 32
    long-billed, 213, 250, 252, *258–59*, 260,
        279, 280, 283, 302, 309, pl. 32
    spectacled, 17, 33, 257, *259–60*, 261, 279,
        283, pl. 32
Greenshank, common, 38, *180–81*, 183,
    pl. 17
Ground-roller, long-tailed, 11, 24, 25, 28, 36,
    244–45, pl. 29
    pitta-like, 17, 33, 35, *242–43*, 244, pl. 29
    rufous-headed, 17, 34, *243–44*, pl. 29
    scaly, 17, 20, *242*, pl. 29
    short-legged, 16, 34, *241*, pl. 29
Guineafowl, helmeted, 11, 12, 117, 137,
    147–48, pl. 14
Gull, gray-headed, 38, *190–91*, pl. 21
    kelp, 24, 38, *189–90*, pl. 21
Gulls, *189*

Hamerkop, *111–12*, pl. 6, 7
Harrier, Réunion, 11, 34, 37, *136–37*, pl. 9,
    12
Harrier-Hawk, Madagascar, *135–36*, 298,
    pl. 11, 12
Hawk, bat, 35, *132–33*, pl. 9, 12
Heron, black, *104–5*, 106, pl. 5, 7
    black-crowned night, 37, 92, *98–99*, 101,
        106, 107, pl. 4, 7
    black-headed, 13, *109–10*, pl. 5

    goliath, 13, 109, *111*, pl. 5
    gray, 38, 105, 106, *108–9*, 110, pl. 5, 7
    green-backed, *103–4*, pl. 4, 7
    Humblot's, 23, 35, 37, 105, 106, 108, 109,
        110, 134, pl. 5, 7
    Malagasy pond, 12, 37, 99, 100, *101–2*,
        104, 106, 107, pl. 4, 7
    purple, *107–8*, 109, 111, pl. 5, 7
    squacco, 92, *99–100*, 101, 102, 104, 106,
        107, pl. 4, 7
Herons, *97*
Hoopoe, *247*, pl. 30

Ibis, glossy, 23, 37, 115, *116*, pl. 6, 7
    Madagascar crested, 33, 35, *116–17*,
        pl. 6, 7
    sacred, 22, *115*, pl. 6, 7
Ibises, *115*

Jacana, Madagascar, 36, *163–64*, pl. 16
Jaeger, parasitic, *188–89*
Jery, common, 37, 213, 214, 252, 257, 270,
    273, 274, *276–77*, 278, 285, 290, 291,
    295, 303, pl. 36
    green, 18, 276, *277–78*, pl. 36
    stripe-throated, 273, 274, 276, 277, *278*,
        279, 290, 291, pl. 36
    wedge-tailed, 18, 34, *278–79*, pl. 36

Kestrel, banded, 36, 37, *140–41*, pl. 11, 13
    Madagascar, *140*, 141, 240, 298, pl. 11, 13,
        28
Kingfisher, Madagascar pygmy, *237–38*,
    pl. 28
    malachite, 237
    Malagasy, 35, *236–37*, pl. 28
Kite, black, *133*, 310, pl. 9, 12

Lark, Madagascar bush, *252–53*, pl. 35
Lovebird, gray-headed, *210–11*, pl. 23

Magpie-robin, Madagascar, 11, *263–64*, 266,
    270, 291, pl. 33
Mannikin, Madagascar, 211, 223, *313*, 314,
    pl. 40
Martin, brown-throated sand, 15, *253–54*,
    pl. 27
    Mascarene, 14, 253, *254–55*, pl. 27
    sand, *254*, pl. 27
Mesite, brown, 16, 34, *150–51*, pl. 15
    subdesert, 11, 24, 25, 28, 36, *151–52*,
    pl. 15
    white-breasted, 22, 35, 36, 137, *149–50*,
    151, pl. 15

Mesites, *149*
Moa, 10
Moorhen, common, *159–60*, pl. 16
Myna, common, 12, *306–7*, pl. 30

Newtonia, Archbold's, 25, 35, 55, 270, *275*,
  pl. 34
  common, 55, 213, 250, 252, 257, 259, 270,
    274–75, 276, 277, 285, 286, 288, 290,
    298, 303, pl. 34, 37
  dark, 18, 33, 55, *273–74*, 276, pl. 34
  red-tailed, 11, 18, 274, *275–76*, pl. 34
Nightjar, collared, *231*, pl. 30
  Madagascar, 11, *230–31*, pl. 30
Noddy, brown, 79, 197, *199–200*, pl. 20, 21
  lesser, 13, 79, *200*, pl. 20, 21

Oriole, European golden, *289*
Ostrich, 9, 10
Owl, common barn, *226*, pl. 26
  Madagascar long-eared, 37, *228–29*, pl. 26
  Madagascar red, 11, 16, 34, *225–26*, pl. 26
  Malagasy scops, 35, *227*, 228, pl. 26
  marsh, *229*, pl. 26
  white-browed, 11, 34, 35, *227–28*, pl. 26
Owls, *225*
Oxylabes, white-throated, 18, 33, 259, 261,
    279, *282–83*, pl. 32
  yellow-browed, 18, 34, 279, *283*, pl. 32

Parrot, greater vasa, *208–9*, 210, pl. 24
  lesser vasa, *209–10*, 307, pl. 24
Parrots, *208*
Partridge, Madagascar, 12, *144–45*, pl. 14
Pelican, pink-backed, 22, *96*, pl. 3
Penguin, *73*
Penguin, rockhopper, *73–74*
Petrel, Barau's, 50, pl. 2
  black-bellied storm, 51, *80–81*, pl. 2
  Bulwer's, *50*, 51
  cape, *77*, pl. 2
  flesh-footed, 47, 49, pl. 2
  great-winged, *49*, 50, pl. 2
  herald, *50*, pl. 2
  Jouanin's, *50*, pl. 2
  Mascarene, 49, *50*, pl. 2
  Matsudaira's, *51*, pl. 2
  northern giant, *49*, 76, pl. 1
  soft-plumaged, *50*, pl. 2
  southern giant, 38, 49, *76–77*, pl. 1
  white-bellied storm, *51*, pl. 2
  white-chinned, 47, 48, pl. 1
  Wilson's storm, *80*, pl. 2
Petrels, *76*, 80

Pigeon, Madagascar blue, 16, 204, *207*, pl. 23
  Madagascar green, 204, *206*, 207, pl. 23
Pigeons, *204*
Plover, black-bellied, *171*, pl. 18
  common ringed, 52, *171–72*, 173, 174,
    187, pl. 18
  crab, 38, 166, 167, *168–69*, pl. 17
  greater sand, 38, 52, 173, *175–76*, pl. 18
  Kittlitz's, *173–74*, 175, 176, 186, 187,
    pl. 18
  lesser sand, *52*
  little ringed, *51*
  Madagascar, 23, 36, 52, *172–73*, 174, 175,
    176, pl. 18
  Pacific golden, *170–71*, pl. 18
  three-banded, 172, 173, *174–75*, pl. 18
  white-fronted, 173, 174, *176–77*, pl. 18
Pochard, Madagascar, 7, 11, 15, 37, 85, *129*,
  pl. 8
Pratincole, Madagascar, 12, *169–70*, 240,
  pl. 22
Prion, antarctic, *78*, pl. 2
Prions, *78*

Quail, common, *145–46*, 153, pl. 14
  harlequin, 13, 145, *146–47*, 153, pl. 14

Rail, Madagascar, 15, 37, *154–55*, 165, pl. 16
  Madagascar wood, 155, *156–57*, pl. 15
  Sakalava, 22, *157–58*, pl. 16
  white-throated, *155–56*, pl. 15
Rails, *154*
Rock-thrush, Benson's, 33, *267–68*, pl. 33
  forest, 17, 33, 35, *265–66*, pl. 33
  littoral, 24, 25, 28, *266–67*, pl. 33
Roller, broad-billed, 13, 140, *239–40*, pl. 28
  cuckoo, *245–46*, pl. 30
Ruff, *187*, pl. 19

Sanderling, *185*, pl. 19
Sandgrouse, Madagascar, 11, 35, *202–3*,
  pl. 23
Sandpiper, common, *182–83*, pl. 19
  curlew, 173, 174, 179, 180, 184, *186*, 187,
    pl. 19
  green, *181*, pl. 19
  marsh, *179–80*, 181, 182
  Terek, 38, *182*, 183, 184, pl. 19
  wood, *181–82*, pl. 19
Serpent-eagle, Madagascar, 11, 16, 34,
    134–35, 137, pl. 10
Shearwater, *76*
Shearwater, Audubon's, *51*, pl. 2
  wedge-tailed, 24, *79*, pl. 2

Skua, subantarctic, *188*, pl. 21
Snipe, greater painted, *164–65*, pl. 16
  Madagascar, 15, 34, 37, 165, *184–85*,
    pl. 16
Sparrow, house, 12, *308*
Sparrowhawk, Frances's, *138–39*, pl. 10, 13
  Madagascar, 35, *137–38*, pl. 10
Spoonbill, African, 37, 106, 113, *117–18*,
  135, pl. 6, 7
Starling, Madagascar, 11, *305–6*, pl. 40
Stilt, black-winged, *166–67*, 168, pl. 17
Stint, little, *185–86*, pl. 19
Stonechat, *264–65*, pl. 34
Stork, African openbill, 22, 36, *113–14*,
  pl. 6, 7
  yellow-billed, *113*, 118, pl. 6, 7
Storks, *113*
Sunbird, long-billed green, 251, 274, 285,
  286–87, 288, 298, 301, 303, pl. 31
  Souimanga, 251, 252, 257, 274, 276,
    285–86, 288, 290, 298, 301, 303, pl. 31
Sunbird-asity, 17, *250–51*, 261, pl. 31
Sunbird-asity, yellow-bellied, 11, 17, 20, 34,
  251–52, pl. 31
Swallow, *255*, pl. 27
Swamphen, purple, 160, *161*, pl. 16
Swift, African black, 13, 14, 234, *235*
  African palm, *233–34*, 235, pl. 27
  alpine, *234–35*, 254, pl. 27
  Malagasy spine-tailed, *233*, 235, 253, pl. 27
  Swiftlet, Mascarene, 13, *233*

Teal, Bernier's, 22, 23, *126*, 127, 128, pl. 8
  Hottentot, 126, 127, *128–29*, pl. 8
  red-billed, 37, 38, 82, 124, 126, *127–28*,
    pl. 8
Tern, arctic, pl. 20, 22
  black, 192, *193*, pl. 20, 22
  black-naped, *51*, pl. 20, 22
  bridled, *196*, 197, pl. 20, 21
  Caspian, 38, 190, *193–94*, 198, pl. 20, 21
  common, *194–95*, pl. 20, 22
  greater-crested, 38, 89, *198–99*, pl. 20, 21
  gull-billed, *193*, pl. 20
  lesser-crested, 38, 89, 198, *199*, pl. 20, 21
  roseate, 38, *195–96*, 197, pl. 20, 22
  Saunders's, *197–98*, pl. 20, 22
  sooty, 195, *196–97*, 199, pl. 20, 21
  whiskered, 38, *191–92*, 193, pl. 20, 22
  white, 13, 193, *200–201*, pl. 20, 22
  white-winged, *192–93*, pl. 20
Terns, *191*

Tropicbird, red-billed, *86–87*, 88, pl. 2
  red-tailed, 24, *87*, 88, pl. 2
  white-tailed, 38, *88*, pl. 2
Tropicbirds, *86*
Turnstone, ruddy, 179, *183–84*, 186, pl. 18
Turtledove, Madagascar, *204–5*, 207, pl. 23

Vanga, Bernier's, 18, 19, 20, 257, 297,
    299–300, 301, pl. 39
  blue, 213, 250, 280, 295, 297, *298–99*,
    301, 302, 303, pl. 37
  Chabert's, 280, 291, 295, *297–98*, 299,
    301, pl. 37
  helmet, 18, 19, 20, 257, 291, 296, 297, 299,
    300–301, pl. 39
  hook-billed, 250, 257, *292–93*, 298, 300,
    pl. 39
  Lafresnaye's, 18, 25, 35, 36, *293–94*, 296,
    pl. 38
  nuthatch, 274, 288, 290, 297, 299, *301*,
    302, pl. 37
  Pollen's, 18, 34, 257, 280, *294–95*, 302,
    pl. 38
  red-tailed, 257, 259, 270, 274, 276, 288,
    290–91, 295, 298, 299, 302, 303, pl. 37
  rufous, 35, 277, *291–92*, 300, 302, pl. 39
  sickle-billed, 35, 36, 292, 293, *295–96*,
    297, pl. 39
  Tylas, 35, 252, 295, 297, 299, 300, *301–2*,
    pl. 38
  Van Dam's, 18, 22, 23, 35, *294*, pl. 38
  white-headed, 250, 257, 260, 280, 291, 292,
    295, *296–97*, 298, 299, 300, 301, 302,
    303, pl. 37
Vangas, *290*

Wagtail, Madagascar, 14, *256*, pl. 35
Warbler, Madagascar brush, 14, 37, 252, 268,
    269–70, 272, 273, pl. 35
  Madagascar swamp, *268–69*, pl. 35
  Rand's, 18, *273*, 278, pl. 36
  Thamnornis, 25, 35, 36, 260, *270–71*,
    pl. 35
Waxbill, common, 12, *313–14*, pl. 40
Weaver, nelicourvi, 19, 257, 261, 279, 283,
    290, *309*, pl. 40
  Sakalava, 211, 270, 290, *309–10*, 313,
    pl. 40
Whimbrel, *178–79*, 184, 186, pl. 17
White-eye, Madagascar, 213, 259, 274, 276,
    285, 286, *287–88*, 295, 298, 301, 303,
    pl. 36

Index of Scientific Names

Italicized numbers refer to the main description.

ablectanea, Agapornis cana, *210–11*
Accipiter francesii, *138–39*
  henstii, *137*
  madagascariensis, *137–38*
Accipitridae, *131*
Acridotheres tristis, 12, *306–7*
Acrocephalus newtoni, *268–69*
Actitis hypoleucos, *182–83*
Actophilornis albinucha, *163–64*
Aepyornis, 9–11
Aepyornithidae, 9
Aepyornithiformes, 9
aequinoctialis, Procellaria, 47, 48
aetherus, Phaethon, *86–87*
aethiopicus, Threskiornis, 22, 26, *115*
affinis, Tyto alba, *226*
africana, Coturnix coturnix, *146*
africanus, Phalacrocorax, 53, *91–92*
Agapornis cana, *210–11*
Alaudidae, *252*
alba, Calidris, *185*
alba, Gygis, 13, *200–201*
alba, Platalea, 53, *117–18*
alba, Tyto, *226*
albigularis, Tylas eduardi, *302*
albinucha, Actophilornis, *163–64*
albospecularis, Copsychus, 11, *263–64*
albospecularis, Copsychus albospecularis, *263–64*
albus, Casmerodius, 53, *106–7*
albus, Corvus, *304–5*
Alcedinidae, *236*
alcinus, Machaeramphus, *132–33*
aldabrensis, Fregata minor, *90*
Alectroenas, *207*
Alectroenas madagascariensis, 16, 21, *207*
aliena, Oena capensis, *205–6*
alleni, Porphyrula, *160–61*
Amaurornis olivieri, 22, 26, *157–58*
amphichroa, Newtonia, 18, 21, *273–74*, 276
anaethetus, Sterna, *196*
Anas bernieri, 22, 26, *126*
  erythrorhyncha, *127–28*
  hottentota, *128–29*
  melleri, 12, *126–27*

Anastomus lamelligerus, 22, 26, *113–14*
Anatidae, *122*
andapae, Phyllastrephus zosterops, *259*, *260*
anderssoni, Machaeramphus alcinus, *133*
Anhinga melanogaster, *92–93*
ankafanae, Phyllastrephus zosterops, *259*, *260*
ankaratrae, Saxicola torquata, *264*, *265*
annae, Leptopterus viridis, *296*, *297*
Anous stolidus, *199–200*
  tenuirostris, 13, *200*
Anseriformes, *122*
antarctica, Catharacta, *188*
antarctica, Sterna, *196*
Apodidae, *232*
Apodiformes, 10, *232*
apolis, Nectarinia souimanga, *286*
apperti, Phyllastrephus, 11, 22, 26, *260*
apricarius, Pluvialis, *171*
Apus barbatus, 13, 14, *235*
  melba, *234–35*
archboldi, Newtonia, 25, 26, *275*
Ardea cinerea, *108–9*
  goliath, 13, *111*
  humbloti, 23, *110*
  melanocephala, 13, *109–10*
  purpurea, *107–8*
Ardeidae, *97*
ardeola, Dromas, *168–69*
Ardeola idae, 12, *101–2*
  ralloides, *99–100*
ardesiaca, Egretta, *104–5*
Arenaria interpres, *183–84*
ariel, Fregata, 13, *90*
arminjoniana, Pterodroma, 47, 49, *52*
arquata, Numenius, *179*
Asio capensis, *229*
  madagascariensis, *228–29*
astrild, Estrilda, 12, *313–14*
astur, Eutriorchis, 11, 16, 21, *134–35*
Atelornis crossleyi, 17, 21, *243–44*
  pittoides, 17, 21, *242–43*
aterrima, Pterodroma, 47, 49, *52*
audeberti, Cuculus, 16, 21, *212–13*
auratus, Hartlaubius, 11, *305–6*
auritus, Nettapus, *125–26*

australis, Treron, *206*
Aviceda madagascariensis, *131–32*
avosetta, Recurvirostra, *167*
Aythya innotata, 7, 11, 15, 21, *129*

bailloni, Puffinus lherminieri, 47, 53
balstoni, Apus barbatus, *235*
bannermanni, Scopus umbretta, *112*
baraui, Pterodroma, 47, 49
barbatus, Apus, 13, 14, *235*
belcheri, Pachyptila, 47, *78*
bengalensis, Sterna, *199*
benghalensis, Rostratula, *164–65*
benschi, Monias, 11, 24, 26, *151–52*
bensoni, Pseudocossyphus, *267–68*
bergii, Sterna, *198–99*
berliozi, Canirallus kioloides, *156, 157*
Berniera, *258*
bernieri, Anas, 22, 26, *126*
bernieri, Oriolia, 18, 21, *299–300*
bernieri, Threskiornis aethiopicus, *115*
bicolor, Dendrocygna, *122–23*
bifrontatus, Charadrius tricolaris, *175*
borbonica, Phedina, 14, *254–55*
Brachypteracias leptosomus, 16, 21, *241*
    squamiger, 17, 21, *242*
Brachypteraciidae, 10, 15, *241*
brachypterus, Buteo, *139*
brunneicauda, Newtonia, 18, *274–75*, 276
brunneicauda, Newtonia brunneicauda, *274,*
    275
brunneus, Dromaeocercus, 17, 21, *272*
Bubulcus ibis, 53, *102–3*
Bulweria, 49
Bulweria bulwerii, 47, *52*
    fallax, 47, *52*
bulwerii, Bulweria, 47, *52*
Buteo brachypterus, *139*
Butorides striatus, *103–4*

caerulea, Coua, *222–23*
Calicalicus madagascariensis, *290–91*
Calidris alba, *185*
    ferruginea, *186*
    minuta, *185–86*
calva, Treron, 206
camelus, Struthio, 9
Campephagidae, *257*
cana, Agapornis, *210–11*
cana, Agapornis cana, *210, 211*
Canirallus kioloides, *156–57*
capense, Daption, 48, *77*
capensis, Asio, *229*
capensis, Oena, *205–6*

capensis, Tachybaptus ruficollis, *83*
Caprimulgidae, *230*
Caprimulgiformes, *230*
Caprimulgus enarratus, *231*
    madagascariensis, *230–31*
carneipes, Puffinus, 49
Casmerodius albus, 53, *106–7*
caspia, Sterna, *193–94*
castanea, Philepitta, 17, 21, *248–49*
Catharacta antarctica, *188*
cauta, Diomedea, 47, 48
Centropinae, *212*
Centropus toulou, *223–24*
cetera, Vanga curvirostris, *292, 293*
chabert, Leptopterus, *297–98*
chabert, Leptopterus chabert, *297, 298*
Charadriidae, *170*
Charadriiformes, 12, 56, *163*
Charadrius dubius, 47, 48, 53
    hiaticula, *171–72*
    leschenaultii, *175–76*
    marginatus, *176–77*
    mongolus, 47, 48, *52*
    pecuarius, *173–74*
    thoracicus, 23, 26, *172–73*
    tricollaris, *174–75*
cherina, Cisticola, *271–72*
chimaera, Uratelornis, 11, 24, 26, *244–45*
Chlidonias hybridus, *191–92*
    leucopterus, *192–93*
    niger, *193*
chloropetoides, Thamnornis, 25, 26, *270–71*
chloropus, Gallinula, *159–60*
chlororhynchos, Diomedea, 47, 48
chrysocome, Eudyptes, *73–74*
Ciconiidae, *113*
Ciconiiformes, *97*
cinerea, Ardea, *108–9*
cinerea, Coracina, *257–58*
cinerea, Coracina cinerea, *257, 258*
cinereiceps, Phyllastrephus, 17, 21, *261–62*
cinereus, Xenus, *182*
Circus maillardi, 11, *136–37*
cirrocephalus, Larus, *190–91*
Cisticola cherina, *271–72*
Collocalia francica, 13, *233*
Colombidae, *204*
Colombiformes, *202*
Columba livia, 12, *204*
comorensis, Cyanolanius madagascarinus, *299*
comoroensis, Terpsiphone mutata, *281*
concolor, Falco, 12, *142–43*
Copsychus albospecularis, 11, *263–64*
coquereli, Coua, *216*

Coraciidae, *239*
Coraciiformes, *236*
Coracina cinerea, *257–58*
Coracopsis nigra, *209–10*
    vasa, *208–9*
corallirostris, Hypositta, *301*
coruscans, Neodrepanis, 17, 21, *250–51*
Corvidae, *304*
Corvus albus, *304–5*
Corythornis cristata, *237*
    vintsioides, 53, *236–37*
Coturnix coturnix, *145–46*
    delegorguei, 13, *146–47*
Coua caerulea, *222–23*
    coquereli, *216*
    cristata, *220–21*
    cursor, 24, 26, *218–19*
    delalandei, 10, 11, 16, 21, *214*
    gigas, 26, *214–15*
    reynaudii, 16, 21, *217–18*
    ruficeps, 26, *219–20*
    serriana, 16, 21, *216–17*
    verreauxi, 24, 26, *221–22*
Couinae, 10, 15, 16, *212*
cowani, Riparia paludicola, *254*
crassirostris, Pachyptila, *78*
cristata, Corythornis, *237*
cristata, Coua, *220–21*
cristata, Coua cristata, 220, 221
cristata, Fulica, *161–62*
cristata, Lophotibis, *116–17*
crossleyi, Atelornis, 17, 21, *243–44*
crossleyi, Mystacornis, 18, 21, 53, *284*
Crossleyia xanthophrys, 18, 21, *283*
Cuculidae, *212*
Cuculiformes, *212*
Cuculinae, *212*
Cuculus audeberti, 16, 21, *212–13*
    rochii, 11, *213–14*
cursor, Coua, 24, 26, *218–19*
curvirostris, Vanga, *292–93*
curvirostris, Vanga curvirostris, 292, 293
cuvieri, Dryolimnas, *155–56*
Cyanolanius madagascarinus, *298–99*
Cypsiurus parvus, *233–34*

dactylatra, Sula, 47, 48, *51*
damii, Xenopirostris, 18, 22, 26, *294*
Daption capense, 48, *77*
debilis, Neomixis tenella, *276, 277*
decaryi, Neomixis tenella, *276, 277*
delacouri, Neomixis viridis, *277, 278*
delalandei, Coua, 10, 11, 16, 21, *214*
delegorguei, Coturnix, 13, *146–47*

Dendrocygna bicolor, *122–23*
    viduata, *123–24*
desolata, Pachyptila, *78*
Dicruridae, *303*
Dicrurus forficatus, *303–4*
diluata, Ispidina madagascariensis, *238*
dimorpha, Egretta, 97, *105–6*
dimorpha, Egretta garzetta, 97, *106*
Dinornis maximus, 10
Diomedea cauta, 47, 48
    chlororhynchos, 47, 48
    exulans, 47, 48
    melanophrys, 48, *75–76*
Diomedeidae, *75*
discolor, Leptosomus, 10, *245–46*
domesticus, Passer, 12, *308*
dominica, Pluvialis, *171*
dominicanus, Larus, 24, *189–90*
dougallii, Sterna, *195–96*
Drepanidae, 10
Dromadidae, *168*
Dromaeocercus brunneus, 17, 21, *272*
    seebohmi, 17, 21, *272–73*
Dromas ardeola, *168–69*
drouhardi, Coracopsis vasa, *208, 209*
Dryolimnas cuvieri, *155–56*
dubia, Pterodroma mollis, 50
dubius, Charadrius, 47, 48, *51*
dumonti, Coua cristata, *220, 221*

eduardi, Tylas, *301–2*
eduardi, Tylas eduardi, *301, 302*
Egretta ardesiaca, *104–5*
    dimorpha, 97, *105–6*
    garzetta, 97
eleonorae, Falco, 12, *141–42*
ellisi, Nesillas typica, *270*
enarratus, Caprimulgus, *231*
epops, Upupa, *247*
erythronotus, Pseudocossyphus sharpei, *265, 266*
erythrorhyncha, Anas, *127–28*
Estrilda astrild, 12, *313–14*
Estrildidae, *313*
Eudyptes chrysocome, *73–74*
Euryceros prevostii, 18, 21, *300–301*
Eurystomus glaucurus, 13, *239–40*
Eutriorchis astur, 11, 16, 21, *134–35*
exulans, Diomedea, 47, 48

falcinellus, Plegadis, 23, *116*
Falco concolor, 12, *142–43*
    eleonorae, 12, *141–42*
    newtoni, *140*

Falco concolor (*continued*)
  peregrinus, *143*
  zoniventris, *140–41*
Falconiformes, 12, *131*
Falculea palliata, *295–96*
fallax, Bulweria, 47, *52*
fanovanae, Newtonia, 11, 18, 21, *275–76*
ferruginea, Calidris, *186*
firasa, Ardea cinerea, *109*
flaviventris, Motacilla, 14, *256*
flavoviridis, Hartertula, 18, 21, *278–79*
fluvescens, Phyllastrephus zosterops, *259, 260*
forficatus, Dicrurus, *303–4*
forficatus, Dicrurus forficatus, *304*
Foudia madagascariensis, 12, 19, *310–11*, 312
  omissa, 19, 22, *311–12*
francesii, Accipiter, *138–39*
francica, Collocalia, 13, *233*
Fregata ariel, 13, *90*
  minor, 13, *89–90*
Fregatidae, *89*
Fregetta, 49
Fregetta grallaria, 48, *51*
  tropica, *80–81*
Fulica cristata, *161–62*
fulva, Pluvialis, *170–71*
fusca, Phoebetria, 47, 48
fuscata, Sterna, *196–97*

Galliformes, 11, *144*
Gallinago macrodactyla, 15, 21, *184–85*
Gallinula chloropus, *159–60*
garzetta, Egretta, 97
Geospizinae, 10
giganteus, Macronectes, *76–77*
gigas, Coua, 26, *214–15*
Glareola ocularis, 12, *169–70*
glareola, Tringa, *181–82*
Glareolidae, *169*
glaucurus, Eurystomus, 13, *239–40*
goliath, Ardea, 13, *111*
gracilis, Cypsiurus parvus, *234*
grallaria, Fregetta, 48, *51*
grandidieri, Zoonavena, *233*
griseus, Puffinus, 47, 49
Gruiformes, 10, *149*
Gygis alba, 13, *200–201*

Haliaeetus vociferoides, 22, 26, *133–34*
halli, Macronectes, 47, 49, 77
Hartertula flavoviridis, 18, 21, *278–79*
Hartlaubius auratus, 11, *305–6*
henstii, Accipiter, *137*
hiaticula, Charadrius, *171–72*

Himantopus, 166
Himantopus himantopus, *166–67*
Hirundinidae, *253*
Hirundo rustica, *255*
hirundo, Sterna, *194–95*
hottentota, Anas, *128–29*
hova, Asio capensis, 229
hova, Mirafra, *252–53*
hovarum, Zosterops, 288
humbloti, Ardea, 23, *110*
hybridus, Chlidonias, *191–92*
Hydrobatidae, *80*
hypoleucos, Actitis, *182–83*
Hypositta corallirostris, *301*
hypoxantha, Neodrepanis, 11, 17, 21, *251–52*
Hypsipetes madagascariensis, 11, *262*

ibis, Bubulcus, 53, *102–3*
ibis, Mycteria, *113*
idae, Ardeola, 12, *101–2*
imerinus, Pseudocossyphus, 24, 26, *266–67*
inceleber, Phyllastrephus madagascariensis,
  259
indicus, Passer domesticus, 308
inexpectatus, Copsychus albospecularis, *263,
  264*
innotata, Aythya, 7, 11, 15, 21, *129*
insularis, Sarothrura, 11, 16, 21, *158–59*
insularis, Thalassornis leuconotus, *130*
interpres, Arenaria, *183–84*
iredalei, Fregata ariel, *90*
Ispidina madagascariensis, 53, *237–38*
Ixobrychus minutus, *97–98*

Jacanidae, *163*

kioloides, Canirallus, *156–57*
kioloides, Canirallus kioloides, *156, 157*

lamelligerus, Anastomus, 22, 26, *113–14*
Laniidae, 10, *212*
lantzii, Nesillas typica, *269, 270*
lapponica, Limosa, *178*
Lariidae, *189*
Larus cirrocephalus, *190–91*
  dominicanus, 24, *189–90*
Leptopterus chabert, *297–98*
  viridis, *296–97*
Leptosomatidae, 10, *245*
leptosomus, Brachypteracias, 16, 21, *241*
Leptosomus discolor, 10, *245–46*
lepturus, Phaethon, *88*
lepturus, Phaethon lepturus, *88*
leschenaultii, Charadrius, *175–76*

leucogaster, Sula, *94–95*
leuconotus, Thalassornis, 23, *129–30*
leucopterus, Chlidonias, *192–93*
lherminieri, Puffinus, 47, 49, *51*
libs, Coracopsis nigra, *209*, *210*
Limosa lapponica, *178*
    limosa, *177–78*
livia, Columba, 12, *204*
Lonchura nana, *313*
Lophotibis cristata, *116–17*

Machaeramphus alcinus, *132–33*
macrodactyla, Gallinago, 15, 21, *184–85*
Macronectes, 48
Macronectes giganteus, *76–77*
    halli, 47, 49, 77
macroptera, Pterodroma, 47, *49*
madagascarensis, Margaroperdix, 12, *144–45*
madagascariensis, Accipiter, *137–38*
madagascariensis, Alectroenas, 16, 21, *207*
madagascariensis, Anastomus lamelligerus, *114*
madagascariensis, Ardea purpurea, *108*
madagascariensis, Asio, *228–29*
madagascariensis, Aviceda, *131–32*
madagascariensis, Calicalicus, *290–91*
madagascariensis, Caprimulgus, 11, *230–31*
madagascariensis, Foudia, 12, *310–11*, 312
madagascariensis, Hypsipetes, 11, *262*
madagascariensis, Ispidina, 53, *237–38*
madagascariensis, Oxylabes, 18, 21, *282–83*
madagascariensis, Phedina borbonica, *255*
madagascariensis, Phyllastrephus, *258–59*
madagascariensis, Phyllastrephus
    madagascariensis, *258*, *259*
madagascariensis, Porphyrio porphyrio, *161*
madagascariensis, Rallus, 15, 21, *154–55*
madagascarinus, Cyanolanius, *298–99*
madagascarinus, Cyanolanius madagascarinus, *299*
maderaspatana, Zosterops, *287–88*
maderaspatana, Zosterops maderaspatana, *288*
maillardi, Circus, 11, *136–37*
Margaroperdix madagascarensis, 12, *144–45*
marginata, Upupa epops, *247*
marginatus, Charadrius, *176–77*
maroantsetrae, Phyllastrephus zosterops, *259*, *260*
Mascarinus, 10
matsudairae, Oceanodroma, 48, 49, *51*
maxima, Coua cristata, *220*, *221*
maximus, Dinornis, 10
melanocephala, Ardea, 13, 109
melanogaster, Anhinga, *92–93*

melanophrys, Diomedea, 48, *75–76*
melanops, Sula dactylatra, 51
melanorhynchos, Casmerodius albus, *107*
melanotos, Sarkidiornis, *124–25*
melba, Apus, *234–35*
meleagris, Numida, 11, *147–48*
melleri, Anas, 12, *126–27*
Meropidae, *238*
Merops superciliosus, 13, 14, *238–39*
Mesitornis, *149*
Mesitornis unicolor, 16, 21, *150–51*
    variegata, 22, 26, *149–50*
Mesitornithidae, 10, 15, 16, *149*
Mesitornithiformes, 10
migrans, Milvus, *133*
Milvus migrans, *133*
minor, Fregata, 13, *89–90*
minor, Phoeniconaias, 13, *120–21*
minor, Ploceus sakalava, *309*, *310*
minuta, Calidris, *185–86*
minutus, Ixobrychus, *97–98*
minutus, Ixobrychus minutus, *98*
Mirafra hova, *252–53*
mitrata, Numida meleagris, *148*
mollis, Pterodroma, 47, 49, *52*
Monarchidae, *280*
mongolus, Charadrius, 47, *52*
Monias, *149*
Monias benschi, 11, 24, 26, *151–52*
Monticola, *268*
monticola, Nesillas typica, *270*
monticola, Newtonia brunneicauda, *274*, *275*
moseleyi, Eudyptes chrysocome, 74
Motacilla flaviventris, 14, *256*
Mullerornis, 9
mutata, Terpsiphone, *280–82*
mutata, Terpsiphone mutata, *281*
Mycteria ibis, *113*
Mystacornis crossleyi, 18, 21, 53, *284*

nana, Lonchura, *313*
nebularia, Tringa, *180–81*
Nectarinia notata, *286–87*
    souimanga, *285–86*
Nectariniidae, *285*
nelicourvi, Ploceus, 19, 22, *309*
Neodrepanis, 10, *248*
Neodrepanis coruscans, 17, 21, *250–51*
    hypoxantha, 11, 17, 21, *251–52*
Neomixis striatigula, 53, *278*
    tenella, 53, *276–77*
    viridis, 18, 21, *277*
Nesillas typica, 14, *269–70*
Nettapus auritus, *125–26*

newtoni, Acrocephalus, *268–69*
newtoni, Falco, *140*
Newtonia amphichroa, 18, 21, *273–74, 276*
  archboldi, 25, 26, *275*
  brunneicauda, 18, *274–75, 276*
  fanovanae, 11, 18, 21, *275–76*
niger, Chlidonias, *193*
nigra, Coracopsis, *209–10*
nigra, Coracopsis nigra, *209, 210*
nigricollis, Turnix, 12, *153–54*
nilotica, Sterna, *193*
Ninox superciliaris, 11, *227–28*
notata, Nectarinia, *286–87*
nubilosa, Sterna fuscata, *196*
Numenius arquata, *179*
  phaeopus, *178–79*
Numida meleagris, 11, *147–48*
Numididae, *147*
Nycticorax nycticorax, *98–99*

obscura, Nesillas typica, *269, 270*
obscura, Porzana pusilla, *157*
occidentalis, Schetba rufa, *291, 292*
oceanicus, Oceanites, 49, *80*
Oceanites oceanicus, 49, *80*
Oceanodroma matsudairae, 48, 49, *51*
ochropus, Tringa, *181*
ocularis, Glareola, 12, *169–70*
Oena capensis, *205–6*
olivaceiceps, Coua ruficeps, *219, 220*
olivieri, Amaurornis, 22, 26, *157–58*
omissa, Foudia, 19, 22, *311–12*
orientalis, Neomixis tenella, *276, 277*
Oriolia bernieri, 18, 21, *299–300*
Oriolidae, *289*
Oriolus oriolus, *289*
Otus rutilus, *227*
Oxylabes madagascariensis, 18, 21, *282–83*

Pachyptila, 49, *78*
Pachyptila belcheri, 47, *78*
  crassirostris, *78*
  desolata, *78*
  salvini, *78*
  turtur, 47, *78*
  vittata, *78*
pacificus, Puffinus, 24, 49, *79*
palliata, Falculea, *295–96*
pallida, Coracina cinerea, *257, 258*
pallidior, Neomixis striatigula, *278*
paludicola, Riparia, 15, 21, *253–54*
parasiticus, Stercorarius, *188–89*
parasitus, Milvus migrans, *133*
parvus, Cypsiurus, *233–34*

Passer domesticus, 12, *308*
Passeriformes, 10, *248*
pecuarius, Charadrius, *173–74*
Pelecanidae, 91, *96*
Pelecaniformes, *86*
Pelecanus rufescens, 22, 26, *96*
pelzelnii, Tachybaptus, 23, *83*
peregrinus, Falco, *143*
personatus, Pterocles, 11, 26, 53, *202–3*
petrosia, Terpsiphone mutata, *281*
phaeopus, Numenius, *178–79*
Phaethon aetherus, *86–87*
  lepturus, *88*
  rubricauda, 24, *87*
Phaethonidae, *86*
Phalacrocoracidae, *91*
Phalacrocorax africanus, 53, *91–92*
Phasianidae, *144*
Phedina borbonica, 14, *254–55*
Philepitta, *248*
Philepitta castanea, 17, 21, *248–49*
  schlegeli, *249–50*
Philepittidae, 10, 15, *248*
Philomachus pugnax, *187*
Phoebetria fusca, 47, 48
Phoeniconaias minor, 13, *120–21*
Phoenicopteridae, *118*
Phoenicopterus ruber, 26, *118–19*
Phyllastrephus, *258*
Phyllastrephus apperti, 11, 22, 26, *260*
  cinereiceps, 17, 21, *261–62*
  madagascariensis, *258–59*
  tenebrosus, 11, 17, 21, *260–61*
  zosterops, 17, 21, *259–60*
pica, Copsychus albospecularis, *263, 264*
pictilis, Phalacrocorax africanus, *92*
picturata, Streptopelia, 53, *204–5*
pileatus, Anous stolidus, *199*
pittoides, Atelornis, 17, 21, *242–43*
Platalea alba, 53, *117–18*
Plegadis falcinellus, 23, *116*
Ploceidae, *308*
Ploceus nelicourvi, 19, 22, *309*
  sakalava, 26, *309–10*
Pluvialis apricarius, *171*
  dominica, *171*
  fulva, *170–71*
  squatarola, *171*
Podicipedidae, *82*
Podicipediformes, *82*
podiceps, Ixobrychus minutus, *98*
poliocephalus, Larus cirrocephalus, *191*
polleni, Xenopirostris, 18, 21, *294–95*
Polyboroides radiatus, *135–36*

Porphyrio porphyrio, *161*
Porphyrula alleni, *160–61*
Porzana, 154
Porzana pusilla, *157*
prevostii, Euryceros, 18, 21, *300–301*
Prionopinae, 213
Prionops retzii, 213
Procellaria aequinoctialis, 47, 48
Procellariidae, *76, 77*
Procellariiformes, 12, 56, *75*
Pseudobias wardi, 18, 21, *280*
Pseudobulweria, 50
Pseudocossyphus, *268*
Pseudocossyphus bensoni, *267–68*
   imerinus, 24, 26, *266–67*
   sharpei, 17, 20, 21, *265–66*
pseudozosterops, Randia, 18, 21, *273*
Psittacidae, *208*
Psittaciformes, 10, *208*
Psittacula, 10
Pterocles personatus, 11, 26, 53, *202–3*
Pteroclididae, *202*
Pterodroma arminjoniana, 47, 49, *52*
   aterrima, 47, 49, *52*
   baraui, 47, 49
   macroptera, 47, *49*
   mollis, 47, 49, *52*
Puffinus carneipes, 47, 49
   griseus, 47, 49
   lherminieri, 47, 49, *53*
   pacificus, 24, 49, *79*
pugnax, Philomachus, *187*
purpurea, Ardea, *107–8*
pusilla, Porzana, *157*
Pycnonotidae, *258*
pyropyga, Coua cristata, 220, *221*
pyrrhorhoa, Gallinula chloropus, *160*

radama, Falco peregrinus, *143*
radiatus, Polyboroides, *135–36*
Rallidae, 149, *154*
ralloides, Ardeola, *99–100*
Rallus madagascariensis, 15, 21, *154–55*
Randia pseudozosterops, 18, 21, *273*
Recurvirostra, 166
Recurvirostra avosetta, *167*
Recurvirostridae, *166*
retzii, Prionops, 213
reynaudii, Coua, 16, 21, *217–18*
Riparia paludicola, 15, 21, *253–54*
   riparia, *254*
rochii, Cuculus, 11, *213–14*
roseus, Phoenicopterus ruber, *119*
Rostratula benghalensis, *164–65*

Rostratulidae, *164*
ruber, Phoenicopterus, 26, *118–19*
rubricauda, Phaethon, 24, *87*
rubripes, Sula sula, *94*
rufa, Schetba, *291–92*
rufa, Schetba rufa, *291, 292*
rufescens, Pelecanus, 22, 26, *96*
ruficeps, Coua, 26, *219–20*
ruficeps, Coua ruficeps, *219, 220*
ruficollis, Tachybaptus, 23, *82–83*
rufolavatus, Tachybaptus, 7, 11, 15, 21, *84–85*
rustica, Hirundo, *255*
rutenbergi, Butorides striatus, *104*
rutilus, Otus, *227*

sakalava, Ploceus, 26, *309–10*
sakalava, Ploceus sakalava, *309, 310*
salomonseni, Pseudocossyphus sharpei, 20, *266*
salvini, Pachyptila, *78*
Sarkidiornis melanotos, *124–25*
Sarothrura insularis, 11, 16, 21, *158–59*
   watersi, 15, 21, *159*
saundersi, Sterna, *197–98*
Saxicola torquata, *264–65*
Schetba rufa, *291–92*
schistocercus, Leptopterus chabert, *297, 298*
schlegeli, Philepitta, *249–50*
sclateri, Chlidonias hybridus, *192*
sclateri, Neomixis striatigula, *278*
Scolopacidae, *177*
Scopidae, *111*
Scopus umbretta, *111–12*
seebohmi, Dromaeocercus, 17, 21, *272–73*
serriana, Coua, 16, 21, *216–17*
sharpei, Pseudocossyphus, 17, 20, 21, *265–66*
sharpei, Pseudocossyphus sharpei, *265, 266*
sibilla, Saxicola torquata, *264, 265*
singetra, Terpsiphone mutata, 281
souimanga, Nectarinia, *285–86*
souimanga, Nectarinia souimanga, *285, 286*
soumagnei, Tyto, 11, 16, 21, *225–26*
Sphenicidae, *73*
Spheniciformes, *73*
squamiger, Brachypteracias, 17, 21, *242*
squatarola, Pluvialis, *171*
stagnatilis, Tringa, *179–80*
Stercorariidae, *188*
Stercorarius parasiticus, *188–89*
Sterna anaethetus, *196*
   bengalensis, *199*
   bergii, *198–99*
   caspia, *193–94*
   dougallii, *195–96*

Sterna (*continued*)
  fuscata, *196–97*
  hirundo, *194–95*
  nilotica, *193*
  saundersi, *197–98*
  sumatrana, 47, 48, *51*
Sternidae, *191*
stolidus, Anous, *199–200*
Streptopelia picturata, 53, *204–5*
striatigula, Neomixis, 53, *278*
striatus, Butorides, *103–4*
Strigidae, *227*
Strigiformes, *225*
Struthio camelus, 9
Sturnidae, *305*
Sula dactylatra, 47, 48, *51*
  leucogaster, *94–95*
  sula, 13, *94*
Sulidae, 91, *94*
sumatrana, Sterna, 47, 48, *51*
superciliaris, Ninox, 11, *227–28*
superciliosus, Merops, 13, 14, *238–39*
Sylviidae, *268*

Tachybaptus, 82
Tachybaptus pelzelnii, 23, *83–84*
  ruficollis, 23, *82–83*
  rufolavatus, 7, 11, 15, 21, *84–85*
temptator, Puffinus lherminieri, 47, 51
tenebrosus, Phyllastrephus, 11, 17, 21, *260–61*
tenella, Neomixis, 53
tenella, Neomixis tenella, *276–77*
tenellus, Charadrius marginatus, *177*
tenuirostris, Anous, 13, *200*
Terpsiphone mutata, *280–82*
Thalassornis leuconotus, 23, *129–30*
Thamnornis chloropetoides, 25, 26, *270–71*
thoracicus, Charadrius, 23, 26, *172–73*
Threskiornis aethiopicus, 22, 26, *115*
Threskiornithidae, *115*
Timaliidae, 15, 18, *282*
torquata, Saxicola, *264–65*
toulou, Centropus, *223–24*
Treron australis, *206*
  calva, 206
tricollaris, Charadrius, *174–75*
Tringa glareola, *181–82*
  nebularia, *180–81*
  ochropus, *181*
  stagnatilis, *179–80*
tristis, Acridotheres, 12, *306–7*
tristis, Acridotheres tristis, *307*
tropica, Fregetta, *80–81*
tsaratananae, Saxicola torquata, *264, 265*

tundrae, Charadrius hiaticula, *171*
Turdidae, *263*
Turnicidae, *153*
Turnix nigricollis, 12, *153–54*
turtur, Pachyptila, 47, *78*
Tylas eduardi, *301–2*
typica, Nesillas, 14, *269–70*
typica, Nesillas typica, *269, 270*
Tyto alba, *226*
  soumagnei, 11, 16, 21, *225–26*
Tytonidae, *225, 227*

umbretta, Scopus, *111–12*
unicolor, Mesitornis, 16, 21, *150–51*
Upupa epops, *247*
Upupidae, *247*
Uratelornis chimaera, 11, 24, 26, *244–45*
urschi, Lophotibis cristata, *117*

Vanga curvirostris, *292–93*
Vangidae, 10, 15, 18, 213, *290*
variegata, Mesitornis, 22, 26, *149–50*
vasa, Coracopsis, *208–9*
vasa, Coracopsis vasa, *209*
verreauxi, Coua, 24, 26, *221–22*
viduata, Dendrocygna, *123–24*
vintsioides, Corythornis, 53, *236–37*
viridis, Leptopterus, *296–97*
viridis, Leptopterus viridis, *296, 297*
viridis, Neomixis, 18, 21, *277–78*
viridis, Neomixis viridis, *277, 278*
vittata, Pachyptila, *78*
vociferoides, Haliaeetus, 22, 26, *133–34*
voeltzkowiana, Terpsiphone mutata, *281*
vulpina, Terpsiphone mutata, *281*
vulsini, Anhinga melanogaster, *93*

wardi, Pseudobias, 18, 21, *280*
watersi, Sarothrura, 15, 21, *159*
willsi, Apus melba, *234*

xanthophrys, Crossleyia, 18, 21, *283*
xenia, Treron australis, *206*
Xenopirostris damii, 18, 22, 26, *294*
  polleni, 18, 21, *294–95*
  xenopirostris, 18, 25, 26, *293–94*
Xenus cinereus, *182*

zoniventris, Falco, *140–41*
Zoonavena grandidieri, *233*
Zosteropidae, *287*
Zosterops hovarum, 288
Zosterops maderaspatana, *287–88*
zosterops, Phyllastrephus, 17, 21, *259*
zosterops, Phyllastrephus zosterops, *259–60*